Gurus of Modern Yoga

Gurus of Modern Yoga

Edited by Mark Singleton

and

Ellen Goldberg

OXFORD
UNIVERSITY PRESS

OXFORD
UNIVERSITY PRESS

Oxford University Press is a department of the University of Oxford.
It furthers the University's objective of excellence in research, scholarship,
and education by publishing worldwide.

Oxford New York
Auckland Cape Town Dar es Salaam Hong Kong Karachi
Kuala Lumpur Madrid Melbourne Mexico City Nairobi
New Delhi Shanghai Taipei Toronto

With offices in
Argentina Austria Brazil Chile Czech Republic France Greece
Guatemala Hungary Italy Japan Poland Portugal Singapore
South Korea Switzerland Thailand Turkey Ukraine Vietnam

Published in the United States of America by
Oxford University Press
198 Madison Avenue, New York, NY 10016

Library of Congress Cataloging-in-Publication Data
Gurus of modern yoga / edited by Mark Singleton, Ellen Goldberg.
p. cm.
ISBN 978-0-19-993870-4 (hardcover : alk. paper) — ISBN 978-0-19-993872-8
(pbk : alk. paper) 1. Gurus—Biography. 2. Yoga—History—20th century.
I. Singleton, Mark, 1976- II. Goldberg, Ellen, 1954-
BL1171.G87 2013
294.5'4360922—dc23
2013035325

9780199938704
9780199938728 (pbk.)

1 3 5 7 9 8 6 4 2

Printed in the United States of America on acid-free paper

CONTENTS

CONTRIBUTORS

Joseph S. Alter has conducted academic research in India since 1981. He teaches anthropology at the University of Pittsburgh and has published a number of books, including *The Wrestler's Body* (1992), *Gandhi's Body* (2000), *Yoga in Modern India* (2004), and *Sex and Masculinity in Modern India* (2011). Beyond the study of yoga in contemporary practice, his interests include the cultural history of nature cure as a system of medicine and the natural history of animals in the human imagination.

Gwilym Beckerlegge studied religions at the Universities of Oxford and Lancaster and is currently professor of modern religions in the Department of Religious Studies at The Open University, United Kingdom. His publications include *Swami Vivekananda's Legacy of Service: A Study of the Ramakrishna Math and Mission* (2006); *Colonialism, Modernity and Religious Identities* (2008), which he edited; and "'An Ordinary Organization Run by Ordinary People': A Study of Leadership in Vivekananda Kendra" (*Contemporary South Asia*, vol. 18, pp. 71–88, 2010).

Jean Byrne conducts research on the intersection between feminist philosophy and nonduality at the University of Queensland. Her recent publications include *Yoga in the Modern World: Contemporary Perspectives* (2008), edited with Mark Singleton. She also runs The Yoga Space in Perth, Australia, and is an authorized Ashtanga Yoga teacher.

Charles I. Flores is adjunct professor at John F. Kennedy University, associate managing editor of the *International Journal of Transpersonal Studies*, and psychotherapist specializing in the field of addiction and at-risk youth. He has written and worked on issues of diversity, social action, and integral psychology for over fifteen years. His most recent scholarly work focuses on what he calls Evolutionary Spiritual Action.

Tara Fraser has studied, practiced, and taught in a number of *haṭhayoga* traditions. For the last thirteen years, her practice has been profoundly influenced by the teaching of T. K. V. Desikachar and his students. She is the author of a number of books on yoga that have been translated into eight languages and sold close to a million copies. She is the founder of the Yoga Junction center, London's only British Wheel of Yoga (BWY)–approved education center, and has served on the BWY Education Committee.

Ann Gleig is assistant professor of religious studies at the University of Central Florida at Orlando. She is also an area editor for the anthropology and sociology of religion at *Religious Studies Review*. Her areas of specialization are Asian religions in America and religion and psychoanalysis. She has recently completed an edited volume, with Lola Williamson, titled *Homegrown Gurus: From Hinduism in America to American Hinduism* (2013).

Ellen Goldberg is associate professor of South Asian studies in the School of Religion, Queen's University, Canada. She is the author of *The Lord Who Is Half Woman: Ardhanārīśvara in Indian and Feminist Perspective,* and has written extensively on yoga including the intersection between yoga and cognitive science. She serves on the editorial board of two journals, *Studies in Religion/Sciences Religieuses* (SAGE) and *Literary Discourses: International Journal of Art and Literature* (Indira Kala Sangeet University, India) and on the steering committee of the American Academy of Religion's Yoga in Theory and Practice Group.

Andrea R. Jain is assistant professor of religious studies at Indiana University–Purdue University Indianapolis. Her research interests include theories of religion as well as religion in relation to the body. More specifically, her research focuses on the transnational construction and global popularization of modern yoga. Her current projects include studies on the intersections of consumer culture and modern yoga as well as modern yoga gurus.

Dermot Killingley studied Latin, Greek, and Sanskrit at Merton College, Oxford, from 1955 to 1959 and Middle Iranian languages in the School of Oriental and African Studies (SOAS) at the University of London from 1959 to 1961. He returned to SOAS in 1968 to study Indian philosophy. He taught in the Department of Indian Studies, University of Malaya, from 1961 to 1968; in the Department of Religious Studies, Newcastle University, from 1970 to 2000, when he retired as reader in Hindu studies; and as visiting professor at the University of Vienna in 2008. He is now joint editor (with Anna King and Lynn Foulston) of *Religions of South Asia*. He has published research on aspects of ancient Indian thought and on modern developments, and has written on Rammohun Roy, Vivekananda, and Radhakrishnan in particular. He has also published a three-volume teaching course, *Beginning Sanskrit* (1995).

Hanna H. Kim is assistant professor of anthropology at Adelphi University, New York. She received her Ph.D. in anthropology from Columbia University,

New York. She is working on a book project based on her long-term ethnographic research with the Bochasanwasi Shri Akshar Purushottam Swaminarayan Sanstha. Her recent article titled "Public Engagement and Personal Desires: BAPS Swaminarayan Temples and their Contribution to the Discourses on Religion" appeared in *International Journal of Hindu Studies* (13: 357–390, 2009).

Suzanne Newcombe is a research officer at Inform, an organization that studies new and alternative religiosity based at the London School of Economics and Political Science, and is associate lecturer at the Open University. Her research focuses on the historical development of yoga and *āyurvedic* medicine in Britain as well as contemporary spirituality and new religious movements particularly among Buddhist and Hindu groups. She received her Ph.D. in 2008 from Cambridge and holds a M.Sc. in religion in contemporary society from the London School of Economics. She has published articles in the *Journal of Contemporary Religion, Asian Medicine* and *Religion Compass.*

Stuart Ray Sarbacker is associate professor of comparative religion and Indian philosophy at Oregon State University. His work is centered on the relationships between the religious and philosophical traditions of Hinduism, Buddhism, and Jainism. He has written extensively on topics related to the theory and practice of yoga (both contemplative practices and bodily disciplines) in traditional, modern, and contemporary contexts, including a book titled *Samādhi: The Numinous and Cessative in Indo-Tibetan Yoga*. He has served as co-chair of the American Academy of Religion's Yoga in Theory and Practice Group, which provides a forum for collaborative academic research on yoga.

Mark Singleton gained his Ph.D. in divinity from the University of Cambridge. His research interests include contemporary South Asian religion, the intersection of religion and politics, and new religious movements, particularly those inspired by Asian practices. He has written extensively on modern, transnational yoga, notably *Yoga in the Modern World, Contemporary Perspectives* (ed. with Jean Byrne, 2008) and *Yoga Body, the Origins of Modern Posture Practice* (2010). He is currently co-chair of the American Academy of Religion's Yoga in Theory and Practice Group. He teaches at St. John's College, Santa Fe, New Mexico.

Frederick M. Smith received his M.A. from the Centre for Advanced Studies in Sanskrit at the University of Pune and Ph.D. from the Department of Oriental Studies at the University of Pennsylvania. He is professor of Sanskrit and classical Indian religions at the University of Iowa. He is known for his work on *Vedic* sacrificial ritual, for his translations from Sanskrit of the devotional and philosophical works of the early sixteenth-century north Indian saint

Vallabācārya, and for his major study of possession titled *The Self Possessed: Deity and Spirit Possession in South Asian Literature and Civilization* (2006). He is currently completing a volume in the series of translations of the *Mahābhārata*, the Indian national epic: *The Mahābhārata: 14. The Book of the Horse Sacrifice. Introduction, Translation, and Annotations* (2012), and is under contract from Cambridge University Press to write a general study of Vedic literature. He has written more than fifty articles (including several on yoga) and nearly two hundred reviews. He has also been an active practitioner of yoga for more than thirty years.

Smriti Srinivas is professor in the Department of Anthropology at the University of California, Davis. Her research focuses on urban space, social, and cultural memory, the body, and religion. Her publications include *In the Presence of Sai Baba* (2008) and *Landscapes of Urban Memory: The Sacred and the Civic in India's High Tech City* (2001). Srinivas is cofounder of Nagara, a center for urban studies, history, and culture based in Bangalore, and currently serves on the editorial board of the *International Journal of Urban and Regional Studies*.

Joanne Punzo Waghorne is professor of religion at Syracuse University. She is currently working on global gurus and their multiethnic following, especially in Singapore and Chennai, India. Her previous publications include *Diaspora of the Gods: Modern Hindu Temples in an Urban Middle-Class World* (2004) and *The Raja's Magic Clothes: Re-visioning Kingship and Divinity in England's India* (1994). During 2007–2008, she was a Fulbright-Hays Faculty research abroad fellow and visiting senior research fellow (sabbatical leave program) in the Asian Research Institute (globalization and religion cluster) at the National University of Singapore.

Maya Warrier is senior lecturer in religious studies at the University of Wales, Trinity Saint David. She is author of *Hindu Selves in a Modern World: Guru Faith in the Mata Amritanandamayi Mission* (2005). Her research interests center on modern manifestations of popular Hinduism in India and overseas. She is currently working on a collaborative project examining public representations of Hinduism in Indian and overseas contexts. The results are to be published in a coedited volume titled *Public Hinduisms*. She is also working on a fieldwork-based project funded by the Wellcome Trust researching the development of modern forms of *āyurveda* in the United Kingdom.

Joan White who operates perhaps the most high-profile yoga studio in Philadelphia, is one of the world's leading teachers of Iyengar Yoga. For many years she has been the director of the Iyengar Yoga assessment committee, the branch of the Iyengar Yoga Association that certifies Iyengar Yoga teachers.

She has taught throughout America, Canada, Europe, and Central America since 1972 and has traveled nearly every year since then to Pune to study with B. K. S. Iyengar at his home studio.

Lola Williamson is associate professor of religious studies and director of peace studies at Millsaps College in Jackson, Mississippi. Her articles and chapter contributions to books and encyclopedias focus on the transmission of Hinduism to America through immigration and missionary activity. She is the author of *Transcendent in America: Hindu-Inspired Meditation Movements as New Religion* (2010) and co-editor, with Ann Gleig, of *Homegrown Gurus: from Hinduism in America to American Hinduism* (2013).

NOTE ON TRANSLITERATION

Transliterations from Sanskrit follow the standard International Alphabet of Sanskrit Transliteration (IAST) scheme, with the following exceptions: (1) place names are generally transliterated without diacritical marks, and modern English-language spellings are preserved; (2) names of authors and well-known persons from the modern period are generally written without diacritical marks, consistent with their or their organization's convention; (3) terms used in quotations are reproduced according to the original source; and (4) specific use of terminology by an organization, a guru, or an informant is reproduced accordingly. Although we have tried to maintain consistency throughout the text, the great variety of ways in which Sanskritic terms are rendered into English (and into the Roman script) across modern guru organizations inevitably results in some variation in spelling. We hope this will not be unduly confusing for the reader.

Gurus of Modern Yoga

Introduction

ELLEN GOLDBERG AND MARK SINGLETON

This book is about gurus in modern yoga. Its sixteen chapters explore the contributions that individual gurus have made to the formation of practices and discourses of yoga in the modern, transnational world, both within India and elsewhere. While our treatment is not intended to be exhaustive (and necessarily excludes important figures), our hope is that these various perspectives will shed new light on the changing role and function of the yoga guru in nontraditional contexts. Transnational yoga (i.e., yoga taught and practiced at a global level) is almost by definition dislocated with regard to localized, sectarian, or grassroots Indian models. This dislocation can be particularly apparent within guru-centered organizations, where either the students or the guru or both might find themselves in a unique hermeneutic encounter with norms and perspectives removed from those of their birth community. The result is adaptation: of the form or substance of the guru's teaching; of the spiritual and cultural affiliations of the students; or (usually) a complex intermingling of both. Many (if not all) of the yoga gurus represented in this book negotiate these cultural spaces.

YOGA AND MODERNITY

Yoga, in its dissemination in the Western world, has undergone radical transformation in response to the differing worldviews, logical predispositions, and aspirations of modern practitioners. These forms were the result of a reframing of practices and beliefs within India itself over the last 150 years in response to encounters with modernity and the West, and of simultaneous and on-going experimentation in a global context. Perhaps a majority of recent forms of English language-based yogas in and out of India bear the clear traces of these processes.[1]

The modern period saw the dawn of new, democratic, scientific modes of yoga practice and teaching. These forms spread beyond the borders of India and were embraced by enthusiasts around the world. This transnational renaissance of yoga came into being as part of a wider dialogue between tradition and modernity. Certain aspects of yoga praxis were eliminated, while others were reconfigured and shaped according to the needs of the day. One such aspect was the guru. Teachings, and gurus, have always adapted to the times and circumstances in which they find themselves. However, the sheer pace of cultural change ushered in by modernity led to some unprecedented innovations in the way gurus present themselves and their teachings, and in the way they are received by their students. The situation is complicated still further when these gurus operate within foreign cultures (such as those of the United States or Europe) where there is no traditional infrastructure for their activities. What happens when Indian yoga gurus come to the West? What happens when their teachings are shaped by modern technology or corporate organizational structures? How do Western teachers of yoga negotiate their elevation to the status of guru? And what abuses can occur as a result of a guru's transplantation from a traditional, conservative environment to the modern, liberal West? These are some of the questions asked in the chapters of this book.

THE CHANGING FACES OF YOGA

Peter Berger (1979) claims that the encounter between modernity and global religions was "cataclysmic and unprecedented" (p. 2), and something similar might be asserted with regard to yoga. Transnational yoga today is not necessarily divorced from premodern Indian forms (or indeed "extramodern" ones, i.e., forms that have been isolated from and therefore not significantly altered by the encounter with modernity). Nevertheless, in many instances the forces and themes that have shaped the modern world have also left their indelible marks on yoga theory and practice: the ascendency of reason, characterized by an emphasis on science, technology, and empirical thinking, or what Wade Clark Roof (1999) calls the "rational basis for truth" (p. 621); secularization and the separation of the private and the public spheres (i.e., religion and state); democratization, leading to the demise of religious monopolies through the rejection of institutional exclusivism; the relativizing of religious beliefs and practices, in conjunction with a profound desire for freedom of choice; the triumph of capitalism and the subsequent commodification of religion (which in turn gives birth to the complex phenomenon of the spiritual marketplace and competition among global religions); and the rise of the modern state, where we see discourses on nation-building, notably in India, adopt and adapt religious themes and practices in the service of the new (or emerging) country. These modern themes, and how they play out through the figure of the modern yoga guru, are variously addressed in the sixteen chapters of this book.

The modern vision of yoga as an empirical science develops not only as an integral part of its formative rationale but also as its culminating narrative. Modernity transforms yoga, for example, in the medicalization of its applications, practices, and goals in an attempt to create a new *somatic science*—to borrow a phrase from David A. Palmer and Xun Liu (2012; see also De Michelis, 2008). The medicalization (and somatization) of yoga is demonstrated, for example, in the work of modern gurus like Kuvalayananda (Alter, 2004) and Yogendra (see Chapter 3 by Alter in this volume). Early modern yoga gurus forged new ground by developing medical applications of *āsanas* and *prāṇāyāmas* (postures and breathing techniques) for the purpose of treating the sick and as a therapeutic aid to cultivate optimum physical fitness and health (see Singleton, 2010a).

Health benefits and the potential for increased longevity are central issues in modern yoga that coincide with the stabilizing and validating rhetoric of medicalization yet retain a sense of *haṭhayoga*'s collective and canonical past (see Goldberg, 2009). Several of the gurus examined in this volume (see Chapters 6 and 7 on Iyengar, Chapter 3 on Yogendra, and Chapter 16 on Swami Ramdev) suffered severe illness in their youth and came to yoga not necessarily to find enlightenment but rather to find a cure. However, we also see embedded in some modern discourses of yoga the notion that the eradication of disease can potentially culminate in the attainment of immortality or the divine body (*divyadeha*), particularly among adept practitioners (see Chapter 8 on Kripalu in this volume). Thus, we find combined the instrumental, scientific emphasis of the modern rational world and the alchemical and metaphysical preoccupations of medieval *haṭhayoga* (see White, 1996).

The encounter with modernity has brought yoga to the forefront of the spiritual marketplace where gurus (must?) compete with each other for disciples and practitioners (see Chapter 9 by Jain and Chapter 13 by Waghorne in this volume). With the aid of teacher training curricula; the sale of yoga clothing, books, and DVDs; and worldwide online access, we see unprecedented innovation not only in the ways that modern gurus market their particular approach to yoga but also in how they mastermind forms of connectivity with devotees in a global context (see, e.g., Chapter 13 by Waghorne, Chapter 14 by Warrier, and Chapter 16 by Sarbacker in this volume). This leads to what Joseph Alter in Chapter 3 calls "transnational refractions of globalized *gurudom*." Moreover, the commercialization and popularization of yoga practice has repositioned modern yoga as a repository of idealized cultural norms that have concretized themselves in such a way that they appear iconic, prototypical, and eternal. Though the strategy of claiming an ancient and primordial past is not new, modern forms of yoga nonetheless emphasize and express it in non-normative and innovative ways—often according to the transmission, authority, and experience of the individual guru (see, e.g., Chapter 1 and Chapter 4 in this volume).

THE GURU TRANSFORMED?

Traditional Indian students had to undergo initiation and extensive training under a qualified guru before they could learn the techniques and practices of yoga. Yoga was often secretive and exclusive, and the relationship with the guru was one of submission and obedience (although not necessarily without interpersonal tensions: see Smith and White, Chapter 6, n.20). Indeed, it was often understood that yoga would simply not work without the grace of the guru (see, e.g., Hayes, 2003; Padoux, 2000; White, 2000b. See also *Kaṭha Upaniṣad* 1.28; *Śvetāśvatara Upaniṣad* 6: 21–23). Today, on the other hand, millions of yoga practitioners around the world appear to carry out their study and practice of yoga perfectly well without ever having had—and even perhaps without ever having wanted to have—a guru. (Some, of course, might dispute exactly how "well" such study and practice is in fact carried out.) In other cases, popular modern gurus open their doors to everyone who wishes to follow their teachings and learn their techniques. Indeed, from the beginnings of yoga's acculturation in the West, students have often readily received teachings and guidance without necessarily being formally inducted into any organized doctrinal or social structure, and without undergoing "traditional" initiation. Such indeed was the case with Swami Vivekananda's students, as Joe Mlecko has observed (1982: 21; see also Chapter 1 by Killingley in this volume).

As such, discipleship under modern Indian gurus takes on new normative features, often reflecting the new technological, ideological, bureaucratic, and spiritual concerns of the day. Some gurus may even seem to outright reject tradition (or, in the inimitable words of Sadhguru Jaggi Vasudev, "all that traditional whatever"; see Chapter 13 in this volume) but nevertheless build on traditional tropes of the guru to create distinctly modern mediations of authority and charisma (see also Chapter 15 in this volume). Conversely, we may still see an ongoing preoccupation with and respect for lineage (*paramparā, sampradāya, saṅgh parivār*) and the transmission of knowledge from guru to disciple, albeit reconceptualized in the context of, for example, nationalist belonging or online transnational community (see Chapters 14, 15 and 16 in this volume). Transmission may no longer be exclusive and private, nor does it necessarily even entail a direct, personal relationship with the guru, especially in large, transnational organizations (see, for example, Chapter 13 in this volume).

Growing standardization within various schools of modern yoga has meant that the line between public and private knowledge has shifted. Institutionalized teaching curricula and standardized, graded courses may reinforce (or at times even replace) the charismatic authority of the living guru, especially when yoga organizations have to adapt themselves to the legal and bureaucratic demands of state law or local government (see Chapter 7, this volume). Alongside this "institutionalization of charisma", we also witness what we might call the "corporatization of charisma", with freshly trademarked rituals and the culture of corporate secrecy displacing more traditional understandings (see Chapter 13 in this volume).

Similarly, the newly invented ritual of community yoga practice held in a dedicated "yoga studio" thrives particularly in the modern urban environment, where teacher training courses are often a substitute for the guru–disciple relationship of the past. Secrecy and privacy have given way to community and public settings, and in some quarters even a programmatic discouragement of private, individual self-practice (see Chapter 10 in this volume). Similarly relevant in this regard is the phenomenon of the Yoga Shivir, the group yoga camps common today in modern India (Alter, 2008; see also Chapters 15 and 16 in this volume).

In place of personal, secretive, one-on-one models, then, we may see a variety of public, democratic, accessible, *one-on-many* modes of teaching and knowledge transmission. Nevertheless, many of the gurus discussed in this volume still reflect the master's ability to transmit the charismatic authority of tradition, genealogy, and lineage. Some resort to traditional means of transmission like *śaktipāta dīkṣā* (see, e.g., Chapters 8–10 in this volume) albeit shorn of the secrecy and exclusivity of traditional practice. Others insist on the mastery of particular postural sequences as a stringent prerequisite to entry into the lineage (Chapter 5). What all have in common to some extent, however, is their dynamic process of adaptation to the new requirements and the new opportunities of the modern world.

GURU AS EXPERT

The changing function and status of the guru is intimately and dialogically linked to changes in the understanding and practice of yoga itself in the modern, globalized world. Similarly, a semantic shift has occurred in the usage of the term *guru* in the English language over the past century. Indeed, the phenomenon of the transnational Indian guru has itself brought into being its own global spiritual nomenclature, which Srinivas Aravamudan (2006) has labeled *Guru English*. To some extent, the new, predominant meaning of guru in popular English-language culture has displaced older significations, in turn (arguably) altering expectations of what it is to be a guru. The Oxford English

Dictionary tells us that guru means "a Hindu spiritual teacher or head of a religious sect. Also in gen. or trivial use: an influential teacher; a mentor; a pundit" (http://www.oed.com, accessed March 1, 2012). The first sense is the one that we might expect to be intended in a scholarly work on yoga (such as this one), and indeed many of the gurus treated in this book are arguably *Hindu spiritual teachers* or heads of *a religious sect*. However, this is by no means always the case: some do not even consider their work *religious* (see, e.g., Chapter 15 in this volume), and nor do they necessarily self-identify as Hindu (see, e.g., Chapter 10 in this volume).

Indeed, some modern gurus most certainly embody features of the guru closer to the second definition of the term—which introduces a fundamental ambiguity into the role and purpose of the guru in the world of modern yoga. Clearly, today's *general/trivial* sense of the word can apply to virtually any field of endeavor and is by no means limited to the spiritual or religious domains. There are parenting gurus, lifestyle gurus, design gurus, computer gurus, business gurus, fitness gurus, sex gurus, and golf gurus. Like another English loanword from the Sanskrit, pundit (Skt. *paṇḍita*, cited, rather confusingly, as part of the OED's second definition of guru), a guru is "an expert in a particular subject or field, *esp.* one frequently called upon to give his or her opinion to the public" (http://www.oed.com, accessed March 1, 2012). These leaders are not necessarily expected to make pronouncements on religious or spiritual matters, although they may. This sense of the word is a metonym of the original, primary meaning, connoting the privileged understanding and authority supposed of the Indian guru, albeit transposed into the secular realm and limited often to purely technological knowledge.

But if the prominence of Indian gurus in the modern world (and ideas about what they do) has given rise to this colloquial English usage, it is also true that the colloquial usage can help us think through what it means to be a guru of modern yoga. In other words, the semantic associations of the word in contemporary, popular parlance—one possessed of technological efficiency and expertise, whose ideas and vision have become influential or authoritative and who can offer definitive advice—may also illuminate the range of functions that the yoga guru is expected to fulfill. The website http://theyogaguru.com (accessed January 12, 2012) presents an eye-catching example. It is the online home of the New Delhi–based Holistic Healthcare Foundation, whose team offers classes and courses on power yoga, corporate yoga, health yoga, kids yoga, call center yoga,[2] dance yoga, dynamic meditation, and memory power development. The founder of the organization, yoga guru Dr. Mohan Kumar, is currently engaged in "Ph.D.-level research" on "yogic science for chronic management with side benefits" and possesses an MA in yoga science, diplomas in yogic science, Scientology, Silva Method of Mind Power, "and other various intensive training programs on yoga and naturopathy" (http://theyogaguru.com/mohanji.htm, accessed January 12, 2012). *Yoga gurus* in this model are presented as highly trained instructors or physicians whose technological expertise makes them eminently qualified to teach. The emphasis is firmly on the scientific demonstrability of yoga's efficacy. What is more, the various classes are clearly inspired by trends in yoga that were developed and popularized in the West (in particular the United States) and that are increasingly influencing Indian conceptions of the place and purpose of yoga (to say nothing of its dress codes). The guru here is the lifestyle coach, personal trainer, and alternative health practitioner who may offer spiritual advice but is authorized by essentially nonmystical, rational-scientific knowledge. Thus, the modern yoga guru may operate in the space between the traditional, Indic sense of the word and the colloquial English one.

ABUSES

The problem of what constitutes a guru, and in particular a yoga guru, is a pressing one. The globalization of yoga has expanded the guru's sphere of influence beyond the boundaries of his or her own immediate cultural community into milieus where the religious affiliations, function, status, and role of the guru may not be well understood—indeed where he or she may also be a stranger. This is surely a significant contributing factor in the many infamous conflicts and abuses that have dogged guru organizations in the West and in India during the twentieth and twenty-first centuries. Examples are numerous and familiar and, it would seem, ongoing, even within the arguably secularized domain of popular, mainstream yoga.[3] Indeed, during the first third of 2012, just prior to the submission of this manuscript to Oxford University Press, there were two more high-profile guru scandals, this time involving American teachers of (respectively) Indian and Tibetan tantra, one of whom had previously been selected as the topic of a chapter for this book.[4] And some months later (October 1, 2012) a new scandal emerged around Kausthub Desikachar, grandson of the legendary modern yoga guru T. Krishnamacharya (Chapter 4, this volume) and head of the Krishnamacharya Healing and Yoga Foundation, who was accused of the sexual, mental, and emotional abuse of students dating back at least to 2007.

The blogosphere has been buzzing with discussion of how adherents of these particular systems, or, more generally, practitioners of yoga and meditation, can come to terms with these events, which in many ways recapitulate similar, famous scandals of the 1960s, '70s and '80s. Guru scandals have deepened the distrust of the guru system among many in the West. Guruship has been diagnosed as one way of assuming dangerous and insidious "masks of authoritarian power," to cite the subtitle of one well-known book on the topic (Kramer & Alsted, 1993), and gurus' "feet of clay" (to cite the title of another: Storr, 1996), have been extensively examined, psychoanalyzed, and criticized.

The rejection of gurus' authority on moral and rational grounds also has a strong history within modern India and includes such eminent figures and associations as the Brahmo Samaj (see Chapter 1 in this volume); Jiddu Krishnamurti (see Chapters 4 and 15 in this volume); the Indian Rationalist Association; and the novelist G. V. Desani (see Chapter 15 in this volume). A strong anti-guru critique also prevails in certain quarters of the press in India today, which often takes particular umbrage at the enormous wealth accumulated by some.[5] Abuses by gurus are not generally the focus of the chapters in this book—although some gurus, such as Sathya Sai Baba, discussed in Chapter 12, and Swami Muktananda, discussed in Chapter 9, have indeed been at the center of major controversy, as has Kripalu's disciple Amrit Desai (discussed in Chapter 8 in this volume; see also Goldberg, 2013). It is nonetheless important to acknowledge that for many in Asia and the West today the guru system has come to appear bankrupt, suspect, or intrinsically corrupt.

It may also be that modern egalitarianism and a strong ethos of self-sufficiency, coupled with a belief in *spiritual empiricism* (where one's own inner and outer experience is all that is needed to ascertain spiritual truth), also contributes to a mistrust of traditional roles of the guru as source, authority, and guarantor of success in the spiritual life. In the individualized realm of Protestant, nondenominational spirituality or of varieties of New Age religion, the guru may in fact be perceived as a threat or an impediment to the process of discovering *one's own truth*.[6] In the words of one Western spiritual seeker encountered in India by one of the editors, one doesn't need a guru because "G-U-R-U [Gee, you are you]." That is, ultimately one must rely upon oneself to find oneself. Such convictions are also prevalent in the teachings of some Western Protestant Buddhists, such as Stephen Bachelor (see Bachelor, 2010). For millions of yoga practitioners around the world today, it is neither necessary nor desirable to have a guru.

MODERN *BHAKTIYOGA*

An assumption is sometimes made that modern yoga has been formulated, standardized, and formatted in a singular or immediately recognizable way: that is to say, the *āsana*-based systems that De Michelis (2004) labels *Modern Postural Yoga*. However, as De Michelis herself makes clear, and as several of our authors ably demonstrate, yoga's various expressions in the modern world cannot be reduced to single monolithic model.[7] The modern development of *bhaktiyoga* (the yoga of intense personal devotion to a guru or god) and *karmayoga* (the "yoga of action", sometimes used synonymously in modern parlance with *sevā*, to mean humanitarian service or engaged practice) are particularly interesting examples. Although often arguably at odds with what is traditionally designated by these terms, such forms allow dedicated practitioners to embrace the teachings of their gurus and to engage in meritorious and charitable acts. To regard modern expressions of yoga only in terms of global forms of posture practice would be to ignore the massive popular growth of *bhaktiyoga* in modern India and the globalized world and to significantly underestimate its profound influence and widespread appeal. Thus, we have made a conscious choice to include several gurus who exemplify the modern traditions of *bhaktiyoga* and *karmayoga* (see Chapter 11 by Kim, Chapter 12 by Srinivas, and Chapter 14 by Warrier in this volume).

CHAPTER OVERVIEW

The chapters in Part 1 examine three of the founding fathers of the modern yoga renaissance: Swami Vivekananda, Sri Aurobindo, and Shri Yogendra. In Chapter 1, Dermot Killingley considers Swami Vivekananda (1863–1902), whose decision to "manufacture yogis" in the United States set the scene for a new global culture of yoga. Local demand for yoga was high, but Vivekananda maintained a critical (and selective) relationship to it. Drawing principally on certain parts of the *Yogasūtras*, and on the *Bhagavad Gītā*, Vivekananda developed two recurrent and interrelated themes: a hierarchy of religions and a distinctive interpretation of the theory of evolution. The inclusion of this chapter comes at a pivotal time as organizations throughout India celebrate the 150th anniversary of Vivekananda's birth. In Chapter 2, Ann Gleig and Charles Flores take as their starting point the scholarly neglect of Sri Aurobindo (1872–1950) and demonstrate the important impacts that he has had on the contemporary yoga climate. The chapter considers the status of physical culture and *haṭhayoga* in his Integral Yoga system, before examining the influence that his *close* and *creative* lineages have had on modern yoga generally. Joseph Alter, in Chapter 3, examines the *magic and modernity* of Shri Yogendra (1897–1989), who was among the first to develop a system of modern yoga physical education in the early 1920s, combining yogic knowledge from his guru with an understanding of contemporary physical culture acquired during several years in New York. While rejecting yoga's superstitious past, he nonetheless invoked the potential of yoga's supernatural power and the authority of mystical gnosis. In this way, he embodies many of the contradictions of the modern yoga guru.

Part 2 examines the lineage of Tirumalai Krishnamacharya (1888–1989), whose enormous effect on the popular Western practice of yoga was mainly due to his influential disciples. In Chapter 4, Mark Singleton and Tara Fraser examine the life and later teachings of Krishnamacharya, as mainly refracted through the writing and teaching of his son, T. K. V. Desikachar (1938–). Krishnamacharya's vision of religious universalism for yoga exists in a complex tension with his profound commitment to his native Śrīvaiṣṇavism. This latter is reflected in the significant elements of *bhaktiyoga* which pervade his yoga teaching. Jean Byrne (Chapter 5) considers the early Krishnamacharya disciple and founder of the popular system of Ashtanga Vinyasa Yoga, Sri K. Pattabhi Jois (1915–2009). Permission to teach in this system (known as *authorization* or *certification*) comes through a direct blessing from the guru rather than as a result of completing a standardized teacher training course (otherwise common in many schools of Modern Postural Yoga). This, argues Byrne, makes Ashtanga as taught by Jois a unique guru *paramparā* within modern yoga. In Chapter 6, Frederick Smith and Joan White examine the career of B. K. S. Iyengar (1918–) as a *yoga guru*. The chapter considers the formation and development of Iyengar's career as a yoga teacher; the influences beyond his teacher, T. Krishnamacharya; his self-perception as a student, teacher, and acclaimed guru; the transformations in his reception as a yoga teacher, master, and guru; and his literary output. In Chapter 7, Suzanne Newcombe compares Iyengar with a less well-known transnational guru, Yogini Sunita (1932–1970), who taught yoga in Britain during the 1960s. This chapter explores how the guru–*śiṣya* (disciple) relationship was institutionalized within a highly bureaucratic, state-funded adult education system, arguing that Sunita failed to create a lasting body of popular yoga because she did not establish institutional structures around her charismatic teachings.

Part 3 considers three influential figures within transnational yoga who have taught within a tantric framework. In Chapter 8, Ellen Goldberg examines the extraordinary life of Swami Kṛpālvānanda, also known as Kripalu (1913–1981), who inspired a transnational community of devotees when his disciple Amrit Desai (1932–) brought him into international prominence in 1977. Goldberg stresses the importance of three core tantric elements in Kripalu's approach that are not typically seen in other schools of modern yoga, namely, *śaktipāt dīkṣā* (defined in the Kripalu community as initiation through the awakening of *śakti* or *prāṇa*); *prāṇayoga sādhanā*; and the attainment of divine body. The publication date of this book coincides with the 100th anniversary of Kripalu's birth. Andrea Jain, in Chapter 9, analyzes Swami Muktananda (1908–1982) as an *entrepreneurial godman*. Jain argues that it was by packaging his religious organization, *Siddha Yoga,* in the accessible form of the Intensive and by actively marketing *śaktipāt* (direct, mystical transmission: lit. descent of power) to mass audiences in the 1970s that Muktananda successfully attracted thousands of spiritual seekers. Though revelations about Muktananda's tantric sexual practices damaged Siddha Yoga's image, the movement survived largely because of strategies to maintain a positive vision of Muktananda. In Chapter 10, Lola Williamson considers John Friend, founder of Anusara Yoga, who established a spiritual system based on rituals of the body that create a sense of community and provide meaning to individuals who have abandoned traditional religion. The chapter considers his role as a modern guru (or, as he refers to himself, an *ācārya*) and explains how

Friend's encouragement of networks of teachers and practitioners helped to establish a tantra-based philosophy and practice in America as well as other countries.

Part 4 considers *bhaktiyoga*. Chapter 11, by Hanna Kim, examines the life of Pramukh Swami Maharaj (b. 1921), current head of the Swaminarayan (Svāminārāyaṇa) organization. Kim explores the relationship of the devotee to guru and to God in the Bochasanwasi Shri Akshar Purushottam Swaminarayan Sanstha (BAPS) and shows that according to the devotees the guru represents god incarnate. Next, in Chapter 12 Smriti Srinivas examines the life of Sathya Sai Baba, who died during the preparation of this book (1926–April 24, 2011). Srinivas argues that at least two different uses of yoga are refracted within Sathya Sai Baba's teachings and writings. These refractions also intersect with other histories, social movements, teachers, and their practices (including Theosophy and Buddhism), creating a wide terrain of significance and giving vitality to theories and practices of yoga in the contemporary world. The Swaminarayan organization and the Satya Sai Baba movement place absolute emphasis on the guru whose living presence provided seekers with a tangible and humanly recognizable template for how to achieve the ontological goal of being in constant communion with the guru through *bhaktiyoga*.

The two chapters in Part 5, Chapter 13 by Joanne Punzo Waghorne and Chapter 14 by Maya Warrier, consider mediation of the guru–student relationship by technology. The setting for Chapter 13 is Singapore, where two gurus—Sri Sri Ravi Shankar (1956–) and Sadhguru Jaggi Vasudev (1957–)—and their organizations offer courses on yoga techniques. Singapore—cosmopolitan, multiethnic, and increasingly the model for development in Asia—presents a fascinating case study of new contexts and new packaging for yogic techniques that offer practical solutions for life in the new fast-paced urban Asia. Chapter 14 (which might equally have been placed in the section on *bhaktiyoga*,) explores the online expression and experience of *bhaktiyoga* in the modern, transnational, devotional enterprise centered on the popular globetrotting guru Mata Amritanandamayi (1953–). It examines the ways this organization uses its vast cyber network to reinforce devotion to the guru and to cement guru–devotee attachment across vast geographical distances. The Internet sustains, enhances, and intensifies devotional experience and gives an immediacy and intimacy to the devotee's engagement with an often physically absent, but always virtually present, guru.

Finally, Part 6 considers two politicized gurus for whom nation-building is a component part of yoga practice. In Chapter 15 Gwilym Beckerlegge examines the role of Eknath Ranade (1914–1982), founder of the lay, service-oriented spiritual movement the Vivekananda Kendra. Ranade determined that yoga should be at the core of the Kendra's activities. Beckerlegge explores the transmission of yoga within the Kendra in relation to its categorization as a *sevā* activity; the role of Eknath Ranade, who was in many respects highly critical of guru culture; and the movement's reliance on its cadre of life workers in promoting its vision of the so-called yoga way of life. In Chapter 16, Stuart Sarbacker considers the controversial contemporary guru, Swami Ramdev (1965–), a central figure in contemporary Indian spirituality and politics. Launched into celebrity status through a popular cable television series, Swami Ramdev has brought the theory and practice of yoga to India and the world on an unprecedented scale. Sarbacker provides an overview of Swami Ramdev's life, philosophy, and social activism, arguing that he can be understood as a modern yoga revolutionary, committed to the transformation of the Indian people, the Indian nation, and ultimately the world through yoga.

REFERENCES

Alter, Joseph, S. 2004. *Yoga in Modern India: The Body between Science and Philosophy*. Princeton, NJ: Princeton University Press.

———. 2008. Yoga *Shivir*: Performativity and the Study of Modern Yoga. In Mark Singleton and Jean Byrne (eds.), *Yoga in the Modern World: Contemporary Perspectives*. London: Routledge, pp. 36–48.

Aravamudan, Srinivas. 2006. *Guru English: South Asian Religion in a Cosmopolitan Language*. Princeton, NJ: Princeton University Press.

Bachelor, Stephen. 2010. *Confession of a Buddhist Atheist*. New York: Spiegel & Grau.

Berger, Peter. 1979. *The Heretical Imperative: Continuous Possibilities of Religious Affiliation*. Garden City, NY: Anchor Books.

Bellah, Robert N. 2011. *Religion in Human Evolution: From the Paleolithic to the Axial Age*. Cambridge, Mass: Harvard University Press.

Bharati, Agehananda. 1976. *The Light at the Center: Context and Pretext of Modern Mysticism*. Santa Barbara, CA: Ross-Erikson.

De Michelis, Elizabeth. 2004. *A History of Modern Yoga: Patañjali and Western Esotericism*. London: Continuum.

———. 2008. Modern Yoga, History and Forms. In Mark Singleton and Jean Byrne (eds.), *Yoga in the Modern World: Contemporary Perspectives*. London: Routledge, pp. 17–35.

Goldberg, Ellen. 2009. Medieval *Haṭhayoga Sādhana*: An Indigeneous South Asian Biotherapeutic Model for Health, Healing and Longevity. *Acta Orientalia* 70: 93–109.

———. 2013. Amrit Desai and the Kripalu Center for Yoga and Holistic Health. In Lola Williamson and Ann Gleig (eds.), *Homegrown Gurus: From Hinduism in America to American Hinduism*. Albany: State University of New York Press, pp. 63–86.

Hanegraaff, Wouter J. 1998. *New Age Religion and Western Culture*. New York: State University of New York Press.

Hayes, Glen Alexander. 2003. Metaphoric Worlds and Yoga in the Vaiṣṇava Sahajiyā Tantric Traditions of Medieval Bengal. In Ian Whicher and David Carpenter (eds.), *Yoga, The Indian Tradition*. London: RoutledgeCurzon, pp. 162–184.

Heelas, Paul. 1996. *The New Age Movement: the Celebration of the Self and the Sacralization of Modernity*. Oxford: Blackwell.

———. 2008. *Spiritualities of Life: New Age Romanticism and Consumptive Capitalism*. Malden, MA: Blackwell.

Levi-Strauss, Claude. 1966. *The Savage Mind*. Chicago: University of Chicago Press.
Kramer, Joel and Diana Alstad. 1993. *The Guru Papers: Masks of Authoritarian Power*. Berkeley, CA: Frog, Ltd.
McKean, L. 1996. *Divine Enterprise: Gurus and the Hindu Nationalist Movement*. Chicago: University of Chicago Press.
Mlecko, Joel D. 1982. The Guru in Hindu Tradition. *Numen* 29 (1): 33–61.
Newcombe, Suzanne. 2009. The Development of Modern Yoga: A Survey of the Field. *Religious Compass* 3: 1–17.
Padoux, André. 2000. The Tantric Guru. In David Gordon White (ed.), *Tantra in Practice*. Princeton: Princeton University Press, pp. 41–51.
Paglia, Camille. 2003. Cults and Cosmic Consciousness: Religious. Vision in the American 1960s. *Arion* 10 (3): 57–111.
Palmer, David A. 2012. Introduction: The Daoist Encounter with Modernity. In David A. Palmer and Xun Liu (eds.), *Daoism in the Twentieth Century: Between Eternity and Modernity*. Berkeley: University of California, pp. 1–22.
Puttick, E. 1995. Sexuality, Gender and the Abuse of Power in the Master–Disciple Relationship: The Case of the Rajneesh Movement. *Journal of Contemporary Religion* 10(1): 29–40.
Rochford, E. Burke, Jr. 2007. *Hare Krishna Transformed*. New York: New York University Press.
Roof, Wade Clark. 1999. *Spiritual Marketplace: Baby Boomers and the Remaking of American Religion*. Princeton, NJ: Princeton University Press.
Singleton, M. 2005. Salvation through Relaxation: Proprioceptive Therapy in Relation to Yoga. *Journal of Contemporary Religion* 20 (3): 289–304.
———. 2007. Modern Yoga. In D. Cush, C. Robinson, and M. York (eds.), *Encyclopedia of Hinduism*. London: Curzon-Routledge, pp. 1033–1038.
———. 2010a. *Yoga Body, the Origins of Modern Posture Practice*. New York: Oxford University Press.
———. 2010b. Modern Yoga. In Knut A. Jacobsen (ed.) *Encyclopedia of Hinduism*. Leiden: Brill, pp. 782–788.
Singleton, Mark and Jean Byrne. 2008. *Yoga in the Modern World: Contemporary Perspectives*. London: Routledge Hindu Studies Series.
Storr, Anthony. 1996. *Feet of Clay, a Study of Gurus*. London: Harper-Collins.
Strauss, Sarah. 2005. *Positioning Yoga: Balancing Acts across Cultures*. Oxford: Berg.
Tamm, Jayanti. 2010. *Cartwheels in a Sari, A Memoir of Growing up Cult*. New York: Three Rivers Press.
White, David Gordon. 1996. *The Alchemical Body, Siddha Traditions in Medieval India*: Chicago: University of Chicago Press.
———. 2000a. (ed.) *Tantra in Practice*. Princeton: Princeton University Press
———. 2000b. Introduction. In David Gordon White (ed.) *Tantra in Practice*. Princeton: Princeton University Press, pp. 3–40.

NOTES

1. The academic study of modern yoga has burgeoned over the past ten years or so, and while we do not have space to summarize that work here readers interested in finding out more about the field might begin by reading the introductory articles and chapters in De Michelis (2008); Newcombe (2009), and Singleton (2007; 2010b) and the foundational books Alter (2004); De Michelis (2004); Strauss (2005), and

Singleton and Byrne (2008a). More resources for the study of modern yoga can be found at http://modernyogaresearch.org.

2. This service is for the many young people in the Delhi area who are employed in call center work, which is, according to the website, resulting in "rising cases of spondilitis [sic], hypertension, insomnia, fatigue, nausea, chronic headache, coronary malfunctions, back pain, computer syndrome and dry eyes" (http://theyogaguru.com/callcenter.htm, accessed January 12, 2012). These complaints cause increased absences from work, which could, claims the website, be reduced through the practice of yoga: "It is scientifically proved that yoga makes call center's employees healthy, productive and alert, taking less medical leaves" (ibid.). This seems a particularly poignant intersection of corporate capital's demand for global outsourcing and the reconfiguration of yoga as a component part of the international (tele-) service industry. It also recapitulates the way that yoga and relaxationism were conceptualized and used by white-collar Americans in the early twentieth century as a means to increase worker efficiency (see Singleton, 2005).
3. See, for example, Kramer and Alsted (1993), Paglia (2003); Puttick (1995), Rochford (2010), and Storr (1996). The website http://strippingthegurus.com, while not an academic source, has useful references for further investigation. Thanks to Suzanne Newcombe for this reference.
4. These were John Friend, founder of Anusara Yoga (see Chapter 10 by Williamson in this volume), and Geshe Michael Roach. For a timeline of the Friend scandals, see http://www.yogadork.com/news/running-timeline-of-anusara-controversy-updates-and-teacher-resignations/ (accessed May 25, 2012). On Michael Roach, see the article by Matthew Remski: http://www.elephantjournal.com/2012/05/psychosis-stabbing-secrecy-and-death-at-a-neo-buddhist-university-in-arizona (accessed May 4, 2012).
5. For example, http://www.siliconindia.com/news/general/SuperRich-Spiritual-Gurus-of-India-nid-110419-cid-1.html (accessed May 25, 2012). See also http://www.indiansceptic.in/index.htm (accessed May 25, 2012). Thanks to Suzanne Newcombe for this reference.
6. See, for example, Jayanti Tamm's (2010) memoir of growing up as a disciple of Indian guru Sri Chinmoy before breaking free. In a newspaper interview, Tamm emphasizes, "It's about finding one's own truth. This is my experience; this is my truth." From http://www.rickross.com/reference/srichinmoy/srichinmoy46.html (accessed May 30, 2012). On New Age as a category, see Hanegraaff (1998) and Heelas (1996, 2008).
7. De Michelis's (2004) other types are Modern Psychosomatic Yoga, Modern Meditational Yoga, and Modern Denominational Yoga (188). For De Michelis, the guru is a predominant feature of only one of her four categories: Modern Denominational Yoga, which "was a later development that seems to have got fully underway only during the 1960s with the appearance of more ideologically engaged Neo-Hindu *gurus* and groups that incorporated elements of Modern Yoga teachings" (p. 189).

PART ONE

Key Figures in Early Twentieth-Century Yoga

CHAPTER 1

Manufacturing Yogis: Swami Vivekananda as a Yoga Teacher

DERMOT KILLINGLEY

INTRODUCTION

Swami Vivekananda (1863–1902), the first teacher of yoga in the West, has been called "the creator of fully-fledged Modern Yoga" (De Michelis, 2004: 90). The words *creator* and *modern* are significant; he did not simply bring yoga from India to the West. He had not been trained in any yoga school, and much of what he said about yoga was developed when he was already in the West. To say this is not to question his authenticity, still less his sincerity, but to point out the complexity of his position in the history of Indian and Western thought and of modern yoga. Before discussing his yoga teaching in detail, we need to look at the circumstances in which it took place: his background in India and his career in the West, starting with the Parliament of Religions in Chicago in September 1893. We should also consider what was already known and thought about yoga in the West, particularly in the United States.

VIVEKANANDA'S LIFE

Vivekananda was born in 1863 among the English-educated bourgeoisie of Calcutta (now Kolkata). His birth name was Narendranath Datta; but he is referred to throughout this chapter as Vivekananda, the monastic name by which he was known when he went to America and for the rest of his life. Soon after he graduated from Calcutta University in 1884, the sudden death of his father, a successful lawyer, plunged the family into poverty, with Vivekananda

Figure 1.1:
Photo portrait of Vivekananda. (Courtesy of WikiCommons.)

as its head. He became a follower of the uncouth but influential saint Ramakrishna (1836?–1886). After Ramakrishna's death, Vivekananda and some other followers became *saṃnyāsins*, and from 1888 to 1893 he wandered through India. In June 1893 he sailed for the United States, where he spoke at the Parliament of Religions in Chicago (Seager, 1995). After his success there, he toured America, giving lectures on Hinduism and building a following, mainly in New York. In August 1895 he sailed to London and gave talks there, returning in December. In April 1896 he sailed again to London; in December he sailed to India, landing in Colombo on January 15, 1897. In May he organized his followers into the Ramakrishna Mission in Belur Maṭh, Calcutta. In 1899 he again visited London and the States, returning in December 1900 to Belur, where he died in 1902.

VIVEKANANDA'S BACKGROUND

Calcutta in the nineteenth century was a marketplace of ideas, offering many of the wares that were current in the British Isles and North America. This was made possible through developments in communications, including printing, steam travel by rail and sea, and changes in the use of vernacular languages. These, together with the growing class of people familiar with English, made possible the all-India lecture tours of the Brahmo Samaj leader Keshub Chunder Sen (1838–1884),[1] his associate Pratap Chandra Mozoomdar (1840–1905), and later Vivekananda.

The education system, in which English was the dominant language, provided a body of knowledge with which a limited, largely urban public could be expected to be more or less familiar. At the same time, communication with India's past was facilitated by philological and archeological research, the printing of Sanskrit and other Indian language texts, translations into European languages, and historical and literary studies. The Buddha and his teachings, which had been known mainly to *paṇḍits* through the refutations found in brahmanical literature, became a serious option for religious seekers.

Like many of his class, Vivekananda spoke and read Bengali and English; he was also fluent in Sanskrit. He became one of the most successful exporters of Indian ideas in modern times, reaching a wider market than his predecessors such as Rammohun Roy or even Keshub. Demand in the English-speaking world, especially the United States and England, for wisdom from the East—which often meant India, the eastern country with which the United Kingdom was most closely connected politically and intellectually—led to his success. This demand motivated the Parliament of Religions of 1893, where Vivekananda had his first public success in the West. "The dichotomy between East and West was an organizing principle" for Vivekananda (Brekke, 2002: 48), but *East* here is hardly a geographical term: he came to Chicago from the west, across the Pacific.

VIVEKANANDA, KESHUB, AND RAMAKRISHNA

As a student, Vivekananda was a member of the Brahmo Samaj, and like other Brahmos he was drawn to Ramakrishna. When his father died, Vivekananda's responsibilities included performing rituals for the dead. This led to a religious struggle within him, since the Samaj condemned these rituals in their traditional form. He turned again to Ramakrishna and became his close follower.

Vivekananda presents himself as Ramakrishna's foremost disciple, authorized by him to give his message to the world, and deriving his doctrines from him. He refers to him repeatedly as his Master, and attributes all his own achievements to him (*The Complete Works of Swami Vivekananda* [hereafter *CW*]: 3.312). In particular, Vivekananda attributes to him several recurrent motifs of his own teaching. One such motif is the harmony not only of all the doctrinal traditions of India (*CW:* 3.233 3.348; 4.107), but of all religions of the world (*CW:* 6.469); these are all paths to the same goal, as Ramakrishna himself has experienced by trying them all in turn (*CW:* 8.79). Another such motif is the use of *advaita vedānta* as the key to reconciling conflicting doctrines; another is the moral imperative to help the poor. This view of the relation of Vivekananda's teachings to those of Ramakrishna is presented in the biographies published by the twin organizations that carry on Vivekananda's work: the Ramakrishna Math and the Ramakrishna Mission.

Critical studies have shown that this view presents an inadequate picture of the personality and influence of Ramakrishna (Neevel, 1976) and of the sources of Vivekananda's ideas (Beckerlegge, 2000; De Michelis, 2004: 91–110). It is especially questioned whether *advaita vedānta*, which for Vivekananda is the ultimate truth underlying all Hindu traditions and all the religions of the world, was the basis of Ramakrishna's thought, and whether Ramakrishna set any value on social action, which is important in the work of the Maṭh and Mission, though Vivekananda's own attitude to it was ambivalent. His thought owes much to the Brahmo Samaj and perhaps even to Freemasonry, which he also joined in his youth (De Michelis, 2004: 97–100). Later, he despised the Brahmos for their conformity to British ways of thinking (*CW:* 8.477-8), and regarded Mozoomdar, who represented the Samaj at the Parliament, as an obstacle to his work in the States (*CW:* 5.31; 6.282). When writing for a Bengali readership, he could nevertheless count the Brahmo Samaj among the great religious movements of India (*CW:* 4.462f.). He contrasted Keshub unfavorably with Ramakrishna (*CW:* 7.16), and the biographies published by the Ramakrishna movement follow him in emphasizing the role of Ramakrishna in his development, at the expense of the Brahmo Samaj. But, as we shall see, some of his ideas match Keshub's, and he presented them in an idiom which Keshub would have recognized, but which Ramakrishna, even if he had known English, would not.

Vivekananda takes liberties with his own biography. In a talk in California in September 1900, for instance, he describes how, when he was about sixteen (*CW:* 8.79), he and a "handful of boys" gathered at the feet of Ramakrishna, "an old man," and were inspired by him to work for "Universal religion" and to have "great sympathy for the poor." But "then came the sad day when our old teacher died" (*CW:* 8.80). Next comes the death of Vivekananda's father. Vivekananda, standing between the "two worlds" of his destitute family and his bereft band of young monks, with their task "for the good of India and the world," found sympathy only from Ramakrishna's widow Sarada (*CW:* 8.81). There followed ten years of wandering, after which he determined to go to Chicago (*CW:* 8.84-5).

The chronology of this touching story is skewed at several points. Ramakrishna was hardly old: he was forty-five, or at most forty-eight, when Vivekananda first met him, and fifty to fifty-three when he died.[2] Vivekananda was not sixteen but eighteen at their first meeting, and twenty-one when he became a full-time follower. That was after his father died, contrary to what his narrative implies. The interval between Ramakrishna's death on August 16, 1886, and Vivekananda's embarkation on June 30, 1893, allows less than seven years of wandering, not ten. (In an earlier speech he claims to have "travelled twelve years all over India"

(*CW:* 3.226).) The chronological liberties entail others: it was to Ramakrishna, not to Sarada, that Vivekananda turned when his father died.

These inaccuracies can be excused by the context: Vivekananda was giving a talk, not writing an autobiography. He had intended to talk about *vedānta* but had been asked instead to talk about his work and what he had been doing. This, he says, is not such an interesting subject to him as to his hearers: "this will have been the first time in my life that I have spoken on that subject" (*CW:* 8.73). This disarming introduction, which itself takes some autobiographical liberties,[3] provides some excuse for lack of precision. The same excuse applies to most of his published works: they are talks taken down by others, and their structure is rhetorical rather than logical. They move quickly from one point to another, as the argument requires, explaining no more than is needed in the context. The context includes the cultural background of the audience, so that Vivekananda says different things to Indian, America and British audiences. Often the same point appears differently in different talks, and we need to compare several versions, each presenting the same point in incomplete form, to understand his argument. As a student he had been omnivorous rather than thorough or methodical (De Michelis, 2004: 96), and this trait appears in his works.

Keshub had already met Ramakrishna in 1875, and it was through the Brahmo Samaj that Vivekananda came to know him in 1881. Keshub's meeting with Ramakrishna prompted an increasing acceptance of Hindu ideas and practices, as shown by his speeches during the last nine years of his life. Vivekananda confesses that he used to object to idolatry—a typically Brahmo attitude—until he learned otherwise from Ramakrishna (*CW:* 3.218). It was Ramakrishna, too, who won him over to the worship of Kālī, after six years of struggle against it (*CW:* 8.263).[4]

In several ways, Vivekananda's methods resemble Keshub's. Both were flamboyant characters who used their gifts for music and drama in their preaching. Both used the opportunities presented by steam travel within India and overseas, by the English language, and by the familiarity of their hearers with some features of Western secular thought, Christianity, various Hindu traditions, and to some extent Buddhism and Islam. Both believed that social problems could be solved only by spiritual means. Both were speakers rather than writers, and their published works have to be examined as rhetoric rather than sustained argument. That is, each not only sets forth the ideas that are in his mind but also manipulates ideas that are already in the minds of his audience. These ideas include the polarity of spiritual East and material West, the harmony of religion and science, human potential, and evolution.

On the other hand, Keshub shows none of Vivekananda's fluency in Sanskrit and extensive knowledge of Sanskrit literature. Nor is he so concerned to anchor his teaching in Hindu tradition. While invoking elements from the Bible and European history as well as from India, he emphasizes the newness of his teaching and its freedom from any ethnic identity. Vivekananda, on the other hand, emphasizes the antiquity of his teaching and claims that while it is to be found in the original forms of all religions, only *vedānta* preserves it in its purity.

While Keshub's treatment of yoga is much more general than Vivekananda's, he gives it an important place. His "New Dispensation" is not only "the harmony of all scriptures and all saints and all sects . . . of reason and faith . . . of the east and the west"; it is also "the harmony of yoga and bhakti" (Scott, 1979: 344). He associates yoga with his own interpretation of the divinity of Jesus, which he says must be framed in Indian terms if Indians are to accept it. Accordingly, "Christ is a true Yogi, and he will surely help us realize our national ideal of a Yogi"; Chaitanya and Guru Nanak embody the same ideal (p. 215). The term *yogi* denotes not only what Christ is but also what his followers are to become. "He will come to you as self-surrender, as asceticism, as Yoga, as the life of God in man, as obedient and humble sonship" (p. 217). Keshub does not tell us with any precision what he means by *yoga*, but it seems that, like Vivekananda, he regards the meaning "join" of the root *yuj* as a key to it, indicating a union of the human with the divine. Yoga is communion (p. 266), and Christ's "life was one continued yoga or communion with the Heavenly Father" (p. 332). The crucifixion "means *Yoga* posture, humanity dead yet alive" (p. 295).

MISSION TO THE WEST

Vivekananda knew the Hindu tradition far more deeply than Keshub, and anchored his teaching much more securely in it. His need to do so follows both from his mission to the West and from the "plan of campaign" (*CW:* 3.207–227), which he announced on his return in 1897: to regenerate India using her own resources. In his first speech to the Parliament of Religions, he announced himself as representing "the most ancient order of monks in the world; . . . the mother of religions; and . . . millions and millions of Hindu people of all classes and sects" (*CW:* 1.3; cf. Chowdhury-Sengupta, 1998: 26). He had been included in the program of the Parliament only as a result of negotiations after his arrival in the States, but his lack of organizational backing marked him as genuinely and universally Hindu, unlike the Brahmo representative Mozoomdar, whose attendance had been arranged in advance.[5] Rather than question the use of the multivalent term *Hindu* to cover the various, sometimes conflicting, religious traditions of India, Vivekananda exploited it as standing for "a religion which has taught the world tolerance and universal acceptance" (*CW:* 1.3).

Vivekananda had not set out for the West with the intention of becoming a yoga teacher.[6] Indeed, he may not have intended to be a teacher at all; at the Parliament of Religions, and in his first lecture tours, he was not so much a teacher as an advocate. He became a teacher during his stay in the States, in response to the reception he found, and he developed his teaching during that time (Raychaudhuri, 1998; Burke, 1966; Killingley, 1998). It has been said that "he had to be an authentic Hindu even if it meant making it up as he went along" (Hatcher, 1999: 48). The idea of teaching yoga may have occurred to him in the course of that development; there is no indication of it in the speeches to the Parliament, or in the admittedly slight records from the time before he crossed the seas.

The evidence for Vivekananda's intentions in 1893 is not entirely clear, but in addition to going to the Parliament he wanted to raise funds for relief work in India (Raychaudhuri, 1998: 4). This is the aim he declared in a confrontational speech to the Parliament: "I came here to seek aid for my impoverished people, and I fully realised how difficult it was to get help for heathens from Christians in a Christian country" (*CW:* 1.20). On his return to India, he said again that he had gone not for the Parliament of Religions but out of a fervent desire to relieve the misery of his people (*CW:* 3.226). Though he eventually stayed in the West for three and a half years, he had not intended to be there for so long. However, after the Parliament ended in September 1893, he made well-paid lecture tours, arranged by an agency (Burke, 1992: 178–179) and reported in enthusiastic, if ill informed, newspaper stories. By March 1894 he was tiring of the lecture circuit, "mixing with hundreds of varieties of the human animal" and having to "suit anybody's or any audience's fads" (letter from Detroit, March 15, 1894, 302–3). Instead, he was "bent upon seeing a little of Boston and New York" (letter from Detroit, March 12, 1894, *CW:* 8.301), rightly expecting more select, stable, and discriminating audiences there. He was also driven by the hostility of the supporters of Christian missions, which grew vehement from late February 1894 (Burke, 1966: 289–313). Accordingly, he moved in April from the Midwest to the East Coast, and participated in the annual conference of liberal Christians in Greenacres, Maine (Jackson, 1994: 28).

From July 1894 he lectured independently to various groups that can be described as cultic:[7] Christian Scientists, Spiritualists, Theosophists, occultists (De Michelis, 2004: 112–119). His motives and impressions are partially revealed in his letters. He tells his fellow disciples in India that he is "the guest of big people here" and "a widely known man" (Bengali letter, summer 1894, *CW:* 6.291), but he is becoming wary of accepting hospitality, especially from the rich (letter from Fishkill Landing, New York, to Mrs. Hale, his "mother," as he called her, in Chicago, July 1894, *CW:* 8.314). The letters show that his purpose in America is shifting. In June 1894 he wrote to India that "primarily my coming has been to raise funds for an enterprise of my own": to "educate and raise the masses" of India (letter from Chicago, June 20, 1894, *CW:* 8.306). But in February 1895 he is "beginning to feel that the old sages were right" in forbidding *saṃnyāsins* to collect funds (letter to Mrs. Ole Bull, February 14, 1895, *CW:* 6.299). In April 1895 he was teaching a Jnana yoga class of 130 students and two other weekly yoga classes of 50 each; soon he would be going to the Thousand Islands (on the St. Lawrence River) to find peace and seclusion with a few of his students and to "manufacture a few 'Yogis'" (letter from New York to Mrs. Ole Bull, April 25, 1895, *CW:* 6.306). Such talks on yoga must have been undertaken in response to a growing American demand for spiritual practices and techniques that would yield results (De Michelis, 2004: 118).

In his letters of this period, Vivekananda seems uncertain about his course of action, sometimes worried about the nascent movement he has left behind in India, and giving detailed instructions to his fellow *saṃnyāsins* there about their work, their finances, and their health. About his own work he can be ambitious, flippant, and despondent by turns. "To tell you the truth, the more I am getting popularity and facility in speaking, the more I am getting fed up" (letter to the Hale sisters, March 12, 1894, *CW:* 8.301). Reading his speeches to the Parliament of Religions and the reports of their reception, one would hardly expect him six months later to show such lack of self-confidence or such a sense of still being a learner. Just as it cost Congress lakhs of rupees to keep Gandhi in poverty, as Sarojini Naidu observed, so it took much mothering by wealthy American ladies to support Vivekananda's manly self-reliance.

In 1895, writing from America to his brother disciples in India about the future expansion of their ashram, Vivekananda proposes "a big hall" for daily readings and classes, "one day for Yoga, a day for Bhakti, another for Jnâna, and so forth" (*CW:* 6.324), evoking the triad of yogas that, with the addition of *rājayoga*, recurs throughout his work. This suggests that his plans for India, as well as his teaching in the West, had been developing in the course of his American tour and in the light of his experience there. However, in his talks and writings in India after his return, there is little on yoga. Even in the "Lectures from Colombo to Almora" of 1897, in which, returning in triumph from the West, he sets out his visions for the regeneration of India, yoga and yogis receive only sporadic mention.[8] Though Aurobindo and Gandhi, in making *karmayoga* part of their schemes for national regeneration, were following Vivekananda (King, 1980: 51–53), he made remarkably little use of *karmayoga* in that context. Two of his talks on the *Bhagavad Gītā* (*BhG*)—one in Bengali in 1897 (*CW:* 4.102–110) and another in English in Calcutta in 1898 (*CW:* 5.246–249)—mention yoga frequently, as might be expected from their subject. But it appears on the whole that scheduled teaching on yoga was for export rather than home consumption.

YOGA IN THE WEST BEFORE VIVEKANANDA

The word *yoga* was already current in English by Vivekananda's time, not only in specialist literature. In 1843 the *Penny Cyclopædia* included an article on yoga (Vol. 27, p. 657), which begins by deriving the word from "the Sanscrit radical *yuj*, 'to join,'" and explaining it as "union with the universal spirit (*Paramâtma*)"—a similar *vedāntic* understanding of the word to Keshub's and Vivekananda's.[9] This was the usual explanation; it was not until 1925 that Edgerton's translation "discipline," justified by the contexts in which the word is used as well as by etymology, became generally available.[10] The word *yogi,* in various spellings, many reflecting the pronunciation *jogi*, had been current much longer, often with disreputable connotations.[11] However, until Vivekananda, yoga had been known in the West as an activity of the other, not as something to which Westerners might aspire. Even when Henry David Thoreau says that "rude and careless as I am, I would fain practice the *yoga* faithfully" and claims to be a yogi "to some extent, and at rare intervals,"[12] his claim is extravagant; he is making a trip to the fabled Orient in his head rather than reporting any actual practice.

Monier-Williams's *Indian Wisdom* (1875) describes yoga on the basis of Patañjali's *Yogasūtras* (*YS*), though he views it negatively as "a mere contrivance for getting rid of all thought" (p. 103) and adds accounts of the "physical mortifications . . . popularly connected with the Yoga system" (p. 103) and impelled by "faith in a false system" (p. 104). He also describes yoga as it appears in the *BhG*, treating it as an eclectic combination of *sāṃkhya*, yoga, *vedānta*, and *bhakti* (p. 137). He translates *yoga* in the *BhG* as "yoking" (p. 142, fn. 3), but follows the usual interpretation as referring to union with God. These passages, in a book intended to give "educated Englishmen . . . an insight into the mind, habits of thought, and customs of the Hindūs" (p. iii), provided an authoritative, though unsympathetic, statement of some aspects of the meaning of *yoga*. They offered no encouragement to take it up.

The Theosophical Society, founded by Helena Petrovna Blavatsky, did much to popularize Indian ideas and Sanskrit words, including the word *yoga*. However, it presented yoga as an occult science. A. P. Sinnett, an English journalist in India, taking his ideas from Blavatsky, described yoga as cultivated by a brotherhood of adepts to be found "all over the East" but mainly in Tibet (Sinnett, 1881: 24). The inaccessibility of Tibet and the relative inaccessibility of "the East" itself, not to mention its lack of geographical location, guaranteed the occult status of this science. Sinnett insists on the difference between yoga and "the loathsome asceticism of the ordinary Indian fakeer, the *yogi* of the woods and wilds" (p. 26). He also distinguishes between "*Hatti yog*" (*haṭhayoga*), which is "mere physical exercises," and "*Ragi yog*" (*rājayoga*), "which is approached by the discipline of the mind, and which leads to the higher altitudes of occultism" (p. 27). However, the Theosophical Society did not encourage the view that anyone, apart from Blavatsky herself and the remote brotherhood of Mahatmas in Tibet with whom she claimed to communicate, could become an adept, so for most Theosophists yoga remained an activity of the other (De Michelis, 2004: 118). Vivekananda repudiated such esoterism (e.g., *CW:* 1.134), insisting on the inherent potential of every person; this fit the ideas of self-improvement that were current in the American circles he addressed.

THE PLACE OF YOGA IN VIVEKANANDA'S MESSAGE

In the Ramakrishna movement, yoga is the practical teaching underpinned by *vedānta*; it is the means to the ultimate goal (Jackson, 1994: 71). Either of these terms could denote Vivekananda's teaching: the book published in

London as *Yoga Philosophy* (Vivekananda, 1896) was republished in the States as *Vedanta Philosophy*.[13] Since he regarded all forms of spiritual striving as yoga, his yoga teaching is not clearly divided from the rest of his teaching. More recent yoga classes have been filmed or ethnographically reported, but Vivekananda's are harder to describe. They are partially recorded in his *Complete Works*, in the form of talks taken down by his followers; after Vivekananda's return to the States from England in December 1895, this was done by the stenographer Josiah Goodwin (*Life of Swami Vivekananda by His Eastern and Western Disciples*, 1965 [hereafter *Life*]: 383).

Vivekananda's first attempt to "manufacture" yogis (*CW:* 6.306, quoted previously) was at Thousand Island Park, the country retreat of his New York follower Miss Dutcher, from June 19 to August 6, 1895. Some talks given there were taken down by one of the participants, Miss S. E. Waldo, and published as "Inspired Talks" (*CW:* 7.3–104). However, because the course lasted several weeks and Miss Waldo found "it was not possible to take notes" (*Life*: 357; but see p. 361), this record is incomplete. The recorded talks include passages loosely based on the *YS* and the *BhG*—the two texts on which Vivekananda relied most for authority in his yoga teaching—and they also refer to other texts.[14] However, they range over many topics, which are developed elsewhere in his works. He taught that all paths lead to "the Whole" (*CW:* 7.6); all prophets teach the same (*CW:* 7.17); Spirit is omnipresent (*CW:* 7.7); truth is beyond books (*CW:* 7.9, 53); truth is within each of us, needing only to be uncovered (*CW:* 7.20, 34, 54, 71); and our efforts cannot benefit the world (*CW:* 7.102) but they benefit ourselves (*CW:* 7.9). He expounded Śaṅkara's commentary on the *Vedānta Sūtra* (*CW:* 7.32) and spoke extensively of Ramakrishna (*CW:* 7.23–25) and of the Goddess (*CW:* 7.26) and here and there of the Buddha and Jesus.

Evidently the manufacture of yogis is not a routine process; indeed, any sort of routine would be contrary to Vivekananda's soteriology as well as his temperament, since the ways to perfection are countless and should be chosen to suit the needs of different people. His classes would hardly be recognized as yoga classes today: as far as we can see, his students sat on chairs in their ordinary clothes.[15] Even in *Râja-Yoga,* posture receives only passing mention (*CW:* 1.137). If he had given them exercises in posture and breathing, his students would surely have mentioned such novelties, but what they report is the "blessed experience" (*Life:* 365), "fraught . . . with unusual opportunity for spiritual growth" (p. 357), of being in his presence and hearing him talk, not forgetting his cookery (pp. 361, 365).

Vivekananda's yoga classes, besides meeting an American demand, served an agenda of his own, which he had announced in Chicago: to show that conflict between religions could be resolved only by Hinduism, or more precisely by *advaita vedānta*—and not by Christianity, as some participants in the Parliament, including some of its organizers, supposed. In his first speech, after extolling Hinduism for its tolerance, he added, "We believe not only in universal toleration, but we accept all religions as true" (*CW:* 1.3). This acceptance, which goes beyond tolerance, he expresses in a free translation of *BhG* 4.11: "Whosoever comes to Me, through whatsoever form, I reach him; all men are struggling through paths which in the end lead to me."[16] He claims that this doctrine is vindicated by the Parliament itself. He contrasts this acceptance with "sectarianism, bigotry . . . fanaticism" (*CW:* 1.4).

In a later speech to the Parliament, he pursues the same theme in more detail. Hinduism embraces a hierarchy of religions, "from the high spiritual flights of the Vedanta philosophy . . . to the low ideas of idolatry" (*CW:* 1.6). The "common basis on which all these seemingly hopeless contradictions rest" (ibid.) is a belief in an infinite and immortal soul and a formless and almighty God, to be worshipped through love and *realized* (a keyword of modern Hinduism, found also in Keshub; De Michelis, 2004: 139) through the pure heart (pp. 1.10–13). "This is the common religion of all the sects of India" (p. 1.3). Before his concluding universal prayer and paean to the "motherland of liberty" (p. 1.20), he congratulates America on "proclaim[ing] to all quarters of the globe that the Lord is in every religion" (p. 1.19). Since this is the message he finds in Hinduism, he is in effect recruiting the Parliament of Religions itself to his cause.

Running through this speech are some of Vivekananda's recurrent ideas, which help to explain his interest in yoga. He claims that his approach, and Hinduism itself, is scientific: it recognizes "the laws of our mental constitution" (*CW:* 1.16) and "the plan of nature" (p. 1.17); the Vedas are not books but "the laws that govern the spiritual world" (p. 1.7); "science is nothing but the finding of unity"; physics seeks "one energy of which all the others are but manifestations" (p. 1.14); "manifestation, and not creation, is the word of science today," an allusion to the conservation of energy and conservation of mass that were axiomatic in the physics of the period. Moreover, this is what the Hindu "has been cherishing in his bosom for ages" (p. 1.15). Since everything is manifested, not created, perfection must be the manifestation of something that already existed as a potentiality. We are therefore not sinners but "heirs of immortal bliss" (*CW:* 1.11); perfection will be reached when the bondage of matter will burst (p. 1.12). This idea was incorporated in 1904 as one of the ten doctrines of the Vedanta Society of San Francisco (Jackson, 1994: 68). It also informs Vivekananda's version of evolution: every being contains in latent form, or *involved* as he termed it,[17] the being into which it will evolve. This version of evolution underlies the Hindu acceptance of all religious paths, whether high or low on the evolutionary scale. *Vedānta*, which is the true Hinduism, embraces *dvaita*—represented by Christianity and Islam—*viśiṣṭādvaita*, and *advaita*, which are "the three stages of spiritual growth in man" (letter to Alasinga, May 6, 1895, *CW:* 5.81).[18] The manufacture of yogis is a way to speed up the process of evolution, "to shorten the time for reaching perfection" (p. 1.157); Vivekananda's task in America is "to create a new order of humanity" (p. 5.82).

In assessing Vivekananda's role as a guru of yoga, we should notice that his attitude to such gurus is ambivalent. While he considers yoga useful, it is only as a means; the true end is *advaita vedānta*. He emphasizes Patañjali's view that yogic powers (*siddhi*) are an obstacle to *samādhi* (*YS* 3.38; Vivekananda, 1886: 197, corresponding to *CW:* 1.281), and he complains that the only yoga taught in Bengal is "the queer breathing exercises of the Hatha-Yoga—which is nothing but a kind of gymnastics" (letter to Akhandananda, *CW:* 6.233). In February–March 1890, he spent some time in Ghazipur, about 40 miles east of Varanasi, visiting a well-known ascetic, Pavhari Baba (p. 6.219). Later, he included stories about him in talks in the West and wrote a brief, largely homiletic, sketch of his life (pp. 4.283–295), describing him as "one of the greatest Masters [I have] loved and served" (p. 4.295). According to a talk in 1902, his intention in visiting him was to learn *haṭhayoga* (though at the time he had called him a "wonderful Raja-Yogi"; p. 6.233), for the purpose of "making this weak body strong," something he had not learned from Ramakrishna (p. 7.242). But Ramakrishna (who had died three and half years previously) repeatedly appeared to him, silently grieving; these visions dissuaded Vivekananda from taking initiation under "another Guru" (p. 7.243). In a letter written nearer the time, he merely said: "I shall not go to Pavhari Baba or any other saint—they divert one from his highest purpose" (Vivekananda to Saradananda and Kripananda, July 6, 1890, *CW:* 6.243). In recounting his visions, Vivekananda seems to repent of approaching Pavhari Baba as an act of disloyalty to Ramakrishna.

THE FOUR YOGAS

One theme of the "Inspired Talks" at Thousand Island Park is the set of four yogas, which runs through all Vivekananda's yoga teaching. Among the countless ways to perfection, these four have a special place: "every way is a kind of Yoga, but . . . Bhakti, Karma, Raja and Jnana-Yoga get over the ground more effectively" (*CW:* 7.71). Vivekananda sometimes uses other terms for these four. "Love [*bhakti*] is higher than work [*karma*], than [*rāja*] Yoga, than knowledge [*jñāna*]" (p. 7.9). This should not be read as a fixed hierarchical order. "The teaching must be modified according to the needs of the taught," which depend on tendencies molded in past lives. In each teaching situation one of the four yogas—"intellectual [*jñāna*], mystical [*rājayoga*], devotional [*bhakti*], [and] practical [*karma*]"—should be made the basis, but the others should also be taught (p. 7.98). As an epigraph to his book *Yoga Philosophy: Lectures on Râja Yoga,* he announces that the goal of manifesting "the divinity within" can be reached "either by work [*karma*], or worship [*bhakti*], or psychic control [*rājayoga*], or philosophy [*jñāna*], by one, or more, or all of these" (Vivekananda, 1896: v, reprinted in *CW:* 1.124).

The four yogas, like other features of Vivekananda's ideas, have a precedent in Keshub, who in 1876 classified his missionaries as "the *Yogi*, or the adept in rapt communion, the *Bhakta*, or the adept in rapturous love of God, the *Jnani*, or the earnest seeker of true knowledge and the *Shebak* [Skt. *sevaka* "server," i.e., the karma yogi]". Another report lists the four "departments" as yoga, gyān [*jñāna*], bhakti, and seba [*sevā*] or karma (De Michelis, 2004: 87).[19] "Yoga" in Keshub's terminology corresponds to "Raja Yoga" in Vivekananda's; Vivekananda himself sometimes uses "yoga" in this sense, as in the aforementioned quotation from *CW*: 7.9, and in the title *Yoga Philosophy*. (This is confusing, as "yoga" in Vivekananda, as also in the *BhG*, often stands for *karmayoga*.)

Among the four, "Raja Yoga" stands out as grammatically different, since unlike the others it cannot be shortened to "Raja." In Vivekananda's usage, and in modern yoga generally, it refers to the *YS* and its doctrines, which he interprets in terms of *advaita vedānta*. This identification, though it has roots in late medieval yoga literature (Birch, 2011: 543), was given currency by Dvivedi's (1885) *Rāja Yoga or the Practical Metaphysics of the Vedānta* and was further popularized by Theosophy (De Michelis, 2004: 178). The opposition between *rājayoga* and *haṭhayoga*, though common from the eleventh century, acquired new meaning when nineteenth-century Indologists associated the latter with self-torture (Birch, 2011: 527–529); it too was popularized by Theosophy (Schreiner, 2011: 765). *Haṭhayoga*, represented as physical and inferior, became a dustbin in which to dump the opprobrium heaped on yoga in the West; purged of this opprobrium, *rājayoga* emerged as spiritual and superior.

Sometimes Vivekananda mentions only three yogas, omitting *rājayoga*. In one of the talks collected as "Karma-Yoga" (*CW*: 1.27–118), he mentions "work" together with the Buddha as an exemplary *jñānī*[20] and Christ as an exemplary *bhakta* but no fourth (p. 1.55). In the same collection he says that "the Yogas of work, of wisdom and of devotion are all capable of serving as direct and independent means for the attainment of Moksha" (p. 1.93), again omitting *rājayoga*; but he also refers to four paths "of work, love, psychology and knowledge" (p. 1.108),[21] where "psychology" stands for *rājayoga*. Vivekananda treats Patañjali's *YS*, his authority for *rājayoga*, as a psychological work; as part of his attempt to recruit Western science in support of his message, he asked the psychologist and philosopher William James to write a preface to *Yoga Philosophy*, but without success (De Michelis, 2004: 171).

Vivekananda describes the *BhG* as harmonizing Yoga (meaning *karmayoga*), *jñāna*, and *bhakti* (*CW*: 4.106). This triad has been used so often as a hermeneutic device by interpreters of the *BhG* that some modern writers attribute it to the *BhG* itself (e.g., De Michelis, 2004; Smith, 2003: 40), though no such triad occurs in it.[22]

In Vivekananda's collected works, the four yogas provide the titles of four sections: *Karma-Yoga* (*CW*: 1.27–118); *Bhakti-Yoga* (*CW*: 3: 31–69); *Jnâna Yoga*, based on talks in London, May 1896 (*Life*: 413) (*CW*: 8.3–35); and *Râja-Yoga*

(*CW:* 1.120–313). They were mentioned in a letter to Alasinga in March 1896: *Karma-yoga* was already out,[23] and *Râja-Yoga* was in press. He seemed to expect *Bhakti-Yoga* to be published in India and *Jñāna-Yoga* in England (*CW:* 7.490; cf. *CW:* 8.373).[24]

Râja-Yoga was published under the title *Yoga Philosophy: Lectures on Râja Yoga* in London while Vivekananda was in New York, and although it was taken down from talks he seems to have prepared the text himself.[25] While working on it, in December 1895 (*CW:* 8.361; Killingley, 1990: 168), he wrote to his English supporter Sturdy to buy him some Sanskrit texts relevant to yoga;[26] this is further evidence that yoga teaching had not been part of his plan in going to the States. *Râja-Yoga* has the clearest structure of Vivekananda's works. An exposition of *aṣṭāṅgayoga,* the "yoga of eight limbs" formulated in *YS* 2.28–3.8, is followed by a "rather free translation" (Vivekananda, *CW:* 1.122) of the *YS* and an even freer commentary. Internal evidence shows that it was conceived as a series of talks. Thus, to exemplify concentration, the author says, "You are listening to me" (Vivekananda, 1896: 8, reprinted in *CW:* 1.130); to show how practice can make actions automatic, he says, "For instance, most of you ladies play the piano" (Vivekananda, 1896: 151, reprinted in *CW:* 1.240).

VIVEKANANDA'S INTERPRETATION OF THE *YOGASŪTRAS*

The *YS*, with the *BhG,* provided the textual authority anchoring Vivekananda in the Hindu tradition, while Ramakrishna provided the personal authority. However, in interpreting these authorities he adapted them to some recurrent themes of his own message and to themes of popular Western thought. His interpretation of the *YS* (*CW:* 1.200–304) uses the ancient commentary *Yoga-bhāṣya* (hereafter *YBh*), attributed to Vyāsa but sometimes ignores it and sometimes takes liberties with the *sūtras* themselves. Textual authority was never absolute for Vivekananda (Rambachan, 1994), and he bases his teaching on his own experiential knowledge; however, "as to what I do not know I will simply tell you what the books say" (*CW:* 1.134). This leaves him free to report doctrines such as the multiplicity of *puruṣas*, without explicitly reconciling them to *advaita vedānta* (*CW:* 1.251).

He claims that Patañjali's yoga is scientific—the claim that he made in Chicago for Hinduism—since it explains the "extraordinary phenomena" that "surface scientists" are unable to explain, and so deny (*CW:* 1.121). He presents it in terms familiar in the popular scientific discourse of his time: matter and energy; solids, liquids and gases; molecules; vibrations; electricity and magnetism. *Oṣadhi* (herbs) is translated "chemical means" (Vivekananda, 1896: 206, reprinted in *CW:* 1.289, on *YS* 4.1). *Saṃskāras,* the traces left by previous karma that affect the predispositions and destiny of each living being, are explained as "waves" (Vivekananda, 1896: 152–156, reprinted in *CW:* 1.241–245, on *YS*

2.9–12); the wave is a recurrent image in this and other works. *Prāṇa* is explained as not merely breath but also the source of "everything we call energy, everything we call force . . . manifesting as gravitation, as magnetism" (Vivekananda, 1896: 31, reprinted in *CW:* 1.147); it is "the sum-total of the cosmic energy" (Vivekananda, 1896: 184, reprinted in *CW:* 1.267, on *YS* 2.49). At the same time, the Hindu tradition is shown to supply what the scientific view lacks. The universe is presented as consisting of "matter and force" but is illuminated by "the Puruṣa" (Vivekananda, 1896: 217, reprinted in *CW:* 1.299, on *YS* 4.18), which is unknown to Western science. The *advaita* cosmology, which runs through Vivekananda's interpretation (despite the *sāṃkhya* dualism presupposed by the *YS*), finds an affinity with popular Western Neoplatonism (De Michelis, 2004: 154).[27]

He claims that "control of Prana" is partially understood by contemporary "sects" such as "Spiritualists, Christian Scientists, Hypnotists, etc." (*CW:* 1.149) but is fully known by the yogi. However, he shows little interest in yogic powers. "Though, as a scientist, Patanjali is bound to point out the possibilities of this science, he never misses an opportunity to warn us against these powers" (Vivekananda, 1896: 115, reprinted in 211, on *YS* 1.17). This affects his translation of *YS* 1.140, which refers to *vaśīkāra,* imposition of one's will. Vivekananda's translation, "The Yogî's mind becomes unobstructed from the atomic to the Infinite," suppresses this reference to yogic powers. In *YS* 4.4, where the *YBh* argues that when a yogi multiplies his body each body has a separate consciousness (*citta*), Vivekananda uses the *sūtra* for a discussion of karma and the inherent perfection of the self (Vivekananda, 1896: 211, reprinted in *CW:* 1.293); he introduces self-multiplication, somewhat obscurely, only in the next *sūtra*. He avoids the subject of clairvoyance (Vivekananda, 1896: 193, reprinted in *CW:* 1.276, on *YS* 3.18–19).

YOGA, REBIRTH, EVOLUTION, AND THE MEETING OF RELIGIONS

Vivekananda sometimes seems uncertain as to whether his hearers are able to grasp all the implications of the doctrine of rebirth, but he takes care to teach it. One of his longer comments is on *YS* 2.9 (Vivekananda, 1896: 150–153, reprinted in *CW:* 1.239–242; cf. 2.220). The *YBh* on this *sūtra* uses the universal fear of death as evidence for previous births: since it cannot result from perception, inference, or report (*pratyakṣa, anumāna, śabda*), it can be explained only by previous experience (*anubhava*) of death. Vivekananda presents a simplified form of this argument (which he had already used in Chicago; *CW:* 1.9) and contrasts it with an idea he attributes to the West—that "this clinging to life indicates a possibility of a future life"—though this is envisaged only for humankind. Digressing from the fear of death, he passes to other indications of previous experience: newly hatched chickens picking up food or fearing hawks;

newly hatched ducklings taking to water. Instinct is only a word, not an explanation; modern scientists attribute it to the body, but he prefers the Indian explanation of experience in previous births. Like the pianist's practice, which has made playing automatic, experience has become *saṃskāra*, "sleeping in the Chitta"; fear of death is another example. These are the *cittavṛttis*, "mind-waves" as Vivekananda characteristically calls them, which yoga sets out to control (*YS* 1.2). What the West calls instinct and attributes to animals rather than to humankind is a product of conscious activities in the past, usually in previous lives. It is "involved reason" (Vivekananda, 1896: 151, reprinted in *CW:* 1.240; *CW:* 2.221), using the term "involved" in Vivekananda's special sense as the opposite of "evolved"; he also calls it "degenerated reason" (ibid.).

He seems more ready to speak in terms of progression through higher and higher births to ultimate perfection, as the Theosophists did, than of low rebirths as punishment for sins, as found in texts such as *Manu* 12.54–81. But he recognized an affinity between the Hindu idea of rebirth, which places humankind in a hierarchy that includes animals and plants below us and various grades of gods above, and the scientific idea of evolution. Evolution, including "Lamarckian notions about the inheritance of acquired characteristics," was "the most powerful scientific vocabulary" of late nineteenth-century and early twentieth-century America (White, 2009: 98). It had become an alternative way of interpreting the universe, and an alternative revelation, challenging the biblical one. Vivekananda—and here again he was preceded by Keshub (Killingley, 1995: 190)—evoked it in many contexts, including his *YS* commentary. Though Darwin is the name he invokes, his view of evolution, with its inheritance of conscious actions, is Lamarckian (Killingley, 1995: 192).

One passage in the *YS* that Vivekananda finds particularly relevant to evolution is *YS* 4.2–3, which uses the analogy of a farmer irrigating a field by breaking a dam to let the water follow its natural course. According to the *YBh,* this analogy shows how a yogi enters another body (Killingley, 1990: 157–159). Vivekananda, ignoring this example of yogic powers, uses the passage to present his version of "the evolutionary theory of the ancient Yogis" (Vivekananda, 1896: 210, reprinted in *CW* 1.292): a melioristic version of evolution, incorporating his concept of involution.

> So all progress and power are already in every man; perfection is man's nature, only it is barred in and prevented from taking its proper course. If anyone can take the bar off, in rushes nature. Then the man attains the powers which are his already. Those we call wicked will become saints . . . All these practices and struggles to become religious are only negative work, to take off the bars, and open the doors to that perfection which is our birthright, our nature. (Vivekananda, 1896: 210, reprinted in *CW:* 1.292)

Evolution and involution are the foundation on which Vivekananda builds his doctrine of the inherent though obstructed perfection—not merely perfectibility—of each person. Having proclaimed this doctrine in Chicago in opposition to the Christian doctrine of original sin, he now applies it to the manufacture of yogis. Each of us, and indeed each living being, has a blissful and infinite essence, which can be released by breaking through the accumulation of karma and *avidyā* (ignorance), which appears to limit us. Yoga—which includes all forms of spiritual striving—hastens this process of evolution. Vivekananda finds authority for this in *YS* 4.2–3, and this is the passage of the *YS* to which he returns most frequently (Killingley, 1990: 156, 160–163).

VIVEKANANDA'S YOGIC LEGACY

The yoga Vivekananda taught was hardly "fully-fledged"; being more interested in doctrine than practice, he left it to later gurus to introduce more formal, and more recognizably yogic, practices. However, he ensured that yoga in the West was no longer only for the other, and he helped to form its vocabulary. He used the word *yoga* very widely to refer to all forms of spiritual striving; he could call any great religious figure, such as Jesus or the Buddha, a yogi. But he also used the word *yogi* in a specific sense, as when he says: "The moderns have their evolution, and so have the Yogis. But I think the Yogis' explanation is the better one" (*CW:* 5.277). Here, he is thinking of "our Yogi Patañjali" (*CW:* 3.406) and in particular of his own interpretation of *YS* 4.2–3. This interpretation, which combines evolution, the innate perfection of each person, a progressive view of rebirth, and a melioristic view of the future, became the foundation of his project of manufacturing yogis.

Vivekananda was a guru in the modern sense: a teacher with a large if ill defined following. His yoga teaching, like his style of lecturing, his showmanship, and his polarization of East and West, owed more than he would like to admit to Keshub Chunder Sen. However, while Keshub's message was a universal religion that drew on all traditions, Vivekananda's was a fulfillment of all traditions that only India could provide, since only India held the unifying truth of *advaita vedānta* and the techniques of yoga. His teaching also owed something to Theosophy and other occult movements. Its claim to be scientific was an appeal not so much to scientists as to those in whom interest in phenomena that science was unable to explain had been aroused by Spiritualism, Theosophy, and the like.

REFERENCES

Beckerlegge, Gwilym. 1998. Swami Vivekananda and *sevā:* taking "social service" seriously. In William Radice (ed.), *Swami Vivekananda*. Delhi, Oxford University Press, pp. 158–193.

———. 2000. *The Ramakrishna Mission: The Making of a Modern Hindu Movement*. Delhi: Oxford University Press.

Birch, Jason. 2011. The Meaning of *haṭha* in Early Haṭhayoga. *Journal of the American Oriental Society* 131: 527–554.

Brekke, Torkel. 2002. *Makers of Modern Indian Religion in the Late Nineteenth Century*. Oxford: Oxford University Press.

Burke, Marie Louise. 1966. *Swami Vivekananda in America: New Discoveries*, 2nd ed. Calcutta: Advaita Ashrama.

———. 1992. *Swami Vivekananda in the West: New Discoveries*, 4th ed., vol. 1.

Chowdhury Sengupta, Indira. 1998. Reconstructing Hinduism on a World Platform: The World's First Parliament of Religions, Chicago 1892. *Radice* 1998: 17–35.

Christy, A. 1932. *The Orient in American Transcendentalism: A Study of Emerson, Thoreau and Alcott*. New York: Columbia University Press.

Colebrooke, H. T. 1858 [1837]. *Essays on the Religion and Philosophy of the Hindus*, 2nd ed. London: Williams & Norgate.

De Michelis, Elizabeth. 2004. *A History of Modern Yoga*. London: Continuum.

Dvivedi, M. N. 1885. *Rāja Yoga or the Practical Metaphysics of the Vedānta*. Bombay: Subodhaprakasha.

Edgerton, Franklin. 1924. The Meaning of *Sāṃkhya* and Yoga. *American Journal of Philology* 45: 1–46.

———. 1952. *The Bhagavad Gītā: Translated and Interpreted. Part I: Text and Translation*. Cambridge, MA: Harvard University Press.

Hatcher, Brian A. 1999. *Eclecticism and Modern Hindu Discourse*. New York: Oxford University Press.

Jackson, C. T. 1994. *Vedanta for the West: The Ramakrishna Movement in the United States*. Bloomington: University of Indiana Press.

Killingley, Dermot. 1990. Yoga-Sutra IV, 2–3 and Vivekananda's Interpretation of Evolution. *Journal of Indian Philosophy* 18: 91–119.

———. 1995. Hinduism, Darwinism and Evolution in Late Nineteenth-Century India. In David Amigoni and Jeff Wallace (eds.), *Charles Darwin's* The Origin of Species: *New Interdisciplinary Essays*. Manchester: Manchester University Press, pp. 174–202.

———. 1998. Vivekananda's Western message from the East. In William Radice (ed.), *Swami Vivekananda*. Delhi, Oxford University Press, pp. 138–157.

King, Ursula. 1980. Who Is the Ideal Karmayogin? The Meaning of a Hindu Religious Symbol. *Religion* 10: 41–59.

Lamotte, Etienne. 1929. *Notes sur la Bhagavadgītā*. Paris: Geuthner.

Life of Swami Vivekananda by His Eastern and Western Disciples. 1965. Calcutta: Advaita Ashrama.

Monier-Williams, M. 1875. *Indian Wisdom: or Examples of the Religious, Philosophical and Ethical Doctrines of the Hindus*. London: W.H. Allen.

Müller, Friedrich Max. 1898. *Ramakrishna: His Life and Sayings*. London: Longmans, Green and Co.

Neevel, Walter G., Jr. 1976. The Transformation of Śrī Rāmakrishna. In Bardwell E. Smith (ed.), *Hinduism: New Essays in the History of Religions*, Leiden: Brill, pp. 53–97.

Penny Cyclopædia of the Society for the Diffusion of Useful Knowledge. 1843. Vol. 27. London: Charles Knight & Co.

Rambachan, Anantanand. 1994. *The Limits of Scripture: Vivekananda's Interpretation of the Vedas*. Honolulu: University of Hawaii Press.

Raychaudhuri, Tapan. 1998. Swami Vivekananda's Construction of Hinduism. In William Radice (ed.), *Swami Vivekananda*. Delhi, Oxford University Press, pp. 1–16.

Sanborn, F. B. 1906. *The Writings of Henry David Thoreau*, vol. 6: *Familiar Letters*. Boston: Houghton Mifflin.

Schreiner, Peter. 2011. Rāja Yoga. In Knut A. Jacobsen (ed.), *Brill's Encyclopedia of Hinduism*, vol. 3. Leiden: E. J. Brill, pp. 760–769.

Scott, David C. 1979. *Keshub Chunder Sen: A Selection*. Madras: Christian Literature Society.

Seager, Richard Hughes. 1995. *The World's Parliament of Religions: The East/West Encounter, Chicago, 1893*. Bloomington: Indiana University Press.

Sinnett, A.P. 1881. *The Occult World*. London: Trübner.

Smith, David. 2003. *Hinduism and Modernity*. Oxford: Blackwell.

Versluis, Arthur. 1993. *American Transcendentalism and Asian Religions*. New York: Oxford University Press.

Vivekananda. 1962–1997. *The Complete Works of Swami Vivekananda*. 9 volumes. Calcutta: Advaita Ashrama.

———. 1896. *Yoga Philosophy. Lectures Delivered in New York, Winter of 1895–6 by the Swâmi Vivekânanda on Râja Yoga, or Conquering the Internal Nature: Also Patañjali's Yoga Aphorisms, with Commentaries*. London: Longman.

White, Christopher G. 2009. *Unsettled Minds: Psychology and the American Search for Spiritual Assurance, 1830–1940*. Berkeley: University of California Press.

Yule, Henry, and Burnell, A. C. 1902 [1886]. *Hobson-Jobson: A Glossary of Colloquial Anglo-Indian Words and Phrases, and of Kindred Terms, Etymological, Historical, Geographical and Discursive*, 2nd ed. London: Routledge & Kegan Paul.

NOTES

1. The Brahmo Samaj ("theistic society") was founded in 1828 by Rammohun Roy, reshaped in 1843 by Debendranath Tagore, and further reshaped in the 1860s by Keshub Chunder Sen.
2. Müller (1898: 30) gives the birthdate as February 20, 1833; other dates are given in early sources. The Ramakrishna movement favors February 18, 1836 (Neevel, 1976: 65).
3. He had talked before about his work and his relations with Ramakrishna in 1895 (*CW:* 5.185–188), 1896 (*CW:* 4.177–187), and 1897 (*CW:* 3.208–213, 218).
4. If we take Vivekananda's chronology seriously (we need not, as shown already), the struggle began in 1878, before Vivekananda's first meeting with Ramakrishna in 1881, and ended mid-1884, two years before Ramakrishna's death.
5. "I came here without credentials. How else to show that I am not a fraud in the face of the missionaries and the Brahmo Samaj?" (letter to India from Chicago, June 28, 1894, *CW:* 8.311). Vivekananda was not the only Hindu speaker, though he was by far the most eloquent and memorable. Others were Manilal Dvivedi (a Theosophist) from Bombay and Narasimhacharya from Madras (Seager, 1995: 81–83, 106; Chowdhury-Sengupta 1998: 24).
6. However, his use in Chicago (*CW:* 1.9) of an argument for rebirth reminiscent of *YBh* 2.9, discussed following, suggests that he was already familiar with *YS* and *YBh*.
7. I follow De Michelis's (2004: 31–33) application of Ernst Troeltsch's typology. A cult and a sect both differ from a church in that membership tends not to be inherited from the family, but a cult is distinguished from a sect in being loosely structured, without defined boundaries, and claiming a spiritual fellowship independent of any human organization.

8. *CW:* 3.103–461. There, he mentions the yogi as an ideal person (*CW:* 3.134, 138), calls the Buddha the greatest Karma-yogi (*CW:* 3.262), and summarizes his idea that the siddhis are already present in everyone and that yoga only makes them manifest (CW: 3.334). On the other hand, he ridicules meditation and breathing exercises, perhaps standing for *haṭhayoga* (*CW:* 3.301). Otherwise there is nothing on yoga.
9. The article describes meditation on the syllable *Om*, asceticism, and the pursuit of magical powers. Part of it is taken verbatim from Colebrooke (1858 [1837]: 158).
10. Edgerton's study of the *BhG*, for a nonspecialist readership, was first published in 1925 and appeared in a revised form as vol. 2 of his 1952 publication. He had already discussed the meaning of "yoga" in detail, translating it variously according to context as "method," "exertion," "disciplined activity" (Edgerton, 1924: 37–46). He observes that his rejection of the meaning "union" matches Charpentier in 1912 (in German) and Tuxen in 1911 (in Danish) (Edgerton, 1924: 39 fn. 44); he implies that it is otherwise novel. Thus, the explanation of yoga as discipline and not union became generally available to the English-reading public in 1925. Lamotte (1929: 86) similarly explains "yoga" as "discipline; méthode de contrôle."
11. Yule and Burnell (1902: 461) quote from Marco Polo onward, variously spelled. They say "the stuff which has of late been propagated in India by certain persons, under the names of theosophy and esoteric Buddhism [Sinnett 1883], is essentially the doctrine of the Jogis" (p. 461). There is no article on "yoga"; this suggests that in 1886 when the book was first published this word was much less current in English than "yogi"/"jogi" or at any rate that it was not part of the "Anglo-Indian" vocabulary that the book records: words current among the British in India, brought by them into British conversation and literature or introduced through trade (p. xv–xvi). It does not cover the vocabulary of Theosophy, which the authors despised as the previous quotation shows; there is no entry for "mahatma" and no mention of Theosophical usage in the article on "chelah".
12. Letter to Harrison Blake, Concord, November 20, 1849 (Sanborn, 1906: 175). The phrases are quoted by De Michelis (2004: 2–3) from Christy (1932: 185, 201); De Michelis describes them as "what seems to be the first recorded affirmation, by a Westerner, that he considered himself a yogic practitioner — after a fashion." The letter quotes an unnamed text on the yogi, "free in this world as the birds . . . united to the nature which is proper to him, he goes, he acts as animating original matter." But it immediately changes the subject and says no more on yoga. The brevity of the passage hardly suggests a serious commitment, and phrases in it ("I would fain"; "to some extent, and at rare intervals") suggest otherwise. Versluis (1993: 79–99) dismisses claims that Thoreau was in any sense a yogi.
13. *Vedanta Philosophy: Lectures on Raja Yoga and Other Subjects, Also Patanjali's Yoga Aphorisms . . .*, Albany, NY: Weed-Parsons, 1897. Reprinted in *CW:* 1.120–313 under the title "Raja-Yoga."
14. Texts are identified by name, without chapter and verse, but allusions can be recognized to *YS* 1.2 (*CW:* 7.61), 1.11, 1.27, 1.30 (*CW:* 7.62), 2.34, 2.38 (*CW:* 7.67), 2.46, and 3.2 (*CW:* 7.68); and to *BhG* 2.47 (*CW:* 7.20), 3.27 or 5.8, 9.27, and 5.10 (*CW:* 7.63). Other texts referred to are the *Nārada Bhakti Sūtra*, Śaṅkara's commentary on the *Vedānta Sūtras*, *Bṛhadāraṇyaka Upaniṣad,* and *Avadhūtagītā*.
15. However, a newspaper report, apparently of 1896, says London ladies sat cross-legged on the floor "for want of chairs" (*Life*: 379). Jackson (1994: 30) says the course at Thousand Island Park included breathing and meditation, citing *Life* (p. 359). Silent meditation is mentioned (*Life:* 364), as well as initiation with a mantra (*Life:* 359, 363) but not breathing. On March 6, 1895 (*CW:* 5.75), Vivekananda asked

his Madras disciple Alasinga to send "some Kushâsanas" (*kuśāsana*), that is, mats of kuśa grass, the seat prescribed for yogis, so he intended students to sit on them.

16. *CW:* 1.4. A closer translation would be "Whoever turn to me in whatever way, I favour them in the same way. People follow my path everywhere." The phrase "through whatsoever form" suggests that he may also be thinking of *BhG* 7.21: "Whoever devotedly tries to worship whatever form with faith, I make that same faith of his firm." Raychaudhuri (1998: 5) identifies the quotation that precedes this in Vivekananda's talk as from the *Śivamahimna Stotra* and gives the Sanskrit text.
17. For example, "instinct is involved reason" (*CW:* 1.240); "every evolution is preceded by an involution" (*CW:* 5.255). This use of "involution" is Vivekananda's innovation; it was developed further by Aurobindo Ghose (Killingley, 1995: 193–196).
18. Though he implies that this is a recent "discovery," it seems to underlie his view of the universality of Hinduism presented at Chicago.
19. *Sevā* is a key term in the Ramakrishna movement and in neo-Hinduism (Beckerlegge, 1998).
20. Elsewhere, the Buddha is an exemplary karma yogi (*CW:* 1.116; *CW:* 3.262).
21. De Michelis (2004: 180, fn. 40), implying that Vivekananda's *Karma-Yoga* refers only to three yogas, seems to have overlooked this passage.
22. The three are never mentioned together. *Karma-yoga* occurs five times, but the other two only once each. Besides these, *buddhi-yoga* occurs three times, *abhyāsa-yoga* twice, and *ātma-yoga, ātmasaṃyama-yoga, dhyāna-yoga,* and *saṃnyāsa-yoga* once each. The hermeneutic device may have originated with the sixteenth-century commentator Madhusūdana Sarasvatī, who divides the *BhG* into six chapters on karma, six on *bhakti* and six on *jñāna*. Lamotte (1929) organizes his interpretation partly around the triad.
23. *Eight lectures/by the Swami Vivekananda, on Karma Yoga, (the secret of work,) delivered in New York, winter 1895–6*. New York: Brentano's, 1896 (Library of Congress Catalog).
24. *Bhakti Yoga* was first published by Vivekananda's English supporter E. T. Sturdy as *Addresses on the Vedanta Philosophy, vol. II: Bhakti Yoga* (London, Simpkins and Marshall, 1896). (The designation "vol. II" implies that Vivekananda (1896) was the first volume in a series.) This embarrassed Vivekananda, as he had already promised publication rights to the Vedanta Society of New York (letter to Sturdy, March 17, 1896, *CW:* 8.374). I am grateful to Dr. Stephen Gregg for information on this publication. *Jñāna Yoga* was published by the Vedanta Society of New York, in 1902.
25. The Sanskrit words are accurately printed, with diacritics. Miss Waldo indicates she took down the commentary, at least, from dictation rather than from class talks (*Life* 1965: 348). This seems to be contradicted by Vivekananda's letter to Sturdy: "These talks are all taken down, and when completed will form the fullest annotated translation of Patanjali in English" (*CW:* 8.361). The text of *Râja-Yoga* in *CW:* 1.120–313 differs in places from Vivekananda (1896) and adds the *sūtras* in Sanskrit.
26. He lists *Kūrma Purāṇa,* which he has not seen but finds frequently quoted in Vijñānabhikṣu's *YS* commentary; *Haṭhayogapradīpikā; Sāṃkhya-kārikā*. The *Kūrma Purāṇa* passage on yoga is translated in *CW:* 1.189–193. He had earlier asked Alasinga for *Vedānta Sūtra* commentaries, "of all the sects" (letter April 4, 1895, *CW:* 5.77).
27. De Michelis (2004: 153–176) examines the cosmology of *Râja-Yoga* in detail and interprets it in relation to other systems popular in the United States at the time.

CHAPTER 2

Remembering Sri Aurobindo and the Mother: The Forgotten Lineage of Integral Yoga

ANN GLEIG AND CHARLES I. FLORES

First-time visitors to the Sri Aurobindo ashram in Pondicherry might well have a difficult time locating it. While they would reasonably assume that the ashram of one of the most influential figures of twentieth-century India would be easily found, it is quite possible, particularly if they are visiting in the hot season when temperatures reach 40 degrees Celsius and the numbers of visitors drop, that they could walk straight past the side or back of the unassuming ashram building. As their search continues, they will be relieved to come upon a twelve-foot bronze statue; here he is, they sigh; I must be close. It will be a shock, then, to discover that the figure is not Sri Aurobindo, but his contemporary, Mohandas Gandhi. This gives one cause to wonder: there is little doubt that Aurobindo's forty-year residency here has firmly planted the former French seaside colony of Pondicherry on the scholastic and devotional map, so where *exactly* is he?

This geographical predicament functions, moreover, as a metaphor of a neglect or amnesia of Aurobindo in modern yoga scholarship. In studies of modern yoga, as with a first visit to Pondicherry, one gets the sense that Aurobindo is somehow both everywhere yet nowhere quite specifically to be found. On one hand, a number of the main studies credit him with playing a major role in the formation of modern yoga. Joseph Alter (2004), for example, acknowledges Aurobindo and Vivekananda as the "two chief architects" of the Indian yoga renaissance and notes that there is little doubt that they defined the broad intellectual context within which it occurred (pp. 26–28). On the other, however, whereas Vivekananda appears as the protagonist of Elizabeth De Michelis's (2004) seminal study of modern yoga, Aurobindo curiously does not even merit a reference in her text. Similarly, while Mark Singleton (2010) labels Aurobindo as "the most famous freedom-fighting yogi" within the physical culture movement that determinatively shaped transnational yoga, he gives few details and only glances at Aurobindo in his pre-guru revolutionary nationalist days (p. 104).

Given the centrality of Aurobindo in the yoga renaissance, his absence from studies on modern yoga is indeed, as Sarah Strauss (2008) puts it, "conspicuous" (p. 72). A similar situation pertains to his status in practitioner circles; well-known scholar-practitioner George Feuerstein (1998) raves that Aurobindo's Integral Yoga is "the single most impressive attempt to reformulate Yoga for our modern needs and abilities" yet also concedes that it is not as widely known amongst contemporary Western practitioners as it deserves to be (p. 73).

This chapter will attempt to rectify the neglect of Aurobindo by both fleshing out his role as a guru in the modern yoga renaissance and recovering some of the concealed but nonetheless important impacts of Aurobindo on the contemporary yoga climate. First, we will offer an outline of the life and work of Aurobindo, as it pertains to his role in the formation of modern yoga. Second, we will reflect on the status of physical culture and *haṭhayoga* in Aurobindo's system of Integral Yoga. Third, we will track the continuing presence of Aurobindo on the contemporary yoga scene through uncovering what we are identifying as *close* and *creative* lineages. Finally, we will reflect on why Aurobindo has been somewhat forgotten and what can be gained through recovering Integral Yoga for a larger audience.

Before proceeding, however, a word on definition is necessary. We are using *Modern Yoga* in a broad sense as an umbrella term to cover the different iterations of yoga provisionally mapped out by De Michelis (2004) and not, as it is now commonly used, as synonymous with *haṭhayoga*. In doing so, we will show that although it is undeniable that the history of *haṭhayoga* "slips past" Aurobindo (Alter, 2004: 27), in other aspects he still remains part, if a somewhat concealed one, of a wider yoga climate.

Making transparent our own location as researchers is also useful and necessary here. One of us (Gleig) writes as a scholar concerned by recent events which this chapter will discuss both in the Integral Yoga community and the American yoga community, which have attempted to erase or undermine the western strands in the construction of modern yoga and claim exclusive Indian ownership over what scholars such as De Michelis (2004) and Singleton (2010) have shown was from the beginning a hybrid creation drawing as much from Western influences as traditional Hindu sources. The other (Flores) is in agreement with the scholarship that documents the construction of Modern Postural Yoga (De Michelis, 2004) and does not believe that the transparent influence of the Western tradition on Integral Yoga can be erased by detractors. He is vocal within the Integral Yoga community against the exclusive ownership the figure of Sri Aurobindo by any group.

AUROBINDO, THE MOTHER, AND INTEGRAL YOGA

Aurobindo Ghose was born in Kolkata, India, on August 15, 1872. His anglophone father, a rationalist physician who had rejected religion, sent him at the age of seven to England for a Western education. Aurobindo spoke only English, and he knew little about India until he attended King's College, Cambridge, where he studied, along with Greek and Latin, Sanskrit and Bengali and read translations of the Upaniṣads. On his return to India in 1893, he immersed himself in the study of Sanskrit and Bengali and classic Indian literary, philosophical, and religious works. This period also saw Aurobindo, who had supported Home Rule since Cambridge, become involved in revolutionary activities, and in 1906 he moved to Kolkata, where he briefly became perhaps the most important leader in the Indian national movement, critiquing the ineffectiveness of Indian National Congress and audaciously championing the

Figure 2.1:
Shri Aurobindo. (With permission of the Sri Aurobindo Ashram Trust.)

notion of complete independence from Britain. He was arrested three times by the British—twice for sedition and once for conspiring to "wage war"—and was imprisoned at Alipore jail for over a year.

It was mainly to obtain powers to help the nationalist cause that Aurobindo began to practice yoga in 1905. In 1908 he received instructions by a guru in the Datttātreya lineage on how to silence the mind and unexpectedly realized the *vedāntic* impersonal Brahman or Absolute. A few months later while in Alipore jail, he experienced the personal godhead in the form of Kṛṣṇa (Krishna). These experiences spiritually radicalized him, and in 1910, when facing further imprisonment, he abandoned politics and escaped to Pondicherry to fully focus on his *sādhanā* or spiritual practices. Between 1908 and 1914, he achieved several profound spiritual realizations, and from these personal experiences and his extensive study of Indian and Western religious, philosophical, and cultural thought he developed his new system of Integral Yoga (Heehs, 2008).

Aurobindo credited much of the development of Integral Yoga to his platonic spiritual collaborator known as the Mother. The Mother was born Mirra Alfassa on February 21, 1878, in Paris to a wealthy family of Turkish, Egyptian, and Sephardic Jewish decent. Trained in art in the Academie Julian, she

Figure 2.2:
The Mother. (With permission of the Sri Aurobindo Ashram Trust.)

was acquainted with numerous famous artists and spiritual figures in Paris at the time. A prodigy of occultism at an early age, in 1906 she went to Tlemcen, Algeria, to study with adepts Max and Alma Theon and taught in occult circles in Paris between 1911 and 1913. In 1914, she traveled with her husband, Paul Richard, a French civil servant, to meet Aurobindo. She immediately recognized Aurobindo as a figure who had appeared to her in visions and declared that she "at once knew that it was he, the Divine" (Roy, 1929). Aurobindo, for his part, eventually honored her as an embodiment of the Divine Mother or *śakti* force. The Richards had to return to France due to the outbreak of the First World War, but in 1920 Alfassa returned alone to Pondicherry and began to collaborate with Aurobindo in the development of Integral Yoga. In 1926, when the Sri Aurobindo Ashram was founded, Aurobindo gave material and spiritual charge of the ashram to her so that he could concentrate on his *sādhanā*, and he remained in the relative seclusion of his room until his death in 1950.

Integral Yoga is an explicitly modern system of yoga that fuses together Indian and Western thought. Aurobindo reinterpreted the Vedas and *vedānta* philosophy through a Western evolutionary lens to produce a spiritual evolutionary metaphysics. He rejected both traditional Indian renouncer paths and Western scientific materialism in favor of an all-encompassing or "integral" model that recognized the partial truths of both "spirit and nature" and postulated an evolutionary teleology that aimed at the radical divinization of matter rather than liberation from the world. To catalyze this evolutionary process, Aurobindo synthesized certain elements of traditional schools of yoga and set them within his wider evolutionary hermeneutic to produce a new system, which he named *Integral Yoga*.

The foundation of Aurobindo's Integral Yoga is a dialectical metaphysics that advances a bipolar model of ultimate reality. Aurobindo (2005) refers to ultimate reality as Brahman and describes it as both static and dynamic, unmanifest and manifest, transcendent and immanent, spirit and nature. Whereas Indian renunciate traditions have focused on the unmanifest aspect of Brahman and reject the manifest as an illusion or a mistake, Aurobindo attempts to reunite the two through the utilization of an involution–evolution or a descent–ascent narrative. This narrative begins with the Upaniṣadic notion that the "one without a second" (p. 458), Brahman, decided to play a game for its own enjoyment, a type of peekaboo that involved a narrowing and amnesia of its own consciousness in an intentional act of involution. Involution refers to the descent of spirit into nature and the progressive emergence of "matter, life and mind," and evolution signifies the reascent of the latter to their spiritual origin, a process that results in a spiritualization of matter and "the divine life." This reascent is not a return to an original state but the unfolding of a fundamentally new manifestation of Brahman as divinized matter (Heehs, 2008: 232–233).

The principle themes of Aurobindo's evolutionary spirituality are set out in his philosophical masterpiece *The Life Divine* (1970 [1914–1919]). The text begins by claiming that the Western scientific materialist perspective that reality is reducible to matter and the Indian ascetic position that only Brahman or pure consciousness exists are only partial truths. In the "completer affirmation" that Aurobindo proposes, matter and spirit are embraced as two different forms of a unitary reality, which is structured as a hierarchical "scale of substance" (Heehs, 2008: 270–276). At the upper hemisphere of the cosmos is the monistic Brahman, the nature of which is *saccidānanda* or being-consciousness-bliss. At the lower hemisphere are matter, life, and mind, which are characterized by division and multiplicity. Situated between the two is what Aurobindo calls the supermind, a level of consciousness that is simultaneously aware of both unity and multiplicity. The supermind is the principle by which spirit and nature are reunited because, unlike the utterly transcendent realms of Brahman, it can act on and divinize the material (ibid.). Brahman's descent was "not a blunder and a fall" but a "purposeful descent" to obtain a "divine existence." The human being is the first species to be on the cusp of a new kind of evolution, one led not by the force of *prakṛti* or nature but by consciousness. With the human being, "evolution has now become conscious," and through the human's "conscious self-transformation" the evolutionary ascension can proceed more rapidly (Aurobindo 1970: 591–592). Aurobindo presents the human as a transitional being, a turning point, and a central instrument in the spiritual evolutionary process. The human "may well be a thinking and living laboratory" in which nature "wills to work out the superman, the god." Essential to this process is what Aurobindo, borrowing a term from the Mother, identifies as the soul or "psychic being." Unique to Integral Yoga, the psychic being or "true individuality" carries forward the developmental gains of one lifetime to another. Its realization is crucial because unlike the transcendent *ātman* it enables a conscious participation in the evolutionary process (Aurobindo, 2005: 3–7).

The psychic being evolves beyond the human to the supermind or supramental consciousness, which will result in the emergence of a spiritualized species and a "divine life" on earth. Aurobindo believes that it is only through the appearance of such perfected beings that there can be a lasting solution to the numerous religious, social, and political problems inflicting humanity (Aurobindo, 2005: 290–291). The spiritualization of humankind is attained through a "revolutionary individual effort" with rare figures such as Aurobindo and the Mother acting as the forerunners of an "evolutionary general progression." In November 1926, Aurobindo had a major experience later reported as the "descent of the Overmind," a preliminary stage in the "ascent to the Supermind" (Heehs, 2008: 347–381). The Mother declared in 1956 that due to both of their efforts the supramental light and force rushed down on the earth in an uninterrupted flow.

Aurobindo (1972) adopted the generic term *yoga* to signify the process and methods of spiritual evolution. It consists of two progressive aspects: a movement into the depths of the self to realize the psychic being; and the upward ascension to and descent of the supermind. At the heart of this process is a threefold practice of surrender, aspiration, and rejection. Surrender is the foundation of the practice: an inner receptivity to the higher forces that allow a human being to transcend the limitations of their "animal nature." The aspiration for the divine is something that is cultivated over time, an unshakable desire for the higher consciousness. Rejection points to an inner discrimination between ignorance and consciousness and a discernment between choices that move one forward toward emancipation rather than those that reinforce bondage.

Integral Yoga incorporates some of the "indispensible" elements of the traditional yogas—*karma, jñāna,* and *bhakti* —yet rejects asceticism and the renunciate goal of absorption in the unmanifest Absolute. As reflected in his motto "All life is yoga," Aurobindo (1999) proposed a householder model, "the Yoga of Self-Perfection," that incorporated all aspects of life into spiritual practice. Like tantric yoga from which it considerably borrows, Integral Yoga aims at the transmutation of the material rather than its renunciation.

PERFECTION OF THE BODY: *HAṬHAYOGA* AND PHYSICAL CULTURE IN INTEGRAL YOGA

Given the contemporary popularity of *haṭhayoga* and the influence of European physical culture in shaping it, a glance at the role of both in Integral Yoga is useful. Statements by Aurobindo (1967) and the Mother on *haṭhayoga* and physical exercise must be situated in the context of the material divinization affected by the supramental descent. Both gurus insisted that the "perfection" of the physical body was essential to this process. Aurobindo stressed that the physical body was the basis and instrument for a "perfection of being" and could not, as in traditional renunciate paths, be discarded. He understood the perfection of the body as resulting in a new body that would transcend its "original earth-nature" and attain a physical immortality. Similarly, the Mother (2004) talked of a literal reconstitution of the bodily cells, a process that had already begun for her and that, moreover, was possible for all bodies.

Aurobindo (1999) originally assumed that the radical transformation of individual and cosmic "Nature" would occur through receptivity to the divine descent, a process facilitated by work, meditation, and devotion. When he and the Mother began to see physical exercises as also increasing receptivity, it was unconventionally sport rather than *haṭhayoga* that was preferred. Aurobindo identified *haṭhayoga* as a method that employs multiple *āsanas* and *prāṇāyāma* for the primary purpose of accessing *prāṇa* or life force and gaining health and longevity (p. 34). His understanding of *haṭhayoga* appears to be descriptive of many forms of Modern Postural Yoga such as those described by Singleton (2010), and he was no doubt describing what he knew of the *haṭha* yogi *fakirs* on the streets of India at the turn of the century, decades before the popularization of yoga by Krishnamacharya and Shri Yogendra, with its infusion of Western physical culture practices. In any case, he saw Integral Yoga as quite distinct from *haṭhayoga*, which he did not view as having the power to effect material divinization. If people in the ashram wanted to practice *āsanas* they were allowed to do so for health, but Aurobindo did not want them to view *haṭhayoga* as a means of spiritual opening. He was against *kriyās* generally for being too mechanical and not giving room for the divine force to act on its own. It is understandable, therefore, why those today who think of yoga as primarily postural have little knowledge of or interest in Integral Yoga.

The Mother (2004) also directly refuted the idea that *haṭhayoga* postures were special and insisted that any "well-planned and scientifically arranged program of system exercise" approached with surrender and aspiration "will become Yogic exercise" (p. 227). Under her direction, a comprehensive and robust program of physical culture developed, including an array of individual and group sports and competitions and the establishment of a playground and gymnasium in the ashram. Although physical culture was soon to be ascribed a great spiritual significance, its origins were rooted in the more prosaic aim of keeping the children of the ashram occupied and healthy with adults permitted but not required to participate.

Over time, however, physical culture came to the forefront of Integral Yoga as the Mother (2004) increasingly began to stress its evolutionary impact in numerous statements such as, "Physical culture is the best way of developing the consciousness of the body, and the more the body is conscious, the more it is capable of receiving the divine forces that are at work to transform it and give birth to the new human race" (p. 204). The primary purpose of exercise became therefore to make one strong and supple enough to "bear the pressure" of the divine influx, thereby increasing receptivity to the supramental force and catalyzing the very infusion of consciousness in the cells of the body.

CLOSE LINEAGES: ORGANIZATIONS DIRECTLY ESTABLISHED BY AUROBINDO AND THE MOTHER

As Heehs (2000b) noted, documents written by Aurobindo between 1911 and 1920 illustrate he had two ways of viewing spiritual community (pp. 209–223). One suggests that Aurobindo originally showed no interest in and remained ambivalent about starting an ashram. Another, however, demonstrates that as early as 1911 he regarded his group in Pondicherry as a "seed plot, a laboratory" for perfecting human society. In either case, Aurobindo (1997) was clearly suspicious about the fate of spiritual communities, noting that after an initial inspiration they often became reified into "a Church, a hierarchy, a fixed and unprogressive type of ethical living, a set of crystallized dogmas, ostentatious ceremonials, sanctified superstitions, an elaborate machinery for the salvation of mankind" (p. 264).

From the onset, then, Aurobindo wanted to create a new type of spiritual community that was free of the common problems such as petty regulations, mechanical observations, and proselytism that he saw as inflicting traditional ashrams. The first of what we are calling "close lineages," those associations directly established by Aurobindo or the Mother, was the Sri Aurobindo Ashram formed in 1926. Located in the middle of Pondicherry, Aurobindo insisted that the ashram was not a place for retreat from the world and that all residents were required to work. Ashramites engaged in both traditional forms of practice such as meditation and study and developed innovative practices such as the ritual distribution of food. All were required to be celibate, yet there were no distinctions based on gender.

Between 1926 and 1934 the number of people staying at the ashram grew from two dozen to around one hundred fifty, and during World War II the numbers rose to four hundred. Some individuals also formed groups for study or practice in other cities, although Aurobindo did not permit any type of missionary or outreach work. After Aurobindo's death in 1950, the ashram witnessed a gradual increase under the direction of the Mother and peaked at around fifteen hundred. An International Center of Education was founded in 1943 for members who joined the ashram as a family, and numerous other enterprises such as a printing press were to follow. The Mother also allowed the establishment of the Sri Aurobindo Society in 1960 to promote Integral Yoga and to engage in educational, medical, and cultural activities.

The most innovative community to develop under the Mother was the utopian "Universal Township" of Auroville. The Mother (2004) envisioned Auroville as a place dedicated to human unity and evolutionary progress where, according to the Auroville Charter, "to live in Auroville, one must be a willing servitor of the Divine Consciousness" (p. 193). It would be a nonsectarian space for living the "divine life" without religious dogmatism or authoritarianism. Such aspiration eventually saw devotees of the Mother create a green oasis and a town from a barren landscape literally with their own hands. After such an inspiring start, however, Auroville was threatened by a decade long battle for control between the Aurobindo Society and the Auroville community, a power struggle imbued with cosmic significance that included violent intimidation from both sides. It was a dark and deeply depressing period that saw many people flee and the Indian government eventually take control of the land.

Against expectations, Auroville survived, and while not without ongoing tensions it has grown into a functioning even flourishing community. It is now populated by eighteen hundred residents from thirty-five countries, all of whom have different relationships to Integral Yoga. Many of the older residents strongly identify as devotees of the Mother, the visitor center very much forefronts the Mother, one finds photos of Aurobindo and the Mother in resident's houses, and much energy is devoted to completing the building of the Matrimandir, the spiritual heart of Auroville. There is also a vocal population in Auroville that wants things to be done exactly as the Mother instructed regardless of other weighty pragmatic considerations such as climate and community resources.

At the same time, Auroville is markedly different from the Sri Aurobindo Ashram. The percentage of Westerners is much higher and the atmosphere decidedly more liberal and progressive. There is no requirement for participants to be devotees of Integral Yoga, although they must be committed to the principles underlying Auroville, and it is not uncommon for participants to have never heard of Integral Yoga before visiting. One will find workshops on t'ai chi and massage alongside Integral Yoga in the eclectic, pluralistic community. Many residents are drawn by the ideals of collective and ecologically sound living, and the numerous tourists passing through are as likely to be attracted by the stunning aesthetics of the Matrimandir as the spiritual principles embodied in its construction.

The current atmosphere at the ashram can be politely described as one of tension and transition. Numerous shifts are under way that appear to have coalesced around a massive controversy regarding the 2008 publication of the seemingly innocuous and scholastically impressive biography *The Lives of Sri Aurobindo* by Peter Heehs, an American who has been an ashram resident and worked in the ashram archives since its founding in 1973. A small but vocal number of ashramites engineered the banning of the book in India and are currently mounting a court case against the ashram's board of trustees who have refused their demand to expel Heehs from the ashram. The charges against the book range from the apologetic to the apocalyptic: some are outraged that the book portrays a human rather than a divine Aurobindo; others more sinisterly see Heehs as an agent of a cosmic plot to thwart the evolutionary work of Integral Yoga. Another complaint is that as the archivist who is supported financially by the ashram, Heehs has betrayed the community by not seeking their approval in how Aurobindo is publicly portrayed.

To think of community here as a monolithic and unitive entity, however, is misguided. To begin with, there is no set body or formal procedure by which this abstract notion of "community" approves documents, and none of Heehs' previous scholarship has elicited any response from ashram members. Moreover, many within the Integral Yoga community do support Heehs and see the charges as reflecting an increasing and deeply troubling "Integral Yoga fundamentalism" within the ashram.

They rightly point out that many of those who have called for the book to be banned have not even read it and that none of the specific charges against it have been substantiated. The situation is a complex one, which reflects many conflicting interests and internal power struggles at the ashram, and to reduce it solely to a clash between Western liberal and Indian conservative currents is a simplification. Yet at the same time many Westerners and Indians have spoken against a fundamental current within the ashram that is imposing an oppressive religious conservatism on others. A growth in worship of Aurobindo and the Mother as avatars is undeniable: over the last forty years there has been a great increase of Aurobindo devotees in Orissa and a corresponding influx of Orissa devotees within the ashram. While some feel such devotional religiosity practiced by these and other devotees is somewhat at odds with Aurobindo's antireligious pronouncements, the problem is less with its appearance and more with its exclusivity. These events have also taken place in a wider context in which Aurobindo has been appropriated by Hindu fundamentalists such as the Bharatiya Janata Party (BJP; see Heehs, 2000a). Taken together such occurrences illustrate the type of increasing Hinduization of the community being seen in modern meditation yoga schools such as Transcendental Meditation (TM; Humes, 2005: 55–79).

Mention should also be made of the small but serious number of Integral Yoga practitioners in the United States. While not a close lineage in the sense of being directly established by Aurobindo or the Mother, this community illustrates how Integral Yoga is practiced transnationally today. Scattered across the country, practitioners come together for an annual conference known as AUM (All US Meeting). In addition, a journal called *Collaboration*, which has a subscription list rate of two hundred but a significantly higher readership, keeps them abreast of community news. A few centers are specifically established for the practice of Integral Yoga, each of which functions independently with no formal ties between each other or the Pondicherry ashram. Two long-term American practitioners founded one of these, an ashram in Lodi, North California, that is modeled on the Pondicherry ashram. As with other decentralized Aurobindo centers, the Lodi ashram requested relics of Aurobindo from the Pondicherry ashram and enshrined them in a ceremony attended by around 225 people. It currently has seven residents, a mix of females and males ranging from ages twenty to eighty, all of whom are required to be celibate and do work or *karmayoga* for the ashram. The ashram hosts retreat, study, and community events that are attended by a mix of Western and Indian students. The latter group includes both those with direct connections to Integral Yoga, such as former residents of Auroville, and those for whom the ashram is visited alongside other Hindu pilgrim sites in the area.

CREATIVE LINEAGES: FROM INTEGRAL YOGA TO INTEGRAL PSYCHOLOGY

Yoga is nothing but practical psychology.

—Aurobindo

Aurobindo's Western legacy is arguably carried not by the sincere but small community of Aurobindo devotees but rather through what we are identifying as a *creative lineage* or assimilation of Integral Yoga. There are numerous avenues through which Aurobindo has creatively entered the contemporary yoga world. Both Sri Chimoy and Mother Meera, two transnational gurus, spent time at the ashram and have related their spiritual projects to Integral Yoga. What we are focusing on with our category of creative lineage, however, are direct adaptations of key concepts of Integral Yoga. An integral model, for example, is being increasingly championed by a wide variety of thinkers and applied to fields as diverse as spirituality, education, business, and science (Esbjorn-Hargens, 2010). It is obviously beyond the parameters of this article to track these multiple assimilations, so we will limit ourselves to the more modest aim of picking up one of the central threads, namely, the shift from Integral Yoga to Integral Psychology.

The development of Integral Psychology from Integral Yoga has occurred within the wider context of psychospirituality, an increasingly popular, modern, and decontextualized form of religiosity that often blurs boundaries between psychological and spiritual growth. If, with the rise of *haṭhayoga*, Aurobindo slipped out of the history of Modern Yoga, he has slipped back into contemporary iterations of East–West spirituality through a lineage of psychologized spirituality that runs from Carl Gustav Jung to transpersonal psychology (Parsons, 2008: 97–123).

Aurobindo never used the term Integral Psychology, but, with his permission, one of his students, former psychology, and philosophy professor Indra Sen began to identify an Integral Yoga Psychology in his work in the 1940s. Sen's Integral Yoga Psychology was not a new system but rather drew out the psychological dimensions implicit in Aurobindo's work and put them in dialogue with depth psychology. After meeting Jung in India in 1928, Sen followed his advice to pursue doctoral studies in psychology in Germany, and he saw many parallels between Jungian psychology and Integral Yoga (Sen, 1986: 145).

Integral Psychology as an Aurobindonian-inspired but fundamentally new system appears with philosophy professor Haridas Chaudhuri, the first Indian to bring Integral Yoga to America. Born in Bengal in 1913, Chaudhuri began a correspondence with Aurobindo while working on his Integral Yoga doctoral dissertation. In 1950, Chaudhuri received a letter from Frederick Spiegelberg inviting him to teach at a newly founded graduate school, the American

Academy of Asian Studies (AAAS), in San Francisco. Spiegelberg was a German professor who had escaped Nazi Germany and taught Asian religions at Stanford University. In 1949, he had experienced a profound transmission while he attended *darśan* ("sight," to see a great or holy being) with Aurobindo, and he later sought an Indian Integral Yoga scholar to join him and Alan Watts at the academy.

With the encouragement of Aurobindo, Chaudhuri moved to the United States with his family in 1951. AAAS was one of the first cultural spaces to introduce Asian philosophy and religion to the American public and the dynamic colloquiums hosted by Spiegelberg, Watts, and Chaudhuri were soon packed with leading figures from the Beat generation. Chaudhuri also founded the Cultural Integration Fellowship (CIF) where, in a building opposite Golden Gate Park, he would eloquently lecture at his popular Sunday morning service. CIF became the first destination in the United States for many visiting Indian gurus, hosted numerous Asian spiritual and cultural events, and functioned as a popular spiritual hub for the emerging counterculture of the 1960s.

Chaudhuri (1977) initially taught Aurobindo's insights through the lens of Western philosophy, but with the advent of humanistic and transpersonal psychology he realized that his audience related to and benefited more from a psychological framework. In 1970, he borrowed the term Integral Psychology and developed his own psychological system that is based on three principles—uniqueness, relatedness, and transcendence—and stresses the need for individual and interpersonal psychological development as well as spiritual transcendence. The basic project of Integral Psychology is an integration of Western depth psychology with Eastern spiritual teachings to develop a more complete model of the human being.

CIF's website declares that it is "inspired by the Integral Yoga of Sri Aurobindo," and the center displays a number of photographs and a bust of Aurobindo as well as using the same symbol as the Pondicherry ashram. There have never been, however, any formal ties between the two. Chaudhuri created CIF as a pluralistic nonsectarian space that promoted universal spiritual principles rather than an official Aurobindo center. Chaudhuri and CIF have undoubtedly had their most influence through acting as a conduit between Aurobindo's Integral Yoga and the Human Potential movement. One can trace a direct line from Integral Yoga through CIF to two of the major centers of the Human Potential movement and the transpersonal psychology field it birthed: Esalen and the Californian Institute of Integral Studies (CIIS).

Michael Murphy and Richard Price, the two founders of Esalen, met while Murphy was living at CIF in 1960. Murphy's connections with Aurobindo had begun much earlier when as a Stanford undergraduate he had stumbled on a life-changing comparative religion lecture delivered by the charismatic Spiegelberg. The fascinating story of Spiegelberg, Murphy, and Esalen has been told well before and does not need to be repeated here (Kripal, 2005:

113–121). The key point to note is that much of Esalen can be interpreted as a selective, creative, and distinctively American assimilation of Aurobindo's integral vision. Through Esalen and his books, Murphy (1992) contributed much to creating an Aurobindo-inspired evolutionary and integral spirituality centered on the full development of human potentials.

In 1968 Chaudhuri began the California Institute of Asian Studies to continue the mission of the American Academy of Asian Studies, which had closed due to loss of financial backing. Renamed as the California Institute for Integral Studies (CIIS) in 1980, it has grown into a thriving university in the heart of San Francisco. CIIS's distinctive signature is the development of an integral education that combines academic scholarship with spiritual transformation and through its student body, faculty publications, and popular public program it has significantly shaped contemporary East–West spiritualities. As with the other main creative lineage centers—Esalen and CIF—CIIS is committed to a pluralistic spiritual vision and its Aurobindonian roots are somewhat hidden. Nonetheless, Robert McDermott, its former president, has written several books on Aurobindo, CIIS has produced a couple dozen dissertations on Aurobindo making it one of the premier higher education institutions to study Integral Yoga outside of India, and it has recently developed ties with close lineage communities. In 2005, it offered its first study-abroad program in Auroville, and CIIS professors Brant Cortright, Bahman Shirazi, and one of the authors of this paper (Flores) have presented at numerous "Integral Psychology" conferences in India and the United States. Cortright (2007) also developed his own sophisticated system of Integral Psychotherapy that synthesizes the full range of Western depth psychology with Integral Yoga.

Perhaps no one, however, has done more to popularize integral psychology and evolutionary spirituality than transpersonal theorist turned integral pioneer Ken Wilber. Wilber's (2006) basic project is the integration of the Great Chain of Being presented by the perennial philosophers with Western developmental models in an evolutionary framework, and his latest offering is the "four quadrants model" (AQAL) and the "integral map". In 1998, Wilber founded the Integral Institute and has been at the forefront of numerous enterprises to promote his integral vision in fields as diverse as education, spirituality, sport, and business. Given the popularity of his prolific corpus, Wilber is arguably the author most responsible for introducing Aurobindo to a wider Western audience.

What type of Aurobindo he has introduced, however, is debatable. On one hand, Wilber credits Aurobindo as the great forefather of his own AQAL theory and reveres him as being a brilliant "philosopher-sage" who pioneered spiritual evolutionary metaphysics. On the other, however, Wilber declares that Aurobindo's insights have already been transcended and included by his own AQAL model. Flores (2010) challenged Wilber's selective misrepresentation of Aurobindo, who never viewed himself as a theorist but rather as a yogi co-creating a new spiritual path of Integral Yoga. So ironically, although Wilber has done the most to popularize the name "Aurobindo" in the West, he has at the same time relegated him to the past and left his contributions to Modern Yoga praxis unacknowledged.

While American guru Andrew Cohen is not in the Integral Psychology lineage proper, he also must be mentioned; he joined forces with Wilber to promote an integral and evolutionary spirituality. Cohen presents himself as a "pioneer of evolutionary enlightenment," a spiritual teaching that places a tantric understanding of nonduality in an evolutionary context. He claims that his teaching is rooted in a spontaneous experiential realization and that he was later astonished to discover strikingly similar insights in Aurobindo's Integral Yoga (Wilber & Cohen, 2004). Cohen credits Aurobindo with a seminal role in the lineage of evolutionary spirituality and through his popular magazine *EnlightenNext,* which is reported to have an international readership of seventy thousand, he is disseminating an essentially Aurobindonian spirituality to a large audience most of whom have likely never heard of Aurobindo before.

With the creative psychospiritual lineage, therefore, we see a much wider dissemination of aspects of Integral Yoga than with its close community. The popularity of Integral Psychology over Integral Yoga in the West is not surprising in a cultural context marked by what Philip Rieff (1966) famously called the "the triumph of the therapeutic". Critics of psychologized spirituality have argued that it dilutes authentic Indian spirituality with Western humanism and reduces yogic practice to capitalist commodities to be peddled in the spiritual marketplace (Carrette and King 2006). While it is important to recognize the real and substantial differences between Integral Yoga and Integral Psychology, however, we are more inclined to a sympathetic reading. To begin with, Integral Yoga is itself a synthesis of Indian and Western religious and philosophical thought, and one could reasonably argue that the integration of psychology continues rather than corrupts the internal spirit of the tradition. There is also a strong pragmatic element to the shift as witnessed in Chaudhuri's embrace of psychology as an effective and necessary translation for Integral Yoga in America. Moreover, it is not just a case of one-way influence, since Aurobindo's schematic hierarchy of consciousness greatly influenced the development of transpersonal psychology (Miovic, 2001). Similarly, a number of Indian devotees of Aurobindo such as A. S. Dalal (2001) have continued the project begun by Chaudhuri to combine Western psychology with Integral Yoga, focusing particularly on the importance of the psychic being in the psychotherapeutic process.

Rather than dismiss Integral Psychology, therefore, a more fruitful approach is to be transparent about what adaptations have been made and why. Such a perspective also allows for discrimination between the different iterations within the creative lineage and an illumination of why certain forms of Integral Psychology have been more popular. Wilber's Integral Psychology, for example, includes multiple spiritual traditions and perspectives, and it makes sense that in a pluralistic society such as the United States it would gain much greater popularity than those forms that focus exclusively on Integral Yoga. While close lineage devotees often problematize Integral Psychology as failing to capture the essence of Integral Yoga, the creative translations do find some grounds in Aurobindo's own writings and resonate with his approach of offering multiple ways into the yoga.

THE FORGOTTEN YOGA: REFLECTIONS ON THE INVISIBILITY OF INTEGRAL YOGA IN THE WEST

Many of Aurobindo's pioneering concepts—the evolution of consciousness, an integral approach to spiritual development, and a socially transformative this-worldly mysticism—permeate contemporary East–West spirituality, yet it is indisputable that Integral Yoga is unknown to a wider Western audience. We want to offer some reflections on its relative invisibility by focusing on the following interrelated areas: (1) publicity and marketing; (2) accessibility; (3) methods; (4) lineage; and (5) conservative currents within the Integral Yoga community.

(1) Publicity and Marketing

The growth of postural yoga has gone hand in hand with a multimillion-dollar industry in which legal battles have been fought over who owns certain postures, styles have been franchised, and trademarks patterned (Singleton, 2010: 3). While perhaps not attaining the heights of *āsana*-oriented yoga, meditational yoga groups have also engineered highly successful marketing and publicity campaigns. The global status of transnational gurus such as Maharishi Mahesh Yogi, Ammachi, and Satya Sai Baba attest to their success in constructing powerful institutional structures to promote their teachings. Studies show that these communities have engaged in careful strategies and marketing innovations to facilitate the growth of their movements in the West (Forsthoeffel & Humes, 2005).

Integral Yoga goes against the grain of the marketing mentality that has facilitated the mass dissemination of many meditational and postural yoga movements in the West. Aurobindo was a reluctant guru who lived in seclusion for the last twenty-six years of his life. In contrast to the American tour undertaken by Vivekanada and the later "world tours" of gurus such as Maharishi Mahesh Yogi, neither he nor the Mother ever left Pondicherry, nor did they encourage any direct form or specific program of "spiritual missionary" activity to the West. In fact, Aurobindo (2011) insisted that in "serious work" propaganda was a "poison" resulting either in a "boom or a stunt" or "a movement" and "a movement in the case of a work like mine means the founding of a school or a sect or some other damn nonsense. It means that hundreds and thousands of useless people join in and corrupt the work or reduce it to a pompous farce from which the truth that was coming down recedes into secrecy and silence" (p. 71). Similarly, while both Aurobindo and the Mother conceded it was necessary to have some organization within the ashram, for the most part they eschewed the type of organizational structures necessary to sustain any expansion or development campaigns. The Mother, for example, insisted that after she passed away Auroville was to have no central authority except that of the "Divine Consciousness."

Aurobindo and the Mother had little interest in promoting Integral Yoga because they believed that it was meaningful only for certain select evolved souls. All that was necessary for the descent of supermind was the participation of a select few, and great numbers of practitioners were not only irrelevant but might well have also been counterproductive since, as Aurobindo (2011) wrote, "nothing depends on the numbers" (p. 310). Following this view, it makes little sense to actively promote Integral Yoga; consequently, the Integral Yoga community in America does very little in the way of publicity. In an inversion of the supermarket spirituality model, many students believe that they do not choose but rather are chosen by Aurobindo and the Mother. Some claim that the gurus have appeared to them in dreams or visions and understand this as a subtle body encounter through which they are initiated into the yoga. A select few have even reported a type of mystical transmission or esoteric encounter with Aurobindo through his writings (Walker, 2008).

(2) Accessibility

For most readers the sheer size of Aurobindo's canon, not to mention his abstract and scholastic Victorian writing style, is intimidating. Aurobindo, simply put, is not an easy read. His prolific and sophisticated corpus demands an intelligent, careful, and committed reader. This helps explain why the concerted attempts of perhaps his most famous American devotee, Margaret Wilson Woodrow, who during her residence at the Pondicherry ashram between 1938 and 1944 became a "one woman publicity machine" sending Aurobindo's texts to scholars and literary figures, yielded little results. Only one short review of his twelve hundred page epic *The Life Divine* appeared, and Aurobindo's books failed to sell well in the United States (Syman, 2010: 143–159). Similarly, although there are numerous books on Integral Yoga, none have ever succeeded in popularizing it for a wider audience, and it has never gained the type of exposure that classic spiritual texts such as Paramahansa Yogananda's *Autobiography of a Yogi* have afforded their communities.

(3) Methods

The popularity of both first-wave and second-wave gurus and guru traditions in America can, in large part, be attributed to their ability to provide practical methods and technologies of transformation to a receptive utilitarian and technologically oriented audience. As De Michelis (2004) noted, much of the success of Vivekananda's Modern Yoga can be attributed to the fact that it delivered efficient methods to a Western esoteric audience that was hungry for them (p. 118). Vivekananda capitalized on the "strong craving for practices" that had arisen in cultic milieus toward the end of the nineteenth century by providing "techniques and methods to achieve immediate, practical and rational goals" (ibid.). Similarly, second-wave guru traditions flourished by supplying the spiritual technologies desired by the new age milieu within which they flowered. Cynthia Ann Humes (2005), for example, shows that much of the appeal of Maharishi Mahesh Yogi's early TM movement was because it offered an easy-to-learn, effective, and cheap meditation technique (p. 57).

Integral Yoga forms a notable counterpoint to the types of practical and result-oriented spiritual technologies that have proven so popular in America. To begin with, neither Aurobindo nor the Mother ever prescribed any specific routine practices that were to be used by all *sādhakas* (spiritual aspirants). They presented Integral Yoga not as a method but rather as a profound and challenging *process* of self-surrender and aspiration for the divine that was to be cultivated over a long period of time. It was, Aurobindo (1972) warned, "an exceedingly difficult aim and difficult yoga; to many or most it will seem impossible" (p. 505). Several practitioners commented on how the lack of specific practical technologies within Integral Yoga has shaped its audience and growth in the West. One participant suggested that Integral Yoga attracts a different type of practitioner from many of the other yoga traditions because it is not oriented around immediate results. She acknowledged that it was a demanding path without a wide appeal and would never become a mass movement. Another stressed that Integral Yoga was about an inner vibrational transformation that was difficult to externally measure and that one had to be immersed in the work to understand it. This type of exclusive insider perspective contrasts with the inclusivism and universalism that marks many of the most popular meditative and postural yogic schools.

(4) Lineage

Within the Indic traditions, the ideal passing on of yogic knowledge is through *paramparā*, the presence of the guru and the live transmission from one person to the next. *Paramparā* highlights the importance of lineage and a personalized embodied example of the teachings over more textual forms of transmission (De Michelis, 2008: 19). Neither Aurobindo nor the Mother appointed any successors, so there is no official lineage or living gurus within Integral Yoga. For some participants this absence of "live embodiment" is not problematic because they feel in contact with the presence of Aurobindo and the Mother. For others, though, this lack of living teachers is a significant obstacle. One long-term on-and-off resident of the Lodi ashram, for example, shared that she had decided to leave the ashram again because she needed more direct guidance and instruction. The lack of living charismatic teachers undoubtedly affects the numbers of newcomers into the community and illuminates why the majority of Western practitioners are over fifty and began practicing before the Mother died.

(5) Conservative Currents

A number of figures have commented critically on the devotional, conservative, and authoritarian currents in the ashram. As early as the 1950s Spiegelberg and Murphy were wary of what they respectively saw as slavish devotionalism in the community in which Aurobindo and the Mother were deified and their every word literalized. The recent controversy around Heehs's (2008) book has amplified what many feel is a troubling fundamentalism in the ashram. Some Auroville residents interviewed felt that the ashram was not a welcoming place for Westerners, others commented on an increasing xenophobia, and the intensely Indian devotional and religious atmosphere around the *samādhi* (the mausoleum of Aurobindo and the Mother) might well intimidate the casual Western visitor. These currents have undoubtedly affected the dissemination of Integral Yoga in the West. Western spiritual seekers are more likely to be drawn to the progressive and pluralistic atmosphere of Auroville and thus less likely to bring a traditional form of Integral Yoga back to the West. One practitioner, for example, stressed that she was not a devotee but a "child" of Aurobindo and the Mother and was inspired by, but not exclusively committed to, their teachings. Such figures tend to be drawn to and develop the type of inspired iterations that we have seen in the creative lineages rather than practicing and preserving the specific tradition of Integral Yoga.

CONCLUSION

Numerous studies have shown that Modern Yoga emerges through a reframing of traditional Indian practices and beliefs in response to the different assumptions and aspirations of Western modernity. Nowhere is this more evident than in Integral Yoga which, from the very body, speech, and texts of Aurobindo to its creative contemporary iterations, is an intentional, explicit, and sophisticated hybrid mix of East–West values and thought. As Kripal (2005) notes, Integral Yoga could not have been created in either the East or the West but exists only as a creative fusion of the two cultural, philosophical, and religious horizons and as a cross-fertilization that aims, moreover, at the birth of new and better selves and worlds (p. 111).

Such integral visions have since fallen out of academic fashion; they have either been dismissed as essentializing "affirmative Orientalism" or have been berated for being historically inauthentic. Such critiques are not entirely without merit: claiming modern iterations as traditional is simply incorrect, and monolithic categories such as East–West can erase internal multiplicity and reinforce binaries when used unreflectively. Although we are fully cognizant of such dangers, perhaps there is no better time not just to remember but also to recover and resuscitate Aurobindo and the Mother and their East–West integral legacy. As we write this piece, a battle over "who owns yoga" blazes across religious communities, yoga studios, academic journals, blogs, and even the *New York Times* (Vitello, 2010). In their campaign to "take back yoga" and reclaim "branding rights," Hindu purists perpetuate bad history and pursue a nationalistic agenda. Christian evangelicals, who rant that yoga is an insidious demonic form of false religion that threatens (an imaginary) Christian America, ironically support them in this purist project. Both parties erase yoga's fluid and dynamic history, reinforce a false opposition between the sacred and secular, and perpetuate religious dogmatism, exclusivism, and fundamentalism.

At a time, then, when Modern Yoga and the Integral Yoga community itself are threatened by fundamentalism, perhaps there is no better moment to fully claim and celebrate the spirit of Aurobindo's East–West integralism and the pluralistic and promising worlds that it has and may still birth. From the dialogical texts of Aurobindo to the cosmopolitan and nonsectarian spaces of Auroville and Esalen, we see glimpses of the secular and spiritual transformative potentials of hybrid East–West yoga. It is, we think, a vision worth remembering.

REFERENCES

Alter, Joseph S. 2004. *Yoga in Modern India: The Body between Science and Philosophy*. Princeton, NJ: Princeton University Press.

Aurobindo, Sri. 1967. *Sri Aurobindo and The Mother on Physical Education*. Pondicherry: Ashram Trust.

———. 1972. *Letters on Yoga, Vol. 1: The Collected Works of Sri Aurobindo*. Pondicherry: Sri Aurobindo Ashram.

———. 1979. *Health and Healing in Yoga: Selections from the Writings and Talks of the Mother*. Pondicherry: Sri Aurobindo Ashram.

———. 1997. *The Human Cycle, Vol. 25: The Collected Works of Sri Aurobindo*. Pondicherry: Sri Aurobindo Ashram.

———. 1999. *The Synthesis of Yoga, Vol. 23: The Collected Works of Sri Aurobindo*. Pondicherry: Sri Aurobindo Ashram.

———. 2005. *The Life Divine, Vol. 21:* The *Collected Works of Sri Aurobindo*. Pondicherry: Sri Aurobindo Ashram.

———. 2011. *Letters to Himself and the Ashram. Vol. 35: The Collected Works of Sri Aurobindo*, Pondicherry: Sri Aurobindo Ashram.

Carrette, Jeremy and Richard King. 2005. *Selling Spirituality, the Silent Takeover of Religion*. London: Routledge.

Chaudhuri, Haridas. 1977. *The Evolution of Integral Consciousness*. Wheaton, IL: Quest Books.

Cortright, Brant. 2007. *Integral Psychology: Yoga, Growth and Opening the Heart*. Albany: State University of New York Press.

Dalal, A. S. 2001. *A Greater Psychology: An Introduction to Sri Aurobindo's Psychological Thought*. New York: Jeremy P. Tarcher/Putnam.

De Michelis, Elizabeth. 2004. *A History of Modern Yoga: Patañjali and Western Esotericism*. London: Continuum.

———. 2008. Modern Yoga: History and Forms. In Mark Singleton and Jean Byrne (eds.), *Yoga in the Modern World: Contemporary Perspectives*. London: Routledge, pp. 17–34.

Esbjorn-Hargens, Sean. (ed.). 2010. *Integral Theory in Action: Applied, Theoretical and Constructive Perspectives on the AQAL Model*. Albany: State University of New York Press.

Feuerstein, George. 1998. *The Yoga Tradition*. Prescott, AZ: Hohm Press.

Flores, Charles. 2010. Appropriation in Integral Theory: The Case of Sri Aurobindo and the Mother's "Untold" Integral View. In Sean Esbjorn-Hargens (ed.), *Integral Theory in Action*. Albany: State University of New York Press, pp. 369–385.

Forsthoeffel, Thomas A. and Cynthia Ann Humes (eds.). 2005. *Gurus in America*. Albany: State University of New York Press.

Heehs, Peter. 2008. *The Lives of Sri Aurobindo*. New York: Columbia University Press.

———. 2000a. *Nationalism, Terrorism and Communalism: Essays in Modern Indian History*. Delhi: Oxford University Press.

———. 2000b. The Error of All Churches: Religion and Spirituality in Communities Rounded or "Inspired" by Sri Aurobindo. In Anthony Copley (ed.), *Gurus and Their Followers*. Delhi: Oxford University Press, pp. 209–223.

Humes, Cynthia Anne. 2005. Maharishi Mahesh Yogi: Beyond the TM Technique. In Thomas A. Forsthoeffel and Cynthia Ann Humes (eds.), *Gurus in America*. Albany: State University of New York Press, pp. 55–79.

IY Fundamentalism: Religious Fundamentalism and Integral Yoga. Available online at http://www.iyfundamentalism.info (accessed November 20, 2011).

Kripal, Jeffrey J. 2005. Reading Aurobindo from Stanford to Pondicherry. In Jeffrey J. Kripal and Glenn W. Shuck (eds.), *On the Edge of the Future: Esalen and the Evolution of American Culture*. Bloomington: Indiana University Press, pp. 113–121.

Miovic, Michael. 2001. Sri Aurobindo and Transpersonal Psychology. In A. S. Dalal (ed.), *A Greater Psychology*. Pondicherry: Sri Aurobindo Ashram Trust, pp. 10–50.

Mother. 2004. *The Complete Works of the Mother*, volume 13. Pondicherry: Sri Aurobindo Ashram Trust.

Murphy, Michael. 1992. *The Future of the Body: Explorations into the Further Evolutions of Human Nature*. New York: Tarcher/Putnam Books.

Parsons, William B. 2008. Psychologia Perennis and the Academic Study of Mysticism. In William B. Parsons, Diane Jonte-Pace, and Susan E. Henking (eds.), *Mourning Religion*. Charlottesville: University of Virginia Press, pp. 97–123.

Rieff, Philip. 1966. *The Triumph of the Therapeutic*. Chicago: University of Chicago Press.
Roy, Anilbaran. 1929. *Diary of Anilbaran Roy*. Pondicherry: Sri Aurobindo Archives.
Sen, Indra. 1986. *Integral Psychology: The Psychological System of Sri Aurobindo*. Pondicherry: Sri Aurobindo Press.
Singleton, Mark. 2010. *Yoga Body: The Origins of Modern Postural Practice*. Oxford: Oxford University Press.
Strauss, Sarah. 2008. Adapt, Adjust, Accommodate: The Production of Yoga in a Transnational World. In Mark Singleton and Jean Byrne (eds.), *Yoga in the Modern World: Contemporary Perspectives*. London: Routledge, pp. 49–73.
Syman, Stefanie. 2010. *The Subtle Body: The Story of Yoga in America*. New York: Farrar, Straus & Giroux.
Vitello, Paul. 2010. Hindu Group Stirs a Debate over Yoga's Soul. *New York Times*, November 28, p. A1.
Walker, Robert. S. 2008. Integral Reading: A Hermeneutic-Phenomenological Study of Reading Differently as Suggested in Sri Aurobindo's "Letters on Yoga." *Dissertation Abstracts International* 69 (02): 1–10.
Wilber, Ken. 2006. *Integral Spirituality: A Startling New Role for Religion in the Modern and Postmodern World*. Boston: Integral Books.
Wilber, Ken and Andrew Cohen. 2004. Following the Grain of the Kosmos: The Guru and the *Pandit*: Ken Wilber & Andrew Cohen in Dialogue. *What Is Enlightenment*? May–July 2004. Available online at http://www.enlightennext.org/magazine/j25/guruPandit.asp (accessed April 25, 2009).

CHAPTER 3

Shri Yogendra: Magic, Modernity, and the Burden of the Middle-Class Yogi

JOSEPH S. ALTER

There are a number of ways modernity produces the conditions under which the status of a guru takes shape as well as ways gurus as public figures reflect paradoxes and contradictions in terms of the development and communication of knowledge. In other words, as a discrete, specialized category of teacher, a guru is defined by modern ways of knowing in relation to a spectrum of discipline-specific designations for expertise, as well as by changing ideas about the limits and nature of knowledge. Although the idea of a guru invokes a sense of deep, profound, and inspired knowledge, the force of this invocation is a function of modernity's infatuation with the authenticity of the past and with ancient wisdom rather than an articulation of archaic history unto itself. In other words, gurus represent modernity, even though they do so indirectly by embodying what modernity seems to have left behind or lost touch with. Gurus are, to various degrees, self-consciously out of sync with the present, both in terms of time and place. This produces their particular authority as well as a range of paradoxes and contradictions.

This chapter is concerned with the paradoxes and contradictions embodied by one of the key figures in the early twentieth-century yoga renaissance, Manibhai Haribhai Desai, who as a guru adopted the title Shri Yogendra—after briefly calling himself Swami Yogananda—to define and teach his brand of yoga physical education in Bombay (now Mumbai) and New York. In ways that will become clear, Desai's role in the yoga renaissance is defined by the interplay of various kinds of knowledge and by the claims that he made in relation to these knowledges rather than by taking on disciples and thereby falling into the "guru slot." Throughout his career Desai remained very independent

Figure 3.1:
Yogendra instructing schoolboys in rhythmic exercise. (With permission of the Yoga Institute, Santa Cruz.)

and published extensively, although almost exclusively under the banner of his own institute (Yogendra & Yogendra, 1939; Yogendra, 1934; 1940; 1966; 1975; 1978; 1997). In 1918 he established the Yoga Institute at the beachfront home of Dadabhai Naoroji. Now located in Santa Cruz, a neighborhood of Mumbai, it is the oldest organized yoga center in the world, a claim that has taken on considerable importance in light of yoga's place both in the contemporary moment of rapid globalization as well as in relation to yoga's claim to an ancient history of ideas and practices.

Thus, broadly speaking, two bodies of literature have a bearing on Yogendra's position and on understanding the development of his career in relation to modernity. One body of literature is concerned with the historical and philosophical identity of yogis, *saṃnyāsins,* and gurus as defined in the classical and medieval literature (see Eliade, 1958; Lorenzen, 1972; 2004; Olivelle, 1992; 1993, 2007; Fort 1996, 1998; White, 1996; 2003; 2009). A second body of literature focuses on the dynamics of Orientalism and the warp and woof of Hindu spirituality and mysticism in the nineteenth and twentieth centuries (see Singleton & Byrne, 2008; Singleton, 2010; Urban, 2003; 2006; Shrinivas 2008; Syman, 2010; Williamson, 2010). Although intimately connected and recursively inspired, these literatures have quite different orientations and intellectual textures, the former being concerned with a delineated understanding of historical texts and the history of ideas, and the latter with a history of the present based on textual analysis. With respect to Yogendra's position in relation to the history of ideas, David Gordon White's 1989 article

"Why Gurus Are Heavy" is a directly relevant example of the former. An examination of White's argument provides critical insight on Desai's struggle with magic, alchemy, and sexuality in relation to his effort to sanitize, secularize, and rationalize the practice of yoga. With regard to the way the idea of a guru fits into contemporary practices—and articulates a dimension of Yogendra's persona—Kirin Narayan's (1993) *Refraction of the Field at Home: American Representations of Hindu Holy Men in the 19th and 20th Centuries* sheds light on how and why the figure of the guru is constructed and deconstructed in the context of modernity. Her analysis provides a frame of reference for understanding where Yogendra fits into the transnational refractions of globalized *gurudom*.

Desai's life is characterized by a number of transformations along lines that define the trajectory of modernity and colonial globalization in general. Desai was born in a village in southeastern Gujarat but lived in the cosmopolitan environment of Bombay. As a young man he traveled to the United States, spending three years in New York before returning to his village home. As the son of a Brahmin farmer and village schoolteacher, his friendship with Homi Dadina, son-in-law of Dadbhai Naoroji, and the philosopher Surendranath Das Gupta, as well as his correspondence with Rabindranath Tagore, characterizes the growth, plasticity, and a particular intellectual orientation of the middle class in early twentieth-century India (Bayly, 1983; Joshi, 2010; Kumar, 1989). After starting his education in the Gandevi village school, Desai's father enrolled him in Amalsad English School and subsequently, with ambitions for the Indian Civil Service, in St. Xavier's College, Bombay. Although Desai never completed his studies, his education brought him into contact with a number of wealthy and well-connected individuals who provided the means by which he was able to become a teacher of *āsana* and *prāṇāyāma* and one of the first individuals to modernize and popularize yoga. Building on interest generated by Vivekananda (Radice, 1998) and Aurobindo (Heehs, 2008; Minor, 1999), he worked to define yoga in terms of science, medicine, and physical fitness as well as in relation to questions of religion, education, and psychology. Perhaps better than any other figure in the yoga renaissance, he embodied an idealized and ultimately paradoxical synthesis of metaphysical fitness and physical philosophy.

Even though Yogendra's primary contribution to yoga was the development of rhythmic exercise regimens and the medical application of *āsana* and *prāṇāyāma*, it is particularly noteworthy that he dramatically embodied the tension between yoga as philosophy and yoga as physical fitness, as these aspects of yoga in practice came to be disarticulated in the context of modernity (see also Kuvalayananda & Vinekar, 1963; Kuvalayananda, 1963; 1972). To some extent this may also account for the fact that although he was very successful in establishing the Yoga Institute, he never achieved the kind of public recognition accorded to individuals like B. K. S. Iyengar (Kadetsky,

2004), Swami Sivananda (Strauss, 2005), K. Pattabhi Jois (Donahaye, 2010), and Swami Yogananda (1946), who more definitively embodied clearly defined roles either as spiritual gurus or as masters of "traditional" *āsana* and *prāṇāyāma*. Yogendra's eclectic, idiosyncratic, and holistic philosophy of evolutionary self-development based on rhythmic exercises proved to be a message with a specific gravity that prevented it from easily rising with the tide of popular globalization.

Desai's encounter with Paramahamsa Madhavadasji in 1916 changed the course of his life. While a student as St. Xavier's College in Bombay, Desai—a self-proclaimed skeptic—went with his roommate to hear a discourse given by Madhavadasji. Very soon he became a follower, leaving Bombay for his guru's ashram in Malsar, on the banks of the Narmada twenty-five miles upriver from Bharuch. Needless to say this abrupt change was not easy, and, with Madhavadasji's support, Desai, an only child, had to persuade his skeptical, worldly father to let him go. At Malsar Desai apprenticed with Madhavadasji, working out a relationship whereby he self-consciously did not become an initiated disciple (*saṃnyāsin*) but served as something like a junior chief of staff, translator, and scribe.

Madhavadasji is in interesting figure. Although details of his early life are vague and probably impossible to pin down (it is said he died at the age of 123 in 1921), he was born into a Bengali Brahmin household in the village of Shantipur, northeast of Calcutta in the Nadia district probably sometime in the late 1830s. He was educated at a missionary school in Calcutta, most likely Scottish Church College in the 1850s, and was trained in law. After practicing law in Bengal, he renounced the world sometime in the 1870s and became an itinerant *saṃnyāsin* teaching a devotional form of mysticism based on the *bhakti* tradition of Chaitanya Mahāprabhu as well as *āsana* and *prāṇāyāma* for the treatment of health problems. According to accounts provided by his disciples, Madhavadasji lived and traveled in the Himalayas for many years and became an enlightened master of *haṭhayoga* based on this experience. Exactly how Madhavadasji reconciled the principles of Gauḍiya Vaiṣṇavism (Mukherjee, 1986; Chakravarti 1996; Broo, 2003; see also Lorenzen, 1995; 1996) with the tantric Śaiva alchemy of *haṭhayoga* (see Briggs, 1938; White, 1996) is unclear, but what he did certainly reflects an innovative synthesis that has become very common in contemporary practice.

Whatever the precise lineage of ideas and practices manifest in Madhavadasji's teaching, there is no question that he embodied the persona of a mystic—full beard; long, matted hair; black robes—and is commonly depicted seated on a tiger skin (although close examination shows it to be a leopard) with a begging bowl, *kamaṇḍalu* (water pot), and *paduka* (sandals) by his side (Azmi, 1994). By Desai's own account it is clear that Madhavadasji's focus was on absolute faith in God as realized through the constant chanting of his name: *Hare Kṛṣṇa, Hare Rām*. As he wrote to Desai in an early letter, providing moral and spiritual support for his conflicted follower, "... Make your mind strong and adamant and abandon your father. What is going on is for the good. Purify yourself, this is a purificatory process. Remember, if you give up firmness of mind it will lead to catastrophe! Be quiet.... start the medicine by chanting the name of God (Shri Hari). Do not let go even for a moment without remembering Him" (Rodrigues, 1982: 42).

Despite the fact that his teachings concern ecstatic devotion to God, both Desai and Jagganath G. Gune, Madhavadasji's other primary "disciple," clearly indicate that their guru used *āsana*, *prāṇāyāma*, and various *kriyā* and *śuddhi* (purification) procedures to treat sick people who came to the Malsar ashram. Yoga is consistently and unequivocally referred to as a *technology*. As Desai's biographer puts it: "Much of the training was related to practical and pragmatic use of Yoga and the application of it in various situations of sickness and suffering. The cause of these problems had to be first studied and an intuitive skill of analysis had to be developed.... Thus the instructions continued from learning and observing to acting and resolving. A round of the 'sick ward' would end up with a wealth of information" (Rodrigues, 1982: 47). Although he was an enlightened mystic who is said to have performed miracles, including magical cures, Madhavadasji seems to have also been one of the very first to integrate much more down-to-earth physiological yoga into the rubric of nature cure as it—a distinctly European system of treatment—became a very popular form of modern alternative medicine in India at the turn of the century (Alter, 2000).

Many features of Desai's life before he met Madhavadasji are interesting, but it is important to note that after a serious bout of typhoid as a child he became an enthusiastic proponent of physical fitness, exercise, and wrestling during his teenage years in Amalsad.

> "The love for physical culture imbibed by Gulababhai's master continued. Mani [as Desai was known in school] got so fond of gymnastics and wrestling that he began to skip the moral science classes to get extra practice in the gymnasium. As he grew in strength his reputation also grew. Mani was hailed as a local Mr. Universe..." (Rodrigues, 1982: 20).

To whatever extent this interest grew directly out of the organization of school sports at the English School, it certainly set the stage for Desai's subsequent development of a program of athletic yoga and the incorporation of yoga physical fitness and ethics into the rubric of muscular Christianity, a broad-based, turn-of-the-century reform movement that linked morals, ethics, and character development to ideals of fitness, fairness, hard work, and self-improvement (Alter, 2004a; 2006; Hall, 2006; Knott, 2000).

To the extent that Desai's athleticism was encouraged by Gulababhai, the principal of the school in Amalsad, one can imagine that as a teenager

Madhavadasji might have had a similar experience some seventy years earlier when the Scottish Presbyterian Alexander Duff (1839a; 1839b; 1854) enthusiastically incorporated sports into the curriculum of his new college to build muscles and morals as a means by which to promote the development of Christianity among the middle-class youth of Calcutta. His legacy certainly had a discernable impact—although with recursive religious twists—on the thinking of two somewhat later, much more famous graduates of Scottish Church College, Narendranath Dutta (Swami Vivekananda), and Mukunda Lal Ghosh (Swami Yogananda).

When Desai left Bombay to join Madhavadasji at the ashram in Malsar, he started practicing *āsana* and *prāṇāyāma*. Although the details of his training can be determined only indirectly, he apparently developed considerable skill and a high level of accomplishment. He became very adept, and it was on the basis of his ability to perform *āsana* and *prāṇāyāma* exercises that he was drawn into the elite circles of Bombay. However, it was the publication of two books of devotional poetry—*Prabhubhakti* (*Devotion to the Lord*, 1917a) and *Hṛdayapuṣpāñjali* (*Prayers from the Heart*, 1917b)—and a Gujarati translation of Rabindranath Tagore's (1918) *Gitāñjali* that brought Desai to the attention of Sir Rustom Pestonji Masani, a prominent member of Bombay society. Masani invited Desai to his home in Versova, and by late 1918 Desai began teaching yoga to a small group, including Homi Dadina a wealthy member of the Pharsi community.

From the very outset, Desai conceptualized his teaching as directly related to health and healing. Founding documents of the Yoga Institute are in the form of medical admission records that show that students were enrolled as patients, Homi Dadina himself suffering from piles and "trouble with uric acid." This follows directly on what Desai had been trained to do in Malsar: "Many cases would be brought to the āśramā for relief and Paramahamsaji would pass on selected ones, at first very simple, to his beloved disciple. On one occasion a wealthy woman from Bombay came seeking help for pulmonary tuberculosis. The usual procedures were followed and one of the āśramā attendants gave the woman a clean piece of cloth (*vastra dhouti*) to swallow partially in order to remove mucous from the oesophagus and stomach" (Rodrigues, 1982: 47).

As letters indicate, Desai was often referred to as Homi Dadina's *yogi* or *swami* and was regarded as something of an exotic curiosity. However, treatment using the "technology" of *āsana* and *prāṇāyāma* proved effective to the extent that the demand for Desai's treatment began to increase. As several letters indicate, the elite of Bombay conceptualized yoga as a branch of nature cure or fit it into the larger bracket of *physical culture*, a fin-de-siècle term that encompassed a spectrum of different kinds of exercise and health regimens. As Morarji Jeram Trikamji puts it after five days of treatment at the Yoga Institute in early March of 1919: "My confidence in nature cure has been doubly confirmed by the wonderful cure on myself within such a short period and I feel that the profound study of Swamiji Mani in the science of nature cure and Yoga . . . will not fail to [restore] health and vitality" (Rodrigues, 1982: 77). Following his success in Bombay, Desai and his benefactors made arrangements for a trip to the United States to promote the "technological Yoga renaissance" by building on the momentum of interest generated by Vivekananda and on sympathy for things Indian generated by Lala Lajpat Rai (Grewal & Banga, 2000; Gupta & Gupta, 1999), who was in exile in New York. Before departure, Desai—who was now referred to as Swami Yogananada—Dadina and Shapurji Sohrabji, another wealthy Pharsi patron, made a trip to Shantiniketan to receive the blessing of Rabindranath Tagore.

Desai and Dadina traveled to the United States via England, where they had very little success generating interest in "yoga therapeutics." However, after a very rough voyage they arrived in New York in mid-December 1919 and were reassured in their project through a chance meeting with Lala Lajpat Rai. Some indication of Desai's mood and motivation can be discerned from letters: "How much easier it would be if I can only induce those sleeping sages of the Himalayas to come to the West and open the eyes of the people who can never take anything for granted without direct perception. They need the bite of a snake before they can realize that it is a snake, and even then the trouble is that they will call it a scorpion. . . . In some ways, however, the Westerners are right. . . . They believe that in preference to a theory against a practice, they would rather have the practice. What is the use of knowing that fire burns, when you try to take a live coal in your hand" (Rodrigues, 1982: 90).

In the United States, Desai sought to promote yoga therapy as a practical form of alternative medicine. He did so by providing the proof of "direct perception" but also by invoking the power of the "sleeping sages." In a letter to Mrs. White, he wrote about yoga as the "Science of Sciences": "It is the oldest philosophy and science that has been known to humanity, formulated by those ancient forest sages of India. Think of five thousand years back when all the nations were in a state of barbarism, and this harmonious system of philosophy was preached in the Indian forests" (Rodrigues, 1982: 82). Significantly, Desai decided to capitalize on the American obsession with the extraordinary (see Syman, 2010) and agreed, in essence, to perform magic based on his yogic abilities to secure backing from the medical community for his goal of building a nature cure sanitarium. A number of leading physicians were invited to the flat where he was staying at Riverside Drive to watch as he inflated one lung at a time, changed the temperature of extremities at will, turned on lights with the electricity from his body, and stopped his watch.

Given how quickly Desai was able to secure help and support from a small cadre of individuals, including Dr. Charles W. Hack of the Life Extension Institute and Dr. A. G. Bell of the Hygiene Reference Board, his performances, along with his philosophical discourses, must have been persuasive. By late spring 1920, a suitable location was found, and an estate was donated. On June 20, the Yoga Institute was formally opened in Harriman, near Tuxedo Park, New York. As in Bombay, the institute—also referred to as a yoga ashram—operated as a sanatorium, with Desai prescribing regimens of *āsana*, *prāṇāyāma*, *dhautī*, and various *kriyās* under Hack's medical supervision.

In the light of his own magical performances, it is not surprising that the treatment provided by Desai at the Yoga Institute is characterized in different ways—rational and scientific based on the principles of yoga technology and also miraculous based on the mystical aura of Swami Yogananda's identity as a guru and swami. Although in some respects difficult to reconcile in practice, Desai was able to bring the rational and the magical together through the use of language and by invoking the wisdom of the past. Under the rubric of the institute he printed a brochure titled "Lost Science of 5000 Years Ago" and used this to promote a lecture tour.

While it is unclear how successful Desai was on the East Coast lecture circuit, titles of the talks that he gave indicate that he identified himself with—but sometimes sharply distinguished himself from—a range of different but closely related "New Age" philosophies, including spiritualism, Theosophy, New Thought (Morrissey, 2002), and Transcendentalism, as well as closely linked systems of health reform, primarily naturopathy, gymnastics, and physical fitness. Thus, he engaged directly with William J. Flagg's (1898) *Yoga; or Transformation* and met or corresponded with the religious studies scholar Dr. A. V. Jackson and Hereward Carrington of the Society for Psychical Research. Lectures titled "The Logic of Gymnastics" and "To Live a Hundred Years" as well as "How they Live in the Forests" seek to relate principles of yoga directly to the way Bernarr MacFadden and Benedict Lust were defining nature cure and physical culture.

In many respects the three years Desai spent in the southern Catskills of New York shaped his philosophy and his orientation toward the practice of yoga, even though his return to India in late 1922 set the stage for a kind of radically recursive reorientation of the subject. This reorientation began, in essence, through a chance encounter with a young scholar of Indian philosophy Surendranath Dasgupta who was returning to India from England onboard the same ship sailing from London to Bombay. Desai and Dasgupta, who had just published the first volume of *History of Indian Philosophy* (1922; see also 1927), had much to talk about. At the end of the voyage Dasgupta invited Desai to visit him in Chittagong where he was to be professor of Sanskrit and Bengali.

While Desai's experience in the United States—healing Catholic priests and teaching mysticism and rhythmic breathing to Boston Brahmins—seems exotic and out of the ordinary, it reflects the larger history of how holy men from India have been integrated into American religious experience (see Williamson, 2010). As Kirin Narayan points out, swamis and gurus like Yogendra played an important if complicated and conflicted role in the history of American spirituality. They were regarded as occult, dangerous, and debauched practitioners of black magic by some and by others as sage wise men offering profound, exotic insights on transcendental consciousness and the nature of God. Against the counter-counterfactual of Vivekananda's physical presence and erudition at the Chicago World's Parliament of Religions 1893, many of the negative opinions against gurus and swamis carried over into the twentieth century from earlier missionary accounts—the bed of nails and hypnotic rope trick being iconic. But whatever the legacy of these prejudices, there was pervasive discomfort with what might be called the *body of the ascetic*—recall the magic performed at Riverside Drive—as this body was understood to animate flesh and blood holy men such as Desai.

An interesting footnote gives some indication of just how common it was for swamis to go on lecture tours during the roaring twenties. Having taken on the title of Swami Yogananda in the United States and using it as an official name upon his return to India, Desai confused his colleagues in New York when they read announcements that a Swami Yogananda was scheduled to give lectures on yoga and psychology in Philadelphia. This Swami Yogananda was, in all probability, Mukunda Lal Ghosh, recent graduate of Scottish Church College and future founder of the Self-Realization Fellowship (see Ghosh 1925, 1934, 1938), who had arrived in Boston from Calcutta in 1920. Ghosh gave lectures on the East Coast from 1921 through 1924, at which point he undertook a cross-country tour ending in Los Angeles. Apart from a brief return visit to India in the 1930s, he remained on the West Coast until his death in 1952.[1] His book *Autobiography of a Yogi* (Ghosh 1946) has become a classic text in the field of popular spiritualism and first-person comparative religion.

In his lectures, and with respect to the practical nature of yoga therapeutics, Yogendra was constantly faced with the problem of defining his uniqueness, claiming authority, demonstrating truth value, and at the same time distancing himself from pretenders of various sorts: one of the most notable was William Walker Atkinson (1902, 1908, 1922a, 1922b), who wrote many popular books on yoga under the pseudonyms Yogi Ramacharka (1903, 1904a, 1904b, 1906, 1909a, 1909b, 1931) and Swami Bhakta Vishita as well as the somewhat less prosaic Theron Q. Dumont. Although Yogendra took issue with "charlatans and demagogues" in the abstract, rarely if ever naming names, he was incensed by the way yoga was, in his view, being exploited, fetishized, mystified, and perverted by those with no direct, personal experience who willfully confused magic with healthy self-development and robust spirituality. In fact, however, there is little that clearly distinguishes Yogendra's writing from the likes of Atkinson, since many people were using yoga in various ways to define their own brand of hygienic spiritualism and metaphysical fitness.

As Kirin Narayan (1993: 495) rightly points out, many of the holy men who came to the United States in the early twentieth century returned again to India. Their encounter with various American traditions and audiences shaped their practice, and this recursive process has played an important role in the development of modern traditions. Upon his return, Yogendra put on *āsana* performances in Chittagong much as he had done in New York—causing a commotion among Dasgupta's middle-class educated colleagues—but he also set off along a track of discovery that follows the trajectory of yoga's purported precolonial history. It is important to understand this in relation to the problem of authenticity encountered in New York, as this brought underlying questions about the nature of Madhavadasji's experience into focus.

Returning to Malsar and Bombay to fulfill family duties following his father's illness, Yogendra became a businessman, marketing a product called YOCO book polish or varnish—sometimes confused with boot polish but a different product altogether—that prevented silverfish and termites from making short work of published material. Whatever else he learned from Dasgupta, the varnish used by the philosopher in the torpid climate southeast of Dhaka had direct, practical significance and textual value. Capitalizing on Dasgupta's innovative invention to preserve his personal library, Desai negotiated deals for the distribution and sale of YOCO, securing an international contract with Oxford University Press. Business deals required travel, and in early 1923 Desai used these trips around India to visit the Bohar and Tilla hermitages in the Punjab as well as sites in Lahore, Jammu, and Kashmir, where he hoped to find ancient yoga manuscripts.

While traveling and searching for manuscripts, Desai was also trying to secure support and find a new location for the Yoga Institute. An arrangement with the founder of Amritdhara Pharmacy in Lahore fell through when Vaid Bhushan *Paṇḍit* Thakur Datt Sharma, the famous *āyurvedic* innovator's son, died unexpectedly. Earlier Prabhanshankar Pattani, the diwan of Bhavnagar State, offered Desai property in Lonavala, but this offer was never formalized. Subsequently Jagganath G. Gune established Kaivalyadhama in the hill station between Pune and Bombay where the diwan had land holdings. Clearly Desai and Gune were in direct competition to secure patronage and public support for their very similar projects. At various points they stepped on each other's toes, Gune—referred to as an imposter by Desai's partisan biographer—being more persistent in his effort to secure support from politicians, princely estates, and captains of industry (Alter, 2004b).

Although it is not clear what Desai found by way of specific manuscripts while traveling in 1923, at the Bohar and Tilla hermitages he "came in contact with the oldest traditional institution of Goraksha and Matsyendra" (Rodrigues, 1982: 124). In a complex way these hermitages represent the illusive essence of the "lost science of five-thousand years"; they seem to locate, in time and space, the forest sages Desai had referenced in his New York lectures.

As detailed by David Gordon White (1996), Matsyendranath's disciple, Gorakhnath, may be given credit for founding the Nāth *sampradāya* in the thirteenth century. The Nāth yogis represent a tantric tradition of embodied alchemical practices that involve esoteric physiological procedures based on the principles of *sāṃkhya* and the internal hydraulic transmutation of channeled sexual fluids. What concerned the Nāth yogis was power, in both natural and supernatural manifestations (Pinch, 2006; White, 2003; 2009). They were bent on purposefully transforming reality. All of the primary *haṭhayoga* texts are directly associated with this alchemical tradition, which is a medieval permutation of older forms of Pāśupata and Kāpālika Śaivite asceticism (Lorenzen, 1972).

While the principles of *haṭhayoga* as internal alchemy have less than might be expected to do with what Desai did in the years following 1924, given that *haṭhayoga* has come to be synonymous with *āsana* and *prāṇāyāma* as regimens of exercise, a brief consideration of the key elements is useful in gaining a perspective on the logic of Desai's inspired creativity as well as on the underlying, persistent contradictions in his role as a modern guru.

In essence, medieval *haṭhayoga* is concerned with magic and magical power and with using the body to change the nature of reality on all levels of experience. *Sāṃkhya* philosophy holds that the body is an evolute of natural elements that devolve through creation to increasing levels of complexity and impure amalgamation. This process reflects the flawed and contingent nature of the relationship between consciousness and things, as this relationship is animated by misperception. Following a logic that is manifest clearly in *sāṃkhya*, *haṭhayoga* seeks to stop the process of transformation that reflects flawed contingency. It does this by means of physiological exercises—on both the most gross and most subtle levels of materiality—that stop and reverse change and delineation. Thus, *haṭhayoga* involves stopping—by purposefully causing it to flow, mix, and transmute—the ejaculation of sexual fluids, stopping the breath, and stopping the flow of consciousness in the mind. As Eliade (1958) pointed out, in terms that are hard to articulate in a field clouded by the politics of Orientalism and nationalism, yoga is profoundly antihuman in the sense that human consciousness reflects the prejudice of humanism as the essence of being. Existential being is the problem. *Prāṇāyāma* involves breathing exercises to control the flow of breath to the point at which it can be stopped; in their numerical proliferation and endless permutation, *āsanas* delineate difference, working the body against the flow of the endless categorization of things. On another level, *āsanas* are said to produce—or perhaps just mirror—the requisite physiological strength and stamina to withstand the force of transcendent changelessness. Stopping the flow of semen stops reproduction, in the full mimetically materialist sense of the word, and captures the problem of consciousness, perception, and things.

As David Gordon White (1989) points out, gurus in the Nāth *sampradāya* are heavy—as the etymology of the title suggests they are—because in essence they embody the condensed, distilled, purified, and subtle form of semen, as semen is cognate with mercury in the natural world. "In terms of physical states, it is the perfecting of the body fluids, the transmutation of the body, and once again, the getting of density, impenetrability and immortality that is the ultimate end" (pp. 61–62). "Sperm is as essential to yoga as mercury is to alchemy. Only from sperm is it possible to obtain the *amṛta* by which the body is rejuvenated and made *siddha*. It is thus very valuable, and the necessity of having an optimum quantity of sperm in the body to fuel the psychochemical process is emphasized in every tradition" (p. 65). Although abstinence from sex obviously preserves sexual fluids, the *vajrolī mudrā* is a much more proactive active technique for refinement and purification. "The Tantric yogins conceived of the *vajrolī mudrā* as follows: by emitting one's semen into a woman and then drawing it back into the penis before withdrawal, one leaves behind the gross matter of the semen, and, in addition to the 'subtle' sperm, the energy of the blood inside the *yoni* or *garbha* is also drawn into the yogin. This is exactly what takes place in the purification, etc. of mercury in sulphur" (p. 66).

While obviously obscure and arcane, the primary *haṭhayoga* texts are unambiguously technical; indeed, their apparent obscurity is, in part, a function of descriptive literalism, a paradox at the very heart of magic. Thus, the *Haṭhayogapradīpikā* provides instructions on how to wash the alimentary canal, perform urethral suction, and cleanse the sinuses, esophagus, and stomach by using water, cotton cord, and cloth. Along with the instruction for these procedures, the medieval texts explain that practice based on secret knowledge will produce magical powers, immortality, and, perhaps most significantly for the modern case in question, good health, immunity from disease, and cures for various ailments.

Unless one can, with complete honesty—and that is the rub—claim to be a perfected immortal and immune from all diseases or to have achieved a state of consciousness wherein one's continued state of being is just a reflection of the will to help others transcend the entanglement of reality, which is the existential if not essential heaviness of the guru's burden, it is difficult to know how to read the medieval literature. If *haṭhayoga* were simply nonsensical duplicity based on the cynical exploitation of credulity, the texts would not matter; *vajrolī mudrā* would not exist to be dismissed, and reproduced across time through a series of perverse erasures, edits, hints and indications. *Vajrolī mudrā* is for humans what YOCO is for texts; both come up short against time-bound consciousness.

In a general sense, albeit indirectly, Desai's insistence on being a householder yogi references the inherent structural logic of procedures such as *vajrolī mudrā* and the sexual alchemy of *haṭhayoga* more generally. In 1927

Desai married and settled in Bulsar. During this time he had children and focused on family matters and business but also continued to work on several yoga-related writing projects. He published several short, inexpensive booklets—*Breathing Methods, Way to Live,* and *Mental Health*—as the Yoga Health Series. In conjunction with this he also wrote several longer books that are very similar in content but appear under different titles: *Rhythmic Exercises* and *Physical Education*. Based on his research experience, *Rhythmic Exercises* contains a simplified program of *āsanas*. It was reviewed and promoted in the first of Bernarr McFadden's exceedingly popular magazines: *Physical Culture*. "This work combines the rarest features of the ancient and modern gymnastics as well as the Eastern and Western physical culture. Here is a scientific course of daily exercises based on the rhythm of breath. It is simple, scientific and workable" (Rodrigues, 1982: 139).

Following on the publication of *Rhythmic Exercises*, Desai continued writing and befriended Dr. John W. Fox, a medical missionary who was put in charge of the Brethren mission hospital in Bulsar. Fox showed great interest in Desai's ideas about yoga and provided helpful medical advice on a manuscript titled *Yoga Personal Hygiene*. Significantly, while they worked on the manuscript Fox invited Desai to observe his surgical work at the hospital, thus allowing Desai to further develop expertise in physiology and healing based on earlier apprenticeship with Madhavadasji and Hack's supervision in New York. *Yoga Personal Hygiene* was published in 1930, two years after *Rhythmic Exercises*, and was more directly concerned with the therapeutic benefits of *āsana* and *prāṇāyāma*. By 1933, while the Yoga Institute was still located in Bulsar, Desai reinaugurated the magazine *Yoga*—originally published in 1931—which carried articles on *āsana* and *prāṇāyāma* as well as on Desai's interpretation of yoga philosophy applied to modern life. This concern with the applied relevance of yoga philosophy to every day life is also reflected in several other books such as *Life Problems*, which contains pithy epigrams on issues such as love, honesty, thrift, anger, and prejudice and on more general topics like religion, politics, and society at large. *Educational Review* compared him to Norwegian playwright Henrik Ibsen, pointing out that the collection of epigrams was iconoclastic: "they are like bombs, intellectual bombs, destroying the old fogyism of reactionaries and hypocrites" (Rodrigues, 1982: 161).

After the death of his father in 1935, Desai made plans to move the Yoga Institute to Bombay, soon finding a location at "Beach View", Chowpatty. At this time the institute's publishing enterprise was at full strength and *Yoga*, in exchange with other similar publications, was going into worldwide circulation. Desai also began to invite public figures, such as the Sanskrit scholar A. B. Gajendragadkar, to give lectures under the auspices of the institute. In turn, he gave lectures at various venues, including the Bhandarkar Oriental Research Institute where he spoke on "Yoga for the Householders." As the national and international reputation of the Yoga Institute expanded, there was need for more space. This again brought Desai into direct competition with Gune who was, by the late 1930s, very closely allied with both local and national politicians. Ultimately Gune, who had built an institute for the scientific study of yoga in Lonavala, in the hills between Pune and Bombay, succeeded in pressing his claim to establish a branch of Kaivalyadhama in Kandivali. It was not until after the war and independence in 1947 that Desai was able to build an expanded institute at a new location in Santa Cruz.

In outline and essence the developmental history of the Yoga Institute shows that Desai was very successful in attracting national and international attention and in promoting practical yoga training for health and education. Very explicitly—although with embodied contradiction, given his robes, long hair, and flowing beard—Desai spurned the designation guru, which he felt carried a heavy weight of formal responsibility and had been sullied by all manner of hypocrites and pretenders throughout history. To some extent the formal activities of the institute directly reflect Desai's identity as a modernizer of traditional yoga. Although he sometimes claimed to be preserving the purity of an ancient, classical tradition, most of what he wrote and did reflects the purposeful modification of practice to fit *āsana* and *prāṇāyāma* into the rubric of therapy and rhythmic exercise. Like Gune he conducted experiments on the physiological effects of *āsana* and *prāṇāyāma*, reporting on these in *Yoga* and in the new editions of his original books, using the results in his clinical work with patients who continued to come to the institute in large numbers.

It is important to note that up to the present the Yoga Institute has continued to evolve and develop as a modern center for research and teaching on yoga. To a large extent Dr. Jayadeva Yogendra and Smt. Hansaji Jayadeva Yogendra embody the modernity of this tradition. As the directors of the institute they have fully adapted Desai's innovations into a modern institutionalized system and represent the complex and dynamic ways the ineffable insight and authority of a guru is integrated into a spectrum of educational formats: workshops, camps, teacher training programs, and corporate seminars.

Desai's first book offering a course of daily, regimented practice appeared in 1928. By 1991 the twenty-fourth reprint was published under the title *Yoga Āsanas Simplified,* and the institute claimed that over 100,000 copies of the book were in circulation. Although Desai's book is not nearly as well known as B. K. S. Iyengar's (1966), the trajectory of popularity reflected in the sequence and rapidity of reprinting traces a line from the early twentieth-century development of physical culture and health reform up through the phenomenal diffusion of *āsana* and *prāṇāyāma* into the matrix of late twentieth-century self-improvement and globalized fitness branding and marketing. In most respects *Yoga Asanas Simplified* is written in the language of early twentieth-century American health reform. Desai's interlocutors are Bernarr McFadden, both directly and indirectly through the magazine *Physical Culture* and through books and pamphlets such as *Brain Energy Building and Nerve-Vitalizing Course* (1916; see also 1895, 1900, 1919, 1935) and *Lecture on the Value of Air in Strength Building* (1909); Walter L. Pyle, who wrote *A Manual of Personal Hygiene: Proper Living upon a Physiological Basis* (1917); George Trumbull Ladd, who published *Elements of Physiological Psychology* (1911); William Lee Howard, who wrote *Breathe and Be Well* (1916a, see also 1910, 1915, 1916b); and R. Tait McKenzie, who published *Exercise in Education and Medicine* (1909). In dialogue with writers such as these, Desai's concern with the link between physiology and both mental and moral hygiene is unambiguously modern, in a distinctly early twentieth-century mode, which is visually reflected in the author as a young man wearing a one-piece bathing costume performing rhythmic *āsana*.

Desai's career from the late 1930s up until his death in 1989 also had a different trajectory that is captured both in his appearance as a sage old man with long hair and beard but also in the way he tried to reconnect mind and body, which had a way of drifting apart and then converging in different ways over the course of the 1950s, 1960s, 1970s, and early 1980s. Desai's vision of yoga as an idealized form of practice was based on the principle of integrated, holistic synthesis and positive, developmental evolution.

As the physiological features of *asana* and *prāṇāyāma* training became more institutionalized and as their performance in various contexts came to define an extremely popular articulation of public culture, Desai grew increasingly concerned that yoga was being misrepresented and misunderstood. This is not to say that he articulated a clear and consistent critique of modern practice but simply that he expressed frustration in the complex, paradoxical, and contradictory role he was forced to play in relation to what he wanted to do on various different levels—practical, financial, and philosophical—what people wanted him to do, and what he was forced to stand for in the public sphere of metaphysical fitness: a discursive space that he played a prominent role in shaping and expanding.

Dogging this trajectory of postcolonial Orientalism are the problems of history, histories of ideas that shape popular, profligate, and more intellectual public understandings of yoga's origins, and the search for origins and authenticity. Toward the very end of his career, Desai turned to the *Yogasūtras* to define a point of reference for his understanding of integrated, evolutionary synthesis. However, his turn to the *Yogasūtras* at the end of his career was in fact a return, for in 1922 he ordered a copy from Oriental Publishers of Lahore and had it sent to him in New York. He first read it while staying at the Union League of Philadelphia and found that it "had surprising similarity to his own thinking" and that he knew the content of this classic work before reading it (Rodrigues, 1982: 222). As Desai's biographer suggests—closing the recursive loop of origins, the history of ideas, and Orientalism—an iconic guru in the tradition of classical yoga had identified a true disciple.

At the same time Desai continued to teach his brand of rhythmic exercises and a breathing technique called *Yogendra pranayama* (Rodrigues, 1982: 204). He also established other name brands: Yogendra Laya and Yogendra Nispanda Bhava (p. 206). He conducted extensive experiments on yoga efficacy, including a series on the treatment of asthma sponsored by a commission set up by the Government of India to establish the scientific basis for the practice of indigenous medicine and to evaluate medical claims (p. 212). However heavily involved in this enterprise and in the project of modernizing yoga Desai was, he remained deeply skeptical, as several books of his collected philosophical essays make clear. Several brief quotations from *Yoga Essays* (1978) and *Facts about Yoga* (1975) provide counterpoints to the many points of contradiction in his weighty career.

> Gurus who deal with yoga specifics are imposters either by design or accident, and in either case do not represent classic yoga which subscribes to the cycle of cause and effect. (1978: 157)
>
> What can a so-called yogin who is neither truthful nor free from emotional and moral depravities represent to the ECG and EEG instrumentation, when exhibiting *āsanas*, *prāṇāyāma*, *kriyās*, *dhyāna* and the oft-quoted *Samādhi*? Of what use are such applications and evaluations based upon dismembered aspects of Yoga which are torn out of context and follow no traditional or classic methodology? As in the human body, none of the parts of Yoga are without relation to the others. . . . It is not for the modern man to upset this balance and call it Yoga; it is better that it be known by any other name so that the real image of Yoga not be distorted in the *pot-pourri* of modern progress. (1975: 46)

REFERENCES

Alter, Joseph S. 2000. *Gandhi's Body: Sex, Diet, and the Politics of Nationalism*, Critical Histories. Philadelphia: University of Pennsylvania Press.

———. 2004a. Indian Clubs and Colonialism: Hindu Masculinity and Muscular Christianity. *Comparative Studies in Society and History* 46 (3): 497–534.

———. 2004b. *Yoga in Modern India: The Body between Science and Philosophy*. Princeton, NJ: Princeton University Press.

———. 2006. Yoga at the *Fin De Siècle*: Muscular Christianity with a "Hindu" Twist. *International Journal of the History of Sport* 23 (5): 759–776.

———. 2011. *Moral Materialism: Sex and Masculinity in Modern India*. New Delhi: Penguin.

Atkinson, William Walker. 1902. *Nuggets of the New Thought: Several Things That Have Helped People*. Chicago: Psychic Research Company.

———. 1908. *Your Greater Self or the Inner Consciousness: A Course of Lessons on the Unexplored Regions of the Mind, the Subliminal Self, the Superconscious Mind, the Subconscious Mind, Automatic Mentation, Intuition, Instinct, Psychic Forethought, and Other Wonderful Phases of the Great Within*. Chicago: Advanced Thought Publishing Co.

———. 1922. *Regenerative Power or Vital Rejuvenation: Personal Power Books, Vol. 12*. Detroit: Personal Power Company.

Atkinson, William Walker, and Edward E. Beals. 1922. *Spiritual Power*. Detroit: Personal Power Company.

Azmi, Tasnim.1994. How Yoga Was Studied. *Yoga* 39 (6): 7–16.

Bayly, C. A. 1983. *Rulers, Townsmen, and Bazaars: North Indian Society in the Age of British Expansion, 1770–1870*. Cambridge: Cambridge University Press.

Briggs, George Weston. 1938. *Gorakhnāth and the Kaṇphata Yogīs*. Calcutta, London, New York: Y.M.C.A. Publishing House.

Broo, Måns. 2003. *As Good as God: The Guru in Gauḍīya Vaiṣṇavism*. Åbo Finland: Åbo Akademi University Press.

Chakravarti, Ramakanta.1985. *Vaishnavism in Bengal, 1486–1900*. Calcutta: Sanskrit Pustak Bhandar.

Dasgupta, Surendranath.1922. *A History of Indian Philosophy*, 5 vols. Cambridge: Cambridge University Press.

———. 1927. *Hindu Mysticism: Six Lectures*. Chicago: Open Court Pub. Co.

Donahaye, Guy, and EddieStern.2010. *Guruji: A Portrait of Sri K. Pattabhi Jois through the Eyes of His Students*. New York: North Point Press.

Duff, Alexander. 1854. *An Address Delivered before the General Assembly of the Free Church of Scotland, at Edinburg*. Washington, DC: H. Polkinhorn.

———. 1839a. *Farewell Address, on the Subject of the Church of Scotland's India Mission*. Edinburgh: J. Johnstone.

———. 1839b. *India, and India Missions, Including Sketches of the Gigantic System of Hinduism, Both in Theory and Practice: Also Notices of Some of the Principal Agencies Employed in Conducting the Process of Indian Evangelization*. Edinburgh: J. Johnstone.

Eliade, Mircea. 1958. *Yoga: Immortality and Freedom*. New York: Pantheon Books.

Flagg, W. J. 1898. *Yoga or Transformation: A Comparative Statement of the Various Religious Dogmas Concerning the Soul and Its Destiny, and of Akkadian, Hindu, Taoist, Egyptian, Hebrew, Greek, Christian, Mohammedan, Japanese and Other Magic*. New York: J.W. Bouton.

Fort, Andrew O. 1998. *Jīvanmukti in Transformation: Embodied Liberation in Advaita and Neo-Vedanta*. Albany: State University of New York Press.

Fort, Andrew O., and Patricia Y. Mumme.1996. *Living Liberation in Hindu Thought*. Albany: State University of New York Press.

Gajendragadkar, A. B.1934. *The Venisamhara: A Critical Study, Critical Studies of Sanskrit Dramas*. Poona: A.B. Gajendragadkar.

Grewal, J. S., and InduBanga.2000. *Lala Lajpat Rai in Retrospect: Political, Economic, Social, and Cultural Concerns*. Chandigarh: Publication Bureau, Punjab University.

Gupta, Visvaprakasa, and MohiniGupta.1999. *Lala Lajapata Raya: Vyakti aura Vicara*. Nai Dilli: Namana Prakasana.

Hall, Donald E. 2006. *Muscular Christianity: Embodying the Victorian Age*. Cambridge: Cambridge University Press.

Heehs, Peter. 2008. *The Lives of Sri Aurobindo*. New York: Columbia University Press.

Howard, William Lee. 1910. *Plain Facts on Sex Hygiene*. New York: E.J. Clode.

———. 1915. *Sex Problems in Worry and Work*. New York: E.J. Clode.

———. 1916a. *Breathe and Be Well*. New York: E.J. Clode.

———. 1916b. *How to Live Long*. New York: E.J. Clode.

Iyengar, B. K. S. 1966. *Light on Yoga: Yoga Dipika*. New York: Schocken Books.

Joshi, Sanjay. 2010. *The Middle Class in Colonial India*. New Delhi: Oxford University Press.

Kadetsky, Elizabeth.2004. *First There Is a Mountain: A Yoga Romance*. Boston: Little, Brown and Company.

Knott, R. 2000. Muscular Christianity: Evangelical Protestants and the Development of American Sport. *Journal of Sport History* 27 (2): 329–331.

Kumar, Ran Vijoy. 1989. *Role of the Middle Class in Nationalist Movement, 1912–1947*. New Delhi: Commonwealth Publishers.

Kuvalayananda, Swami. 1966. *Pranayama; Popular Yoga*. Bombay: Popular Prakashan.

———. 1972. *Popular Yoga: Asanas*. Rutland: C.E. Tuttle Co.

Kuvalayananda, Swami, and S. L. Vinekar.1963. *Yogic Therapy: Its Basic Principles and Methods*. New Delhi: Central Health Education Bureau.

Ladd, George Trumbull, and Robert Sessions Woodworth. 1911. *Elements of Physiological Psychology; a Treatise of the Activities and Nature of the Mind, from the Physical and Experimental Points of View*. New York: C. Scribner's Sons.

Leviton, Richard. 1990. How the Swamis Came to the States (A Comprehensive History of Yoga in the US from Swami Vivekananda in 1893 to Prospects for Hathayoga in the 1990s). *Yoga Journal* 3–4: 40–56.

Lorenzen, David N.1972. *The Kāpālikas and Kālāmukhas: Two Lost Śaivite Sects*, Australian National University Centre of Oriental Studies Oriental Monograph Series. Delhi: Thomson Press.

———. 1995. *Bhakti Religion in North India: Community Identity and Political Action*. Albany: State University of New York Press.

———. 1996. *Praises to a Formless God: Nirgunī Texts from North India*. Albany: State University of New York Press.

———. 2004. *Religious Movements in South Asia, 600–1800*. New Delhi: Oxford University Press.

Macfadden, Bernarr.1895. *Mcfadden's System of Physical Training*. New York: Hulbert Bros. & Co.

———. 1900. *Virile Powers of Superb Manhood: How Developed, How Lost: How Regained*. New York: Physical Culture Publishing Company.

———. 1916. *Brain Energy Building and Nerve-Vitalizing Course*. New York: Physical Culture Publishing Co.

———. 1919. *Making Old Bodies Young*. New York: Physical Culture Publishing Company.

———. 1935. *Man's Sex Life*. New York: Macfadden Book Company, Inc.

McKenzie, R. Tait. 1909. *Exercise in Education and Medicine*. Philadelphia: W.B. Saunders Company.

Minor, Robert Neil. 1999. *The Religious, the Spiritual, and the Secular: Auroville and Secular India*. Albany: State University of New York Press.

Morrissey, Mary Manin (ed.). 2002. *New Thought: A Practical Spirituality*. New York: Jeremy P. Tarcher/Putnam.

Mukherjee, A. M.1986. *Vaishnavism in Assam and Bengal: A Comparative Study*. Belari, Bardhaman: Granthana.

Narayan, K. 1993. Refractions of the Field at Home—American Representations of Hindu Holy Men in the 19th and 20th Centuries. *Cultural Anthropology* 8 (4): 476–509.

Olivelle, Patrick. 1995. *Rules and Regulations of Brahmanical Asceticism: Yatidharmasamuccaya of Yūdava Prakāśa*. Albany: State University of New York Press.

———. 1992. *Saṃnyasa Upaniṣads: Hindu Scriptures on Asceticism and Renunciation*. New York: Oxford University Press.

———. 1993. *The Aśrama System: The History and Hermeneutics of a Religious Institution*. New York: Oxford University Press.

Pinch, William R. 2006. *Warrior Ascetics and Indian Empires*. New York: Cambridge University Press.

Pyle, Walter L. 1917. *A Manual of Personal Hygiene: Proper Living upon a Physiologic Basis*. Philadelphia: W.B. Saunders Company.

Radice, William. 1998. *Swami Vivekananda and the Modernization of Hinduism*. Delhi: Oxford University Press.

Ramacharaka, Yogi. 1903. *The Hindu-Yogi Science of Breath: A Complete Manual of the Oriental Breathing Philosophy of Physical, Mental, Psychic and Spiritual Development*. Chicago: Yogi Publication Society.

———. 1904. *Fourteen Lessons in Yogi Philosophy and Oriental Occultism*. Chicago: Yogi Publication Society.

———. 1904. *Hatha Yoga*. Chicago: Yogi Publication Society.

———. 1906. *A Series of Lessons in Raja Yoga*. Chicago: Yogi Publication Society.

———. 1909. *The Science of Psychic Healing*. Chicago: Yogi Publication Society.

———. 1931. *Hatha Yoga: Or Yogi Philosophy of Physical Well-Being. With Numerous Exercises, Etc*. Chicago: Yogi Publication Society.

Ramacharaka, and Harry Houdini. 1909. *The Hindu-Yogi System of Practical Water Cure: As Practiced in India and Other Oriental Countries: A Condensed System for Self Treatment*. Chicago: Yogi Publication Society.

Rodrigues, Santan. 1982. *The Householder Yogi, Life of Shri Yogendra*. Bombay: Yoga Institute.

Singleton, Mark. 2010. *Yoga Body: The Origins of Modern Posture Practice*. Oxford and New York: Oxford University Press.

Singleton, Mark, and Jean Byrne. 2008. *Yoga in the Modern World: Contemporary Perspectives*. London: Routledge.

Srinivas, Smriti. 2008. *In the Presence of Sai Baba: Body, City, and Memory in a Global Religious Movement*. Leiden: Brill.

Strauss, Sarah. 2005. *Positioning Yoga: Balancing Acts across Cultures*. Oxford: Berg.

Syman, Stefanie. 2010. *The Subtle Body: The Story of Yoga in America*. New York: Farrar, Strauss and Giroux.

Urban, Hugh B. 2001. *Songs of Ecstasy: Tantric and Devotional Songs from Colonial Bengal*. Oxford: Oxford University Press.

———. 2003. *Tantra: Sex, Secrecy Politics, and Power in the Study of Religions*. Berkeley: University of California Press.

———. 2006. *Magia Sexualis: Sex, Magic, and Liberation in Modern Western Esotericism*. Berkeley: University of California Press.

White, David Gordon. 1989. Why Gurus Are Heavy. *Numen* 31: 40–73.

———. 1996. *The Alchemical Body: Siddha Traditions in Medieval India*. Chicago: University of Chicago Press.

———. 2003. *Kiss of the* Yogini: *"Tantric Sex" in Its South Asian Contexts*. Chicago: University of Chicago Press.

———. 2009. *Sinister Yogis*. Chicago: University of Chicago Press.

Williamson, Lola.2010. *Transcendent in America: Hindu-Inspired Meditation Movement as New Religion*. New York: New York University Press.

Yogananda, Paramahansa. 1925. *East–West*. Los Angeles: Yogoda and Sat-Sanga Headquarters.

———. 1934. *Inner Culture*. Los Angeles: Self-Realization Fellowship (Yogoda and Sat-Sanga Society).

———. 1938. *Inner Culture for Self-Realization*. Los Angeles: Self-Realization Fellowship.
———. 1946. *Autobiography of a Yogi*. Nevada City: Crystal Clarity Publishers.
Yogendra. 1917. *Prabhubhakti*. Prathamavrtti (ed.). Amadavada: Manibhai Haribhai Desai.
———. 1966. *Yoga in Modern Life*. Bombay: Yoga Institute.
———. 1975. *Facts about Yoga*. Bombay: Yoga Institute.
———. 1978. *Yoga Essays*. Bombay: Yoga Institute.
———. 1997. *Yoga Asanas Simplified*. Mumbai: Yogendra Publications Fund, Yoga Institute.
Yogendra, Shri. 1934. *Life Problems (Memorabilia)*. Bombay: Yoga Institute.
———. 1940. *Yoga Personal Hygiene*. Bombay: Yoga Institute.
Yogendra, Shri, and RabindranathTagore. 1918. *Gītāñjali: Suvikhyāta Kāvya*. Prathamavrtti (ed). Amadavada: Parikha Devidasa Chaganalala.
Yogendra, Shri, and Sita Devi Yogendra. 1939. *Science of Yoga*. Bombay: Yoga Institute.

NOTES

1. A further example of how crowded and confusing the field was is as follows. From 1919 through 1923 there was supposedly a Swami Yogendra Mastamani living on Long Island and teaching yoga in New York (Leviton, 1990). He is said to have founded an American branch of Kaivalyadhama, an institute that was established by another one of Paramahansa Madhavadasji's disciples, Swami Kuvalayananda. It is unlikely that Yogendra Mastamani is, in fact, Shri Yogendra, since at the time there was no "Shri Yogendra," only two different Swami Yoganandas. In any case there is probably no direct connection between the (mythical?) Yogendra Mastamani and Kaivalyadhama, since Kuvalayananda's institute was not founded in India until 1924.

PART TWO

The Lineages of T. Krishnamacharya

CHAPTER 4

T. Krishnamacharya, Father of Modern Yoga

MARK SINGLETON AND TARA FRASER

Every day there must be something new.

—Krishnamacharya, cited in Srivatsan (1997: 40)

INTRODUCTION

T. Krishnamacharya (1888–1989) is one of the most well-known gurus of transnational yoga today. He is often referred to as the father of modern yoga, and his reputation as the source and originator of yoga in the modern world is well established in many practitioner circles, especially those foregrounding popular modern varieties of *haṭhayoga*. This reputation is largely due to the enormous influence of several of his students at the global level and also to the energetic promotion of his teachings by family members and the organizations founded in his name. These students include B. K. S. Iyengar (1918–), who has perhaps done more than anyone else to popularize a posture-based, global culture of yoga;[1] K. Pattabhi Jois (1915–2009), who taught the dynamic "jumping" system of postural yoga known as Ashtanga Vinyasa;[2] Indra Devi (1899–2002), a Latvian woman who studied with Krishnamacharya in the 1930s and subsequently helped to popularize yoga in America with the help of her high-profile Hollywood students like Gloria Swanson and Greta Garbo; and Krishnamacharya's son, T. K. V. Desikachar, who studied with his father from 1961 until the latter's death in 1989 and who established the Krishnamacharya Yoga Mandiram (KYM), Chennai, in his father's honor in 1976. This organization continues to be the main mouthpiece for Krishnamacharya's teachings.

Thirty years later, T. K. V. Desikachar, along with his son, Kausthub Desikachar, founded the Krishnamacharya Yoga and Healing Foundation (KYHF), specifically to provide training for and regulation of teachers and therapists working in the Krishnamacharya tradition. In recent years, T. K. V. Desikachar's involvement in the KYM and KYHF has become minimal, apparently due to serious health issues. The management of these organizations largely fell to Kausthub Desikachar, who has enthusiastically promulgated the legend and teachings of his grandfather. The establishment of KHYF, with its bold mission statements and international ambitions, heralded a major shift in pace and style that gained many new recruits but also saw established devotees, teachers, and students distancing themselves from the organization. In October 2012, Kausthub Desikachar stepped down from the KYM and KHYF due to allegations of sexual abuse.[3] Some months later, however, two new organizations emerged out of Chennai: the Sannidhi of Krishnamacharya Yoga (apparently founded by T. K. V. Desikachar and Menaka Desikachar), and Yoga Makaranda, The Essence of Yoga, which promotes the teaching of Kausthub Desikachar.[4]

In this chapter, we consider Krishnamacharya's place as a guru of modern, transnational yoga. We begin with a brief summary of his life and move on to an examination of the core principles of his mature yoga teaching. We then consider some of Krishnamacharya's pronouncements concerning the role of the guru before examining his relationship to his own gurus. We discuss the importance of his native Śrī Vaiṣṇavism and the apparent tension between his commitment to that faith and the discourse of religious universalism that pervades KYM teaching on yoga. Krishnamacharya's own role as a guru and his creative adaptation and rewriting of tradition are then examined, followed by a consideration of the importance in Krishnamcharya's yoga teaching of *bhakti* (devotion). T. K. V. Desikachar is also considered, since Krishnamacharya's later teachings are in many respects indistinguishable from Desikachar's interpretations and mediations of those teachings, insofar as he was, for several decades, the public and transnational voice of the Krishnamacharya organization.

LIFE

There are two principal biographies of Krishnamacharya, the first by his later student, Mala Srivatsan (1997), and the second, to a large extent derivative of Srivatsan's work, by Kausthub Desikachar (2005). T. K. V. Desikachar's (1998) book *Health, Healing and Beyond* also contains useful biographical information. We do not intend to reproduce Krishnamacharya's biography in any detail here. It is worth noting, however, that Krishnamacharya was apparently reluctant to talk about himself (Desikachar, 1982: 1), and there are significant gaps in our knowledge of his life. Moreover, his relation of the

Figure 4.1:
Portrait of T. Krishnamacharya. (With permission of Ganesh Mohan.)

facts of his life would often change, resulting in some contradictory accounts. For instance, in interviews conducted in anticipation of his hundredth birthday, Krishnamacharya listened to stories that he himself had told about his life, sometimes denying them, sometimes adding ("malicieusement," as the French interviewer puts it) the "latest version," and sometimes just smiling without replying (Dars, 1989: 11, author trans.).

This mischievousness with regard to his own history, combined with the sometimes creatively hagiographical accounts of his recent biographers, makes it difficult to offer a definitive version of his life. It also makes clear that Krishnamacharya is complicit in the creation of his own myth. A thorough, academic study of Krishnamacharya's life and teaching has not yet been undertaken. However, it is also worth recognizing that while the scholar may seek biographical fact the hagiographer "has often blended those facts into an intricate mix of myth and legend" (Rinehart, 1999: 3), which in turn becomes its own dynamic, shifting history that influences the guru's status and function within his own or his followers' milieu (for our purposes, transnational modern yoga). Furthermore, this interplay can reveal much about the dynamics of guru apologetics in the ever-evolving modern yoga scene, since "the mix of myth and history itself is central to the purposes of hagiography and tells us a great deal about how the followers of a saint construct and preserve his or her memory" (ibid.). The management of Krishnamacharya's memory as it plays out in the various portrayals of his life, in other words, sheds light on the concerns and values of modern yoga itself (as well as its power politics) regardless of the historical veracity of the various accounts.

We present here a very condensed version of the now orthodox Krishnamacharya legend. Other aspects of Krishnamacharya's life and work, particularly as they pertain to the guru, will be considered later in the chapter. Born in Muchukundapuram, Karnataka State, Tirumalai Krishnamacharya was the eldest child of a distinguished Vaiṣṇava Brahmin family. From a young age his father began to initiate him into this culture and to instruct him in yoga. He divided his early studies between Benares and Mysore. He studied for seven and a half years with Rammohan Brahmacari in a cave near Lake Mansarovar in Tibet. At the end of his apprenticeship, this guru instructed him to go back to India, start a family, and teach yoga. In accordance with these instructions he returned to Mysore in 1925, married a young girl called Namagiriamma, and for the next five years toured the region promoting the message of yoga (Chapelle 1989: 30).

In 1931 he was invited by the maharaja to teach at the Sanskrit College (*paṭhaśālā*) in Mysore and two years later was given a wing of the Jaganmohan Palace in which to teach yoga. It was during this time that B. K. S. Iyengar and Pattabhi Jois studied under him. Patronage, however, came to an end soon after Independence and the *yogaśālā* closed forever. In 1952 Krishnamacharya was invited to Chennai by a leading jurist and took over the evening yoga classes at the Vivekananda College there (Chapelle 1989: 31). He remained in Chennai until his death in 1989. In 1976 his son T. K. V. Desikachar established the Krishnamacharya Yoga Mandiram in his honor, and it remains the principal organ for the dissemination of Desikachar's vision of his father's teaching.

TEACHING PRINCIPLES

> He has developed so much in his teaching, made so many changes, that I don't think anybody can identify "Krishnamacharya's style." One person will say one thing, and a few minutes later somebody else will say, no, no, this is what he taught me.
>
> —Desikachar (1982: 10)

Krishnamacharya taught yoga over a period of nearly six decades, during which time his methods and ideas matured and developed around a set of core themes. These developments are evident in the diversity of approaches taken by his most influential students in their own teaching. The changes in Krishnamacharya's style during the decades separating the student days of, for example, K. Pattabhi Jois (1930s and 1940s) and T. K. V. Desikachar (1960s and 1970s) show a significant progression in the application of yoga techniques.

Here we focus mainly on Krishnamacharya's post-1960 teachings, which have been comprehensively articulated for a Western audience by T. K. V. Desikachar, his son and primary student over the last three decades of Krishnamacharya's life. These teachings, which remain central to teaching at KYM today, find one of their most complete expressions in Desikachar's 1995 book *The Heart of Yoga*. The following account will mainly draw from this text as well as from Krishnamacharya's *Yoga Rahasya* ("the secret yoga"), which he is said to have received from a vision of Nāthamuni in 1904 at the age of sixteen and which was eventually published by the KYM in 1998. Regardless of how one regards the debatable derivation of this work (discussed in more detail below), the text does provide a kind of manifesto for Krishnamacharya's mature work: here we can see his concern for the health of the physical body (both of men and women), an emphasis on the correct use of *bandha* (physical locks) and *prāṇāyāma* (breathing practices), and a firm belief in the value of faith (Krishnamacharya, 1998:140), the necessity of the teacher, and "devotion to the guru" (ibid.).[5]

Krishnamacharya foregrounded the use of *āsana* throughout his career, and his teaching shows a highly structured approach to this branch of practice. He used the term *vinyāsa krama* ("specially ordered steps") to describe a threefold scheme of preparation, main focus, and then release or restoration of balance (Desikachar, 1995: 25). His initial experiments with *vinyāsa krama* seems to have begun in the early 1930s,[6] with the series of dynamic *āsana* sequences that later came to be known as Ashtanga Vinyasa.[7] In this style, the term *vinyāsa* indicates the repeated sequence of "jump back," from a posture, partial, or complete *sūryanamaskar* (known as half or full *vinyāsa*", respectively), and "jump forward" to the next posture (see Singleton, 2010: 182 for a visual representation of these movements). In later teachings, such as those presented by Desikachar, however, this single, unvarying *vinyāsa* between each posture is less in evidence, and individually tailored programs predominate (see Desikachar, 1995: chapter 4).

This individualized approach requires considerable modification and variation of postures to meet the needs of students with varied physical skills and capabilities. T. K. V. Desikachar (2005: 50) describes modification as an attempt to retain the "principle" of the pose while giving accessibility to a body that may not easily bend into the ideal–typical shape. For more able students, variations of the key poses add interest, intensity, or challenge. Krishnamacharya devised his individualized approach based on each student's constitution, needs, capacity, and circumstances. Which practice is given depends on a number of factors: "Before yoga is taught, the teacher should consider the time, surroundings, age, nature of employment, energy and strength of the person and his power of comprehension" (Krishnamacharya, 1998: 38).

The choice and use of postures are further varied by performing them in not just the familiar static form (usually considered more intense) but also in groups of dynamically linked sequences, accompanied by breathing ratios. A series of dynamic postures may be used as a preparation for holding one of those poses statically. This might then typically be followed by one or more poses that reduce any potentially negative effects from the *āsana* by countering the body shape with an opposing one in a less intense form. This, known as *pratikriyāsana* ("counter pose"), allows the benefits of the key pose to remain while any potentially negative effects are moderated, reduced, or removed. Counter poses are generally easier than the pose they follow, usually symmetrical and performed dynamically. (For a detailed description of the principles of *pratikriyāsana*, see Desikachar, 1995: 26–37.)

One of the strongest threads in Krishnamacharya's teaching is the use of specific breathing techniques during *āsana* practice; unlike some other methods inspired by Krishnamacharya (such as those of B. K. S. Iyengar), "The first step of our Yoga practice is to consciously link breath and body" (Desikachar, 1995: 19). *Ujjayi prāṇāyāma* (an audible, gently rasping breath) is employed in *āsanas*, with breath ratios building in intensity according to the skill of the student. This is combined with what Desikachar calls *directional breathing*, in which the abdominal wall remains taut on inhalation while the rib cage expands to its near maximum, lifted by the external intercostal muscles. According to M. D. David Coulter (2001: 133), this leads to a "celebratory" mental state. Desikachar (2005: 22) describes "consciously contracting the abdomen on exhalation," which gives the impression that air is expelled from the lower to the upper part of the body, with the last air being expelled from the top of the lungs. Desikachar believes these techniques "have the great advantage of stretching the spine and straightening the back" (ibid.).

Prāṇāyāma exercises in this tradition follow the same developmental *vinyāsa krama* pattern as the *āsana* practice, building step by step and then easing off to create a smooth arc of controlled practice. *Prāṇāyāma*, which can be quite forceful in some traditions, is characterized here by great subtlety, gentleness, and refinement. The classical ratios are considered unsuitable as basic exercises for beginners, but all students are offered some kind of breath awareness and breath control practice (see Desikachar, 1995: chapter 6). Krishnamacharya combined mantra practice with *prāṇāyāma* in a therapeutic modality: "According to the capability and faith of the person he should think of different mantras while doing the *prānāyāma*. *Prānāyāma* done along with mantra has a role to play in the therapy of all kinds of diseases" (Desikachar, 1998: 64).

Bandhas are used to some extent in Krishnamacharya's post-1960s teaching, but less intensively than in earlier teaching methods such as Ashtanga Vinyasa. *Bandhas* are regarded as extremely powerful techniques and are treated with great care. As T. K. V. Desikachar (1995: 73) writes, "*A word of caution:* Do not use bandhas through the entire asana practice. Like all other yoga techniques, bandhas should be practiced artfully and not obsessively. The help of a good teacher is essential." They are linked explicitly with the use of breath ratios and *vinyāsa krama*. In Krishnamacharya's *Yoga Rahasya*, the emphasis is primarily on using *uḍḍiyāna bandha*; however, in practice teachers in this tradition lay most emphasis on the initial use of *jālandhara bandha* (throat lock), and only when this is done safely and securely are the other *bandhas* taught (Fraser, field observation).

Philosophical discussion on an individual basis between student and teachers is encouraged. In some cases this might be supported by the memorization of texts, chanting, and meditation. Whichever method is used, it must be appropriate for the student and take account of his or her background, skills aptitude, and interests. The second part of *The Heart of Yoga*, titled "The Understanding of Yoga," gives some of the common themes that might be topics of discussion between students and teachers as a way of beginning to develop a capacity to use yoga as a philosophical framework for daily life. Typical topics include the notion of *duḥkha* (suffering), *yama* and *niyama* (moral and ethical guidelines), and the *kleśas* (causes of suffering), all of which are central to Patañjali's *Yogasūtras* (*YS*). Often, and perhaps especially in the hands of Western students, such discussion can take on the flavor of contemporary psychotherapeutic discourse (see, e.g., the thematic suggestions for discussion of Patañjali in Bouanchaud, 1997).

Chanting and sound play an important role in practice in the later Krishnamacharya tradition. Sound is introduced as a way of monitoring the breath in *āsana*, both as a preparation for *prāṇāyāma* and as a *sādhanā* in itself. Material for chanting may come from the *YS*, the *Haṭhapradīkipā*, the *Bhagavad Gītā*, the *Yogayājñavalkya Saṃhitā*, and other Indian texts or, where more appropriate, from the student's own religious or cultural tradition. Chanting may also take the form of simple open vowel sounds without meaning attached. Although heavily used by perhaps all teachers in this tradition (Fraser, fieldwork observation), chanting is not treated in Desikachar's *The Heart of Yoga*, which in all other respects is a fairly comprehensive statement of the teaching tradition. A long-term Desikachar student David Charlton suggests that this is because at the time of publication Desikachar associated chanting with the Vedic tradition and had not found yet found a way to "de-Indianize" and secularize it sufficiently for consumption by a Western audience (personal communication, April 2012).

By the end of his life Krishnamacharya had honed his teaching style—characterized by its individually tailored approach and its therapeutic focus—into a complex interdisciplinary model combining elements of *āyurveda*, astrology, music, and *haṭhayoga*. The mind should be constantly engaged through counting breath ratios in *prāṇāyāma*, considering philosophical questions, or chanting *ślokas*.

KRISHNAMACHARYA ON THE GURU

Krishnamacharya insisted often during his life that training under the guru for a reasonable amount of time is a vital condition if one is to see the fruits of yoga (Srivatsan, 1997: 47). He believed, moreover, that the guru is "the only guiding force who could lead one in the right direction" (p. 74). He consistently emphasized the continued presence of the guru in his own life, from placing his guru's sandals on his head as part of his daily ritual to attributing all his learning and achievement to his guru, effectively effacing his own innovations and contributions. He was known to declare, "I don't say anything, I close my eyes and it is the guru in me who says all those things" (Krishnamacharya Yoga Mandiram 1988: 9). According to A. V. Balasubramaniam, who studied with Krishnamacharya around 1982, the master used to declare that when the guru teaches he sows a seed within the student and thus is personally responsible for the way he or she develops: the guru "gives a part of his *sadhana* to his students" (in Desikachar 2005: 227).

While the student owes a profound debt to the guru for the learning received from him, the guru also takes on the responsibility for the future development of the student, in a relationship of ongoing mutual obligation and aide, even in physical absence from each other or long after the guru has left his body. The guru must meet the needs of the student but, as Krishnamacharya puts it in an interview carried out in his ninety-ninth year, "should nevertheless always keep the initiative" by judging the right moment and appropriate form for the teaching (Dars 1989a: 75, author trans.). He tells the story of the day when he kept the maharaja of Mysore, who was his yoga student, waiting for twenty-five minutes while he finished his own practice of *japa* (repetition of a mantra or the name of God). Another day, he insisted that the maharaja come for his lesson at 5 a.m. instead of at the hour requested by the maharaja. As Krishnamacharya comments, "That day, the rank of guru took precedence over the rank of king. That's entirely as it should be" (ibid.). In Krishnamacharya's view, sustained contact with the guru is the single, vital, and indispensable element for safe progress and success in yoga, which is otherwise dangerous (the same goes for music, medicine, and dance: Srivatsan, 1997: 101). The presence of the guru enables a communication of knowledge that cannot be grasped through mere words on a page, and, as he puts it, "It is only by remaining constantly in the guru's company that the student—thanks to the presence, the look, the sacred contact and the words of the guru—is able to grasp the essence of these words and to gain clarity of mind" (Dars 1989a: 75, author trans.).

RAMMOHAN BRAHMACARI, THE "YOGA GURU"

According to Srivatsan (1997: 40), Krishnamacharya had many teachers during his years as student but "only one guru in yoga practice." Little is known about Krishnamacharya's yoga guru, Rammohan Brahmacari. According to *Paṇḍit* Rajmani Tigunait, the current head of the respected Himalayan Institute of Yoga Science and Philosophy (founded by Swami Rama in 1971), Rammohan Brahmacari may also have been the guru of Swami Rama's guru, Bengali Baba.[8] According to his own account, and as already noted, Krishnamacharya spent seven and a half years learning from him in a cave near Mount Kailash in the Himalayas (between about 1914 and 1922). He had been directed there by his preceptor in Benares, Ganganath Jha, who told him that Rammohan Brahmacari was the only person capable of giving him mastery of yoga and revealing to him "the complete meaning of the Yoga Sūtra of Patañjali" (p. 23). Upon meeting Rammohan Brahmacari, the recognition was instant (p. 25; see also Desikachar 2005: 57), and Krishnamacharya began learning under his guidance.

His guru was a harsh taskmaster, and, as Krishnamacharya himself put it, "every slackening of effort [relâchement] was punished, every emotion banished" (Dars 1989a: 61–62, author trans.), an uncompromising attitude mirrored in Krishnamacharya's own tough teaching style.[9] Srivatsan (1997: 27) summarizes the stages of this apprenticeship: "The first three years he was made to memorise the Yoga texts in the form of an adhyayanam. His focus was in the study of the Yoga Sūtra, Vyāsa Bhāṣya and the Sāṃkhya Darśana. In the next three years he practiced Yogābhyāsa and for the next one and a half years he studied the śikṣaṇa Krama and the cikitsā krama." After his sojourn with his guru, Krishnamacharya had absorbed "all of the philosophy and mental science of Yoga; its use in diagnosing and treating the ill; and the practice and perfection of *asana* and *pranayama*" (Desikachar, 1998a: 43). On completing his training, as the well-known story goes, the guru instructed Krishnamacharya to return to India, to raise a family, and to popularize the practice of yoga. In the mid-1970s, T. K. V. Desikachar related to senior US teacher Gary Krafstow that Krishnamacharya was in contact with Rammohan Brahmacari for many years but lost contact in 1959 after the Chinese invasion of Tibet. At that time he was reputed to be 180–200 years of age (personal communication with Gary Krafstow, May 30, 2012).

It is said that the guru taught from a Gurkhali language text called *Yoga Kurunta*, which contained "practical information on yoga and health" (ibid.). According to K. Pattabhi Jois, this text laid forth the dynamic *vinyāsa* sequences taught to him by Krishnamacharya in Mysore in the 1930s, known today as Ashtanga Vinyasa Yoga (Jois, 1999: xv–xvi). However, Krishnamacharya's grandson Kausthub Desikachar (2005: 60) challenges this notion, referring to writings by Krishnamcharya indicating that the text contained practical instructions on modifying *āsana* and *prāṇāyāma* for individual healing, sometimes using props. For a summary of the various statements regarding the *Yoga Kurunta*, see Singleton (2010: 184–186). It is worth noting that two senior Indological scholars have independently suggested to the authors that the word *kuruntam* (variously spelled *karunta, korunta, kuranta, gurunda*) is likely a Tamil (or other Dravidian) variant of the Sanskrit word *grantha* (which means "book") rather than a Gurkhali term.[10] Yoga Kurunta would therefore simply mean "Yoga Book." The generic name (and the conflicting accounts of its contents) may indicate that the *Yoga Kurunta* was one of Krishnamacharya's ever evolving, inspired "teaching texts," much like the *Yoga Rahasya* (see Singleton, 2010: 185).

The Dravidian origin of the book's title may support Norman Sjoman's (1996) thesis that Krishnamacharya's yoga apprenticeship took place in South India rather than in Nepal/Tibet as commonly supposed.[11] It may also indicate, as T. K. V. Desikachar stated, that Rammohan Brahmachari was from South India (personal communication with Gary Krafstow, May 30, 2012). Also pointing to his country of origin is the use of the title "Sjt," which appears preceding his name in the first edition of Krishnamacharya's *Yoga Makaranda* and which Sjoman understands as an abbreviation of *ciranjivi*, a South Indian form of address (contra Singleton, 2010: 223, n.16, who reads it as an abbreviation of *serjeant*, a common spelling of "sergeant" prior to the First World War).

In an interview at the Omega Institute Conference in 2000, then *Yoga Journal* contributing editor Fernando Pagés Ruiz—following up on Sjoman's thesis—asked T. K. V. Desikachar whether it was true that Krishnamacharya had in fact studied in South India with Rammohan Brahmacari and not in Tibet. According to Ruiz, Desikachar affirmed this and said that he repeated the story about the cave in Tibet "to honor his father," who would have "wanted it [told] that way" (Ruiz, personal correspondences, October 7, 2000, with Norman Sjoman; June 2, 2012, with Mark Singleton). However, none of the senior teachers we interviewed for this chapter had heard this account from Desikachar, and these statements did not appear in the *Yoga Journal* article that Ruiz (2006) was researching.[12]

Whether Krishnamacharya apprenticed in South India or in Tibet, it is clear that "Seven Years in Tibet" is a familiar trope in twentieth-century esoteric historiographies of gurus (as Hollywood well knows).[13] Anthony Storr (1996: xv), in his psychoanalytic study of gurus *Feet of Clay*, declares, "Travels to parts of Central Asia or Tibet inaccessible to ordinary mortals have, in the past, been promoted as prologues to the acquisition of esoteric knowledge and mystical experiences." In this, and regardless of the truth of the various accounts, Krishnamacharya's popular biography conforms closely to the standard mythopoeic conventions of the time.

THE "KRISHNAMACHARYA LINEAGE," ŚRĪ VAIṢṆAVISM, AND THE SPIRITUAL MASTER

The "Krishnamacharya lineage," which is foregrounded in much of the KYM's teaching today, however, refers primarily not to Krishnamacharya's relationship to his yoga guru, Rammohan Brahmacari, but to his purported descent from the patriarchs of the Ṣrī Vaiṣṇava *sampradāya*, Nammalvar and Nāthamuni. Chapter 1 of Kausthub Desikachar's (2005) biography lays out the importance of Śrī Vaiṣṇavism in South India before presenting Krishnamacharya as an immediate successor of this lineage, not only in terms of blood but also as a result of the direct, transhistorical transmission of knowledge from Nāthamuni. Just as the ninth-century saint had revived the declining Ṣrī Vaiṣṇava teachings thanks to a vision in which Nammalvar "helped him recover" the lost verses of the *Divya Prabhandam*, so Krishnamcharya revived the practice of yoga after a vision in which Nāthamuni dictated to him the verses of his lost text, the *Yoga Rahasya*. Both visions occurred under a tamarind tree in the village of Alvar Tirungari where Nammalvar is said to have meditated. Completing the circle of revelation, Kaustubh Desikachar's (2005: 35) biography of his grandfather was itself also conceived while sitting in meditation under the same tree after, as he puts it, "maturity [had] dawned in me."

As Kaustubh Desikachar (2005: 52) summarizes, "The incident at Alvar Tirunagari changed Krishnamacharya's life forever. It was clearer than ever to him that he was destined to play a role in resurrecting the glorious tradition of yoga just as his ancestor, Nathamuni, had revived Sri Vaisnava Sampradayam centuries before." In this presentation, Krishnamacharya's yoga (and hence Kausthub Desikachar's also) is invested with the authority of the Śrī Vaiṣṇava patriarchs through blood and through mystical transmission.

Krishnamacharya's teaching is sometimes presented as a synthesis of the North Indian yoga teachings represented by Rammohan Brahmacari and the South Indian teachings of the Āḷvārs, but it seems clear that the "Krishnamacharya lineage" is primarily associated with the latter, in spite of the apparent fact that "[yoga] does not seem to play an important part at all with the Āḷvārs" (Nevrin, 2005: 74). As Srivatsan (1997: 95) sums up, "The Guru Paramparā that had its auspicious beginning in the 9th century still continues and will continue with the guiding spirit of our pūrnācārya ['complete, or completely accomplished teacher']." We have been able to find no indication that Rammohan Brahmacari also belonged to this *guru paramparā*.

Furthermore, it seems that when in later life Krishnamacharya speaks of his guru, it is with reference not to Rammohan Brahmacari but to Shri Vagisha Brahmatantra Parakala Swami, head of Krishnamacharya's ancestral religious home, the Parakala Maṭha in Mysore, and his own great-grandfather, with whom he studied at the age of twelve, after the death of his father (Srinivasa Tatacarya, who had taught him Vedic chanting and *āsana*). His great-grandfather, and then his successor, Sri Krsna Brahmatantra Swami, taught the child Sanskrit grammar, *vedānta*, and logic.[14] It was to this childhood family guru that Krishnamacharya would offer such great devotion in later life. For example, before accepting an interview with senior T. K. V. Desikachar student Claude Maréchal, Krishnamacharya is said to have become absorbed in meditation as he asked his guru and spiritual master Shri Brahmatantra Parakala Swami to give his agreement to the interview. In response to an inquiry about his reluctance to give the interview, Krishnamacharya states, "Since my guru, Shri Vagisha Brahmatantra Parakala Swami, is no longer alive, he can't derive any benefit from fame" (Maréchal, 1989b: 76).

A verse prayer in Sanskrit, composed by Krishnamacharya at his students' request "so that they could pay their respects to him before beginning their studies" (Krishnamacharya, 1995: 67), summarizes this lineage: "I salute my teacher (T. Krishnamacharya) who was initiated by Sri Kṛṣṇa Brahmatantra Parākal Swāmi, who studied the Sri Bhasyam under Śrī Vagiṣa Brahmatantra Parakāla Swāmi and who underwent the ritual signifying surrender to the Lord under the guidance of Śrī Raṅganātha Brahmatantra Parakāla Swāmi" (Desikachar n.d.).[15] The lineage that is being formally praised by Krishnamacharya's (and T. K. V. Desikachar's) students is not just therefore markedly Śrī Vaiṣṇava but is also hereditary and does not (perhaps surprisingly for many practitioners who situate themselves within a "Krishnamacharya lineage") include his yoga guru Rammohan Brahmacari.[16] The lineage of Krishnamacharya's family religion, comprising so-called pontiffs dedicated to the dissemination of Śrī Vaiṣṇavism, hail from an institution that is, in Kausthub Desikachar's (2005: 31) words, "as important to the *Sri Vaisnava Sampradayam* as the Vatican is to Christianity." This of course raises interesting questions about the relationship between Krishnamacharya's yoga teaching and his native religion as well as the division of labor between yoga guru and spiritual master, and the place of Śrī Vaiṣṇavism within his system of yoga.

RELIGIOUS UNIVERSALISM

Contrary to what one might expect given the prominence of this very specific Śrī Vaiṣṇava devotionalism in their yoga teachings, Krishnamcharya, T. K. V. Desikachar, and the KYM commonly assert yoga's essentially nonreligious nature, such as in the sentiment attributed to Krishnamacharya by

Srivatsan (1997: 51–2), that "yoga was not merely doing āsana-s [sic] nor has it anything to do with religion. This was how Krishnamacharya saw and taught yoga." Krishnamacharya did not insist that his foreign students adopt his sectarian allegiance and instead adapted practices to suit the culturally influenced needs of the individual. For example, the French woman Yvonne Millerand, who studied with Krishnamacharya in the mid-1960s, learned how to properly pronounce the name "Nārāyaṇa" under his guidance but was then encouraged by Krishnamacharya "to find in your own culture the name which you want to invoke in the depths of your heart" (in Desikachar 2005: 207; see also Srivatsan, 1997: 75). While he remained a devout Śrī Vaiṣṇava throughout his life, Krishnamacharya did not insist that his yoga students adopt his hereditary faith (although respect to the lineage was due). Like his older contemporaries Swami Kuvalayananda and Shri Yogendra (Alter 2004; see also Alter this volume), and Vivekananda before them (Killingley, this volume), Krishnamacharya presented a form of yoga that could be open and accessible to all, beyond religious sectarianism, gender, caste, or nationality. In the year before his death, he declared, "We need to de-Indianize yoga in order to try to universalize it . . . the work of Nāthamuni is of great usefulness for the human community as a whole" (Dars 1989a: 73, author trans.). The unmatched global popularity of yoga forms that he inspired speaks to the success of this mission. In the last decade of his life, the willingness to bend the exclusivist strictures of Vedic orthodoxy even extended to the teaching of Vedic chanting, which Krishnamacharya feared was dying out. What he had formerly considered the province of men only was now made available also to women, provided they fulfilled certain preliminary disciplines (Srivatsan, 1997: 75).[17] (It is also worth noting, however, that while this measure demonstrates Krishnamacharya's openness to change and adaptation it also makes clear how important orthodox Vedic religion is in his yoga system.)

T. K. V. Desikachar's close and enduring early association with the famous antiguru and radical thinker Jiddu Krishnamurti (1895–1986), to whom he taught yoga beginning in 1964, may also have contributed to the kind of universalism apparent in the post-1960s Krishnamacharya tradition. Desikachar's contact with Krishnamurti, in his own words, "opened [his] mind to fresh thinking" and made him "question the relevance of what [he] was learning and doing with [his] teacher [Krishnamacharya]" (Desikachar, 1998: 3).[18] Krishnamurti offered at the time to fund Desikachar's full-time study with his father (Srivatsan, 1997: 80). Many years later Desikachar (1995: v) dedicated his influential book *The Heart of Yoga* to Krishnamurti who, he declares there, "taught [him] to be a good yoga student." According to Ranju Roy, a longtime student of Desikachar, "Desikachar was enormously influenced by Krishnamurti. I remember him often quoting Krishnamurti as telling him 'don't be another performing monkey.' In other words, don't pretend—as Krishnamurti was insinuating many other gurus do—to be other than you are. I think Desikachar's 'ordinariness'—his refusal to shave his head, to wear religious markings, the way he distanced himself from the Temple etc.— are all indications of his closeness to Krishnamurti" (personal communication, April 18, 2012).[19]

When he met Krishamurti, Desikachar was twenty-seven years of age and had only recently given up an engineering career to study yoga with his father. Krishnamurti was sixty-nine years old and had been a world-famous spiritual teacher since at least 1929, when he delivered his renowned speech "Truth Is a Pathless Land" after refusing the position of World Teacher within the Order of the Star, for which he had been groomed by the Theosophical Society (see Lutyens, 2003). He was in some respects the polar opposite of the orthodox, Vedic Krishnamacharya. Given such a formative early contact with the charismatic, iconoclastic, unorthodox, and antiorthodox Krishnamurti, it is perhaps not surprising that Desikachar (1995: xxvii) insists on the universality of his father's work, which "helps us make sense of all religious traditions and spiritual points of view and practice."[20] It is not surprising either, perhaps, that he emphatically refused the role of guru for himself.[21] Desikachar's universalistic emphasis in the presentation of Krishnamacharya's teaching may also derive in part from his early exposure to non-Hindu spiritual teachers for whom he felt affinity,[22] from his Western education (of which his father was very proud: see Maréchal, 1989: 22–23), and from the fact that Krishnamacharya adapted his teaching to suit the needs of his modern, Western-educated son and his liberal, ecumenical ideas about religion.[23] This has certainly colored the post-1960 teaching of Krishnamacharya, as formulated and popularized by T. K. V. Desikachar, although (as we shall see) the Śrī Vaiṣṇava element is never entirely absent.

Faith and commitment to the lineage of T. Krishnamacharya are fundamental aspects of training at the KYM (see especially Young, 2006: 33–42), but in practice this faith is multivalent and can signify "faith in the tradition, in the teacher or in God, or humbly accepting our duty to society, or even devotion to the sun or some other 'higher force'" (Nevrin, 2005: 73). This multivalency provides "an effective rhetorical strategy" and makes the teachings available to those for whom devotion to Nārāyaṇa—or to any god at all for that matter—is not appealing (ibid.).

READING AND WRITING TRADITION

From one point of view, Krishnamacharya's attribution of all his learning and innovation to his guru is a standard trope in Hindu religious transmission. As P.-S. Filliozat (1992: 92, author trans.) explains, "The orthodox *paṇḍit* is not in the least concerned to restore an ancient state of affairs. If he were to point out the diachronic differences between the base-text and his own epoch, he would have to reveal his own share of innovation and his individuality. He prefers to keep this latter hidden. For him, the important thing is to present the whole of his knowledge—which contains both the ancient heritage and his new vision—as an organized totality." However, this obscuring of innovation is not merely a question of masking one's individuality to present a seamless whole of tradition. It is also, in A. K. Balasubramaniam's understanding, that each innovation is an expression of the pure truth manifested in the guru–*śiṣya* relationship (in Desikachar 2005: 227). Once Krishnamacharya had entered into a true relationship with the guru, self-generated innovation became in some respects literally impossible, insofar as it was considered to be the seed of the guru at work within him.

Krishnamacharya never ceased to innovate within this framework and was presenting new teachings even a few years prior to his death. As T. K. V. Desikachar states in 1982 with regard to *āsanas*, "He continues to discover new postures, in fact I am unable to keep track of his new discoveries" (p. 32). One of the senior-most teachers in the tradition, Maréchal (who made forty trips to India to study with his teacher Desikachar and indirectly with Krishnamacharya between 1969 and 2002) similarly declares: "A large number of postures, notably most of the standing postures, no doubt come to us directly from Prof. Krishnamacharya, who developed them in response to the needs of the modern age" (1989a: 47, author trans.).[24] Although the metaphorical basis of the terms is different in the two accounts (discovery vs. development), it seems clear that a similar process is envisaged here. In a recent interview with Mark Singleton, Maréchal elaborated on his earlier statement, recounting that when Krishnamacharya arrived in Mysore he observed the physical education routines of a regiment of British soldiers stationed there and "saw very clearly that the standing postures should be an important element of yoga" (Interview, June 23, 2012, Singleton trans.). Krishnamacharya was a renovator, he borrowed [French: "reprit"] things, and "he himself invented postures" (ibid.).

His use of textual material proceeds along similar lines and was similarly innovative. The *Yoga Rahasya*, which, as we have seen, was purportedly received in a vision of Nāthamuni when Krishnamacharya was sixteen, is a practical guide on how to adapt yoga to the individual and formed "the basis on which he established his principles of yoga practice and lifestyle" (Srivatsan, 1997: 15). It is held by some scholars to be a patchwork of other, better-known texts plus Krishnamacharya's own additions[25] and was subject to constant variation through his teaching career (see Ramaswami, 2000: 18). Perhaps surprisingly for some, the original *Yoga Rahasya* appears to have been written by Krishnamacharya in Telugu and not in Sanskrit as commonly believed.[26] It was only in later years that Krishnamacharya translated it into Sanskrit, in which form it was eventually published by the KYM in 1998, without reference to its Telugu prototype. What is more, senior Desikachar student Paul Harvey recalls that a very different "origin story" was told in the early days of his apprenticeship in Chennai. In this version, Krishnamacharya was wandering in Afghanistan when a mysterious stranger approached him and handed him a bundle of pages, saying "This is for you." It turned out to contain the *Yoga Rahasya* (personal communication, September 26, 2012). These examples further demonstrate the plasticity and evolving nature of Krishnamacharya's text-based teaching as well as the element of creative variation in his own myth formation, albeit firmly within the mythopoeic conventions of the mystical East.

The mysteriously vanished *Yoga Kurunta* may also have been subject to Krishnamacharya's creative adaptation (if not his very authorship), as the varying views of its contents suggest (see Singleton, 2010: 184–186; also discussed herein in a previous section). He also selectively eliminated elements of *haṭha* texts, rejecting the purificatory practices (*ṣatkarmas*) and five of the *mudrās* of the *Haṭha Pradīpika* (which nevertheless remains a core teaching text within the KYM) and challenging the authority and reliability of the *Gheraṇḍa Samhitā* and the *Śiva Samhitā* (Maréchal, 1989a: 44–45).[27] Similarly, he "corrected and filled up the gaps" in the manuscripts of the *Yogayājñavalkya Saṃhitā* (trans. Desikachar 2000: xi) and "correct[ed] certain passages of the famous commentary by Vyasa on the third book of the YS," which he judged to be too theoretical, difficult to understand, and responsible for confusion (Maréchal, 1989a: 41; more follows on his adaptive use of the *YS*). It is clear that Krishnamacharya is engaged in a dynamic and creative relationship with the textual tradition on which he draws for his teaching.

Where a "diachronic," cultural historicist study of Krishnamacharya's teaching career might emphasize the difference that results from ongoing adaptation and innovation in the face of modernity, for Krishnamacharya this is secondary and perhaps irrelevant when set beside yoga's perennial sameness. As he himself puts it, "Whatever place, whatever time, the ancestors have framed the yoga practices to suit them all. Only the attitudes and circumstances of human beings change. Time and space do not change. The same sun shines as ever" (Srivatsan, 1997: 11). "New" techniques, texts, and teachings are never invented, but always discovered, and thus the new is never really new but is a reframing of the ancient and unchanging logos of yoga. Through the relationship with the guru and the lineage, innovation becomes the manifestation of the continuing tradition, and empirical historicity or textual philology are rendered inconsequential by authentic and authoritative performativity. In other words, the very instant of the guru's enactment and utterance of the new is also its transformation into the synchronous present of timeless tradition. From this standpoint, constructivist studies that work from the premise that yoga is the contingent product of the (fallible) human imagination through time, with distinctly different and occasionally irreconcilable expressions at different points in history, are therefore suspect insofar as they fail to recognize the transcendent and perennial sameness that always underlies the *appearance* of difference in the guru's teaching. What the historian may see as revisionism is in fact conservatism: there is nothing new under the guru's sun. And this sun is itself the always already present source of the guru's authority.

BHAKTI

The declarations of universalism within the Krishnamacharya school can seem somewhat ambivalent given the obvious importance of Śrī Vaiṣṇavism in Krishnamacharya's life and the way this colors his understanding of yoga. The most visible practical manifestation of this is the pronounced devotionalism, which pervades the yoga teaching of the KYM: as A. K. Balasubramaniam puts it, "If I were to describe [Krishnamacharya] in one word, I would choose the word, 'Bhakta,' or devotee, rather than a scholar, healer, or anything else" (Desikachar 2005: 229). As we have seen, Krishnamacharya considered himself a lineage holder of Śrī Vaiṣṇavism through Nāthamuni, and his daily *sādhanā* consisted of *āsana, prāṇāyāma* and ritualistic devotional practices (*pūjā*) to Nārāyaṇa. He was scrupulous to observe every last detail in his practice of ritual, especially in his later life (Desikachar, 1998a: 141). This devotionalism remains a vital component in the teaching of his organization and informs many other aspects of practice. For example, *prāṇāyāma* practice may itself be conceived as a form of devotion to Nārāyaṇa: "Inspiration is like an inspiration from God himself. Retention is some sort of meditation, because you are with Him. Exhalation is some sort of movement towards God, and retention after exhale is like surrender to God" (Desikachar, 1982: 34–35). Therapeutics and healing, which are central rationales for the practice of yoga in Krishnamacharya's system, are also conceptualized within a religious, devotional framework, setting this method apart from more secular, medicalized yoga systems (such as those of Kuvalayananda and Yogendra) that predominate in the modern period and emphasize the purely scientific basis of yoga's healing properties. Krishnamacharya's paradigm of healing is markedly theistic rather than merely biological/mechanical. As T. K. V. Desikachar (1982: 20) puts it, "Faith in God is absolutely necessary for any healing."

Krishnamcharya's reading of the *YS* also reveals his religious and devotional convictions. The *YS* was Krishnamacharya's most important teaching text: if the *Yoga Rahasya* was the practical manual of his craft, the *YS* was the source and authority for this practice. Srivatsan (1997: 43) writes: "In his teaching every aspect of yoga, [sic] would rely on the authority of the Yoga Sūtra of Patañjali: he would validate everything he taught with the appropriate sūtra." The YS were for him "the only yoga text that has any clear presentation of yoga" (Desikachar, 1982: 35). The YS continues to retain its central status in the teaching of the KYM, and its verses are routinely chanted in the same way as Vedic texts, which as Klas Nevrin (2005: 71) notes, "considerably elevates the status of the *YS* vis-à-vis the Vedas." Moreover, the *YS* are conceived in Krishnamacharya's hands as instruction on *bhakti*. The atheistic, dualistic outlook of Sāṃkhya, perhaps most often considered as the primary metaphysical underpinning of the text (Bronkhorst, 1981; Larson, 1989; 1999), is here superseded by a devotional, theistic emphasis. Indeed, in later life, "the essence" of Krishnamacharya's thinking was that "the yoga of Patañjali is the only means to develop *bhakti*" (Desikachar, 1982: 1). A similar message is put forth in the verses of the *Yoga Rahasya*, where "the yoga of eight limbs (Patañjali's aṣṭāṅgayoga) is proclaimed as Bhakti yoga" (Krishnamcharya, 1998: 17). *Yoga Valli*, Krishnamacharya's final commentary on the YS, dictated to T. K. V. Desikachar, gives "an entirely devotional interpretations to the text as a whole" (Maréchal, 1989a: 42).

Perhaps the clearest instances of Krishnamacharya reading against the Sāṃkhya grain of the *YS* is his interpretation of *sūtra* I.23 (*īśvarapraṇidhānādvā*), where the particle *vā* is interpreted to mean "only" rather than the more commonly accepted "or." He thereby makes meditation on (or submission to) the Lord the *only* means to reach the goal of yoga and no longer simply one option among the several laid out in the first chapter of the *YS* (e.g., I.34–39). *Īśvara* is the final object of yoga and is certainly not simply an expedient or psychological "transitional object" toward liberation as many have understood it.[28] For Krishnamacharya, such was "the interpretation relevant to the kaliyuga (our present age)" (Srivatsan, 1997: 91), and one that is in keeping with the qualified nondualism of his tradition.[29]

CONCLUSION

For many practitioners in the West today, Krishnamacharya is considered the source of and authority for yoga practice. His reputation as the father of modern yoga is increasingly widespread, while other innovators in the modern *haṭhayoga* revival, such as Yogendra and Kuvalayananda, are largely eclipsed in the popular transnational yoga psyche—and this in spite of their arguably much wider renown and deeper influence on yoga's development during the first half of the twentieth century. As we have already proposed, this is no doubt in large part because of the global impact of Krishnamacharya's students and because of the energetic promotion in recent years of the "Krishnamacharya legend" by third- and fourth-generation practitioners and teachers in the various modern (sub-)traditions that, to a considerable extent, dominate transnational yoga today. Even yoga students who have not heard of Krishnamacharya may well often be practicing a form that has developed directly or indirectly from his work (such as the various popular styles deriving from Ashtanga Vinyasa, like Power Yoga and Vinyasa Flow).

Sarah Dars (1988: 12) noted that, in spite of his considerable innovations, "[Krishnamacharya's] theories now constitute in themselves a new orthodoxy." A quarter of a century later, after the massive boom in postural yoga's popularity during the 1990s and 2000s, this is all the more true, and at much more of a global level. Transnational postural yoga's orthopraxis (i.e., the right way of practicing) and belief frameworks (i.e., the theory and rationales used to explain practice) have been radically shaped by Krishnamacharya's work and legend. Moreover, over the last two decades (and increasingly in recent years) Krishnamacharya himself, as guru, has become the focus of worldwide reverence among (mainly) non-Indian yoga students. It may be significant in this regard that the biographical portion of Desikachar's (1995: 41) book *The Heart of Yoga*, written "for the purpose of introducing Krishnamacharya's yoga teachings to a wide audience," is confined to a mere ten pages near the end (219–229) and contains little mention at all of Krishnamacharya's Śrī Vaiṣṇavism. This is perhaps in keeping with Krishnamacharya's own "reluctance to talk about himself," Desikachar's consequent hesitation to write about him (see Desikachar, 1982: 1), and Desikachar's concern that the universalistic elements of his father's teachings be emphasized. While information about Krishnamacharya's life and religious affiliation is by no means suppressed there, it is rather minimal when compared with the more recent cult of personality that has grown up around Krishnamacharya. The presentation is certainly in contrast with Kausthub Desikachar's (2005) book, which, as we have seen, foregrounds the Śrī Vaiṣṇavism and the mythopoeic elements of Krishnamacharya's lineage.

For some today, indeed, especially perhaps in the United States, it would seem that the story of yoga as a whole begins and ends with Krishnamacharya.[30] His enormous significance in the development of recent globalized yoga cannot be underestimated, but it is also true that a posthumous, revisionist history of modern yoga itself is under way, with Krishnamacharya as the principal, beatified protagonist. As a final example, the trailer for a new film about Krishnamacharya and his students (in particular B. K. S. Iyengar and Pattabhi Jois), titled *Breath of the Gods: A Journey to the Origins of Modern Yoga*, bluntly states the matter: "Modern yoga originated in South India in the early twentieth century, a creation of Indian savant Tirumalai Krishnamacharya" (Schmidt-Garre, 2012). Such history may well strike scholars of yoga as exaggerated, partial or exclusionary in its account of how yoga developed within India and transnationally during the twentieth century: all the more so, perhaps, because of the uniquely elevated status afforded to Ashtanga Vinyasa Yoga and Krishnamacharya's early years in Mysore. Krishnamacharya is, says the voiceover, "the man who in the 1920s and 30 turned yoga into what it is today" (ibid.).[31] Nevertheless, assertions like these are symptomatic of the enormous influence of Krishnamacharya today and suggest that the rehearsal of his legend is an essential aspect of belonging to the imagined community of yoga practitioners.

REFERENCES

Bouanchaud, Bernard. 1997. *The Essence of Yoga: Reflections on the Yoga Sutras of Patañjali*. Portland OR: Rudra Press.

Bronkhorst, Johannes. 1981. Yoga and Seśvara Sāṃkhya, *Journal of Indian Philosophy* 9: 309–20.

Coulter, David. 2001. *Anatomy of Hatha Yoga, Body and Breath*. Honesdale, PA: Body and Breath.

Dars, Sarah. 1989. "Au pied de la montagne," *Viniyoga, Shri T. Krishnamacharya, La Traversée d'un siècle* 24: 4–13.

———. 1988a. "Entretiens," *Viniyoga, Shri T. Krishnamacharya, La Traversée d'un siècle* 24: 56–75.

Desikachar, T. K. V. 1982. *The Yoga of T. Krishnamacharya*. Madras: Krishnamacharya Yoga Mandiram.

———. 1993. Introduction to the Yoga Makaranda. *Krishnamacharya Yoga Mandiram Darśanam* 2(3): 3–5.

———. 1995. Yoga Makaranda, for the Attention of the Readers. *Krishnamacharya Yoga Mandiram Darśanam* 3(4): 4.

———. 1998. *In Search of Mind*. Chennai: EastWest Books.

———. 1998a. *Health, Healing and Beyond, Yoga and the Living Tradition of Krishnamacharya*. New York: Aperture.

———. n.d. A Prayer to Krishnamacharya. Sheet circulated to KYM students.—(trans.). 2000. *Yogayājñavalkya Saṃhitā, The Yoga Treatise of Yājñavalkya*. Krishnamacharya Granthamala Series 4. Chennai: Krishnamacharya Yoga Mandiram.

Gurum Prāsayet Dhīmān, Shri T. Krishnamacharya, The Legend Lives On . . . 1998. Madras: Krishnamacharya Yoga Mandiram.

Iyengar, B. K. S. 1978. *Body the Shrine, Yoga thy Light*. Bombay: B.I. Taraporewala.

Jois, K. Pattabhi. 1999. *Yoga Mala*. New York: Eddie Stern.

Krishnamacharya, Tirumalai. 1995. *Yogāñjalisāram*. Chennai: Krishnamacharya Yoga Mandiram.

———. 1998. *Yoga Rahasya*. Chennai: Krishnamacharya Yoga Mandiram.

KYM. 2006. *T.K.V. Desikachar, A Tribute*. Chennai: Krishnamacharya Yoga Mandiram.

Larson, J.G.1989. An Old Problem Revisited: The Relation between Sāṃkhya, Yoga and Buddhism. *Studien zur Indologie und Iranistik* 15: 129–46.

———. 1999. Classical Yoga as Neo-Sāṃkhya: A Chapter in the History of Indian Philosophy, *Asiatische Studien* 53(3): 723–32.

Lutyens, Mary. 2003. *J. Krishnamurti: The Open Door. A Biography*. Bramdean: Krishnamurti Foundation Trust.

Maehle, G.2006. *Ashtanga Yoga: Practice and Philosophy*. Innaloo City: Kaivalya Publications.

Marechal, Claude. 1989. Guru-Shishya, Père et fils, Interview de T.K.V. Desikachar, *Viniyoga, Shri T. Krishnamacharya, La Traversée d'un siècle 24*, 1989: 20–26

———. 1989a. Enseignements. *Viniyoga, Shri T. Krishnamacharya, La Traversée d'un siècle* 24: 40–51.

———. 1989b. La Demarche du Yoga, Interview de Shri T. Krishnamacharya par Claude Marechal, *Viniyoga, Shri T. Krishnamacharya, La Traversée d'un siècle* 24: 76–79.

Nevrin, Klas. 2005. Modern Yoga and Sri Vaishnavism. *Journal of Vaishnava Studies* 14(1): 65–93.

Ramaswami, Srivatsa. 2000. *Yoga for the Three Stages of Life*. Rochester, VT: Inner Traditions.

Rinehart, Robin. 1999. *One Lifetime, Many Lives: The Experience of Modern Hindu Hagiography*. Atlanta: Scholars Press.
Ruiz, F. P. 2006. Krishnamacharya's Legacy. Available at http://www.yogajournal.com/wisdom/465_4.cfm, accessed March 6, 2006.
Schmidt-Garre, Jan. (Dir.) 2012. *The Breath of the Gods, A Journey to the Origins of Modern Yoga*. Berlin: PARS Media.
Singleton, Mark. 2010. *Yoga Body, The Origins of Modern Posture Practice*. New York: Oxford University Press.
———. 2010a. *Yoga Makaranda* of T. Krishnamacharya. In D.G. White (ed.), *Yoga in Practice*. Princeton, NJ: Princeton University Press, pp. 337–352.
Singleton, Mark, and Jean Byrne (eds.). 2008. *Yoga in the Modern World: Contemporary Perspectives*. London: Routledge Hindu Studies Series.
Smith, Benjamin. 2008. With Heat Even Iron Will Bend: Discipline and Authority in Ashtanga Yoga. In M. Singleton and J. Byrne (eds.), *Yoga in the Modern World: Contemporary Perspectives*. London: Routledge Hindu Studies Series.
Srivatsan, Mala. 1997. *Śrī Krishnamacharya the Pūrnācārya*. Chennai: Private Printing, Vignesha Printers 1997.
Storr, Anthony. 1996. *Feet of Clay, a Study of Gurus*. London: Harper-Collins.
Young, Jane W. 2006. *Passing on a Tradition of Teaching: A Naturalistic Study of Yoga Therapy at the Krishnamacharya Yoga Mandiram*. Chennai: Krishnamacharya Yoga Mandiram.

NOTES

1. Writing in 1997, Krishamacharya's son, T. K. V. Desikachar, wrote: "If Śrī Krishnamacharya is now known all over the world, the credit must go to [B. K. S. Iyengar]" (Srivatsan, 1997: 3).
2. Pattabhi Jois claimed, "I was the first one to make Krishnamacharya's name famous in America" (Schmidt-Garre, 2012).
3. In September 2012, news emerged that four women from the European branch of KHYF had filed formal complaints with the Austrian police against Kausthub Desikachar, accusing him of "sexual, mental, and emotional abuse," including "the misuse of his position as a yoga mentor by utilizing his knowledge of personal histories of sexual and emotional trauma in an attempt to initiate sexual relations." Other, similar allegations date back to at least 2007. See Sonia Nelson, Chase Bossart, Kate Holcombe, and Dolphi Wertenbaker, letter to the American KHYF: http://www.yogadork.com/news/kausthub-desikachar-krishnamacharyas-grandson-accused-of-sexual-mental-emotional-abuse/, accessed October 1, 2012. In an email dated September 18, 2012, sent by two of his senior British students to KHYF's UK members, he was said to be "full of remorse and shame and is seeking help from different directions, to change his behaviour" (ibid.). Thus far, at least one senior Indian teacher in the lineage has called for the dissolution of the KYM and KHYF in response to these events. Insofar as Kausthub Desikachar is the grandson of Krishnamacharya himself, and in some respects the primary lineage holder and senior executive of the Krishnamacharya institutions worldwide, this is clearly of significance for our study of the Krishnamacharya lineage. Unfortunately, this latest turn of events will have to remain largely unexamined here due to publishing schedules and space restraints.

4. The Sannidhi of Krishnamacharya Yoga is intended to be "the medium through which the whole range of the teachings of T Krishnamacharya will be extended into the current century in a traditional manner, yet relevant to the modern era" (publicity email received by the authors, January 23, 2013). Through the organization Yoga Makaranda, The Essence of Yoga one can "begin or sustain your Yoga Journey with Dr. Kausthub Desikachar" (publicity email received by authors May 27, 2013). Courses include Divine Feminine Chant, and Yoga for Pregnancy (ibid.). It is not entirely clear what the relationship of these two organizations is to each other, but it is noteworthy that they share a common Chennai postal code, a common mailing list, and a common mail-shot system (https://madmimi.com).
5. Some of the comments on practice in this section come from Tara Fraser's direct experience with teachers of this lineage over the past thirteen years.
6. "In the beginning of [Krishnamacharya's] teaching, around 1932, he evolved a list of postures leading towards a particular posture, and coming away from it" (Desikachar, 1982: 33).
7. On Ashtanga Vinyasa Yoga, see K. Pattabhi Jois (1999), *Yoga Mala*; Byrne, this volume; Maehle (2006); Smith (2008).
8. Thanks to Gary Krafstow for this information (personal communication, May 30, 2012). Although we received this information too late to be able to develop it in this chapter, it is clear that if true it would be of great significance for the study of modern lineages of yoga.
9. B. K. S. Iyengar (1978: 5) recalls, for instance, that Krishnamacharya's "presence was like a frightful nightmare." See Newcombe, this volume, and Desikachar (2005: 188).
10. Thanks to Frederick M. Smith and Dominik Wujastyk. There are only a handful of manuscripts called *Yogagrantha* in the as-yet-unpublished "Y" volume of the *New Catalogus Catalogorum* being prepared at the University of Madras. We have not had time to consult them. We thank Dr. Siniruddha Dash, University of Madras, for providing these references.
11. Sjoman (1996: 66) believes that references to Rammohan Brahmacari's apparent location on the banks of the Gandaki River in Nepal actually refer to a river in Northern Karnataka, also known as the Gandaki. He cites from the original preface to Krishnamacharya's *Yoga Makaranda* (1934), which refers to "Sjt Ramamohan Brahmacari Guru Maharaj of Mukta Narayan Ksetra (Banks of the Gandaki)" (1996: 61).
12. This may point to the varying levels of discursive censorship that operate within the yoga media as well as to the loosely enforced narrative conformism that may be characteristic of certain Krishnamacharya lineage groups (see Byrne, this volume, on discursive self-policing within Ashtanga Vinyasa Yoga and the telling comment by Ruiz that while researching Krishnamacharya's life he felt like he was "investigating Watergate"; personal communication with Norman Sjoman, October 15, 2000).
13. We refer here, of course, to the 1997 blockbuster movie "Seven Years in Tibet," directed by Jean-Jacques Annaud and starring Brad Pitt. This was a Hollywood remake of the 1956 movie of the same name directed by Hans Nieter. See http://www.imdb.com/find?q=seven+years+in+tibet&s=all, accessed March 12, 2012.
14. See T. K. V. Desikachar (1998a: 34) and Kausthub Desikachar (2005: 31). See *Gurum Prāsayet Dhīmān* (1988) for an outline of this period of his life.
15. The prayer appears in a Devanagari script in Krishnamacharya's *Yogāñjalisāram* (1995: 67) with T. K. V. Desikachar's aforementioned comment. The translation by

Desikachar (n.d.) is from a sheet circulated by him to students and in widespread use in the KYM. Thanks to senior British Wheel of Yoga teacher and longtime KYM student Wendy Haring for providing a copy.

16. Moreover, it is not the *Yogasūtra* that is referenced but Ramānuja's commentary on the *Brahmasūtras*, the *Śrībhāṣya*.
17. It is in fact this very aspect of Krishnamacharya's teaching that is singled out in T. K. V. Desikachar's introduction to the Sanskrit prayer in praise of Krishnamacharya (in Desikachar n.d.): "Through this verse, we remember and honour T. Krishnamacharya, who opened the doors of vedic chanting to everyone."
18. See Krishnamacharya Yoga Mandiram (2006: 23–25) and Srivatsan (1997: 80) for accounts of Desikachar's encounter with Krishnamurti.
19. Roy also points out that Desikachar has been critical of Krishnamurti for not teaching a clear methodology or practice (ibid.).
20. Desikachar acknowledges three major influences in his life: "that of my father who represented the Vedic tradition, that of J. Krishnamurti, an extraordinary Indian personality who represents everything that is other than the Vedic tradition of India—and Mr. Gerard Blitz from the West who introduced me to Buddhism, Zen and all that" (Desikachar, 1998: 4).
21. Leslie Kaminoff has recently spoken of his teacher Desikachar's emphatic refusal to be treated as a guru; his refusal to offer easy, formulaic answers; and his dramatic dissolution of the organization founded on the basis of his teachings. "Reaction to the Anusara situation and the idea of the Guru", YouTube, http://www.youtube.com/watch?v=f1qD0_ewm-s&feature=youtube_gdata_player, accessed May 14, 2012. One can't help but be struck by the close echoes with Krishnamurti's own history (in particular his dissolution of the Order of the Star) and self-presentation.
22. "I have known a great many teachers of many different traditions, and I have never felt strange in their presence. I think this is a tribute to my father's teaching I have never felt myself to be against somebody . . . I was with J. Krishnamurthi [sic]. I was with U. G. Krishnamurthi. I have been with great theosophists, with great *ācāryas* [teachers]. I have friends who are devoted Muslims and others who are Christians. My own experience has taught me that my father's teaching is universal; it helps make sense of all religious traditions and spiritual points of view and practice" (Desikachar, 1995: xxvii).
23. "I am a Western-educated person and he was a traditional teacher. He saw that I was different so he adapted his teachings to me" (Desikachar, 1995: xxi).
24. Significantly, this assertion is made seven years before Sjoman's (1996) controversial study *The Yoga Tradition of the Mysore Palace*, which makes a similar claim regarding standing postures.
25. Somadeva Vasudeva, personal communication, March 2005. See also Smith and White (this volume, fn. 6): "It might be harsh to call [the *Yoga Rahasya*] spurious, but it is written in rather unfortunate Sanskrit and is little more than a projection into antiquity of a modern description of and justification for the primacy of *āsana* practice."
26. Krishnamacharya showed the original Telugu manuscript directly to Claude Maréchal (Interview, June 23, 2012).
27. On Krishnamacharya's critical stance toward *haṭhayoga* methods, see Singleton (2010a); Srivatsan (1997: 109) also records Krishnamacharya's view that "Gorakṣa Samhitā and Haṭhayoga Pradipikā contain certain practices such as nauli, dhauti, basti, Kuṇḍalini cālana, etc. These are no[sic] consistant [sic] with the spirit of the

yama and niyama of the Yoga Sūtra." Desikachar (2005: 231) notes that *ṣatkarmas* are also absent from *Yogayājñavalkya Saṃhitā*, another important text of the KYM tradition.

28. See Nevrin (2005: 81) for some examples.
29. As Klas Nevrin (2005: 76) summarizes: "With reference to Nāthamuni himself, Krishnamacharya legitimates and authorizes a set of practices and doctrines that combine Patañjali's YS with his version of Shri Vaishnavism, as well as with various Haṭha-yogic practices, healthistic ideologies and Neo-Vedāntic interpretations of classical Hinduism."
30. A very good example is the video made by American yoga teachers titled "The Story of Yoga," YouTube, http://www.youtube.com/watch?v=r4Iewghkixw, accessed January 10, 2012. The pietistic tone and the presentation of Krishnamacharya as the sole modern authority on yoga are in some respects typical of recent hagiographical accounts.
31. In an interview on the film's website, Schmidt-Gare elicits "the paradox of a practice thousands of years old formed only recently by one single man [i.e., Krishnamacharya]." http://www.breathofthegods.com/interview/, accessed May 8, 2012.

CHAPTER 5

"Authorized by Sri K. Pattabhi Jois": The Role of *Paramparā* and Lineage in Ashtanga Vinyasa Yoga

JEAN BYRNE

In the ever-growing yoga marketplace, where the practice is used to sell everything from cars to yogurt, a consumer might feel a certain reassurance when undertaking classes with teachers endorsed as "authentic." As a result, instructors who claim to be "authorized" or "certified" in Ashtanga Vinyasa Yoga enjoy a special kind of capital, and their promotional materials often display this status. Ashtanga Vinyasa Yoga (also known simply as Ashtanga Yoga or just Ashtanga)[1] has an aerobic character because of the component known as *vinyāsa*, a dynamically performed, repeated series of linking movements between each posture, synchronized with the breath. This practice of *vinyāsa* forms the basis of many styles of yoga we see today, such as Power Yoga or Dynamic Yoga. But unlike other *vinyāsa* yoga systems, Ashtanga Yoga is handed down in a rather traditional, even perhaps premodern, way. Its teacher certification process is an exercise in *paramparā*, a mode of transmission[2] by which a student becomes a recognized "lineage holder". This happens through many years of daily practice and extended trips to Mysore, India, to study with Krishna Pattabhi Jois, considered to be Ashtanga's founder, or (since Jois's death in 2009) with his grandson Sharath Rangaswamy (now Sharath Jois) who has succeeded him. Commonly, so-called lineage holders promote their classes with the phrase "authorized/certified in the tradition of Sri K. Pattabhi Jois." Such claims hold currency due to the perceived purity of the teachings imparted by those with this status. The discourse around and enactment of *paramparā* in Jois's Ashtanga Yoga is distinctive, especially in comparison with certain other forms of Modern Postural Yoga, to use De Michelis's (2004) terminology. This uniqueness may account for its tremendous popularity around the world, particularly in Western urban centers like London, New York, and Los Angeles. This paper weaves the voices of Ashtanga practitioners and teachers into qualitative analyses of the historical basis for *paramparā*, its functioning in Modern Yoga, and the complexity of the practitioner lineage in Jois's method. What results is a thick description of the ways heritage and innovation work to the benefit of Ashtanga practice.

To gain a cross section of views on what it means to be an authorized or certified Ashtanga Yoga teacher, a research abstract and questions were emailed to authorized and certified teachers. To some, the direction of the research as outlined in the abstract seemed misguided. The questions were "wrong," and one teacher advised that I should not write the paper in this way or on this topic at all. This kind of "self-policing" is fairly typical. On occasion, research or personal experience that doesn't subscribe to the orthodox view is discouraged or disallowed within the Ashtanga community. Even when scholars may reach balanced conclusions regarding the elasticity of tradition in yoga lineages, informed by the correlation of various primary sources (e.g., Singleton's, 2010 *Yoga Body*), authors at times discourage readers from taking work such as this seriously since the researchers are modern scholars who have "barely dipped their toes in the ocean of yoga" (Maehle 2009: 55). Unfortunately, what is lost is a dialogue that could "prove of virtually immediate use and benefit to both academic institutions and modern yoga milieus alike" (De Michelis, 2008: 27). For those who are beholden to any particular orthodoxy, the discussion here may appear offensive, but it is written with an appreciation and respect for the teachings of Krishnamacharya and an understanding that the popularity of his successors' yoga teachings worldwide are testaments to the system's authenticity and power, regardless of the process one must undertake to become a teacher in that lineage.

The discussion here is additionally informed by personal experience as an authorized Ashtanga Yoga teacher. My own experience is not explicitly interwoven into the essay; instead, I serve as an interlocutor in a discussion with other Ashtanga Yoga teachers and students about the complex currency of what it means to be "authorized by Sri K. Pattabhi Jois." While such an affiliation may seem an insurmountable obstacle to objective writing on this topic, we must acknowledge that, in any field of inquiry, the subjective can never be removed from the construction of knowledge. Rather, what is needed is a level of reflexivity and, perhaps, honesty instead of impartiality, which, as some have argued, is a questionable aim.[3] Consequently, as is the case for many writing in the field of Modern Yoga Studies, my own work can be understood as that of a scholar-practitioner.

ASHTANGA VINYASA YOGA'S "MODERN" METHOD

Jois's Ashtanga Yoga is characterized by the use of *vinyāsa*, the dynamic linking of postures and the synchronization of the breath. Many practitioners believe that Ashtanga Yoga originated in a text named the *Yoga Kurunta*, imparted to Jois by his guru Krishnmacharya, to whom it was imparted by his own guru, Rammohan Brahmachari. According to Jois, the *Yoga Kurunta* states, "Oh Yogi, don't do *āsana* without *vinyāsa*." The existence of the *Yoga Kurunta*, however, is hotly debated in a variety of camps. Even if we are to believe that the text existed, it is necessary to describe it as "imparted," as it is unclear whether the text was physically passed down from guru to student; perhaps each student received the knowledge but not any physical volume.[4]

In *vinyāsa*, movements are linked to specific inhalations and exhalations. This matching of breath and motion is thought to produce a detoxifying sweat that cleanses the body, nervous system, and sense organs.[5] As Benjamin Smith (2008: 140) reports, many practitioners understand this profuse sweat to have both physical and metaphysical meanings in the Ashtanga Yoga context.[6] The practice of *vinyāsa* in Ashtanga Yoga is also accompanied by a garland (*mālā*) of postures (*āsana*), gaze points (*dṛṣṭi*), specific breathing (*ujjayi prāṇāyāma*), and muscular locks (*bandha*). Taken as a whole, the *vinyāsa* sequence is understood to have specific therapeutic effects: the *bandhas*[7] seal *prāna* in the body, and *dṛṣṭi* assists with concentration and the cultivation of mental stillness to which practitioners may aspire. The postures of Ashtanga Yoga are generally split into six series, all with differing intended effects. Most students practice the Primary Series of Ashtanga Yoga, known in Sanskrit as *yoga cikitsā*—yoga therapy. All of the Ashtanga sequences begin with the *sūryanamaskāra* (salutation to the sun) sequence and end with back-bending postures and a finishing sequence that consists of inverted postures (such as shoulderstands and headstands). Following the sequence, Jois advises students to "take rest" rather than to lie down for *śavāsana* (corpse pose, as is taught in many modern yoga classes). For Jois, *śavāsana* is an esoteric practice, not simply "relaxation."

Ashtanga Yoga is practiced in a number of formats. Classes can be led, meaning that the teacher guides the class, or be conducted Mysore style, which is unique to Jois's yoga and has its origins in his teaching in Mysore, India, where the teacher directs the students' practice individually as they silently move through the Ashtanga Yoga sequence.

This style of practice and teaching allows all levels of students to practice together, whether they are beginners learning *sūryanamaskāra* or experienced students who have been returning to the Krishna Pattabhi Jois Ashtanga Yoga Institute (KPJAYI) for many years. Each Friday, which is the end of the practice week, students in Mysore come together to practice the primary series in a synchronized, "counted" class. Here the emphasis is on performing the correct *vinyāsa* linking postures. The practice week begins on a Sunday, with another led, Primary Series class, followed by a separately led Intermediate Series class.[8] Saturdays are traditionally a day of rest, as are the new and full moons, when it is thought that the heightened energy makes spiritual practice inauspicious.

The Mysore-style classroom features an individual relationship between teacher and student: the postures and sequences are undertaken at the discretion of the teacher, and the selection differs by student. While students practice side by side in the *śālā* (as the KPJAYI yoga center is called by students), they move according to their own rhythm, working on which ever postures the teachers have deemed appropriate. Students are given individual physical adjustments and instruction as necessary: at times, the adjustments are verbal or minor (e.g., the positioning of the hands), but sometimes they are physically and mentally intense, bringing students to the threshold of pain or fear. Due to their discomfort, such adjustments require that students have some level of faith in the teachers. Failing that, it is unlikely that students would put themselves in the position of receiving such adjustments day after day. This connection between teacher and student is the hallmark of Ashtanga Vinyasa Yoga as Jois taught it and a key part of *paramparā*, or the passing of knowledge, as it occurs between teacher and student. Although Pattabhi Jois did not call himself a guru, the trust and obedience his students reserved for him demonstrate that, even after his death, he is understood to be the central guru, or teacher, of Ashtanga Yoga.

JOIS'S BIOGRAPHY

Krishna Pattabhi Jois was born into a Brahmin family in the small village of Kowshika, Karnataka, on the full moon of July 1915, a day known as *Guru Pūrṇimā* (the full moon of the guru).[9] This is often understood as an omen of his future teaching destiny as the guru of the Ashtanga Yoga lineage. In 1927, at the age of twelve, Jois witnessed a *yogāsana* demonstration by Tirumalai Krishnamacharya in the nearby village of Hassan and was drawn to study with him. After much questioning by Krishnamacharya, Jois was accepted as his student. So, the story goes, upon becoming a student of Krishnamacharya, for two years Jois walked 5 kilometers each morning before school to study at the guru's house. Later, he would come to describe Krishnamacharya as "a very good man, a strong character. A dangerous man" (Medin, 2004: 7).[10] After two years, Krishnamacharya left Hassan to teach elsewhere.

In 1932, Jois once again met his teacher during a yoga demonstration that Krishnamacharya was giving at Mysore University. Jois studied with him for many more years and taught yoga at the Sanskrit University in Mysore until he became a professor in the 1950s. He married Savitramma and had three children—Manju, Ramesh, and Saraswati. In 1948 he established the

Ashtanga Yoga Research Institute in his home and worked therapeutically with Mysore residents whose ailments ranged from asthma to diabetes. In 1964 his home expanded as he opened the doors to Western students. Over time his small yoga *śālā* became very busy, and in 2002 he established a larger *śālā* and home in the Mysore suburb of Gokulum but still returned to teach students in the mid-morning at his old residence. He passed away on May 18, 2009, in Mysore and is succeeded by his grandson, Sharath Jois (formerly Sharath Rangaswamy). His nonbiological lineage is carried on by the students that he officially authorized and certified.

PARAMPARĀ: LINEAGE FROM TEACHER TO STUDENT

Paramparā literally means "proceeding from one to another". It denotes the succession and passing of knowledge from teacher to student in Hindu culture and religion. Its key aspect is the ongoing relationship between teacher and student (guru and *śiṣya*) wherein the student comes, over time, to embody the knowledge that the master conveys through tutelage. As De Michelis (2008: 19) explains, *paramparā* is one of the cornerstones of premodern yoga: "As for the passing on of yogic types of knowledge, the emphasis, in a way ideally, but very often also in practice, is on live transmission "from one [person] to another" which further contributes to keeping the whole structure decentralized." *Paramparā* can be found in Indian music, dance, and art traditions. Whatever the field of study, student and teacher "embark on a relationship which is at once psychologically and emotionally intimate and spiritually profound" (De Saram, 2003: 133).

Paramparā can be recognized as a key component in many Upaniṣads. In the *Praśna Upaniṣad*, for example, pupils come to ask questions of the sage Pippalada. Before he answers their questions, he requests that they spend a period of time performing meditation and austerities. It is only when a student conforms to Pippalada's requirements that he offers his wisdom. It is this close relationship between teacher and student that is core to *paramparā* in whichever context it is found (religion, art, music). Just as the etymology of the term *upaniṣad* suggests, students must sit at the foot of the guru and devote themselves to learning from the guru's words and actions. The learning is not necessarily something that is quantifiable, although at times students will need to learn certain texts or practices. Students also learn from being in the guru's presence, so that over time they imbibe the teachings of the guru and learn not just from the guru's words but also from their actions. The relationship between student and teacher, as well as the passing of knowledge via this relationship, is also central to Jois's Ashtanga Yoga. While students are not asked to perform the same austerities as Pippalada's disciples, very clear remnants of *paramparā* tradition persist nonetheless.

In spite of its arguably modern elements (see Singleton, 2010), Ashtanga Yoga retains the remnants of premodern traditions by holding central the guru–*śiṣya* relationship. The prominence of lineage is at the forefront of many so-called Ashtangis' minds, and the commitment to returning to Mysore (the "source") to develop a guru–*śiṣya* relationship with Sharath Jois, and previously his grandfather Pattabhi Jois, is great. In fact, for authorized/certified teachers and aspiring teachers, regular study trips to the KPJAYI are mandated. Within contemporary modern yoga, the focus on *paramparā* that we find in Jois's Ashtanga Yoga has no exact parallel and therefore confers a rare "spiritual currency" upon those who can claim to be "authorized/certified by Sri K. Pattabhi Jois."

Because *paramparā* lies at the heart of Jois's Ashtanga Yoga, students are encouraged to have faith in the method and their teacher to discover the benefits of the Ashtanga practice. For example, Sharath Jois explains that faith (or *śraddhā*) is "surrendering your sense organs, your body, your everything, surrendering to the practice" (Stern & Donahue, 2010: 191). This faith in the practice, and the importance of *paramparā* in becoming an Ashtanga Yoga teacher, means that Ashtanga students worldwide will routinely travel to the source in Mysore, India. The website for the KPJAYI provides a very clear outline of *paramparā*:

> Knowledge can be transferred only after the student has spent many years with an experienced guru, a teacher to whom he has completely surrendered in body, mind, speech and inner being. Only then is he fit to receive knowledge. This transfer from teacher to student is *paramparā*.
>
> The dharma, or duty, of the student is to practice diligently and to strive to understand the teachings of the guru. The perfection of knowledge—and of yoga—lies beyond simply mastering the practice; knowledge grows from the mutual love and respect between student and teacher, a relationship that can only be cultivated over time.
>
> The teacher's dharma is to teach yoga exactly as he learned it from his guru. The teaching should be presented with a good heart, with good purpose and with noble intentions. There should be an absence of harmful motivations. The teacher should not mislead the student in any way or veer from what he has been taught.

The bonding of teacher and student is a tradition reaching back many thousands of years in India and is the foundation of a rich, spiritual heritage. The teacher can make his students steady—he can make them firm where they waver. He is like a father or mother who corrects each step in his student's spiritual practice.

In attempting to acquaint the prospective student with the institute's mode of teaching, the website essentially outlines the way, according to *paramparā*,

Figure 5.1:
Student prostrates before Pattabhi Jois at his ninetieth birthday celebration. (Photo by Graeme Montgomery, 2005.)

the student should approach Ashtanga Yoga practice at the KPJAYI—and how teachers should convey what they have been taught. It is clear that having numerous teachers is understood to be detrimental to students, and during their period of practice at the KPJAYI students are encouraged to undertake yoga studies only there and not with other local yoga teachers (with one or two exceptions, such as for Sanskrit study and chanting). Pattabhi Jois would often explain that more than one teacher equals the death of the student, and his daughter, Saraswati Rangaswamy, reiterates this point: "Something that is very important is to learn one method, from one teacher and not to learn many methods at the same time with many different teachers. That will be confusing" (http://aysnyc.org/index.php?Itemid=184&id=175&option=com_content&task=view, accessed January 8, 2011). Pattabhi Jois also warned against learning from books or pictures (which can be dangerous) and insisted on the need for a qualified guru (Jois, 1999: 29).

As paramount to Ashtanga as the relationship between teacher and student is, Pattabhi Jois didn't seem to understand or represent himself as a guru. As he explains in the documentary *Guru* (Wilkins, 2006), he disputed this status and insisted that he himself was a student. As certified teacher Mark Darby corroborates, "He's never said he's a guru" (Interview with author, July 2005). His wife, Joanne Darby, also a certified teacher, recalls Pattabhi Jois saying, "Me teaching *āsana*, *prānayāma*, some *pratyahara*, then you go see someone else" (Interview with author, July 2005). Pattabhi Jois demonstrated his commitment to his studenthood by receiving ongoing instruction from his own guru, Krishnamacharya, with whom he studied for a number of decades.[11]

In the wake of Pattabhi Jois's death in 2009, the lineage remains intact through his grandson, Sharath Jois. The responsibility for the lineage was clearly and gradually handed over to Sharath Jois through an extensive period of assistant directorship of the KPJAYI. Following the death of a guru, there is often debate about who takes over the lineage. In this case, however, it was very clear that Jois wished his grandson Sharath to be considered the institute's new director. There have been protests in the blogosphere against certain features of the new order,[12] but for the most part the transference of leadership to Sharath Jois has been without the loud objections and infighting that many spiritual communities experience during these transition periods. This may be seen as a testament to the strength and functionality of this *paramparā*.[13] For some Ashtanga Yoga practitioners, the founder's death and the passing of the lineage to Sharath Jois has made their part in the transmission of Jois's teaching more real. Authorized Ashtanga Yoga teacher Mitchell Gould, for example, states that with Pattabhi Jois's death his and others' part in transmission "has become more real, more substantial" (E-mail correspondence, December 14, 2010).

Just as Jois studied with his teacher, Krishnamacharya, for many years, he expected his students to undertake regular study with him in exchange for his permission to teach. Indeed, the moment at which they will finally be entrusted with the Ashtanga Yoga lineage through authorization is never readily apparent to a student. Authorization is offered when the KPJAYI director (now Sharath Jois) deems it appropriate for the student; on rarer occasions, students will ask to be authorized.

Until 2009, there was no formal teacher-training program within Ashtanga Yoga. While many students visit the KPJAYI as aspiring teachers, it is very clear that class attendance at KPJAYI is primarily for the purpose of studying Ashtanga Yoga at its source and does not constitute teacher training. The KPJAYI website states that "students traveling to Mysore should not come with the expectation of obtaining authorized or certified status."[14] Only after numerous visits, demonstrated proficiency in *āsana*, and possession of the correct attitude may students be granted such status.

This, however, is simply the beginning of the journey of Ashtanga Yoga teaching. The teacher always remains a student, and authorized teachers are expected to return to KPJAYI every eighteen months for a minimum of two months of intensive study. In this way, *paramparā* is maintained, and the students dedicate and orient their lives to being not just teachers but also learners. It takes a considerable effort, time, and financial investment for teachers to return regularly to India to further their studies.

Professional development requirements such as these are arguably some of the most stringent found in Modern Postural Yoga lineages, and they derive directly from the emphasis that both Pattabhi and Sharath Jois have placed on *paramparā*. This emphasis is evident in Pattabhi Jois's correspondence with his teachers in 2008, in which he explains: "This type of lineage is called *paramparā* and is obtained only from long, dedicated study with your guru. In each succession, it is the obligation of the new teacher to pass on this method undiluted and unaltered to their students" (letter, August 11, 2008). To ensure that the lineage is transmitted "undiluted" according to *paramparā*, teacher training in Ashtanga Yoga has become more formalized in recent years. Once students become recognized lineage holders, insofar as they have studied for numerous months and on many occasions at the KPJAYI, they are invited to a training course conducted at KPJAYI. Before such an invitation is offered, the students already have a relationship with the director of KPJAYI and have made their dedication to the lineage apparent to him through ongoing study. The training course doesn't have an application process; rather, students whom the director decides are ready will be invited to complete the training. The guru–*śiṣya* relationship and *paramparā* are already in place before the training begins.

The training course is an opportunity for teachers to understand more explicitly what it means to share the lineage of Ashtanga Yoga with others. The training covers yoga philosophy, hands-on adjustments, and teaching technique; overall, it focuses on correct ways of sharing Pattabhi Jois's teachings. Once again, the focus here is on *paramparā*, and the course is designed for those "committed to passing on the Ashtanga system precisely as Pattabhi Jois has taught it."[15] Teachers "should maintain a yoga room or shala to allow for daily, preferably morning, Mysore-style practice and should honor Saturdays and the full/new moon days as rest days."[16] In keeping with the recommendation of the institute, many yoga schools that have KPJAYI teachers often follow somewhat similar structures.

For David Roche, certification signaled "that I was committed to [Pattabhi Jois] as my guru as well as committed to the teaching the Ashtanga system as he and other of his disciples had taught it to me." It also meant "love for me through inclusion into the guru-disciple family" (E-mail correspondence, December 13, 2010). For another teacher, Mitchell Gould, "authorization was acknowledgment by my teacher that I was ready to teach." It wasn't that he had achieved technical competence but that something had ripened in him: "this teaching is something organic, precious, that we hold and sow in others where the soil is fertile" (E-mail correspondence, December 14, 2010).

Becoming an Ashtanga Yoga teacher is not so much about completing set requirements or graduating from any specific training program. While there are some general minimum requirements to becoming a teacher—i.e., a number of study trips to the KPJAYI and completion of the Primary Series for authorization, and of Advanced A, also known as Third Series, for certification—authorization and certification are often understood as acts of faith on behalf of teacher and student. Thus, certified teacher Hamish Hendry describes being an Ashtanga Yoga teacher as "an honor with a lot of responsibility" (E-mail correspondence, December 14, 2010). The words of teachers themselves fill out our understanding of *paramparā*. Joanne Darby spoke of Pattabhi Jois as family and the practice as "deep energy," remarking, "It's amazing how one touch, or one word or one look can have such an effect" (Joanna Darby, interview with author, July 2005). Mark Darby talked about how Pattabhi Jois's mere presence was a transmission, or a "knowledge that comes out, just kind of oozes out of his body as he walks past" (Mark Darby, interview with author July 2005).

Common to the previous accounts is an underlying or explicit respect for *paramparā* in Ashtanga Yoga and for Pattabhi Jois. There is a sense of the unquantifiable in students' relationships with their guru. Each experiences a sense of closeness with Jois, and their shared perception of his character as generous, warm, and humble plays a key role in the guru status that the community assigns him.

Jois himself certainly thought that the guru–*śiṣya* arrangement was paramount—indeed, he defined yoga in those terms: "The real meaning of yoga is to get self knowledge about our inner Self, realising what we are. So if that is not there, it is more physical, you know, and everybody has their own system which does not come from *paramparā*. Only a few people are there that are teaching from *paramparā*" (Stern & Donahue, 2010: 187). The modernity of the practice of Ashtanga Yoga lies in sharp contradistinction with the system by which its practitioners become recognized teachers. Unlike some other forms of Modern Postural Yoga, Ashtanga upholds certain aspects of traditional Hindu culture. The way *paramparā* is maintained in the Ashtanga Yoga system is unique among modern yoga systems, which tend to offer curriculum-based teacher-training courses.

Teachers and students of Ashtanga Yoga are marked by their understanding of and commitment to perpetuate *paramparā*, particularly in making the transition to becoming teachers, or lineage holders.[17] The prominence of *paramparā* within other Krishnamacharya lineages varies considerably and has a correlation with the processes by which teachers are trained within their organizations. For instance, in T. K. V. Desikachar's Krishnamacharya Yoga Mandiram and its teaching branches, there is an emphasis on the completion of curricula, with the help of a mentor.[18] The mentoring seems to foster a form of guru–*śiṣya* relationship. However, the contact between T. K. V. Desikachar himself and the trainees is minimal, if it exists at all. What the lineage gains from this setup is a standardized training. What is lost is that certain *je ne sais quoi*, or transmission (as Ashtanga teacher Mark Darby referred to it, interview, July 2005), that comes from a guru–*śiṣya* arrangement like that of Ashtanga Yoga, whose key feature a continuous, personal relationship sustained over many years.

Iyengar Yoga (see Smith and White, this volume) also has highly structured and standardized curricula for teacher trainees. Teachers granted permission to call themselves Iyengar yoga teachers are understood to represent his work. Certified Iyengar teachers also have numerous responsibilities and restrictions regulating how and what they teach in their classes.[19] Local organizations enact teaching guidelines, at least for introductory teaching levels. This means that aspiring, "introductory" teachers do not need to meet Iyengar to attain certification, although they may. In this sense, the relationship that is cultivated over an extended time of direct contact between teacher and student is often missing in the progression from student to teacher in Iyengar Yoga. Unlike in Ashtanga Yoga, which requires students to travel to the KPJAYI in Mysore, India, one can advance to the high levels of Iyengar certification without meeting him in person.[20]

So Jois's teachings are spread in ways quite different from Desikachar's and Iyengar's, whose transmission systems also differ from one another. There is no prescribed Ashtanga curriculum, and study cannot be undertaken anywhere other than Mysore. While assessments have been introduced more recently with the teacher training that KPJAYI offers, it is a brief part of the overall journey to becoming a KPJAYI-recognized Ashtanga Yoga teacher. Of course, this arrangement does mean that teachers can graduate without studying anatomy or gaining senior certification in first aid, both of which are required by many global yoga organizations. Yet it also means that, compared with some other forms of Modern Yoga, Pattabhi and Sharath Jois have actively chosen to maintain a formalized guru–*śiṣya* relationship with their teachers rather than decentralize this authority by allowing governing bodies (e.g., Iyengar Association of Australia) to determine who has the right to be a recognized teacher in the lineage. The point here is not that a particular lineage is more or less authentic than another but that Ashtanga Yoga, which often faces severe criticism because it is more aerobic and therefore perceived as modern (and therefore less authentic), paradoxically maintains a strong sense of *paramparā* and emphasizes the importance of a traditional guru–*śiṣya* relationship when training teachers.

Ben Smith (2008: 154) argues that the discipline and authority of Pattabhi Jois are often internalized by Jois's students and can be found in their own classes worldwide. Further, Smith suggests that the authoritative presence of Pattabhi Jois—and by implication, the "correctness" of the yoga being taught and practiced—is also made manifest through photographs or pictures of Pattabhi Jois that are commonly displayed on a shrine or on the wall of Ashtanga Yoga schools throughout the world (ibid.). While Smith certainly has a point regarding the authority resulting from the guru–*śiṣya* relationship, what may add to his analysis is the evident fondness for Jois that Ashtanga Yoga teachers and students describe, which implies that Ashtanga *paramparā* is not simply about authority or discipline but also engenders an element of *bhakti*—devotion. In all the personal accounts of *paramparā* elicited for this paper, this sense of warmth toward Jois is central, as it is for senior teacher Richard Freeman, who was initially impressed by Jois's "sweetness" and who was "swept off [his] feet" (in Stern & Donahue, 2010: 272). Students often report experiencing his playful admonishments—"bad lady," for example, or "fifty dollar fine!"—as acts of love and gentle guidance. These comments clearly carried his authority as a teacher but were delivered in such a way that they could hardly be read as harsh. Through devotion to Jois as a teacher, the practice and lineage of Ashtanga Yoga are personalized rather than abstract. As such, students are better enabled to maintain their inspiration to undertake the rigorous, daily *āsana* that Jois prescribed.

De Michelis (2008) mentions the visibly acrobatic and aesthetic character of Ashtanga Yoga as a driving force behind its popularity. However, here I have attempted to present an alternative or complementary account that stresses the interplay between obvious differences with other popular Modern Postural Yoga forms and the centrality of the KPJAYI to the Ashtanga Yoga teaching lineage. Other Krishnamacharya-derived yoga methods achieve their ubiquity through decentralized and depersonalized training and accreditation systems; Ashtanga's formula depends on a sense of love and devotion not just to its method but also to Pattabhi Jois the man—teacher, friend, father, husband, grandfather, and great-grandfather.

REFERENCES

Alter, Joseph. 2008. Yoga Shivir. In Mark Singleton and Jean Byrne (eds.), *Yoga in the Modern World*. London: Routledge, pp. 38–48.

KHYF Curriculum. Available at http://www.khyf.net/khyf/curriculum.aspx (accessed February 20, 2011).

De Michelis, Elizabeth. 2004. *A History of Modern Yoga: Patañjali and Western Esotericism*. London: Continuum.

———. 2008. Modern Yogas: History and Forms. In Mark Singleton and Jean Byrne (eds.), *Yoga in the Modern World*. London: Routledge, pp. 17–35.

De Saram, Amila Joseph. 2003. The Guru Disciple Relationship. In John Huntington and Dina Bangde (eds.), *The Circle of Bliss: Buddhist Meditational Art*. Ohio: Columbus Museum of Art and Serindia Publications, pp. 133–134.

Desikachar, T. K. V. 2001. *The Viniyoga of Yoga: Applying Yoga for Healthy Living*. Chennai: Krishnmacharya Yoga Mandiram.

Hether, Christine. 1986. A Garland of Postures. *Yoga Journal* 67: 44–47.

Iyengar Yoga Australia. 2011. Iyengar Yoga Australia Teacher Training Certification. Available at http://www.iyengaryoga.asn.au/teacher-training-certification/teacher-training/ (accessed January 5, 2011).

Jois, K. Pattabhi. 1999. *Yoga Mala*. New York: North Point Press.

McLean, Bethany. 2012. Yoga-for-Trophy-Wives Fitness Fad That's Alienating Discipline's Devotees. *Vanity Fair*. Available at http://vanityfair.com/business/2012/04/krishna-pattabhi-trophy-wife-ashtanga-yoga (accessed April 28, 2012).

MacDonell, Arthur. 2004. *A Practical Sanskrit Dictionary*. Delhi: Motilal Barnasidas.

Maehle, Gregor. 2006. *Ashtanga Yoga: Practice and Philosophy*. Novato: New World Library.

Medin, Alex. 2004. 3 Gurus, 48 Questions. *Namarupa* 3(2): 6–18.

KPJAYI. 2011. Parampara. Available at http://kpjayi.org/the-practice/parampara (accessed February 15, 2011).

Prabhavananda, Swami. 2003. *The Spiritual Heritage of India*. New Delhi: Indigo Books.

Singleton, Mark. 2010. *Yoga Body: The Origins of Modern Posture Practice*. New York: Oxford University Press.

———. 2008. The Classical Reveries of Modern Yoga: Patanjali and Constructive Orientalism. In Mark Singleton and Jean Byrne (eds.), *Yoga in the Modern World*. London: Routledge, pp. 77–99.

Smith, Ben. 2008. "With Heat Even Iron Will Bend": Discipline and Authority in Ashtanga Yoga. In Mark Singleton and Jean Byrne (eds.), *Yoga in the Modern World*. London: Routledge, pp. 140–160.

Stern, Eddie. 2011. Hoysala Brahmin: Sri K Pattabhi Jois. *Namarupa* 13(4): 3–8.

Stern, Eddie and Summerbell, Deirdre. 2002. *Sri K Pattabhi Jois: A Tribute*. New York: Eddie Stern.

Stern, Eddie and Donahue, Guy. 2010. *Guruji: A Portrait of Sri K Pattabhi Jois through the Eyes of His Students*. New York: North Point Press.

Teachers Information. 2011. Teachers. Available at http://kpjayi.org/the-institute/teachers (accessed February 15, 2011).

Wilkins, Robert (Dir.). 2006. *Guru: Discover What It Means To Be and to Have a Guru*. London: Guruthemovie.com

NOTES

1. Ashtanga Vinyasa Yoga (another being Astanga Yoga) is the most common spelling for this style of yoga, which references (but is not identical with) the *aṣṭāṅga* (eight-limbed) yoga of Patañjali.
2. Transmission here, as we shall see, does not convey any sort of magical conference of "energy." As Kimberly Flynn explains: "Guruji (Pattabhi Jois) often spoke out against teachers who claimed to impart yoga and knowledge through touch or 'shaktipat' (Skt: *śaktipāta*) saying that a teacher who made such claims is a 'mesmerism man' and that yoga could only be known through study and practice" (E-mail correspondence, December 15, 2010).
3. As Marilyn Gottschall (2002: 81) writes: "The objective knower (a Cartesian cogito), who employs an uncontaminated reasoning process in order to produce true knowledge of a coherent, and ultimately knowable, 'real' world is no longer defensible."
4. For example, Eddie Stern (2002: xv–vi) reports that Jois has not seen the text but rather received the teachings verbally from his guru Krishnamacharya. Other sources purport that the *Yoga Kurunta* was found in a Calcutta library and that both Jois and Krishnamacharya extensively studied the manuscript (Hether, 1986: 45). For a fuller account on the controversy and conflicting information see Singleton (2010: chapter 9) and Singleton's chapter in this volume.
5. See http://kpjayi.org/the-practice (accessed March 3, 2011).
6. However, there is no biological basis for understanding the sweat that is produced from Ashtanga Vinyasa yoga practice as detoxifiying. Ashtanga Yoga practitioners

make a connection between the physical heat created in their practice and the concept of *tapas*, by which the practitioner exerts effort to achieve physical and spiritual purification. *Tapas*, heat, and sweat become interrelated in a process by which the practitioner "burns up" negative emotion, thoughts, and habitual patterns that are not aligned with what they consider to be the goal of their yoga practice.

7. The more esoteric nature of *bandha* is not often taught in Ashtanga Vinyasa Yoga classes.
8. There is a certain element of performativity to these led classes at the KPJAYI. During the Intermediate Series–led class, other KPJAYI students gather in the entrance to sit and watch their fellow practitioners move through the sequence. For further discussion of yoga and performativity and spectacle see Alter (2008) and Singleton (2010).
9. Unless otherwise stated, this account of Pattabhi Jois's life is taken from the official website, http://kpjayi.org/biographies/k-pattabhi-jois (accessed January 30, 2011). For a more detailed account of the village life into which Jois was born see Stern (2011). In this paper, while I refer to Patabhi Jois as a guru, it is very important to understand that he never claimed to be one. Instead, this is a status his students ascribed to him. He describes himself as a teacher, teaching what his teacher taught; and most importantly he explains that he is a student of yoga (see Wilkens, 2006).
10. Other students of Krishnamacharya have spoken of his "dangerous" character. See, for instance, the chapters by Smith and White and by Newcombe in this volume. See also note 11.
11. Pattabhi Jois's grandson, Sharath Jois, has this to say about his grandfather's experience with Krishnmacharya and the level of faith required for him to maintain his commitment: "Guruji left his family and everything . . . he came to Mysore and he had to go through so many difficulties, but he had faith. In learning from Krishnamacharya too. Krishnamacharya used to hurt his students. So many of them. When he started he had one hundred students, but in the end there were only three or four students. I don't say or know what happened to them or what difficulty they had, but the amount of *shraddha* that Guruji had to learn yoga was immense. He went there, learned, surrendered himself, and see how he has become now" (Stern & Donahue, 2010: 191).
12. See Kimberely Roberts, *Designer Yoga*, available at http://www.elephantjournal.com/2010/09/designer-yoga-kim-roberts/ (accessed February 21, 2011).
13. However, a recent *Vanity Fair* article, "Yoga-for-Trophy-Wives Fitness Fad That's Alienating Discipline Devotees," does highlight some emerging unrest in the Ashtanga Yoga community because of a new chain of studios and boutiques using the name "Jois Yoga" (McLean, 2012).
14. KPJAYI website, available at http://kpjayi.org/the-institute/teachers (accessed February 15, 2011).
15. Sharath Jois, personal correspondence with author, January 2009.
16. KPJAYI website, available at http://kpjayi.org/the-institute/teachers (accessed February 15, 2011).
17. As Ben Smith (2008: 148) points out, there "are numerous claims to orthodoxy within Ashtanga Yoga, which often are quite divergent. Usually these claims refer to the authority of a certain text, Pattabhi Jois's teachings or personal experience through practice."
18. Available at http://www.khyf.net/khyf/curriculum.aspx (accessed February 20, 2011). See also Singleton and Fraser's chapter in this volume.

19. See BKS Iyengar Yoga Association of Australia *Teachers Certification Handbook*, available at http://www.iyengaryoga.asn.au/teacher-training-certification/teacher-training/ (accessed January 5, 2011).
20. For example, to progress to the senior or advanced level of certification, Iyengar assesses students' applications, but there is no requirement that students undertake training with him.

CHAPTER 6

Becoming an Icon: B. K. S. Iyengar as a Yoga Teacher and a Yoga Guru

FREDERICK M. SMITH AND JOAN WHITE

INTRODUCTION

For the last sixty-five years, B. K. S. Iyengar has been the most visible and influential figure in the development and expansion of *haṭhayoga* (i.e., postural yoga); indeed, it would not be wrong to state more categorically that his position and influence are paramount within yoga itself, adjectives and typologies aside. Regardless of what one's personal yoga lineage or affiliation might be or the specific name and identity of one or another yoga practice (or teaching), there is general (even if occasionally grudging) recognition that Mr. Iyengar is the single Indian yoga master who has changed the face of both the practice and the presentation of yoga. This has been an ongoing and evolving process for him. On a teaching trip to China in June 2011, at the age of ninety-two, he was queried by a student in Guangzhou, "I've been practicing for seven years, but feel I can't improve." Mr. Iyengar offered little comfort. "I've been practicing yoga for seventy-six years," he said, "and I'm still learning" (Krishnan, 2011). This unpretentious, and doubtless helpful, admission for a man remarkably active at the age of ninety-four (as of August 2013) is testimony to the power of the yoga that he continues to practice assiduously for several hours every day at his studio in Pune. As a result of his practice habits, his lifetime of dedication to refining his teaching, and a renown that has proven to be self-generating, it is unsurprising to discover that Iyengar is both the patriarch of a family that has dedicated itself to yoga and the central figure of a yoga lineage that bears his name. During these decades, however, he has only gradually adopted the persona of a guru and adjusted to the expectations of this position.

Here we explore some of the dynamics involved in Mr. Iyengar's growth from yoga teacher to yoga guru: how the response he has evoked over the decades from those around him has straddled the line or, more accurately, spread across the expansive gray area separating the enthusiastic, dedicated, and highly skilled and disciplined student from the fully devoted disciple. Wherever possible, we supply his own thoughts on his own transformation. We also inquire, more generally, given the increasingly broad and diffuse audience that has become attracted to his practices, what does it mean to be a yoga guru in today's world? This essay is not intended to be biographical, even if it will occasionally comment on autobiographical statements that Mr. Iyengar made in conversation in January 2011, in statements appearing in various publications throughout the decades, or in comments reported by his daughter Geeta or son Prashant, whose unique perspectives are irreplaceable.

Unavoidably, the material presented here is also based on the authors' longtime knowledge of and personal association with B. K. S. Iyengar. This assumes their familiarity with the evolution of his teachings, the changing profile of his students, and the dynamics and structures of the (usually national) organizations that Mr. Iyengar has closely overseen that are responsible for teaching Iyengar Yoga.

We asked him, crucially, to reflect on the meaning of his own "guruship." What does it mean to him to be a yoga guru? How did this come about? What role did students play in transforming him from a professional yoga teacher, struggling to make ends meet to support himself and his family, to a highly acclaimed yoga guru? We asked him about his experience of this journey from a poor if upper-caste South Indian childhood to his adolescent period of study under his guru in Mysore to his comportment as a yoga guru in today's bewildering world of mass-marketed, prepackaged culture and instant availability of everything from dog food to chemotherapy medicine to esoteric doctrines and exercise regimes. In addition to speaking to Mr. Iyengar about these matters, we interviewed Geeta and Prashant. As a matter of full disclosure, we are obliged to mention that we have known both of them well for several decades. To repeat, however, this not a biography, nor can it be considered a textbook ethnography. It is simply an inquiry into Mr. Iyengar's career as a yoga teacher and yoga guru.

We are grateful to the Iyengar family for their cooperation, but we are also aware that in a very long career Iyengar has met many more people than we can hope to contact, a fair number of them passed on by now. It is normal, perhaps, for any individual with a long, complicated, and colorful life history to give slightly different accounts of various crucial events to different people and to emphasize different facets of a particular well-known experience for didactic or conversational purposes, often to people whose observations and personal histories might be very different from our own.[1]

We attempt to move beyond the usual reportage of students or disciples, whose assertions of faith, gratitude, and humility, true and sincere though they may be, share a discursive repetitiveness, a predictability based on previous models. Some of these models are shared territory of Sanskritic culture, but their repetition, unfortunately, does not reveal very much from the guru's point of view.[2] Because the influence of Indian gurus is very often tied in with their writing, with formal and widely distributed presentations of their teachings[3]—and this has certainly been true in Mr. Iyengar's case—we have placed a brief annotated bibliography of his important works at the end of the article.

IYENGAR'S LIFE AND DEVELOPMENT OF HIS YOGA

"Mr. Iyengar," as he is often addressed, was born into a family of highly respected, if far from wealthy, Tamil-speaking Śrīvaiṣṇava Brahmans in the village of Bellur in Kolar district in the southeastern part of the state of Karnataka on December 14, 1918.[4] This respectful term of address, Mr. Iyengar, is commonly used by yoga students who appear in his classes, especially those who feel cultural discomfort calling him *Guruji*, the pervasive honorific for "honored" or "revered guru" (the Hindi suffix *-ji* denoting the sense of reverence). He has often recounted his early life: he suffered from malaria, typhoid, and tuberculosis and was, therefore, decidedly weak in addition to being undernourished.[5] At the age of five his family moved to nearby Bangalore, and in 1934, when he was fifteen, he moved to Mysore to live with one of his elder sisters. It so happened that this sister was married to Sri T. Krishnamacharya,[6] an experienced yogin and yoga master who founded the lineage of yoga practice that Mr. Iyengar and others further developed. Krishnamacharya had as his patron Krishnaraja Wodiyar IV, the Maharaja of Mysore, one of the most powerful men in South India (Singleton, 2010: 175–179). Krishnamacharya lived 101 years (1888–1989), a testimony to a lifetime of yoga practice and strict lifestyle observances. He was not only Mr. Iyengar's teacher but also the mentor of his own son, the well-known Chennai yoga guru T. K. V. Desikachar (b. 1938), the Mysore yoga master K. Pattabhi Jois (1915–2009), and the lesser known but equally gifted Srivatsa Ramaswami of Chennai (b. 1939).[7] Mr. Iyengar was, however, Krishnamacharya's best-known student, and the innovative style of yoga he developed is now known as Iyengar Yoga. Krishnamacharya's life cannot be discussed here, except to say that he was unusual because he was a householder head of a yoga school (*yogaśālā*) that taught regular members of the community.[8]

Krishnamacharya's yoga, the development of his *yogaśālā*, and the reasons that his yoga gained acceptance and a modicum of visibility among the householder middle classes, contrary to the prevailing tradition of yoga in India as a renunciate practice,[9] have been ably discussed by Mark Singleton

(2010), Norman Sjoman (1996), Joseph Alter (2004; 2005a; 2005b), and Elizabeth De Michelis (2004).[10] The personal magnetism and natural abilities of Krishnamacharya aside, the reasons for this, according to these authors who have written convincingly, are the effective integration of British physical fitness regimes, including gymnastics; an attractive Western esotericism that helped domesticate yoga to a rising, outward-looking middle class, separating it from the domain and control of renunciate ascetics; the influence of locally constituted wrestling traditions; and the institutional support of the Mysore (Jaganmohan) palace, including Krishnaraja Wodeyar, the Maharaja himself.[11]

Regardless of these forces, however, and wholly unaware of them in his youth, Mr. Iyengar studied in a yoga culture in which Krishnamacharya spoke glowingly of a history, not so very ancient—an imagined history, it turns out—of thousands of *āsanas* or yogic postures.[12] This culture surely had a lasting effect on him: his discourse of yoga and self-presentation as a yoga guru are thoroughly permeated by references to classical religious narrative. The burgeoning number of *āsanas* presented in *Light on Yoga*—his path-breaking book on postural yoga that first appeared in 1966—may well be a reminiscence of the halcyon days of thousands of *āsanas*, which are, rather suggestively, named for figures from classical Hindu mythology, including deities and sages.[13] Not only are the *āsanas* so named, however, but Mr. Iyengar's discourses and writings are similarly bursting with such references.[14] It is in the names of the *āsanas*, however, and in his personal presence that Mr. Iyengar's empiricism becomes indistinguishable from his spiritual authority, from his power as a guru.

As he has aged and allowed his hair to flow into a long mane, he has unmistakably come to resemble Narasiṃha, the lion man of Hindu mythology who bursts forth from a pillar to slaughter a powerful demon,[15] as well as Hanumān, the monkey devotee of Rāma who is widely worshiped as the exemplar of physical strength.[16] One yoga teacher commented that he is "a larger than life character, really of mythic proportions."[17] Certainly his physical presence encourages this attitude. Physically, pedagogically, and thoroughly in command of his knowledge, he exudes both personal power and spiritual authority. By presenting the nuggets of his teaching, namely, the *āsanas*, in mythic terms, he has spiritualized, historicized, and naturalized his yoga. In other words, he has actualized his yoga by linking it with his formidable physical presence, which must now include his long lifespan and remarkable lucidity. His physical presence itself, along with his reputation and well-known personal history, has augmented this naturalized link between the *āsanas* and classical Indian cultural and religious imagery. He himself, then, has become not just an iconic figure but also an icon. His empirical genius coupled with this iconic status and gift for systematization now more than ever demarcates his yoga, animating it with historical and spiritual presence. An aspect of his

Figure 6.1:
B. K. S. Iyengar in later years. (Photo by Jake Clennell.)

command and confidence is the clear fact that he has enjoyed, and continues to enjoy, thinking about the links between postures and the activities of figures from classical narrative.[18]

Publicly, as well as in his writings, Mr. Iyengar has spoken very little of this narrative empowerment of yoga, preferring to limit his discussion of his early years and the development of his pedagogy to his more pressing life experiences, including his oft-repeated assertion that training in yoga as a teenager enabled him to overcome the debilitating effects of respiratory disease. He also, evidently, had a natural gift for yoga that complemented an equally natural facility for hard work.

Mr. Iyengar has recounted his relationship with Krishnamacharya, under whom he studied for no longer than a year and a half. He states: "I am grateful to my guru, who sowed the seed of interest in me in his own rough and tough way" (Iyengar, 2002: 228). Despite their troubled history—what might be regarded optimistically as tough love or severe testing—Mr. Iyengar has unfailingly honored Krishnamacharya as his guru.[19] Their contentious and clearly competitive relationship is reminiscent of both the normative rules for a disciple as expressed in the classical Indian literature such as the *Laws of Manu*

(*Mānavadharmaśāstra*) and the testiness of guru and disciple relationships often recorded in the *Mahābhārata*. Both of these texts were composed about two millennia ago and appear to speak from different perspectives of the same spiritual culture, one in which errant disciples studied under very strict gurus, sometimes with extremely dire consequences.[20] Mr. Iyengar reports that quite early in his apprenticeship Krishnamacharya asked him to become a yoga "demonstrator," short of conferring on him the position of teacher. He would demonstrate poses when Krishnamacharya taught classes (2002: 224). Iyengar states that "in 1935 I simultaneously started practicing and teaching yoga" (p. 228), which is to say at the age of sixteen.[21] Shortly thereafter, in 1936, he accompanied Krishnamacharya on a tour of northern Karnataka to propagate yoga (p. 293). In August 1937, Krishnamacharya sent Mr. Iyengar, then only eighteen years old, to Pune to teach yoga.[22] Although Mr. Iyengar initially felt exiled and humiliated, he was forced to quickly adapt to his situation.

He recollects that he arrived in Pune for the first time in his life, with little practical knowledge of English and none of Marathi. He spoke Tamil and Kannada, but these were of no use in Pune. He writes: "There I did not possess the language nor have the community, family, friends, or even safe employment" (Iyengar 2006b: 7–8). He confesses a strong admiration of Krishnamacharya's athleticism, a masculinity that was part of a cultural response to British occupation, and a Hindu response to several centuries of Islamic hegemony that preceded the British. Indians under the British and Hindus under the Mughals were often depicted as weak, soft, and easily ruled. This masculine response, then, became idealized in certain (non-Gandhian) sectors of India's independence struggle.[23] It is thus perhaps not coincidental that Mr. Iyengar admits to having been somewhat ashamed of his own physical appearance.

Mr. Iyengar recalls Pune as a city of wrestlers and practitioners of *mallakhamb*, a variety of physical culture derived from wrestling practice, performed with poles and hanging ropes.[24] Yoga, in his experience, barely existed in Pune when he arrived. "The idea in the minds of the people then was that yoga was for those who had lost their head, or had some misunderstandings with their parents or who walk on fire, swallow flaming match sticks and so on" (Iyengar, 2008: 225). He states that there were only half a dozen yoga teachers in the entire Bombay presidency at the time.[25] He does not mention Swami Kuvalayananda, founder of Kaivalyadhama in Lonavala, halfway between Pune and Bombay, and how his presence and influence shaped the popular perception of yoga. Both Mr. Iyengar and Krishnamacharya did, however, willingly undergo certain early scientific experiments on yoga that were the hallmarks of Kaivalya Dham in the 1920s and 1930s.[26] What led to his breakthrough in Pune was, unsurprisingly, the prodigious skill, precision, and enthusiasm that defined his practice at that time and his exploration and insight into medical yoga. While the former have remained intact for the last seventy-five years, his yoga assisted healing abilities, borne of his insight into the mechanics of the human body, have continued to develop. [27]

Thus it happened that Mr. Iyengar inherited from Krishnamacharya the mantle of professional yoga teacher at an early age, a vocation that was virtually nonexistent at the time. Kuvalayananda had a few students in Lonavala, as did Swami Sivananda in Rishikesh, but it was not a viable career path in the first half of the twentieth century.[28] Success in the world came gradually for Mr. Iyengar. He did not burst forth into a ready-made yoga world with a network of contacts, videos, chic clothing, and endorsements, as is often the case today, but was forced to endure a succession of hardships during the first decade and a half of his career in Pune. He has described his vicissitudes as a yoga teacher in several articles and books, narrating just how slowly his clientele built up, his teaching developed (especially medical yoga), and his reputation increased.[29] He has never suggested that he had any desire to assume the historical trajectory of a yogin, namely, becoming a renunciate armed with esoteric doctrines and complicated philosophies, aspiring to collect around him a handful of carefully selected disciples. In any case, his Śrīvaiṣṇava background excluded this; it offers practically no institutional mechanism for the kind of renunciation that one finds in most religious sects in India, including Vaiṣṇava sects throughout the country[30] and Śaṅkarite (Smārta) sects in the South, such as the Sringeri and Kanchi *maṭhas*.[31] His householder status was never in question, and in the early 1940s he married a sixteen-year-old girl from his same Śrīvaiṣṇava community named Ramāmaṇī, after whom his institute in Pune was named in 1975 following her death. He fathered six children with her, including the eldest, Geeta (b. December 6, 1944), and later Prashant (b. July 2, 1949).

During his first years in Pune, Mr. Iyengar wrote a number of letters to Krishnamacharya, asking him how to teach people with challenging physical, psychological, or mental conditions. Krishnamacharya wrote back that he should send such people to him in Mysore. Iyengar took this as a challenge, as his guru's blessings (*āśīrvāda*)[32]; he felt that he could teach these people just as well himself if he relied on his own knowledge and creative powers. At the same time he decided to develop his pedagogical skills, to "present the subject with liveliness" (Iyengar, 2008: 224). It was after this, he says, that he began to be regarded as a teacher. On this evolutionary process, he says, "From a practitioner I grew to become a demonstrator, then an instructor. After this, with experimentation I became a teacher" (p. 225). He states that only after practicing and teaching yoga for eight years, including his first three years in Pune working for the public school system, did he give himself the freedom to become a true *śiṣya* or disciple. Before that, in spite of his years teaching, he regarded himself as a beginner.

At this time he began teaching private medical classes, which became the most important turning point in his thinking as well as in his teaching. This

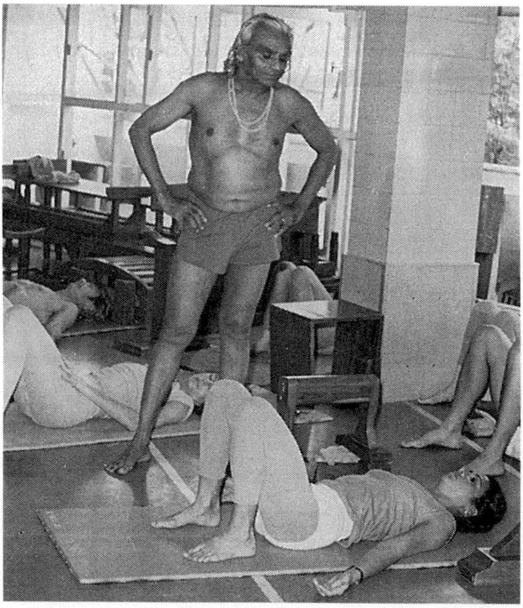

Figure 6.2:
Iyengar teaching in Pune, 1982. (Photograph by Chandru Melwani, Soni Studio.)

was the first real transformation for him from disciple to teacher and eventually to guru. Well before that, however, he began examining the microscopic effects of *āsanas*, and figuring out how to apply them to individual physical or other problems. At this time, still in the 1940s, people began calling him *masterji*. "People never used to call me even Mister. It took people decades to consider me from a demonstrator to *masterji*" (Iyengar, 2008: 226). After a period as *masterji*, people begin to call him *ustād*, an Urdu term for a virtuoso musician, because they felt his yoga flowed like a *rāga*, or musical scale. Because of his skill in healing through yoga alone, rather than through yoga and a separately identified medicine, including *āyurveda*, some referred to him as a *mantravādin*, a term used (especially in South India) for a magician or one who heals through the power of mantras and ritual. In North India many would use the term *tāntrik* for such an individual; however, that term has a harder edge to it, and Mr. Iyengar never suggests that he was referred to with this term. His yoga and healing were much too thoroughly grounded in body mechanics and explicable empiricism for this to have been the case. The next step on his path of recognition occurred when he became known as a *yogācārya*, a more formal Sanskrit title for yoga master. This transpired because a number of well-known renunciate teachers of yoga and meditation consulted with him about their own teaching and practice.[33] This occurred increasingly from the 1950s to the 1970s, by which time he was regularly referred to as a yoga guru

(2002: 227). He claims that the transformations in his practice took fifty years, that it was only then that he became a yoga guru.

It was also at about this time, it appears, that Mr. Iyengar began to look seriously into the classical texts of yoga and to see Patañjali and Vyāsa as his gurus, every bit as much as Krishnamacharya. He understood that his life was irrevocably dedicated to yoga, and as a result he increasingly and instinctively envisioned himself within the classical Sanskritic lineage. He never formally undertook the study of Sanskrit, but he gained enough control of the language to read the *Yogasūtras* (*YS*), a few well-known *haṭhayoga* texts such as the *Haṭhayogapradīpikā*, and the foundational Upaniṣads. No one today claims to belong to an unbroken guru–disciple lineage dating to Patañjali or Vyāsa, the earliest and most important commentator on the *YS*, probably dating from the third to fifth centuries CE). But Mr. Iyengar and many others have positioned themselves in this lineage through the classicization and narrativization processes that have served the purposes of legitimization for at least a thousand years. Thus, regardless of the identity of his actual lineage predecessors, which is to say Krishnamacharya and his teachers, Mr. Iyengar equally appropriated Patañjali and Vyāsa as his gurus.

This is entirely in keeping with the standards of Indian religious culture. It cannot be regarded as a mistaken, contrived identity marker or a quirky and quixotic fabrication. Whatever historical lines of descent one might map out that conclusively demonstrate that Mr. Iyengar cannot be descended from this lineage, the power of his personal identification with it is both sufficient objective justification for it and crucial in locating the meaning of his life and his yoga. This is why he can honestly begin his talks, as he did on Guru Pūrṇimā 2007, with the statement, "I salute my guru and the guru of all gurus in yoga—Vyāsa and Patañjali" (Iyengar, 2008: 221). To him the psychological reality of *anuśāsana* or teaching (*YS* 1.1) overrides the historical facticity of fragmented lineages and "rationalism" (Iyengar, 2008: 221).[34] Simultaneously, the power of classical narrative, such as the story of the birth of the sage Vyāsa from the sage Parāśara and the celestial nymph Satyavatī,[35] holds great power for him. It relates a history of Vyāsa, the redactor of the great Indian epic, the *Mahābhārata*, whom Mr. Iyengar equates with the *YS* commentator Vyāsa.[36] In establishing this history, Mr. Iyengar is able to connect himself with a lineage that descends from divine and semidivine figures.

In this way, Mr. Iyengar considers his own personal history as a *yogācārya* or yoga guru to be wholly explicable in terms of the teacher–disciple (guru–*śiṣya*) relationship, and has therefore taken responsibility for examining this relationship. As a yoga guru, he thinks about discipleship; without the disciple, he understands, there can be no guru. For this he draws from the *Haṭhayogapradīpikā* and the *Gheraṇḍa Saṃhitā*, the two most often cited texts on *haṭhayoga*, which, he says, divide students into four categories. The first is called *ārambhaka*, the beginner, which he equates with the category of practitioner called *mṛdu* or mild in *YS* 1.21. The second is *ghaṭāvasthā*, the condition of being a container. After understanding that the body is a mere container, the student becomes a disciple (*śiṣya*). The third stage, Mr. Iyengar reports, is called *paricaryāvasthā*, the state of being an attendant or devotee, in which the student understands how to "dominate his body through his intelligence" (Iyengar, 2008: 223), in which "the mind introduces each and every part of the body to the intelligence" (ibid.). In the realization of this state, the intelligence completely engulfs the body, after which the student becomes a true *śiṣya*. The fourth stage, on which Mr. Iyengar offers no direct comment, is called *niṣpatti*, or completion.[37] The only statement we were able to find that might explain his views of this stage is found further in the same article: "When all the sheaths of the body are connected by intelligence with the Self, then the *sādhaka* has reached a state where he becomes the *guru*" (p. 229). Mr. Iyengar does not explicitly state that this is *niṣpatti*, but we must assume that the *sādhaka* (practitioner) is the advanced *śiṣya* and that he is indeed referring to the state of *niṣpatti*.[38] The sheaths are the five interlocking and contiguous bodies described in Chapters 2 and 3 of the *Taittirīya Upaniṣad*. Mr. Iyengar prefers this description of the subtle physiology to the standard yogic and tantric descriptions of the *cakras*, *nāḍīs*, and *kuṇḍalinī*.[39]

His teaching developed as he observed an increasing number of students with physical problems, disabilities, and varying levels of natural skill. He gradually attracted well-known students, including, crucially, a well-known cricket star (and Sanskrit scholar) from Pune named Dinkar Balwant Deodhar in the 1940s, whose knee problems were rectified through Iyengar's guidance,[40] and, beginning in 1952, the well-known violinist Yehudi Menuhin, who sought his help after "he had problems with his playing" (Iyengar, 2002: 307). Menuhin later wrote a preface to the first edition of *Light on Yoga*.[41] Many early yoga enthusiasts from Europe also studied under him in the mid-1960s; the Americans followed in the early 1970s.[42] It was, however, *Light on Yoga* that brought him major international acclaim and quickly made him the most celebrated teacher of postural yoga in the world. Many other non-Indians learned under him before the appearance of *Light on Yoga*; indeed, Mr. Iyengar initially traveled to the United States in 1954 and thus began nearly yearly journeys abroad, which, he now says, have concluded with the China trip in 2011.

THE STUDENTS' (OR DISCIPLES') POINT OF VIEW

One measure of a teacher's status or identity as a guru is the reception of his or her students. This is not simply an issue of concern to the students themselves for their own sake, but it is the students' perception of this delicate issue reflected back to the teacher that helps determine his or her self-presentation as a guru. It is part of the heaviness (*gurutva*) of the guru,[43] because it helps guide the teacher's deployment of authority and power in the guru–*śiṣya* relationship. More germane to the present case, we might further ask whether Mr. Iyengar's students regard him as a guru whose influence extends beyond the mechanics of his teachings to eventually empower their lives as a whole? Do they participate in the rituals of veneration that are appropriate to a sect or specific lineage? To what extent are they able to modify their cultural predispositions (if that is in fact an issue for them) to embrace the notion of a guru as distinct from a teacher? Does the word *disciple* flow easily from their lips? Is the guru–*śiṣya* relationship as found among students (or disciples) of Mr. Iyengar a peculiarly Western construction? Is it a mediated construction in which both Mr. Iyengar and his students have given equal ground? Or is it constituted along lines that are (almost) entirely recognizable within Indian cultural history? If the latter, it would indicate that the students (or disciples) have given much more ground in this peculiar intercultural negotiation than Mr. Iyengar has, which is to say they have accommodated themselves to the Indian cultural construction of this relationship and that Mr. Iyengar's adjustments to his students' expectations and goals would have been minor in comparison. Even if one might observe that both have made major adjustments and met somewhere in the middle, these are big questions that cannot be answered in a paragraph or two but require a serious anthropological inquiry that can hardly be undertaken here to arrive at a cogent and definitive answer. Mr. Iyengar is not a teacher who demands devotional loyalty of his students; he is not a *bhakti* guru, so to speak. His students make this decision for themselves in much the same way they practice their yoga—diligently and over time. Given this history, what we can do here is provide impressions based on decades of familiarity, observations that might help others follow up on this in the future.

Through the decades Mr. Iyengar's returning students, including yoga teachers from the West, have become more experienced and sophisticated in their practice and have developed a better understanding of the assumptions and socialization processes of Indian spirituality. This has led many, perhaps most, of the advanced teachers who have been returning to Pune for the last forty years into an acknowledgment of their dedication not just to his teachings or form of yoga or to him as an exquisitely skillful teacher but to him as their guru. It is a fact that most of the advanced teachers are non-Indians, primarily because yoga remains a difficult and slightly onerous career path in India. It generally requires knowledge of English, and most young English speakers possess career options that offer greater security and prestige. For better or worse, the language of modern yoga in India is either English or modern Indian languages mixed with English. Indeed, most of the books used in teaching yoga in modern Indian languages have been either derived from or translated from English. Thus, the culture of modern yoga in India is undeniably cross-cultural and even transnational.

Among the deeply acculturated Indian words that have impacted the present comportment of Iyengar yoga on the highest organizational levels is *Guruji*. What does it mean that nearly all accredited Iyengar yoga teachers now refer to Mr. Iyengar as Guruji rather than as Mr. Iyengar? One can sense awkwardness in either of them as deployed by Iyengar yoga teachers. But each individual must make a choice based on cultural use, available precedent, or social standing within the organization. In the early 1980s it was unusual to hear anyone except local students in Pune or Bombay address Mr. Iyengar as Guruji, but this has now become commonplace. Most of the longtime returning students will explain this by admitting that regardless of the socialization processes that have occurred to facilitate this, their own personal resistances to using the term Guruji have faded as they have themselves grown to feel a genuine and sincere devotion to him as a guru. In sum, as Mr. Iyengar has shifted his own comportment from the model of the harsh master manifested by Krishnamacharya to one who is stern but eminently approachable, his established students have shifted their stance from one of reserved practicality with extreme skepticism of the cultural accouterments of Indian yoga to one of growing admiration for the vision and cultural narratives of yoga that still demarcate yoga, despite the eclectic roots that Singleton, Sjoman, and others have correctly noted.

Mr. Iyengar has spawned and tightly overseen a large number of yoga centers that bear his name. He has established specifications for a lengthy list of certification procedures that include thirteen levels from Introductory I to Senior Advanced II, each of which requires extensive training and testing before a student can progress to teaching any of the poses or *prāṇāyāma* practices that define these levels.[44] In spite of this high degree of specificity there is no "testing" or inquiry at all into a student's devotional commitment. Mr. Iyengar has never claimed for himself the status of divine incarnation (*avatāra*) or resorted to any of the popular discourses that associate the guru with God (or with a particular god).[45] Even among his students who have accorded him the honorific Guruji, there has been no perception or subsequent discussion of him as endowed with inborn sainthood or divinity that exceeds that of any of his students or disciples. He emphasizes above all that dedication, thoroughness, and acutely focused consciousness from skin to bone, from external to internal, are what he represents as an exemplar or guru.[46] As a guru he unfailingly asserts his humanness, not his divinity or exceptionalism.

REFLECTIONS

We conclude with a few words on the guru–*śiṣya* relationship and the clientele that Iyengar yoga has attracted. As discussed, Mr. Iyengar is a strong advocate of hard work, of self-effort (*svataḥ-prayatna*), a category into which yoga fits without controversy. Within Indian religious systems, this is contrasted with cultivation of an attitude of devotion, considered the "effort of another" (*parataḥ-prayatna*), which is to say grace bestowed causelessly by a guru or deity who is effortlessly honored through song, chant, service, or other related practices.[47] This is not to say that Mr. Iyengar's yoga practice or the presentation of events in his yoga studio are devoid of the worship of deities such as Hanumān, Viṣṇu, or a deified Patañjali.[48] Indeed, the worship of embodied deities is nearly always in evidence in his presence. He has perhaps never been seen in public without his Śrīvaiṣṇava *nāman* or prominent U-shaped sectarian mark on his forehead, and he surely always performed *pūjā* (or has employed others to do this on his behalf) on his carefully installed images, including Hanumān. But he has separated this from his yoga teaching, and generally from his self-presentation as a yoga guru, for the sake of mentoring his multireligious and multinational clientele.

That said, his iconic status as the monkey deity Hanumān or the powerful Narasiṃha or Man-Lion of classical mythology, replete with the forehead mark identifying him as an aspect of Viṣṇu, is, as mentioned already, impossible to miss, which suggests that he has few inhibitions in allowing this aspect of his life and personality to passively leak into and permeate his yoga teachings and persona as a guru. Although he has not dwelled on this, neither has he denied it. He has rarely, if ever, discussed in a class or other scheduled discourse his background in Śrīvaiṣṇava doctrines and practices of the twelfth-century saint Rāmānuja (and his successors) and almost never mentions the more tantric aspects of *haṭhayoga* that became part of the standard discourse of yoga from the twelfth century onward. For example, he has never spoken of Rāmānuja's qualified nondualism (*viśiṣṭādvaita*) as more authoritative than other forms of *vedānta*; or of the delicate *sāṃkhyayoga* dualism found in the *YS* as a "lesser" form of knowledge; or of *nāḍīs*, *cakras*, or *kuṇḍalinī* as historically linked more closely to Śaiva-inspired Nāth yoga.[49] He has not encouraged his highly trained teachers to learn the catechism of Śrīvaiṣṇava devotional practice (*bhakti*); read the texts on which it is based (e.g., the *Bhāgavata Purāṇa* and the Tamil poetry of the fifth to tenth centuries CE); visit the well-known Śrīvaiṣṇava temples at Tirupati, Srirangam, or Melkote; or study the doctrines of *viśiṣṭādvaita* as they are found in Rāmānuja's commentaries on the *Bhagavad Gītā*, the *Brahmasūtras*, or other learned Śrīvaiṣṇava treatises.

We asked Mr. Iyengar in an interview how he reconciles the doctrines espoused in his familial Śrīvaiṣṇava practice with the doctrines espoused in the *YS*. Although these two philosophical systems abound with important differences, Mr. Iyengar sees himself as a disciple of both Rāmānuja and Patañjali. He answered, first, that he understands god (*īśvara*) defined in *YS* 1.24 as a "special person" (*puruṣaviśeṣa*) to be Viṣṇu, and, second, that he harkens back to the sage Nāthamuṇi, a predecessor of Rāmānuja, who supposedly wrote a treatise on yoga.[50] Mr. Iyengar sees himself as a yogin and a *vedāntin* and moves easily between the dualistic cosmology presented in *sāṃkhya* and yoga with the more deistic and nondual ontologies of *vedānta*.[51]

Similarly, and arguably of greater consequence for the practice of Iyengar yoga and for Mr. Iyengar's standing within the community of yoga gurus, is that he has largely sequestered *prāṇāyāma* or breath control from his *āsana* teaching. This represents a sharp departure from the practice and teachings of the other students and disciples of Krishnamacharya. It appears that the historical reason Mr. Iyengar did not integrate *prāṇāyāma* more fully into his *āsana* practice and teaching is that he did not study it with Krishnamacharya before he left Mysore for Pune in 1937. He developed his *prāṇāyāma* practice many years later, largely on his own, with no more than a few pointers from Krishnamacharya and others after he had already settled in Pune. He therefore integrated it differently into his yoga practice than did other students of Krishnamacharya such as Pattabhi Jois or T. K. V. Desikachar, who studied with Krishnamacharya for a much more sustained period. Mr. Iyengar explains most of this in his autobiographical accounts, even if he attributes some of his early hesitation on *prāṇāyāma* to his guru's lack of confidence in him (Iyengar, 1978; 1990). However, various Iyengar yoga teachers are slowly reintroducing *prāṇāyāma* into *āsana* practice, which indicates that some of the fundamental practices of Iyengar yoga are undergoing a shift.[52] It is certain that this has not affected Mr. Iyengar's status as the supreme authority in postural yoga among his longtime followers. They have shown every indication over the decades of attempting to learn—and teach—according to the most recent developments and innovations that they have picked up from Mr. Iyengar in their regular or semiregular visits to Pune, even if these are occasionally at odds with what is stated in *Light on Yoga*.

It should be mentioned again that the names of an overwhelming number of the *āsanas*, many of which Mr. Iyengar and other contemporaries have developed, are drawn from narrative Hindu lore, and annual celebrations such as Guru Pūrṇimā[53] and Mr. Iyengar's birthday (which have become increasingly important over the years) are also framed in religious and cultural narratives and ideals. As a yoga teacher, Mr. Iyengar's authority has virtually never been challenged and has remained unchanged, but as a guru his status has expanded through the years as certain nontechnical aspects of his teachings have emerged, including his teachings deriving from cultural narratives and his attention to the *YS* and allied scholarly discourse, which are now a regular part of his teaching. Mr. Iyengar's concerns both with assiduous goal-oriented work and with sharpening his learning is what anthropologist David Gellner (2010: 174) attributes to "the rising middle-class obsession with education and the constructive use of time."[54]

In sum, Mr. Iyengar presents a complex image of style and substance and of harshness and ease, even if most of his established students now understand this harshness as a legacy of his own guru's more egregious excesses. He is strict with his students but mixes easily with them in his library every afternoon. He is not trailed by retinues of saffron- or white-robed Sanskrit *paṇḍits* or politicians seeking his worldly or divine favor, nor has he placed himself on a dais, garlanded with flowers and surrounded by institutional identity markers. He expresses a parochialism born of devotion to his inherited culture and a worldly sophistication born of extensive travel. His public presence and charisma are evident from the outset. One always knows when he is in the room, even if he does not demand a special status because of it. A good deal of this is his presence and oft-told personal history, which has now stretched well into its tenth decade. This longevity, along with his remarkable clarity, has itself become part of the story, part of the iconicity that has taken on a life of its own, as previously described. His authority and power as a yoga guru lie not only in the mythic stature he has achieved as well as his influence and permanence but also in his organizational skill: he has raised two, or perhaps by now three, generations of dedicated, intelligent, and sensitive teachers who are capable of articulating the subtleties and complexities of his yoga. On how he has conducted himself as a yoga teacher, and subsequently as a yoga guru, he states: "I first worked to make them accept it [yoga] as an art. I made them understand it as a science, and then made them absorb it as a philosophy or way of life" (Iyengar, 2002: 229). Thus, he has a unique ability to weave, in a single class, the precise details of anatomy, the mechanics of movement, traditional narrative, and philosophy to allow him to stand out as perhaps the most paradigmatic yoga guru of the last seventy-five years.

BIBLIOGRAPHIC NOTES ON THE WORKS OF B. K. S. IYENGAR

Light on Yoga. New York: Schocken Books, 1977 [1st ed. 1966]. The definitive book on the *āsanas* of *haṭhayoga*. It includes step-by-step instructions, deep anatomical discussion, hundreds of photographs of poses, and a large number of suggested sequences.

Light on Prāṇāyāma. London: George Allan & Unwin, 1981. This occupies the same position among books on breath control (*prāṇāyāma*) that *Light on Yoga* does on the practice of *āsanas*. It gives acutely detailed instructions, with attention to physiological and mental processes.

Yogavṛkṣa: The Tree of Yoga. Ed. by Daniel Rivers-Moore. Oxford: Fine Line Books, 1988; Boston: Shambhala Press, 1989. Edited from numerous talks in the 1980s, this book uses the metaphor of yoga as a tree with many branches to describe the practice and application of yoga in daily life.

Light on Life: The Yoga Journey to Wholeness, Inner Peace, and Ultimate Freedom. With John J. Evans and Douglas Abrams. London: Rodale Press, 2005. An advice book in nontechnical language using as a template the principals of yoga. Chapters and sections are conceived according to the divisions of the five *kośas* (sheaths) of the Upaniṣads (body, breath, mind, wisdom, bliss; e.g., *Taittirīya Upaniṣad*, chapter 2), *sāṃkhya* cosmology (e.g., *puruṣa, prakṛti, manas, ahaṃkāra*), and the eight limbs of yoga described in chapters 2 and 3 of the *YS*

Light on the Yoga Sūtras of Patañjali. London: Aquarian Press, 1993; New Delhi: HarperCollins, 1993. A translation and explanation of every *sūtra* of the *Yogasūtras*. This volume is used extensively by Iyengar yoga teachers to comprehend the basic doctrines of yoga.

In the last several years Mr. Iyengar has produced a number of books that are spinoffs and refinements of his earlier books. None of them will achieve canonical status but will be interesting to beginners. This list is not exhaustive, but Mr. Iyengar stated (August 2011) that the last two in this list will be his final books.

The Art of Yoga. Delhi: HarperCollins India, 2005.
Yoga Wisdom and Practice. Delhi: DK Publications, 2009.
Yaugika Manas. Mumbai: YOG Publications, 2010.
Yoga Sūtra Anusandhāna: The Yoga Sūtras Re-Arrayed (forthcoming).
Pātañjala Yoga Sūtra Paricaya—Formal Introduction of Pātañjala Yoga Sūtras. (forthcoming).

In addition, frequent short articles, transcriptions of lectures, interviews, and other brief notices have been published over the years and have been collected in (so far) nine invaluable volumes titled *Aṣṭadaḷa Yogamālā* [The eight-petaled garland of yoga]. Volume 8 of this series contains an extensive and helpful index of all the previous volumes. Student's articles and extracts from Iyengar's own work regularly appear in local and national in-house yoga newsletters, journals, and conference magazines. For example, *Yoga Rahasya* is published in Pune four times annually. In addition, countless translations of many of Iyengar's works have appeared in languages from Marathi and Hindi to virtually every European language.

REFERENCES

Akers, Brian Dana. 2002. *The Hatha Yoga Pradipika*. Woodstock, NY: YogaVidya.com.
Alter, Joseph S. 1992. *The Wrestler's Body: Identity and Ideology in North India*. Berkeley: University of California Press.

———. 2004. *Yoga in Modern India: The Body between Science and Philosophy*. Princeton, NJ: Princeton University Press.

———. 2005a. Modern Medical Yoga: Struggling with a History of Magic, Alchemy and Sex. *Asian Medicine*, *1*(1), 119–146.

———. 2005b. Yoga at the Fin de Siecle: Muscular Christianity with a "Hindu" Twist. *International Journal of the History of Sport*, *23*(5), 759–776.

Birch, Jason. 2011. Modern and Traditional Yoga: Is There a Connection? American Academy of Religion Annual Meeting, San Francisco, November.

Bühnemann, Gudrun. 2007. *Eighty-four Āsanas in Yoga: A Survey of Traditions*. New Delhi: D. K. Printworld.

Busia, Kofi. 2007. *Iyengar: The Yoga Master*. Boston: Shambhala.

Clark, Matthew. 2006. *The Daśanāmī-Saṃnyāsīs: The Integration of Ascetic Lineages into an Order*. Leiden: Brill.

De Michelis, E. 2004. *A History of Modern Yoga: Patañjali and Western Esotericism*. London: Continuum.

Desikachar. T. K. V. 1980. *Religiousness in Yoga: Lectures on Theory and Practice*. Lectures edited by John Ross Carter and Mary Louise Skelton. Lanham, MD: University Press of America.

———. 1999. *The Heart of yoga: Developing a Personal Practice*. Rochester, VT: Inner Traditions.

Forsthoefel, Thomas, and Cynthia Ann Humes (eds.). 2005. *Gurus in America*. Albany: State University of New York Press.

Gellner, David N. 2010. Initiation as a Site of Cultural Conflict among the Newars. In Astrid Zotter and Christof Zotter (eds.), *Hindu and Buddhist Initiations in India and Nepal*. Ethno Indology, Heidelberg Studies in South Asian Rituals. Gen. ed. Axel Michaels, vol. 10. Wiesbaden: Harrassowitz.

Gharote, M. L. 2007. *Encyclopaedia of Traditional Asanas*. Lonavla: Yoga Institute.

Gold, Daniel. 1987. *The Lord as Guru: Hindi* Sants *in North Indian Tradition*. New York: Oxford University Press.

Gonsalves, Michael. 2011. Master of the Body. *Financial Chronicle,* August 4. Blog: http://www.mydigitalfc.com/art-and-culture/master-body-739.

Idea Exchange. 2011. Yoga Is a Spiritual Subject and Should Not Be Mixed with Politics. B. K. S. Iyengar interview with staff members of the *Financial Express*, Mumbai, September 4, p. 5. http://epaper.financialexpress.com/11222/Financial-Express-Mumbai/4-September-2011#p=page:n=5:z=2.

Iyengar, B. K. S. 1977. *Light on Yoga*. New York: Schocken Books. (Original publication London: George Allen & Unwin, 1966.)

———. 1978. *Iyengar. His Life and Work*. Bombay: B.I. Taraporewala.

———. 1990. My Yogic Journey. In *70 Glorious Years of Yogacharya B. K. S. Iyengar (Commemoration Volume)*. Bombay: Light on Yoga Research Trust, pp. 1–19.

———. 1993. *Light on the Yoga Sūtras of Patañjali*. London: Aquarian Press.

———. 2002. *Aṣṭadaḷa Yogamālā* (Collected Works), Vol. 3. New Delhi: Allied Publishers Pvt. Ltd.

———. 2006. *Aṣṭadaḷa Yogamālā* (Collected Works), Vol. 6. New Delhi: Allied Publishers Pvt. Ltd.

———. 2008. *Aṣṭadaḷa Yogamālā* (Collected Works), Vol. 8. New Delhi: Allied Publishers Pvt. Ltd.

Iyengar, Geeta S. 1990. Guru-Shishya Parampara: The Guru-Disciple Tradition. In *70 Glorious Years of Yogacharya B. K. S. Iyengar (Commemoration Volume)*. Bombay: Light on Yoga Research Trust, pp. 375–385.

———. 2000. *Yoga in Action. Preliminary Course*. Mumbai: Yog Publications.

Krishnamacharya, T. 2002. *Śrī Nāthamuni's Yogarahasya*. English version by T. K. V. Desikachar. Chennai: Krishnamacharya Yoga Mandiram.

———. 2006. *Yoga Makaranda or Yoga Saram (The Essence of Yoga)*, First Part. Trans. by Lakshmi Ranganathan and Nandini Ranganathan. Privately distributed. Kannada edition 1934, Tamil edition 1938. Madurai: C.M.V. Press.

Krishnan, Ananth. 2011. An Indian Yoga Icon Finds Following in China. *The Hindu*, June 23. http://www.hindu.com/2011/06/23/stories/2011062365930700.htm.

Lester, Robert C. 1994. The Sāttāda Srivaisnavas. *Journal of the American Oriental Society* 114: 39–53.

Lutgendorf, Phillip. 2007. *Hanuman's Tale: The Messages of a Divine Monkey*. Oxford: Oxford University Press.

Mallinson, James. 2004. *The Gheranda Samhita: The Original Sanskrit and an English Translation*. Woodstock, NY: YogaVidya.com.

Mohan, A G. 2004. *Yoga Therapy: A Guide to the Therapeutic Use of Yoga and Ayurveda for Health and Fitness*. Boston: Shambhala.

———. 2010. *Krishnamacharya: His Life and Teachings*. Boston: Shambhala.

Nemec, John. 2009. When the *Paramparā* Breaks: On Gurus and Students in the Mahābhārata. In *The Anthropologist and the Native: Essays for Gananath Obeyesekere*. Ed. by H. L. Seneviratne. Firenze: Società Editrice Fiorentina, pp. 35–64.

Prasad, Leela. 2006. *Poetics of Conduct: Oral Narrative and Moral Being in a South Indian Town*. New York: Columbia University Press.

Ramaswami, Srivatsa. 2000. *Yoga for the Three Stages of Life*. Rochester, VT: Inner Traditions.

———. 2005. *The Complete Book of Vinyasa Yoga*. New York: Marlowe & Company.

Ramaswami, Srivatsa, and David Hurwitz. 2006. *Yoga Beneath the Surface*. New York: Marlowe & Company.

Sarma, Deepak. 2003. *An Introduction to Mādhva Vedānta*. Aldershot: Ashgate Publishers Ltd.

Singleton, Mark. 2010. *Yoga Body: The Origins of Modern Posture Practice*. New York: Oxford University Press.

Sjoman, N. E. 1996. *The Yoga Tradition of the Mysore Palace*. New Delhi: Abhinav Publications.

Smith, Frederick M. 2005. The Hierarchy of Philosophical Systems According to Vallabhācārya. *Journal of Indian Philosophy*, *33*(4): 421–453.

———.2011. *Yogasūtras* II.25 and the Conundrum of *Kaivalya*. In J. Duquette and P. Penumala (eds.), *Classical and Contemporary Issues in South Asian Studies: In Felicitation of Prof. T.S. Rukmani*. New Delhi: D.K. Printworld (P) Ltd., pp. 66–78.

Staal, Frits, 1993. Indian Bodies. In Thomas P. Kasulis, Roger T. Ames, and Wimal Dissanayake (eds.), *Self as Body in Asian Theory and Practice*. Albany: State University of New York Press, pp. 59–102.

Stephan, Karin. 2004. Memories of Mr. Iyengar Abroad 1972–1976. http://www.yogamacro.com/karin_profile/ks_writings/memories/nmemories.htm (accessed June 24, 2013).

Vasudeva, Som Dev. 2011. "Haṃsamiṭṭhu: 'Pātañjalayoga Is Nonsense.'" *Journal of Indian Philosophy*, *39*(2): 123–145.

Vidyasankar, S. 2000. Conflicting Hagiographies: The *Bṛhat, Prācīna, Anantānandagīriya*, and *Mādhavīya Śaṅkaravijaya*. *International Journal of Hindu Studies*, *4*(2): 109–184. Available at: http://indology.info/papers/sundaresan/.

White, David Gordon. 1984. Why Gurus Are Heavy. *Numen*, *31*(1): 40–73.

———. 2009. *Sinister Yogis*. Chicago: University of Chicago Press.
White, Hayden. 1981. The Value of Narrativity in the Representation of Reality. *Critical Inquiry*7: 5–27.

NOTES

1. The interviews were conducted by Joan White in Pune in January and February 2011, with a follow-up by Frederick Smith in August 2011. Joan has been a close student of Mr. Iyengar's for forty years. She has traveled to India to study under him nearly every year during that time, is one of his senior teachers, and has served as a member of the board of the Iyengar Yoga National Association of the United States (IYNAUS) for more than four years, chair of the certification committee for more than six years, and chair of the ethics committee for four years. Frederick Smith studied under Mr. Iyengar for six years while a student and academic researcher in Pune in the 1980s and 1990s, and, like Joan, became friendly with the Iyengar family. We would also like to thank Rajiv and Swati Chanchani for their insights, good company, encouragement, and use of their private library for many years.
2. For example, the *Guru-Gītā*, a late addition (in the early nineteenth century) to the *Skanda Purāṇa*, contains a great deal of the language that is widely deployed in praise of the guru. This text is not a part of the Iyengar yoga canon, as the *YS* is, but the discourse that appears there has permeated India-based spiritual movements, including yoga.
3. Examples are Śaṅkara in the eighth century, Jñāneśvar and Rāmānuja in the twelfth century, and Aurobindo, Yogananda, Shivananda, and Vivekananda in the last century or so. Few have eschewed literary production yet still obtained major stature. Examples are Chaitanya in the early sixteenth century, Ramakrishna Paramahamsa in the nineteenth century, and Sai Baba of Shirdi in the late nineteenth and early twentieth centuries. But all of them were surrounded by others who closely documented their lives and teachings.
4. The letter B as the first initial of his name is for Bellur. An important identifier in South Indian nomenclature is placing the name of one's home or ancestral village as the first initial of a full name. Following South Indian naming practices, the second letter, K, represents his father's name, Krishnamachar, while the third letter, S, is his given name, Sundararaja. The name *Iyengar* is a community of Tamil-speaking Śrīvaiṣṇava Brahmans. On this name, see Lester (1994).
5. He writes: "I was in Mysore in 1934–35. A doctor examined me in school. My height then was 4 feet 10 inches. I weighed 70 pounds. My chest measurement was 22 inches and chest expansion was only half an inch" (Iyengar, 1978: 7). This article should be read by anyone who wants details of Mr. Iyengar's early life.
6. Although he seems to have written quite a bit, his renown was as a teacher rather than an author. But what he did write is of more than antiquarian interest. His most important available work is the first part of the *Yoga Makaranda*, published in Kannada in 1934 and then in Tamil in 1938. It was translated into English only in 2006 and, in a slightly different version, privately distributed in 2010 (Krishnamacharya 2006). Another work is the *Yogarahasya*, which he asserts he received in a vision from the shadowy semimythical Śrīvaiṣṇava founder Nāthamuni. It might be harsh to call it spurious, but it is written in rather unfortunate Sanskrit and is

little more than a projection into antiquity of a modern description of and justification for the primacy of asana practice (Krishnamacharya, 2002).

7. See Desikachar (1980; 1999) for his philosophical perspective; see also Ramaswami (2000; 2005) and Ramaswami and Hurwitz (2006). Krishnamacharya had many more students whose names are known, such as A. G. Mohan, who wrote a (rather uncritical) biography of Krishnamacharya (Mohan 2010) and a book on healing through yoga (Mohan, 2004). Pattabhi Jois and (especially) Desikachar emphasize Sanskrit chanting more than Mr. Iyengar does. Desikachar and Ramaswami emphasize active use of breath more than Mr. Iyengar does. Mr. Iyengar has (on the whole) emphasized a quiet, even meditative, precision, with considerable variation in pose sequencing rather than active yoga-inspired calisthenics with relatively fixed series of poses (*vinyāsa*). See Singleton (2010) for a thoroughly researched and illuminating discussion of the character of modern yoga as a product of an early twentieth-century effort, largely based in Mysore, to integrate *haṭhayoga*, British calisthenics, and other European cultural influences. The history of modern yoga has received great impetus in the last two decades, from Sjoman's (1996) landmark study, which required great familiarity with the history of the Mysore palace, to De Michelis's (2004) study of the influence of Western esotericism on modern yoga to Alter's (2004; 2005a; 2005b) many studies and of course to Singleton's (2010) recent volume.
8. Krishnamacharya (2006: 17) wrote: "Everyone has a right to do yoga. Everyone—brahmin, kshatriya, vaishya, sudra, gnani, strong, women, men, young, old and very old, the sick, the weak, boys, girls, etcetera, all are entitled to *yogabhyasa* with no restrictions on age and caste." The photos in the book show no women or girls, and it remains to be researched whether he did in fact teach all of those whose eligibility he extols here. But see "Children Practicing Yoga with Krishnamachary—1938 Film SILENT," available at http://www.youtube.com/watch?v=9-EcePRXOP4 (accessed May 30, 2012). One of the keys to Mr. Iyengar's success is that he has in fact taught members of all classes, communities, religious affiliations, and, of course, women.
9. This was the case irrespective of whether or not the renunciate yogins were supported by religious institutions such as temples or monastic organizations.
10. See White (2009) for an account of why, before the advent of Krishnamacharya, and still in much of India outside the domestic (and domesticated) lineages of modern yoga, *sinister yogis* have been the norm.
11. Royal patronage has always proven to be crucial in the spread of religious or philosophical practices in India: for example, rituals performed by kings mentioned throughout the Vedas, the spread of Buddhism under the emperor Aśoka in the third-century BCE, and so on through the millennia. Although Mr. Iyengar has in general favored the agendas of the Indian political right wing (as is common among Brahmans in Pune), he has not adopted the style or substance of the politics of yoga, for example in the valorization of *sūryanamaskār*, or sun salutations (he includes it as an afterthought; Iyengar 1977: 468; but see Geeta Iyengar, 2000: 105–107). The *sūryanamsakār* appears to be an innocuous practice, but since the early twentieth century its performance has been linked with nationalist ideologies (Alter, 2004; Singleton, 2010: 179–184).
12. Krishnamacharya writes: "In Nepal, living in Muktinarayanakshetra, Sri Rama Mohana Brahmachari Guru Maharaj has mastered/(brought into his experience) 7000 *asanas*. I have seen this directly and through his guidance and advice, I have mastered 700 *asanas*. Nowadays (in present times), there are only 84 *āsanas*

illustrated in the books available and it is the same with some renowned yogis" (*Yogamakaranda*, p. 25). On the number eighty-four for *āsanas*, see Bühnemann (2007).

13. See, for example, the descriptions of *kūrmāsana* (Iyengar 1966: 288) and *hanumānāsana* (ibid., 352).
14. It should be mentioned that, in spite of the clear reconstitution of postural yoga as a result of the external influences that Singleton and others cite, Singleton was recently critiqued by Jason Birch (2011), who points out that several relatively unknown and little read precolonial and early colonial period yoga texts contain many more yoga postures than are found in the well-known lists (see Bühnemann, 2007). The evidence from these texts, such as the *Yogāsanamālā* (1789 CE), which lists 109 *āsanas*; the *Kapālakuraṇṭakahaṭhābhyāsapaddhhati*, most likely from the nineteenth century, with 112 poses, and the *Āsananāmāni*, with 500 poses, in part substantiates the assertions of Krishamacharya and others that they drew more from classical yoga in their astonishingly large number of poses. However, unless a mechanism can be established between the texts that Birch cites and Krishnamacharya, his conclusions remain in doubt. We remain skeptical of the methodology followed by Gharote (2007) in his enumeration of classical poses.
15. Images of Narasiṃha and his special form as Yoga Narasiṃha can be found in many places with a simple Google search.
16. It is noteworthy that Hanumān is not only the most popular deity in India (see Lutgendorf, 2007) and ubiquitous in Kiṣkindha, the home of Hanumān in the Rāmāyaṇa and very close to Iyengar's home in Karnataka, but is also the primary deity of wrestlers and others who prioritize physical culture (Alter, 1992; Lutgendorf, 2007). Hanumān has always been celebrated for his strength and is almost always depicted as powerfully built. This was necessary to fulfill his exploits in the Rāmāyaṇa, which were associated with his defeat of the ten-headed demon Rāvaṇa, who had abducted Sītā, the wife of the Hanumān's guru and lord, the righteous king Rāma.
17. Nancy Footner of Iowa City (e-mail message, August 2011). Joan White recalls that upon meeting Mr. Iyengar at a dinner party in 1973, "I was surprised that he was so friendly, humorous and a wonderful raconteur. The following day in my first class with him he assumed mythic proportions seemingly larger than life with his commanding presence, his razor sharp vision and his profound knowledge of the subject."
18. Mr. Iyengar's deployment of classical (usually Sanskritic) narrative fits with Hayden White's distinction between narrative and storytelling, with narrative being more open-ended; see White (1981).
19. Geeta Iyengar notes in a Guru Pūrṇimā talk (July 12, 1987) that Krishnamacharya would stand on pupils' abdomens while they were in upward bow pose (*ūrdhvāsana*; see *Light on Yoga*, p. 357) or pigeon pose (*kapoṭāsana*; see *Light on Yoga*, pp. 367–372). Mr. Iyengar confirmed this in an interview with Joan White in January 2011. He recalled that once, during a yoga lecture in which Iyengar was demonstrating poses, Krishnamacharya stood on his stomach for eighteen minutes while Iyengar was in pigeon pose, while his legs and arms rested on broken glass. Geeta (1990: 378) acknowledges that Krishnamacharya's guru, Ram Mohan Brahmachari, was also known for his "harsh method." Nevertheless, Geeta recalls that in 1961 Krishnamacharya came to Pune and presented Iyengar with a very fine gift, honoring him highly (ibid., 379).
20. See Nemec (2009), who brings this out well. For example, according to *Manu* the student was to revere the master at all costs, never argue with him, become

completely disciplined in body and mind, and must maintain eternal loyalty. But, as the *Mahābhārata* often narrates, strong-willed disciples were occasionally slighted, which could lead to disaster or, at any rate, to breaks in the tradition, as Nemec calls them. Nemec's article sheds a good deal of light on yogic and spiritual lineage behavior of the present, not just of the period he is directly addressing.

21. In a recent interview in the *Financial Times* (Idea Exchange, 2011; see next note) he says he began studying yoga in 1934. Thus, there is some variance in his reports.
22. Mr. Iyengar stated in an interview with Joan White in January 2011 that Krishnamacharya sent him to Pune to teach yoga at a girl's school because he felt Mr. Iyengar would not be attractive to young girls, but more importantly, Krishnamacharya added, it was important to teach ladies and girls separately from men, especially elderly men. This, of course, is consistent with long-standing Indian cultural patterns. Currently the schedule of classes at the Institute in Pune includes two weekly classes for women and one for men only, but the rest of the schedule accepts both men and women, including the weekly, overcrowded *prāṇāyāma* class.
23. See Alter (1992) on this. The Rashtriya Svayamsevak Sangh (RSS), which was both Hindu nationalist and anti-British, developed conditioning regimes that were very close to British calisthenics. It may be mentioned that Mr. Iyengar has stayed away from the political arena (but see note 11). As will be noted here, he has always maintained a welcoming attitude to people of all communities, never favoring one or another person because of his or her background, except in the case of his own family, which he regards as the inheritors of his Institute in Pune. Notably, he has encouraged his son Prashant to develop his own practices.
24. Staal (1993) discusses this, with illustrations and photos of its current practice, which was little changed from pre-Independence India. (Both of the current authors have also observed this distinctly local method of physical conditioning at a school in Pune.) Mr. Iyengar never discloses the extent to which the ropes and poles influenced his own propensity to employ yoga props, which are one of the primary features of Iyengar yoga.
25. Before the division of independent India into the current system of states in 1959, Bombay Presidency contained all of Maharashtra, and half of present-day Gujarat, Karnataka, and Andhra Pradesh.
26. On this, see Alter (2004: 73–108). Alter demonstrates that Kuvalayananda's "scientific nationalism," rooted in the body, was transformed by the end of his life into a more universalistic humanism. The nationalistic undertones to Krishnamacharya's yoga are much more accessible than in Mr. Iyengar's.
27. The best and most gripping personal account that Mr. Iyengar gives of his own life is found in a transcript of a talk he gave on December 11, 1988, in Pune, as part of his seventieth birthday celebration (Iyengar, 1990). For another available account, see Busia (2007: introduction) and Gonsalves (2011), with details of his coming to Pune and his initial trials and eventual successes there. Mr. Iyengar enjoys telling his life story; see most recently an interview in the *Financial Express*, September 4, 2011 (see Idea Exchange, 2011). The degree to which stories of Mr. Iyengar's life are repeated, with certain variations, with virtually no cross-referencing, is reminiscent of Alter's (2004: xviii) observation that "many authors write as though they are the only person writing on the subject [of yoga] with any authority, and that what they are saying is new. Yet if there is one single thing that characterizes the literature on Yoga, it is repetition and redundancy in the guise of novelty and independent invention." Alter calls this literature "the discursive field of yogic pulp nonfiction" (p. xix).

28. Kuvalayananda and Sivananda presented their teachings almost entirely in English.
29. He discusses his past frequently. Many of these discussions are now scattered throughout the eight volumes of *Aṣṭadaḷa Yogamālā*, a series that has collected together Mr. Iyengar's various lectures, minor writings, and ephemera, a project that will probably continue.
30. Although renunciation is permitted in the Śrīvaiṣṇava sect, it is practically never undertaken. At present, according to Lakshmi Tatacharya of Melkote, near Mysore, one of the great living scholars among Śrīvaiṣṇavas, no more than half a dozen people (all men) are alive today who have taken the Śrīvaiṣṇava vows of renunciation. All of them are administrators in important temples, including two at the great Śrī Veṅkateśvara temple at Tirumala, in Andhra Pradesh (personal communication, August 2011).
31. For the Sringeri *maṭha* and Kanchi *maṭha* histories, see Vidyasankar (2000) on the authenticity of their lineages; Clark (2006) on renunciation; and Prasad (2006), whose observations on narrative, storytelling, and moral authority are germane, as they may be extended to the individual. But this is not the place to enter further into this interesting discussion. It is sufficient to state that the Śaṅkara *maṭhas* in Sringeri and Kanchipuram have a long history of support for Vedic recitation and ritual and for *vedāntic* approaches to yoga practice.
32. On the poetics and cultural meaning of *āśīrvāda*, see Prasad (2006: 163–174).
33. Among those he mentions are Swami Sivananda and Swami Chidananda (from Rishikesh), Swami Satyananda, Swami Dayananda (from Coimbatore), and Swami Satchidananda (who was based in the United States for several decades).
34. Guru Pūrṇimā talk, Pune, July 2007, "From a Śiṣya to a Guru" (2008: 221–232).
35. From *Mahābhārata* 1.57.
36. For a number of reasons that we need not enter into here, this equation cannot bear the weight of historical scrutiny.
37. Cf. *Haṭhayogapradīpikā* (*HYP*) 4.69. In spite of Mr. Iyengar's reading *paricarya*, the various editions (e.g., Akers, 2002) read *paricaya*, "heaping up, accumulation" as the third stage. In either case, Mr. Iyengar's interpretation appears to be his own. The *HYP* discusses these four stages entirely in terms of the internal sounds heard during the integrated practice of *āsana*, *prāṇāyama*, and *mudrā*.
38. In our reading of his many writings, we have not discovered any instances of Mr. Iyengar using the word *niṣpatti* as part of a self-description.
39. Mr. Iyengar provides an interesting and expanded chart of the sheaths in Iyengar (1993: 133).
40. Gonsalves (2011) writes of this. Deodhar lived to the age of 101 (d. 1993).
41. Iyengar (2002: 294); see Iyengar (2006: 279–329), a transcript of a long interview of Mr. Iyengar with Mark Tully, the well-known former chief India correspondent with the BBC, conducted in Pune on April 7–8, 1999. In this interview Mr. Iyengar discusses at length his association with Menuhin. Another early student of Mr. Iyengar's, Karin Stephan, wrote the following:

    > For several years Menuhin would give concerts in Gstaad, Switzerland, the beautiful ski resort tucked away in the mountainous Alps, and Mr. Iyengar would go there and give him private classes. There is no better person to express to what degree Iyengar taught Menuhin how the body itself, like the violin, is a beautiful instrument in its own right which one could play. Below is the eloquent eulogy to that power written by Menuhin himself in the preface to *Light on Yoga*: "The practice of Yoga induces a primary sense of

> measure and proportion. Reduced to our own body, our first instrument, we learn to play it, drawing from it maximum resonance and harmony. With unflagging patience, we refine and animate every cell as we return daily to the attack, unlocking and liberating capacities otherwise condemned to frustration and death" [1977: 11]. In addition to Menuhin, Gstaad and its neighboring town, Sanaan, would also be host to another great luminary as well—the renowned Indian thinker and philosopher, J. Krishnamurti. (Stephan, 2004)

Among some others who came to him in the 1950s were the well-known Indian Freedom Fighter and politician Jayaprakash Narayan and the queen mother of Belgium (Iyengar, 1990: 15–16, 2002: 307).

42. Mary Palmer from Ann Arbor, Michigan, studied in India with Mr. Iyengar in 1971. She subsequently invited him to Ann Arbor in 1973, where he was introduced to many yoga enthusiasts, including Joan White.
43. Drawing from the title of an article by David White (1984). Although White dealt with an entirely different topic than we are covering here, the notions of the heaviness of hierarchical relationships and masculinity are important to both his and our study. We cannot here open up these topics to full inquiry but can only mention them.
44. See http://www.bksiyengar.com/modules/Teacher/certeach.htm for the entire list. In September 2011, the list of certified Iyengar yoga teachers is 2453, ranging from 595 in England, 824 in the United States, and (very far down the list) 19 in India and 1 in China. Adding to the United States and England total, there are 193 from Australia, 97 from Canada, 73 from Scotland, 40 from New Zealand, 14 from Wales, 59 from South Africa, and 16 from Ireland. At least 1911 of the teachers are mostly likely native English speakers, or 78% of the total of 2453 (http://www.bksiyengar.com/modules/IYoga/noteach.htm). Thus, it is easy to conclude that Iyengar yoga is largely an Anglophone phenomenon and largely, we can assume, educated upper middle class. It would be interesting to compile much broader demographic data on Iyengar and other yoga movements. The trends may be clear, but surprises cannot be ruled out.
45. Examples of this are common in Indian religion. To mention just a few, disciples of Sathya Sai Baba (1926–2011) and Meher Baba (1894–1969) regarded their guru as God fully incarnate or as an avatar, because they made such claims for themselves; the followers of the Puṣṭimārga regard their lineage holders (descendants of Vallabhācārya, 1479–1531) as saints because Vallabhācārya was regarded as a partial incarnation (*mukhāvātara*) of Kṛṣṇa (Barz 1976). A very good account of sainthood and the role of the guru in an established lineage is Gold (1987). For reflections on contemporary gurus who have come to the United States and what it means to be a guru, see Forsthoefel and Humes (2005), even if it is necessary to point out that none of the figures highlighted in that book can be considered yoga gurus. In addition, an enormous popular devotional literature on gurus and tens of thousands of websites are easy to find, which we cannot take into account here, excepting http://www.bksiyengar.com/modules/guruji/guru.htm, the official site of Iyengar yoga.
46. "We reach a state when skin consciousness moves toward the centre of being, and the centre radiates toward the periphery" (Iyengar, 1993: 66).
47. This is a theme often addressed in Indian religion; see, for example, Smith (2005). See *Bhāgavata Purāṇa* 7.5.23 on the nine aspects of *bhakti*: (1) hearing (*śravaṇam*) the names and stories of Viṣṇu; (2) singing his praises (*kīrtanam*); (3) meditating

on him (*smaraṇam*); (4) serving his image (*pādasevanam*); (5) offering worship to him (*arcanam*); (6) prostrating to him (*vandanam*); (7) dedicating one's actions to him (*dāsyam*); (8) cultivating friendship with him (*sakhyam*); and (9) dedicating one's entire life and being to him (*ātmanivedanam*).

48. In fact, his studio has prominent images of Hanumān and Patañjali next to the entrance to the main yoga hall. Because of his Śrīvaiṣṇava background, his main shrine in his home has an image of Viṣṇu.
49. Prashant Iyengar has adopted this discourse much more openly in his classes and lectures, of which thousands of hours have now been recorded. Krishnamacharya has a very interesting discussion of ten *cakras* quite early in *Yoga Makaranda* (Krishnamacharya 2006: 10). He also discusses *nādīs* (2006: 36). All of this is a prelude to detailed descriptions of *bandhas*, *kriyās*, and 42 *āsanas*. Mr. Iyengar's *āsana* practice can clearly be seen in Krishnamacharya's poses and descriptions, shorn of the non-*āsana* material.
50. YS 1.24 reads: *kleśakarmavipākāśayair aparamṛṣṭaḥ puruviśeṣa īśvaraḥ* Iyengar translates this, "God is the Supreme Being, totally free from conflicts, unaffected by actions and untouched by cause and effect" (Iyengar, 1993: 73). He does not link Īśvara with Viṣṇu in his commentary on this *sūtra*. On the shadowy figure of Nāthamuṇi, see above note 6. Interview conducted by F. Smith, August 2011.
51. See Vāsudeva (2011) and Smith (2011) on the *vedāntic* appropriation of yoga in the second millennium CE. Mallinson (2004: xiv), perhaps the leading scholar on *haṭhayoga*, writes explicitly, "The early texts of hatha yoga showed no trace of Vedanta; their doctrinal framework was Tantric. As Hatha Yoga and its proponents, the Naths, gained in popularity and patronage, the religious orthodox, amongst whom Vedanta had become the predominant ideology, had to sit up and take notice. As they had done with other heterodox movements that threatened their hegemony (e.g., renunciation and vegetarianism) they claimed Hatha Yoga as their own."
52. Although Mr. Iyengar himself has initiated some of this, it is Prashant Iyengar who has reintroduced breathing practices into his yoga teaching, with the full acquiescence of his father. It is through Prashant's influence that *prāṇāyāma* as a part of *āsana* is trickling down into the Iyengar yoga community of teachers. Nevertheless, what Prashant teaches is rather differently constituted from the breathing practices found in the teachings of Pattabhi Jois, Desikachar, and the other disciples of Krishnamacharya. Thus, in spite of strict certification requirements largely intended for non-Indians, Iyengar Yoga is, apparently, amenable to modification. One measure of Mr. Iyengar's gradual development of *prāṇāyāma* in *āsana* practice is its near complete absence in *Light on Yoga*. Conversely, Mr. Iyengar is barely muted in his criticism of certain yoga gurus, including, pointedly, Swami Ramdev, who primarily teaches *prāṇāyāma*, and in Mr. Iyengar's view makes unsubstantiated claims for it (Idea Exchange, 2011).
53. The full moon day of the Hindu month Āṣāḍha, usually in mid-July.
54. Gellner, who specializes in Nepal, was addressing children's prepuberty rituals that featured several days of play, which were recently suspended and replaced with rituals of education, including reading, writing, Buddhist catechism, and other modern goal-oriented activity.

CHAPTER 7

The Institutionalization of the Yoga Tradition: "Gurus" B. K. S. Iyengar and Yogini Sunita in Britain

SUZANNE NEWCOMBE

The guru–*śiṣya* (guru–disciple) relationship is often considered an essential aspect of the transmission of yoga. Yet at the beginning of the twenty-first century, intense one-on-one yoga tuition from master to pupil is exceptional. There are now millions who describe themselves as practicing yoga, the majority of them in group classes (Carter, 2004). Is it possible to have transmission of an authentic yoga tradition without an immediate guru–*śiṣya* relationship? In this chapter I will argue that an important characteristic contributing to the successful popularization of Modern Postural Yoga (De Michelis, 2005: 188) as a global phenomenon has been the institutionalization of charisma away from a direct guru–*śiṣya* interaction. My argument is based on a comparison between two key figures in the spread of yoga in 1960s Britain: B. K. S. Iyengar and Yogini Sunita. Both cases are examples of how personal charisma in teaching yoga were incorporated into a highly bureaucratic, state-funded adult education system. I will argue that the way Iyengar institutionalized his charisma was a direct contributing factor to his system's worldwide popularization. In contrast, Sunita's exceptional charisma was not successfully institutionalized into a globally known system and has now been virtually forgotten. In the 1960s the British adult education system was faced with a demand for yoga teaching, but without any established means of assessing the quality or qualifications of a yoga teacher. As early as 1965,

Birmingham City Council was concerned about the proper qualifications for yoga practitioners. In an article reported in the London *Times*, the Council was said to be concerned about the "hundreds" who had enrolled for yoga in adult education venues. Apparently, there had been an attempt at "methodological investigation" of yoga, but this was found to prove "an irritating business" ("Birmingham Tries to Size Up All This Yoga," 1965). The article described how one popular Birmingham yoga teacher had Keep-Fit qualifications but had learned yoga from books, while another teacher was a woman of Indian origin who "appeared to know quite a lot" but had not "graduated from a yoga academy" (likely Yogini Sunita). The article questioned, however, "If there were yoga graduates, would they, on the whole, be quite the sort of people one really wants?" (ibid.). Both Sunita and Iyengar were able to convince the local educational authorities in Birmingham and London, respectively, that they had the necessary skills and expertise to be a safe choice for state-funded yoga. From reading contemporary reports, both Sunita and Iyengar had an exceptional ability to give an almost immediate experiential understanding of what they termed *yoga* to many with whom they interacted, although the means to obtain this aim were somewhat different for each. According to Max Weber's (1947: 328) theories, this type of authority could be termed *charismatic*. Weber characterized charismatic authority as the motivating force for change in society, an inherently unstable, potentially revolutionary force that is "foreign to everyday routine structures" (ibid.). For any lasting organization to be created from charismatic authority, Weber argued that charismatic authority must be "radically changed," and he termed this process the "routinization of charisma" (ibid., p. 364).

In this chapter I focus on the importance of the routinization of charisma for creating global Modern Postural Yoga. However, this discussion is not intended to deny that the charisma of a guru remains an important reference point for many yoga practitioners. The transformative potential of an intense teacher–student interaction remains an integral aspect of many people's experience of yoga. But by drawing attention to the process of how charisma was routinized (or not), the tension between the emphasis on yoga teaching qualifications and the transformative experience of a guru–*śiṣya* relationship can be better understood.

THE POPULARIZING CHARISMA OF YOGINI SUNITA IN BIRMINGHAM

The majority of yoga practitioners in Birmingham in the early 1960s were inspired by a woman called Yogini Sunita (1932–1970). Sunita dedicated herself to popularizing yoga between her arrival in England in 1960 and her death in 1970. As she is now an unknown figure, it is necessary to briefly outline

Figure 7.1:
Portrait from Yogini Sunita's self-published *Pranayama Yoga*, 1965. (Photo courtesy of Kenneth Cabral.)

her background. She was raised with the name Bernadette Bocarro in Bandra, a wealthy Catholic suburb of Bombay. English was spoken at home, and the family described itself as devoutly Catholic and of Brahmin caste (Robins, 1961). Rejecting an arranged marriage at the age of sixteen, Bernadette Bocarro joined a Franciscan order of nuns. She explained to a newspaper reporter in 1961 that at first she idealized religious renunciation. However, when she refused to keep writing to her mother for gifts of antique furniture for the convent (the Bocarro family ran an antique shop in Bombay) she became suddenly unpopular. The sparse food and rigorous discipline began to affect her health. Eventually, she walked out of the convent without permission, returning to her parents' home (Robins, 1961).

After leaving the convent, Bernadette described her only comfort as solitary walks by the seashore. On one of these walks Sunita claims that she encountered a yogi, apparently well-known locally, named Narainswami who was believed to have cured leprosy, tuberculosis and many other diseases; he offered to teach Bernadette yoga (Robins, 1961). Through the practice of what Narainswami called "Pranayama Yoga," Bernadette reported that confidence and peace of mind returned (Cabral, 2002a: 67; and personal interview with K. Cabral, July 17, 2007). I have not been able to trace any sign of Narainswami in the public record, and there is no outside source of confirmation for this period of Bocarro's life. But whomever taught her and whatever the method of transmission, by the time Bernadette reached England she felt confident teaching Pranayama Yoga as well as Japanese massage (ibid.). Sometime after she left the convent, the Bocarros were able to arrange a marriage for Bernadette to Roydon Cabral, another Catholic Indian of Portuguese ancestry, who worked as a printer for *The Times of India*. Bernadette accepted this marriage and had two children while in India. She took employment as a secretary for the Italian Embassy in Bombay and also claimed to have taught yoga in schools (Cabral, 2002a: 57). During the 1950s, the Cabrals began to think that the situation for Anglicized Indians was becoming precarious and felt their children would have a better education abroad; the family decided to emigrate to England.[1] In late 1959, Roydon Cabral found work as a printer in the North Birmingham area. Bernadette initially attempted to return to a career as a pianist, and casually taught yoga to a few friends. These friends encouraged others to try yoga, and Bernadette found that her knowledge of yoga was in more demand than her skill on the piano (Robins, 1961; personal interview with K. Cabral, July 17, 2007).

By mid-1961, Bernadette Cabral, a Westernized Indian, had transformed into Yogini Sunita, a sari-clad Indian yoga teacher. As Sunita, she became a living promotion for Pranayama Yoga. Her dress and manner excited curiosity from onlookers and encouraged interest. An interviewer described meeting Sunita in September 1961:

> I met Yogi Sunita at a smart West End hotel. She was wearing a flame-coloured sari, sandals and long silver earrings with her dark hair swept back in a chignon. She was young and attractive and as she took off her sandals and sat cross-legged on the floor, I wondered how she had become interested in yoga (Cabral, 1961).

Dressed characteristically in a sari, Sunita usually squatted or sat on the floor for her media interviews, which increased her intrigue. Having got her audiences' attention with her unusual appearance, Sunita impressed her listeners with a calm authority and skill in guiding them into an experience of relaxation ("Talk on Relaxing Yogi Style," 1963; "Yogi Sunita Visits Rotarians," 1967).

Especially considering that she was a newly arrived immigrant, Sunita's activities in establishing yoga in England were impressive. In August 1961, Bernadette Cabral registered a business in the name of Yogi Sunita Clinic in central Birmingham (Cabral, 1961; Business Registration Certificate 1168078). In autumn 1963, Sunita began yoga classes in the Women's Section of the Birmingham Athletics Institute (BAI), a kind of subsidized health club for Birmingham residents. These classes proved very popular, and she continued to teach classes at the BAI, some with hundreds of pupils, throughout the 1960s (BAI 1963–4). Also during 1963, Sunita "beat the panel" in the popular BBC television program "What's My Line?" in which a panel attempts to guess the profession of a guest (BBC Television Diploma, 1963).

When Sunita was interviewed for the BBC Radio in 1961, the interviewer commented, "I had always thought of yoga as mind over body, you know, the practice of physical exercises to achieve complete control of the body" (Cabral, 1961). However, the interviewer went on to explain, "Yogi Sunita teaches only relaxation of the *mind* and has made a record of the relaxing formula." While the transcript does not record Sunita's words, it is likely that she repeated her "slip second" on the radio. This is a mental exercise, which should take a minute and a half to perform, in which all those people and situations that require personal attention and involvement are brought to mind. Then one tries to let all of these attachments and worries go—just for one second. According to Sunita this practice will relax the mind and allow one to engage with all the demands of life more effectively. Sunita claimed that one slipped second was equivalent to eight hours of perfect sleep. Sunita advocated that her students practice this exercise thrice daily: upon waking; between noon and 2 p.m.; and before sleep at night (Cabral, 1961; Cabral, 2002a). She also maintained that hearing the teacher's voice was necessary for beginners to learn this method and made recordings for this purpose (Cabral, 1961; Cabral, 2002b).

An important part of her charisma for the middle-class women who attended her classes was her ability to "do it all" and stay relaxed and calm (Newcombe, 2007). Sunita worked in schools, tutoring immigrant children who spoke no English. She taught yoga and Indian dance in some of the schools of the area, in addition to the evening yoga classes at the BAI. Her oldest child, Kenneth, recalled Sunita's hectic schedule during his childhood, which he estimates would have meant she rose at 5:30 a.m. and often worked on the typewriter well past midnight (Cabral 2007). Sunita's heavy workload and apparently successful negotiation of her responsibilities as a wife and mother, combined with a presence that inspired calm and relaxation in those around her, were an important part of her charismatic authority. Her personal example was both pedagogically important and an inspiration to her students.

The *āsanas* that Sunita taught consisted of movements, which were a series of interconnected *āsanas* flowing from one posture to the next. The idea of movements might relate to musical conventions, and Sunita had a keen interest in piano and classical Indian dance, which she taught in Birmingham schools (Cabral, 2002a: 61). Sunita illustrates only two movements or sequences of postures and *prāṇāyāma* in her self-published book, although she implies that there are many more movements to Pranayama Yoga and that more exercises could be attempted with personal instruction. The first movement of Pranayama Yoga relies heavily on variations of *padmāsana,* commonly known as the lotus pose, where the legs are folded at the knee so that the foot is in the opposite groin. The relative difficulty of this position for average Western hips might also account for the limited popularity of this sequence of *āsanas*. However, Sunita did not emphasize the flexibility so evident in her surviving photographs but taught that it is the slip second and a full experience of the present moment that contains the essence of Pranayama Yoga (and yoga more generally). According to Sunita, "A moment of complete peace" is what marks the essence of yoga—but notes in capital letters that this experience "CANNOT BE TAUGHT" (Cabral, 2002a: 51).

Stemming from her resounding popularity at the BAI and other Birmingham venues, Sunita trained a group of about twenty pupils to become Pranayama Yoga teachers within the adult education course structure in 1969 (Cabral, 2002a: 58). Unfortunately, little remains of her notes from this course, and there are no class plans that could have been used for future training courses. Her son explained that she was more interested in nurturing the holistic understanding of each individual than in developing an articulated proficiency that could be measured by external assessors (personal interview with K. Cabral, July 17, 2007). Sunita did not intend that her course would provide an automatic qualification for her students to teach yoga in adult education:

> Assuming a student takes the Teachers' Course, and a Yogi is confident that some of the students will be able to teach, it may well be that the Education Authorities do not select a single one from this group to teach for them. In this case a teacher will teach privately . . . on average, one in every thousand is chosen to work for Education. (Cabral, 2002a: 57)

She expected adult education officials would choose from among Pranayama Yoga teachers those that had the characteristics necessary to transmit the tradition of Pranayama Yoga in this context. This method of integrating yoga within adult education was very dependent on the personal charisma of future teachers. Yogini Sunita's means of transmitting her knowledge ensured a continuation of the tradition of Pranayama Yoga as a tradition but not its popularity.

It is hard to know if Sunita's system of yoga might have become more influential, had she lived longer. In 1970, at the age of thirty-eight, Yogini Sunita was hit by a car and killed as she crossed a road on foot (General Register Office, 1970). Her son believes that at the time of her death, Sunita had concrete plans with television producers and contacts in the United States to further popularize her yoga teaching (personal interview with K. Cabral, July 17, 2007).[2] But best-selling books and TV contracts alone do not make for a lasting method of transmitting yoga, as the cultural forgetting of Richard Hittleman—whose series on yoga was syndicated on over forty U.S. television channels by 1970—demonstrates (Kent, 1971).

Immediately after Sunita's death, the teachers she trained were able to carry on the established classes at the BAI, which continued to be popular through the 1970s (BAI Annual Report 1970–71: 2). Sunita was influential enough to create a tradition that continues to this day—as of 2006, there were between fifty and sixty Pranayama Yoga teachers (personal interview with K. Cabral, July 17, 2007). Pranayama Yoga does continue to be taught, but it remains uninstitutionalized and, therefore, less visible than other forms of yoga. Sunita taught that Pranayama Yoga was a way of life, of doing one thing at a time, in the present moment, without anxiety. It was never her intention to make yoga teacher training fully integrated into a bureaucratic qualification. During Sunita's lifetime, she judged whether the student had embodied the yoga enough to be able to transmit the tradition to others. However, there is perhaps a sense in which a person's competency to transmit a yoga tradition is not easily judged. The ability to impart an experience of a kind of personal transformation, which Sunita's students clearly reported in their comments about her teaching (Cabral, 1965: 17), is perhaps the essence of the yoga tradition. Is it possible to package this experience of yoga away from the personal interaction with the master?

THE CHARISMATIC POPULARIZATION OF YOGA BY B. K. S. IYENGAR

In contrast to Pranayama Yoga, a yoga tradition as taught by B. K. S. (Bellur Krishnamachar Sundararaja) Iyengar (1918–) is now globally recognized. In 2004, Iyengar was one of *Time* magazine's one hundred most influential people in the world, and Iyengar Yoga entered the Oxford English Dictionary. Iyengar Yoga could be characterized by its attention to anatomical detail and precision in the placement of the body in various *āsanas*, perhaps epitomized by Iyengar's *Light on Yoga* (1966). However, Iyengar Yoga is very much a living tradition. Much of Iyengar's teaching (and that of his children) since the 1960s has focused on making the postures in *Light on Yoga* more accessible for those with limited physical ability. In Iyengar Yoga, the teacher's instructions are concentrated on positioning the body into correct alignment and on directions of actions (e.g., rotation and extension). In Iyengar Yoga, movement between postures is less standardized than in Pranayama Yoga or in Pattabhi Jois–inspired "Vinyasa" sequences (see Burger, 2006) and does not involve the verbatim scripting of a Bikram Yoga franchise (see Fish, 2007). Nevertheless, Iyengar Yoga places great attention on sequences of postures and how actions and movements link postures together. In the Iyengar Yoga tradition, attention toward and research into the physiological effects of the practice on the physical body is connected with an observation of the effects of the practice on the mind. The ultimate goal for Iyengar, the "cessation of the fluctuations of the mind" (see Patañjali's *Yogasūtras* I.2), is essentially the same as Pranayama Yoga's cultivation of a "moment of complete peace" (Cabral, 2002a: 51).

While in many ways Iyengar has created a new Modern Postural Yoga tradition (to use the typology of De Michelis 2004), Iyengar very much attributes his authority in teaching yoga to study of the *Yogasūtras* of Patañjali (see Singleton, 2008) and to the instruction of his personal guru (and brother-in-law), Tirumalai Krishnamacharya (1888–1989), who lectured in Indian philosophy (yoga, *sāṃkhya*, and *mīmāṃsā*) and taught *āsana* and *prāṇāyāma*, under the sponsorship of the Krishna Raja Wadiyar IV (1884–1940), Maharaja of Mysore (Sjoman, 1999). Iyengar's understanding of yoga was developed within a traditional guru–*śiṣya* interaction, but he was also taught in a yoga school (*yogaśālā*) inside the Jaganmohan Palace in Mysore (Singleton, 2010; Sjoman, 1999: 175–210).

B. K. S. Iyengar was born the eleventh of thirteen children to a poor Tamil-speaking Brahmin family in rural Karnataka. Iyengar's mother was affected by the worldwide influenza epidemic at the time of his birth. Iyengar believes that his mother's illness while she was pregnant weakened him physically and slowed his mental development (Iyengar, 1988: 2). Iyengar was a sickly child who was not able to concentrate on his studies. After his father died when Iyengar was nine years old, the financial and practical responsibility for the younger children was split between the elder siblings. In spring 1934, Krishnamacharya (Iyengar's brother-in-law) asked B. K. S. Iyengar, then sixteen, to go to Mysore and stay with his wife (Iyengar's sister) during Krishnamacharya's absence on a short trip (Iyengar, 1978: 113). This temporary visit extended to three years.

Krishnamacharya had a traditional authority over Iyengar as his brother-in-law and benefactor, but he also had considerable personal charisma. Krishnamacharya trained Iyengar, who was living in his home, to obey his commandments unquestioningly. On his seventieth birthday Iyengar recalled:

> My Guru is a man of unpredictable knowledge with unpredictable moods. It was not easy to read his mind. If he said one thing at one time, he used to contradict the same at other time [sic]. We were made to accept and obey him without questioning. If I sit in the ordinary cross legs with the left leg first, he would say, take the right first. If the right is placed first, he would say, take the left first. If I stand, he would say "is that the way to stand?" If I change, he would say "who asked you to change?" . . . Life became perplexing to me. Difference in age set fear in my heart and his presence was like a frightful nightmare. (Iyengar, 1978: 5)

Similar to Yogini Sunita's experience, the guru's instruction in yoga was not about religious dogma or specific beliefs but rather an approach to life. Krishnamacharya pushed Iyengar into a physical practice and a way of dealing with his ego that eventually led into the zeal of self-discipline.

Iyengar has claimed that personal instruction in *yogāsana* with Krishnamacharya was limited to three intense days, but Iyengar also practiced regularly in the *yogaśālā* with the other students (Iyengar undated: 1–2). By October 1935 Iyengar reported that he was judged to have given the best performance of all of Krishnamacharya's students in all three grades of "elementary, intermediate, and advanced courses" of *yogāsana* (Iyengar undated: 3).[3] This experience of a *yogaśālā* might have been important to the later institutionalization of Iyengar's yoga teaching. Iyengar has not written about the impact of practicing in the group environment that Krishnamacharya established in Mysore, but group teaching was certainly significant for Iyengar's *āsana* development while in Mysore and was also the type of teaching Iyengar was initially asked to provide by Krishnamacharya.

Having failed to achieve a school-leaving certificate and having learned no other trade, Iyengar felt he had no alternative but to teach yoga for a living (Iyengar undated: 3). At first Iyengar attempted to work in other parts of Mysore. However, he did not receive any viable employment. In September 1937, Iyengar accepted a request that was sent to Krishnamacharya to train college students in Pune for a six-month period (ibid., p. 4). Although he found it difficult to earn a living in Pune after his initial contract had expired, Iyengar decided to stay on in the city: "The freedom had come to me by chance which I did not like to lose at any cost. If I go back, I have to join my Guruji only. That means to live in the web of constant fear" (Iyengar, 1988: 16).[4] After he left Mysore, Iyengar primarily taught himself by a close observation of his own *āsana* practice (ibid.). Slowly he built up a successful clientele in Pune, partially by addressing individuals with medical conditions for which local biomedical doctors felt they could offer only limited help (ibid., p. 17).

Iyengar's yoga teaching expanded internationally through the personal influence of violin virtuoso Yehudi Menuhin (1916–1999). In 1952, Menuhin gave a tour in the newly independent India, and one of Iyengar's students was a member of the official welcoming party. B. K. S. Iyengar was asked to give a demonstration to the famous violinist, which turned into a regular teaching arrangement. Menuhin brought Iyengar to Europe in 1954 and the United States in 1956 (where Iyengar did not again teach until 1973) (Magidoff, 1973: 256–7). Every year between 1960 and 1974, Iyengar spent at least a month in London at Menuhin's expense, first to give the violinist private lessons in his home and second to popularize yoga more widely (Menuhin, 1996: 259). What began as a traditional guru–*śiṣya* arrangement between Menuhin and Iyengar eventually became the catalyst for transforming the transmission of a yoga tradition.

Iyengar gave public yoga demonstrations and received good press coverage on his visits to London in the early 1960s. For the first few years, Iyengar only had a dozen or so regular students, most connected personally to Menuhin ("Working for Health", 1961; *Daily Mail,* 1961; Marris, 2005).

Figure 7.2:
Throughout the 1970s Iyengar taught teachers in intensive, relatively small classes in London. This photograph was taken in the early 1980s at the Iyengar Yoga Institute in Maida Vale, London.

The small size of these early classes created an intense personal interaction between the keen yoga students and Iyengar, similar to the traditional guru–*śiṣya* transmission of the yoga tradition. Individual feedback was very important for many of Iyengar's early students, and they could ask Iyengar directly for advice about how to deal with particular problems. Diana Clifton, along with several of these first students, corresponded with Iyengar regularly during the '60s and '70s and exchanged news of their families as well as receiving Iyengar's advice on yoga. For example, Clifton sent a series of photographs of herself practicing *āsanas* to Iyengar for comment, and in reply he wrote: "I went through all the pictures and remarked in the back. In the whole you have made a good progress. For your husband standing postures and twistings are good. . . . Hope members of the yoga class are fine" (Iyengar, 1962).

In 1962, one of Iyengar's London students provided Gerald Yorke, a publishing agent, with Iyengar's manuscript for a comprehensive instructional guide to *yogāsana*. Over the next few years, Yorke made extensive suggestions for revisions to this work, and in 1966 it was eventually published by Allen & Unwin as *Light on Yoga*. It quickly came to be referred to as the bible of *yogāsana* (Iyengar, 1993: xx–xxi; Tuft, 1971). The publication of *Light on Yoga* and the media association between Menuhin and Iyengar were important in raising the visibility of Iyengar yoga in Britain (see, e.g., "Yehudi Menuhin & His Guru", 1963).

The publication of *Light on Yoga* was also a significant influence for the acceptance of Iyengar's teaching into the Inner London Educational Authority (ILEA). The ILEA coordinated all publicly funded education classes in Inner London on subjects that ranged from sewing to car mechanics, foreign languages, and swimming. Across the country Local Educational Authorities (LEAs) promoted these classes to reeducate the population in the period between the close of World War II and Margaret Thatcher's cuts to public services in the 1980s. The transformation of Iyengar's teaching required by the educational authorities created something new in the tradition of Modern Postural Yoga.

In contrast to Birmingham (which introduced Yogini Sunita's classes to the public in 1963), an experimental yoga class was not approved in the ILEA until 1967.[5] By this time, the ILEA could be seen as jumping on an established cultural bandwagon of interest in Indian spirituality.[6] At this time, the chief inspector for physical education at the ILEA was a man called Peter McIntosh. McIntosh was something of a physical culture visionary—he was involved in forming the U.K. Sports Council and the International Council of Sport, Science and Physical Education (Huggins, 2001). He was an enthusiastic advocate of sport for "its own sake" and firmly championed the importance of physical culture, linking it with classical Greek ideals (McIntosh, 1968: 114). It was McIntosh who took a personal interest in introducing this new subject of yoga to the physical education curriculum for London.

While the experimental class in London was a success, the committee in charge of physical education at the ILEA wanted yoga classes to be safely and respectably institutionalized. While excited about the potential of yoga, particularly for the elderly and those with limited physical ability, the ILEA officials wanted to identify a suitably qualified teacher:

> Owing to the growing demand for classes there is a tendency for well-meaning enthusiasts—some perhaps not so well-meaning—to push themselves forward as teachers. Inspectors of physical education do not have the experience in this particular subject necessary to ensure good standards of teaching and work. (ILEA, 1969, Report No. 11)

The committee considered establishing yoga associations, and McIntosh visited "a number of [yoga] classes" but apparently did not find what he was looking for in what was going on elsewhere in the country (ILEA, 1969, Report 25.1.69). Apparently fortuitously, McIntosh happened to speak with Yehudi Menuhin's sister, Hephzibah Hauser, who felt that she had benefited from Iyengar's teaching (Marris, 2005). McIntosh then spent a period investigating and discussing yoga as a subject with Iyengar. McIntosh reported that he discussed with Iyengar "the difficulties in the way of ensuring that those who offer themselves as teachers at Hatha Yoga are competent and reliable" (ILEA,

1969, Report No. 11). The ILEA officials were impressed by *Light on Yoga* describing it as "probably the most reliable English text on the subject [of Hatha Yoga]" (ibid.). In Iyengar, McIntosh found a quality of instruction in yoga in which he felt confident. In late 1969, ILEA agreed to approve "gurus trained by Mr. B. K. S. Iyengar, the author of 'Light on Yoga,' a recognized authoritative book on this subject" as qualified to teach yoga on public funds throughout inner London. In doing this, Iyengar-trained teachers received a bureaucratic authority in addition to an implicit requrement of having charismatic authority required to inspire trust and interest in potential yoga students (ILEA, 1969, Report No. 11). It is interesting that the ILEA report called the Iyengar-approved teachers "gurus"; I have found no other evidence of guru being used in the Iyengar movement except with reference to Iyengar himself as Guruji.

The agenda of ILEA shaped how Iyengar was teaching yoga in two main ways: (1) Iyengar was explicitly asked to teach physical aspects of yoga and avoid discussion of religion or spirituality[7]; and (2) there was an emphasis on safety and avoiding physical injury in the students. The ILEA agreement with Iyengar specified that yoga was to be taught only "provided that instruction is confined to 'asanas' and 'pranayamas' (postures and breathing disciplines) and does not extend to the philosophy of Yoga as a whole" (ILEA, 1969, 25.11.69). Regarding the safety of yoga classes, the ILEA medical advisor assessed Iyengar's teaching and recommended that those with "five types of disorder" (unnamed in the report) should be excluded from general yoga classes to avoid possible harm (ILEA, 1969, Report No. 11). The yoga classes in ILEA were expected to benefit healthy participants' levels of fitness and flexibility; any further benefits were not to be promoted.

These two stipulations of yoga teaching under ILEA clearly continue to resonate with what is expected of yoga teacher training programs in the twenty-first century. Emphasis is placed in most teacher training programs on how to keep students safe from injury. Although many yoga teacher training programs now include yoga philosophy, this is often explored in a non-confessional context that was only beginning to become established in the 1970s. The situation in ILEA reflects an attempt to control the more spiritual, ineffable, and unpredictable aspects of the yoga tradition within something that was safe and beneficial within the context of adult, physical education. It was a utilitarian compromise that angered other yoga groups in Britain. This was particularly true of the British Wheel of Yoga, a national association of yoga teachers, who argued at this time that yoga was more properly a philosophy than a physical discipline, and that classes in adult education should consist equally of postures, *prāṇāyāma*, meditation, and philosophy (Newcombe, 2008: 62–79).[8]

The ILEA format was a curious meld between bureaucracy and charismatic authority. The "gurus approved by Iyengar" to teach in ILEA were subject to the "prior approval of the Senior Inspector of Physical Education" (then Peter McIntosh) and therefore nominally subject to a "quality control" at ILEA's discretion. Iyengar himself lived in Pune and came to London only once a year. In practice, from 1971 to 1979, both teachers and would-be yoga teachers for ILEA attended a weekly class run by Silva Mehta (1926–1994) at the Physical Education College in Paddington. Iyengar would approve future yoga teachers by watching participants in the class on his annual visits (Finesilver, 1999; personal interview with John and Ros Claxton, December 5, 2004). For the first few years there were no standardized syllabi of postures or contraindications for specific medical conditions. However, within a few years Iyengar developed three grades of progressively more difficult *āsanas* for the ILEA classes. By 1979 approximately two hundred yoga teachers had been trained on this course (Mehta, 1983).

Participants remember Iyengar's annual visits as resulting in a "tough" and "highly charged" experience (personal interview with John and Ros Claxton, December 5, 2004). Iyengar attempted to give his students control over both their minds and bodies by demanding precision in *āsanas* ("The Sutras of Iyengar" c.1970s: 11). Much of Iyengar's instruction was focused on details of how to work in the basic postures (Herremans, 1974–5). In response to criticisms that he only taught physical postures, Iyengar described his approach as a pragmatic expedient: "Better life can be taught without using religious words. Meditation is of two types, active and passive. I took the active side of meditation by making students totally absorbed in the poses" (Dale undated). Iyengar attempted to give his students control over both their minds and bodies by demanding precision in *āsana*.

Some of the students experienced that elusive moment of peace, as one student articulated:

> He never warned us or prepared us for special experiences. He simply led us, all unawares, into an altered state of consciousness and then called our attention to it when we were already there . . . my mind had been like a deep pool, unruffled by random thoughts and fancies. If I had the slightest expectation that he was going to lead us into that sort of experience, I would have been so greedy for it that I would have missed it altogether. (Herremans, 1974–5).

At least some of Iyengar's English students reported experiencing personal transformations, which they attributed to Iyengar's charisma and skill in yoga. Although the ILEA extracted some compromises for the teaching of yoga in London, the teacher training system for Iyengar Yoga in the ILEA was similar to the system that Sunita developed, in that it was primarily reliant on Iyengar's personal charisma in deciding who embodied the yoga tradition enough to teach it.

THE INSTITUTIONALIZATION OF IYENGAR YOGA

Iyengar's tradition of yoga became fully institutionalized only when it developed a form of transmission that was not dependent on Iyengar's charismatic authority. It was in Manchester during the 1970s that a system developed aimed at isolating a syllabus and principles for qualifying teachers. Part of the catalyst for this change was logistical; Iyengar's annual visits were based in London. Iyengar first came to Manchester in 1968 at the invitation of two women who were already teaching yoga in the LEA evening classes (Maslen, 1992).[9] Iyengar's demonstration popularized yoga, and to meet the demand for more yoga teachers in the LEA structure the Manchester and District Iyengar Yoga Institute was established and a course for training yoga teachers was designed ("East Manchester Area of Further Education: Yoga Demonstration", 1968; "Indian Yoga Expert at Spurley Hey", 1968; Maslen, 1992). This institute had no official premises but used the LEA premises (often school buildings) for evening classes and teachers did administration from home.

The Manchester-based teacher training program started in 1971–72. It was open to those who had taken yoga classes under a recognized teacher for at least two years. The course lasted thirty-four weeks at four hours per week, with an emphasis on physiology and anatomy to "safeguard against physical injury which can be incurred if the complicated posture exercises are taught by a person uninstructed in this direction" (MDIIY, 1972: 6). The successful passing of both a written exam and practical teaching assessment assessed by both yoga instructors and "educational experts" would result in a diploma "recognised by the Manchester Education Committee" (ibid.). While Iyengar did not personally select teachers (as he did in London), he was consulted on the syllabus, which facilitated the growth of a bureaucratic means of transmitting Iyengar's understanding of yoga. Due to the physical distance between Iyengar and his English students, a system of assessing standards of teaching *yogāsana* developed that was not personality dependent. This development was crucial to the global popularization of yoga in the Iyengar tradition and has influenced the shape of other traditions of yoga teaching.

As the 1970s progressed, Iyengar teachers in England began to work together to create a national assessment body that issued certificates. In 1975 it was reported to Iyengar that two people in Oxford had been "taken to hospital from yoga classes" reported to be taught by another yoga association's teachers (Iyengar, 1975). As a result of this, it was requested that a pupil of Iyengar conduct three teacher training classes at the Oxford College of Further Education. In response to this request Iyengar chose one of his first English students, Diana Clifton. In consultation with Iyengar, Clifton designed a set of syllabuses with "an emphasis on safety" and sent it to Iyengar for approval. The course in Oxford involved observing a yoga class for beginners. Later the teachers would be taught "to assist so as to get an understanding of how to teach beginners" (ibid.). This teaching method—to observe and correct incorrect physical action in *asana*—quickly became the focus for the Iyengar teaching method in Britain.

From 1978, formal assessments of all Iyengar-trained teachers in Britain were standardized on a national level by the formation of a professional organization, the B. K. S. Iyengar Teachers' Association. At the end of a training period, potential Iyengar Yoga teachers were assessed by a panel of qualified teachers whom they did not know personally. Emphasis on safety and avoiding harm rather than on the personal transformation of the pupil became the overall standard for teaching beginners. A focus on physical actions also made it easier to reduce the teaching of yoga into a syllabus. In June 1978, ILEA was informed that Iyengar was now issuing certificates to teachers qualified in his system at three levels: elementary, intermediate, and advanced (BKSITA, 1978: 1). Elementary and intermediate levels were assessed in Britain, while advanced certificates were issued by Iyengar personally in India (Assessments for Teaching Certificates, 1979–1980, no page numbers). This decentralized authority away from Iyengar but maintained a place for his charismatic oversight at the top of a pyramid of teaching.

Since the late 1970s in Britain, and increasingly throughout the world, a generation of teachers is being guided in how to teach Iyengar Yoga without any personal contact with Iyengar. The facilitation of these international networks of Iyengar's students was made possible by the model of distance teaching developed by Iyengar in the 1970s for his English students who were working within the already established structure of state-funded adult education classes. Iyengar began regular trips to Southern Africa from 1968, and there has been a formally organized association for the region since the late 1970s.[10] Iyengar made his second visit to the United States in 1973; the BKS Iyengar Yoga National Association of the United States (IYNAUS) began assessing teacher training candidates in 1985. In the 1990s, Iyengar Associations and teacher training organizations were founded in Canada, throughout Western Europe, Israel, and New Zealand, while even more recently institutionalized Iyengar yoga has spread to Eastern Europe, South America, and East Asia.[11]

At the head of this bureaucratic pyramid, there is still a charismatic element in the transmission of Iyengar Yoga. In 1976, Iyengar's international students funded the opening of a yoga center in Pune, and this became the center of the global Iyengar network. Senior students worldwide began traveling to Pune for a month or more of intensive daily lessons with Iyengar, his daughter Geeta, and his son Prashant. This ensured that students continue to have a personal relationship with Iyengar as a teacher and that teaching is controlled and standardized at one source. Those who train Iyengar Yoga teachers locally are also expected to have been taught yoga at the Iyengar

Institute in Pune. As of 2012, Geeta, Prashant, and Iyengar's granddaughter Abi all teach classes at the Institute in Pune, while Iyengar supervises from a distance. As Iyengar ages, the charismatic authority has been transferring to a dynastic linage of sorts in Pune. Presently, it appears that Iyengar has developed a successful method of institutionalizing his yoga tradition and ensuring the continuation of his influence.

Iyengar's work in England provides an example of a particular kind of routinization of charisma. Rather than independently establishing a bureaucratic system of transmission, Iyengar melded his charismatic yoga teaching with the already established institution of adult education. The resulting method of transmission involved standard syllabi and teacher training courses that were successfully exported globally. The further transmission of this method of teaching (i.e., the subject of Iyengar yoga) has become something independent of the dynastic linage. However, it remains to be seen how the compromise between bureaucratic and charismatic authority in the Iyengar tradition will transform in the twenty-first century after Iyengar's death.

CONCLUSION

Sunita and Iyengar show two different trajectories for charismatic authority and the continuation of a yoga tradition. While Yogini Sunita was highly popular during her lifetime, her approach was personal, and she never developed—or intended to develop—a bureaucratic framework for transferring her knowledge that was not ultimately dependent on a guru's intuition. Despite training a group of Pranayama Yoga teachers, Sunita never separated the knowledge contained within her tradition of yoga from the guru–*śiṣya* model. Her tradition has continued, but with teachers of Pranayama Yoga currently numbering between fifty and sixty Sunita's tradition has faded as a social movement (personal interview with K. Cabral, July 17, 2007).

In contrast, Iyengar's teaching has been institutionalized to the extent that his understanding of *āsana* can be (largely) transmitted in his personal absence. This transformation occurred in the process of adapting his teaching to the needs of the state-funded adult education system in Britain. This environment created teacher training syllabuses that could produce Iyengar quality-controlled teachers in the absence of Iyengar's physical presence. In the stages of getting yoga approved in the ILEA and Manchester areas, Iyengar effectively routinized his charisma so that a recognizable teaching of yoga could continue in his absence. This system has spread Iyengar Yoga worldwide, and this form of teaching now influences *āsana* in most other forms of Modern Postural Yoga worldwide (De Michelis, 2005: 187).

The contemporary experience of yoga is not defined primarily by a relationship with a charismatic personality. While this development has made yoga more accessible, it has also made yoga teachers' effects more safe and predictable. Of course, they can still exert considerable charisma within the institutionalized structures of international coordinating associations. However, the very structures that promote greater popularization, reliability, and safety in yoga teaching (e.g., ethical standards and professional accountability practices) also sanitize the guru–*śiṣya* relationship.

Iyengar and Yogini Sunita's personal biographies emphasize the transformative relationship with a guru. Iyengar's transformation from sickly child to determined *āsana* practitioner would not have been possible within an adult education class. Likewise, one wonders if Bernadette Cabral would have been so profoundly affected by her guru's teachings had she herself learned yoga at the Birmingham Athletics Institute. The institutionalization of yoga might promote the greater good in terms of safety and the benefits of health and relaxation commonly ascribed to contemporary yoga practice, and the lack of explicit religiosity offends neither contemporary humanistic ideology nor the ideal of a human right to individual religious freedom while learning a skill. However, global participation came at the cost of losing the more extreme elements in the dynamic, unpredictable, transformative, and possibly abusive guru–*śiṣya* relationship. In this, the institutionalization of charisma marks a significant new chapter in the thousands of years of yoga history. As the Birmingham city officials lamented in 1965, it is an irritating business to find a qualified yoga teacher. Even early in the twenty-first century when there are a plethora of organizations offering accreditation and ethical frameworks for qualified yoga teachers, it can remain a struggle for a student to find a yoga teacher that is both safe and is able to offer profound physical, psychological, and spiritual transformation. As Sunita's legacy demonstrates, is unlikely that Modern Yoga could have become a global phenomenon on the strength of interpersonal, charismatic interactions alone. A tension between keeping a tradition viable through institutionalization and maintaining the possibility of a transformational experience through contact with an inspirational teacher has been a theme in the global expansion of Modern Yoga—and this tension shows no signs of reaching a resolution in the foreseeable future.

REFERENCES

Assessments for Teaching Certificates November 1979 and March 1980. 1979–1980. In the Archives of the Iyengar Yoga Institute, Maida Vale, London.

BBC Television diploma certifying that on the night of Sunday 10 March 1963, Mrs Sunita Cabral "Beat the Panel" in "What's my Line?" at the BBC Television Theatre, London W12. 1963. Certificate in the possession of The Lotus and The Rose Publishers, Beehive Cottage, Nafford Road, Eckington, Worcs WR10 3DH.

Birmingham Tries to Size Up All This Yoga: Should Prana Force Teaching Come out of Rates? 1965. *The Times* (London), February 23, p. 7, col. c.

Birmingham Athletics Institute (BAI). 1964. *Annual Report 1963–4*. Birmingham Athletics Institute (BAI) Women's Section, Annual Reports 1951–1975, MS 1468/3/1. Birmingham Central Library, Chamberlain Square, Birmingham B3 3HQ.

———. 1971. *Annual Report 1970–71*. Birmingham Athletics Institute (BAI) Women's Section, Annual Reports 1951–1975, MS 1468/3/1. Birmingham Central Library, Chamberlain Square, Birmingham B3 3HQ.

B. K. S. Iyengar Teacher's Association Newsletter (BKSITA). 1978. June.

Burger, Maya. 2006. What Price Salvation? The Exchange of Salvation Goods between East and West. *Social Compass* 57(4), pp. 81–95.

Business Registration Certificate No. 1168078. 1961. Certificate in the possession of The Lotus and The Rose Publishers, Beehive Cottage, Nafford Road, Eckington, Worcs WR10 3DH.

Butler, M. 1992. Helpful Advice on How to Get through the "Bad Patches." *Yoga & Health*, March 30.

Cabral, Sunita. 1961. Unbilled Extra on Woman's Hour. Interview No. 26. Broadcast, September 27, 14.00–15.00. Interviewed by Christopher Young Venning, British Broadcasting Corporation Written Archives Centre (BBC WAC), Reading, United Kingdom.

———. 1965. *Pranayama Yoga: The Art of Relaxation*. Self-Published. In the possession of Kenneth Cabral.

———. 2002a [1972]. *Pranayama Yoga: The Art of Relaxation*, 3rd ed. Worcester: Lotus and the Rose Publishers.

———. 2002b. *The Art of Relaxation*. Audiocassette. Eckington, Worcester: Lotus and the Rose Publishers.

Carter, M. 2004. New Poses for Macho Men. *Times* (London), May 22.

Daily Mail, 1961. Newspaper clipping in the archives of the Iyengar Yoga Institute, Maida Vale, June 16.

Dale, Julie. undated B. K. S. Iyengar: An introduction by one of his students. Manuscript in the library of the Ramamani Iyengar Memorial Yoga Institute in Pune, India.

De Michelis, Elizabeth. 2005. *A History of Modern Yoga*. London: Continuum.

East Manchester Area of Further Education: Yoga Demonstration. 1968. Advertisement. *Manchester Evening News*, June 27.

Finesilver, Sally. 1999. Letter to Lorna Walker dated 26 November in response to a request for memories of "Iyengar's early days in the UK." Held in the archives of the Iyengar Yoga Institute, Madia Vale, London.

Fish, Allison. 2007. The Commodification and Exchange of Knowledge in the Case of Transnational Commercial Yoga. *International Journal of Cultural Property* 13(2), pp. 189–206.

General Register Office. 1970. Certificate of Death for Bernadette Cabral OBDX 771214, County Borough of Walsall, April 17, Entry No. 193.

Herremans. 1974–5. Notes Taken at Classes Held by Mr. Iyengar in London in May 1974 and in Poona in January 1975. Archives of the Iyengar Yoga Institute, Maida Vale.

Huggins, M. 2001. Walking in the Footsteps of a Pioneer: Peter McIntosh—Trail-Blazer in the History of Sport. *International Journal of the History of Sport* 18(2), pp. 136–147.

Indian Yoga Expert at Spurley Hey. 1968. *Gorton and Openshaw Reporter* (Manchester) July 12, 1.

Inner London Educational Authority (ILEA). 1969. Further and Higher Education Sub-Committee Papers Oct-Dec 1969, ILEA/CL/PRE/16/24, London Metropolitan Archive.

Iyengar, B. K. S. Undated. Typewritten autobiographical manuscript. (Account from birth to 1954, but written after 1958.)

———. 1962. Letter to Diana Clifton. February 13. In the archives of the Iyengar Yoga Institute, Maida Vale, London.

———. 1975. Letter to Diana Clifton. October 19. In the Archives of the Iyengar Yoga Institute, Maida Vale, London.

———. 1978. *Body the Shrine, Yoga thy Light*. Bombay: B.I. Taraporewala.

———. 1988. My Yogic Journey: A Talk Given by Guruji on His 70th Birthday, December 14, at Tilak Smarak Mandir, Pune, 5. Archives of the Iyengar Yoga Institute, Maida Vale, London.

———. 1993. *Light on the Yoga Sutras of Patañjali*. London: Aquarius Books.

Iyengar Yoga News. 2007. No. 10 (Spring).

Jackson, Ian. 1978. "Running" in Body the Shrine, Yoga Thy Light BKS Iyengar 60th Birthday Celebration Committee eds. Bombay: B.I. Taraporewala, pp. 136–46.

Kent, Howard. 1971. Yoga for Health—A Breakthrough Television Programme. *Yoga & Health*, Vol. 1.17.

Magidoff, Robert. 1973 [1955]. *Yehudi Menuhin: The Story of the Man and the Musician*. London: Robert Hale & Company.

The Manchester and District Institute of Iyengar Yoga (MDIIY). 1972. No. 1 March.

Marris, Angela. 2005. Personal Interview. June 30.

Maslen, Jeanne. 1992. The Early Years. *Manchester and District Institute of Iyengar Yoga 25th Anniversary Magazine*.

McIntosh, Peter. 1968. *Sport in Society*. London: C.A. Watts & Co. Ltd.

Mehta, Shyam. 1983. "A Brief History of Iyengar Yoga in England and The South East England Iyengar Yoga Institute," March 19. Archives of the Iyengar Yoga Institute, Maida Vale, London.

Newcombe, Suzanne. 2007. Stretching for Health and Well-Being: Yoga and Women in Britain, 1960–1980. *Asian Medicine* 3(1), pp. 37–63.

———. 2008. *A Social History of Yoga and Ayurveda in Britain*, PhD Dissertation, Faculty of History, University of Cambridge.

Robins, J. 1961. East or West—There Are Some Things Every Woman Wants—Youth and Happiness—Here's a Wife with the Secret of Both. Newspaper clipping, *Sunday Mercury*, March 12.

Singleton, Mark. 2010. *Yoga Body: The Origins of Modern Posture Practice*. Oxford: Oxford University Press.

———. 2008. The Classical Reveries of Modern Yoga: Patanjali and Constructive Orientalism. In Mark Singleton and Jean Byrne (eds.), *Yoga in the Modern World: Contemporary Perspectives*. London: Routledge, pp. 77–99.

Sjoman, Norman E. 1999. *The Yoga Tradition of the Mysore Palace*, 2d ed. New Delhi: Shakti Malik.

The Sutras of Iyengar. c. 1970s. Anonymous typewritten manuscript in the archives of the Iyengar Yoga Institute, Maida Vale, London.

Talk on Relaxing in Yogi Style. 1963. *Derby Evening Telegraph*, April 19.

Tuft, N. 1971. Standing on Her Head to Face the Day. *Daily Telegraph*, December 31.

Unbilled Extra on Woman's Hour. 1961. No. 26, September 27, 14.00–15.00 Yogi Sunita interviewed by Christopher Young Venning, British Broadcasting Corporation Written Archives Centre (BBC WAC).

Weber, Max. 1947. *The Theory of Social and Economic Organization*, trans. A. M. Henderson and Talcott Parsons, ed. Talcott Parsons. London: Macmillan.

Working for Health. 1961. *Hampstead and Highgate Express and Hampstead Garden Suburb and Golders Green News*, July 7, p. 4.

Yehudi Menuhin and His Guru. 1963. Transmitted August 21, 10.25–10.55 p.m., T32/1,870/1 BBC WAC.

Yogi Sunita Visits Rotarians. 1967. *Sutton Coldfield News*, January 12.

NOTES

1. Conventional wisdom has held that the US Immigration Act of 1924 (which limited immigration to 2% of the number of immigrants already present from a given nation—seriously limiting immigration from Asian countries) prevented the global spread of yoga before the 1960s. However, there were no restrictions on Indian residents as members of the Commonwealth who entered Britain as full citizens before 1962—after which date immigration restrictions began to be enforced. Therefore, more factors need to be considered in the question of why yoga did not become more popular a practice outside of India prior to the 1960s.
2. The BBC lunchtime program Pebble Mill at One produced a regular yoga feature with teachers who had studied with Yogini Sunita during the 1970s.
3. These might be earlier versions of the sequences that have become Ashtanga Vinyasa Yoga as taught by another of Krishnamacharya's students, Pattabhi Jois.
4. These challenges were not insignificant. In addition to having little money, Iyengar (a Tamil) spoke neither of the local languages (Hindi and Marathi), and his English had not been good enough to achieve his school-leaving certificate.
5. Alan Babington gave the first "experimental" yoga class in Inner London Adult Education at the Clapham Institute. He later moved to the independent Mary Ward Centre in Bloomsbury where he developed Albion Yoga.
6. Perhaps most significantly, the Beatles' well-publicized association with the Maharishi Mahesh Yogi from August 1967 to summer 1968 raised the profile of meditation and yoga for many who had previously never considered the subject.
7. It is likely that Iyengar's teaching could have included more explicit references to Indian religiosity had ILEA not requested this approach. For example in 1961 descriptions of public yoga demonstrations by Iyengar ("Working for Health", 1961; *Daily Mail*, 1961) make it seem that Iyengar was referencing scripture at this time.
8. Another important British "guru" of modern yoga in this context was Wilfred Clark who, through the British Wheel of Yoga, worked tirelessly to have yoga considered as philosophy (or at least not solely as physical education) in the British adult education system.
9. One of the women, Pennrell Reed, had learned yoga in Birmingham (probably from Sunita Cabral) and the other (Jeanne Maslen) transferred from teaching Keep Fit to teaching yoga after seeing Ms. Reed demonstrate yoga at the end of a Keep Fit class in the mid-1960s.

10. For a short basic history of countries and dates see http://www.bksiyengar.co.za/html/history.html (accessed April 29, 2012). Australia began institutionalizing Iyengar Yoga in the 1980s.
11. Iyengar Yoga Association of South East & East Asia (IYASEEA) established in 2009; in 2012, if living in Southeast Asia, one could train as an accredited Iyengar Yoga teacher in Bali, Hong Kong, Indonesia, Singapore, and Macau. Available at http://iyengaryoga.asia/index.php?option=com_content&task=view&id=35 (accessed April 29, 2012).

PART THREE

Tantra-Based Gurus

CHAPTER 8

Swami Kṛpālvānanda: The Man behind Kripalu Yoga

ELLEN GOLDBERG

INTRODUCTION

In 1977, Swami Kṛpālvānanda (1913–1981; also known as Kripalu or Bapuji) moved from western India to live in silence (*mauna*) and continue his life of *prāṇayoga sādhanā* in a small house (*kuṭīr*) on the property of the Kripalu Yoga ashram located in the rural area of Sumneytown, Pennsylvania. He inspired a transnational community of devotees when his lay disciple Amrit Desai (b. 1935; see Goldberg, 2013) brought him into international prominence not only by naming his center and his style of yoga in his honor but also by adopting and adapting Kripalu's life and teachings as the basis of his Kripalu approach. Yet in spite of the global popularity of the Kripalu name and the fact that he galvanized the growth of the Kripalu yoga ashram—today one of the most successful yoga centers in North America with 2011 revenues estimated at $30.6 million dollars—the life of Swami Kṛpālvānanda (hereafter referred to as Kripalu) is little known and has yet to receive scholarly attention.[1]

In this paper I provide a portrait of Kripalu's life as relayed by his principle disciples: Swami Rajarshi Muni (1931–) in a short hagiography (1974) and a longer version (2002); Swami Vinit Muni (1938–1996) through conversations in India and in Canada between 1989 and 1996; and Amrit Desai during interviews conducted in 2010 at his ashram and home in Salt Springs, Florida,[2] and supplemented by Kripalu's profoundly autobiographical commentary of the fifteenth-century *Haṭhayogaprādīpikā* (*HYP*) of Svātmārāma called *Rahasyabodhinī* (Secret Treatise, 1974). What becomes clear is that Kripalu's transmission of yoga is based essentially on an encoded performative

Figure 8.1:
Kripalu. (Courtesy of Muni Mandal Ashram Trust, India.)

reenactment of his own personal journey to reach *nirbīja samādhi* (pure consciousness). He focuses on three core elements not typically seen in other modern approaches, namely, *prāṇotthāna* (the partial awakening of *prāṇa* or life force) through *śaktipāt dīkṣā* (initiation through the awakening of *śakti*), *prāṇayoga sādhanā* (also referred to as *sahajayoga* and *siddhayoga*), and the attainment of immortality or divine body (*divya deha, siddha deha*). The importance of these core elements is reinforced repeatedly in Kripalu's commentaries on particular Hindu scriptures including the *Bhagavad Gītā*, the Upaniṣads, and various *haṭhayoga* root (*mūla*) texts.[3] Here we observe what Benjamin Richard Smith (2008) and Mark Singleton (2008) refer to as the *circular construction of authority*. Within the Kripalu lineage, this implies that yoga experiences are considered authentic insofar as they accord with Kripalu's life as outlined in his biography, hagiography, and autobiography. The various narratives and commentaries set forth by Kripalu are held to be definitive and, as such, set the standard by which yoga experience is measured particularly within the monastic community (*saṃnyāsins*).

I argue, too, that the goal of Kripalu yoga *sādhanā* for himself and his principle disciples is primarily mystical—not in the sense that De Michelis (2004) employs the term but rather as it pertains to the attainment of the final limb (*aṅga*) of yoga *sādhanā* (spiritual practice) called *nirbīja samādhi*. In this sense Kripalu's approach offers an interesting counterpoint to the schools of Modern Postural Yoga that emerge, for example, from the teachings of the Krishnamacarya lineage (e.g., B. K. S. Iyengar, K. Pattabhi Jois, T. K. V. Desikachar) as identified by De Michelis (2004) and Singleton (2010). When performed voluntarily, the practice of postures or *āsanas*—what Kripalu refers to as *cit-sādhanā*—is considered a necessary though preliminary stage of yoga required primarily for the purification (*śodhana*) of the body-mind and for arousing *prāṇa*. Kripalu applies this strategy to advance a simplified methodology specifically for householders and nonmonastics (*pravṛtti-mārga sādhaks*)[4] that syncretizes *āsanas* and *prāṇāyāma* with elements from the *bhakti* tradition (e.g., repetition of mantra; practice of guru-*sevā*, or service to the guru), the vernacular tradition in Gujarat (e.g., chanting *bhajans* or devotional songs), *dharma* and ethics (e.g., the practice of *yama* and *niyama*), and modern science (e.g., psychology and anatomy). What emerges is a living and fully engaged alternative yoga lifestyle that exemplifies what Paul Heelas (2008) recently referred to as *inner-life spiritualities*. For Kripalu this implies practicing a gradual path of postural yoga framed by an ascetic paradigm that has been modified and modernized exclusively for nonmonastics, including his closest lay disciple Amrit Desai, and it embraces what Gregory P. Fields (2001) calls *religious therapeutics*, meaning basic spiritual "principles and practices that support human well-being" (p. 1).

For monks and nuns (*nivṛtti* or *prāṇa-mārga sādhaks*), Kripalu insists on a performative reenactment of *haṭhayoga sādhanā* as outlined in his commentaries on medieval Nāth yoga root texts, specifically the *HYP*. What becomes evident, as we will see further on, is that for adept practitioners the tantric elements of the *haṭhayoga* tradition, including the full awakening of *kuṇḍalinī* and advanced practices such as *khecarī mudrā*, replace *āsanas* as the core practices leading to *nirbīja samādhi*. The adept thus follows a step-by-step reenactment of Kripalu's own history of *prāṇayoga sādhanā* as a way to cultivate the tantric goal of an immutable and immortal body.

Within the Kripalu lineage, the internal logic of a two-stage approach that requires monks and nuns to follow a much closer reading of medieval *haṭhayoga* treatises than householders seems neither arbitrary nor idiosyncratic. Nor is it surprising that the exoteric (public and communally practiced) postural limbs (*aṅga*) rather than the more esoteric (subjective, privately practiced, and therefore secretive) mystical limbs of Kripalu's teachings on yoga are most widespread particularly among the majority of his nonmonastic disciples. We see that in more advanced stages, Kripalu's approach to yoga is deeply tied to the logic of renunciation (*saṃnyāsa, vairagya*) and taking a vow of celibacy (*brahmacarya*) is mandatory. Whether this makes it more authentic is a question that modern scholars (see, e.g., Alter 1997) and practitioners of yoga and tantra could debate, but for Kripalu the answer is perfectly clear.

A BRIEF SKETCH OF KRIPALU'S EARLY LIFE

To understand the significance that *śaktipāt*, *prāṇayoga sādhanā* and divine body play as well as the defining role that Kripalu's life as a source of authority and authenticity holds within the Kripalu lineage particularly among *saṃnyāsins*, a look at his life as told through the narratives of his disciples and through his commentary on the *HYP* is necessary. In this section I outline briefly the background on the early life of Kripalu. In the following sections I provide a tripartite structure that discusses each of the three key features of his approach to modern yoga, namely, *śaktipāt*, *prāṇayoga*, and divine body, and situate them within the context of his extraordinary life story.

Kripalu was born January 13, 1913, into a Kayāstha Brahmin community in Dahboi, Gujarat, under the given name Saraswati Chandra Majmudar (affectionately known as Hariprasad). Dabhoi is the modern name of the ancient town of Darbhavati in the Vadodara district near Baroda. In the early 1900s, Maharaja Sayaji Rao Gaekwad III ruled throughout the state. And though noted scholars have suggested his princely government was "ideal and progressive" due to the implementation of social, political, and constitutional reform based on Western modernization, Manu Bhagavan (2001: 387) argues that Gaekwad advanced a number of Western initiatives as a strategy to "reclaim" and "redeploy" them in an Indian setting and thus "challenge the presumed normality of the colonial way of life." According to Bhagavan, Gaekwad's reforms included radical legislation in 1902 to allow Hindu widows to remarry (p. 390), and in 1904 he signed the Infant Marriage Prevention Act. He reformed primary education in Baroda by making vernacular education in Gujarati free to all citizens. He also created international scholarships, developed a public library system, and challenged the prevailing status of women as second-class citizens. He initiated charities for the poor, opened hospitals, provided access to clean water through the construction of public wells, and, perhaps most relevant to our discussion, advocated that Indians master modern Western science and technology—all in the interest of the modern Indian nation (p. 391). We see several of these modern ideas embraced as normative in Kripalu's own life and in his approach to yoga, particularly the role that science and gender equity play. By the time Kripalu was born, Baroda had modernized its social, intellectual, political, and financial institutions primarily as a mode of resistance against colonial forces (see Bhagavan, 2001 for more details).

On a personal or familial level, there is little historical evidence of Kripalu's childhood. His parents, Jamnadas and Mangalaba, are portrayed in his hagiography as pious Vaiṣṇavas. His father worked as a cleric in a lower court of law but died when Kripalu was only seven years old, leaving his mother and a family of nine children in financial ruin. Mangalaba managed to educate Kripalu until grade seven, but when poverty overcame the family he was forced to leave school to find work at age fourteen. All we know from the scant material available is that as a young boy Kripalu dreamed of becoming either a musician or an actor and, like many still today, made his way in 1930 to Bombay (now Mumbai) to find fame and fortune. However, he sank into depression and despair, felt his life was worthless, and attempted suicide several times.

ŚAKTIPĀT DĪKṢĀ (INITIATION)

In 1930, the young Kripalu met a "mysterious man" named Swami Pranavananda (also known as Dadaji) who became his *sadguru* (true guru). During *ārtī* (the ceremony of light) at the Mahālakṣmī Temple in Bombay,[5] Kripalu visualized committing suicide by throwing himself off the Sandhurst Bridge onto an oncoming train. According to Rajarshi Muni's (1974: 3) hagiographical account, Kripalu cried out, "I don't want to live a futile and loveless life. I don't want to live." Strangely enough, at that precise moment a saffron clad holy man (*sādhu*) carrying a water pot (*kamaṇḍalu*) entered the temple and sat down beside Kripalu; he took his hand gently and said, "Don't cry my son" (ibid.). The *sādhu* called Kripalu *sādhak* (spiritual aspirant) and asked him to come see him the following day at his ashram. When Kripalu arrived half an hour late on January 15, 1931, Pranavananda's disciples were still waiting for him. It seems that four months earlier Pranavananda had predicted his coming. When he arrived, Pranavananda called him *swami*, but Kripalu politely corrected him by saying that he was not in the least bit interested in becoming a *saṃnyāsi* (monk)—he said he had neither the inclination, given that he was only eighteen years old, nor the requisite purity (ibid.).

Nevertheless, over the next fifteen months Pranavananda instructed Kripalu in various aspects of yoga during two daily one-hour meditation sessions in the morning and evening. He taught Kripalu about nonattachment, equanimity, introspection, giving, patience, compassion, and selfless love (*prema*). Pranavananda initiated Kripalu into the ancient and esoteric teachings of yoga through *śaktipāt dīkṣā*, ordained him as a *yogācārya* (yoga teacher), and installed him as the third *kūla*-guru in the modern day Pāśupata lineage of Lord Lakulíśa (we will say more about this further on). Few details are available except to relay that in preparation for initiation Kripalu fasted for forty-one days, lived in seclusion in a completely enclosed room, took *darśan* with Pranavananda twice daily, and confessed that he desired "wealth, women, and fame" (Rajarshi 1974: 15).

Śaktipāt dīkṣā defines a profound turning point and moment of spiritual transformation in Kripalu's life, as it does in the spiritual lives of many Kripalu devotees. Douglas Brooks (1977) draws on similar experiences within the Siddha Yoga community. He refers to *śaktipāt* initiation as energy unleashed by the guru or as the guru's "grace bestowing power (*anugraha-śakti*)" (p. xxxviii). Paul Muller-Ortega (1997: 407) writes that *śaktipāt* is a "deeply secret and mystical notion of spiritual awakening" and is considered the "highest form of spiritual initiation, an initiation that bestows immediate and spontaneous entry into spiritual life." Regarding the Siddha Yoga lineage, Muller-Ortega claims that *śaktipāt* is "the rarest form of esoteric or secret initiation" (ibid.) given by the guru, and he argues that there are no living sources of *śaktipāt* initiation in India before Swami Muktananda (1908–1982; see Jain, in this volume). However, we know without a doubt that Pranavananda initiated Kripalu in 1931 through *śaktipāt* and that Kripalu as a guru of modern yoga in turn initiated others, implying that *śaktipāt* is not as "rare" or as "unavailable" as Muller-Ortega claims.[6]

One possible reason for the error could lie in the modern usage of the term *śaktipāt*, as June McDaniel (2009) points out. The *Kulārnava Tantra* refers to *śaktipāt* by the earlier name *vedha dīkṣā,* meaning initiation by piercing, and it describes five basic types of initiation, namely, *varṇa dīkṣā* (the placement of Sanskrit letters on the body), *samaya dīkṣā* (initiation by ritual), *sparśa dīkṣā* (initiation by touch), *vāk dīkṣā* (initiation by word or mantra), and *dṛksāñjana dīkṣā* (initiation by sight or gaze) (McDaniel, 2009; see also *Śiva Pūraṇa, Vāyavīyasaṃhitā* 15.7–10). So too, David Gordon White (2009) describes the tantric initiation of "co-penetration" (known as *samāveśa)* where the guru "penetrates the body of his [or her] disciple via the mouth, eyes, or heart, through the conduits of 'rays' or 'channels,' to transform the latter from within, thereby ensuring his [or her] future release from this world" (p. 140). Although the exact details of Kripalu's initiation are hard to pin down, it is evident from his autobiographical writings that he received *śaktipāt* from Pranavananda by sight and touch. The penetration or transmission of *śakti* through the rays that emanate from the eyes are a direct source of the guru's power, as White notes, and thus an effective conduit for giving and receiving *śaktipāt* initiation.

Kripalu describes *śaktipāt* as a profoundly embodied experience signaling the partial awakening of *prāṇa* or energy of *kuṇḍalinī śakti*. For Kripalu, *śaktipāt* initiation does not indicate the full awakening of *kuṇḍalinī* as commonly believed (see, e.g., Brooks, 1997: xxxviii). The *sādhak* or *sādhakā* (male or female student) who receives *śaktipāt* directly from the guru typically experiences a variety of spontaneous movements or preliminary signs (*lakṣaṇa*) called *kriyās* that could include shaking, spontaneous postures, crying, dancing, chanting, or visions in his or her meditation. This is arguably an intrinsic part of purification and spiritual refinement that, according to Kripalu, signals entry into a beginner stage of yoga only and is a requisite condition for higher initiations. Kripalu is unambiguous in his conviction that stories told by disciples of uncontrollable shaking, trembling, crying, movements such as *bandhas* (locks), or visions are primary experiences resulting from what he calls *prāṇotthana*—or the partial awakening of *kuṇḍalinī* due to *śaktipāt*. In an unpublished letter to John White dated October 29, 1977, Kripalu writes:

> In this modern age the partial awakening of the pranic energy (*prāṇotthāna*) is believed to be *kuṇḍalinī*. This is not in accordance with the ancient scriptures. My own experience is in agreement with this. The awakening of pranic energy is different from the awakening of *kuṇḍalinī*. The occurrence of various physical manifestations is not the awakening of *kuṇḍalinī*. This opinion of mine is totally different compared to modern *yogis*. (Muni Mandal Ashram Trust, India)

Furthermore, although Kripalu claims there is only one process of *śaktipāt*, he does distinguish between *śaktipāt* for extraordinary disciples (*saṃnyāsis*) and group *śaktipāt* for nonmonastics and states quite clearly that group *śaktipāt* is not "true" *śaktipāt* but rather a special relaxation technique (Rajarshi 2002: 234). Kriplau was thoroughly aware that various modern gurus initiated large groups en masse via *śaktipāt*, and although he tried to avoid this method of initiation and discern for himself the fitness of each individual devotee, he was persuaded by Rajarshi Muni to hold several *śaktipāt* meditation retreats at his ashram in Malav, Gujarat. On one occasion in 1970 ninety-five people attended, and many began to experience various automatic movements (*kriyās*) from the release of *prāṇa* (*prāṇotthāna*). In 1971 Rajarshi organized three more meditation retreats where "nearly five hundred men and women

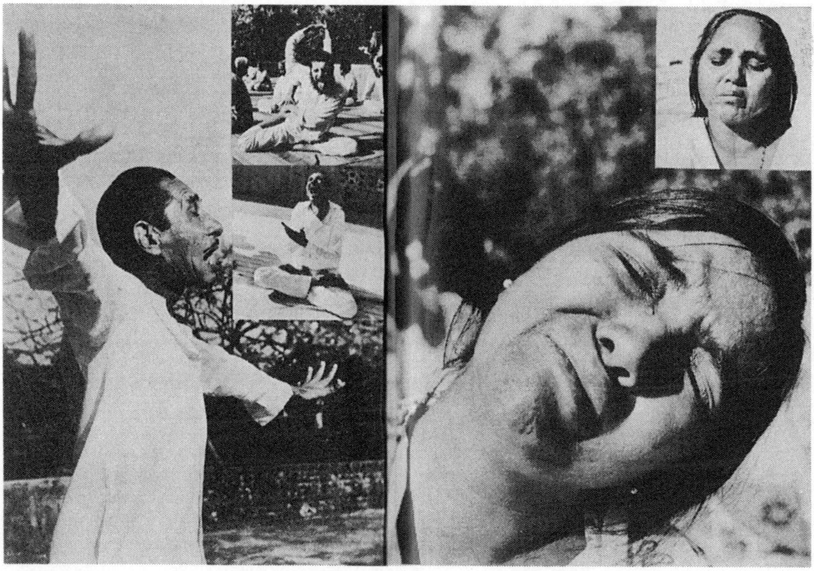

Figure 8.2:
Śaktipāta Initiation. (Courtesy of Muni Mandal Ashram Trust, India.)

received *shaktipat* initiation" (p. 245) with similar results. Kripalu and members of his lineage (e.g., Amrit Desai) attracted large followings because of their charismatic ability to bestow *śaktipāt dīkṣā* (see Goldberg, 2013).

PRĀṆAYOGA SĀDHANĀ

Śaktipāt bestows initiation into *prāṇayoga sādhanā*—or what I would describe as the defining feature of Kripalu's approach to yoga and the key to understanding his role as *guruji* (beloved guru) and *bapuji* (father) in a lineage that bears his name.

After a brief pilgrimage to Mathura, Pranavananda disappeared suddenly, leaving Kripalu on his own. He returned to Gujarat in 1932 where he studied classical vocal music from a disciple of the legendary musician Ustad Faiaz Khan of the Baroda Royal Court. He became a classically trained music teacher, traveled throughout western India on foot giving music lessons and singing *bhajans*, and, by all accounts, became quite popular in the small towns and villages around Baroda. In 1941 when his family thought it was time for him to marry, he broke off the engagement and took *saṃnyāsa dīkṣā* (monastic ordination) in 1942 on the banks of the Narmada River at Rajpipla from Swami Shantananda of the Udasin lineage and was given the name Swami Kṛpālvānanda (bliss of compassion).

After his initiation, Kripalu traveled to Haridwar where he studied Hindu scriptures at the Munimandal Ashram, the principal center of the Udasin lineage founded by Swami Keshavananda, Shantananda's guru. Shortly thereafter, Kripalu moved to the forests of the Himalayan foothills, lived in isolation in a simple hut in Rishikesh, bathed each day in the Ganges, begged for his food, and absorbed himself in meditation. During the 1940s, Rishikesh was populated mostly by *sādhus* and yogis, and the town, as Sarah Strauss (2005: 26) observes, provided the embarkation point for pilgrimage to the four auspicious sites of the Garhwal region, Kedarnath, Badrinath, Gangotri, and Yamunotri, collectively referred to as Char Dham.[7] These pilgrimage sites, as Strauss points out, are the abodes of various gods and goddesses of Hindu mythology. Thus, the Garhwal region offered Kripalu an ideal setting to seek self-realization.

During this time, Kripalu experienced a series of visions (*darśans*) of his guru in what he refers to as his *true* or *divine form*. In the first vision, Pranavananda appears to Kripalu as a handsome, nineteen-year-old saint. He explains to Kripalu how he entered the corpse of an old *sādhak* named Pranavananda[8] before coming to Bombay and that the form Kripalu was now seeing is his *true form*. Two years later, on *guru pūrṇimā* (festival of homage to one's guru), Kripalu experienced a second vision. Rajarshi Muni recounts how a "divine light shooting straight from the darkness of space came directly toward him," and before Kripalu could "jump in surprise, he found Dadaji [Pranavananda] standing right before him in his 'true form'" (Rajarshi 1974: 39). In the vision, Dadaji (or Pranavananda) bestowed his blessing on Kripalu through what June McDaniel (2009) calls "the mystical transmission of a hidden lineage" and instructed him in the advanced method of *prāṇayoga* (or *sahajayoga*) through the subtle power of his yoga *siddhis* (powers, perfections). The very next day Kripalu moved into a hut in a remote village near Baroda and started *prāṇayoga sādhanā* for ten hours a day—a schedule he adhered to for more than two decades. He changed his diet following the strict yogic practice of moderation (*mitāhāra*). At night he often went into states of deep ecstasy and wandered naked through the village. Devotees were posted at the gates of the town to watch over him in case he wandered away, which he often did.

Then, in December 1955, the villagers of Kayavarohan[9] invited Kripalu to give a lecture on the *Bhagavad Gītā*. They took him on a tour of the Brahmeshwar Mandir, and when he saw the Śiva *liṅgam* enshrined in the temple he immediately identified the face of the young man carved in the black meteoric rock as the *true form* of his *sadguru* as he had experienced him during *darśan* while in the Himalayas—he was Lakulish (or Lakulīśa, c. early first–second century CE), the twenty-eighth incarnation (*avatāra*) of Śiva and the founder of the Pāśupata sect (Kṛpālvānanda, 1972).[10] The *Viśvakarmāvatāra-vāstu-śāstra* identifies Lakulīśa as a young, naked, *ūrdhvaretas* (ithyphallic) yogi seated in a type of lotus posture (*padmāsana*), holding a citrus fruit (*mātuliṅga*) in his right hand and a club (*daṇḍa* or *lakula*) in his left hand (Bhandarkar, 1904–07: 166, also cited in Lorenzen, 1972: 177). The codified description of Lakulīśa that we find in the *vāstu-śāstras* matches with the *mūrti* located in the Brahmeshwar Mandir at Kayavarohan and with Kripalu's *darśans* of Lakulīśa during meditation.[11]

The *Kāravaṇa-māhātmya* is probably the most useful primary source for our purpose of recording the intersections between Lakulīśa and Kāyāvarohaṇa. It recounts the story of Śiva who incarnated as the son of a brahmin couple in the village of Ulkāpurī (modern-day Avākhal). As a divine infant he performed miraculous deeds (*siddhis*), but he died when he was only seven months old. His mother immersed him in the waters of a nearby *tīrtha*, as was the custom in traditional infant burial. As the story goes, he was taken by tortoises to the Jāleśvara *liṅgam* and then brought back to life as Lakulīśa by entering the corpse of a chaste brahmin student found on the cremation grounds at Kāyāvarohaṇa (see White, 2009: 193). In another version of the story, Śiva as Lakulīśa enters the body of a young brahmin ascetic to propagate Pāśupata *dharma*. David Lorenzen (1972: 176) refers to a thirteenth-century record from Somnātha showing that Śiva came to Lāṭa and lived at Kāyāvarohaṇa as Lakulīśa "in order to bestow favor on the universe." The central message in these narratives, as well as several inscriptions found near Udaipur, is the descent of Śiva-Lakulīśa, founder of the Pāśupata sect in the twenty-eighth *yuga* (age), at Kāyāvarohaṇa (*kāyā* + *avarohaṇa* translates as *descending of the body*). As we will see further on in the chapter, the Nāth tradition that develops approximately eleven hundred years later absorbed aspects of the Pāśupatas,[12] and therefore it is not at all surprising that *haṭhayoga* plays such a defining role in Kripalu's approach to modern yoga *sādhanā*.

However, there is still more to this story. In c. 1024 CE, Muslim invaders under Mahmud Ghazni raided and destroyed the Somnātha Temple located near Veraval in Junagadh District, considered the original home of the Pāśupatas, on the Arabian Sea. Legend has it that Anant Sarvagna, who was installed as the Pāśupata teacher at Kāyāvarohaṇa, received instructions during meditation to protect the temple's statue (*mūrti*) of Lakulīśa by burying it in an underground pit. Shortly thereafter (c. 1025 CE), Muslim invaders continued on to Kāyāvarohaṇa, one of the 68 *tīrthas* in India, looted the temple, and left only ruins behind. The *liṅgam* of Lakulīśa that had been buried by Sarvagna surfaced in a farmer's field approximately eight hundred years later in 1866, but the villagers had no knowledge of its historical significance and referred to it as Raja-rajeshwara (Rajarshi 1974). It was not until 1955, when Kripalu visited Kayavarohan, that he immediately identified the *mūrti* not only as the original *liṅgam* of Lakulīśa but also as the *true form* of his guru Pranavananda.

What transpired on a deeply personal level for Kripalu is that during evening meditation he received a third vision of Lakulīśa-Pranavananda. He was instructed in this vision to revive Kayavarohan as a modern pilgrimage center and to create an institute of modern yoga "open to men and women of all races, religions and nationalities" (Rajarshi 1974: x). When the temple eventually reopened in 1974, a prospectus was circulated at the inaugural ceremony introducing the future home of the Shri Lakulish Institute of Yoga. It was advertised as a non-profit, non-sectarian university open to all aspirants regardless of their sex, caste, creed, race, religion, or nationality. Course offerings included physiology, psychology, biochemistry, parapsychology, and sociology to prepare students for the modern scientific study of yoga (Prospectus, 1974). The brochure addressed the future goals of Kayavarohan based on the global appeal and institutionalization of Kripalu's biography (and hagiography), which was at the time being publicized widely by his lay disciple Amrit Desai as spiritual director ("Gurudev") of the Kripalu Yoga center in the United States. It also underscores the defining role Kripalu's life as an adept yoga-guru played in establishing what I referred to earlier as the *circular construction of authority* within the tradition for future generations of lay and monastic disciples East and West.

Immediately after he recognized his guru as Lakulīśa, Kripalu began to experience advanced yogic techniques automatically in meditation—that is, *prāṇayoga sādhanā*— including *khecarī mudrā* (discussed in detail further on in the paper) and *kevala kumbhaka* (spontaneous cessation of breath) by the sheer force (*haṭha*) of fully awakened *kuṇḍalinī*. In his commentary on the *HYP*, Kripalu describes how his capacity to restrain the modifications of the mind (*citta-vṛtti*) became effortless. He refers to this state as the *samādhi* of *haṭhayoga* (known as *sabīja samādhi* or concentration with seed) and as the beginning stage of *rājayoga*. Although David Gordon White (2003: 81) offers an alternative reading of the term *rājayoga*, Kripalu explains that entrance into *sabīja samādhi* occurs when the adept experiences spontaneous *khecharī mudrā* and *kevala kumbhaka* due to the force of fully awakened *kuṇḍalinī*, meaning it ascends upward from the *ajña cakra* (command center) located in between the eyebrows to the *sahasrāra* or crown *cakra*—hence the use of the term *rājayoga*. The fundamental point in Kripalu's approach is that the power of *prāṇa* harnessed in the body ascends naturally (*sahaja*) by means of its own inner intelligence and force. Kripalu distinguishes *prāṇa*-induced or self-arising alchemical techniques such as *khecarī mudrā*, *śāmbhavī mudrā*, *unmani mudrā*, *śakticālana mudra*, and *vajrolī mudrā*, from voluntary or *citta*-induced practices such as the *āsanas* that he typically associates with the beginning stages of yoga *sādhanā*. Kripalu also distinguishes *prāṇa*-induced *mudrās* and *bandhas* from voluntary *mudrās* and *bandhas* (e.g., the *bandhas* required in the modern-day Ashtanga Vinyasa Yoga; see Chapter 5, in this volume), and he discusses this point at some length in his commentary on the *HYP*. He bases his tiered *pravṛtti*- and *nivṛtti-mārga* approach to yoga on this critical and little-known distinction.

What we see (or perhaps what Kripalu would like us to see) in his particular discussion of *prāṇayoga sādhanā* is a modern yoga-guru's reenactment of the hidden lineage of the Pāśupatas as a forerunner to the medieval *sampradāya* of Nāth Siddhas, particularly with reference to the practices of *haṭha* and tantric yoga for alchemical transmutation and perfection of the body, a point of importance noted in White's (1996: 97, 122) historical analysis of the Nāth tradition. Kripalu's emphasis on the intensification and spontaneous movement of *prāṇa* beyond the initial and partial awakening (*prāṇotthāna*) experienced during *śaktipāt dīkṣā* provides a central thesis. Through his own autobiography, he reveals how *prāṇa* moves by the grace and compassion (*kṛpā*) of the *sadguru* to produce perceptible signs of health and healing in the body including slimness, radiating aura, and luminous eyes (the "rays" that enable the guru to give *śaktipāt*), extraordinary strength, bliss, and restraint of the senses, to name just a few, leading the adept gradually to divine body or immortality (*jīvanmukti*, *divya deha*). For Kripalu, the metaphysics of modern *haṭhayoga* are preoccupied with purification, self-cultivation, rejuvenation, and longevity. Although these are concrete goals they are never viewed as ends in themselves; rather, they are linked to a broader template of adept strategies that he believes remove ignorance (*avidyā*)—the root cause of illness and suffering—and furthermore produce an internal elixir of immortality (*amṛta*) capable of bestowing long life and liberation.

Khecarī mudrā and *kevala kumbhaka* are two essential practices that bring about this transformation and, in Kripalu's view, distinguish the adept from the beginner. *Khecarī mudrā* refers to the difficult *haṭhayoga* practice or *siddhi* of elongating the tongue through a process of milking (*dohana*), moving (*cālana*), and striking (*tāḍana*). These actions spontaneously sever the tongue from the *frenum linguae* by the sheer force of *prāṇa,* without the use of external instrumentation, so that it can be inserted fully into the "three-peaked mountain" or cavity called the "diamond bulb" (*Khecarīvidyā of Adināth (KV)* 3: 50) located behind the soft palate in the region above the uvula (*rājadanta, HYP* 3: 32–53; *KV* 3:1, 15). When accompanied by the spontaneous restraint of the breath (*kevala kumbhaka*) and the three *bandhas* (*mūla, uddīyāna,* and *jālandhara*), *khecarī mudrā* facilitates the preservation and drinking of *candrājala* (also known as *amṛta* and *somarasa* or the nectar of immortality) by physically sealing off the cavity above the uvula with the severed tongue (*HYP* 3: 47–50; *KV* 3: 20–25). The *mudrā* prevents the nectar of immortality from being consumed by the lower *cakras*, particularly the *maṇipūra cakra* (or third *cakra* located in the navel region and referred to as *sūrya* or sun). As a result, the adept "cheats" death, as the *KV* states, and he or she attains an immortal body (*KV* 3: 10–20). This *siddhi* also enables the yogi to enter the body of another being at will.

As to the therapeutic benefits, the *HYP* states there is no more hunger, thirst, old age, disease, or death for the adept who knows the secret rejuvenation practice of *khecarī mudrā*, nor is the adept subject to the mundane laws of time (*kāla*) or *karma* (*HYP* 3: 38–40; *Śiva Saṁhitā* [SS] 3: 66). The *Gorakṣaśataka* (*GŚ*) makes the explicit claim that *khecarī mudrā* alone renders the body immortal (*GŚ* 131–148; cited in Mallinson, 2007). The *KV* and the *HYP* also explain, as Kripalu stated earlier, that the experience of *khecarī mudrā* enables the yogi or yogini to still (*nirodha*) the fluctuations of the mind (*citta-vṛttis*) to such an extent that he or she enters deeper and deeper states of meditative absorption (*laya*). Thus, *khecarī mudrā* accompanied by *kevala kumbhaka* announce the attainment of *sabīja samādhi*, and are interpreted by Kripalu as the onset of *rājayoga*. They provide corporeal evidence that the *haṭhayoga* stage is complete.

IMMORTALITY AND DIVINE BODY (*DIVYA DEHA*)

In 1959 Kripalu took a vow of silence that he maintained for over twenty years. In 1965 he relocated from Malav to Kayavarohan and devoted himself to the restoration of the temple and to his *sādhanā*. On May 3, 1974, the *liṅgam* of Lakulīśa was ceremoniously (re)-installed (*prāṇa-pratisṭhā*). Over twenty-five thousand people attended the opening ceremony including a large contingent from Canada and the United States led by Desai. Then, in 1977, Kripalu left

India with one of his principle disciples, Swami Vinit Muni, and traveled to Canada, specifically Toronto and Montreal where he met with devotees, and the United States where he lived for four years in a small house called *Muktidham* (abode of liberation) that is still maintained by disciples on the original ashram property of the Kripalu Center. Kripalu remained in silence and continued to do *sādhanā* in seclusion while in the United States, though twice yearly he offered talks (read aloud by Desai) and led *satsang*. He describes how groups of 250, 500, and 1000 (referred to as "brothers and sisters") poured into the Kripalu Center for programs and retreats (Kṛpālvānanda 1981).

On October 1, 1981, Kripalu returned to India where he died in Ahmedabad, Gujarat, at approximately 6 o'clock the morning of December 29. He was hailed not only as a great guru but also as a saint, and thousands of devotees East and West claimed he did not die "a usual death" but rather chose to leave his body and enter *mahāsamādhi* (final liberation). There are of course considerable reasons to doubt this account, but I will not pursue this thinking here. What is significant is that Kripalu fervently believed until the very last moment that his body was being transformed alchemically due to *sādhanā* rather than being consumed by death. He refused medical treatment including alternative therapies. Nevertheless, his *mahāsamādhi* (ritual ceremony) was held in Malav, Gujarat, on the sixteenth day after his death in accordance with Indian tradition. The details of his last days are recorded in a Kripalu Yoga ashram pamphlet called *Guru Prasad,* April 1982.

One framework that is useful for us to understand the role that Kripalu's life plays as both model and measure of what constitutes authentic yoga experience is based on the core elements directly issuing from his aspiration to attain immortality. Although the Kripalu approach to *haṭhayoga* was modified for beginners, Kripalu himself emphasized *prāṇayoga sādhanā* (once *śaktipāt* and the awakening of *kuṇḍalinī* sufficiently matured) as the *only* way for adept disciples to attain spiritual liberation through divine body—even though he himself was ultimately unsuccessful. For Kripalu, it is clear that the merging of the physical and the mystical dimensions of yoga manifest in the living body only to the extent that the adept experiences marked health and therapeutic benefits. On this point, not only does he follow a decidedly pragmatic approach and makes few distinctions between the system of physical yoga and its metaphysical or mystical correlates or between macrocosm and microcosm, but he also places much more emphasis on the mystical dimensions of yoga than many of his contemporaries.

By physical yoga, I refer primarily to advanced and spontaneous experiences of various *mudrās* or fire-generating (*yogāgni*) practices arising from *prāṇayoga sādhanā* such as *mahā, mahāveda, khecarī, vajrolī, sahajolī, amarolī, yonī,* and *śakticālana,*[13] accompanied by spontaneously arising *bandhas* such as *mūla, uḍḍiyāna,* and *jālandhara, prāṇāyāmā,* most notably *kevala kumbaka,* stages of *anāhata nāda* (inner sound) including drum, cymbal, and *vīṇā* sounds, and the final stages of *sabīja* and *nirbīja samādhi*. The meaning here is that Kripalu engages the psychophysical culture of *haṭhayoga* as a radical biotherapeutic strategy to remove disease, decay, and ultimately even death so that the material body (*sthūla śarīra*) becomes completely transformed (*para śarīra*) or transubstantiated. In the process, Kripalu never loses sight that *haṭhayoga's* final aim of liberation (*mukti, mokṣa*) is conceived in terms of a perfect body that is free from old age, disease, and death (*HYP* 1: 29; 2: 16, 20; 3: 6–7, 40–44; 4: 13, 27, 70, 74; see also *KV* 1:1, 15; 3:10, 45, 55).[14] He believes the adept yogi can cultivate the ability to enter another's body at will. Why? For Kripalu the liberated body is a living body or *jīvanmukti* that is not bound by the mundane laws of time (*kāla*) and *karma*. Just as his *sadguru*, now identified as Lakulīśa-Pranavananda, was not limited, it seems, by ordinary or conventional consciousness or constrained by the limits of death and could enter another person's body at will—Kripalu too sought the *siddhi* of divine body.[15] To this end I am told that he had his body photographed regularly and that he kept records of his hair, teeth, and nails to track any physiological changes or potential signs of alchemical transformation. On more than one occasion he announced publicly to his disciples, "if I do not attain a divine body, consider me an ordinary *sadhak*" (Kṛpālvānanda, 1977: viii).[16] Even in the final moments before death, the hope of attaining divine body lingered, and he falsely attributed the changes occurring in his body to alchemical transformation.

We see that for Kripalu health and healing are prefigured in the performative and experiential dimensions of adept yoga practice—there is a causal link.[17] However, even though the adept's body becomes a somatic vehicle of spiritual and mystical transformation that unveils the inscribed metaphysical map of tantric yoga philosophy by using techniques that could to some extent be described as Modern Postural Yoga (MPY), this only creates the physical and hygienic conditions requisite for deeper spiritual training. For Kripalu, *haṭhayoga* as physical culture is a means—not an end—leading to divine body. This does not diminish his contribution to Modern Postural Yoga (as per De Michelis's, 2004 category) insofar as he provides the novice with what he calls "the proper" introduction necessary for deeper spiritual understanding and development, but it does call attention to the pervasive overlap of adept tantric *sādhanā* not typically found in other modern posture-identified approaches. To best accomplish this goal, as I stated at the outset, Kripalu identifies three key elements found within the more esoteric traditions of *haṭha* and tantric yoga, namely, *śaktipāt dīkṣā* and *prāṇayoga sādhanā*, since in his own experience they perfect the receptivity of the human body to create and sustain conducive circumstances for a direct understanding of what transcendence ultimately means—immortality. These three elements, as far as I can see, are not taught in conjunction in other modern approaches and, as I have argued, they summarize the measure of what constitutes "authentic" yoga not only for Kripalu's disciples but also for Kripalu himself as a guru of modern yoga par excellence.

CONCLUSION: WAS KRIPALU SUCCESSFUL?

In this paper I presented a sketch of Kripalu's life based on the biographical, hagiographical, and autobiographical material available. Furthermore, I structured this portrait to illuminate two important issues. First, Kripalu's life provides a circular construction of authority within the Kripalu lineage. That is to say, his yogic experiences as guru (and as *bapuji*) within the Kripalu community mark the standard by which all yoga experiences are measured. Second, I framed his life narrative around three central features, namely, *śaktipāt dīkṣā, prāṇayoga sādhanā,* and the attainment of divine body. These factors, as I stated at the outset, are unique in the overall context of the transnational phenomenon of modern yoga.

One difficult question that I have not asked but that yet seems critical is whether Kripalu was successful. If we measure his success by his own criterion—to attain a divine body—then Kripalu has failed to achieve his goal, though as June McDaniel (2009) recently said, he "set the bar rather high." Even if we approach the notion of divine body as part of an esoteric or symbolic landscape that is uniquely subjective and highly mystical, from Kripalu's own point of reference he did not achieve his goal—he was not able to enter another body at will. If, however, we measure the success of Kripalu through the lens of his guru's request during *darśan* to reestablish Kayavarohan as a place of pilgrimage and to teach yoga as a modern spiritual practice to women and men of all races, religions and nationalities, then by galvanizing a transnational community of yoga teachers and practitioners located today across twenty-seven countries, Kripalu fulfilled his guru's instructions. Finally, if we look at whether he was successful from the point of view of the Kripalu disciple and devotee, then we see that Kripalu left the tradition of modern yoga with a rich legacy and a paradigmatic figure of the modern guru whose authoritative two-stage approach to yoga has only begun to be understood, studied, and practiced.

REFERENCES

SANSKRIT TEXTS

Khecarīvidyā of Adināthа: A Critical Edition and Annotated Translation of an Early Text of Haṭhayoga. Sanskrit with English. Trans. James Mallinson. London: Routledge, 2007.

Gheraṇḍa Saṁhitā. Sanskrit with English. Trans. S. C. Vasu, 1914–15. Reprint, Delhi: Oriental 6 Books, 1980.

Gheraṇḍa Saṁhitā. Sanskrit with English. Trans. James Mallinson. Woodstock: Yogavidya.com, 2009.

The Haṭhayogapradīpikā of Svātmārāma with the Commentary Jyotsnā of Brahmānanda and English Translation. Sanskrit text, commentary and English translation, by S. Iyangar. Madras: Adyar Library and Research Centre, 1994.

Pāśupata Sūtram with Pañchārtha Bhāṣya of Kauṇḍinya, ed. Haripada Charkraborti. Calcutta: Academic Publishers, 1970.

Śiva Purāṇa. Delhi: Motilal Banarsidass, 1988.

Śiva Saṁhitā. Sanskrit and English. Trans. James Mallinson. Woodstock: Yogavidya.com, 2007.

Śiva Saṁhitā. Sanskrit with English. Trans. S. C. Vasu, 1914–15. Reprint, New Delhi: Oriental Books, 1979.

OTHER SOURCES

Agarwala, R. C. 1965. Two Standing Lakulīśa Sculptures from Rajasthan. *Journal of the Oriental Institute Baroda* 14: 388–391.

Alter, Joseph. 1992. Seminal Truth: A Modern Science of Male Celibacy in North India. *Medical Anthropology Quarterly* 11 (3): 275–298.

Bhagavan, Manu. 2001. Demystifying the "Ideal Progressive": Resistance through Mimicked Modernity in Princely Baroda, 1900–1913. *Modern Asian Studies* 35 (2): 385–409.

Bhandarkar, R. G. 1904–1907. An Ekliṅga Stone Inscription and the Origin and History of the Lakulīśa Sect. *Journal of the Bombay Branch of the Royal Asiatic Society* 22: 151–165.

Brooks, Douglas Renfrew. 1997. Introduction: The Experience of Perfected Yogis. In Douglas Renfrew Brooks et al. (eds.), *Meditation Revolution: A History and Theology of the Siddha Yoga Lineage*. New Delhi: Muktabodha Indological Research Institute, pp. xix–xlix.

Dasgupta, Surendranath.[1922] 1988. *A History of Indian Philosophy, Volume 5: The Southern Schools of Śaivism*. Delhi: Motilal Banarsidass.

De Michelis, Elizabeth. 2004. *A History of Modern Yoga: Patañjali and Western Esotericism*. London: Continuum.

Eliade, Mircea. 1969. *Yoga: Immortality and Freedom*. Trans. Willard R. Trask. Princeton, NJ: Princeton University Press.

Fields, Gregory P. 2001. *Religious Therapeutics: Body and Health in Yoga, Āyurveda, and Tantra*. Albany: State University of New York Press.

Goldberg, Ellen. 2003. *The Lord Who Is Half Woman: Ardhanārīśvara in Indian and Feminist Perspective*. Albany: State University of New York Press.

———. 2009. Medieval *Haṭhayoga Sādhanā*: An Indigenous Bio-therapeutic Model for Health, Healing and Longevity. *Acta Orientalia* 70: 90–101.

———. 2013. Amrit Desai and the Kripalu Center for Yoga and Health. In Lola Williamson and Ann Gleig (eds.), *Homegrown Gurus: From Hinduism in America to American Hinduism*. Albany: State University of New York Press, pp. 63–86.

Hara, Minoru. 1958. Nakulīśa-Pāśupata-Darśanam. *Indo-Iranian Journal* 11: 8–10.

———. 2002. *Pāśupata Studies*. Edited by Jun Takashima. Vienna: Institut für Südasien, Tibet, und Buddismuskunde.

Heelas, Paul. 2008. *Spiritualities of Life: New Age Romanticism and Consumptive Capitalism*. Oxford: Blackwell.

Kṛpālvānanda, Swami. 1974a. *Haṭhayogapradīpikā*. Sanskrit and Hindi. Pransali: Kripalu Muni Mandal Trust.
———. 1972. *Re-manifestation of Shri Lakulish: A Commentary by Swami Kripalvanandaji*. Sumneytown, PA: Kripalu Center.
———. 1977. *The Science of Meditation*. Pransali: Kripalu Muni Mandal Trust.
Lorenzen, David N. 1972. *The Kāpālikas and Kālāmukhas: Two Lost Śaivite Sects*. Delhi: Motilal Banarsidass.
Mallinson, James. 2007. *The Khecarīvidyā of Ādinātha: A Critical Edition and Annotated Translation of an Early Text of Haṭhayoga*. London: Routledge.
McDaniel, June. 2009. Spiritual Biography/Autobiography: Response. American Academy of Religion Meeting in Montreal, November 10.
Muller-Ortega, Paul E. 1997. Shaktipat: The Initiatory Descent of Power. In Douglas Renfrew Brooks et al. (eds.), *Meditation Revolution: A History and Theology of the Siddha Yoga Lineage*. New Delhi: Muktabodha Indological Research Institute, pp. 407–444.
Prospectus. 1974. Kayavarohan: Shri Lakulish Institute of Yoga.
Rajarshi Muni. 1974. *Light From Guru To Disciple*. Summneytown: Kripalu Yoga Ashram.
———. 2002. *Infinite Grace: The Story of My Spiritual Lineage*. Vadodara, Gujarat: Life Mission Publications.
Reddy, Venkata M. 1982. *Haṭharatnāvalī of Srinivasabhatta Mahyogindra*. Sanskrit and English. Arthamuru: Ramakrishna Reddy.
Sanderson, Alexis. 2006. The Lākulas: New Evidence of a System of Intermediate between Pāñcārthika Pāśupatism and Āgamic Śaivism. *Indian Philosophical Annual* 24 (2003–05): 143–217.
Sastri, Ananthakrishnan, R. (ed.). 1940. *Pāśupata Sūtras with Pañchārtabhāṣya of Kauṇḍinya*. Trivandrum: University of Travancore.
Singleton, Mark. 2008. The Classical Reveries of Modern Yoga: Patañjali and Constructive Orientalism. In Mark Singleton and Jean Byrne (eds.), *Yoga in the Modern World: Contemporary Perspectives*. London: RoutledgeHindu Studies Series, pp. 77–100.
———. 2010. *Yoga Body: The Origins of Modern Posture Practice*. Oxford: Oxford University Press.
Smith, Benjamin Richard. 2008. With Heat Even Iron Will Bend: Discipline and Authority in Ashtanga Yoga. In Mark Singleton and Jean Byrne (eds.), *Yoga in the Modern World: Contemporary Perspectives*. London: Routledge Hindu Studies Series, pp. 140–161.
Strauss, Sarah. 2005. *Positioning Yoga: Balancing Acts Across Cultures*. Oxford: Berg.
White, David Gordon. 1996. *The Alchemical Body: Siddha Traditions in Medieval India*. Chicago: University of Chicago Press.
———.2009. *Sinister Yogis*. Chicago: University of Chicago Press.

NOTES

1. In 2010, an earlier version of this chapter appeared in *Religions of South Asia* 4 (1): 67–88. Since 1994, Amrit Desai is no longer associated with the Kripalu center. However, their current Website claims that it has welcomed over one million visitors since it opened its door in the early 1970s, and it boasts a roster of high profile patrons and international teachers. As stated, in 2011 the Kripalu center reported revenues totaling over $30.6 million dollars under its charitable, tax-exempt status, making it one of the largest and most successful spiritual organizations in North America (see IRS public tax return, http://www.guidestar.org/FinDocuments/2009/231/718/2009-231718197-065128bd-9.pdf (accessed June 24, 2013)).

2. In 1989 I conducted field research on various sites relevant to Kripalu's life including the Brahmeshwar Mandir in Kayavarohan, his *mahāsamādhi* in Malov, and the Munimandal Ashram of the Udasin lineage in Haridwar. In 2002 I stayed at Kripalu Muni Mandal Ashram in Pransali located near the well-known Śiva temple at Somnath.
3. The heritage of yoga scriptures in India is vast. Kripalu was selective and focused primarily on medieval Nāth *haṭhayoga* texts such as *Haṭhayogapradīpikā* (*HYP*); *Haṭhapradīpā* (*HD*); *Gorakṣa Saṁhitā*; *Gorakṣa Paddhati*; *Gorakṣaśataka* (*GŚ*); *Gheraṇḍa Saṁhitā* (*GS*); *Khecarīvidyā* (*KV*); *Yoga Bīja*; *Śiva Saṁhitā* (*ŚS*); and *Haṭharatnāvalī*, to name just a few. This genre of Sanskrit literature concentrates primarily on a prescriptive regimen of corporeal practices that facilitate *samādhi* and longevity. Goraknāth of the Nāth yoga *sampradāya* first used the technical term *haṭha* in the *Haṭhadīpikā* (*HD*). See also Reddy (1982) for more details on two unpublished manuscripts of the *HD* in the Darbar Library, Nepal and Government Manuscript Library Bhubaneswar, Orissa. See also White (1996) for an excellent study of Nāth tradition in India.
4. Kripalu's *pravṛtti mārga* for non-renouncers emphasizes *citta* over *prāṇa* meaning that *āsanas* and *prāṇāyāma* (breathing practices) are learned and practiced voluntarily. The practice remains steady, and the energy is restrained. In more advanced or adept stages, *āsanas* and other *kriyās* arise spontaneously (*sahaja*), involuntarily, or naturally through the intense force of awakened *kuṇḍalinī*.
5. The Mahālakṣmī Temple was completed in Bombay c. 1785. Considering Kripalu's own visionary experiences at Kayavarohan, the temple has an interesting story. The chief engineer of the Hornby Vellard named Ramji Shivji was having a difficult time building the exterior sea wall. It had collapsed on more than one occasion. However, the goddess Lakṣmī came to him in a dream and told him to look under the sea for three buried statues (of Lakṣmī, Sarasvatī, and Kālī). He led a search, found the three statues, and built a temple to house them.
6. Kripalu claims if a guru gives *śaktipāt* it does not necessarily mean that he is a perfect yogi (*mahātma*. For example, Amrit Desai, as a householder or lay disciple, bestowed *śaktipāt*). Tibetan *lamas* also employ a variant of *śaktipāt* during certain ritual initiation ceremonies or *wongkurs*.
7. After returning from a field trip to the Amarnath caves in 1989, I traveled this particular pilgrimage route with Swami Vinit Muni, Kripalu's principle disciple, and visited the Udasin headquarters in Haridwar as well as the site of a small Kripalu ashram on route to Gangotri, Badrinath, Kedarnath, and Yamunotri.
8. Kripalu refers to this as *nirmānadeha* or the historical or emanation body that appears in time and space.
9. The modern day town of Kayavarohan is variously referred to as Kārvan, Kāyāvarohaṇa, Kāyāvatāra, Kārohana, and Kāyārohaṇa, as well as Medhavati. For more details see Lorenzen (1972: 177). Kripalu (1972) adds that although Kayavarohan was located only 25 kilometers from his home in Dabhoi, he knew nothing of its history as an ancient pilgrimage center, nor had he visited it before this invitation.
10. The name Lakulīśa means "lord who holds a club" (*lakulin*): it is a compound of *lakula* "club" with the possessive suffix *-in*, and *īśa* "lord." Variants of this name include Nakulīśa, Lakuleśa, Lakulin, and Lakulīśvara (Lorenzen 1977: 177; see also Dasgupta [1922], 1988). Manuscripts of the Pāśupatas including the *Pāśupatas Sūtras* with the *Pāñcārtha bhāṣya* (commentary) of Kauṇḍinya (also referred to by Mādhava as the *Rāśīkara bhāṣya* and published in 1940 in the Trivandrum series; see Sastri, 1940), and the *Gaṇakārikā*, are attributed to the early Gupta period (c. 280–550 CE) and were rediscovered in the 1930s. We see monistic as well as

monotheistic elements in this literature with a theoretical emphasis placed on grace (*kṛpā*), compassion (*karuṇā*) and *karma*—we also see references to *śaktipāt*. Furthermore, the Pāśupatas hail originally from Gujarat given several references in the *Kāravaṇa-māhātmya* to the temples at Somnātha and Kāyāvarohaṇa as important centers of the early Pāśupata sect. We also see references to Lakulīśa's personal history at Kāyāvarohaṇa in the *Vāyu, Kūrma, Skandha, Śiva (SP),* and *Liṅga Purāṇas.* For example, the *SP* lists twenty-eight *yogācāryas* each having four disciples. The last *yogācāya* born at Kāyāvarohaṇa is listed in the *SP* as Lakulish.

11. Although R. C. Agarwala (1965) identifies two unusual standing poses from Rajasthan, Alain Danièlou argues that standing poses are considered normative (cited in Lorenzen, 1972: 177). The *mūrti* of Lakulīśa in the Brahmeshwara Mandir at Kayavarohan is in seated posture, though not *padmāsana.*
12. As White (1996: 146) argues, "We may quite safely characterize the emergence of the Nātha Siddhas as a marriage between Nāthas (i.e. Śaiva groups—Pāśupatas, Kāpalikas, and Śaktas—for whom Śiva had long been called Nāth, "Lord") and Siddhas (Maheśvara and Rasa Siddhas and Sittars, as well as Buddhist Siddhācaryas) which took the institutional form of the Nātha *sampradāya.*" It is also significant that the teachings of the Pāśupatas were traditionally kept secret and revealed only to initiates based on strict caste rules until a householder path evolved from the earlier monastic orders. Today, the Somnātha Temple is still one of the most revered and active sites of the Pāśupatas in India. In the seventh century, Varanasi was also a popular site for Pāśupata tradition, and in the literature one finds stories that explain clashes between Varanasi and Kayavarohana. Since the eighth century, Pāśupatinātha Temple in Nepal has become a central place of pilgrimage. For more details on the Pāśupata sect, see Sastri (1940), Minoru (1958, 2002), Kripalu (1972), Lorenzen (1972); Sanderson (2006), and White (2009).
13. For this reason, do-it-yourself instructions on how to practice *mudrās* (seals) are typically omitted from *haṭhayoga* treatises, suggesting to Kripalu that they must be learned as he did, either through direct transmission from an accomplished guru or through spontaneous *yoga-kriyās*. See Goldberg (2002) and White (1996).
14. As Mircea Eliade (1969) observes, the human body is valorized in the *śaivāgamas* (e.g., *haṭhayoga* root texts) in ways unknown before in the history of Indian religions. Purification, rejuvenation and longevity, eradication of all disease, recognition of the human body as homologous to the cosmos, and the acquisition of a transfigured body beyond the grasp of death are among the possible *siddhis* (perfections, powers) declared attainable through *sādhanā*.
15. There are countless stories in Hindu, Buddhist, and Daoist literature of immortals, *siddhas* or transcendents who have obtained longevity or bodily immortality through alchemy or *yoga*.
16. Elsewhere he makes reference to the *Bhagavad-Gītā* 7:29, claiming that only a yogi who has attained divine body is a *siddha yogi*.
17. The lists of remedial cures and benefits include but are not limited to corrective movements in the body, increased endurance and strength, the release of afflictive or painful emotions *(kleśas)*, the cessation of hunger and thirst (*HYP* 1: 32; 2: 55, 58; GS 3: 28), the eradication of deadly diseases (*HYP* 1: 28–29, 31; *GS* 1: 16), balancing the three humours (*dośas*, i.e., bile, phlegm, and wind); eliminating the signs of old age such as deteriorating health, gray hair, and wrinkles (*HYP* 3: 29), radiance (*GS* 1: 18–19), endurance (*SS* 3: 54), the extension of one's lifespan, and the transfiguration of the body (*GS* 3: 4–30; *SS* 4: 25, 28, 41, 51, 56)—also revealing deeper and subtler states of consciousness (*samādhi*).

CHAPTER 9

Muktananda: Entrepreneurial Godman, Tantric Hero

ANDREA R. JAIN

INTRODUCTION

In 1975, a nineteen-year-old living in a small city in Florida spent much of his time experimenting with meditation methods.[1] One day, during meditation, he had a profound vision. The student "saw" himself "sitting under a mountain of shit." And he knew what it meant:

> It was clear that all of this shit came from inside of me, and that in order to reach God, or to become enlightened, or whatever other name that I wanted to give to what it was that I was seeking to attain, that I was somehow going to have to dig my way up through this mountain of filth that covered me. But I also knew that this task was impossible—there was just too much there. There was no way in hell that I could ever hope to dig myself out using my own efforts. (Anonymous Source)

He called out for the help of a guru.

Within a couple of days, he came across a flyer posted on trees throughout the campus of a nearby university. It pictured Swami Muktananda (1908–1982). On it was the message, "Meditate on Yourself. Worship Yourself. God Dwells Within You as You," and a phone number to call for more information. Muktananda was the guru of a growing Hindu movement, Siddha Yoga, based on ideas and practices primarily derived from tantra and promising God-realization through the *kṛpā* or "grace" of the guru. Muktananda was believed to be a *Siddha* or "perfected one" and therefore equivalent to God.

Figure 9.1:
Muktananda. (Courtesy of William Carter.)

But the conception of God in Siddha Yoga was not one of a distant god, far removed from the reach of his worshippers. In fact, the young man was attracted to what he had heard was Muktananda's democratic experiential approach to God—God, according to this guru, was within *everyone*—and the immediate experience of God that the guru allegedly offered. This experience came in the form of *śaktipāt dīkṣā*, or initiation through the descent of *śakti*. *Śaktipāt dīkṣā* is a form of religious initiation through the spontaneous awakening of the previously dormant feminine divine energy believed to reside in all beings (Muller-Ortega, 1997: 426–428; see Goldberg, in this volume). In Siddha Yoga, *śaktipāt* is transmitted by the guru to the devotee in an initiatory ritual involving a look, a touch, or Muktananda's method of choice, a strike on the head with a wand of peacock feathers. Muktananda would deliver *śaktipāt* during Intensives, or choreographed retreats hosted by the guru and his devoted disciples.

The young man needed a guru, and this one was compelling. He scraped together what for him was the steep price of thirty dollars to attend the upcoming Intensive at a suburban home right there in his own city. On the day of the Intensive, he arrived at 8 a.m., paid his thirty dollars, and joined about thirty or forty others sitting on the floor as they awaited the guru's arrival.

After a series of talks by devotees, Muktananda arrived, dressed in his recognizable orange silk and wool ski cap, and addressed the disciples as they eagerly awaited *śaktipāt*. Finally, the time came for the highlight of the Intensive, and Muktananda walked up and down the rows of initiates, striking each on the head with his wand of peacock feathers. The nineteen-year-old describes his *śaktipāt* experience: "My consciousness dramatically shifted inside of me almost immediately after those feathery whacks and the firm, rather intense, pressure of his finger on my forehead. The shift wasn't subtle" (Anonymous Source). This experience forever altered his worldview and life trajectory. He eventually became one of Muktananda's monastic disciples and lived in the guru's Indian ashram for several years until he returned to the United States to earn a Ph.D. in religious studies.

This young man's story raises questions regarding the ways that Muktananda so effectively constructed Siddha Yoga in response to his audiences' desires and needs. How, after all, did a guru from the village of Ganeshpuri in the state of Maharashtra, India, attract a nineteen-year-old American from Florida in the 1970s? I ask and attempt to answer some of those questions by evaluating Muktananda as an entrepreneurial guru who consciously constructed and introduced Siddha Yoga in the 1960s and successfully disseminated it to mass audiences in the 1970s by associating it with his own godman persona as well as spiritual wares that were attractive to large target audiences of late twentieth-century spiritual seekers.

Muktananda's goal was to bring about a *meditation revolution*. He largely succeeded at that in his role as entrepreneurial godman, attracting thousands of people from urban areas across the world to Siddha Yoga. In the last year of his life, however, there were major gaffes in the guru's path toward a meditation revolution. He also played the role of a tantric *vīra* or "hero" who transgressed the normative ethical standards that Siddha Yoga prescribed when he engaged in sexual rituals involving young women and girls. And in that role, he almost destroyed Siddha Yoga. With accusations of improprieties, its popularity declined. Muktananda's persona as the paragon of virtue was key to disciples' uncompromising commitment to the organization. In their attempts to repair damage to its image, Muktananda's successor, Chidvilasananda (b. 1954), and her disciples have adopted a strategy of denial that attempts to maintain the perception of Muktananda as a "perfect" being according to normative standards.[2] The aim in all of this is to continue the mission of their guru to bring about a meditation revolution through the mass dissemination of Siddha Yoga.

MUKTANANDA AS DISCIPLE AND SUCCESSOR

Only when I lost myself in the ecstasy of Nityananda did I realize who he was. He is the nectar of love which arises when everything, sentient and insentient, becomes one.

–Muktananda, Secret of the Siddhas

When evaluating the life of Muktananda, it is difficult to distinguish between the details that are historical and the details that are hagiographic. Muktananda, named Krishna upon his birth in 1908, is believed to have been raised in a wealthy family near the town of Mangalore in the southern Indian state of Karnataka. Stories of his birth and early childhood include a miraculous conception story involving the intervention of a form of Śiva and a vision of Kṛṣṇa (Durgananda, 1997: 25–26). At some point in his early teens, while at school, he had an intimate encounter with the man who would become his guru, Nityananda (d. 1961), when the guru approached the boy in his schoolyard, embraced him, and affectionately stroked his cheek (pp. 26–27). At that moment, Krishna decided that he wanted to become like Nityananda. Six months later, the boy left his home in total secrecy lest his parents thwart his plans. He abandoned his family and belongings. The boy was in pursuit of God.

Krishna spent the early stages of his pursuit alternating between the roles of devoted disciple and mendicant wanderer. Having renounced conventional life, it was not long before he arrived at the town of Hubli in Karnataka, where he encountered the renowned guru and devotee of Śiva Siddharudha Swami. He taught a version of *advaita vedānta* to many monastic disciples at his traditional ashram. Krishna joined them and eventually took full initiation into the Sarasvati Order of renouncers. Upon initiation, he was granted a new name, Muktananda, meaning "bliss of liberation." In 1930, having prepared himself for yet another stage in his pursuit of God, he left Siddharudha's ashram and began a period of wandering by foot during which he made visits to many pilgrimage sites across India and to many gurus, including several visits to Nityananda, the guru who instigated his religious pursuit.

After over a decade of wandering, Muktananda finally settled down at Nityananda's ashram in Ganeshpuri. There, he fully devoted himself to Nityananda. Muktananda considered Nityananda to be God himself according to the vision of God found in *advaita vedānta* and Kashmir Śaivism, a school of tantra. God, according to those systems of thought, underlies all of reality: God is everyone and everything. Muktananda adopted the tantric vision of the union of Śiva, divine masculinity, and Śakti, divine femininity, as a representation of God's transcendence of duality.

So Muktananda envisioned Nityananda as God, but he envisioned all of reality as God. Nityananda was special because in his perfected state—he was believed to be a *Siddha*—he transcended the illusion of duality and achieved permanent direct knowledge of his identification with God. Through devotion to Nityananda, Muktananda sought to also achieve and maintain that perfected state. In the words of one of Muktananda's monastic disciples, Swami Durgananda:

> Muktananda identified his guru's enlightened consciousness with the pure consciousness that Vedanta calls Brahman, the source and substratum of the universe. Therefore, when he identified himself with his guru, when he meditated on his guru, he experienced not a merging into a separate person but a merging into his own higher consciousness. (Durgananda, 1997: 35)

In addition to the philosophical nondualist dimension of Muktananda's religiosity, there was also a practical nondualist dimension called *kuṇḍalinī* yoga. The Sanskrit term *kuṇḍalinī*, derived from the term *kuṇḍala* or "to coil," is used in tantric literature to refer to the divine feminine energy, *śakti*, that lies dormant, coiled like a serpent located at the base of the human spine, in the subtle body. The *kuṇḍalinī's* sleep represents the ignorance of most beings, as they reside in the illusion of duality. Once *kuṇḍalinī* is awakened, she rises through the subtle body along the spine, successively penetrating energy centers, as she gets closer and closer to the top of the head. There, she penetrates the highest center where divine masculinity, Śiva, resides. Here, their union within the individual represents the same transcendence of duality that exists within God. When the tantric hero or heroine achieves this inner state, he or she experiences total bliss and awakens to the identification of *ātman*, the individual self, with *Brahman*, the God who underlies all of reality.

Kuṇḍalinī yoga comprises a complex *sādhanā* or system of practical techniques. Though some tantric traditions prescribe practices that are consistent with normative ethics of behavior, including postures, breathing exercises, chanting, *bhakti* or devotion, and meditation, other tantric traditions also prescribe transgressive techniques meant to jolt the practitioner out of dualist thinking, which is believed to be perpetuated by normative social guidelines. Some tantric traditions, for example, prescribe various sexual rituals whereby intercourse serves to represent nonduality and to arouse *kuṇḍalinī*. In Siddha Yoga, meditation is preeminent, and none of the Siddha Yoga gurus have ever publicly prescribed transgressive rituals, though, as I will discuss, such rituals played a role—albeit a secret one—in the last year of Muktananda's life.

According to Siddha Yoga, *kuṇḍalinī* yoga is often initiated by a guru through the bestowal of *śaktipāt dīkṣā*. Paul E. Muller-Ortega (1997: 409) describes the function of that initiation:

> When the essential, enlightened consciousness of the *sadguru* [true guru] enters the disciple, shaktipat occurs. And it is thought to destroy the root or foundational impurity of spiritual ignorance. In this way, shaktipat ignites the fire that will culminate in the achievement of liberation and enlightenment.

For Muktananda (1994b: 12), "the grace of the Guru" is *śaktipāt*. On August 15, 1947, he received that grace from his guru, Nityananda. Muktananda (2000: 74) describes the experience:

> A ray of light was coming from his pupils, and going right inside me. Its touch was searing, red hot, and its brilliance dazzled my eyes like a high-powered bulb. As this ray flowed from Bhagavan Nityananda's eyes into my own, the very hair on my body rose in wonder, awe, ecstasy and fear. I went on repeating his mantra Guru Om, watching the colors of this ray. It was an unbroken stream of divine radiance. Sometimes it was the color of molten gold, sometimes saffron, sometimes a deep blue, more lustrous than a shining star. I stood there, stunned, watching the brilliant rays passing into me.

Muktananda's "vision shifted" as he began to perceive "the presence of god in everything" (Durgananda, 1997: 36). Though this initial enlightenment was fleeting, Muktananda spent the next nine years slowly and painfully working toward the permanent awareness of nonduality and the unitive God who underlies all of reality until he finally attained that perfect state and thus became a *Siddha*.

Nityananda immediately acknowledged that Muktananda had achieved that perfect state. And as his *mahāsamādhi* (i.e., his physical death) neared, he publicly and privately acknowledged Muktananda as his successor (Durgananda, 1997: 42). First, after his disciples built a temple in which to worship God once their guru was gone, Nityananda told them to install Muktananda as the God to worship there. Many of his disciples considered this Nityananda's public acknowledgment that Muktananda was his successor (ibid.). Then, according to Muktananda's account, while Nityananda lay on his deathbed in 1961, in a secret encounter between guru and disciple, the guru thrust his hand down Muktananda's throat, transferring the lineage to him (pp. 47–48).[3]

Following Nityananda's death, Muktananda laid the foundations for a movement that would eventually go global at his ashram, the Shree Gurudev Ashram (later renamed Gurudev Siddha Peeth) in Ganeshpuri. He came to refer to his teachings as *Siddha Yoga*.

MUKTANANDA AS ENTREPRENEURIAL GODMAN

Today, with my Guru's command and grace, I am going away from India for some time. Owing to our limited vision, we consider various countries as different. For God, all countries are His and all beings are His. In God's house there is no particular region or sect or faith. To Him all are the same. I am going abroad to initiate a revolution, a meditation revolution.

–Muktananda, February 26, 1974, to a crowd of thousands of people at Bombay's Santa Cruz Airport

Scholars have suggested that we consider Siddha Yoga an example of the transplantation of a religious movement from the Indian context to the Euro-American one where it underwent a number of assimilative processes (Caldwell, 2001; Williamson, 2005: 149). Siddha Yoga, however, began to take form long before its dissemination beyond India. It did not develop in response to transplantation or as a result of cultural negotiations between a static Indian culture and a static Euro-American one. It was, in fact, a movement that developed in response to transnational cultural developments.

By the 1960s, urban areas across the world had assimilated to an emergent transnational culture that featured a consumer-oriented approach to worldviews and practices as individuals chose from a variety of such to construct individual lifestyles. *Godmen* (and *godwomen*), defined by C. J. Fuller (2004: 177–81) as contemporary ascetic figures who find fame within and sometimes beyond India and are revered and worshiped as divine, were in particularly high demand in the global spiritual market.[4] Fuller's case studies of late twentieth-century popular gurus suggest that the rise in demand for godmen illustrates how devotional traditions adapt to sociological change (Kakar, 1983; Swallow, 1982; Babb 1986; Fuller, 2004; Gombrich & Obeyesekere, 1988). Such studies suggest that the godmen appealed to contemporary urban middle-class and wealthy individuals who felt threatened by social environments that they no longer controlled in the face of globalization and other modern social processes (Kakar, 1983; Swallow, 1982). Godmen broke into the competitive spiritual market with wares that they prescribed as solutions to the perceived problems of excess and chaos associated with modern life (Swallow, 1982; Kakar, 1983: 191–92). They also provided group identity to otherwise uprooted individuals along with a reenchantment or remystification of the world through what were believed to be their divinity and miracles (Babb, 1987; Gombrich & Obeyesekere, 1988).

Indian godmen first responded to the growing demand by marketing themselves and their products to the masses throughout India. In 1960s India, Muktananda lived as a guru more akin to a modern entrepreneurial godman than to a traditional guru, such as Nityananda.[5] He adopted a godman persona and an exoteric dispensation. Selecting from the teachings of Nityananda and from *vedānta* and Kashmir Śaivism, he consciously constructed a unique persona and set of tantric spiritual commodities that he packaged as *Siddha Yoga.*

Muktananda introduced Siddha Yoga to disciples at his ashram, Shree Gurudev Ashram, in Ganeshpuri. The ashram came to resemble a European- or American-style retreat center more than a traditional, bare ashram and hosted large numbers of disciples from around the world. Disciples visiting or living at the ashram could choose the extent of their commitment to Siddha Yoga. Choices ranged from becoming a fully initiated monastic member of Muktananda's community where Siddha Yoga functioned as an all-encompassing worldview and system of practice, to incorporating it into one's spiritual repertoire as one part of an eclectic path toward God- or self-realization. Peter Brent (1972: 236) describes the ambiance of Muktananda's ashram prior to the guru's world travels:

> The ashram stands in some seventy acres of its own ground. The forecourt is backed by the main building where the offices and the audience hall are. Above and to the left, in a newer building, are the apartment of Swami Muktananda and the women's quarters. Behind this there are gardens, splendid with bougainvilia [*sic*], and a caged white peacock named Moti. To the left of the first, walled garden is a cluster of buildings and courtyards—the halls where men and women eat, the kitchens, a new guest house still under construction and so on—while in the main garden, mostly scattered about a water tower to the right, stand the chambers and dormitories where male visitors or those permanently on the ashram sleep, their washrooms and lavatories, stone benches for their occasional relaxation. A narrow double door in the back wall of this garden leads to a causeway which divides two patchwork stretches of small paddy fields. Beyond, on a low hill, there stand a cluster of well appointed bungalows and the marble lined meditation hall. This last is bare, very still; there is no motion in its air, sounds die within its walls. Its marble floor gleams faintly. A picture of Swami Nityananda dominates it, and others of him line the walls. The hill is quiet, bright with sunshine and bougainvilia [*sic*]. There are low, spear leaved guava trees . . . on the slopes, two or three of the ashram's Westerners work at some improving task—improving for them; it seems to have no value in itself. Outside the bungalows, long chairs stand on the terraces, prepared for the comfortable conversation of the faithful.

Though contact with Muktananda still required substantial effort, since disciples had to travel to Ganeshpuri to meet him in the isolated context of the Shree Gurudev Ashram, Muktananda reached out to them by consciously creating a space that would be attractive to a wide range of Indian, European, and American disciples. As the Shree Gurudev Ashram Trust, which has administered the financial and legal affairs of the ashram since 1962, accumulated funds, the ashram continued to grow. Since Brent's visit to the ashram, the trust has added an open-air pavilion capable of holding hundreds of people at a time, additional housing, classrooms, large auditoriums, and several dining facilities.

Muktananda also reached out to disciples by encouraging an exoteric discourse about the transformative experiences triggered by initiation into Siddha Yoga. He functioned as a model of that discourse by publicly sharing his own experiences. Siddha Yoga was one among many types of yoga available in the spiritual marketplace, so the accessibility of testimonials about its effectiveness could serve to attract disciples as they shopped around and calculated the pros and cons of the various gurus and spiritual wares available to them. The discourse was dominated—and continues to be dominated today—by testimonials of *śaktipāt*, that exoteric initiatory ritual that the guru, in this early period of Siddha Yoga's history, delivered to his disciples one at a time.

The global market for spiritual goods required marketers to calculate the costs for products associated with unpopular ideas or practices, so, in his efforts to reach out to large audiences, Muktananda publicly embraced the exoteric, popular dimensions of tantra (e.g., devotion and meditation) rather than the esoteric, antinomian dimensions (e.g., the use of intoxicants or sexual rituals) that required the practitioner to deliberately violate normative ethical and purity standards for the sake of awakening to the reality of nonduality.[6] In short, Siddha Yoga was the product of a process of carefully selecting from tantra and *vedānta* as well as contemporary dominant ethical standards for marketability. For example, Muktananda selected from tantric scriptural sources, embracing exoteric dimensions while eschewing esoteric, antinomian ones. Describing Muktananda and his successor Chidvilasananda's use of one tantric scripture, the *Kulārṇava Tantra*, which includes certain left-hand elements, Brooks (1997: 334) adds that they "cite frequently *but selectively*," since "ethical preconditions create criteria that inform the Siddha Yoga guru's scriptural choices."

Muktananda also chose the dominant normative ethical standards of late twentieth-century urban environments where democratic religious ideals prevailed. Theoretically, Siddha Yoga was a democratic movement. Although the disciple relied on the grace of the guru, all individuals were equally dependent in this way. Furthermore, all individuals had equal access to Siddha Yoga teachings and practices, were required to perform right actions out of self-effort, and were viewed as having God within them.[7] Muktananda thus argued that Siddha Yoga stood out from traditional or "orthodox" yoga systems. The following excerpt from one of Muktananda's published books succinctly captures the guru's general attitude about the democratic nature of the practice:

> Our time is different from the orthodox era when certain people were prohibited from studying the scriptures . . . recently, the sage Dayananda broke the bonds of the orthodox attitude toward women and people of lower caste . . . It is obvious that the orthodox restrictions are not applied in Siddha Yoga Dham; everyone chants the *Rudram*, which is a portion of the *Rig Veda*. Everyone should read and understand the scriptures. By performing good actions, a person should make himself a pure temple of God and worship the Lord of the Self within. (Muktananda, 1985: 189)

In the 1970s, Muktananda's active steps toward the mass dispensation of Siddha Yoga expanded to other parts of the world, especially to the United States. As Muller-Ortega (1997: 410) articulates, this move toward making *śaktipāt* readily accessible to a global audience was radical:

> Because of shaktipat's historical rarity and relative unavailability, the notion that Swami Muktananda should have made shaktipat attainable on a wide scale around the world is quite noteworthy. After many centuries of barely being available even in India, its sudden and relatively easy accessibility marks an unprecedented and significant historical shift. It is only when we fathom the rarity of what Swami Muktananda professed to be offering to the world that we can begin to appreciate the boldness and genius of his decision to bring shaktipat out of its millennial obscurity.

The timing was ideal. Although legal restrictions had made twentieth-century immigration from India to the United States and Europe rare, they were lifted in the 1960s, leading to an influx of Indian residents to the United States, Britain, and France. The 1960s also witnessed the British–American counterculture, which called for a religiosity radically distinct from what was perceived as the oppressive, puritanical orthodoxies of the previous generation. Many participants in the counterculture eagerly looked to Indian gurus for religious insights and techniques. For these reasons, yoga had become a popular product desired for its perceived ability to improve everyday life as well as for its soteriological benefits.

All of these variables had everything to do with the timing of Muktananda's world tours, which involved three trips: one in 1970; one from 1974 to 1976; and one from 1978 to 1981. The very method through which people learned Siddha Yoga changed when, instead of relying on one-on-one transmission through the traditional guru–disciple relationship in the isolated context of the guru's ashram, Muktananda went out in search of disciples, actively marketing Siddha Yoga, which was now immediately accessible to vast numbers of spiritual seekers. In 1970, he began his mission. By 1974, he was confident that his dissemination would instigate a global meditation revolution and thus that this practice would survive and even grow long after his death.

Figure 9.2:
Muktananda. (Courtesy of Prem Chadha.)

Accessibility also increased when Muktananda first introduced the Intensive in 1974, making the bestowal of *śaktipāt* to hundreds—and today, thousands—of people at a time efficient, cost-effective, and available for immediate consumption.[8] Making *śaktipāt* readily accessible in this way was a key step in developing Siddha Yoga as a global movement. To be initiated, all the individual had to do was drop out of conventional life for a couple of days and drop in to an Intensive, hosted in their own city. Unlike the usual modes of initiation in tantric traditions in which disciples often had to permanently renounce established forms of life and adopt a systematic program of preparation for initiation into the esoteric core of the tradition, Muktananda's bestowal of *śaktipāt* was available to the masses for immediate consumption, and the guru dispensed it independent of the extent of individuals' commitment to the movement.

As Siddha Yoga's practitioners suggest, many individuals, however, did make extensive, long-term commitments to the practice. Siddha Yoga provided a remystification of the world. Spiritual seekers associated Siddha Yoga with Muktananda, who was perceived as a *Siddha*, an enlightened master, and with *śaktipāt*, which involved an experience of nothing less than God.

Through Siddha Yoga, individuals realized that God was *them*. Return to the young man from Florida and consider his description of his profound insight as he received *śaktipāt* at an Intensive in 1975:

> Then, at last, I almost jumped when the peacock feathers, firmly but with a soft weightiness, hit me repeatedly on my head, and then gently brushed my face as Swamiji, with a quiet rumbling in the back of his throat, powerfully pressed one of his fingers into my forehead, at a spot located just between my eyebrows . . . Here's where I feel like I need to begin to step very carefully. I'm honestly somewhat reluctant to write about what happened next because I know that whatever I say will inevitably diminish it, will make it sound as if it were just another "powerful experience." This was not an experience. This was THE event of my spiritual life. This was full awakening. This wasn't "knowing" anything, because you only know something that is separate from you. This was being: the Ultimate—a fountain of Light, a dancing, ever-new Source. Utter freedom, utter joy, swirling with unfettered delight at the center of it all, the Heart of the cosmos, pouring out everything from my own Self, yet always having More. Completely fulfilled, completely whole, no limits to my power and love and light. The Lord of the Universe. This was my true nature. Eternally. Always. I never have been anything different than this, ever, not even in a dream. Not even when I forget. (Anonymous Source)

Muktananda transformed the world of his disciples not only through *śaktipāt* but also through the transfer of (if not always direct) contact with his powerful persona. Muktananda was the paragon of virtue, the transmitter of power and knowledge, and the perfected master. Publicly, he held himself to standards beyond that of ordinary individuals, arguing that "the Guru should possess every virtue . . . He cannot be a true Guru if he engages in business, in different material pursuits or therapies . . . or if he indulges in sense pleasures. A disciple who discovers such behavior in a guru can only benefit by considering him a worm of bad conduct and rejecting him" (Muktananda, 1985: 10). In another context, he asserts:

> Just as we expect a disciple to be high and ideal, we should expect a Guru to be high and ideal. The Guru should have the power to cause an inner awakening in his disciple. He should be well versed in all the scriptures, he should be able . . . to transmit knowledge directly. He should have extraordinary skill in instructing his disciples. This is what a true Guru is like. (Muktananda, 1994a: 371)

Muktananda was considered the perfect model of what all disciples strove to be, especially for monastic disciples, who were expected to be celibate and to perfectly conform to rigorous standards of ethical behavior.

Disciples were drawn to this model of perfection. One disciple actually resorts to gravitational metaphors to describe the disciple's relationship to Muktananda:

> The concept of the relationship between Guru and shishya is that of gravitation, in which the larger body attracts the smaller one. With that gravitational pull, the Guru draws you towards him. When we go a little further, we find that we don't know the nature of this gravitation, how and why it works; we know in what manner gravitation works, but why we do not. (Brent, 1972: 237)

Disciples were drawn to Muktananda, yet for most of them direct contact with him was rare. This was increasingly the case as the movement grew. As we saw already, Muktananda was invested in the growth and stability of Siddha Yoga. Perhaps most importantly, he supported the establishment of Siddha Yoga centers that would provide a sense of group identity to uprooted individuals who could not regularly interact with him. The young man referred to in the introduction describes his first encounter with the Siddha Yoga community at a center in his small city in Florida:

> As I ambled around the house a bit, I was immediately struck by the love and energy that I felt in his devotees' eyes. His disciples were just so enlivened and plugged in as they bustled around the house preparing for his visit. And their energy was infectious: before I knew it, I found myself out front mowing the lawn, loving every minute of what, in another context, might have simply been a chore. (Anonymous Source)

In 1975, Muktananda took a number of additional steps toward fortifying Siddha Yoga, including establishing the Siddha Yoga Dham Associates (SYDA) Foundation in South Fallsburg, New York, which was responsible for the financial and organizational structure of the practice outside of India. Organizational developments also included the introduction of courses and teacher training programs as well as the establishment of departments for the publication of Siddha Yoga books. Durgananda (1997: 95) describes the consequences of such developments:

> The birth of SYDA Foundation marked a major organizational shift from a system in which most ashram decisions were referred directly to Swami Muktananda, to a departmental system with regulated channels of communication. The Siddha Yoga centers, which had to date been independent and as idiosyncratic as each individual who ran them, also fell under the governance of SYDA Foundation, which began now to set up standards, structures, and systems of accountability for the dissemination of teachings.

All of this was possible because Muktananda was willing to give chosen disciples power in the Siddha Yoga movement.

Benton Johnson (1992: S12) explains that a founder of a religious movement who facilitates its *routinization* by giving selected disciples the power to meet the "material needs of the movement" enables its survival. Such leaders "are like entrepreneurs with novel products and bold visions who turn out also to be accomplished chief executive officers of an expanding firm" (p. S8). By establishing the SYDA and granting his disciples the power to establish Siddha Yoga centers so that it could build and spread, Muktananda facilitated the establishment of a normative structure that met the economic and other practical needs of the movement as a whole. In this way, Muktananda was like other popular yoga gurus of his time, such as Maharishi Mahesh Yogi, founder of Transcendental Meditation, who "attended to the long-term advancement of his movement in a calculating manner" (ibid.).

Muktananda marketed Siddha Yoga, which signified a virtuous life, a remystification of the world, and a strong sense of belonging to an organized community. And he made initiation into the Siddha Yoga life readily accessible in the form of *śaktipāt*, conveniently delivered by means of the Intensive, where up to hundreds of people at a time could have direct contact with the godman himself. In these ways, Muktananda created for his disciples what Sarah Caldwell (2001: 17), scholar and former Siddha Yoga disciple, describes as "the blissful, perfect, ordered life of utter dependency and spiritual bliss." Siddha Yoga, unsurprisingly, was in high demand. By the time of Muktananda's death in 1982, Siddha Yoga ashrams and centers had been established in India, the United States, Europe, Canada, and Australia.

MUKTANANDA AS TANTRIC HERO

I began to realize that it was Tantra that spoke of the awakening of the Kundalinī energy; of opening the chakras, of Shaktipat. While in Dada's [Muktananda's] yoga it appeared that most of the relationship with sexual energy happened symbolically rather than literally (there weren't any sexual orgies going on in the ashram, as far as I could tell), but still, it was clear to me that there was an overt acknowledgment on this path that sexuality was powerful, and that if it was transmuted, that it could become a type of spiritual "rocket fuel" that could provide tremendous energy to a person's spiritual blastoff into the transcendent stratosphere of Self-Realization.

–The young disciple from Florida on his sense that sex played a powerful, though symbolic, role in Siddha Yoga prior to the public revelations concerning Muktananda's secret and literal sex life

Following Muktananda's death, the "blissful, perfect, ordered life" of Siddha Yoga fell apart. Caldwell (2001: 28) describes the state of the movement:

> After Baba's [Muktananda's] death, chaos reigned in the ashram. Sexual scandals broke out everywhere. All discipline broke down. George Afif, a close devotee of Baba, and an intimate of Swami Chidvilasananda in the years following Muktananda's death, was accused of raping a 16-year-old girl; Swami Nityananda, one of Baba's two successors, was deposed in 1986 due to charges of sexual misconduct. Swamis (including some of my close friends) were leaving right and left to marry their girlfriends. Others, feeling that they were following Baba's lead, experimented openly with sex while living in the ashram. Passion had swept everyone away. Baba had unleashed a tide and was no longer there to control it. It was a dark time.

The Siddha Yoga movement was at risk.

These events following Muktananda's death were actually set in motion by Muktananda's own choice toward the end of his life to embrace certain esoteric tantric dimensions of yoga that were not previously a part of his public persona. Of course, proponents of Siddha Yoga insist that the movement is free of the deliberate transgression of normative ethical behavior (Brooks, 1997a: 327). The Siddha Yoga guru is no exception:

> What is a *siddha* guru, according to Siddha Yoga, and how are we to understand the experience of spiritual awakening that empowers the guru to act as he or she does? Suffice to say for now that Siddha Yoga is not a convention-defying path that eschews the ethical standards of the world nor is it one that *relies on* a double standard for guru and disciple. Again, this is not to say that the *same* standards apply to guru and disciple, but only that there is no deliberate effort to abuse the notion of having standards in order to assert the siddha's perfect freedom. (Brooks, 1997b: xxxvi)

Evidence suggests, however, that Siddha Yoga has not, in fact, been free of deliberate "convention-defying" practices. In the last year or so of his life, Muktananda engaged in secret sexual rituals with several of his young female disciples—some of whom were teenagers—that were meant to transmit *śakti* to the tantric hero. Evidence also suggests that Muktananda's guru, Nityananda, spent part of his early life in the South Indian ashram of a tantric guru, Śivananda, known for his engagement in esoteric sexual rituals (Caldwell, 2001: 22). It is likely, therefore, that Muktananda had been initiated into the path of the tantric hero at some point in his career as Nityananda's disciple and that he embraced that path in the last year or so of his life.

Based on the testimonials of women who participated in Muktananda's sexual rituals, Caldwell (2001: 25) argues that Muktananda "revered" the esoteric tantric path "as the innermost core of his power." Although he prescribed yoga practices for his disciples that were compatible with the normative ethics of the general populace, Muktananda considered himself a perfected master who could "move effortlessly among all forms of Tantric *sādhana*, picking from regimes of austere discipline, ecstatic devotion, formless direct perception of the absolute, and sexual intercourse with young women in his ashram, like so many items at a banquet" (p. 35).

With regard to the development of new religious movements, Johnson (1992: 6) suggests that, as a movement increasingly depends on disciples to function as mediators to the public, the founder of a religion can become increasingly "insulated from the corrective strictures of ordinary life." A tripartite differentiation emerges among the world of ordinary members, the world of advanced disciples "to whom the founder delegates the chores of keeping the movement going," and the world of the founder and his most intimate circle (ibid.). This differentiation poses a problem for the movement's survival. Johnson explains: "A closed, cocoon-like environment such as this gives a pampered leader free rein to entertain all sorts of ideas and indulge all sorts of wishes with apparent impunity . . . In a protected environment a leader can set events in motion that would be shocking to the membership if discovered or could jeopardize the movement's very existence" (ibid.). This is exactly what happened to Muktananda, and the events he set in motion damaged the very image of the Siddha Yoga movement that he had worked so hard to fortify, causing many disciples to abandon it entirely.

Certain dimensions of tantra are esoteric. In both the premodern and the modern periods, esoteric rituals violated the ethical standards of normative society, though for different reasons. In premodern India, tantric ritualists kept secret what they knew would offend *brahmanic* orthodoxy's standards of purity. In the modern period, Muktananda kept secret what he knew would offend the modern, urban, democratic idealists to whom he marketed, primarily because of what would be perceived as the exploitation of women and girls.

Disciples who remained committed to Siddha Yoga following Muktananda's death could not denounce Muktananda if the movement was to survive and thrive. After all, Muktananda's persona was a significant part of what made it so desirable. As Johnson (1992: 11) argues, "The more solidly established the founder's claim to unique spiritual authority the harder it will be to form the coalition needed to carry out an expulsion, and the harder it will be to legitimate the dirty deed in the eyes of the members." Muktananda had established his claim to authority. Disciples of Siddha Yoga, therefore, did not denounce Muktananda, but they did not legitimate his transgressive actions either. Rather, they simply adopted a strategy of denial, as explained in the following two examples.

The first example is drawn from the actions of Chidvilasananda, the current Siddha Yoga guru. In 1985, she denounced and deposed Muktananda's other successor, who was also her brother, Nityananda (b. 1962), for allegedly participating in antinomian sexual rituals. Chidvilasananda publicly described how she punished Nityananda for his behavior, allowing the women he exploited to slap him with a stick (Caldwell, 2001: 28). Other witness accounts claimed that he was beaten until he was black and blue and could hardly move (p. 29). By focusing her denunciation and even violent punishment on Nityananda, Chidvilasananda, albeit in a convoluted fashion, asserted the normative ethical standards upheld by Siddha Yoga by denouncing sexual transgressions in general while simultaneously ignoring those that were a part of Muktananda's religious life. In short, she made Nityananda into an expedient scapegoat.

The second example of the Siddha Yoga strategy of denial is drawn from the collective project of six disciples, who in 1997 contributed to an edited volume on the history and theology of Siddha Yoga called *Meditation Revolution: A History and Theology of the Siddha Yoga Lineage*. The text ignores the part of Siddha Yoga's history involving Muktananda's sexual transgressions. In a review essay evaluating books on Hindu gurus in North America, Jeffrey J. Kripal (1999: 236) makes the following assessment of *Meditation Revolution*:

> My overwhelming impression while reading this massive volume was that I was not so much reading a critical treatment of the history of the movement as I was witnessing the actual construction of that history; that I was witnessing not a discussion about canon but the actual formation of a canon; that I was encountering not a group of scholars writing about shaktipat and *kuṇḍalinī-yoga* but a group of colleagues who had actually experienced the awakened energies of this "descent of power" and were now offering their testimonies "from within" that gnoseological or Gnostic perspective (even though none of them actually discuss their own experiences); and finally, that this is not a historical-critical book about the Siddha Yoga lineage at all—it is a scholarly legitimation, systematization, and canonization of the Siddha Yoga lineage, the tradition made text . . . None of this, of course, would be a problem if the authors did not explicitly present themselves as historians of religions and their essays as acts of both scholarship and devotion, thus leaving readers who are scholars but not devotees feeling very uncomfortable with the tones and—more importantly—with the silences of their texts.

Caldwell (2001: 34) adds that the denial of Muktananda's sexual exploits in *Meditation Revolution* replicates the "dissimulation" that has always been key to tantra.

As both Kripal (1999) and Caldwell (2001) point out, it is not surprising that Siddha Yoga disciples would write about the movement and its gurus in favorable ways and would consciously ignore details that might damage the organization's image. Religious literature is filled with hagiographies that situate important figures within what is perceived as an authentic, legitimate tradition and ignore historical material that would suggest otherwise. Surprisingly, however, five of the six authors of *Meditation Revolution* are accomplished scholars who are otherwise committed to the historical-critical method of scholarship and, in its Forward, are described as "sophisticated and critical scholars" who contributed to a hagiographic account of Muktananda's life and an apologetic account of Siddha Yoga theology. What this suggests is that, for these Siddha Yoga disciples, the need to manage its public image takes precedence over a historical-critical account of the movement.

CONCLUSION

Muktananda was an entrepreneurial godman who constructed and marketed a set of spiritual wares as well as his own persona under the name *Siddha Yoga*. The guru pursued the global dissemination of Siddha Yoga as the demand for yoga exploded in the increasingly competitive global market.

Numerous late twentieth-century events were significant portents of Siddha Yoga's success. Muktananda introduced it to the world as an ideological and practical movement that, especially for disillusioned urban dwellers and countercultural participants who rejected their inherited orthodoxies, could resolve feelings of chaos and displacement and, most importantly, reenchant an otherwise disenchanted world. He made Siddha Yoga especially marketable to spiritual seekers by packaging it in the easily accessible and immediately consumable forms of the Intensive and *śaktipāt*. Furthermore, the very method through which people adopted Siddha Yoga changed when, instead of relying on transmission through the traditional guru–disciple relationship in the context of an ashram, Muktananda left his ashram, traveled to urban areas across the world, and actively marketed Siddha Yoga to mass audiences.

Reaching out to the masses in urban areas across the world, Muktananda succeeded in attracting thousands of spiritual seekers to Siddha Yoga. His successor, Chidvilasananda, inherited her guru's innovative and ambitious entrepreneurial style and continues to market Siddha Yoga to the masses to this day. Though revelation about Muktananda's esoteric sexual practices in the last year of his life significantly damaged Siddha Yoga's public image, the movement has survived. Because of Muktananda's end-of-life transgressions and the relationship of his persona to Siddha Yoga's image, strategies of denial, meant to maintain the vision of Muktananda as a paragon of virtue according to normative standards of ethical behavior, have been put in place since Muktananda's death to maintain its place as a viable option in the mass market for spiritual wares.

REFERENCES

Babb, Lawrence A. 1987. *Redemptive Encounters: Three Modern Styles in the Hindu Tradition*. New Delhi: Oxford University Press.

Brent, Peter. 1972. *Godmen of India*. New York: Quadrangle Books.

Brooks, Douglas Renfrew. 1997a. The Canons of Siddha Yoga: The Body of Scripture and the Form of the Guru. In Douglas Renfrew Brooks, Swami Durgananda, Paul E. Muller-Ortega, William K. Mahony, Constantina Rhodes Bailly, and S.P. Sabharathnam (eds.), *Meditation Revolutions: A History and Theology of the Siddha Yoga Lineage*. South Fallsburg, NY: Agama Press, pp. 277–346.

———. 1997b. Introduction. In Douglas Renfrew Brooks, Swami Durgananda, Paul E. Muller-Ortega, William K. Mahony, Constantina Rhodes Bailly, and S.P. Sabharathnam (eds.), *Meditation Revolutions: A History and Theology of the Siddha Yoga Lineage*. South Fallsburg, NY: Agama Press, pp. xix–l.

Caldwell, Sarah. 2001. The Heart of the Secret: A Personal and Scholarly Encounter with Shakta Tantrism in Siddha Yoga. *Nova Religio: The Journal of Alternative and Emergent Religions* 5(1): 9–51.

Durgananda, Swami. 1997. To See the World Full of Saints: The History of Siddha Yoga as a Contemporary Movement. In Douglas Renfrew Brooks, Swami Durgananda, Paul E. Muller-Ortega, William K. Mahony, Constantina Rhodes Bailly, and S.P. Sabharathnam (eds.), *Meditation Revolutions: A History and Theology of the Siddha Yoga Lineage*. South Fallsburg, NY: Agama Press, pp. 3–161.

Fuller, C.J. 2004. *The Camphor Flame: Popular Hinduism and Society in India*, Revised and Expanded Edition. Princeton, NJ: Princeton University Press.

Gombrich, Richard and Gananath Obeyesekere. 1988. *Buddhism Transformed: Religious Change in Sri Lanka*. Princeton, NJ: Princeton University Press.

Johnson, Benton. 1992. On Founders and Followers: Some Factors in the Development of New Religious Movements. *Sociological Analysis* 53(S): S1–S13.

Kakar, Sudhir. 1983. *Shamans, Mystics and Doctors: A Psychological Inquiry into India and its Healing Traditions*. Boston: Beacon Press.

Kripal, Jeffrey J. 1999. Inside-Out, Outside-In. Existential Place and Academic Practice in the Study of North American Guru-Traditions. *Religious Studies Review* 24(3): 233–238.

Muktananda, Swami. 1985. *The Perfect Relationship: The Guru and the Disciple*. South Fallsburg, NY: SYDA Foundation.

———. 1994a. *From the Finite to the Infinite*. South Fallsburg, NY: SYDA Foundation.

———. 1994b. *Light on the Path*. South Fallsburg, NY: SYDA Foundation.

———. 2000. *Play of Consciousness*, 3rd ed. South Fallsburg, NY: SYDA Foundation.

Muller-Ortega, Paul E. 1997. Shaktipat: The Initiatory Descent of Power. In Douglas Renfrew Brooks, Swami Durgananda, Paul E. Muller-Ortega, William K. Mahony, Constantina Rhodes Bailly, and S.P. Sabharathnam (eds.), *Meditation Revolutions: A History and Theology of the Siddha Yoga Lineage*. South Fallsburg, NY: Agama Press, pp. 407–444.

Swallow, Deborah A. 1982. Ashes and Powers: Myth, Rite and Miracle in an Indian God-man's Cult. *Modern Asian Studies*16: 123–158.

White, David Gordon. 1999. Tantric Sects and Tantric Sex: The Flow of Secret Tantric Gnosis. In Elliot R. Wolfson (ed.), *Rending the Veil: Concealment and Secrecy in the History of Religions*. New York: Seven Bridges Press, pp. 249–270.

Williamson, Lola. 2005. The Perfectibility of Perfection: Siddha Yoga as a Global Movement. In Thomas A. Forsthoefel and Cynthia Ann Humes (eds.), *Gurus in America*. New York: State University of New York Press, pp. 147–167.

NOTES

1. The account of the young man from Florida, which I will return to in other parts of this chapter, is taken from an anonymous source to whom I am indebted and express my tremendous gratitude. I chose to draw from this particular account by one of Muktananda's disciples rather than that of other former disciples who have written openly and publicly on their experiences with Siddha Yoga because I think it best conveys the truly transformative and enriching power of Muktananda. I want to convey these aspects of the guru's power while simultaneously accounting for various sociological dimensions of Siddha Yoga's success. I am confident that the contrast between the academic voices in this chapter and the voice of this account does just that. I am also confident that I am getting closer to the truth of who Muktananda was as a guru by citing an account that conveys the profoundly positive effects he had on many of his disciples.
2. Among disciples, Chidvilasananda is also affectionately known as *Gurumayi*, which means "Guru Mother" in Marathi or "one who is filled with the guru" in Sanskrit. Durgananda, "To See the World Full of Saints," note 247.
3. Durgananada quotes the 1980 interview with religious writer Lex Hixon (1941–1995) in which Muktananda recalled the experience.
4. Fuller was not the first scholar to use *godmen* in reference to South Asian guru figures. Peter Brent uses it in an earlier text, *Godmen of India* (1972).
5. Brent (1972: 230–282) includes an account of Muktananda as godman prior to his first world tour.
6. Caldwell (2001: 25) suggests that Muktananda's selective strategy is analogous to what David Gordon White calls the dissembling strategy of Abhinavagupta, the medieval Kashmiri Shaiva who reformulated the tantric Kula tradition. Abhinavagupta relegated the transgressive dimensions of the Kula tradition to secrecy to win over the "hearts and minds of the general Kashmiri populace" (White, 1999: 255).
7. Theoretically, Siddha Yoga was democratic in these ways, but, beginning in 1974, initiates had to pay for admission to an Intensive where they would receive *śaktipāt*, thus making *śaktipāt* inaccessible to those who could not afford the price of admission.
8. The current Siddha Yoga guru, Chidvilasananda, makes *śaktipāt* and Siddha Yoga celebrations available to thousands at a time via webcasts.

CHAPTER 10

Stretching toward the Sacred: John Friend and Anusara Yoga

LOLA WILLIAMSON

PROLOGUE

Research for this chapter was conducted in 2010 and 2011. During the final editing stage in February 2012, a scandal surfaced about John Friend that involved several allegations, including questionable financial practices, sexual relations with several married female employees (through a Wiccan coven), use of marijuana, as well as the placement of employees in legal jeopardy by having them unknowingly transport marijuana. On March 20, 2012, Friend wrote a letter of apology to the community of Anusara Yoga practitioners in which he stated that he took full responsibility for "being out of integrity" in intimate relationships with married women. Other allegations were dismissed as being untrue (although he did not address the issue of using marijuana). The consequences of Friend's behavior are still surfacing. At present, a new structure without Friend's leadership is being developed: the organization may survive the crisis. The present chapter should be viewed as a snapshot in time, during which Anusara was at a peak. The juxtaposition of this prologue with direct quotes within the chapter will likely elicit a sense of irony for the reader. I would like to offer one observation: witnessing the devastation felt by many followers of the Anusara path, it appears that Friend played a stronger "guru role" than I present in this chapter.[1]

INTRODUCTION

We physicalize virtue.

— John Friend

John Friend launched his unique style of yoga, Anusara, in 1997.[2] Now, fourteen years later, it is one of the fastest-growing forms of *haṭhayoga* in North America and is rapidly expanding on a global scale as well. Anusara Yoga is experienced variously by different people, depending on their level of involvement. For practitioners who take a weekly class at a local studio, it may be simply a technique for toning muscles and relaxing the mind. For serious students, such as the more than one thousand practitioners who have become teachers or who are pursuing Anusara teacher training, it is a spiritual practice (*sādhanā*) that touches every aspect of their lives.

This chapter locates Anusara Yoga within the context of developments in Modern Yoga and places Friend within the category of modern gurus. The term *Modern Yoga* comes from Elizabeth De Michelis (2004: 2), who defines it as ". . . a technical term to refer to certain types of yoga that evolved mainly through the interaction of Western individuals interested in Indian religions and a number of more or less Westernized Indians over the last 150 years." The term *modern guru* refers to both Indian and Western leaders of the various movements that have shaped Modern Yoga. De Michelis (2004: 187–89) developed a typology of four major categories of Modern Yoga: (1) Psychosomatic, with a focus on the development of mind, body, and spirit based on Vivekananda's (1863–1902) early formulations of yoga and containing few doctrinal limitations; (2) Denominational, which became prevalent in the West in the 1960s, and in which gurus play a strong role in establishing doctrine; (3) Postural, with an emphasis on physical yoga; and (4) Meditational, with a focus on mental practices.

Each of the four categories of Modern Yoga may include gurus, but each understands the guru's qualifications and roles differently. For example, Denominational Yoga regards the guru as superhuman and expects complete submission and exclusive loyalty from followers. The idea of guru lineage (*paramparā*) is important for both Psychosomatic and Denominational Yoga. Postural and Meditational Yoga, emphasizing physical or mental techniques, often employ the word *teacher* rather than *guru*. De Michelis (2004) acknowledges that these four categories are ideal types, developed for comparative and heuristic value. In reality, overlap exists. Groups may also change, beginning as inclusive with less emphasis on fidelity to a guru and becoming more exclusive over time. Transcendental Meditation founded by Maharishi Mahesh Yogi is an example of this type of development. A group may also shift the other way. An example is provided by Gurumayi, the guru of the Siddha Yoga movement, who attempted in the 1990s to change her role from *guru* to *teacher*, hoping that *students* (no longer *disciples*) would take more responsibility for their own development.

Anusara Yoga fits most readily under the Postural Yoga type, yet it contains elements of the other three as well, which will be explained in the chapter. With its emphasis on physical postures, its leader, John Friend, is understood more as a teacher than as a guru. Since one meaning of the word guru is teacher, technically the two could be used interchangeably. However, connotations of these words often place guru on a super-mundane level and teacher on a more ordinary human level. Another Sanskrit word, not used as commonly in the West, is *ācārya*. Again, there is little difference between the terms guru and *ācārya*, as both refer to spiritual guides who teach about scriptures and who initiate. However, the root of guru is *gṛ*, which means "to invoke or praise," thus giving it an exalted connotation. The root of *ācārya*, on the other hand, is *car*, which, when combined with the prefix *ā*, simply means "to approach." Friend prefers the term *ācārya* to guru when referring to himself as well as to meditation teachers with whom he associates. *Ācārya* is more distinguished than teacher, with its mundane association in the West. Simultaneously, it is a more apt term than guru, which, besides having an exalted connotation incompatible with egalitarian values, contains a negative undertone with its implication of a mandate to surrender critical thinking.

This chapter is based on ethnographic research and employs phenomenological methodology. I went to a retreat led by one of Friend's meditation

Figure 10.1:
John Friend Teaching in Tucson, February 2009. (Courtesy of Anusara, Inc.)

teacher associates, Paul Muller-Ortega, during summer 2010, which was primarily attended by Anusara Yoga instructors. In informal conversations and later through more formal phone interviews, I gained a sense of their motivation not only to study with Friend but also to go beyond *haṭhayoga* proper to learn meditation and the philosophy of tantra. I then attended master classes with Friend at an Anusara Yoga Grand Gathering in Estes Park, Colorado, in fall 2010. This was followed by several phone interviews with Friend. Unless otherwise noted, all direct quotes are from these interviews. While at the Grand Gathering, I also attended classes with more of Friend's associates who teach meditation or tantric philosophy. Additionally, I attended Anusara Yoga classes at local centers and spent time in an ashram in the 1990s where Friend taught and where I experienced his teaching style at an early stage before the founding of Anusara Yoga.

The chapter is divided into four sections. The first provides background on Friend, including influences on his philosophy of life and development of Anusara Yoga. My thesis is that John Friend, as founder and luminary of Anusara, has established a system based on rituals of the body that creates a strong sense of community and provides meaning to individuals who have abandoned traditional institutionalized religion. Thus, the second section explores Anusara as *kula,* a word Friend chose to represent the "family" of Anusara practitioners. *Kula* literally means "a grouping together," which could refer to family, school, or lineage. Other meanings include the human body, the world, embodied cosmos, and divine creative energy. The word *kula* links together different social and cosmic levels of reality and thus aptly represents what Anusara Yoga attempts to do. Friend holds the *kula* together and, therefore, this section will give further consideration to his role as a modern guru or *ācārya.*

A secondary thesis of this chapter is that while Anusara Yoga is a tightly defined system in itself, it also plays the role of linking students to ideas and practices that go beyond postural yoga through creating a network of teachers, both of postural yoga and of meditational yoga, all of them loosely connected through Friend. Friend's encouragement of these networks is helping to establish a tantra-based philosophy and practice in America as well as in other countries as Anusara expands. The third section explores this network and the tantra philosophy it espouses. The final section places Anusara Yoga within the framework of Modern Yoga and speculates on why it has attained popularity at this particular historical moment.

JOHN FRIEND

The first thing to point out about Friend is his Americanism. Although he has visited India and been influenced by several renowned Indian gurus, his alliance is primarily with American religious and cultural traditions. As Friend constructs the narrative of his life to create an arc of meaning, he emphasizes key moments and people who have influenced his direction. The first and primary influence on him was his mother. It is significant that in shaping his life story Friend begins with an early memory that is iconically American: the assassination of John F. Kennedy.

Friend was just four, at home recovering from an illness, when Kennedy was shot. He watched the drama unfold on TV for several days, and this, he states, marked the beginning of his quest for meaning. He went to his mother for answers, and she, an intellectual who had long been interested in yoga and the occult, became his guide in an adventure of learning that would last a lifetime. First she read to him, then she gave him books, and then she put him on trains and planes to study with Sufis, yogis, Theosophists, and New Thought teachers. Friend was particularly drawn to magic and the idea of developing powers (*siddhis*). One of the early readings he recalls from his mother was from the magazine *Fate: Stranger than Fiction*. She also read him books about yogis' supernatural powers. In an interview with Stephen Cope, scholar-in-residence at the Kripalu Center for Yoga & Health, Friend said, "As an eight-year-old hearing about guys who could dematerialize and then show up somewhere else—well, they were the greatest superheroes you could imagine. It was better than reading a Superman comic book actually" (Cope, 2003: 225).

Friend began the study of *haṭhayoga* at the age of thirteen with a woman named Margaret from Youngstown, Ohio, where he lived at the time. She joined Friend's mother in becoming a catalyst for exposure to a variety of teachings and worldviews, including those of the Theosophical Society, Wicca, Sufism, and Buddhism. Friend spoke about how these different paths and practices continue to influence him:

> Margaret opened me to whole other worlds that I still value and still practice. Although I no longer participate in the Theosophical Society, they influenced me to present Eastern thought to Westerners. From Wicca I learned about alignment with nature; for example, knowing what effect the sun's waxing during the summer solstice has on us. Recognizing how to behave in alignment with nature brings freedom from suffering and brings happiness and expansion of consciousness, which is what I teach. From Sufism I learned my first mantra practice. Some of my first mystical experiences were with Sufism in my early teens. I still incorporate that in my meditation practice, and even use dance to find my center through whirling in a mindful and sacred way. It's not that easy, but I do play with it. Buddhism is very organized in its analysis of the mind, so I use a lot of the Buddhist paradigm for my understanding of the mind and for my practices. Metaphysically, I'm aligned with *Vajrayāna* [Tibetan Buddhism]. For me it's mostly about compassion, loving-kindness, and the interconnectedness of all things. It's also about recognizing the ephemeral nature of the phenomenal world and why non-clinging is so important if you want to be happy.

Friend was significantly influenced by Paramahansa Yogananda (1893–1952), author of *Autobiography of a Yogi*, which was to become a spiritual classic for yogis worldwide but particularly for American yogis. Friend's inspiration to pursue the practice of yoga and meditation came, in large part, from Yogananda's autobiography, which he read in the late seventies. He then began the practice of *kriyāyoga* taught by Self-Realization Fellowship, the organization Yogananda founded. Yogananda and Friend would seem to have little in common at first glance. Yogananda was an Indian renunciate who established his own order of renunciates after coming to the United States, a far cry from Friend's tantric emphasis on finding God in the world. Yet while Yogananda's and Friend's lives and spiritual aspirations are worlds and generations apart, similarities can also be found. Yogananda was centered in devotion, or *bhakti*, as is Friend. Both were drawn to the throbbing quality of love that Friend today espouses as the essence of postural and meditational practice.

Friend eventually received degrees in finance and accounting from Texas A&M University, married, and worked as a financial consultant. In 1987, however, he left his work as a financial analyst behind and became a full-time yoga instructor. *Haṭhayoga* was to become his venue for spreading his philosophy of life, which, as his Anusara mission statement puts it, is a "celebration of the heart." He first taught under the auspices of Iyengar Yoga and served on the organization's board of directors. Besides being a student of B. K. S. Iyengar, Friend spent periods of time under the tutelage of other masters of the twentieth century, including T. K. V. Desikachar (Viniyoga style), and Patabbhi Jois (Ashtanga Yoga style), as well as with each of their top students. He also apprenticed under Indra Devi, the "First Lady of Yoga" in America.

Over the years of taking classes, he noticed that most teachers described each yoga position with contrasting terminology and also treated each student differently. As he took notes to use them in his own classes, he saw patterns emerging and began to question these teachers' approach. He realized that "there was a deeper order and intelligence to the entire system of the body and the mind, and it was like a hologram between everybody. No matter what unique qualities each individual had, they could still be guided into the universal form of nature."

Out of all the teachers Friend studied with, none affected him as deeply as Gurumayi Chidvilasananda, spiritual head of the Siddha Yoga path. He met her while he was a student of Iyengar, and, like many who came in contact with this *śaktipāt* guru in the eighties and nineties, Friend was captivated by her charisma and grace.[3] He received a spiritual awakening in her presence and shortly thereafter began teaching yoga courses for her devotees. For most of Siddha Yoga's history since its founding in the sixties, *haṭhayoga* was, at best, an ancillary practice for this predominately guru yoga path.[4] However, by the late eighties *haṭhayoga* began to receive more attention. What was already beginning to blossom came to full bloom when Friend began teaching at Gurumayi's ashram. His buoyancy and humor delighted the huge crowds that visited Shree Muktananda Ashram in upstate New York throughout the nineties. Gurumayi had instituted week-long and month-long silent retreats involving intense *sādhanā* practices that began before the sun rose and ended late at night. In the early morning, Friend would lead a group of perhaps five hundred people in *haṭhayoga* and breathing exercises (*prāṇayāma*) as part of these courses. Gurumayi later commissioned the building of a *haṭhayoga* studio. The beautiful seven thousand square foot, wood-floored studio was soon used throughout the day, with classes for children, teens, and adults. Friend definitely had an impact on the milieu of Siddha Yoga. What had been an optional practice became foundational. Furthermore, his style of teaching with humor softened the intensity that had permeated the ashram, adding a quality of lightness and fun.

While Friend changed the ashram, the ashram changed Friend. Gurumayi invited him to be part of a Teachers and Scholars Department. There he befriended some of the more scholarly minded swamis as well as professors who had been invited to the ashram to teach. Some of these professors were as transformed by the spiritual energy of the ashram and of Gurumayi as Friend was, and they soon began to identify themselves as Siddha Yoga scholars. They eventually wrote a book, *Meditation Revolution* (1997), which laid out the history of Siddha Yoga and the tantric-based philosophy on which it rested. Friend described his time with these swamis and professors: "When I went to the ashram in the early nineties, I opened my world to amazing people and brilliant minds and people that have had an incredible influence on me: Douglas Brooks, Paul Muller-Ortega, Bill Mahony, Sally Kempton [then Swami Durgananda], and Carlos Pomeda [then Swami Gitananda]. What a blessing it was to have spent so much time with them! I was so fortunate to be part of the Teachers and Scholars Department. I had close association with all of these people as we worked on the programming. And I spent time in the library where they also worked."

For Friend, being exposed to the tantric philosophy of Kashmir Śaivism was electrifying: "After studying everything, tantra is not only the most elegant and sophisticated system, but it's the one that aligns with my heart because it sees that the very essence of life is joy or love and that there's a goodness to life. Freedom is at the essence of everyone and everything. That is super fundamental tantric philosophy. For me, it's just yes!" Friend went on to explain that the yes also has a no. While his understanding of tantric philosophy embraces goodness and freedom, it also emphasizes boundary and discipline. Anusara is not a neo-tantric movement that espouses freedom from social mores. Ethical guidelines and specific systems for checks and balances within the Anusara organization are outlined on the Anusara website.

Although tantra is a complex system that belies definition, different tantric schools share the basic viewpoint that the way to liberation is not through transcending the world but through embracing it. According to André Padoux, tantra is "an attempt to place *kāma*, desire, in every sense of the word, in the service of liberation . . . not to sacrifice this world for liberation's sake, but to reinstate it, in varying ways, within the perspective of salvation" (quoted in White, 2006: 15). While *kāma* is embraced in Anusara Yoga, the ultimate goal is to evolve from individual, ego-driven desire to alignment with divine desire, or divine will, known as *icchā*.

Friend began to develop his own style of yoga when he realized that his approach stood in contrast to that of his teacher, Iyengar, who embraced the philosophy of *sāṃkhya* found in the *Yogasūtras*. *Sāṃkhya* is a dualistic system that divides the world into an unchanging, pure, yet conscious spirit (*puruṣa*) and an active yet nonconscious matter (*prakṛti*). *Sāṃkhya* privileges *puruṣa* and thus tends to devalue the physical world. After studying with Gurumayi and other proponents of Kashmir Śaivism, Friend intended to incorporate a nondual tantric approach into his style of yoga. At the same time, he wanted to bring heart-opening language into the classroom. Positively affirming his students with lightness and humor quickly became the hallmark of Friend's teaching style. He then franchised this style by developing instructions for how to teach in an uplifting and friendly manner. The *Anusara Teacher Training Manual* (2009), for example, includes instructions on how to stand while teaching—"For the most part, keep your arms by your sides and your heart lifted"—and how to use one's voice —"The tone of voice needs to originate more from the heart than from the head." Classes usually begin with an invocation of grace in the form of mantras or simply with the sounding of *om*. Instructors build a class around a theme that is both spiritual and practical. The theme is specific to something the teacher has experienced and contemplated that week: for example, the need to pause throughout the day to enjoy the moment. Friend systematized the patterns he saw in his studies with different teachers into what he calls Universal Principles of Alignment, "a set of biomechanical principles that can be applied to all physical positions and postures in order to bring the body into alignment with the Optimal Blueprint" (Friend, 2009: 39). These are integrally connected to his foundational principles: attitude, alignment, and action. His emphasis on the "celebration of the heart" is immediately apparent in the first principle. Before any movement begins, an Anusara practitioner "opens to Grace." Grace, or as Friend puts it, "the power of the heart," is understood to be the revelatory power of spirit that animates the postures; it is a life force that opens one's body, mind, and spirit. The practitioner learns to balance surrender with self-effort, softening the heart with engaging "muscular energy." The second foundational principle, alignment, requires knowledge of "how various parts of ourselves are integrated and connected." The third principle, action (or *kriyā*), concerns "the natural flow of energy in the body" (p. 25). He also developed a way of talking about cycles of physical and subtle energies of the body called *loops* and *spirals*. All of these ideas distinguish Anusara Yoga from other types of postural yoga. However, what is more important from a religious studies perspective are the ways Anusara Yoga might be viewed as a "spiritual system" that provides comfort to those who have become alienated from traditional institutional religion. This system is built on rituals of the body that create a sense of community.

ANUSARA YOGA AS *KULA*

Since both ritual and community are strong indicators of a system being classified as *religious*, let me begin by stating why I call Anusara Yoga a *spiritual* system. The first and most obvious reason is common usage. Religion is increasingly connected with traditional established world religions that one might encounter in an Introduction to World Religions book. *New Religious Movement* is another term that might apply to Anusara Yoga. However, this moniker often has a pejorative connotation, being viewed in popular imagination as ephemeral and therefore not to be taken as seriously as its implicit opposite: legitimate religion. The term spirituality has found a permanent home in the English lexicon, and while it is diffuse and vague, one might argue that it is no more so than the term religion. Modern spirituality arose in opposition to established creeds, rituals, and hierarchies of religious denominations. In the twentieth and early twenty-first centuries, it has been used to refer to an inner realm of life that each person can experience without the help of outside mediators such as priests, texts, or institutions. Paul Heelas (2008: 1–2) argues that the spiritual in current conceptions is connected with "the free expression, and thus development, of what it is to be 'truly' human." Spirituality may also refer to a path, the culmination of which is an experience of unity with a larger cosmic or divine reality as well as with humans and the natural environment.

Anusara Yoga differs from religion in other ways as well. The community that Anusara provides for its followers is not the same as the community found in places where churches or synagogues provide a social mode for taking care of one another's physical, emotional, and spiritual needs as well as a support system for acting in concert to help others during local, national, or international crises. One Anusara teacher stated, "Organized religion exists through a family or a local community. This is different. You meet people at yoga workshops or festivals. Then you may stay in touch on Facebook." Another practitioner complained that she missed community and was considering joining a church: "If I belonged to a church, I'd have someone to help me as I get older or if I'm sick. Someone might bring me dinner or give me a ride. That's the upside of organized religion. With yoga a lot of people do it for a while and let go. I had a conversation with someone about the possibility of yoga retirement homes. But that person has quit, so I guess she's not going to drive me anywhere." On the other hand, another practitioner stated that two Anusara groups had recently formed in her city to support one another socially. They go out together in the evenings for dinner or entertainment and organize meals for people who are in need. It appears that the movement is in transition and that it may well be headed toward fulfilling community needs in a more immediate and personal way than is possible in the virtual world.

I use the term *system* in concert with spiritual because, in contrast to the idea that spirituality allows each individual to define ultimate truth for herself, Anusara Yoga proffers a doctrine that unifies individual, social, and cosmic levels of reality based on the philosophy of Kashmir Śaivism. Furthermore, it has created an organized structure based on a corporate model for disseminating that doctrine. Jeremy Carrette and Richard King (2005: 5), in their book *Selling Spirituality,* would call this *corporate hijacking*: "What is being sold to us as radical, trendy and transformative spirituality in fact produces little in the way of a significant change in one's lifestyle or fundamental behavior patterns." Friend defends his position by stating that spirituality and capitalism do not have to be in conflict with each other. In another time or place, spiritual groups might have survived through a system of donations; today they survive through charging for classes and workshops. Early Buddhism, for example, prospered through donations of land from wealthy patrons that were used to establish pleasure parks (*ārāmas*) and rural settlements (*avāsā*) used for three-month annual retreats (*vassa*). Friend argues that his primary motive, as with early Buddhists, is not profit, but rather spiritual growth.

The concept of "shri" (*śrī*: beauty and abundance) is one of Anusara's leitmotifs and is said to unite spiritual and worldly aspirations. The fact that some people are able to earn a living from teaching Anusara Yoga or from developing or selling Anusara products does not conflict with tantric philosophy, which affirms both worldly and spiritual goals. Evidence of economic and material benefits can exist alongside evidence that many people receive deep spiritual benefit through their encounter with Anusara Yoga. These changes are elicited through the meaning system created through rituals of the body that connect the individual to a larger cosmic reality. Furthermore, practitioners of Anusara Yoga gain a community, even if in an altered form from traditional religious communities.

Paul Connerton (1995: 95) argues that bodily memory is more lasting than verbal: "Habit is a knowledge and a remembering in the hands and in the body; and in the cultivation of habit, it is our body which 'understands.'" Connerton goes on to state that performing bodily actions together creates a group memory. As Anusara practitioners engage in the same postures, accompanied by slow rhythmic breathing, a powerful ritual is created, which becomes even more powerful when it is accompanied by words that are meant to link the body to the heart. Friend uses the metaphor *heart* to create a unity of body, will, mind, emotion, and cosmic awareness for his students. At the same time, the metaphor creates openness and warmth toward the instructor and toward others in the class. The first instruction Friend (2009: 101) gives about teaching a class is to "communicate with the students on a personal or heart level, not to their outer bodies on an impersonal level." In a particular posture, instructions may begin, "Lift your heart," which means to open in the chest while allowing the "shoulder blades to melt down the back." As the opening epithet makes clear, the ritual of performing the postures is intended to enhance more than the physical body's well-being; it is to instill virtue. Friend guides his teachers to choose words carefully to do this: "From your belly, *with steady courage,* extend down through your back leg into the earth until your hips become level. Keeping the legs steady, extend *triumphantly* from your focal point in your pelvis up through your core through your fingers" (p. 109, italics added for emphasis). The body becomes the *axis mundi* toward which all levels of reality coalesce and which elevates the physical toward the spiritual.

Beginning the practice by opening to grace and with instructions ringing in their ears—open your heart; now ground your feet into the earth; accept yourself wherever you are; release feelings of weakness and allow the power that surrounds you to support you—practitioners begin to embody the attributes of softening, acceptance, and equanimity, along with courage, enthusiasm, and steady effort. One meaning of the word *tantra* is a loom or a warp and is connected to the meaning of *tan* as to "spread, be diffused (as light) over, shine, extend toward, reach to" (Monier-Williams, 1995 [1899] : 435–36). Thus, the title of this chapter, "Stretching toward the Sacred," is emblematic of two key attributes of Anusara: extending one's limbs and muscles during practice and viewing the Anusara path as learning to shine forth from one's inner light.

During the ritual of body movement, Friend often refers to analogies he learned through his study of Kashmir Śaivism, thus drawing the student from the domain of the body into a larger cosmic orbit. For example, he might explain how everything is made of the same pulsating consciousness. For this reason, a person should not think of the body as something separate from the mind and heart that needs to be manipulated. Instead of controlling one's body, the student can learn to experience the natural balance between *muscle energy*, which creates stability, and a subtler life force called *organic energy*, which creates expansion. In this way, students are exposed to the idea that everything is made of one consciousness. When these words are heard over and over in connection with movement, a transformation of understanding occurs. Thus, the ritual of body movement and postures, performed regularly, becomes part of a spiritual system.

When I asked practitioners whether they practiced alone, they usually replied "rarely," and when they did it was a poor substitute for group practice. Several spoke about going out for tea or coffee together after class. Developing a community, or *kula*, was a goal for Friend from Anusara's foundation.

Feeling a sense of belonging attracts people to Anusara. One person spoke about driving across the country. Whatever town he stopped in, he looked up the Anusara studio. He received invitations from people he had never met before not only to visit classes but also to have dinner and even to spend the night.

Community is also maintained through virtual reality. Video streaming classes, Facebook, and Twitter help to keep people connected. Outdoor festivals that combine yoga, hooping, music, and other forms of entertainment are becoming increasingly popular.[5] People attending these connect with their own yoga community through Twitter. An interviewee described it thus:

> You go with your friends. Once you're there, you find people who have something in common—the same teacher. With Internet, there's constant communication through iPhones. Twitter is huge. When I went to Wanderlust [festival], there were tags for Twitter, and you were instantly connected. We knew exactly where to meet up. Then afterward, thousands of pictures from Wanderlust were posted on Facebook. In fact, I wonder if we'll look back on this time as some kind of awakening, like tent revivals or the sixties. I go to maybe a dozen events like this in a year.

Another spoke about the sense of community as the main attraction for her:

> I have the biggest group of friends that I've ever had in my life. Almost all my friends in San Francisco are through Anusara. It's amazing because I did a variety of yoga practice before, and I met a couple of people, but Anusara emphasizes *kula*. That's one reason I like to go to class. It's hard to argue with going somewhere where I get kisses and hugs every time I go.

Anusara Yoga coincides with contemporary religious aspirations of Americans as outlined by Wade Clark Roof (1999: 38) in *Spiritual Marketplace*, particularly as he describes religion today as more diffuse, and persisting "largely as a result of loosely bound networks of practitioners, the publishing industry, and the media." He warns, similarly to Carrette and King, that this fluid spirituality based on "creative transformation of the self" does not encourage loyalty to organizations and structures. Without this commitment, he asserts, "it is difficult to regularize religious life around a set of practices and unifying experiences, to mobilize people around causes, or even to sustain personal religious identity" (p. 39). Even though the personal experiences of the majority of those I interviewed provided evidence that the Anusara community was supportive, criticisms may be justified as evidenced in the earlier quote in which a practitioner worried that nobody would be around to bring her a meal when she was old or sick. Alternately, this may change as yoga becomes a more stable part of American society. There is a particularly strong rally for green changes by yoga practitioners and many support liberal causes and candidates, either individually or in groups. The Anusara website states:

> Anusara yoga community members also offer themselves in service to life, in all communities both locally and globally, in order to reduce suffering and bring greater happiness and health. Kula members regularly volunteer to provide yoga and other services to those in need and less privileged. For instance, Anusara yoga teachers throughout the world raised tens of thousands of dollars for Tsunami relief programs by organizing local fund-raising classes.[6]

They also raise money locally for teachers who are ill or whose studios need repair.

A final point in considering Anusara Yoga as a spiritual system is the charismatic moment that occurs when students gather with a teacher who inspires them. This may be Friend or one of his trained instructors. For the purposes of understanding Friend as a guru, I will consider some definitions of the word and then draw on examples from people who have experienced Friend's charisma.

For a Hindu perspective on the definition of guru, we might turn to the famous exponent of nondualism, Śaṅkarācārya (788–820), who described the guru as "one who is the supreme consciousness; one whose mind is rooted in the highest reality; one who has a pure and tranquil mind" (Grimes, 1996: 133). Turning to a Western framework, the definition of charisma finds resonance with Śaṅkarācārya's description. Sociologist Max Weber (1947 [1924] : 329) states that charisma is "a certain quality of an individual personality by virtue of which he is set apart from ordinary men and treated as endowed with supernatural, superhuman, or at least specifically exceptional qualities. . . . [that] are regarded as of divine origin." In folk etymology, the word guru derives from *gu*, which stands for darkness, and *ru*, which represents the removal of darkness. These roots can be traced to the *Pāṇini-sūtras*: *gu saṁvaraṇe* and *ru hiṁsane*, which indicate concealment and its annulment (Grimes, 1996: 133).

Many people today have witnessed those who have been exalted as superhuman fall from grace through scandal or through an admission, such as the one Rajneesh/Osho made late in his life, that he had not attained a state of enlightenment after all. In short, many are wary of the term guru. For this reason, Friend does not ordinarily use the word and, in fact, makes fun of it by calling himself a *gugu*: "I take my students from darkness to darkness," he quips, and his students laugh, turning the definition of *heavy*, which is one translation of guru, on its head. The solemnity that normally surrounds the guru–disciple relationship is missing in an Anusara gathering. Friend does admit, however, that when advanced students whom he has worked with for a number of years refer to him as their guru, he does not object. For Friend, this means that they are committed to learning from him and will devote substantial time and effort to be with him and to pass his system on to others.

Although some of Friend's students place him on a pedestal and thus are disillusioned when they see his faults, Friend does not claim that he has attained a state that makes him superhuman. On the other hand, he does view himself as having divine origin. Since divinity infuses every aspect of life according to the tantric philosophy Friend holds, everyone has divine origin. The idea of enlightenment, however, is not stressed in Anusara. Though not in the foreground, Friend still holds it as a possibility and teaches that it is a goal but claims it needs to be defined in a way that is compatible with worldly goals, saying:

> I see it as a heart connection, an open delight and love for life. We experience moments of divine beauty. It doesn't have to occur after twelve hours of meditating; it can be a moment with family, doing something very simple, and suddenly we dissolve in love. When these moments grow and become regular, and we become established in love and wisdom, then that's enlightenment.

When asked who has attained enlightenment, he said he was not aware of anyone—except maybe Jesus or Buddha. This admission seems to place the goal of enlightenment on precarious ground. If Friend thinks it has occurred only for two people who lived two or two and a half millennia ago, is it really a practical goal for Anusara practitioners? Apparently it is not, which is why one interviewee stated, "Attaining enlightenment is not part of the lingo."

While the ideas of enlightenment and of gurus are downplayed in Anusara, something special seems to occur at Anusara gatherings, and more so when Friend is teaching the class. One understanding of guru is the ability to bestow *śaktipāt*, an awakening of spiritual energy. *Śakti* means power, strength, ability, energy; *śaktipāt* literally means "prostration of strength" (Monier-Williams, 1995 [1899] : 1044). This awakening often manifests as spontaneous movements, inner visions, special insights, and laughter or tears (see Chapter 8 in this volume). These types of manifestations occur at Anusara gatherings and are among the reasons people make sacrifices to attend Anusara workshops and conferences. Consider the following examples. One person spoke of how Friend inspires a class to perform well in the worst of conditions as, for example, when the temperatures are very hot and the class is being held outside: "I've studied with a lot of teachers, and no one can lift a group's energy like John." I observed a woman in her late sixties who attended the Anusara Grand Gathering in Estes Park, Colorado, in which about six hundred people had gathered to study with Friend and his associates. Upon coming down from a handstand, she began to cry. I asked her if she was okay, and she replied that she was just incredibly happy and that she had been crying ever since she arrived at the conference. Another woman told me in an interview about an experience she had after being used as a model for demonstrating a pose in which Friend had his hand on her spine. Because he was explaining to the class how to touch people when adjusting them, contact was longer than it would have been if he had simply been assessing her spine. She reported, "As I went back to my place, suddenly everything was neon. I felt like I was on a cloud. People's clothing was more vivid. I felt like Dorothy in *The Wizard of Oz*. I was the most stunned person because it was so unexpected." I asked her what she thought it was, and she replied, "I interpret it as his energy causing it, like when you get a transference of energy from Reiki. Other than that, I have no idea." It should be noted that Friend does not seem to be viewed as the source of spiritual awakening. Even the woman whose vision was "neon" after being touched by Friend interpreted the experience as something that any person could be trained to do. Friend admitted that awakenings do occur in his classes, but he also does not attribute it to any type of special power he has, stating, "*Śaktipāt* happens in the classes in a variety of degrees. Some people have mild openings and some have stronger openings. I think of *śaktipāt* as a recalibration of their energy bodies and their minds through the essence of love and the intersection of themselves with life."

A spiritual atmosphere that fosters awakening may occur at master classes and "grand gatherings." While a guru might be a particularly open conduit for bringing about these experiences, it is also possible that the group energy of people coming together with a strong intention to grow spiritually creates

Figure 10.2:
John Friend Teaching in Los Angeles, April 2009. (Courtesy of Anusara, Inc.)

the atmosphere for awakening experiences. While Weber's explanations of the charismatic personality certainly can be evidenced in many cases, perhaps Emile Durkheim's model better describes what occurs in group rituals such as an Anusara class. The guru or other leader is a catalyst by establishing an atmosphere conducive to an enlivening of spiritual energy. However, the experiences occur as a result of the intentions and rituals of the group gathered together. Durkheim (1995 [1912]: 9) argued that "religion is an eminently social thing. Religious representations are collective representations that express collective realities." According to Durkheim, the purpose of religion is primarily to anchor people in a community, and rituals are able to do this better than intellectual assent to a belief system. He referred to the intensity that produces a charismatic moment as a type of "effervescence that alters the conditions of the psychic activity. . . . the vital energies become hyper-excited, the passions more intense, the sensations more powerful; there are indeed some that are produced at this moment. Man does not recognize himself; he feels somehow transformed and in consequence transforms his surroundings" (p. 424). This seems to adequately describe what sometimes occurs in master classes with Friend or with one of his teachers and which Friend describes as *śaktipāt*, or a "recalibration of the energy body."

THE ANUSARA NETWORK

In August 2004, Friend had just completed an Anusara teacher training course at Gurumayi's ashram in upstate New York when he was informed that this would be the last program at the ashram. Neither Friend nor any of his scholar friends knows exactly why Gurumayi decided to close the ashram to visitors, but the professors were suddenly without an audience. Certainly they had their college classes, but these students were not the same as yoga practitioners, eager to learn what they had to offer. By this time, Swamis Durgānanda and Gitānanda had already discontinued formal association with Siddha Yoga and had become teachers of meditation and yogic philosophy on their own. Friend already had a large following of students when he began to invite some of his former Siddha Yoga colleagues to speak at yoga conferences. This was the beginning of a more formal and in-depth connection between the *haṭhayoga* of Anusara and the philosophy of tantra.

One might refer to the various teachers and movements associated with Friend as the Anusara Network. A consideration of the total picture of Anusara is not possible without examining this network. Viewed as a whole, the Anusara Network is having an impact on the development of American neo-Hinduism.[7] These new forms incorporate Western esoteric philosophy, broad understandings of tantra yoga, and a large emphasis on disciplines of the body.

The former Siddha Yoga scholars and swamis are associated with Friend in varying degrees. Some simply receive Anusara students at their own conferences and retreats. Others associate more regularly with Friend but are also deeply involved with other yoga groups. Sally Kempton, for example, leads her own courses and retreats, has a group of students who consider her their main spiritual teacher, has worked closely with Ken Wilber's Integral Life Practice, and is a regularly featured writer for *Yoga Journal*. She is also a featured speaker at Anusara mega-events, where she uses the Anusara terminology, such as *śrī*, meaning beauty and wealth, and *kula*, referring to the Anusara community. Christopher Wallis, a younger scholar of Sanskrit and tantra who was raised in the Siddha Yoga milieu, is having a large impact on some Anusara yoga students and teachers. The following excerpt from an interview with a lecturer at Stanford University provides an example of how an association between Anusara and a scholar of tantra might progress:

> I first met Hareesh [Christopher Wallis] through doing an "immersion" [one of the steps in becoming a teacher of Anusara, in which students learn not only alignment but also yoga philosophy]. Now I'm studying the tantric text, *The Heart of Self-Recognition,* with him. We repeat all the *sūtras* [verses] in Sanskrit, and I do a meditation for twenty-five minutes every day called *tattva bhāvanā*, in which I try to feel all the impressions: sensations, noises, and everything. I also do some awareness practices throughout the day, like thanking Śiva for coming to me in a certain form. The more you study the texts, the more you see how it is part of the philosophy that winds through Anusara classes. Hareesh is a total academic nerd, yet he's got this room full of people totally in love with him. Normally, people in the United States don't do this kind of study outside of the university. In France, people pay to go hear Derrida, but they don't do that here. And yet Hareesh [who his currently working on his doctorate] may not have to even teach in a university.

Students and teachers of yoga are creating a new space for learning that combines practice with the study of theories and goals of yoga. Certainly, this was already occurring before Anusara's rise in popularity, yet Friend has provided impetus to the movement of studying texts of Hinduism. Tantric scriptures are prominent features of the Anusara spiritual system. Even a person with casual interest will find a recommended reading list on Anusara's webpage with twenty-six books on tantric philosophy compared to only six on anatomy, physiology, and kinesiology.

The person will also find ethical guidelines from the *Yogasūtras* explained, beginning with behavioral restraints (*yamas*) and internal restraints (*niyamas*) and extending to institutional procedures for a breach in ethical behavior. It would be odd if the *Yogasūtras* were not a part of the required reading list for those pursuing Anusara teacher training since it has become an essential text for those studying the Hindu yoga system. This has been true since the mid-nineteenth century when Western Orientalists and Hindu *paṇḍits* collaborated to ensure its inclusion in the formulation of Hinduism for modern times. Yet when I asked Friend about the scriptures that had most influenced him, his lack of enthusiasm for the *Yogasūtras* was obvious. The books that affected him strongly were of two types: those with a devotional orientation, such as the *Bhagavad Gītā* and the *Śrīmad Bhāgavatam*; and those from the tantric tradition of Kashmir Śaivism, such as the *Spanda Kārikās* and the *Vijñāna Bhairava*. It seems that the decoupling of tantra and *haṭhayoga* that first occurred in neo-Hindu developments of the mid-nineteenth and early twentieth centuries has been reconnected by Anusara. Simultaneously, *haṭhayoga*'s ties to Patañjali's classical yoga and to *vedānt*a (another classical philosophical system based on the Upaniṣads), so carefully drawn by the titans of Modern Yoga—Vivekananda in the early twentieth century and B. K. S. Iyengar in the late twentieth century—are, to some extent, being dismantled by Anusara. These changes indicate that Friend is taking *haṭhayoga* in a new direction.

In addition to devotional and tantric texts, Friend has also been influenced by Christian, Buddhist, Taoist, Sufi, Wiccan, and New Thought books and teachers. Add to these his many years of study with Indian *haṭhayoga* masters (most notably Iyengar), his friendship with several scholars of Hindu philosophy, and his time teaching yoga in Siddha Yoga ashrams where he experienced a community of people who, in his words, "lived from the heart," and we have a picture of the eclectic potpourri of ideas and practices that find their way into Anusara Yoga.

As part of the Anusara Network, some "scholar-practitioners" combine teaching in a college setting with teaching in yoga studios or in their homes; others find they are able to retire from university teaching because they have enough financial support from fees and donations from their yoga students; still others, like Christopher Wallis, may never have to teach in a university setting full time. While all of this is occurring outside an academic setting, it is also possible that an accredited college may emerge from the uniting of practice and theory that Anusara Yoga encourages. This would not be the first of its kind in the United States. Maharishi Mahesh Yogi established Maharishi International University, today called Maharishi University of Management, in Fairfield, Iowa, where students bring together traditional academic study with meditation practices. Chogyam Trungpa founded Naropa University because he thought that education and mindfulness training should be combined, and, more recently, Lama Marut (a.k.a. Brian K. Smith) established the Asian Classics Institute. It remains to be seen if the collaboration among scholars, former swamis, and *haṭhayoga* practitioners will one day become another such college for contemplative education.

Currently, Friend is in the process of creating The Center in Encinitas, California, which will combine artistic expression with yoga philosophy. To understand Friend's motivation, we might consider the resonances he felt when he encountered literature that is filled with drama, such as the *Bhagavad Gītā* and the *Śrīmad Bhāgavatam*, as well as his exposure to practices that bring together devotion and movement, such as Sufi dancing. We must also consider Friend's main inspiration: Kashmir Śaivism. Abhinavagupta (950–1020) is the most celebrated philosopher of Kashmir Śaivism, famous not only for his explication of tantra in his opus magnum, the *Tantrāloka*, but also for his contribution to the philosophy of art, which connects aesthetic experience to transcendence of the limited sense of self and thus to the experience of bliss. In Abhinavagupta's commentary on the *Natyaśāstra* by Bhārata Muni, he expands on the theory of *rasa* (taste or essence). A *rasa* is an emotional quality evoked through a work of art, such as love, compassion, or disgust. With the strong influence this literature has had on Friend, it is only natural that he would choose to create a center that links yoga and the arts. Combining yoga with artistic expression can also be seen in the Anusara Network of musicians. Various traveling musicians of Indian music and chanting (*kīrtana*) have been associated with Friend over the years, including Krishna Das, Benjy and Heather Wertheimer (known as Shantala), and MC Yogi.

Anusara allows its boundaries to become porous enough to influence and be influenced by other forms of postural yoga. Cheryl Crawford, founder of Grounded Kids, illustrates the balance of uniqueness and flexibility often found in Anusara Yoga that allows it to expand at the edges, so to speak. After becoming a certified Anusara Yoga teacher, Crawford developed a system of yoga for children and teenagers that is being used in some of the Atlanta-area public schools and is rapidly spreading to surrounding areas as well. She and her business partner are now training teachers throughout the United States and Europe. Grounded Kids is not Anusara Yoga per se since it has its own language and principles specifically developed for children, but Friend supports the effort; it is "Anusara approved." Crawford's system illustrates the organic growth of the Anusara movement and its life-affirming philosophy. Grounded Kids includes more than physical exercises. Crawford teaches her young students to look for the best in others, and classes keep lists of events during the day that "melt their hearts"—attitudes and phrases taught in Anusara Yoga. In this way, Friend strikes a balance between flexibility and rigidity, encouraging Anusara's influence on other forms of yoga, while also maintaining the integrity of his system through only allowing the name Anusara Yoga to be used by those who have gone through the rigorous Anusara Yoga teacher training sequence. Organizations such as Grounded Kids provide yet another example of an expanding network.

ANUSARA'S PLACE IN MODERN YOGA

How do we account for Anusara Yoga's popularity at this particular time? To answer this question, we must examine the qualities of Anusara that are attractive to a global cosmopolitan population as well as the technological, psychological, and religious ambience of contemporary life in developed countries.

Anusara Yoga, and yoga movements in general, is particularly amenable to transnational expansion in the twenty-first century. Simply put, spirituality that is based on the body and breath is transportable because everyone has a body and everyone breathes; a spirituality based on feeling good is attractive because everyone wants to feel good. Yoga brings together the different goals of psychological, physical, and spiritual healing and thus embodies a paradigm of holism that had previously been lost in the modern world. In traditional cultures and tribal societies, healing and religion were intimately connected. As Robert C. Fuller (1989) points out, holistic health movements have arisen, in part, as a response to the separation of the body from the rest of one's self in modern times. Holistic movements often draw on Eastern religious practices because they offer a "legitimation of their belief in the existence of 'subtle energies' and the efficacy of certain meditational states of consciousness in opening individuals to wide ranges of experience unattainable through reason or sensory awareness alone" (p. 96).

Wade Clark Roof (1999), Robert Bellah (1996 [1985]), and others have suggested that contemporary American life could be characterized as a therapeutic culture. We seek wellness above all else. This therapeutic ambience is now becoming globalized. Since scientists have legitimized *haṭhayoga* as an effective holistic therapy, it is gaining support in India, for example, where it was once eschewed as a practice for ascetics who lived on the fringes of society. Today Swami Ramdev draws thousands to his weekend yoga camps where he combines herbal medical treatments with *haṭhayoga*, and Jaggi Vasudev attracts the very wealthy to his Isha Yoga centers around the world (see Chapter 16 and Chapter 13 in this volume). Satellite television is also helping to spread the therapeutic culture as Oprah Winfrey, Dr. Oz, and Dr. Phil reach audiences around the globe. And of course the Internet joins communities from around the world with similar interests. Anusara Yoga, now established in over seventy countries, appeals to people who have been prepared by exposure to yoga as an ideal therapy. Anusara yogis from Japan to Mexico share the branding words that Friend, with his keen business sense, has limited to a handful: grace, divine flow, *śrī*/beauty, and goodness. These are words many long to hear in today's fragmented world.

With its life-affirming attitude, Anusara Yoga aligns its followers with a form of American religion and culture that developed in the nineteenth century and that historian of American religion Sydney Ahlstrom dubbed *harmonial religion*. Ahlstrom (1972: 1091) states, "Harmonial religion encompasses those forms of piety and belief in which spiritual composure, physical health, and even economic well-being are understood to flow from a person's rapport with the cosmos." This religious form is alive and well today. In an article for the *New York Times* (July 21, 2010), Mimi Schwartz compared Friend to Christian evangelist Joel Osteen. Although followers of both sides of this equation might be offended by the comparison, it seems that Schwartz has tapped into the heart of American religion. The harmonial religious strain is not limited to any particular group or religion. It is flexible enough to find expression in a mega-church as well as in a mega-yoga retreat. It fits well with the American dream of "having it all." Americans seek a form of religion that encompasses all aspects of life, accords with laissez-faire ideals, and at the same time develops a sense of physical and spiritual wellness.

De Michelis's (2004) typology can be employed to understand Anusara's place in Modern Yoga. A primary difference between modern Psychosomatic Yoga, which characterized the early transmission of Modern Yoga to the West, and Modern Denominational Yoga, which was a hallmark of the wave that arose in the 1960s, is the degree of inclusivity, with the later Denominational Yoga marking a move toward stricter doctrinal claims, greater exclusivity, and more dependence on sources of authority. As Anusara Yoga continues to evolve as a network, it seems to be returning to the psychosomatic model. Although Friend has chosen the postural model as his forte, he encourages his students to study meditation and to read scriptures of tantra. In doing this, they study with different teachers in the Anusara Network, thus reducing the exclusivity claims of Modern Denominational Yoga. If Anusara is to continue to be a strong force in the development of a transnational neo-tantric form of spirituality, this expanding network would have to continue.

At the same time, some parameters need to exist so that the movement does not become so diffuse that it melds into New Age spirituality, which is too vague to create meaningful community. Rodney Stark (1987: 15–17) argues that for a religion (here taken as spiritual system) to succeed it must combine clear organization and doctrine with some distinction from its environment but not too much to seem radical. In other words, a balancing act between inclusivity and exclusivity and between distinctiveness and diffuseness needs to occur. Focus on a single guru or organization limits a group and makes it ripe for dissolution upon the guru's disgrace or death. On the other hand, if a group is too broad or diffuse, it is difficult to distinguish its ideas and practices from other groups and might also cause its demise.

Friend realizes that an organizational structure must be created so that others can carry on Anusara's work when he retires. The organization, like the teaching, functions to delineate the uniqueness of the movement. In the modern world, this is accomplished by creating trademarks and copyrights—a venture fraught with the danger of losing the very spiritual essence that the leaders want to protect by creating the organization in the first place. The stakes become even higher when the goal of the teacher or guru is to expand a spiritual system globally. In fact, the corporate nature of the enterprise of expanding Anusara Yoga has attracted critics: "pressing of the discipline into a Business Plan," as one blogger put it.[8] And "big business" it has become, with two million dollars a year in revenue and a prediction of this being doubled by 2012.

In the final analysis, whether Anusara Yoga will survive and continue to expand will depend on how well the organization can maintain a balance between providing a coherent structure and tradition that is worth passing on to one's children, on one hand, and allowing enough flexibility to evolve when encountering and assimilating new cultures, new teachers, and new ideas, on the other. Erring too far on either side might be its downfall. The ultimate test, however, will be whether Anusara can continue to provide what many seem to yearn for—a heart connection. People attend an Anusara Yoga retreat to practice yoga but also to connect with others through interpersonal and psychotherapeutic types of exercises. At these gatherings they meet and learn from more than a single person; they encounter a gold mine of meditation teachers, scholars of tantra, and well-trained yoga instructors: the Anusara Network. If Anusara continues to facilitate this type of interaction and collaboration while still maintaining the integrity of the system Friend developed, then it is likely that it will sustain itself.

REFERENCES

Ahlstrom, Sydney E. 1972. *Religious History of the American People*. New Haven, CT: Yale University Press, 1972.

Bellah, Robert, et al. 1995 [1985]. *Habits of the Heart*. Berkeley: University of California Press.

Brooks, Douglas, et al. 1997. *Meditation Revolution: A History and Theology of the Siddha Yoga Lineage*. South Fallsburg, NY: Agama Press.

Carrette, Jeremy R. and Richard King. 2005. *Selling Spirituality: The Silent Takeover of Religion*. New York: Routledge.

Connerton, Paul. 1995. *How Societies Remember*. New York: Cambridge University Press.

Cope, Stephen (ed.). 2003. *Will Yoga and Meditation Really Change My Life? Personal Stories from 25 of North America's Leading Teachers*. North Adams, MA: Storey Publishing.

De Michelis, Elizabeth. 2004. *A History of Modern Yoga: Patañjali and Western Esotericism*. London: Continuum.

Durkheim, Emile. 1995 [1912]. *The Elementary Forms of Religious Life*. Trans. Karen E. Fields. New York: Free Press.

Friend, John. 2009. *Teacher Training Manual*, 12th ed. The Woodlands, TX: Anusara Press.

———. 2012. John Friend, *Anusara Yoga in the Community*. Available at: http://www.anusara.com/index.php?option=com.content&view=article&id=45%90&itemid=112 (Accessed March 14, 2012).

Fuller, Robert C. 1989. *Alternative Medicine and American Religious Life*. New York: Oxford University Press.

Grimes, John. 1996. *A Concise Dictionary of Indian Philosophy*. Albany: State University of New York Press.

Heelas, Paul. 2008. *Spiritualities of Life: New Age Romanticism and Consumptive Capitalism*. Malden, MA: Blackwell Publishing.

Monier-Williams, M. 1995 [1899]. *A Sanskrit-English Dictionary*. Delhi, India: Motilal Banarsidass Publishers.

Roof, Wade Clark. 1999. *Baby Boomers and the Remaking of American Religion*. Princeton, NJ: Princeton University Press.

Schwartz, Mimi. 2010. Yoga Mogul. *New York Times*. July 21. Available at: http://www.nytimes.com/2010/07/25/magazine/25Yoga-t.html?pageswanted=all (accessed April 7, 2012).

Stark, Rodney. 1987. How New Religions Succeed: A Theoretical Model. In David G. Bromley and Philip E. Hammond (eds.), *Future of New Religious Movements*. Macon, GA: Mercer University Press, pp. 11–29.

Weber, Max. 1968. *On Charisma and Institution Building*. Chicago: University of Chicago Press.

———. 1947 [1924]. *The Theory of Social and Economic Organization*. Trans. A.M. Henderson and Talcott Parsons. New York: Oxford University Press.

White, David Gordon. 2006 *Kiss of the Yogini: "Tantric Sex" in Its South Asian Contexts*. Chicago, IL: University of Chicago Press.

Williamson, Lola. 2010. *Transcendent in America: Hindu-Inspired Meditation Movements as New Religion*. New York: New York University Press.

NOTES

1. For more recent information on the scandal and Anusara Yoga's subsequent restructuring under new leadership, see http://www.has.vcu.edu/wrs/profiles/Anusara.htm
2. Anusara publications translate *anusara* as "flowing with grace, flowing with nature, or following your heart." *A Sanskrit-English Dictionary* (Monier-Williams, 1995 [1899]) glosses *anusara* as "going after, following; custom, usage; nature, natural state or condition of anything; prevalence, currency; received or established authority, especially of codes of law; accordance, conformity to usage; consequence, result." The apparent discrepancy might be explained in this way. Douglas Brooks, a professor of religion who collaborated with Friend, came up with the name while in the process of translating a text of Kashmir Śaivism called the *Kulārnava Tantra*. He translated a particular sentence as, "By stepping into the current of grace, the student becomes capable of holding what is of value from the guru." The word *anusara* comes from *saras*, which means flowing. The entire phrase *śaktipātānusarena* would more aptly be translated as "flowing with grace," or as Brooks (1997) put it, "stepping into the current of grace," than *anusara* alone.
3. A *śaktipāt* guru is said to be able to awaken the *kuṇḍalinī*, or subtle spiritual energy, through touch or simply through willing it (see Chapter 8 and Chapter 9 in this volume). According to Muktānanda, Gurumayi's guru, it can also occur as a sort of contagion. Just being close to someone whose *kuṇḍalinī* is awakened can cause a similar awakening.

4. Guru Yoga emphasizes attaining realization through devotion and surrender to the guru, believed to be in a state of "God-realization."
5. Hooping, similar to the hula-hoop fad of the 1950s, has been growing in popularity among *haṭha yogins* in the past ten years. It is a form of exercise and entertainment. Some people are adept at keeping many hoops going at various times around different parts of the body. At night, hoops are lit for added drama.
6. John Friend, *Anusara Yoga in the Community.* Available at: http://www.anusara.com/index.php?option=com_content&view=article&id=45&Itemid=112 (accessed March 14, 2012).
7. First articulated by German Indologist Paul Hacker, the term *neo-Hinduism* contrasts with traditional Hinduism. For a concise description of the differences between the two, see Williamson (2010: 17–20) or De Michelis (2004: 38–40).
8. *Anusara Yoga, Class #5.* Available at: http://www.redroom.com/blog/shumit/ansara-yoga-class (accessed March 14, 2012).

PART FOUR

Bhaktiyoga

CHAPTER 11

Svāminārāyaṇa: *Bhaktiyoga* and the *Akṣarabrahman* Guru

HANNA H. KIM

śravaṇam kīrtanam viṣṇoho smaraṇam pādasevanam
arcanam vandanam dāsyam sākhyam ātmanivedanam

–*Bhāgavata Purāṇa* (VII, 5.23)[1]

In this Satsang fellowship, those devotees seeking their own ultimate liberation cannot fulfill that aim by *ātmā*-realisation alone; nor can they fulfill that aim by lovingly offering the nine types of *bhakti* alone . . .

–*Vacanāmṛta* Gaḍhaḍā I-19: 2

On the day their guru, Pramukh Swami Maharaj, was departing from London to India, on November 11, 1997, *satsaṅgis* (men and women devotees) followed his entourage to Heathrow Airport to have a final *darshan* (*darśana*).[2] One young woman mentioned that, in spite of school, the trip to the airport was important because of the "increased chance of good darshan." Pramukh Swami first did his morning *pūjā* at London's Bochasanwasi Shri Akshar Purushottam Swaminarayan Sanstha (BAPS) Shri Swaminarayan *mandir* before leaving: the assembled audience was noticeably subdued and many were huddled within their winter clothing. Around me, in the *mandir havelī*, the air of excitement and happy anticipation that had been present among these women before their guru's arrival was gone. Many of the women around me were quietly weeping. Others reassured themselves that "Bapa," as he is lovingly called by *satsaṅgis*, would be returning to London soon, though no one quite knew when given his less than robust health. Afterward, when I

Figure 11.1:
Pramukh Swami Maharaj, c. 2007. (Courtesy of BAPS Swaminarayan Sanstha.)

spoke with several young women who had gone to Heathrow, they breathlessly exclaimed: "*Darshan* of Bapa at Heathrow was amazing. His wheelchair almost ran over our feet! *Darshan* of Bapa was so unbelievable that I could see the detailing on Bapa's *cappals*, the wavy lines in the shoes."[3] Each woman vowed that she would never tire of following Bapa to the airport despite London rush-hour traffic and the cost of petrol. Like the spoken words of their guru, Pramukh Swami Maharaj, that the women had listened to during his London visit, these moments of *darshan* would remain in their mind and remind them of Swami's physical form and of the noticeable effect that seeing their guru has had on their behavior. Something about Swami had stirred within them a desire to maintain his presence in their lives though he was no longer physically present in London. This desire could now be transmitted into various devotional practices, all involving recollections of Swami's presence, from his smallest gestures to his gentle lessons on how to become more focused on serving God. In this concatenation of emotions, desires, perceptions, and practices, the women experienced a way of being not as dependent on the needs of the desiring self but on a profound desire to cultivate a particular relation to the guru. What began as a "felt" sensation was now a conviction, one that could be translated into actions, all oriented toward "pleasing my guru."

Who is Pramukh Swami Maharaj? Who is this man, born December 7, 1921, and revered by one million BAPS followers? How is it possible that Pramukh Swami, in noticeable frail health and no longer able to walk vigorously, is credited by *satsaṅgis* as being the sole inspiration for significant transformations in their personal and family lives? How was Pramukh Swami able to inaugurate the largest number of Hindu temples in the world, a feat recorded in *The Guinness Book of World Records*? For his followers, Pramukh Swami is indisputably beyond an ordinary human being. He is not God, yet according to devotees God resides within him. And he is perpetually oriented in service toward God and his own guru's commands (*ājñā*).[4] If devotees are able to emulate his ceaseless devotional stance by sustaining an uninterrupted devotion to God and their guru, this would halt the need for rebirth following death. Pramukh Swami is thus, as any video footage of him with devotees conveys, both the object of intense devotion and the one whose devotional postures and practices are closely followed and recognized by devotees as examples par excellence of the ideal servant of God. Pramukh Swami's quiet personal presence, nonostentatious behavior, and strict adherence to codes of behavior for ascetics do not suggest a "president" or boldly charismatic leader of a global Hindu community. Yet as guru he has nurtured the development of a transnational religious community whose temples have attracted widespread attention and whose publications, charitable services, order of ascetics, temple activities, and large volunteer base are easily recognizable and well appreciated by followers and those they have served.

This chapter provides an introductory overview of the roles that Pramukh Swami, as guru and as president (*pramukh*), fulfills in Swaminarayan *bhaktiyoga*. Relying on ethnographic field research and textual sources that include mediated correspondence, via male BAPS volunteers, with Swaminarayan *sādhus* (male ascetics) and research materials connected to the forthcoming dissertation by Sadhu Paramtattvadas, this chapter explores the role of the Swaminarayan guru and his contribution to the making of a contemporary devotional community.[5] We shall see what motivates Swaminarayan devotees to engage with their guru in particular ways and how this relationship, supported by Swaminarayan *bhakti*, makes possible a multiplicity of ways for devotees to express their individual devotional commitments. Swaminarayan *bhakti* rests on appreciating the relationship of devotees to guru and to God and on recognizing that each is also a distinct ontological entity. These entities are *Parabrahman*, *Brahman* (also *Akṣara* and *Akṣarabrahman*), *Māyā*, *Īśvara*, and *Jīva*. Informed by the dissertation research by Sadhu Paramtattvadas (forthcoming), this chapter suggests one way that Swaminarayan *bhaktiyoga* can be conceptualized is by examining the basis of the devotee's relationship to God. Within this framing, Swaminarayan *bhaktiyoga* can be seen as having two forms, *sādhan bhakti* and *sādhya bhakti*. Both forms are offered by the devotee to God, with *sādhan bhakti* being offered by devotees seeking to acquire the qualities that will make possible the performance of *sādhya bhakti*. As "the means," *sādhan bhakti* serves to help Swaminarayan devotees achieve the desired ontological state, known as *brahmarūpa*, that will make possible an eternal offering of devotion, *sādhya bhakti*, to God. Only after attaining *brahmarūpa* can the devotee experience the bliss of serving God eternally. This is "the end" or "what is to be attained" and what corresponds to *sādhya bhakti* (Sadhu Paramtattvadas, forthcoming). The ultimate objective of the Swaminarayan devotee is therefore to become *brahmarūpa*, the ontological state where the *jīva*, or eternal self, is freed from the cloak of *māyā* and liberated from *saṃsāra*. In this liberated state, the *jīva*, now referred to as the *ātmā*, is able to identify with *Akṣarabrahman* and offer a continuous and most "pure" form of *bhakti*, namely, *sādhya bhakti*, or the offering of eternal love and adoration to God. To achieve this state, one that is only possible after the recognition of the *jīva* as distinct from the body, the *Akṣarabrahman* guru is indispensable.

In Swaminarayan *bhaktiyoga*, thus, a connection is made between devotees' knowledge of their ontological state, the degree of identification with *Akṣarabrahman*, and the form of *bhakti*, *sādhan bhakti*, and *sādhya bhakti*, that can be offered to God. It is the guru who provides the possibility for devotees to attain the necessary knowledge to become *brahmarūpa*. The guru is the link, experientially and ontologically, between the devotee and God. In terms of actual devotional praxis, both guru and God are the focus of devotion in Swaminarayan *bhakti*. The guru is the focal point of devotion for being *Akṣarabrahman*, that is, the "'vessel' in whom God resides, works through, and accepts devotees' bhakti."[6] And it is the guru who makes possible devotees' desired position of offering devotion to God by helping them attain the state of *brahmarūpa* in which they realize their *ātmā* to be distinct from the physical, mental, and causal bodies and are able to identify with *Akṣarabrahman*.[7] In practice, thus, it is the guru who guides and instills the knowledge necessary for serving God eternally.

In BAPS Swaminarayan teachings, offering *bhakti* to the guru and recognizing his relationship to God is a means to achieving liberation from *saṃsāra*, or the cycle of birth and death. The guru occupies a dominant focus in *satsaṅgis'* daily lives for it is he who "holds the pure, complete presence of God" and he who is "the gateway to *mokṣa*."[8] By serving the guru and striving to overcome the limitations to ontological knowledge posed by the sensing and sensory body, devotees can hopefully attain the goal of identifying with *Akṣarabrahman* and serving God for eternity in his abode known as Akshardham.[9] This is the desired culmination of Swaminarayan *bhaktiyoga*, to be able to transition from performing *bhakti* to God while still identifying oneself with the body (*sādhan bhakti*) to offering ceaseless devotion and service to God from the position of a released *ātmā* (or soul) that has identified itself with *Akṣarabrahman* (*sādhya bhakti*). This latter ontological state, of the liberated soul, can be both postmortem while "dwelling eternally in the abode of God" (but which is therefore not possible to ascertain) and achievable while alive on earth as well.[10] In this striving to become *brahmarūpa*, that is, like *Akṣarabrahman*, the role of the *Akṣarabrahman* guru, is paramount.[11]

Figure 11.2:
Line drawing of Bhagwan Swaminarayan (right) and Aksharbrahman Guru. (Courtesy of BAPS Swaminarayan Sanstha.)

Swaminarayan *bhaktiyoga*, in its emphasis on the devotee offering devotion to the guru and striving to identify with the guru's expression of perfect devotion to God to achieve the state of *brahmarūpa*, makes possible certain innovations in *bhakti*.[12] Devotees have a need to offer *bhakti* as a means to acquire a desired ontological knowledge, and it is this impetus that perhaps accounts for BAPS's contemporary expressions of Hindu practice (Kim, 2009). *Satsaṅgis*, in other words, are primed to please their guru in their present lifetime.[13] They seek ways to promote and strengthen their identification with the qualities of the *Akṣarabrahman* guru that will help them move ever closer to the state of being *brahmarūpa* and correspondingly weaken their identification with or attachment to the physical body. In this teleological dynamic, of aiming to offer adoration to God eternally and doing so through the emulation and acquisition of qualities exemplified by the *Akṣarabrahman* guru, the devotional emphasis is on supporting this desire while devotees are living in the world. Perhaps it is not surprising then that the BAPS organization is engaged in efforts to maximize *satsaṅgis'* opportunities to progress toward the desired state of becoming *brahmarūpa*. More notable is BAPS's pragmatic orientation to seek ways to ensure the transmission of its teachings that are effective for its contemporary membership and their everyday social realities. BAPS is, for example, consistently generating new translations of its central texts and creating innovative ways to cultivate, sustain, and share Swaminarayan teachings. The results are visible in the successful and prolific BAPS publishing house, its network of transnational members and temples, and even its thriving ventures in vegetarian foods and *āyurvedic* products.

In the context of contemporary guru and yoga movements, Swaminarayan *bhaktiyoga* is also intriguing for its use of new technologies and the creative incorporation of large-scale festival celebrations and charitable service to support the relationship among devotee, guru, and God. Ethnographically, this chapter is necessarily limited to the terrestrial dimensions of Swaminarayan *bhakti*; however, it is both the observable and the beyond worldly dimensions of Swaminarayan *bhaktiyoga* that can provide a sense of why and how BAPS has become an important contributor to the contours of globalizing Hinduism.

The chapter is organized as follows. We begin with a brief introduction to the BAPS Swaminarayan community, followed by a discussion of BAPS ontological principles. Then we examine two types of *bhakti*, *sādhanā* and *sādhya bhakti*, that can be seen to characterize Swaminarayan *bhaktiyoga*, and we focus on the connection between ontological states and their associated type of *bhakti* practice. We then explore some of the ways devotees translate the teaching of their guru into actions that serve their devotional growth. The chapter concludes with reflections on how Swaminarayan *bhakti* fosters an aspirational orientation, one that is contributing to a distinctive and successful expression of globalizing Hinduism.

THE BAPS COMMUNITY TODAY

With over eight hundred temples, one million followers, and an order of male ascetics numbering more than eight hundred, the BAPS Swaminarayan community has come to exemplify a new kind of global Hindu community, one that can be characterized by its embrace of technological and communication advances and its commitment to sustaining its teachings and traditions on a transnational scale. Ritually and textually, BAPS is usually categorized within the Vaiṣṇava Hindu tradition, but its understanding of the ultimate existential entity is not one that is necessarily shared by those outside of the BAPS community. Administered via a network of temples and centers, including its important headquarter in Ahmedabad (also Amdavad) in Gujarat, the BAPS organization and its many layers of religious and lay administration and volunteer support make possible an extensive global community that counts devotees in most continents and in many countries (see, e.g., the "Global Network" page on http://www.swaminarayan.org).[14] The largest numbers of *satsaṅgis* are in India, followed by North America and England. Most are of Gujarati origin or heritage and come from all caste and class backgrounds.

Founded in 1907, the BAPS Swaminarayan Sanstha, or fellowship, as BAPS publications sometimes translate, must be distinguished from other Swaminarayan sects or communities, some more well known than others. The various Swaminarayan groups recognize the historical person of Sahajanand Swami (1781–1830 CE), who is the founder of the Swaminarayan *sampradāya*, but there are differences in the interpretation of Sahajanand Swami's ontological position, whether as God, *avatāra*, or guru. In the BAPS community, Sahajanand Swami is the same as the ultimate existential entity, Bhagwan, commonly translated as "God." All Swaminarayan sects embrace several texts, produced or written during the time of Sahajanand Swami's life, including the *Vacanāmṛta* (hereafter *Vachanamrut*), a collection of discourses given by Sahajanand Swami and compiled by his ascetic followers.

The guru is the highest point of religious leadership in BAPS. Below him are the male ascetics, or *sādhus*, and below them are the lay leaders, men and women, who fill numerous volunteer positions. Many of the lay leaders have administrative positions in BAPS that provide them with extensive organizational authority; this however, should not be confused with the religious authority of the guru and *sādhus*. Below the religious leadership layer is an international group of "core" followers, an estimated 55,000 *satsaṅgis*, who regularly volunteer at Swaminarayan temples and participate in large-scale festivals organized by BAPS. The vast majority of *satsaṅgis* are not active volunteers but those who visit the temple for the weekly assembly (*sabhā*) and on major Hindu calendrical days.

Among the more well-known and more noticeable aspects of BAPS is its temple-building activities, including the Gandhinagar, Gujarat, and New Delhi Akshardham temple complexes (Kim, 2007). These structures have certainly drawn much notice and from a wider variety of visitors than just BAPS devotees. Also attracting the curiosity of the wider public are the *śikharbaddha mandiras*, or pinnacled temples, including those constructed outside of India, such as the five in North America and the famed London (more precisely the Neasden) BAPS Shri Swaminarayan *mandira* (more commonly spelled as *mandir*). These edifices, with their lavishly carved exteriors and extensive assembly and other interior spaces, have prompted many observers to assume that BAPS is poised to become—if it has not already—a dominant voice in global Hinduism. While this has prompted some critics to allege that BAPS is establishing its visibility through its striking temples possibly to subsume other expressions of Hindu tradition, this is not the motivation behind the temple-building projects, neither from the devotees' nor the religious and lay leaders' perspectives (Kim, 2012).[15]

Another area of BAPS public presence is its role in humanitarian and charitable activities. Though *sevā*, or volunteer work, has been a hallmark of the Swaminarayan *sampradāya* from its early days, the scale of BAPS activities and its ability to mobilize its own volunteer corps have facilitated its ability to help many within and beyond Gujarat. From the volunteers' perspective, BAPS activities, whether in temple building, festival events, or humanitarian work, provide opportunities to promote devotees' awareness of performing *bhakti* to Bhagwan and doing so through service to their guru. As committed *satsaṅgis* often point out, to seek opportunities to do *sevā* is to emulate the ways of the guru who is always in service to God. It is the same guru on whom *jīvas* are dependent for their liberation.

SWAMINARAYAN ONTOLOGICAL PRINCIPLES

Keeping this in mind, all of our *satsangis* should develop the following singular conviction: we also wish to join the ranks of the *aksharrup muktas* and go to Akshardhām to forever remain in the service of God.

–*Vachanamrut*, Gadhada I-21: 8

For *satsaṅgis*, the *Vachanamrut* is seen as Sahajanand Swami's distillation of the classical Hindu texts, the Vedas, Upaniṣads, *Bhagavad Gītā*, Dharmaśāstras, Purāṇas, and Itihāsas, into the lessons that are crucial for those hoping to leave the cycle of death and rebirth. It is also the central text from which the founder of BAPS, Shastriji Maharaj, located the source of his interpretation of Sahajanand Swami as Bhagwan (God) and the *Akṣarabrahman* guru, or "god-realized saint," as the existential entity through which aspirants could attain the ontological state of *brahmarūpa* and come to comprehend the nature of God. The *Vachanamrut* explicates the relationships between the BAPS ontological entities, and it guides the *satsaṅgi* toward acquiring the realization necessary to become an ideal devotee. Without this realization, as even the youngest *satsaṅgi* knows, one cannot spend eternity in the presence of God, in a permanent state of bliss and devotion to him, but must rather endure rebirth.

In the *Vachanamrut*, Sahajanand Swami explains that there are five permanent existential entities: *Parabrahman, Akṣarabrahman* (also *Akṣara* and *Brahman*), *Māyā*, *Īśvara*, and *Jīva*.[16] None of these entities ever merges into the other or into *Parabrahman* who is unique and the "uncaused of all causes" (Dave, 2000: 18). From the Swaminarayan perspective, *Parabrahman* is the ultimate existential reality and, as the creator of all, he is immanent in all. He is also called *Puruṣottama* (more commonly spelled as *Purushottam*) and Bhagwan, and all are translated as "God" by BAPS. *Parabrahman* is independent, eternal, and infinite, and, for BAPS devotees, he has a divine human-like form (*sākāra*) and is known as Bhagwan Swaminarayan or Sahajanand Swami. By his grace, according to *satsaṅgis*, Bhagwan Swaminarayan appeared on earth between 1781 and 1830. And though Bhagwan Swaminarayan returned to his heavenly abode, his ontological presence as *Puruṣottama* remains continuously on earth in human-like form through the penultimate existential entity, *Akṣarabrahman*.

Akṣarabrahman is subordinate only to *Puruṣottama*. Known also as *Brahman* or *Akṣara*, *Akṣarabrahman* is existentially unique but has several roles. One role is the *dhām*, or abode of *Parabrahman-Purushottam* and of the *akṣara muktas*, the *jīvas* released from rebirth. This abode is known as Akshardham. Another role, and one that contributes to the distinctiveness of BAPS *bhakti*, is the equation of *Akṣara* with the *parama ekāntika bhakta* or one who is the perfect devotee of God and in whom God resides. The *parama ekāntika bhakta* exemplifies *ekāntika dharma* wherein *dharma*, *jñāna*, *vairāgya*, and *bhakti* are perfectly upheld for the sole purpose of pleasing God. As the upholder of *ekāntika dharma* and as one who is beyond the influence of *māyā*, *Akṣarabrahman* is synonymous with the *guṇātīta satpuruṣa*, that is, he who is eternally perfect and transcends the *guṇas* of *māyā*. In BAPS, the *parama ekāntika bhakta* and *guṇātīta satpuruṣa* is the guru.[17]

Akshardham, in Swaminarayan teaching, is the abode of God. The form of *Akṣara* that manifests as the human-like *guṇātīta satpuruṣa*, or guru, is also the "residence" of *Parabrahman* on earth. The ontological principle that *Parabrahman* and *Akṣarabrahman* are unique and forever distinct and where *Parabrahman* resides in Akshardham is simultaneously reproduced in an earthly context where *Parabrahman* resides in *Akṣara, or* the guru. In BAPS, there is a lineage of gurus (*guru paramparā*) dating to the time of Sahajanand Swami's historical presence in Gujarat. The current form of *Akṣarabrahman* or *guṇātīta satpuruṣa* is Pramukh Swami Maharaj.

Māyā, according to BAPS teachings, is known also as *prakṛti*. It is eternal, nonsentient, and constituted of three *guṇas* that influence all beings. In BAPS theology, *māyā* can be understood as "anything that hinders devotion and worship of God" and therefore requires the guidance of the *guṇātīta satpuruṣa*, the guru, who helps devotees transcend the influence of *guṇas* so they may attain the ontological state of *brahmarūpa*, or of becoming like Brahman (Sadhu Vivekjivandas 2010: pt. 2, 203).

Īśvaras are eternal and sentient entities who have powers to create, sustain, and destroy. While *īśvaras* are in control of their domain of the universe, they nevertheless are ensnared in *māyā* and subject to *saṃsāra*. In BAPS teachings, *īśvaras* need to attain a state of being like *Brahman*, or *brahmarūpa*, to attain liberation. For this, they too need the intervention of *Akṣarabrahman* or *Parabrahman*.

Jīvas are eternal and sentient entities that are bound by *māyā*. Their powers and abilities to control parts of the universe are far more limited than those held by *īśvaras*. *Jīvas* are clothed in physical bodies and go through death and rebirth. In BAPS teachings, the *jīva*, if reborn into a human body, can associate with Bhagwan or a *guṇātīta satpuruṣa* and thereby have the possibility of being freed from *māyā*. Swaminarayan devotees know that their individual *jīva*, owing to its subservience to bodily senses (*indriyas*), bodily sensory capacities of taste, touch, smell, sight, and sound (*pāñcaviṣayas*) and to the capacities of the mind (*antaḥkaraṇa*),[18] requires the intervention of the guru. By giving devotional service to the *guṇātīta satpuruṣa* (also guru) and to God, the *jīva* can possibly be freed of bodily desires and ignorance. In this state of *brahmarūpa* (also *akṣarrūpa*), the *jīva* no longer becomes attached to the physical body of its birth or to the assumption that the body is synonymous with the self. This is an objective of all Swaminarayan *satsaṅgis*, to be freed from the ignorance of identifying the eternal *jīva* with the temporary form of the human body. Freed of *māyā* and therefore liberated from *saṃsāra*, the *jīva* is referred to as *ātmā*. The final objective of the *satsaṅgi* is, in the state *brahmarūpa*, to offer one's *ātmā* eternally in service to *Parabrahman*, who is also *Paramātmā*, the supreme of all existential beings.

To summarize, the relationship among God (*Parabrahman, Puruṣottama, Paramātmā*), guru (*Akṣarabrahman, Akṣara, Brahman*), and the devotee (*jīva*) is an intertwined one that rests on each ontological entity remaining distinct from the other and where the association of *jīva* with *Akṣara* makes possible the opportunity to remain eternally with *Akṣara* in the company of *Puruṣottama*. In practice, this relationship is experienced against the background of *māyā* and the latter's capacity to orient the bodily self toward fulfilling sensory and worldly desires. In Swaminarayan *bhaktiyoga*, the devotee who seeks or becomes attached to the *guṇātīta* guru, within whom God resides, has the opportunity to discard the influence of *māyā* and, in being freed of *māyā*, recognize the limitless greatness of God. In this state of *mukti* (liberation), the *jīva* enters Akshardham where all entities remain distinct while offering devotion to God. This is the central motivation for following Swaminarayan *bhaktiyoga*, to forever offer love and service to God, and thereby eternally receive his grace.[19]

SWAMINARAYAN *BHAKTIYOGA*

For one who follows Yoga, the luminous, divine form of God which resides in Akshardhām at the time of *ātyantik-pralay* [final dissolution] is worthy of being meditated on forever.

–*Vachanamrut,* Panchālā 2: 9

In the *Vachanamrut*, Sahajanand Swami mentions yoga numerous times. Depending on context, yoga has varying meanings, including yoga in contrast to *sāṃkhya darśan* and yoga as a means to gain control of the physical and mental self and therefore experience *samādhi* and yoga as a way to attain the highest awareness of God through realization of the *ātmā* and *Paramātmā*. It is this latter usage that is synonymous with the objective of *satsaṅgis*, namely, to attain the ability to offer constant and eternal devotion to Bhagwan Swaminarayan in Akshardham through realization of *ātmā* and *Paramātmā* rather than through other means such as breath control (*prāṇāyāma*). Yoga becomes synonymous with the realization of God's greatness from the perspective of being a released *jīva*. The Vachanamrut also emphasizes that the only way to attain the realization of God is by becoming *brahmarūpa* and thereby possessing the qualities of *Akṣarabrahman*. From this ontological state, of being an *ekāntika bhakta*, the devotee can offer the "purest" form of *bhakti*, or what Swaminarayan *sādhus* refer to as *sādhya bhakti*.

The majority of *satsaṅgis* in the BAPS community would likely admit that they have not yet attained the status of *brahmarūpa*. As they perform their daily devotional activities, attend *mandir* events, and contribute their resources to BAPS temple construction and other projects, *satsaṅgis* hope that these actions will contribute to an awareness of their *jīva* as an indivisible entity that is merely temporarily tethered to their bodies. *Satsaṅgis*, in other words, are offering service and devotion and acquiring *satsaṅga* knowledge as part of their *sādhanā*, or endeavors toward the goal of one day sitting in Akshardham and serving God directly. This effort of the devotee is called *sādhan bhakti*, or that which is performed in the process of becoming *brahmarūpa*. *Sādhan bhakti* entails following rules of *dharma* (moral and ethical conduct), seeking *jñāna* (knowledge), observing *vairāgya* (nonattachment to objects and desires other than those directed to God), and performing *bhakti* (offerings, services, and expressions of love) with the intention to please God. In the Vachanamrut, these four endeavors are part of Swaminarayan *sādhanā* (religious praxis) and collectively are referred to as *ekāntika dharma*. The devotee who successfully possesses *dharma*, *jñāna*, *vairāgya*, and *bhakti* and who realizes the unparalleled greatness of God is an *ekāntika bhakta*. The living guru is understood by Swaminarayan devotees to be the perfect example of an *ekāntika bhakta* and is therefore *parama ekāntika bhakta* (see *Vachanamrut*, Gadhada III-13).

The virtues of *dharma*, *jñāna*, *vairāgya*, and *bhakti* are not dissimilar to the teachings in the *Bhagavad Gītā* where the path to God-realization can occur in several ways, via *jñānayoga* (knowledge), *karmayoga* (actions), and *bhaktiyoga* (acts of devotion and love). In BAPS though, the pathways of knowledge, action, and devotion are all necessary for pleasing God and realizing his greatness. And, according to the *Vachanamrut*, all actions, when motivated by the desire to know God, contribute to the performance of *bhakti* (see *Vachanamrut*, Gadhada II-32 and Gadhada II-65).[20]

To summarize, Swaminarayan *bhaktiyoga* can be seen as having two forms, *sādhan bhakti* and *sādhya bhakti*, and both reflect the central significance of *Akṣarabrahman's* qualities. Those who desire to attain liberation will perform *sādhan bhakti* to attain the ontological state of *brahmarūpa*, one that does not mean becoming *Akṣarabrahman* but realizing the qualities of this eternal existential entity. And for those who have attained the state of *brahmarūpa* through the emulation and adoration of the *Akṣarabrahman guru* and who, having demonstrated their realization of *jīva* as distinct from the body, are identified with *Akṣarabrahman*, they are now able to perform *sādhya bhakti*. As the highest form of *bhakti* from the Swaminarayan perspective, *sādhya bhakti* makes possible the permanent offering of "perfect love" directly to God.[21] *Sādhya bhakti* is the same as *ekāntika bhakti*, where the *Akṣara mukta*, that is, the liberated *jīva*, is a permanent servant of God, able now to thoroughly direct the virtues of *dharma*, *jñāna*, *vairāgya*, and *bhakti* toward serving God on earth and in Akshardham, God's heavenly abode. From the perspective of Swaminarayan theology, *sādhya bhakti is* yoga, or the fullest recognition of God as reigning supreme (*sarvopari*), having a divine form (*sākāra*), being the all-doer (*sarva-kartā*), and forever manifesting in the form of the *guṇātīta* guru (*pragata*).

THE GURU IN ETHNOGRAPHIC CONTEXT

> . . . Intense love for the Satpurush is the only means to realising one *ātmā*; it is the only means to realising the greatness of the Satpurush; and it is also the only means to having the direct realisation of God.
>
> –*Vachanamrut*, Vartal 11: 12

The form of *Akṣara* as manifested in the living guru and his immense role in Swaminarayan *bhaktiyoga* is what distinguishes BAPS from other branches of the Swaminarayan *sampradāya*. BAPS *satsaṅgis* see God as present within and working through *Akṣara*, the *brahmasvarūpa* (possessing the form of *Brahman*) guru. As the clearest and most concrete example of how an *ekāntika bhakta* performs devotion, the guru is the object of extraordinary devotion and expressions of surrender. Wherever one meets a Swaminarayan *satsaṅgi*, one will hear much about Pramukh Swami. In day-to-day living, *satsaṅgis* turn to Bapa or Swamishri, as he is lovingly called, to help overcome or address the challenges of living as a *satsaṅgi*. Bapa is the means to achieve the desired state of shedding *māyā*, but there are, as *satsaṅgis* readily share, many obstacles to overcome when trying to attain the state of *brahmarūpa*. *Satsaṅgis* wish, as they say, to "become like Swamishri" while living fully in the world: they hope, in other words, to attain his qualities of offering uninterrupted devotion to God, of being unhindered by the mind and body, and of remaining nonattached to material needs and goods.

Perhaps, for the non-*satsaṅgi*, it is difficult to appreciate the effect the guru has on the *satsaṅgi*, one that often converts to hours of *sevā* and the dedication of personal resources, including monies, to BAPS. For the outsider, Pramukh Swami may not appear to be overtly charismatic. His usually short speeches may not seem to be cleverly constructed or smoothly delivered, and he may not appear to be worldly. Yet Pramukh Swami and the BAPS organization have constructed temples, schools, hospitals, and hostels throughout

Gujarat and elsewhere. For *satsaṅgis*, it is not how their guru sounds but what he says, the qualities of the *parama ekāntika bhakta* he possesses, and who he embodies that draws them to him. As for the monies spent on temple construction, these are donations inspired by Pramukh Swami Maharaj and are not intended to glorify either his or BAPS's indisputable organizational skills but to foster and sustain devotees' own practice of Swaminarayan *bhakti* and *upāsanā* (philosophy and theology). *Satsaṅgis* see Pramukh Swami's unswerving attention to serving God, literally, in the form of the *mūrti* of Bhagwan Swaminarayan that is always with him. And they see his "self-less dedication" to serving the *satsaṅgi* so that devotees too could achieve the knowledge necessary to become *ekāntika bhaktas*. Though elderly and beset by serious health issues, Pramukh Swami, as all *satsaṅgis* know, maintains an unceasing schedule of activities to serve the *satsaṅga*; and he is without holiday, without privacy, and certainly without a permanent residence. Thus, in their *sevā*, devotees frequently mention that their guru works tirelessly to serve them, his guru, and God, and therefore they must do the same for their guru and God.

Many stories of self-transformation illustrate how doing *sevā* is a critical means to realizing the distinction of the *jīva* from the body. Many trace the beginning of their commitment to BAPS by recalling their first *sevā*. Others share that it is only with Pramukh Swami Maharaj's inspiration that they are able to actually work with other *satsaṅgis* and realize that the desires and needs of the body and mind are very difficult to eradicate.

Just as compelling as the accounts of self-transformation that are catalyzed by *sevā* are those that *satsaṅgis* have of being physically touched by Pramukh Swami (males only) or of being in the "right place at the right time" and having the opportunity for an exceptional darshan of their guru. On November 2, 2005, before the inauguration of the New Delhi Swaminarayan Akshardham complex, *satsaṅgis* from around the world were enjoying the privilege of experiencing the complex before its opening to the public. While waiting to enter an exhibition, I met several young men who had come from London. Each had a story to tell about how he had become a *satsaṅgi*. One story, though not unique, nevertheless remained in my mind, perhaps as the narrator himself seemed still astonished by what had happened to him.

> Let me tell you . . . in university, I got in with a bad crowd. I was smoking and drinking and everything. I tried to quit, believe me, many times. On August 18, 2004, Bapa was at London mandir. After *sabha* [*sabhā*], you know how people run up to Bapa, to get to him before he is whisked to his quarters. There, where the *sadhus* [*sādhus*] stay, there is high security. Well, I went to *santos*' quarters after *sabha*.[22] Security let me pass through. I went to Bapa. Few *haribhaktos* were there. Just a few. Bapa took my hand and talked to me for seven minutes. You know how long that is! He put *vartman* [*vartamān*] in my hand and said to stop what I was doing. He talked and I couldn't say anything. From that day, I quit

> smoking and drinking. I have not had even any urges. Viveksagar Swami told me, I had an instant transplant, a shortcut. Like the Government NHS [National Health Service] where Viveksagar [Swami] said that if you break a finger, you have to wait your turn for surgery. And [expression of amazement], I was bumped to the front of the queue!

As he shared this *prasanga* (story), my interlocutor was surrounded by two friends who listened as intently as I to a story that they had undoubtedly heard more than once. Then each also shared his personal account of realizing the "power of Swamishri" and of undergoing instant self-transformations that included changing eating and other habits. One of the young men said, "My family is not *satsangi* . . . then one day I met Swami. All he did, he didn't say anything. He just [pauses, and in demonstration, extends his hand, placing it palm down on the top of my head] and that's it. That's all it took."

The power of Pramukh Swami Maharaj to motivate young men to suddenly transform their ways of life is one that cannot be explained by material reasons alone. From all caste and class backgrounds, Gujarati men and women, in India and much beyond, have found BAPS Swaminarayan Hindu practices and teachings appealing to them. Potential *satsaṅgis* attend *mandir* events and of those who decide to become more regular attendants and those who become regular volunteers, they do so for many different reasons. What remains consistent though is the response that hundreds of *satsaṅgis* have shared with me: they are in BAPS "because of my guru." Were it not for Pramukh Swami's presence, guidance, and quiet inspiration, they would not necessarily remain in *satsaṅga*. Whether due to dissatisfaction with fellow *satsaṅgis* or the ways their temples are organized, or other issues not uncommon in large organizations with a central administrative structure, the *satsaṅgis* who confided some of their misgivings about BAPS noted that only someone like their guru, "truly a *gunatit satpurush* and not a normal human being" could possibly cope with the inevitable problems that would affect the operation of an extensive transnational community.

Indeed, many Hindus have certain expectations of guru-led movements. These assumptions can be traced to long-standing or more recent traditions of guru movements arising in the Indian subcontinent and elsewhere. Perhaps what makes the BAPS guru-led movement appear to be different is not necessarily its ontological system consisting of five eternal entities but the ways in which the real-time relationship between these entities fosters ways of being that, in turn, have contributed to the expansion of this devotional community. The activities of *satsaṅgis*, in other words, rest on an epistemic foundation that accounts for the external expressions of the BAPS *satsaṅga* as well as supporting, from the devotees' perspectives, their goal of becoming *brahmarūpa*. "Inspired by our guru," *satsaṅgis* contributed to the design, construction, and staffing of two Akshardham complexes; for the New Delhi

Akshardham, they have created a large-screen format film in India, one that entailed thousands of preproduction, filming, and postproduction hours and which showcases the story of Bhagwan Swaminarayan; they have organized festivals, some lasting one month or more and where all guests were provided with meals; they have established a successful diaspora of *satsaṅgis*, with temples, centers, publications, teaching materials, and ritual items for the maintenance of devotional practice; they have created a management structure that connects all temples and religious and lay leaders to the institutional center in Ahmedabad, Gujarat. These and many other accomplishments have made possible a global religious community wherein some who have never been to Gujarat or even India, or others who have never had a personal encounter with their guru, nevertheless feel an enormous desire to be a part of BAPS and to "achieve communion" with its president and guru.

BHAKTIYOGA AND ITS WORKING PARADOXES

This is possible because of Bapa.
Everything you see here is all due to our wish to please him.
Whatever Swamishri says, I will do it to the best of my ability.[23]
—Shared by BAPS *satsaṅgis*

In India, with the success of the New Delhi Swaminarayan Akshardham temple complex, BAPS has achieved visibility and a certain amount of notoriety as well. Though beyond the focus of this chapter, scholars and others have critiqued the location, design, content, and even visitor rules for the Delhi Akshardham complex (Brosius, 2010; Singh, 2010; Srivastava, 2009). And critics have also commented on the expenditure of monies on temple construction projects that could have gone to other charitable purposes such as education and health welfare programs for women and children. There is, not surprisingly, a significant chasm between the perspectives of BAPS critics and its devotees. The former are more likely to assess *satsaṅgis* as motivated by needs of nostalgia, power, immigrant nationalism, Hindu nationalism, and middle-class aspirations that promote exclusion and political conservatism. And, among devotees, there are undoubtedly those who are sympathetic to and otherwise supportive of Hindu nationalist agendas, those who are seeking expressions of an "authentic Hinduism," and many more who are keen to join the fabled ranks of the Indian middle class. Yet for the devotees who have willingly donated their time and monies to BAPS and in some instances, have become full-time volunteers or given permission for sons to become fully dedicated to BAPS as *sādhus*, there is only one reason that accounts for the modern-day achievements of BAPS: the desire to please and offer worship to guru and God. For the nondevotee, the relationship between devotee and guru and God is not always a comprehensible one, or perhaps it is one that some choose not to comprehend. In either situation, the visible accomplishments and activities of BAPS are analyzed in exclusive terms of materiality, history, political and economic processes and pressures, and the clash of discourses on religion, Hinduism, and immigrant needs that affect many Hindu movements and not just BAPS. These analyses can go far in helping us to understand the efflorescence of BAPS and they illuminate the on-the-ground challenges of sustaining a devotional movement in the context of shifting materialities. But the chasm remains between these analyses and the understanding of Swaminarayan *bhakti* from the *satsaṅgis'* perspectives.

BAPS *sādhus* themselves are aware that the Swaminarayan *satsaṅga*, particularly since the time of Pramukh Swami's leadership, beginning in 1971, has metamorphosed into a global organization with an efficient ability to coordinate a wide range of temple-based activities and projects. In BAPS texts and in communication that I have received from *sādhus* (always through a male BAPS volunteer serving as an intermediary), they share that they and their guru are frequently asked how BAPS has managed to build so many temples, run large festivals, and cultivate a strong volunteer base. How does a guru with seemingly nonworldly interests appear nevertheless to be overseeing a transnational organization with corporation-like efficiency? In one text focused on highlighting the virtues of guru Pramukh Swami, Sadhu Aksharvatsaldas (2008: 181) writes: "It is near impossible to describe how Swamishri is able to motivate and inspire these volunteers, how he is able to get them to dedicate their lives and livelihoods to better society, and how he is able to satisfy and manage all of them. There is only one word that describes this unachievable task: *kauśalam*." As one of the thirty-nine virtues of God described in the *Bhāgavata Purāṇa*, *kauśalam* as defined by Sadhu Aksharvatsaldas is "efficiency, excellence, and perfection," the qualities also present in the *guṇātīta* guru (p. 179). When devotees and *sādhus* see their guru, in his ascetic's robes, focused on devotion to God and without possessions, they attribute this to his impeccable state of being beyond *māyā*, of being *guṇātīta*, and therefore of having no desires other than to please God. For those outside of BAPS, this explanation, rooted as it is in Swaminarayan *upāsanā*, is less than persuasive. One American graduate student and devoted *satsaṅgi* commented to me, "For those who have not been attracted to BAPS or guru Pramukh Swami, there is no way you can understand what it is to crave the Satpurush's *rajipo* [*rājīpo*], until you have started on that path. . . ." *Rājīpo*, as another *satsaṅgi* sketched out for me, is an "innermost blessing," or what "springs forth spontaneously" and is connected to the "guru's approval and favor."[24] Similarly, Sadhu Mangalnidhidas writes, "*Rajipo* can be defined as the spiritual happiness of one's guru. When the guru is pleased with you, you have earned his *rajipo*."[25] In other words, without already being predisposed toward Swaminarayan *bhakti*, the desire to please guru and to receive in return his pleasure and grace is something that one must be open to experiencing. Constituted of its own categories and informing discourses, its own assumptions and ontologies, Swaminarayan *bhakti* does demand that devotees recognize the pre-eminent role of the guru and the presence of God within him. Indeed, many long-time *satsaṅgis* still express wonder that they somehow managed to find the "perfect guru," the same who is unaffected by living in the world, unconcerned about satisfying his bodily needs, and undisturbed by the attention and distraction arising from being the leader of BAPS.

In their correspondence reflecting on Swaminarayan *bhaktiyoga*, the *sādhus* write, "The guru as the ideal *bhakta* provides a 'devotional compass' in a constantly changing world."[26] As society and culture are ever changing, the living guru remains unaffected by these realities and directs his focus to serving God. But the guru is still able to address the hardships and predicaments of *satsaṅgis* who are very much in the world. Swaminarayan *bhakti* does not proscribe worldly activities but enjoins that the pursuits of wealth and attributes of success, if directed toward serving guru and God, are rewarding to the devotee's own devotional goals. For *satsaṅgis*, the ability of guru Pramukh Swami both to live very much in the world and to show no evidence of being attracted to sensory pleasures is testament to how they should strive to live to become *brahmarūpa*. It is thus possible to pursue the goals of being human, of seeking wealth and satisfying the senses, but these should not interfere with the primary goal of directing the "fruit of actions" toward serving God and their guru.

As *satsaṅgis* face the challenge of maintaining the commandments (*ājñā*) of their guru while living and working in contexts that may impede their devotional goals, the present living guru has kept apace by sustaining Swaminarayan *bhaktiyoga* through numerous means. Pramukh Swami has embraced new technologies and initiated institutional strategies that support the reality of *satsaṅgis'* lives, and he recognizes that many increasingly live where Hindu traditions are not in the majority. In addition to *mandir* building projects, there are Hinduism exhibitions, varieties of weekend events in temples, multimedia products, and publications geared toward different levels of *satsaṅga* knowledge; there are also classes for children and youth that address subjects from Swaminarayan *upāsanā* to public speaking and learning Gujarati. Pramukh Swami and BAPS, while using the latest strategies for meeting the needs of the BAPS membership, from the *satsaṅgi* perspective are confirming that a devotional community predicated on the teachings of a nineteenth-century manifestation of God can indeed thrive in the twenty-first century world.

In Swaminarayan temples, there are gymnasiums and computer centers. In the occasional international BAPS festival celebrations, there are crowd-pleasing cultural performances as well as booths to purchase vegetarian fast food and to exchange foreign currency. On the http://swaminarayan.org website, there are pages for *mūrti darśana*, for hearing Pramukh Swami's lessons, and for seeing photos of the guru which document the range of his devotional activities. For many, these aspects of BAPS are puzzling for their easy integration of leisure and entertainment, their apparent commodification of religion, and the seeming promotion of middle-class trends under the umbrella of a religion. Since these creative ways of enhancing the experience of devotees and visitors to Swaminarayan events could probably not occur against the wishes of guru Pramukh Swami, both he and the BAPS organization appear to tacitly acknowledge that Swaminarayan *bhaktiyoga* can and must coexist within multiple and no doubt competing demands of contemporary life. Furthermore, though the core devotional ideals and practices of BAPS *upāsanā* have not, according to its *sādhus*, changed over the past century,[27] the guru and the BAPS organization's range of projects and activities seem to reflect their strategies to ensure the maintenance of Swaminarayan *bhakti* wherever it has settled. For committed *satsaṅgis*, perhaps the more relevant concern is how to help non-*satsaṅgis* see the guru as a powerful guide for living with ease in the modern world. The *sādhus*, in their correspondence, share:

> One can become confused as to how one *might* practice devotion in a modern setting or when one's devotional values seem in conflict with a modern situation. But seeing how the guru reacts in that same modern world or learning how he wishes for the devotees to act in such situations provides a fresh, relevant, and effective ideal for them to emulate. Importantly, this also provides devotees with timely and vital spiritual confidence and consolation.[28]

Pramukh Swami's role is both one of "spiritual guide" and administrative head of BAPS, and his noticeable abilities in both arenas have contributed to the global presence of BAPS. As a devotional movement arising in colonial India, BAPS's metamorphosis from a regional Gujarati devotional community into a transnational one is also an account of Swaminarayan *bhaktiyoga* and its transformation into a portable framework for ethical living. Guided by a guru whose behavior has inspired many followers to flourish as citizens of the world, the visible success of BAPS can also be read as the material expression of an ontological change within devotees: as *satsaṅgis* seek to acquire increasing knowledge of the unbounded self and perform *sādhan bhakti*, their association with the *Akṣarabrahman* guru and Swaminarayan *upāsanā* continues to inspire them toward further opportunities to serve their guru and God. One *satsaṅgi*, having made the decision to dedicate himself full-time to BAPS and having received permission from his wife and family to pursue this path, noted that he had everything to live comfortably, including the ability to support his wife. With his grown children not yet married, a situation that for some might preclude dedicating oneself to full-time volunteer work, he nevertheless felt drawn to serve Pramukh Swami Maharaj and thereby serve many more people than just "me and my family." A young recently married woman whose husband approved of her volunteer work at Delhi Akshardham, added, "I could have gone out and worked . . . but where could I go improve my relationship to Pramukh Swami? I feel like I am giving something back to Bhagwan and guru."

On the surface, the BAPS Swaminarayan community appears to some to be built on the pilings of class, immigration, conservative politics, and a veiled aggressiveness to assert a singular vision of Hinduism for the consumption of all. Moreover, following Steven Vertovec's (2000) work on the South Asian diaspora, BAPS can be seen as a "cosmopolitan" Hindu group, one that consciously aims to sustain itself via flexible strategies that are attuned to context, geography, and dominant society's expectations. Yet neither the outward achievements of BAPS, such as temple construction nor the personal acts of introspection and devotional offerings can be understood separately from Swaminarayan *bhaktiyoga*. Swaminarayan devotees seek to please their guru and to develop a relationship with him that will sustain their long-term goal to become like him in terms of his "divine characteristics."[29] The actions of *satsaṅgis* are thus not merely gestures of seeking and providing adoration: they are the means of *sādhan bhakti*, of trying to emancipate the *jīva*, the eternal self, from the bondage of identification with the body and thereby attain the ability to identify with *Akṣarabrahman* and attain the objective of Swaminarayan *bhaktiyoga*, namely, offering *sādhya bhakti*, where there is no desire for objects or needs other than to be the adoring servant of *Puruṣottama*.

GURU MIMESIS

Is it truly in one's own hands to see one's own self? If it is, why does the *jiva* remain ignorant?

–*Vachanamrut,* Gadhada I-20: 9

In a broad historical sense, the questions answered by Swaminarayan *bhaktiyoga* are ones that have been asked for millennia: What is the self, and what is the body? What lies beyond the self and body? Are there eternal entities? Is there an eternal component within the physical body? How does the self acquire knowledge about what is eternal? How does the self reconcile its position in relation to the body? Where does the eternal component within the body, if any, go following the disintegration of the body? The BAPS devotional community, supported as it is by devotees' dependency on their guru and his upholding of *ekāntika dharma* as a prerequisite for attaining liberation from *saṃsāra,* is a highly aspirational model. Devotees seek to attain the qualities of the guru, for he is the tangible, visible, and indisputable example of how both to achieve the state of living within the world and to remain fully engaged with devotion to Bhagwan Swaminarayan. This dynamic, in its support of self-transformation for the purpose of a desired ontological objective, generates a religious subjectivity that, in some respects, appears to complement assumptions about modern subjectivity while nevertheless challenging the commonly unquestioned dichotomy of the traditional and the modern. Swaminarayan devotees are described by themselves and others as industrious, hardworking, and organized. Many are exemplars of worldly success and no doubt many more are striving to achieve the same. Yet the desire for material success is motivated, as *satsaṅgis* share, by a determination to translate the actions of everyday life, including educational accomplishments, financial stability, and social recognition, into service to "the manifest form of God," the *Akṣarabrahman* guru. The noticeable aspirational orientation of *satsaṅgis* is thus not solely aligned with the wish to become materially comfortable or to gain social status. Rather, there is a parallel motivation, that the focus and drive to succeed must be applied to the bodily self so that the eternal self, the *jīva*, can be distinguished from the transient body and its many needs and desires. *Satsaṅgis*, in their daily lives, are thus not grappling with how to balance the traditional or the modern. They are trying to live a life fully engaged in the world while yearning to earn the grace of God. For the BAPS devotee, the template for how to achieve this is the *Akṣarabrahman* guru whose qualities of being beyond *māyā*, of being fully devoted to God, and of being humble, compassionate, and eternal are the very same that must be emulated. As the Swaminarayan *sādhus* affirm, ". . . If one truly wishes to form a firm conviction of God infused with the knowledge of his greatness, one must first recognise and understand the true greatness of Aksharbrahma."[30]

To return to the philosophical and existential, the in-built guru mimesis in Swaminarayan *bhaktiyoga* reveals a relationship between *jīva* and *Puruṣottama* that is fostered through the *Akṣarabrahman* guru. Devotees are the seekers who wish to develop their mimetic faculty, and to copy and attain the qualities, characteristics, and actions of the *guṇātīta* guru. The guru is fundamentally an Other in whom the *jīva* of the devotee never merges. To attain the qualities of *Akṣarabrahman* is, according to Swaminarayan *bhakti*, to have the "eligibility" of serving *Parabrahman* in his abode.[31] The Akṣarabrahman guru is one without faults and who is in constant communion with God. As devotees try to mimic their guru and as they are more able to channel their actions, bodily postures, and sensory responses to serving the guru, they move closer to living in the world while possessing his attributes. Through mimesis then, devotees transform themselves and align their beings toward another subjectivity. Michael Taussig (1993) argues that mimesis offers a template for understanding behavior that neither excludes culture nor depends on cultural constructionist arguments. Rather, mimesis is "the nature that culture uses to create second nature" and makes possible "the compulsion to become the Other" (pp. xiii, xviii). For Taussig, the interplay between mimesis and alterity is an arena that problematizes easy associations of the "primitive" and their imitative capacities. The focus on this relationship between the alignment and alterity highlights the need to consider what is being mimicked and who is the Other that occupies the space of difference and desire. Out of the mimetic efforts, relationships are developed and sustained through the very desire to copy. In Swaminarayan *bhaktiyoga*, a result of guru mimesis is the reconceptualizing of relationships and material reality to sustain the profound transformations that are so palpably attainable, so nearby in the form of the guru. No wonder, then, that Swaminarayan devotees are quick to please their guru, to direct their skills and resources to serve him, and to build the temples that sustain Swaminarayan *upāsanā*. By emulating the qualities and devotional actions of their guru, devotees receive knowledge of their real selves, something that seems both profoundly mysterious and yet so graspable.

Whether at home, at the office in front of the computer, or in the temple, the devotee who strives to recall, reflect on, and attain the guru's qualities and devotional actions toward God can determine for herself if these behaviors bring a measure of peace and satisfaction in the present. Swaminarayan *bhaktiyoga* is firmly grounded in the material form of the *Akṣarabrahman* guru, his visible form and actions, and the devotee's capacity to find reasons to emulate him. Mimesis is dependent on a motivating force, and in Swaminarayan *bhaktiyoga* that force is present in the form of the guru and his perfected devotional stance. For the devotee who is able to discern what should be emulated and how this might be sustained through a bodily repertoire of mental and physical postures, the rewards are both real and imaginable. Into this matrix, of potentiality and contingency, where each devotee has the opportunity to access the knowledge for bliss on Earth and beyond, it is the guru who provides the scaffolding for this ontology and metaphysics to endure. Swaminarayan *bhaktiyoga* offers a framework for being where the potential for achieving a seemingly distant goal rests in embracing the possibilities for self-transformation. This is a process that itself depends on the self-conscious efforts to attain someone else's defining qualities. More than anything else, it would matter who that someone else is.

REFERENCES

Brosius, Christiane. 2010. *India's Middle Class: New forms of Urban Leisure, Consumption and Prosperity*. New Delhi: Routledge.

Dave, Ramesh M. 2000. *Navya-Viśiṣṭādvaita: The Vedānta philosophy of Śri Swāminārāyaṇa*. Mumbai, India: Akṣara Prakāśana.

Kim, Hanna H. 2007. "Edifice complex": Swaminarayan bodies and buildings in the diaspora. In Anjoom Mukadam and Sharmina Mawani (eds.), *Gujaratis in the West: Evolving Identities in Contemporary Society*. Newcastle, UK: Cambridge Scholars Publishing, pp. 59–78.

———. 2009. Public Engagement and Personal Desires: BAPS Swaminarayan Temples and Their Contributions to the Discourses on Religion. *International Journal of Hindu Studies* 13 (3): 357–390.

———. 2012. The BAPS Temple Organisation and its Publics. In J. Zavos, P. Kanungo, D. Reddy, M. Warrier, and R. B. Williams (eds.), *Public Hinduisms*. New Delhi: Sage, pp. 417–439.

Sadhu Aksharvatsaldas. 2008. *Eternal Virtues: Spiritual Attributes of Pramukh Swami Maharaj*. Trans.Yogi Trivedi. Ahmedabad, Gujarat: Swaminarayan Aksharpith.

Sadhu Paramtattvadas. Forthcoming. Identifying and Locating Hindu Theology in the Svāminārāyaṇa Vedānta Tradition. Ph.D., diss. [submitted January 2013], Oxford Centre for Hindu Studies and Maharaja Sayajirao University, Baroda.

Sadhu Vivekjivandas. 2010. *Hinduism: An Introduction, part 1 and 2*. Ahmedabad, Gujarat: Swaminarayan Aksharpith.

Singh, Kavita. 2010. Temple of Eternal Return: The Swaminarayan Akshardham, Complex in Delhi. *Artibus Asiae* 70 (1): 47–76.

Srivastava, Sanjay. 2009. Urban Spaces, Disney-divinity and Moral Middle Classes in Delhi. *Economic and Political Weekly* 27 (June): 338–345.

Taussig, Michael. 1993. *Mimesis and Alterity: A Particular History of the Senses*. New York: Routledge.

Vachanāmrut: Spiritual Discourses of Bhagwān Swāminārāyan. 2001. Amdavad, Gujarat: Swaminarayan Aksharpith.

Vertovec, Steven. 2000. *Hindu Diaspora: Comparative Patterns*. London: Routledge.

NOTES

1. These are the nine forms of offering *bhakti,* mentioned in the *Bhāgavata Purāṇa*, that Prahlāda directs toward Viṣṇu as God: listening to accounts of God; chanting and singing devotional songs; remembering Viṣṇu as God; offering service; performing devotional rituals to the image or icon; prostrating oneself; offering oneself as a servant; cultivating the relationship of friendship; and surrendering the *ātmā* (self).
2. In this chapter, non-English words spoken by interlocutors who are otherwise mostly speaking in English will not include diacritics to better approximate the speakers' informal tone. These non-English words are spelled as they most commonly appear in English language materials of BAPS. Proper nouns such as Pramukh Swami Maharaj [Pramukh Svāmī Mahārāja], Sahajanand Swami [Sahajānanda Svāmī], and Bhagwan Swaminarayan [Bhagavān Svāmīnārāyaṇa] are also without diacritics as this is how they appear in BAPS materials.
3. This speaker did not distinguish between the category "shoes" and *cappal*, generally a backless shoe or sandal.
4. This is more commonly romanized as *agna* or *āgnā* [*āgñā*] in BAPS texts.
5. The ethnographic data provided in this chapter comes from fieldwork conducted during 1997–2007 in BAPS communities around the world and from ongoing correspondence via telephone and email. All direct quotations and references to Swaminarayan *sādhus* in this chapter come from documents and email that I received between June 2010 and April 2012, via male intermediaries (BAPS volunteers), from Sadhu Manganidhidas in Edison, New Jersey, several *sādhus* based in Sarangpur, Gujarat, and from portions of Sadhu Paramtattvadas's doctoral thesis in progress. Without these contributions this chapter would not be possible. I wish to acknowledge the

generosity of the *sādhus* and their willingness to share their own work, reflections, and critique with me via male BAPS volunteers. I also owe thanks to the BAPS volunteers who have served as intermediaries between me and the *sādhus*. Not least, I thank the men and women *satsaṅgis* of BAPS who so readily shared their thoughts with me. I take full responsibility for errors as well as arguments and interpretations that may not be the ones held by some or all BAPS *satsaṅgis and sādhus*.

6. Correspondence from Sadhu Mangalnidhidas, through a male BAPS volunteer, March 27, 2012.
7. Correspondence from Sarangpur *sādhus* and Sadhu Paramtattvadas, through a male BAPS volunteer, December 20, 2010, and from Sadhu Mangalnidhidas, through a BAPS male volunteer, March 8, 2012.
8. See *Vachanamrut*, Gadhada I-54 (Correspondence from Swaminarayan *sādhus*, through a BAPS male volunteer, March 8, 2012).
9. Akshardham in BAPS is given several meanings. These include, the heavenly abode (*dham*) of the entity *Parabrahman*. Thus, in this sense, *akshardham* is a theological concept and devotional term for BAPS. More recently, we see the connection to the monument-temple complexes in Gandhinagar, Gujarat and Delhi, which bear the name "Akshardham".
10. Correspondence from Sadhu Mangalnidhidas, through a BAPS male volunteer, March 8, 2012.
11. Correspondence from Swaminarayan *sādhus*, through a BAPS male volunteer, March 27, 2012.
12. There are many other ways to understand Swaminarayan *bhakti* such as looking at the relationship between a guru and his own guru and former gurus or focusing on the dynamics of *dāsa bhava*, *ātmanivedanam*, or *anuvṛtti bhakti* (Correspondence from Sadhu Mangalnidhidas, through a male BAPS volunteer, March 27, 2012).
13. It should be noted that the guru also desires to please his guru (Correspondence from Sadhu Mangalnidhidas, through a BAPS male volunteer, March 8, 2012).
14. BAPS is working on a new website, http://www.baps.org. When the new site is completed, http://www.swaminarayan.org will be taken offline, and visitors to this old site will be directed to the new one (correspondence from Sadhu Mangalnidhidas, through a BAPS male volunteer, March 30, 2012.)
15. See Singh (2010) for a variation on this argument, one that suggests BAPS is trying to subsume not just Hindu but other indigenous traditions.
16. In BAPS texts, these terms, when written in Roman letters, are without diacritics and appear as *Aksharbrahman*, *maya*, *ishwara*, and *jiva*.
17. In BAPS texts, these terms, when written in Roman letters, are without diacritics and appear as *param ekantik bhakta* and *gunatit satpurush*.
18. More commonly, the BAPS romanization for *antaḥkaraṇa is antahkaran*.
19. Recent research by Swaminarayan *sādhus*, including Sadhu Paramtattvadas's dissertation, argues that BAPS Swaminarayan theology exemplifies *Brahma-Parabrahma-Darśana*, or more simply *Svāminārayāṇa Darśana*. I thank Sadhu Mangalnidhidas who shared this insight through a male BAPS volunteer (March 8, 2012). This perspective is in contrast to earlier research that characterized BAPS *bhakti* as Navya Viśiṣṭādvaita or neo-modified nondualism in the Vaiṣṇava tradition (see Dave, 2000).
20. In this sense, as Swaminarayan *sādhus* have noted, Swaminarayan *bhaktiyoga* appears to be synonymous with *karmayoga*. However, all actions must be those undertaken solely to please God rather than to satisfy the needs of the bodily self (Correspondence from Swaminarayan *sādhus*, through a BAPS male volunteer, December 20, 2010).

21. Correspondence from Sadhu Mangalnidhidas, through a male BAPS volunteer, April 3, 2012.
22. Among *satsaṅgis*, *santo* (plural for ascetics or *sādhus*, sg. *sant*) is used as an informal form of address. This speaker adds the English plural –s to the already plural *santo*, a not uncommon occurrence among English–Gujarati speakers.
23. These are common sentiments shared by various BAPS devotees. Such statements can be heard on those occasions that prompt devotees to reflect on some dimension of a completed or not yet completed *sevā* project.
24. Personal communication, March 5, 2012.
25. Correspondence from Sadhu Mangalnidhidas, through a BAPS male volunteer, March 8, 2012.
26. Correspondence from Swaminarayan *sādhus*, through a BAPS male volunteer, December 20, 2010.
27. Correspondence from Sadhu Mangalnidhidas, through a BAPS male volunteer, March 8, 2012.
28. Correspondence from Swaminarayan *sādhus*, through a BAPS male volunteer, December 20, 2010.
29. Ibid.
30. Ibid.
31. Correspondence from Sadhu Mangalnidhidas, through a BAPS male volunteer, April 3, 2012.

CHAPTER 12

Sathya Sai Baba and the Repertoire of Yoga

SMRITI SRINIVAS

In summer 2010, I sit once again for several long and exhausting hours at the hermitage of the guru Sathya Sai Baba (1926–2011) in Puttaparthi, Andhra Pradesh, waiting for *darśan*.[1] This ritual moment of seeing and being seen by the guru-deity is a crucial part of the sacred sensorium in the devotional world centered on Sathya Sai Baba, one of South Asia's most well-known gurus whose devotees worldwide are said to number about ten million—a highly visible group including scientists, judges, intellectuals, government officials, teachers, politicians, and the urban middle class. Devotees have arrived at Prashanti Nilayam (Abode of Eternal Peace) hoping desperately to touch "Swami's" feet, speak to him, or receive ash (*vibhūti*) from his hands—forms of tactility, communication, and exchange that have been noted as significant in guru-based movements in modern South Asia.[2] This summer, long queues form, morning and evening, for his *darśan,* but for most he will remain a distant but distinctive speck dressed in a flame-colored gown with a halo of crinkly hair, being wheeled around in an upholstered armchair. For several decades since the 1950s, before a hip injury confined him to a wheelchair after 2003, Sathya Sai Baba would walk informally amid his devotees giving *darśan* to the thousands gathered either at Prashanti Nilayam or his other hermitage at Bangalore called Brindavan—an allusion, of course, to the earthly dwelling of the deity Kṛṣṇa (Krishna).

Although *darśan* is an important feature of the movement, it is important to recall that Sathya Sai Baba has stressed other spiritual practices such as remembering or hearing the name of the divine. A somatic and organic idiom is employed in his speeches and writings, suggesting the significance of the

Figure 12.1:
Sathya Sai Baba. (Photo courtesy of the author.)

name as a mode of corporeal and mental reform: devotion can be compared to "water" that washes away the "dirt" of egoism and possessiveness; the "soap" is the repetition of God's name (*Sathya Sai Speaks*, Vol. I: 19). The devotional songs or *bhajans* performed by college students at the hermitage during *darśan* time also emphasize this aspect of Sathya Sai Baba's auditory theology, and several well-known musicians and artists in India have performed for him during key festivals. Baba also inaugurated a music college for students in 2000 at his educational campus.

Sathya Sai Baba traces his immediate genealogy to Sai Baba of Shirdi (d. 1918), a mendicant from neighboring Maharashtra identified with many Sufi, devotional, and ascetic traditions in the subcontinent. However, these practices, including the insistence on the recollection of the divine name, the importance of the guru, congregational singing, and musical performance, also link the Sathya Sai Baba movement with older *bhakti* or devotional movements dominated by poet-saints from about the sixth or seventh century onward.[3] Indeed, the words *bhakti and bhajan* share the same Sanskrit root, *bhaj*, including meanings such as partaking of, to share, or enjoy, and the concept of nine steps on the path of devotion (listening to the Lord's glory, singing of him, thinking of him, serving his feet, performing his worship, saluting him, serving him, friendship with him, and surrendering to him) expressed in the *Bhāgavata Purāṇa* and are common to devotees and poet-saints from several traditions. For Tyagaraja (1767–1847), the south Indian musician-composer and saint, music was the medium and message of divinity as well as a spiritual practice (Jackson, 1991). In fact, Sathya Sai Baba's discourses often began with a few lines in Telugu from Tyagaraja's songs that framed his discourse for the day to the thousands gathered to hear and focus on his singing and speaking voice.

Sathya Sai Baba can easily be identified as a guru of modern *bhaktiyoga*, or the path of human salvation through devotion and concentration on a chosen deity or guru, an idea most popularly linked to the *Bhagavad Gītā*—a dialogue between Kṛṣṇa as the charioteer and the epic hero Arjuna. While this connects him with other exponents of modern Hinduism or neo-Hindu traditions such as the Swaminarayan gurus or Mata Amritanandamayi (b. 1953), in this chapter I explore how in Sathya Sai Baba's teachings or in the Sathya Sai Baba movement a broader repertoire of ideas of yoga appear, some of which have a long history in the South Asian subcontinent preceding what we identify as modern Hinduism. In this exploration, I am guided by scholars such as Joseph Alter, Mark Singleton, and David Gordon White (see, e.g., Alter, 2004; Singleton & Byrne, 2008; White, 2012), whose work reminds us that yoga has a huge semantic, somatic, philosophical, and institutional range and that it has been constructed in many ways from its earliest textual uses in the *Ṛg Veda* (c. fifteenth century BCE) to its deployment by global gurus such as Vivekenanada (1863–1902), Paramahansa Yogananda (1893–1952), or Sathya Sai Baba. Following a brief history and outline of Sathya Sai Baba's career as publicly constructed and narrated in authoritative biographies, I will show how at least two different uses of yoga are refracted within Sathya Sai Baba's teachings and writings and within the movement at large. These refractions also intersect with other histories, social movements, teachers, and their practices (including Theosophy and Buddhism), creating a wide terrain of significance and giving vitality to theories and practices of yoga in the contemporary world.

SAINT, GURU, AND AVATAR: THE LIFE OF SATHYA SAI BABA[4]

Sathya Sai Baba was born on November 23, 1926, to the Sathyanarayana family from the Puttaparthi village in Andhra Pradesh (Kasturi, 1962: 7). His father, Pedda Venkappa Raju, and mother, Easwaramma, lived with other members of the Raju family, known by the caste name of Bhat Raju for their role in "interpreting and popularizing sacred literature" (Padmanaban, 2000: 11). Sathya seems to have had a fairly normal childhood, although biographers and oral accounts claim a number of mysterious events at the time of his birth such as the sound of musical instruments playing (Kasturi, 1962: 7). As a young boy, he seems to have possessed some intuitive powers like being able to divine lost articles of value, including a horse that a Muslim carriage driver had lost (p. 31). There were also prosaic moments such as his earning money from the merchant Kote Subbanna during his school years by composing attractive songs and ditties to be sung on the streets to launch a new article or boost sales (pp. 25–26; see also Padmanaban, 2000: 57–60). In fact, many of the aphorisms that circulate in the movement today have the quality of street signs and slogans such as, "Hands that serve are holier than lips that pray."

During his school years, he went through a prolonged period of "illness" and erratic behavior after apparently being stung by a black scorpion sometime around 1940 (Kasturi, 1962: 31–39).[5] After this, he refused to speak for long periods of time, would break into laughter, weeping, and song, and sometimes recited Sanskrit verses. The family took him to various doctors and even an exorcist to drive out the "evil spirit" possessing him, to no avail. On May 23, 1940, after a prolonged period of illness, Sathya declared: "I belong to Apasthamba Suthra [*sūtra*, thread, aphoristic rule, a reference to rules attributed to Apastamba]; I am of the Bharadwaja Gothra [*gotra*, lineage]; I am Sai Baba; I have come to ward off all your troubles; keep your houses clean and pure" (p. 39).

Not all villagers were able to grasp the reference to Sai Baba of Shirdi, who had attracted a number of followers in his lifetime in Hindu, Parsi, and Muslim communities and was often compared to the medieval figure of Kabir. Shirdi Sai Baba exhibited a number of characteristics in common with certain Sufi orders in Maharashtra and north Karnataka and the Nāth tradition, a yogi tradition of considerable significance.[6] Shirdi Sai Baba passed away without explicitly naming any successors; however, a number of contemporary gurus such as Upasni Maharaj (1870–1941) and Meher Baba (1894–1969) have claimed some sort of spiritual genealogy to him.[7]

A few months later, Sathyanarayana (another name of Sathya Sai Baba) cast off his school books and reiterated that he was no longer the Sathya they knew but Sai: "I am going; I don't belong to you; Maya [illusion] has gone; My Bhaktas [devotees] are calling Me; I have My work; I can't stay any longer" (Kasturi, 1962: 44). He stayed initially in the garden of an excise inspector's bungalow in Uravakonda village and attracted a small following. He taught what is recalled as his first devotional song, "*Maanasa bhajare gurucharanam, dusthara bhava saagara tharanam*," translated as "Meditate in thy mind on the feet of the guru; that can take you across the difficult sea of Samsara [world]" (p. 44). He returned to Puttaparthi and after some time shifted to the house of a brahmin woman, Subbamma (Padmanaban, 2000: 165–169). In these early years—a slim teenager with bountiful hair—he continued to compose songs and hold *bhajan* sessions, carried out acts of healing and exorcisms, went into trances, materialized ash, and met devotees who were beginning to arrive from surrounding villages and towns in Andhra Pradesh and the nearby city of Bangalore. He also visited Bangalore, Mysore, and Madras for the first time in 1944 and later went to other south Indian urban centers gathering followers outside of the region in which he was born (pp. 47–76; see also Padmanaban, 2000: 165–177, 183–222). At the same time, there seem to have been objections and doubts about him in his village, and he was impelled to move out of Subbamma's house to a small residence constructed for him on land donated by her on the western bank of the Chitravati River; he also seems to have lived in caves near the river for several months (Padmanaban, 2000: 237, 241).

Through the support of devotees, a building was finally constructed for him in 1945—known today as the Old Mandir (temple)—on the edge of the village (Kasturi, 1962: 59). From this point onward, his mission began to achieve architectural form accompanied by ritual activity. The first ever recorded public procession carrying two images of Shirdi Sai Baba and Sathya Sai Baba took place on the occasion of the inauguration of the Old Mandir (Padmanaban, 2000: 255). Sathya Sai Baba also carried out regular worship within the temple where the main images were busts of Shirdi and Sathya Sai Baba made of concrete, and he would lead the community in *bhajans* (Padmanaban, 2000: 259, 263). The Dassera festival and Baba's birthday were celebrated in Puttaparthi for the first time in 1946. During the Śivarātri festival the following year, Baba is reported to have manifested a spheroid *liṅgam* from his mouth (Padmanaban, 2000: 323, 331, 345), emphasizing his identification with Śiva, an aspect reproduced in popular prints today, in addition to his identity with Shirdi Sai Baba. Four main festivals have been celebrated since the early years—Sathya Sai Baba's birthday, Śivarātri, Gurupūrṇimā (dedication to the guru), and the autumn nine-day Dassera festival culminating in Vijayādaśamī. Today, a number of others—his mother's birthday, Christmas, the birthday of Buddha, New Year festivals based on various calendars, Rāma Navamī, and many more—have been added to the list, and the forms of many of the older festivals have also become more elaborate.

This period of his growing ministry was marked by the appearance of elite devotees such as the royal families of Sandur, Mysore, Venkatgiri, and Chincholi and landlords, merchants, and government officials from various cities. Their support resulted in the construction of the expanded hermitage, Prashanti Nilayam, inaugurated in 1950 (Kasturi, 1962; Padmanaban, 2000: 536). The second hermitage, Brindavan, came up subsequently in Whitefield near Bangalore in addition to a summer retreat in the hill station of Kodaikanal in Tamil Nadu. From the late 1950s, Baba's public role as a pan-Indian guru became more pronounced, and although he was still accessible to devotees, he began to tour urban centers in north and south India and to address various forums such as the Divine Life Society of Swami Sivananda. He also reinforced the fact that he had not come to create a new religious path: "I will never force you to take up a particular Name or Form of the Lord. . . . The Lord has a million Names and a million Forms, and He wants that faith and attachment should be evoked in you by any of them, as you recite the names or contemplate the Forms" (*Sathya Sai Speaks*, Vol. I: 218).

In concert with this project, the newsletter *Sanathana Sarathi* ("The Eternal Charioteer,"), devoted to the moral and spiritual upliftment of humanity through truth, righteousness, peace, and love, was inaugurated during the Śivarātri festival in 1958 (Kasturi, 1962: 204). Sathya Sai Baba also inaugurated an academy for the study of the Vedas and Sanskrit in Prashanti Nilayam and an all-India academy of Vedic scholars in the early 1960s (Kasturi, 1968: 41, 52–53).

This period has been described as one in which Sathya Sai Baba seems to have retreated into orthodoxy and indulged the religious sentiments of landlords and Hindu sympathies (Aitken, 2004: 100–101). However, sometime around the mid-1960s, he seemed to be moving away from this posture, and publicly the paradigm of the pan-Indian teacher was absorbed by the representation of the global avatar. On Gurupūrṇimā day in 1963, for instance, after a stroke and paralysis of his left side, which he later "cured," he made a startling announcement:

> I am Siva-Sakthi . . . born in the gothra of Bharadwaja according to a boon won by that sage from Siva and Sakthi. Sakthi Herself was born of the gothra of that sage as Sai Baba of Shirdi; Siva and Sakthi have incarnated as Myself in his gothra now; Siva alone will incarnate as the third Sai in the same gothra in Mysore state. (Kasturi, 1968: 84)

In other compilations, such as in Kasturi's original compilation and translations of Baba's speeches, this claim is reported differently.[8] Whatever the sequence, this declaration not only invoked descent through Bhāradvāja but also made explicit links to Śaiva and Śakti traditions as well as divine androgyny: the Sai "trinity" includes not only Shirdi Baba, the avatar of the female (or male, depending on the version) principle of divinity, but also Sathya Sai Baba, the unity of both male and female principles, and Prema Sai, another future avatar of the male (or female) principle of divinity.[9] It is important to also recall here that Sathya Sai Baba's triple incarnation scheme—Shirdi Sai Baba, Sathya Sai Baba, and Prema Sai Baba—"mirrors Dattatreya's triadic typology" (Rigopoulos, 1998: 251) and that many believed Shirdi Sai Baba was an incarnation of Dattātreya, an important figure in the Nāth tradition.

The announcement accompanied the incipient international status of Sathya Sai Baba and the beginnings of a world organization dedicated to service (*sevā*). The First All-India Conference of Sai Seva Organizations was held in Madras in 1967 (Kasturi, 1968: 231). At the First World Conference of Sai Seva Organizations at Bombay (now Mumbai) in 1968, Baba announced that he was the embodiment of every divine entity and that he had come to establish eternal religion or *Sanātana Dharma* (Kasturi, 1972: 3–21; *Sathya Sai Speaks*, Vol. VIII: 99–100). In June of the same year, he left for a tour of East Africa, his first and only foreign visit, assuring the Africans and South Asians gathered there in several discourses that he had not come to speak on the behalf of any particular path such as the Hindu *dharma*: "I have no plan to attract disciples or devotees into My fold or any fold. I have come to tell you of this Universal unitary faith, this *Aathmic* principle, this path of love, this *dharma* of *prema*, this duty of love, this obligation of love" (*Sathya Sai Speaks*, Vol. VIII: 118).

This world mission and vision has had two interrelated aspects since the 1960s. First, several civic institutions emerged through the active encouragement of Sathya Sai Baba. The most prominent of these were men and women's colleges founded in the 1960s and 1970s and the Sri Sathya Sai Institute of Higher Learning (now a university), which opened its doors in Puttaparthi in 1981; also significant were medical institutions including specialty hospitals called the Sri Sathya Sai Institute of Higher Medical Sciences, established in Puttaparthi (1990–1991) and Bangalore (2001). Second, Sathya Sai Baba's role as a public speaker and commentator-interpreter of philosophical texts and Indian religious traditions underwent steady growth.[10] This renarrativization of scripture, philosophical texts, or themes in Indian religious culture by Sathya Sai Baba has parallels with the activity of other pan-Indian leaders and gurus in the twentieth century such as Dr. B. R. Ambedkar (1891–1956), C. Rajagopalachari (1878–1972), or Aurobindo (1872–1950), who, like Sathya Sai Baba, were reinterpreting India's place and the place of its traditions in a postcolonial and global world.

THE SENSE OF THE BODY

On March 28, 2011, Sathya Sai Baba was hospitalized at the Sri Sathya Sai Institute of Higher Medical Sciences in Puttaparthi following heart problems and multiorgan failure.[11] A pacemaker was installed, and he was treated with other procedures including kidney dialysis. As devotees around the world conducted prayers, meditated, and waited anxiously for further news (a story that was followed closely in Indian national newspapers and various internet websites), a devotee and member of the organization, Prof. G. Venkataraman, reminded followers of another incident in 2003 when Baba had to undergo surgery for a fracture. At the Gurupūrṇimā festival that year Baba had urged devotees to be courageous and not worried. He stated:

> What is My medicine? The intense prayers of the devotees are My medicine. During this period . . . devotees have intensified their prayers and spiritual

> activities . . . It is as a result of such fervent prayers that I am able to stand before you and address you today.
>
> Neither did I want this suffering nor did I desire its cure. You wanted this body to be cured of the pain, and you achieved it through your prayers. This body is not Mine. It is yours. Hence, it is your responsibility to look after this body. I am not the *deha* (body); I am the *Dehi* (Indweller).[12]

These extracts, a reminder to devotees of the reciprocal bond that links them with the guru, also signal a specific understanding of the relationship between the divine or the self and the body. As we shall see in detail, they refract some of the earliest meanings of the term *yoga* as well as the central principle of yoga as an analysis of perception and cognition (see White, 2012). In the *Ṛg Veda*, one of the primary meanings of yoga is "yoke," and this is then expanded to the chariot, the team of horses, and so on. In the *Kaṭha Upaniṣad*, these ideas emerge in a new form so that the relationship of the self to the body, for example, is compared with the rider and his chariot. Other elements were introduced in this text that become part of the yoga repertoire in the centuries that followed including the separation of the body and the in-dwelling person, who is identified with the universal Person or absolute Being, and the hierarchy of constituents of the mind–body including the senses and mind (see White, 2012: 3–4). Yoga then becomes a "regimen or discipline that trains the cognitive apparatus to perceive clearly, which leads to true cognition, which in turn leads to salvation, release from suffering existence" (p. 7).

As a close reading of the vast corpus of speeches and writings reveals, Sathya Sai Baba's somatic philosophy is rooted in this old epistemological distinction between the body (*deha*) and its resident (*dehin*), separate but related. The former is likened to a vehicle, chariot, a car, a temple, or a mansion, while the latter refers to the driver, charioteer, in-dwelling spirit, or deity. One therefore should not identify with the body but should develop the correct vision about the relationship between the body and its resident: "Without the power of the Divine, the eyes cannot see or the ears hear or the mind think" (*Sathya Sai Speaks*, Vol. XVII: 61). In several talks and texts, Sathya Sai Baba elaborated on the relationship between the senses, the body, and intelligence or will. For example, the senses are regarded as unruly horses yoked to the body–chariot that must be controlled by the charioteer. The purpose of the body is to serve as a means for realizing divinity, liberation, or truth.

In the Gurupūrṇimā lecture cited earlier, he stated emphatically: "You are not the body; you are the embodiments of the *Atma* [divine self]. The physical body comes and goes. Only the body has suffering, not the *Atma*."[13] However, a healthy body is a requisite means for spiritual discipline. "The body is the vehicle which you have to use for attaining the state of bliss and so, it has to be kept safe and strong for that high purpose" (*Sathya Sai Speaks*, Vol. V: 211).

Anything that comes in through the senses is also regarded as "food" for the body and therefore affects one's mental, emotional, and physical health:

> As is the food, so is the mind;
> As is the mind, so are the thoughts;
> As are the thoughts, so is the conduct;
> As is the conduct, so is the health. (*Sathya Sai Newsletter*, 18: 4, 1994: 4)

For Sathya Sai Baba, as the previous aphorism suggests, food is a critical medium. "Moderation in food, moderation in talk, and in desires and pursuits; contentment with what little can be got by honest labor, eagerness to serve others and to impart joy to all" are tonics for health (*Sathya Sai Speaks*, Vol. I: 176). In various writings and speeches, foods such as milk, yoghurt, or fruits, which are "pure" (*sāttvika*), are strongly recommended, but Sathya Sai Baba also states that we need to pay attention to the company or the state of mind in which we eat and the emotions of the person who has cooked the food. Mild fasting once a week and a vegetarian diet is advocated: the food one consumes determines one's thoughts and meat eating promotes animal qualities, but it is also cruel to kill other living things that are sustained by the same five elements as human beings. Other recommendations include avoiding white sugar, promoting the use of uncooked foods, drinking large quantities of water before and after a meal, and always offering food to the divine before eating. All types of intoxicants or stimulants (and especially alcohol and tobacco) should be given up because they reduce the power of the will. Physical exercise is important but, like food, requires moderation. Sathya Sai Baba has spoken of the salutary effects of five types of baths—mud, sun, water, air, and ash. Emphasis is also given to correct posture, the amount of sleep needed at different ages, and maintaining physical cleanliness.

This careful attention to diet and other practices is reminiscent of Gandhi's *Key to Health,* first published in 1948. For Sathya Sai Baba and Gandhi (1869–1948), practices such postures, breathing exercises, vegetarianism, or various types of baths for increasing self-control have value. However, as Alter (2000: 13–14) points out, Gandhi was influenced by forms of healing that were derived from nineteenth-century Western European systems of naturopathy and hydrotherapy rather than purely Indic therapeutics and he remained skeptical of *āyurveda*. For Sathya Sai Baba, on the other hand, allopathic treatment and *āyurveda* have to be coordinated for better results. The ideas of the body expressed by Sathya Sai Baba's also show continuity with those in circulation in the early twentieth century among the Arya Samaj, the Theosophical Society, and other organizations, whose ideas were based on traditions of humors, wrestling and martial cultures, practices of celibacy, and the Indian interest in Baden-Powell's Boy Scout movement (see Watt, 2005: 130–170).

What is critical here is that while Baba's ideas of the body clearly reflect the centrality of a yoga repertoire, the terms of this somatic philosophy not only influence ideas of illness, health, and healing but also go beyond physical culture, diet, or sexuality to include nature (and human nature). Health is regarded as being based on the laws of nature, at once spiritual and natural, inner and outer. When the laws of nature are violated, sickness and pollution occur. Thus, we need to purify the environment around us by increasing the planting of trees, reducing the use of automobiles, controlling the emission of harmful effluents, reducing wastefulness through the Ceiling on Desires Program (which recommends that time, food, energy, and money should not be wasted), and engaging in practices such as community singing that produce waves of vibrations that purify the polluted atmosphere.

Within the Sathya Sai Baba movement, social institutions for healing such as the Sri Sathya Sai Institute of Higher Medical Sciences have also been established based on the idea that hospitals, the medical profession, and medicine must rest on a spiritual vision:

> Health is both an issue of compassion and economics. The main emotion that pours out to the suffering and the afflicted is compassion . . . When compassion covers the best of skills, the best of medical technology, and is given with love and kindness, it transforms mere medicare from the process of disease curing to complete healing. This, when made into a movement to provide such care free of cost to the masses, becomes a potent force, and brings health and dignity to many for whom it would otherwise have been beyond reach. (C. Sreenivas, *Mano Hriday*, Vol. 2, 1, 2002: 7)

Thus, within the movement, not only is Sathya Sai Baba's role as a healer–physician documented in countless devotees' narratives (which speak of the guru's therapeutic touch, look, words, and personal presence as well as the curative powers of ash and other objects given by Baba such as gems and crystals, rings, necklaces, icons, rosaries, lockets, and other talismans), but also attempts are made to provide specialized medical knowledge free of cost to the economically disempowered, to disengage it from the principle of profit, and to locate it within a framework of service.

SERVICE TO MAN IS SERVICE TO GOD

The emphasis on service or *sevā* emerged as early as the 1960s within the Sathya Sai Baba movement. Local chapters of the Sri Sathya Sai Seva Organization are known as *samiti* in India or Sai Centers overseas, and their main function is to undertake spiritual, educational, and service activities. A center or *samiti* usually begins as a locus for singing devotional songs and prayer and gradually encompasses organizational directives applicable to three wings: the service wing may carry out relief work for the poor, provide educational scholarships, deliver medical care through free dispensaries and camps, or sponsor village development activities. The educational wing includes courses for children's moral development and the Education in Human Values Program. The spiritual wing is concerned with devotional singing, study circles, prayers, and meditation.

The first Sai *samiti* was registered in 1965 in Bombay, although there were a number of informal devotional groups already in existence by that time. Within a few years of the first *samiti*'s registration in Bombay under the Societies Registration Act in 1965, Sai Centers began to be formed outside India: in Sri Lanka (1967), the United States (1969), the United Kingdom (1969), Canada (around 1970), South Africa (1973), Italy (1974), Mauritius (1978), Australia (1978), and the West Indies (1983). By 2000, Asia was the largest organizational venue of the Sathya Sai movement (including 8324 centers and groups) with India as its hub (7961), followed by Europe (569), Central and South America and the Caribbean (380), Africa (282), North America (266), and Austronesia (204). Currently, there are over nine thousand official centers and groups of devotion in India and over two thousand in 130 countries outside India.

While aims and procedures of the organization have crystallized over time, one constant theme that has run through it over the years is the centrality of *sevā*. Although Sathya Sai Baba has elaborated on the concepts of *karmayoga, bhaktiyoga, jñānayoga,* and *rājayoga* in several of his speeches and texts, the idea of *sevā* is not collapsible into these categories. Instead, it appears that *sevā* itself is a kind of worship of the divine and, moreover, a means of union, a path of yoga. This stems directly from Sathya Sai Baba's teachings that the body is a means for realizing the self and is mediatory between the individual and society, inner nature and external nature: "Service to man is service to God, for He is in every man and every living being and in every stone and stump" (*Sathya Sai Speaks,* Vol. IV: 251).[14] One of the primary goals of a healthy body, mind, and will is that they should be directed toward civic service. Alternately, the direction of mind, senses, and other activities toward service leads to well-being and liberation.

On one hand, it is evident that this emphasis on service derives from the terms of Baba's somatic philosophy. It might also be possible to trace its genealogy to ideas of yoga as the raising and expanding of consciousness through inquiry, meditative practice, or attention to the breath (White, 2012: 8). The description of Kṛṣṇa's universal body in the *Bhagavad Gītā* as well as Vivekananda's emphasis on the *Yogasūtras* is linked to these ideas. On the other hand, this idea of *sevā* as yoga in the Sathya Sai Baba movement has explicit linkages with the early nineteenth century when new vocabularies for the idea of serving the guru or God began to emerge in many South Asian religious movements in the context of colonialism.

Sahajanand Swami or Swaminarayan (1781–1830), the founder of the Swaminarayan tradition, encouraged social welfare works and manual labor by ascetics such as digging wells, repairing roads, building temples and residences, or providing famine relief, which continues to be a model today (see Williams, 2001; on other aspects of the Swaminarayan tradition, see Chapter 11 by Kim in this volume). The first organized expressions of service in the Ramakrishna movement emerged from the novel response of Vivekananda (1863–1902) to famine and disaster relief (see Beckerlegge, 2000). The Arya Samaj, the Theosophical Society, Servants of India Society, and the Seva Samiti of Allahabad in the first two decades of the twentieth century all "drew on dynamic and deep-rooted 'living traditions' while also being influenced by contemporary Indian social conditions and global developments in the realms of organized philanthropy and civics" (Watt, 2005: 13). Older ideas were given new connotations and embedded social service efforts: for example, the concept of service changed from individual acts of piety or homage to a guru or deity to include social service explicitly by linking the word *sevā* with the words such as *sabhā* or *samiti* (see pp. 97–129). The dress adopted by Sathya Sai Seva volunteers and active workers that includes a scarf with the emblem of the Sai organization also seems inspired by Baden-Powell's Boy Scout movement and Indian national service cadres.[15] The model of service as spiritual praxis in the Sathya Sai Seva Organization is also shared with other contemporary gurus and movements such as Mata Amritanandamayi and engaged Buddhist movements such as Sarvodaya in Sri Lanka (see Warrier, 2005; see, also, Chapter 14 by Warrier in this volume; on Sarvodaya, see Bond, 1996; 2004).

At the heart of the Sai organization is an anthropocentric idea of civic reform; it is humanistic insofar as the understanding of humanity is that divinity is inherent within, and service activities are carried out in civic collectives that nest into each other—family, village or community, nation, and then the world. While such service work is believed to have a cumulative effect, ultimately its rationale does not lie within a developmental model of social change. A female devotee in Bangalore reflects on the way unexpected grace can infiltrate service activities through the presence of Sathya Sai Baba:

> The first time that Sai Darshan [one of the Bangalore *samitis*] was inaugurated, we needed money for Narayana Seva [literally "service of God," the gift of food to the poor]. Mr. Kushalappa and I were sitting on the steps wondering what we could do. As I was saying that we could all contribute to this amount, Neelu came with 750 rupees, which is exactly what was needed. It seems that one lady had brought money to Swami for service purposes. He took it and gave it to Neelu and said: "Give it to Sai Darshan." Swami sent it to us through Neelu. If you start a good program, Swami provides. (Interview, September 22, 1999)

As this account describes, the logic of *sevā* is not simply the external action accompanying inner devotion or the unintended social consequences of piety. The daily life of an active devotee carrying out *sevā* is also reciprocally penetrated by the paranormal powers of the guru, miraculous events, and synchronicities.

THE BODIES OF BHAKTI

Sathya Sai Baba's "miracles" or paranormal abilities, both in the early part of his life and in later years, have attracted a great deal of attention. While such powers may be accepted in India as natural extensions of the (yogic) powers of holy men, some teachers and traditionalists have frowned upon the exhibition of such powers, and rationalists and skeptics have branded him as a magician or charlatan. In devotees' narratives, these miracles appear time and again as signposts in their relationship with Baba, signaling the first encounter, a turning point in their lives, an event when all hope was lost, or an answer to a crisis. His cited abilities (described not as *siddhis* but as *vibhūtis*) include the materialization of objects ranging from candy and fruit to watches, ash, or *liṅgams*, "mobile material vehicles" of his power and "magic" that is transferred to the devotee (Babb 1987: 178; see also Babb, 1983). His powers also include acts of healing, teleporting, being knowledgeable about devotees' lives or many languages, or appearing in distant places and in dreams to give guidance as the following narrative shows:

> I was studying in college in Madras in the mid-1980s and staying at the YWCA hostel when I started reading about Sathya Sai Baba. I had already begun to have experiences in which he came into my life in odd ways. For instance, I remember that a young teacher, Christian by faith and a sort of energy-healer came one evening to my room. I did not know her then but she was also staying in the hostel and she used to ride in the electric train with me daily. At that time, I was suffering from very bad migraines and that evening I was having one of my attacks. The teacher said that she had a dream where she was directed by Baba—who appeared connected somehow with snakes—to come and help me. She was not a devotee as far as I know.
>
> I was also very tearful in those days, feeling separated from Baba, and not knowing how to reach him. The event that I remember most vividly happened one night while I was reading Howard Murphet's book on Baba called *Man of Miracles*. I was lying on my bed, it must have been about midnight or 1 AM in the morning, and it was dark and quiet outside. I had a small altar near the bed where there was a picture of Swami. Suddenly, I felt a presence in the room and when I looked up I saw bright golden light streaming into the room. The light was so powerful that my body gave a jerk as if touched by electricity. Slowly it cleared and Baba walked into my room. He sat on a chair and I sat near his feet. He asked me why I wept so much these days. We talked for a while about

> my feelings and headaches. He then took me to a large room, a temple of some kind which I had never seen before, where all kinds of framed pictures of gods and Baba were hanging from the wall on all sides. In the center was an image of Shirdi Sai Baba. When we returned, I rushed out of my room to call someone and let them know that Baba was here. Instead, I found that it was daylight and I was in my bed. I had been dreaming.
>
> The next morning, taking the train to my college, I sat with a young girl who was wearing a locket with an image of Baba. Out of the blue, she asked me if I knew the Guindy Sai temple—which I did not—and proceeded to tell me how to get there . . . I followed the girl's direction to the temple. It was about noon on Thursday and the priests were just completing their rituals. I stepped inside. It was the room to which Baba had taken me in my dream with pictures on the wall and an image of Shirdi Sai Baba. (Interview with a female devotee, November 3, 2005)

A fuller discussion of this interview and its framing appears elsewhere (Srinivas, 2008: 101–102). Here I wish to signal how this strong belief by devotees in Baba's abilities to travel across time (including dream-time) and space—whether we might legitimately discuss these powers as rooted in yogi perception or as supernatural products of yoga (see White, 2012: 9–12) or simply the characteristics of an avatar—are critical for the future transmission of charisma.

After nearly a month of Sathya Sai Baba lying in critical care, the Sai organization announced to a global network of devotees praying intensely for their guru's recovery: "Bhagawan Sri Sathya Sai Baba is no more with us physically. He left his earthly body on April 24, 2011 at 7.40 a.m. due to cardio-respiratory failure."[16] As the news of his passing on Easter Sunday spread rapidly (being reported by every newspaper and agency including *The Hindu*, BBC, Reuters, Xinhua, the *Wall Street Journal*, and *Los Angeles Times*), approximately half a million people (including grieving members of the organization, Andhra villagers, the Indian Prime Minister Manmohan Singh, and the cricketer Sachin Tendulkar) converged on Prashanti Nilayam to have *darśan* of the guru. The body lay in a casket for public viewership for a couple of days, and on April 27—an event that was broadcast on national TV channels in India and via webTV programs—it was interred in the same area where Sathya Sai Baba had given *darśan* practically every day since 1950. This event was accompanied by *bhajans* sung by students and the classical vocalist Pandit Jasraj; state honors including the national flag being draped over the casket; Vedic rituals; the recitation of verses by representatives of Sikh, Buddhist, Muslim, Jewish, and Christian traditions; and the pious hope that as in "the case in Shirdi, this Tomb of the Avatar of the Age would start speaking to His chosen devotees" from now on.[17]

The relationship of devotees to their guru's entombed body and institutional future of the movement are tied to a number of issues that I cannot explore in depth here. However, I will highlight one aspect here that has significance for the transformation of guru *bhakti*. As the words carried on the website of the organization as Baba's body was laid to rest indicate, the sensorium of *bhakti* in the movement is based on the ontology of multiple presences, even multiple bodies. While devotees longed to have *darśan* of their guru while he was in the body, away from his physical form his presence could also be conveyed and experienced through ash, images, dreams, and other mediums including electronic media as I have discussed elsewhere (see Srinivas, 2008). This experience is rooted in Sathya Sai Baba's claim of being an avatar and incarnation of Shirdi Sai Baba, descriptions of his miraculous powers, and various statements over the years about the nature of his being: for instance, that his birth did not occur through conception but through descent or that he chose his own birth and mother. This ontology creates several presences and bodies—the physical and historical body, a universal divine essence, and a kind of apparent, immaterial, or fabricated body that travels in time, space, or dreams. This has parallels with Gnostic beliefs, Mahayana and Vajrayana Buddhism, and also resonances in various yoga traditions. Thus, within the cosmology of the movement, Baba has always been credited with the ability to communicate without being confined in his earthly body. After his departure from his Earthly body there has emerged a cache of stories of "messages" from Baba to devotees. As my conversations with several devotees also reveal, even in the midst of grief and a sense of loss, through the ontology of multiple presences and bodies, the passage from Baba's physical body to noncorporeal presence is relatively fluid.

REFERENCES

SERIAL PUBLICATIONS

Mano Hriday
Sathya Sai Speaks
Sathya Sai Newsletter
Summer Showers in Brindavan

SECONDARY WORKS

Aitken, Bill. 2004. *Sri Sathya Sai Baba: A Life*. New Delhi: Penguin Books/Viking.
Alter, Joseph S. 2000. *Gandhi's Body: Sex, Diet and the Politics of Nationalism*. Philadelphia: University of Pennsylvania Press.
———. 2004. *Yoga in Modern India: The Body between Science and Philosophy*. Princeton, NJ: Princeton University Press.
Babb, Lawrence A. 1981. Glancing: Visual Interaction in Hinduism. *Journal of Anthropological Research* 37: 387–401.

———. 1983. Sathya Sai Baba's magic. *Anthropological Quarterly* 56 (3): 116–124.

———. 1986. *Redemptive Encounters: Three Modern Styles in the Hindu Tradition*. Berkeley: University of California Press.

Beckerlegge, Gwilym. 2000. *The Ramakrishna Mission: The Making of a Modern Hindu Movement*. New Delhi: Oxford University Press.

Bond, George D. 1996. A.T. Ariyaratne and the Sarvodaya Shramadana Movement. In Christopher S. Queen and Sallie B. King (eds.), *Engaged Buddhism: Buddhist Liberation Movements in Asia*. Albany: State University of New York Press, pp. 121–146.

———. 2004. *Buddhism at Work: Community Development, Social Empowerment and the Sarvodaya Movement*. Bloomfield, CT: Kumarian Press, Inc.

Goldberg, Ellen. 2002. *The Lord Who Is Half Woman: Ardhanārīśvara in Indian and Feminist Perspective*. Albany: State University of New York Press.

Hawley, John Stratton, and Mark Juergensmeyer. 1988. *Songs of the Saints of India*. New York: Oxford University Press.

Jackson, William J. 1991. *Tyagaraja: Life and Lyrics*. Delhi: Oxford University Press.

Juergensmeyer, Mark. 1991. *Radhasoami Reality: The Logic of a Modern Faith*. Princeton, NJ: Princeton University Press.

Kasturi, N. 1962. *Sathyam Sivam Sundaram*. Mangalore: Sanathana Sarathi.

———. 1968. *Sathyam Sivam Sundaram*. Prasanthi Nilayam: Sanathana Sarathi.

———. 1972. *Sathyam Sivam Sundaram*. Bombay: Sri Sathya Sai Education Foundation.

———. 1980. *Sathyam Sivam Sundaram*. Prasanthi Nilayam: Sri Sathya Sai Books and Publications Trust.

Lorenzen, David (ed.). 2004. *Religious Movements in South Asia 600–1800*. New Delhi: Oxford University Press.

Padmanaban, R. 2000. *Love Is My Form: A Biographical Series on Sri Sathya Sai Baba*. Vol. I. Bangalore: Sai Towers Publishing.

Peterson, Indira Viswanathan. 1989. *Poems to Śiva: The Hymns of the Tamil Saints*. Princeton, NJ: Princeton University Press.

Raj, Selva J. 2004. Ammachi, the Mother of Compassion. In Karen Pechilis (ed.), *The Graceful Guru: Hindu Female Gurus in India and the United States*. New York: Oxford University Press, pp. 203–218.

Ramanujam, A.K. 1973. *Speaking of Siva*. Baltimore, MD: Penguin.

———. 1981. *Hymns for the Drowning: Poems for Visnu by Nammalvar*. Princeton, NJ: Princeton University Press.

Rigopoulos, A. 1993. *The Life and Teachings of Sai Baba of Shirdi*. Delhi: Sri Satguru Publications.

———. 1998. *Dattātreya the Immortal Guru, Yogin, and Avatāra: A Study of the Transformative and Inclusive Character of a Multi-faceted Hindu Deity*. Albany: State University of New York Press.

Schomer, Karine, and W. H. McLeod (eds.). 1987. *The Sants: Studies in a Devotional Tradition of India*. Delhi: Motilal Banarsidass.

Shepherd, Kevin 1985. *Gurus Rediscovered: Biographies of Sai Baba of Shirdi and Upasni Maharaj of Sakori*. Cambridge, UK: Anthropographia Publications.

Singleton, Mark, and Jean Byrne (eds.). 2008. *Yoga in the Modern World: Contemporary Perspectives*. London: Routledge.

Srinivas, Smriti. 2008. *In the Presence of Sai Baba: Body, City, and Memory in a Global Religious Movement*. Leiden: Brill and Hyderabad: Orient Blackswan.

———. 2002. Cities of the Past and Cities of the Future: Theorizing the Indian Metropolis of Bangalore. In John Eade and Christopher Mele (eds.), *Understanding the City: Contemporary and Future Perspectives*. Oxford: Blackwell, pp. 247–277.

———. 2001. The Advent of the Avatar: The Urban Following of Sathya Sai Baba and Its Construction of Tradition. In Vasudha Dalmia, Angelika Malinar, and Martin Christof (eds.), *Charisma and Canon: Essays on the Religious History of the Indian Subcontinent*. Delhi: Oxford University Press, pp. 293–309.

———. 1999. The Brahmin and the Fakir: Suburban Religiosity in the Cult of Shirdi Sai Baba. *Journal of Contemporary Religion* 14 (2): 245–261.

Warren, Marianne. 2004. *Unravelling the Enigma: Shirdi Sai Baba in the Light of Sufism*. Revised edition. New Delhi: Sterling Publishers.

Warrier, Maya. 2005. *Hindu Selves in a Modern World: Guru Faith in the Mata Amritanandamayi Mission*. London: Routledge Curzon.

Watt, Carey Anthony. 2005. *Serving the Nation: Cultures of Service, Association, and Citizenship*. New Delhi: Oxford University Press.

White, Charles, S. J. 1972. The Sai Baba ovement: Approaches to the Study of Indian Saints. *Journal of Asian Studies* 31: 863–878.

White, David Gordon (ed.). 2012. *Yoga in Practice*. Princeton, NJ: Princeton University Press.

Williams, Raymond Brady. 2001. *An Introduction to Swaminarayan Hinduism*. Cambridge, UK: Cambridge University Press.

NOTES

1. This chapter is based on my long-term research on the Sathya Sai Baba movement (Srinivas, 1999; 2001; 2002; see especially Srinivas, 2008). There is an extensive scholarly, devotional, and journalistic literature on Sathya Sai Baba and his constituency, which I cannot reference here but do so in these other works.
2. See, for example, Babb (1981; 1986), Juergensmeyer (1991), Selva Raj (2004), and Warrier (2005).
3. There is a fairly large literature on these saints, and a comprehensive bibliography is not possible here. See, for instance, Hawley and Juergensmeyer (1988); Lorenzen (2004); Peterson (1989); Ramanujam (1973; 1981), and Schomer and McLeod (1987).
4. There are several biographies and numerous hagiographies of Sathya Sai Baba. N. Kasturi's account has the most authoritative status in the movement as the earliest sanctioned biography of Sathya Sai Baba (Kasturi, 1962; 1968; 1972; 1980). A more recent biography and documentary history based on field research and detailed interviews dealing with the years between 1926 and 1950 is *Love Is My Form* (Padmanabhan 2000). See also Srinivas (2008: 49–75) for a fuller treatment of Sathya Sai Baba's life and also for a discussion of why the "real" personhood of Sathya Sai Baba, who he is as a private individual, or the truth or falsity of his claim to divinity cannot be the focus of a sociological or anthropological analysis.
5. Padmanaban (2000: 95–103, 128–129) suggests it could have been around 1943.
6. According to most accounts, Shirdi Sai Baba began his long period of residence at Shirdi (a small village in Ahmednagar district of Maharashtra) in 1858. He stayed in a dilapidated mosque and acted in the manner of many Muslim holy men and healers and attracted local villagers. In 1897, the practice of holding a festival in commemoration of the death of a Muslim saint (*urs*) was begun at Shirdi. In 1912, certain devotees decided to hold a Rama Navami festival to celebrate the birth of the deity, Rama, along with the *urs* since the two coincided, and this became an annual feature at Shirdi. The context of this shift deserves mention here: by

the end of the first two decades of the twentieth century, the construction of the Godavari-Pravara canals transformed the famine-prone Ahmednagar district into the prosperous Sugar Belt. The devotees who began to gather at Shirdi in increasing numbers included a number of rich businessmen, administrators, and a growing middle class. There was a gradual layering of Baba's largely Sufi practices with Hinduized forms that coincided with the creation of an industrial-commercial economy. In 1918, Baba had an attack of fever and passed away on Vijayādaśamī day (the final day of the nine-day autumn Dassera festival). A dispute followed about where he should be buried: the Muslim devotees wanted him to be interred in an open place and a tomb constructed over it, whereas the Hindus wished for his body to be placed in a building where a Kṛṣṇa idol was to have stood. It was decided after a plebiscite to place him in the building (see Rigopoulos, 1993; Shepherd, 1985; Warren, 2004).

7. For a fuller discussion of these pathways and the life of Shirdi Sai Baba, see Srinivas (2008: 23–48) and White (1976).
8. "Siva said that They would take Human Form and be born in the Bharadwaja lineage or Gothra thrice: Siva alone as Shirdi Sai Baba, Siva and Sakthi together at Puttaparthy as Sathya Sai Baba and Sakthi alone as Prema Sai, later" (*Sathya Sai Speaks*, Vol. III, original edition: 22). Within the Sai movement, including the new revised and enlarged Indian edition of *Sathya Sai Speaks* and the website of the International Sri Sathya Sai Organization, the later version is the one followed.
9. See Goldberg (2002).
10. Most of his speeches have been collected in *Sathya Sai Speaks*. A separate set of books called *Summer Showers in Brindavan* comprises a compilation of speeches given by him to college students during courses held for them. Many additional discourses have found their way into *Sanathana Sarathi*. There are also works penned by Baba: one set of written works include individual texts called *Prema Vahini, Dharma Vahini, Jnana Vahini, Sutra Vahini, Prasanthi Vahini, Upanishad Vahini*, or *Dhyana Vahini*, which were articles written by Baba in Telugu and first published in the *Sanathana Sarathi* serially. They are essays on specific themes such as love, righteousness, knowledge from the *Brahma Sūtras*, and peace and meditation from the *Upaniṣads*. There are also retellings of different scriptures: the *Geetha Vahini* is an interpretation of the *Bhagavad Gītā*; two of his works—the *Bhagavata Vahini* and the *Ramakatha Rasavahini*—are based on the *Bhāgavata Purāṇa* and the *Rāmāyaṇa*, respectively.
11. Parts of this section and the next are derived from Srinivas (2008: 111–161).
12. "Special Musing Concerning Swami's Health," posted by Prof. G. Venkataraman on Radio Sai on April 6, 2011; http://media.radiosai.org/www/musings_on_Swami_health.html (accessed April 6, 2011).
13. Ibid.
14. It is possible to read this statement as not being inclusive of women or the (divine) feminine, but in many cases Sathya Sai Baba's discussions of gender (difference) depends on the context and his rendition of particular classical texts and popular religious traditions. His own construction of 'his' divine identity as Shiva-Shakti makes it difficult to postulate a singular understanding of gender within the movement or organization. It is probably somewhat accurate to say that his and devotees' public presentation is one of complementarity between genders.
15. See Watt (2005) on the convergence between older service organizations and the Boy Scout movement.

16. "News of Swami," updates and medical bulletin posted on the website of the International Sathya Sai Organization; http://www.sathyasai.org/swamihealth/swaminews.html (accessed April 25, 2011).
17. "News of Swami," updates and medical bulletin posted on the website of the International Sathya Sai Organization http://www.sathyasai.org/swamihealth/laidToRest.html (accessed April 27, 2011).

PART FIVE

Technology

CHAPTER 13

Engineering an Artful Practice: On Jaggi Vasudev's Isha Yoga and Sri Sri Ravi Shankar's Art of Living

JOANNE PUNZO WAGHORNE

Even though I have a deep appreciation of Sanskrit, I never bothered to learn it because my own vision had never failed me and I did not want to read ancient texts written in Sanskrit and clutter myself with all that traditional whatever.

–Sadhguru Jaggi Vasudev

Sadhguru Jaggi Vasudev, with long flowing robes, embroidered shawl, and saffron turban, offered the final prayers at the night-long celebration of Mahashivaratri (*Mahā Śivarātrī*, "the great night of Śiva") at the Isha Yoga Center near the industrial city of Coimbatore in South India. Still onstage with him were an array of American drums with a long Indian drum (*mṛdaṅgam*) from a night of "Vedic Rock," which mixed with the sounds of mantras and periods of quiet meditation during this all night vigil celebrated by over a thousand seated participants, with many thousands watching on huge video screens outside and many more thousands watching the live television broadcast in India or the live webcast linking the worldwide Isha organizations. A few weeks later in the massive Suntec City International Convention Center in Singapore, His Holiness Sri Sri Ravi Shankar spoke to over three thousand ethnic Chinese and Indian Singaporeans on "Practical Wisdom for Personal Excellence." While the audience sat in padded seats in this comfortable convention center, Guruji, dressed also in flowing white robes with equally flowing hair and beard, sat on his richly decorated divan. As he rose to speak in

Figure 13.1:
Sadhguru Jaggi Vasudev. (Photo courtesy of Dick Waghorne with the kind permission of the Isha Foundation.)

his fluid, elegant English, and later led the audience in a mass meditation, the video camera beamed his image onto two huge screens on either side of his dais.

Such newly emerging guru-centered movements are especially popular in the rapidly globalizing cities of Asia, new hubs of the technological world both as manufacturers of advanced hardware and as new sources of information specialists, engineers, and scientists. In the new cities of East Asia, this often unrelenting reliance on expertise means an emphasis on education with proficiency in English, including what are now called *study mothers* (from China) and *Wild Geese mums* (from South Korea), who leave their husbands far behind to enroll their children in prestigious English-medium institutions in Singapore.[1] *The degree*, especially in engineering, technology, or business management, increasingly functions as the major route to the coveted status of *middle-class professional* in Asia—and the membership card of the global economic sphere. In this new technocentric Anglophone world, the old issue that dominated the Euro-American world at the turn of the twentieth century—the struggle between scientific rationality and religious faith—has morphed in twenty-first century Asia into a case of cozy borrowing. Gurus incorporate scientific language, academic registers, and business and media savvy into the development of a new kind of religious association and a new kind of religiosity that adapts and reinvents *yoga* for this rising middle class.

The reach of these new forms of yoga is global, but the setting for this chapter will be Singapore, where many of the new global guru-centered movements thrive within this very cosmopolitan, business-centered city-state. Given the compact size of Singapore, many of these movements compete for and often share the same adherents. Some Singaporeans, from both Chinese and Indian heritages, belong to multiple movements and attend introductory sessions to compare, choose, or add to their repertoire of "spiritual"[2] practices. Thus, these movements as a whole share a common modus operandi and quite literally a common language—English is the major language of both government and education. Within this broader yoga-inspired milieu, I will focus on the very popular *Inner Engineering* offered by Sadhguru Jaggi Vasudev's Isha Yoga and the equally popular *Sudarshan Kriya* (practice for proper vision)[3] developed by His Holiness Sri Sri Ravi Shankar as part of the Art of Living (usually abbreviated as AOL). Both techniques are offered by teachers in the form of courses, which run for a few intensive days over a weekend, or a week of evening classes. In Singapore, and in much of Southeast and East Asia, similar practices, usually called the kriya (*kriyā*), tend to be understood as yoga in these and many other guru-centered movements. The teachers of Isha and AOL are trained at the respective headquarters and primary residences of Jaggi Vasudev or Sri Sri Ravi Shankar located in South India: Sadhguru Jaggi in his idyllic ashram near Coimbatore; and Guruji Sri Sri in his ashram in bustling Bangalore. Because most Indians now settled in Singapore migrated from South India, these English-speaking but also Tamil-savvy gurus are especially popular.[4] Singapore—ultramodern, cosmopolitan, deliciously multiethnic, and increasingly the model for development in Asia[5]—presents a fascinating case study of new contexts and new packaging for yogic techniques. Residents of this city-state, both ethnic Chinese and Indians, remain especially open to new practices that offer practical solutions for life in the new fast-paced urban Asia.

Neither Isha nor Art of Living relies solely on the postural yoga now ubiquitous in the United States (Singleton, 2010; Syman, 2010) but rather on a combination of movement and studied stillness with chanting, breathing, and visualization meditations. Members of these organizations consider their particular combination of practices (i.e., the formula for the kriya), as emerging from the unique insight of the founding guru. Neither Sadhguru Jaggi Vasudev nor His Holiness Sri Sri Ravi Shankar belongs to a lineage (*paramparā*), and neither claim to have learned his unique kriya from a living master.[6] Both studied at some point with traditional teachers of Vedic philosophy and philology, but both have university degrees: Sri in physics; and Jaggi Vasudev in English literature[7] (also see Gautier, 2008; Subramaniam, 2010).

My attempts to delineate the nature of these inventive forms of yoga uncovered a complex interrelation between the past and the present, centered on the guru. However, for the members of these organizations such practices often appear seamless, especially in Singapore. The majority of early nineteenth-century migrants—most from southern China and south India—came as laborers with religious roots in popular ritual practices; those from wealthier trading communities centered their practice in temples, Buddhist, Hindu, or Taoist-Confucian (Sinha 2005, 2011; Tong 2008).[8] Few Hindu Brahmins or Chinese Buddhist priests settled permanently in Singapore (Clothey 2006: 58). In other words, classical and once elite practices like traditional yoga did not migrate. Now the new wave of contemporary émigrés from India are graduates in engineering, computer programing, and business administration whose experience with yoga, if any, began in India with some of the same new movements—not from the remaining traditional practitioners whom I will mention here.[9] Not surprisingly, then, innovative adaptations from the modern educational and business styles inform many similar guru-centered organizations that I followed in Singapore, including Jangama Dhyana Meditation (Shivarudra Balayogi (1954–); Shivabalayogi (1935–1994); Sri Kaleshwar (Sri Kaleshwar, 1973–2012); Amriteswari Society (Mata Amritanandamayi 1953–; "Hugging Guru," see Warrier, this volume); Rajayoga Power Transcendental Center (Yoga Jnana Sitthar, 1954–); Oneness Blessing/Meditation Group Singapore (Sri Bhagavan, 1949– and Sri Amma, 1954–); Sathya Sai Organization (Sathya Sai Baba, 1926–2011; see Srinivas, this volume); Sahaja Yoga Meditation (Shri Mataji Nirmala Devi, 1923–); and Ramakrishna Mission (Sri Ramakrishna, 1836–1886).[10] These innovations are, at the same time, entwined with many older forms of yogic practices: sometimes the fusion is acknowledged as with Jaggi Vasudev (1957–), who traverses "seamlessly from the ancient to the ultramodern" (http://www.ishafoundation.org/Sadhguru/sadhguru.isa); sometimes the sutures remain concealed as with Sri Sri Ravi Shankar (1956–), whose Sudarshan Kriya "came like an inspiration" during a long period of silent mediation (http://www.artofliving.org/sudarshankriya-origin).

To introduce the complexity of this rapid process of borrowing, integrating, and innovating, I will offer several vignettes from my recent experiences in Singapore to set the milieu as well as the modalities of these now very popular forms of spiritual practice.

SCENE 1: CHAIR YOGA AND MINDFULNESS

On May 3, 2008, I sat with an ethically diverse audience at the Chinese Chamber of Commerce—which included several Euro-Americans working in Singapore and a considerable percentage of Chinese heritage Singaporeans—to take part in a one-day yoga workshop offered by the Art of Living Foundation. This workshop included a PowerPoint presentation by a professor in the business school of the National University of Singapore, who was also an AOL member. A session in Chair Yoga followed this well-attended lecture. From the lecture style of the presenter to his use of PowerPoint to the rows of chairs in a hall to the registration desk and the books for sale, I could not immediately distinguish this event from the many academic conferences I have attended. Even the content of the talk remained within an academic frame of reference, with footnotes included on the PowerPoint and carefully delineated models of research. Unsurprisingly, with a professor of business at the podium, the workshop combined an academic model with styles popular in contemporary business workshops offered by human resources personnel for executives or sales staff. I have seen this workshop–lecture format used in many other such religious-spiritual events in Singapore.

During a carefully prepared PowerPoint presentation, "Well Being, Mindfulness, and the Secret of Breath," Professor Narayanan, who later told me he likes interaction with his students, told his audience this was dialogue not a monologue. He focused on the practices leading to mindfulness, especially working with the breath, which he said was not about concentration but rather "de-concentration, allowing the mind to rest in the present moment." He emphasized that forms of mindfulness are not just for monks but "are skills for people in everyday life" with well-documented benefits for those in business and other professions. Dressed in a dashing tan *kurtā* (long tunic) and pants, the professor began by invoking William James and mixing examples from science and popular media, with the teachings of "Sri Sri"—as Sri Sri Ravi Shankar is often called. Stating that modern science is only now awaking to the value of meditative practice, Prof. Narayanan predicted, "In the future this will be part of the school curriculum." He used data from research done at business schools and in departments of psychology (especially parapsychology in some recognized universities), which I was later able to confirm.[11] Beginning by affirming the common search for happiness, he argued that research shows that happiness is 50 percent genetic disposition and 50 percent personal choice. "Sri Sri says past is destiny and future free will." We need to deal with destructive tendencies in our minds. Ruminating on the past "is a disease, a killer"—increasing heart rate and blood pressure. How do we deal with such problems? Not by being passive but by making a choice not to "chew on it [i.e., the past]." Finally, he turned to the issue of the breath. Many old masters, he continued, recognized with remarkable insight how the breath controls the mind and body. So within the AOL, breathing techniques are crucial to finding this mindfulness. He added that there was good evidence emerging in peer-revered journals showing that these kriyas can redirect and transform activities of the mind.[12]

The Chair Yoga that followed fit seamlessly into the venue and the tastes of the audience. The Yoga Dance Team filed onstage wearing matching black tights and white T-shirts with "www.artofliving.org.sg" underneath vertical ideographs of yoga poses that resembled Chinese letterings on the back. As the speakers blared pulsating music, the team performed a quick-paced combination of dance and yoga postures. Then, remaining onstage, they sat down on white chairs identical to those occupied by the audience below. Adam, a young man of Indian origin, took the microphone and verbally instructed the audience on the yoga poses while the team demonstrated the positions on stage. Everyone in the audience remained firmly seated but actively clapping our hands and mirroring these rapidly changing postures to the beat of very New Age contemporary music with bells and drums—a bit Japanese, Balinese, and jazzy. With such pulsating music, I could see that many older members of the audience like me enjoyed the exercise but savored the security of our chairs.

This scene of Chair Yoga introduces several key elements in the innovative forms of yoga, not only in Art of Living but also in a wide variety of similar movements in Singapore. The venue in the Chinese Chamber of Commerce suited this session well. The entire building resembled a Chinese temple yet also had the feel of a well-worn social club: a good setting for a program that also combined an informal yet carefully structured program with a spiritual ambiance. During the program my eyes moved to the old photographs that lined the back wall—all successful Chinese businessmen standing or seated in rows. They seemed to watch over the proceedings. The very style of the yoga and its presentation by Professor Narayanan mirrored the setting, and I imagined that these old boys of the Chamber of Commerce approved. While many gurus, past and present, would have begun with quotations from Hindu texts, followed by an exposition on these quotations, in this engaging lecture Professor Narayan never quoted or even mentioned a Hindu sacred text by name. His choice of clothing, however, did gesture to something traditional. Here was a new kind of proof texting not using isolated quotations from a sacred text to establish his proposition but instead invoking data from the emerging world of neuroscience and cognitive studies. Such an appeal to the legitimacy of science interestingly mirrors the rise of serious interest in cognitive science and neuroscience within the academic study of religion.[13]

An interesting form of secularization was at work here, not only in the offer of scientific proof but also in the relocation of the practice of breath control and meditation to "people in everyday life"—meaning the largely middle-class contingency of the program. Everything was done to make this diverse middle-class audience comfortable, from familiar registration and elegant brochure to Chair Yoga. This yoga moved between entertainment, education, and practice, which in the eyes of Art of Living clearly enhances rather than dilutes the effectiveness.

Why do contemporary popular gurus adopt this amalgam of academic and business models? The familiarity of the forms created an odd predicament: here were familiar, recognizable spaces and procedures, but these same spaces and procedures clouded the meaning of terms like *study, research, course*, and even *education*. This convergence between an academic *style* and the many new guru-centered religious-spiritual movements, I began to realize, is not seamless: this yoga blurs lines between the academic and the guru, who increasingly appears to move into the role of university *teacher*. In some cases, like that of Professor Narayanan, the guru's surrogates are in fact university professors—only the tweed jacket is replaced with the *kurtā*, which is rather chic in Singapore as formal attire.

This confusion between the teacher of AOL or Isha on one hand and the "professor" on the other leads to some surprising issues. When I first began my research, I presented my business card as I introduced myself to leading members of several of these organizations, expecting my hard-won title of "Professor of Religion" in a "Department of Religion" to impress my potential "informants." Instead, these well-educated people looked at my card and repeatedly told me that they liked neither my title nor the name of my department. I had several enlightening but uncomfortable sessions when my interlocutors turned the tables and asked me to explain what I was doing there and what I could possibly have to "teach" about their spiritual movement if I did not approach the guru and the organization as a devotee or disciple? At one point a young teacher in Isha Yoga asked me what I expected to gain by this research and suggested that if I attended the advanced program of Bhava Spandana (an advanced meditation program usually conducted by Sadhguru Jaggi)[14] I would really *understand*. In contrast, during previous years of research on Hindu temples, my position as a writer-scholar remained clear: I was a welcomed outsider with an appealing empathic interest in Hindu institutions. But with the guru movements, the closer the language came to my own work, the more ambivalence I felt from and toward those sitting with me in the same room and those speaking earnestly from the seat of authority. The changing function of the guru as teacher is complex.

SCENE 2: AN UNCOMFORTABLE CONFRONTATION

One moment that vividly revealed differences between the academic and the guru's acolyte occurred during one of the many meditation or yoga "courses" I attended during the year—strongly suggested or required as a preliminary to my interviewing anyone in the organization. Most of the guru-centered movements offer a basic course lasting from two to seven days, which serves as an introduction to its teachings and practices, especially the kriya, and initiation into membership in the organization. No other criteria for admission applied—no *adhikāra,* the classic Sanskrit concept of prior fitness to study. The only requirements to take these courses, based once again on the model of a university extension course, are to register and usually to pay a fee. The registration forms ask *only* for name, address, profession or work, e-mail address, and contact number. However, unlike registering for a class, these organizations asked all participants to sign or verbally accent to a confidentiality agreement promising not to reveal the processes of the kriya to anyone. Such nondisclosure agreements are common in business where processes for the production of products are kept as trade secrets[15] rather than as patents, which would protect the product or processes from replication but nonetheless render them public information.[16] Once, as I was seated for the yoga mediation session, the young instructor—a Euro-American dressed in a saffron shawl—explained that the agreement prevented unauthorized teaching of this powerful kriya for illegitimate profit. Prior to the session I had given this instructor my business card and explained my purpose as both an interested participant and a research scholar. I had brought my camera and very small digital recorder, which I turned off as soon as we began learning the secret techniques. The course combined instruction in technique with explanations of spirituality and meditation. During one of these explanations, when the instructor told us how to explain the importance of these techniques to curious friends and family, I turned on my recorder. Suddenly, the instructor shouted from the stage that someone had been spotted recording and that the person had already violated the confidentiality agreement. Stunned at this public pronouncement rather than a quiet personal reproof, I e-mailed the instructor that night to explain my situation: I had carefully policed myself and had done nothing to reveal the technique and had recorded what was presented as a public explanation. The next day he asked me to destroy the recording: his authoritative tone would normally have been very inappropriate given the difference in our age and education. I had the feeling that in the eyes of the instructor my status as a mere academic professor of religion was trumped by his status as a spiritual teacher of a powerful technique. I began to ponder this interesting juxtaposition between secrecy, authority, and the academic-like model of a "course open to all."

I could continue with more very specific stories, but this complex array of parallels and paradoxes between the academic–business world and the rhetoric, public practices, and organizational styles of the rising global gurus needs some basic formulation. All of these changes move the meaning of the *guru* as teacher from older models of discourse and techniques in the millennium-old Indian mystical traditions into a direct convergence (and potential collision) not only with the teaching techniques of the academic world but also with practitioners of the older procedures.[17]

FROM *GURUKUL* TO CLASSROOM AND BACK AGAIN

Typically a course offered by Isha Yoga or Art of Living in Singapore numbers from six to forty students. Instruction in Inner Engineering as a meditation technique has very recently moved online, but prior to this change, which I will discuss in the final vignette, Isha Yoga instructors offered this foundational course about every three months. The teachers (the English term is the default) who are sent directly by Sadhguru from his ashram near Coimbatore in South India receive considerable respect from the Isha volunteers and meditators—the term used in decided preference to *followers* or *disciples*[18] for those who have taken the basic course and come to the monthly meetings or Sathsang[19] (*satsaṅga*, together with truth, or true company). Each teacher undergoes special training offered only at the ashram and usually conducted by Sadhguru in person. Currently in Isha, the teachers continue to offer initiation in the Shambhavi Mahamudra[20] (*śambhavī mahāmudrā*, formal kriya or practice that includes yoga postures) during a weekend for those who have completed the online course. Art of Living courses are sometimes smaller but are always offered by a teacher to a group and never to an individual. In AOL the instructors also go for training at the ashram of Sri Sri Ravi Shankar in Bangalore. In both cases the training methods are kept confidential, but one young Isha teacher, Maya, shared some of her experiences: Sadhguru, by his special methods, guided her to an inner confrontation with her limitations and potentials. Her articulate discussion echoed popular psychology mixed with concepts that I knew to be Hindu inspired (see Williamson 2010) but never named as such. Speaking of both her guru and his teaching, she told me, "Even now I cannot say who he is, what he is. It just makes sense, not logical sense but sense in terms of life." Both movements (until recently) offered their beginning course in a class-with-teacher format, but the advanced courses switched to a small group encounter with the guru that nonetheless, as many attest, feels like a one-on-one experience for each participant. As Maya explained, "How wonderful he was with every person, when he is talking with you, you feel he is totally there for you—with every person he is like this." Very recently Sadhguru initiated an online Inner Engineering program (which will be the last scene for this chapter).

Contemporary gurus teach their massive following a common kriya during group sessions and usually via appointed surrogates. Sometimes the gurus teach in person, either at their ashrams in special program or more often in very public contexts such as the two events that opened this chapter: Sri Sri Ravi Shankar's talk in the convention center in Singapore where he led thousands in mediation and Jaggi Vasudev's massive celebration of Mahashivaratri. Sri Sri lectures in Singapore every year, and recently Sadhguru visited for a public lecture (interestingly held at the National University of Singapore's University Cultural Center), now available on YouTube.[21] Gone are old models of the guru–*śiṣya* relationship so frequently portrayed in romantic sketches of the traditional *gurukul* (residence of the teacher where students lived and studied). Idealized versions of this relationship can be seen on the covers of many school notebooks in India, which represent one or two disciples sitting next to their guru under the shade of a huge tree. However, these more traditional methods continue and offer a contrast to these new globally oriented organizations. In a conversation with a young teacher of yoga in Pudukkottai in southern India, I asked directly about the difference between the traditional methods of yoga he had learned from his still-practicing nonagenarian grandfather and the current practices of Isha Yoga, which also had come to this small former capital of the erstwhile princely state in Tamil Nadu. Selvaraj explained that because Isha Yoga is taught in large groups, an instructor can never be certain that each person is doing the *āsanas*, or yoga postures, properly. "How can they see each person and know?" he said. "This group teaching is not yoga but only exercises." When his grandfather taught him yoga, he attached a large ball to his grandson's stomach so the young man could begin to understand how a pregnant woman might feel doing yoga. In this way, his grandfather made him aware of each of his students and told him that a program of yoga must be adapted to each student's needs and abilities. As both a traditional teacher of yoga and a student pursuing a Ph.D. at a local university, Selvaraj remained unconvinced that yoga could or should be taught in the large groups of twenty-five or thirty students common in Isha classes even in Pudukkottai.

Far more than borrowing from the academic world, this move from the *gurukul* to the classroom is intertwined with multiple changes in the understanding of the kriya. I have heard many assertions from practitioners that doing the kriya en masse increases the power for each participant. While both AOL and Isha expect their meditators to do the kriya alone at home each morning, both enjoin meditators to come regularly to group sessions. For AOL, the "long" Sudarshan Kriya must be done once a week and always in a group. For Isha, all meditators are urged to attend the monthly Sathsang where the Shambhavi Mahamudra Kriya is practiced together. In these contexts the classroom becomes a more literally "coming together" (Sathsang), fostering a new kind of congregation that enhances solitary practice but never replaces it. These Sathsangs function like a classroom and sometimes are literally in a classroom but simultaneously retain shades of the esoteric, with the guru's powerful *presence* emanating through his or her voice or face, not always in the flesh but on DVD or YouTube. Again, Maya, the Isha teacher in Singapore, spoke of a presence that she experience in his living person but that I noticed translated very well in the visually oriented media world: "just a gesture, the way he moves, absolute grace, absolute, and he is making it available to us." It is important to remember that the academic form of a class, in the hands of the global guru, transforms into much more than a teaching tool.

FROM DISCOURSE TO DVD AND DATA VIDEO PROJECTION

When Isha volunteers set up a classroom for the Inner Engineering program, they arrange a curious combination of objects in the front of the room. A large white banner with the words "Inner Engineering—Peak of Wellbeing" and a rough red triangle enclosing the words "Welcome to the Silent Revolution of Self Realization" hangs on the wall. A framed photograph of Sadhguru Jaggi Vasudev perching on the back of a chair draped in white cloth stands next to a glass-covered flaming lamp surrounded by flowers. Far to the right a huge video monitor stands also draped in a white cloth. That digital screen will carry footage of the guru, elegantly dressed in turban and flowing robes, teaching a small group of devotees: the location of this class is never specified. The DVD becomes a key part of the instruction that evening.

When Sri Sri Ravi Shankar lectured on Practical Wisdom for Personal Excellence in the Suntec City in Singapore, most of the audience saw him close up via two huge video screens at both sides of the dais surrounded by huge vases and pots of flowers. When he rose to speak, he often moved to the edge of the dais, leaned over the railings, and looked at those who were close enough to see him face to face. He also frequently addressed his remarks to those at the very back of this auditorium, gesturing in their direction. However, the only hope of their actually seeing his face was via these screens. Interestingly, the videographer often played creatively with the video projections so that while the live image of Guruji, which I caught on my camera, shows his body melded

Figure 13.2:
Sri Sri Ravi Shankar. (Photo by Joanne Punzo Waghorne.)

into a mélange of plants, flowers, signs, and human heads, the videographer eliminated all this. The majority of the audience saw Guruji's intense profile shadowed onto a pure blue background.

Both Sadhguru Jaggi Vasudev and His Holiness Sri Sri Ravi Shankar teach in a style that mirrors the popular professor in a large classroom or the celebrity writer giving a sold-out talk. But the guru's discourse reaches a level of media savvy that surpasses the professor and her PowerPoint or the writer addressing his devoted fans. These are deeply religious (they would say spiritual) events where the media enhances the power of both the guru's person and message. I have seen PowerPoint and data video projectors used during regular Sathsangs of organizations as seemingly different as the Amriteswari Society of Amritanandamayi (the Hugging Guru) to meeting of the many Satya Sai Baba organizations in Singapore. The most literal adoption of the classroom format, however, was a session of Sahaja Yoga Meditation, a method for self-realization based on the inherent energy within the body, which was held in a classroom of a business school in a modern commercial building. Shri Mataji, one of the earliest of the female gurus and a Christian by birth, spoke to her multiethnic following in Singapore via DVD. Seated in rows of chairs in this up-to-date business classroom, Indian and Chinese Singaporeans sat next to each other and performed the complex meditation practices. The ever-present data video projector of modern university classrooms, which allow instructors to reach and interest otherwise bored students in necessarily large classes, are now the tools for spiritual instruction. Moreover, the data video projector, and sometimes Web streaming direct from the ashram, creates a mediated sense of intimacy between the guru and the students that defies space and even time.

FROM *SĀDHANĀ* TO "RESEARCH"

Many of the global gurus claim that they undertook long intense spiritual practices (*sādhanā*) as part of their deep resolve (*saṃkalpa*) to find a modern means for their followers to achieve peace and happiness. From these austerities emerged the insight, the revelation, of their particularly powerful form of kriya. Yet at the same time most gurus also provide or refer to "scientific evidence" on their websites or in their discourses that proves the effectiveness of their practices on the health and well-being of their adherents—a very popular trope in New Age movements (see Heelas, 2008). Sadhguru Jaggi Vasudev punctuates many of his engaging discourses, available to the public on DVD or to his meditators during both the Sathsang and his courses, with constant references to contemporary physics or physiology. The same is true of H. H. Sri Sri Ravi Shankar whose references, however, emerge as much from psychology as physics. In the introductory lecture for the Art of Living previously mentioned, Professor Narayanan drew carefully documented parallels between Guruji's meditation techniques and studies of the effectiveness of "mindfulness" on success both in business and in daily social life.

Ironically, one of the most conscious cases of borrowing academic discourse—again mostly from the sciences—occurred at the meditation session, Kundalini Awakening, held in Johor Basu, a city in Malaysia just north of Singapore, on May 4, 2008. Yoga Jnana Sitthar Om Sri Rajayoga Guru, usually called His Divine Grace or HDG, conducted the session speaking only in Tamil. This increasingly popular guru is usually understood by his adherents as a master *siddhar* (Tamil: *cittar*; Skt.: *siddha*), a difficult term to translate: perhaps "wizard" in the Harry Potter sense is closest. HDG was introduced by one of his disciples who described him as achieving the equivalent of a "Ph.D. in metaphysics and parapsychology." His address and those of others who followed were all simultaneously translated into English and Mandarin via headphones. As I listened to both the translation and the Tamil, I asked the Tamil–English translator, who held a Ph.D. in the sciences, about the terminology. He assured me that when he translated the description of His Divine Grace's twenty-seven years of "research" (Tamil: *ārāycci*)[22] into the yogic practices, his translation was as literal as possible. In a later e-mail clarifying this, I began to realize that the term research meant that the guru *experimented* or, as my kind respondent put it, "practically tested the meditation techniques, discovered the subtle secrets and any shortcomings in the methods, and then modified the methods so that common people like us can use the yoga shakti power."[23] In his formal address, His Divine Grace also affirmed, "I have done research—not out of a book but out of experience." Later in the program, a session explicitly detailed evidence (through a carefully prepared English-language PowerPoint presentation) that the power of such forms of meditation and yoga on human health and wellbeing are scientifically verifiable.

Yoga Jnana Sitthar's evocation of science is not new. From the early twentieth century in Europe and America, beginning most prominently with William James, religious experience was sporadically associated with the natural sciences (Taves, 2009: 4–8).[24] As Joseph Alter (2004: 30) reveals, yoga advocates and teachers in India modeled their practices "on the hegemonic image of science" by the 1920s and 1930s. Practices drawn from many old yogic postures and meditation continue to gain legitimacy as scientifically verifiable techniques. However, in the twenty-first century in Asia, with the rising status of the academic degree, the gurus' research with such techniques, traditionally called *sādhanā* (leading to a goal, guiding),[25] are affirmed as equivalent, even surpassing, the kind of knowledge conferred by a Ph.D. These borrowed terms from the world of academics also become tools, though, for a critical assessment of the failure of the university systems to provide any real knowledge beyond the description and manipulation of the gross material world.

MODIFYING THE NATURE OF SECRECY

At the heart of the courses and the kriya lies a tension between secrecy and the avowed desire of the contemporary global gurus to update the ancient yogic practices and to make these widely available beyond ethnic or national borders. In his early study of a "Holy Man" in the sacred city of Ayodhya, Daniel Gold writes of the "complementarity between the hidden and the revealed" (Gold, 1988: 21). Gold's purpose is to provide a broad comparative framework that ultimately reveals some crucial feature of the Hindu holy man, which he also terms the guru, in relationship to the publicly revealed Hindu traditions. Several aspects of this complex study are relevant here. Categories of revealed and hidden run through most of the major world traditions with certain aspects usually confined to those with special access, be they priests or rabbis, or those monastics who "ponder esoteric mysteries hidden deep within their heritage" (p. 24). The holy man, however, frequently rejects or carefully negotiates these mainstream systems and offers "hidden esoteric help, the inner riches that the guru gives" (p. 25).

With Isha Yoga and the new global gurus, this hidden esoteric help appears to be both revealed yet *mysterious*, both a matter of business practices to preserve trade secrets and at the same time a force that moves many to tearful silence. When I questioned instructors in the guru movements about the requirement to sign confidentiality agreements as a routine part of the course, most explained that such secrecy protected the kriya both from illicit attempts at profit and from endangerment to any person who learns this powerful practice secondhand. Such confidentiality agreements are directly borrowed from a business paradigm. When a company wishes to protect, for example, their formulas for a cosmetic, or as in the case of Apple Corporation (Marshall, 2012) their nascent products, employees are required to sign these trade secret agreements. Such agreements are a very different form of safeguard from either copyright or patents, as explained earlier in this chapter. In adopting the trade secret model rather than copyright, new yoga movements aptly glide from the esoteric to new business models of secrecy. Included in this business-like secrecy were the restrictions on photography as well as voice or video recording to prevent unauthorized pirating for profit or for exposé. I sometimes kindly received permission to photograph, but under the condition that the digital card in the camera be immediately given to whoever directed the publicity to screen for photos perceived to be unflattering or potentially controversial. In the United States, photographers understand *adhikāra* when working within private property; signed "model releases" are required before any photo is made public. However, in the less global and more local ashrams in India that I have visited, such requests to photograph or record never become legal matters but remain personal—meeting the guru face to face in a far older mode of personal intimacy that global gurus continue to *claim* as part of their own mores.

In addition, there were warnings against dangerous secondhand transmission from neophyte learners. Transmission of such potent practices must be confined to the guru or carefully chosen and trained teachers. I heard multiple stories of improperly transmitted yoga or, even worse, self-help "book yoga" that has resulted in endless failure at best or serious mental and physical damage, even death. Only a true guru could transmit the practice with that special *something* that went beyond the normal intellect, beyond rationality. As Sadhguru Jaggi Vasudev (2008: 252) puts it, "This is the subjective technology that cannot be grasped objectively, hence all the mystery."

The *mystery*, indeed, infused the practices of guru-centered movements but in seemingly incongruously open ways. The Sathsangs of Isha always include personal testimonies of meditators who had traveled to the ashram in India to take the Bhava Spandana Program (BSP), which Sadhguru always conducted personally. The four-day residential program is limited to those who have completed an introduction program but also implicitly require the time, funds, and the persistence to pursue this vigorous program. At the Sathsangs, moving testimonies from women and men usually ended in tears with the constant refrain that the experience of BSP was "beyond words." I heard a young man in his thirties divide his life in two phases: "*before* BSP and *after* BSP." Like the Inner Engineering and other programs, the Bhava Spandana Program also enjoins secrecy, and I have hesitated here to relate many details about the testimonies. Yet ironically in these days of YouTube, Web streaming, and personal blogs, vivid private accounts of these experiences from BSP to Inner Engineering appear frequently—sometimes on individual sites but also officially via the Isha Foundation.

Here, issues of the mysterious power of face-to-face interactions confront the reality of contemporary media, where the *feel* of intimate space can be publicly broadcast to a multiplicity of persons listening or seeing in a strangely public privacy—either in a Sathsang carefully closed to all but meditators or via closed-circuit webcasting or even more ironically in the old-fashioned tell-all book with its own public intimacy. Sadhguru's recent book, *Midnight with the Mystic* (2008) written with an American meditator, records his personal discussions in the dead of night on a lake in North Carolina with two ardent meditators. Here Jaggi Vasudev shows once again his mastery of remaining in the dark, of keeping the milieu of midnight esotericism on the lighted page, or under a spotlight on a darkened stage as in the opening vignette of the Mahashivaratri, that long night of Śiva at the ashram in South India.

SCENE 3: INNER ENGINEERING NOW ONLINE

I received the usual e-mail announcing the monthly Isha Sathsang. However, the message for Sunday June 12, 2011, contained some startling news:

> From a 13 day program 5 years ago, to a 7 day program and now an Online program! Online??? Yes! Don't worry, we will not be teaching Yoga online: This will be offered as a 7 class (each class is an hour and a half) online with Sadhguru himself as the teacher, and guided meditations at the end of every session. After completing these 7 sessions (they have 30 days to go through it), in the privacy of their homes, at their own pace, they will have the option to register for a 2 day program (over the weekend) that we will organize in Singapore. In this 2 day program, they can learn the kriyas, step by step and get initiated into Shambhavi Maha Mudra.

Those of us interested in this online program and in the upcoming visit of Sadhguru Jaggi Vasudev to Singapore could attend a special meeting before the Sathsang. Fortunately I was in Singapore and made plans to attend the volunteers meeting and the subsequent Sathsang program.

The venue for all meetings for the Isha organization in Singapore changed from a cultural hall in the crowded but purposefully picturesque ethnic enclave of Little India[26] to a venue in a mixed residential-industrial area. I took a taxi to the Chai Chee Technopark—a series of five tall buildings with little character. I finally found the multipurpose room, which was located off a car park. I arrived at 4:30 and met the convener of the Sathsang and another active young woman who with her husband had just come to Singapore from San Francisco. She told me that they had lived in Arizona and other places in the United States for about seven years but wanted to be closer to India and would move back to their family in Coimbatore whenever an employment opportunity opened. Very active in Isha in the United States, she had quit her job eighteen months before to devote her time to Isha as a volunteer.

I was in time for the meeting about the online classes, which began with planning for Jaggi's visit to Singapore, just confirmed for September 11. About twenty people were sitting on the floor in Indian style—as usual for Isha, men outnumbered women. We began and ended this meeting with the opening and closing mantras. Sadhguru had set a target of five thousand people for the public, "ticketed" talk. Interestingly, Sri Sri Ravi Shankar, who comes every year to Singapore, usually draws about three thousand people to Suntec City. Prior to the public talk Sadhguru would hold a Sathsang exclusively for meditators—those who had completed the Inner Engineering program and had been initiated. Volunteers were needed to help with the "marketing" of the event.

Then the same new volunteer who had recently relocated to Singapore from the United States explained to us that the program began in America and then introduced the new online program. Called Inner Engineering Online, it offered a sequence of lessons meant to take seven days, but each registered participant had thirty days to complete the set. The "course" for each day took ninety minutes, as she emphasized, "learning directly from Sadhguru who begins by giving instruction on how to sit and eat prior to the lesson."

Apparently the rules about eating are not so strict because there is no kriya taught, meaning now that none of the yoga postures were included. She spoke of the course giving "tools" for living, and each session had a topic similar to the formal courses we had taken in the past. At the end of each session there was an "empowerment process," which I assumed to be a form of guided meditation and chanting. I noted to myself that the kriya as bodily yogic work appeared to be deemphasized. She continued to explain that at the end of each course session there was "homework" as in the old system and that "teachers" would review this at the ashram. Isha now recommended that the practitioners use earphones and find a private space; family members must do the program as individuals and register separately. Practices—here meaning the former kriya—could not be taught on video or online, so these must be still learned from a teacher because someone must be there to correct any problems. After a person completes the online program, they may choose to attend a daylong session on either a Saturday or Sunday from 7 a.m. to 7 p.m. During this long program, a fully trained teacher from the ashram imparts the kriya and the shambhavi initiation. When Sadhguru presides personally over the initiation into the kriya and the mantra, he holds one session usually on a Saturday evening teaching the kriya and then another session in the morning of the next day to impart the Shambhavi Maha Mantra.

Then I asked the assembled mediators what happened to the former concern for secrecy. The convener of the meeting said that Sadhguru realized people were already using small recorders during the session so it has been "given away already." They noticed that other organizations were already copying some of their style and terminology "very closely," so obviously the secrets were already out. Now Sadhguru simply said, "OK, let it spread." For any person wishing to register for the online course in the United States, the cost was $150. If that person chooses to attend the day-long session with a teacher, then an additional $150 was requested for the instruction in the kriya and the mantras. If Sadhguru presides over the kriya and mantra initiation, then the additional charge was $250. At this point after all my attempts to keep confidentiality, I now felt free to write openly about my experiences—hence, this account of the meeting and the Sathsang. However, I have not included any aspects that I still feel should be confidential.

I asked about the potential loss of community, and someone said that the Sathsang would provide that. When I asked if there was any questioning or open concern among members, one woman then turned to me and said that she had done it both ways and had felt no difference, but some at the meeting did voice concerns. At one point our leader did say that those who had done the online course and then attended the Sathsangs were surprised at the noises they heard from those practicing the traditional forms of the kriya[27] and did not like this. Others, though, said that they had gradually learned to accept all versions of the practices.

Clearly, Jaggi Vasudev, now in his sixties, continues to evolve his Isha with maddening swiftness for anyone trying to write about the organization. On the new sophisticated website for the online program, "Isha Inner Engineering Online with Sadhguru—Technologies for Wellbeing," Sadhguru openly defines the nature of kriya.[28]

Even in the initial e-mail and the conversation at the meeting, the kriya continued to be equated with yoga—some form of bodily practices. Now a separate section on the website appearing with a banner reading "Isha Kriya™ designed by Sadhguru, is a simple yet powerful tool to move from untruth to truth." Sadhguru explained his vision in an accompanying video:

> Isha means that which is the source of creation, kriya mean an inward action toward that, karma means outward action—if you perform action with your body or your mind, or your emotions or your physical energies we call this karma, if you perform an inward action which does not involve any of these then we call this kriya. What is a kriya? It is an extremely simple powerful process, a powerful tool to constantly move from untruth to truth . . . generally all of the spiritual processes which move a person in this direction involve physiological changes, whenever physiological changes are involved it is extremely important that the teacher is substantially trained. . . . But those aspects, those processes, which do *not* involve any kind of physiological change but bring about a spiritual transformation—which are very few—those can be taught en masse.

Almost divining the objections of the Pudukkottai yoga master, Sadhguru has kept his public teaching only to "tools" that can be taught in this mass medium, which appear to be breath control, chanting, and meditation—with very limited use of the "physiological." The current website now describes the kriya as a "powerful guided meditation"(http://ishausa.org/ishakriya). I have not registered for the online course, but from the detailed description I have deduced that the power of the program resides in what resembles talk therapy—a series of discourses, usually engaging, along with practices that can be done in the comfort of participants' homes and at their own pace. Gone are the many rules about not eating three hours before the course, sitting without a break for over three hours or asking questions and having group discussions. Instead, as one online participant told me, "It's like hosting Sadhguru in your own home. He is right there talking to you."

However, along with his simplified online course, the Sathsang that June evening defied any simplistic analysis that Isha had lost its esoteric edge—its mystery. At 6:20 our master of ceremonies stood at the microphone and, instead of leading the Sathsang, turned on a CD player. A "voice" came over the sound system directing those who do the two major forms of the kriya to begin now and those from the online program to "sit with eyes closed and chant." The result was about thirty minutes of cacophony of sounds—with the animal-like noises and the heavy breathing and then at the end the final harmony of *oṃ* chanting. As usual, many mediators rose and came to the microphone to witness to the effects that Sadhguru and the practices had on their lives; many were in tears.

After a brief break, Sadhguru's voice—at first very gently—asked us to close our eyes. When we all settled into a quiet space, his almost seductive voice coaxed us to imagine ourselves in a totally desolate place and imagine ourselves desolate inside and outside. Then a soundtrack began emitting eerie noises akin the sound effects of a science fiction thriller. Sadhguru's voice commanded, as I remember his words:

> Imagine your body getting lighter and lighter, floating higher and higher above the desolation, feel it, look down at the desolation. You begin to move—feel the wind in your face. . . . You see a little clearing in a forest; you descend and then slowly touch ground. . . . You spot a little hut—just a simple little hut and something attractions you. You are drawn to a door and walk in—there you see on a pedestal your Spiritual Master—you are in awe, he says to you, "The Infinite will not come to you, you must come to the Infinite, surrender to It."

At points Sadhguru sang and chanted in a sonorous voice; finally, as the drums beat faster and faster, as mediators cried out in ecstasy, his voice intoned the *mahāmantra*, *oṃ namā śivāya*. I could feel my own reluctant body swaying as I heard the undifferentiated sobs and passionate cries of "Shiva, Shiva." Abruptly the sound track stopped, eyes opened, and complete normalcy returned as we filed out to eat the waiting potluck dinner.

PUTTING UNIVERSITY EDUCATION IN ITS PLACE

Sadhguru Jaggi's discourses excel in the art of using, yet critiquing, the academic world often within a single paragraph.[29] In *Mystic's Musings*, Sadhguru discusses the difference between philosophy—in this case Hindu—and his way of being:

> There is a different kind of understanding in you. When you intellectually understand, it leads only to these deceptive states. When you experientially know, it is different. . . . A philosophy like that will give you some semblance of balance in your life, but it does not liberate you from deeper karma. . . . But slowly if a person does this philosophy . . . slowly they will become joyless. They will become reasonably balanced and stable; at the same time they will slowly become lifeless. (2008: 185)

Enfolded together into this paragraph, the more classical forms of Indian intellectual pursuits as well as the university's "intellectual" methods are contrasted with a better epistemology—*experience*. Often Sadhguru's emphasis on experience versus intellectualism (sometimes described as book learning in the discourses of many other gurus) conjoins experiment in science with experiential learning. Yet philosophy (and much of what we would call the humanities) is often glossed a joyless and stultifying pursuits or is ignored completely.[30]

I suspect that the misconceptions about my own research in many of the guru-centered organizations were exasperated by my questions. I did not ask for data or statistics of the organization only—that is, a truly external and objective view—but rather inquired about *understanding* the effect of the practices and the power of guru in their lives. I was asking about *experience,* about the inner as well as the external life of participants. Frequently, I was personally distressed when I heard Isha Yoga instructors tell students not to "philosophize" when they ventured to ask for the meaning or the symbolic sense of any of the yogic postures that we were learning. The Art of Living course nevertheless did include sophisticated philosophical explanations of the meaning of the practices, although the instructor presented these as preliminary to "practices." For this AOL teacher the weight of the practices ultimately rested in the person of the guru, "He is an example of his teaching because whatever he says, he does—the charity, the service projects, because he *is* his knowledge." I heard almost the same words from an Isha teacher, who told me of Sadhguru, "He is saying the truth, and every aspect of him is like truth."

Within these intensely devotional statements lies a difference between the guru as teacher and a college professor. Years ago the philosopher and historian of religions, Joachim Wach, confronted this issue. In "Master and Disciple," he succinctly writes, "The teacher gives of his knowledge and ability, the master gives himself" (Wach [1925] 1988: 30). However, much of this distinction may be challenged as an inadequate portrait of the power of the professor especially of religious studies[31] (Kripal, 1999; 2007), the guru's person continues to dominate even the most modern forms of yoga practices. Looking back on the vignettes here, contemporary technology and modern media—with its ability to enhance and project public personalities—all added (not subtracted) from the power of the guru's personality. The new online Inner Engineering actually diminishes the role of the much revered teachers who once acted as Jaggi Vasudev's surrogates. Now his face alone, his voice alone, in this new form of one-to-one relationship will be the only personality that that new mediators encounter on a deep level.

REFERENCES

Alter, Joseph S. 2004. *Yoga in Modern India: The Body between Science and Philosophy.* Princeton, NJ: Princeton University Press.

Clothey, Fred W. 2007. *Ritualizing on the Boundaries: Continuity and Innovation in the Tamil Diaspora*. Columbia: University of South Carolina Press.

Gold, Daniel. 1988. *Comprehending the Guru: Toward a Grammar of Religious Perception*. Atlanta: American Academy of Religion, Scholar's Press.

Goldberg, Ellen. 2005. Cognitive Science and *Haṭhayoga*. *Zygon* 40 (3): 613–629.

———. 2007. Cognitive Science and Hinduism. In Sushil Mittal and Gene Thursby (eds.), *Studying Hindusim: Key Concepts and Methods*. New York: Routledge, pp. 59–73.

Heelas, Paul. 2008. *The Spiritualities of Life: New Age Romanticism and Consumptive Capitalism*. Oxford: Blackwell.

Kripal, Jeffrey J. 1999. Inside-Out, Outside-In: Existential Place and Academic Practice in the Study of North American Guru-Traditions. *Religious Studies Review* 25 (3): 333–338.

———. 2007. *The Serpent's Gift: Gnostic Reflections on the Study of Religion*. Chicago: University of Chicago Press.

Marshall, Gary. 2012. Apple's Secrets. *Mac Life*, May 12.

Taves, Ann. 2009. *Religious Experience Reconsidered: A Building-Block Approach to the Study of Religion and Other Special Things*. Princeton, NJ: Princeton University Press.

———. 2011. 2010 Presidential Address: "Religion" in the Humanities and the Humanities in the University. *Journal of the American Academy of Religion* 79 (2): 287–314.

Vasudev, Jaggi, Sadhguru. 2003. *Mystic's Musings*. New Delhi: Wisdom Tree.

Vasudev, Jaggi, Sadhguru, and CherylSimon. 2008. *Midnights with the Mystic: A Little Guide to Freedom and Bliss*. Charlottesville, VA: Hampton Road Publishing.

Gautier, Francois. 2008. *The Guru of Joy: Sri Sri Ravi Shankar and the Art of Living*. Carlsbad, CA: Hay House.

Subramaniam, Arundhathi. 2010. *Sadhguru: More Than a Life*. New Delhi: Penguin Books.

Syman, Stefanie. 2010. *The Subtle Body: The Story of Yoga in America*. New York: Farrar, Straus and Giroux.

Singleton, Mark. 2010. *Yoga Body: The Origins of Modern Posture Practice*. New York: Oxford University Press.

Wach, Joachim. 1988. *Essays in the History of Religions*. Ed. Joseph M. Kitagawa and Gregory D. Alles. New York: Macmillan Publishing. (From essay in German from 1925 to 1952).

NOTES

1. Professor Kang Yoonhee of Nanyang Technological University, Singapore, is currently researching this pattern of Korean educational migration. Also see "Plight of the Wild Geese Families," *Straits Times*, March 16, 2009.
2. In Singapore, the term *religion* often equates with a citizen's ascribed ethnoreligion, which the Government of Singapore recognizes on identity cards and applications for employment. These are the four recognized ethnic groups, each usually associated with specific religious tradition: Islam for Malays, Hinduism (with some Islam) for Indians, and Buddhism or Daoism for Chinese. Christianity is the wild card here, with many birthright Christians within Chinese and Indian communities but with increasing numbers of newly converted evangelicals.

3. Guriji translates this as "'Su' means proper, 'darshan' means vision, and 'Kriya' is a purifying practice." The Sudarshan Kriya is therefore a purifying practice, whereby one receives a proper vision of one's true self (http://www.sudarshankriya.net).
4. I followed the movements in Chennai in 2008 and briefly in 2009. However, Singapore remains the major site of my research conducted in summers 2005 and 2006, with a year funded by a Fulbright-Hays Faculty Research Abroad Fellowship and Visiting Senior Research Fellow (sabbatical leave program), Asian Research Institute (Globalization and Religion cluster), National University of Singapore, August 2007 to August 2008. Recent follow-ups in May–June 2010, 2011, and 2012.
5. Both China and India have looked to Singapore for Asian models in housing, transportation, and education.
6. Although Jaggi Vasudev revealed late in his career that he had a master in a former incarnation. See Swami Nisarga's introduction to *Mystic's Musings* (Vasudev, 2003: iii).
7. The Art of Living Website mentions that at age seventeen Sri Sri Ravi Shankar completed his "traditional studies in Vedic literature and a degree in modern science" (http://www.srisri.org/biography/timeline). Jaggi Vasudev gives a fuller account of his unorthodox studies at university but nonetheless mentions his immersion in European classics (Vasudev, 2008: 140–151).
8. Much of this information is well presented at the National Museum of History in Singapore in the Singapore History Gallery. See the gallery online at http://www.nationalmuseum.sg/.
9. I interviewed leaders of both Isha and Art of Living, many of whom were more recent migrants from India but with the intention to make Singapore their home. No one mentioned experiences with traditional practitioners of yoga, some had begun Isha or AOL courses in India or while in the United States on assignments. Several mentioned becoming interested in "spirituality" through reading books by and about gurus. They confirmed that most new migrants from India were in technology or business.
10. I worked with many additional guru-centered groups that remained devotional in nature and centered on gurus who had attained *mahāsamādhi* (they died as enlightened beings): Shirdi Sai Baba Spiritual Center (Shirdi Sai Baba, d. 1918); Sri Raghavendra Society (Swami Raghavendra 1595–1671); Krishna Mandir (Swami Prabhupada, founder of ISKCON 1896–1977); Ramakrishna Mission (Sri Ramakrishna, 1836–1886); Sri Aurobindo Society (Sri Aurobindo 1872–1950). The Ramakrishna mission teaches meditation and yoga and belongs as both devotional and yoga centered; hence, I list it twice.
11. A simple Web search shows the following universities engaged in some form of this research in the United States: The Center for Consciousness Studies at the University of Arizona; Princeton University; Princeton Engineering Anomalies Research (PEAR) [recently closed], with a focus on the "Scientific Study of Consciousness-Related Physical Phenomena" including paranormal studies and remote perception; Duke University's Rhine Research Center is "an Institute for the Study of Consciousness, and offers many psi-related courses, workshops, and seminars" (http://www.hollowhill.com/ghost-hunting/parapsychologydegree.htm, accessed June 8, 2008).
12. Jayanth Narayanan has his Ph.D. from the London Business School. During the talk he referred to research out of the University of Wisconsin, which I have found mentioned in Dan Gilgoff, "Can Meditation Change Your Brain? Contemplative Neuroscientists Believe It Can," CNN Belief Online,

October 26, 2010. Available at: http://pagingdrgupta.blogs.cnn.com/2010/10/26/can-meditation-change-your-brain-contemplative-neuroscientists-believe-it-can/.

13. At the 2010 Annual Meeting of the American Academy of Religion, the presidential address by Ann Taves emphasized the newer "subject-oriented" nature of the field (Taves, 2009; 2011). See also Goldberg (2005; 2007) for an introductory review of cognitive science, neuroscience, and yoga.
14. The website defines and explains the term. "Bhava Spandana Program (BSP) is a four day, three night residential program offered to those who have been initiated into Shambhavi Mahamudra. . . . The word *bhava* literally means 'sensation.' *Spandana* can be loosely translated as 'resonance.' Through powerful processes and meditations, the Bhava Spandana Program creates an intensely energetic situation, where individuality and the limitations of the five sense organs can be transcended, creating an experience of oneness and resonance with the rest of existence" (http://www.ishayoga.org/advanced-programs/bhava-spandana).
15. The unique kriyas taught in each of these courses often appear with a registered trademark on website and printed pamphlets: for example, *Sudarshan Kriya* (Sri Sri Ravi Shankar) and *IAM Technique* (Integrated Amrita Meditation Technique) of Mata Amritanandamayi. All are protected as "trade secrets," including Sadhguru Jaggi Vasudev's *Shambhavi Maha Mudra Kriya* and Jnana Sitthar's *Rajayoga Power Transcendental Meditation of Yoga*.
16. Much information is online about these agreements including templates. For a clear explanation see David V. Radack, "Understanding Confidentiality Agreements." Available at: http://www.tms.org/pubs/journals/jom/matters/matters-9405.html.
17. Angela Rudert, my co-advisee at Syracuse, just defended her dissertation, "'She's an All-in-One Guru': Devotion to a 21st Century Mystic" (April 26, 2012) on Gurumaa, a rising female guru who draws on much of this North Indian mixed tradition. Rudert reminded me in a recent e-mail, "There are definitely gurus out there right now who are the scholarly type. Obviously the scholar/guru is a long established institution in India, and it still thrives. For this reason, I wonder if it might be interesting to juxtapose the modern new age gurus with the more traditional scholar/gurus" (Personal communication, May 27, 2009). An essay on the wide range of ways that old and new gurus interact with the models of scholarship would be very valuable. In South India, the Shankaracharyas fall into this category with their publication of more folksy discourses but also scholarly commentaries.
18. In an interview with one of the leading members of Isha, the term *follower* was specifically rejected as failing to convey the continuing sense of choice within the organization.
19. Sanskrit terms, when used within the Tamil language, are frequently transliterated with a *th* or *dh* to distinguish these within the logic of the Tamil alphabet. Hence for Isha, satsang becomes Sathsang (capitalized).
20. This is a complex term. The Isha website defines it as "Shambhavi Mahamudra is a powerful kriya, or internal energy process, distilled from the yogic sciences to effect a profound self-transformation" (http://www.ishausa.org/programs/basic/inner-engineering/shambhavi/). The Sanskrit term *śambhavī mahāmudrā*, refers to Śiva as Śambu, a tantric-estoteric form; this feminine form with the final "ī," links to the goddess Śambhavī.
21. http://www.youtube.com/watch?v=Sdm_U6ZivZA.

22. Indeed, the term comes from the root *ārāy*, which means "research, critical study" and is related to legal investigations (see the *Tamil Lexicon* published by the University of Madras, 1936 edition).
23. From an e-mail sent May 6, 2008. I do not have formal permission to use my correspondent's name.
24. But Taves (2009: 16–17) points out that these attempts to give personal experience a scientific context were in competition with another more prevalent model—religion as *sui generis*, an aspect of life not reducible to any other modality.
25. The term in the famous old Monier-Williams, *Sanskrit-English Dictionary* (Oxford: Clarendon Press, 1899) also carries the meaning of conjuring, closely relating these practices to that complex designation "magic." In the case of Yoga Jnana Sitthar, his stress on *siddhi* power closely parallels this nexus of science, magic, and experience.
26. The Government of Singapore tore down most of the old neighborhoods to put up the many well-built Housing Board high-rise flats. The ethnic diversity of these building is carefully controlled with each ethnic group assigned a portion of the apartments according to the percentage of that group in the total popular of the city-state. However, areas like Little India and Chinatown were left as much for tourist interest as for the cultural continuity of each ethnic group.
27. Jaggi Vasudev has changed the form of the kriya. An earlier form included shouting sounds somewhat like a rooster.
28. http://www.innerengineering.com/home.php.
29. While many of his discourses on DVDs are not available for public use or even quotation, many other discourses have been published in print or as DVDs. Increasingly, such DVDs appear on YouTube, and more and more of his lectures are openly online.
30. Part of this assessment of higher education can be explained using new revelations about Sadhguru's experiences with the educational system during the 1960s. *Midnights with the Mystic*, reveals young Jaggi refusing to go to college despite his father's desire that his son also become a doctor like him. When the young mystic finally relented, he chose to major in literature. In his disgust with "teachers who read from prepared notes, he simply requested that they let students photocopy the lecture notes so that they would not waste precious time and energy in class." In spite of their initial anger, the faculty allowed Jaggi to read on his own, "So I planted myself in the college garden and people started coming to me to share their problems" (2008: 146). Here, I can attest that Sadhguru's reactions to the system were not simply the acts of an overconfident youth. I taught English for a year at a college in South India during the same period, and I was equally frustrated by the rote learning at the time.
31. With all of the emphasis on the university degree and the importance of education in Asia, I never heard—until recently—education described as "A Place of Discovery, Creativity, and Imagination" (http://thecollege.syr.edu/about/index.html). Religious studies programs are very new to Asia and must tread more carefully than the more typical American programs, which often promise the opportunity for personal engagement with religious issues. The minor in religious studies at the National University of Singapore (NUS) describes its program thus: "Religion has always been a prominent force in human life, and, despite predictions to the contrary, it remains one today. In this region, it is impossible to understand our society or those of our neighbors without understanding the religions that permeate them. Moreover, by virtue of its secular state and pluralistic society, Singapore

is well positioned to take a leading role in the study of religion. Religious studies at NUS will involve the scholarly exploration both of the phenomenon of religion and of different specific religious traditions. Religious studies, as a scholarly and intellectual discipline, transcends individual disciplines to consider beliefs, practices, texts, history, and social functions of religion from a variety of disciplinary perspectives. This program will train students to discuss—with respect and grace—some of the most volatile issues of our time" (http://www.fas.nus.edu.sg/acad/subjects/religion-minor.html).

CHAPTER 14

Online *Bhakti* in a Modern Guru Organization

MAYA WARRIER

Bhakti, or *bhaktiyoga*—intense personal devotion and love to a chosen deity or guru, understood as a path to spiritual enlightenment—is one of the most popular aspects of Hindu faith and practice in the present day. *Bhakti* is mass mediated in different ways across the Indian subcontinent and beyond—through public rituals and festivals; music, theater, dance, and recitation performances; the circulation of mass-produced devotional texts and printed images; and film and television.[1] Over the last couple of decades, the Internet too has come to play a significant role in facilitating, mediating, and sustaining forms of *bhakti* across vast geographical distances, not just in "real" but also in "virtual" space and time.

The growing accessibility of the Internet, and the scope for online interaction, present interesting possibilities for the use of this medium in facilitating *bhakti.*[2] These possibilities have increasingly been explored by a number of modern guru-led *bhakti* organizations in India and overseas, many of whom attract a geographically dispersed following.[3] Some use it mainly to provide information about themselves and publicize their tradition-specific forms of *bhakti*; others additionally enable website visitors to participate online in spiritual practice and interact with fellow visitors. The use of the Internet for facilitating the mediation and practice of *bhakti* raises important questions for contemporary scholars of modern forms of yoga. Does mediation via the Internet transform the expression and experience of *bhakti* in any way? Does *bhakti* acquire new characteristics as a result of its Internet mediation or is online *bhakti* best understood merely as an extension of its offline manifestation?

These are some of the questions I explore in this paper with respect to *bhaktiyoga* in the Mata Amritanandamayi Math (MAM). This transnational organization, headed by the vastly popular female guru, Mata Amritanandamayi (b. 1953), uses the Internet extensively to facilitate and sustain guru *bhakti* among its globally dispersed followers. The MAM's significant web presence serves to instill in followers a particular attitude of wondrous love for the guru, known to her devotees as Amma (mother). It enables followers to sustain and express their *bhakti* to this guru in a manner that is participative and interactive. Most importantly, it engenders a sense of virtual proximity to the guru (even in the guru's physical absence) in ways that help nourish the one-to-one guru–devotee bond that is the cornerstone of this organization. In what follows, I shall explore in some detail these aspects of Internet-mediated *bhakti* in the MAM before returning to the question of whether or not Internet mediation in this organization can be understood to have a transformative effect on the expression and experience of *bhakti*.

MAM'S PRESENCE ON THE WORLD WIDE WEB

The Mata Amritanandamayi Math and Mission Trust, founded in 1981, has its headquarters in Amritapuri, a small coastal township in the south Indian state of Kerala, which houses the Mata Amritanandamayi ashram. Amritapuri, named after the guru, marks her birthplace. The organization has a number of centers both in Kerala and in other parts of India as well as in parts of Africa, the Americas, Europe, Australia, Southeast Asia, the Middle East, and the Far East. Between February and September–October each year the guru, now in her late fifties, travels across the globe widely, appearing at public programs where devotees can see her, seek her advice and blessings, and experience her love in the form of an intimate physical embrace, which she bestows individually on the thousands of followers she meets each day.[4]

The main paths of spiritual seeking emphasized by the guru are those of *bhaktiyoga* and *karmayoga*. While the guru encourages *bhakti* to whichever deity best suits the needs and preferences of each individual, the most widely shared form of *bhakti* in the MAM is in fact that addressed to the guru. This *bhakti* is expressed through rituals worshiping the guru as well as through acts of *sevā* (selfless service) to the guru and her mission. The MAM places great emphasis on humanitarian activity, particularly poverty alleviation, and, increasingly, disaster relief. Service to society, understood as *karmayoga*, is a key aspect of this organization, and the guru encourages her devotees to contribute actively to such service. Because of the strong humanitarian and philanthropic agenda of the guru, *sevā* to the guru (*bhaktiyoga*), and *sevā* to society (*karmayoga*) fade imperceptibly into one another: to serve the guru is to serve society and vice versa.

In addition to acts of worship and service to the guru, devotees orientate themselves toward the guru in their everyday lives by observing daily spiritual practices prescribed by her, familiarizing themselves with her simple teachings compiled in volumes published by the MAM, subscribing to the organization's journals and newsletters, and coming together with fellow devotees locally to participate in shared acts of worship, devotion, and service. These activities are supported by the thriving publications unit of the MAM, which produce a range of books and pamphlets intended for the spiritual seeker. The organization also produces music CDs and DVDs carrying footage of the guru's public events, and operates an Indian satellite channel, Amrita TV, named after the guru.

It is only since the early 2000s that the MAM has cultivated a presence on the World Wide Web. The Mata Amritanandamayi Math now makes extensive use of the Internet to reach out to its adherents across the world and notionally unite them in what can best be described as a *community of sentiment* (Appadurai, 1996) centering on the guru.[5] The hub of the MAM's international Web presence is the voluminous website (http://www.amritapuri.org) maintained by the headquarters of the organization at Amritapuri. This website is in English and provides links to separate websites maintained by the MAM's regional centers in India and the rest of the world.[6] No two websites are alike, and the MAM headquarters would seem to leave decisions on web content and design to the initiative, imagination, skills, and preferences of technophiles at the regional centers. All regional websites maintained by centers within and outside India provide a link to the central MAM website at Amritapuri. This paper focuses in the main on the Amritapuri website managed at the MAM's headquarters in India; it also makes references to particular aspects of websites maintained in the United States and the United Kingdom.

The Amritapuri website provides information about the guru, her teachings, her vision and mission, the organization, its activities, and its global spread. Much of this information is hagiographical in tone and is couched in the language of *bhakti*. This is not simply information for its own sake but, more importantly, information that expresses a particular religious attitude or sentiment directed at the guru. The website thus provides not so much a representation of *bhakti* but an expression of it; it is shaped by *bhakti* sentiments and is therefore, in most respects, a devotional artifact. The tone of the writing is largely informal, friendly, and accessible, as the following lines from the website's "Who Is Amma" page demonstrate:

> If we look at Amma's life, this is what we see—someone who has offered her every thought, word and deed for the benefit of others. Giving is the essence. It's just that when the homeless come crying for shelter and Amma gives them a house, we call her a "humanitarian." And when the sorrowful come crying for

> emotional solace and she gives them love, we call her a "mother." And when those thirsty for spiritual knowledge come earnestly seeking and she gives them wisdom, we call her a "guru." This attitude of selflessly serving all creation, knowing others to be extensions of one's own self, Amma refers to as vishwa matrutvam—universal motherhood. And it is to this pinnacle of human existence that Amma is trying to awaken the world through her life, teachings and *darśan* [divine embrace]. . . .[7]

The tone of this excerpt is representative of that used throughout much of the website. The use of the first-person plural suggests that the views expressed are those of the guru's followers. This narrative would seem to be addressed to those who have not yet had an experience of the guru and want to know more about her. By reading passages like this one, the visitor learns not just about the guru but also about how to experience her; thus, an individual interested to enter the world of this guru and her devotees accesses not just information but an entire world of sentiment and emotion centering on the guru.

Gurudarśan, visually feasting on the image (or person) of the guru, is a central aspect of *bhaktiyoga* in this organization. To stand in the presence of the guru and to behold her, to see her and be seen by her, is of utmost importance to devotees of Mata Amritanandamayi. Real-life *darśan* of this guru, however, is not merely a visual experience but also a physical one—to "have" *darśan* of the guru is to be enfolded in her embrace. For one who has previously not had real (as opposed to virtual) *darśan* of the guru, the meaning of such *darśan* is explained on the "Darshan" webpage thus:

Figure 14.1:
Mata Amritanandamayi. (Courtesy of D. English, MA Center.)

> In India Amma has been known to individually embrace over 20,000 people in one day, sitting sometimes for over 22 hours. Over the past thirty five years, She has embraced over 26 million times! . . .
>
> Hers is an unconditional love which expresses itself through the unique vehicle of Her darshan: being ushered into the awesome presence of a Master, the sheer power of Her gaze, the indescribable sweetness of Her smile, the hug that ensconces one in eternity, the earthy voice whispering words of assurance, the gentle nuzzle on the cheek, and the gift of prasad.
>
> Each person's darshan is a fresh experience because Amma Herself is ever fresh – spontaneous. Amma listens to our spoken words and unspoken thoughts, hugs the devotees and whispers a word or two in their ears. She knows exactly our need of the moment. With a pause here, a glimpse there, She instills moments of transformation. This is the testimony of thousands.[8]

This text is accompanied by photographs of the guru holding devotees in a close embrace, her head pressed against theirs, in an attitude of motherly love for her children. While the website makes no effort to simulate the guru's embrace electronically for its visitors, these visitors can still experience the divine hug vicariously by seeing images of the guru holding other devotees in her arms. In addition to still photographs, the website also makes good use of video footage to capture the love and intimacy of the guru's embrace. Thus, one can have *darśan* of a moving, smiling figure, who invariably appears swamped by crowds of devotees in different settings and who is seen to reach out individually to each of the thousands queuing up for a few precious moments in her arms.

For most part of the year, as noted earlier, the guru is on tour—first on her annual India tour and then on a yearly world tour. In the course of these tours, her time is spent with devotees, who cherish the opportunity to see her in person, feast on her sacred form visually, and receive her embrace. The websites play a crucial role in keeping followers across the world up to date with the guru's movements. They provide detailed itineraries of her tours. Within days of her visit to a given location, the website posts video footage of the visit, thus bringing alive the guru's day-by-day passage across vast geographic distances.

Visitors to the website can thus have virtual *darśan* of the guru touring the world. The posts that accompany both the photos and the videos are a verbal celebration of the guru—they dwell on the comfort she brings her waiting devotees, the joy they feel in her presence, the glow that they experience as she leads them through *bhajan* and meditation sessions, and the pain of separation when she departs. The visuals and accompanying text reinforce the message that a "universal mother" is at work, serving "all creation" in an attitude of selfless love and transforming the world through her care. They enable newcomers to learn the cultural habitus of *bhakti* in this organization and facilitate their immersion in a virtual community of sentiment with the guru at its center.

In the course of a day, a number of different images of the guru appear on the home page, and none is ever repeated. Thus, every experience of accessing the guru via her website is new. However, it is not simply "newness" that devotees are after. Often, their desire for *darśan* is a desire to relive cherished moments from the past. The websites enable this reliving of *darśan* by making video footage from past events available online. An online "Amma Shop," maintained by volunteers from North America and Europe, for instance, directs visitors to a link where they are invited to "Catch glimpses of Amma's 2010 World Tour over and over again and relive your favorite memories."[9]

The Amritapuri website enables interested devotees to follow the guru's activities on a daily basis via Facebook and Twitter and to subscribe to RSS feeds and SMS and e-mail alerts to keep abreast of the latest news updates.[10] The tweets logged by the website are referred to as "Amma chimes." The following chimes, which appeared (in reverse order of their sequence) on the website on March 17 and 18, 2011, and relayed updates on Amma's activities at a public program in India's capital city of Delhi when Amma was on her annual visit, are fairly typical of those routinely posted on the website:[11]

> Darshan is over @ Delhi. At the end Amma sang 3 songs and played Holi with everyone. 18 March 2011 | 12:44 a.m. (UTC [Coordinated Universal Time])
> After a wonderful Holi dance by the students Swamiji started bhajans with Amriteswari Ma . . . 17 March 2011 | 7:19 p.m. (UTC)
> Amritavidyalayam children presented different cultural performances 17 March 2011 | 7:17 p.m. (UTC)
> Darshan started @ Delhi 17 March 2011 | 5:00 p.m. (UTC)
> All are singing Arati. 17 March 2011 | 4:51 p.m. (UTC)
> Amma also sang- Me Khadi, Vraj Me Aya Basant, Kalam Kanalu, Jhala Jhalavena, Karm Ki Nadiya, & Jinki Karuna 17 March 2011 | 4:43 p.m. (UTC)

The Amritapuri website also invites its visitors to write to the guru and to offer thoughts and prayers to her on an online form.[12] This form, addressed "To beloved Amma," requires the visitor to make three entries under the headings: "subject," "your name" and "your message." Once the message has been submitted by clicking a button marked "I offer unto YOU," a text box containing the words "Your Thoughts Reached the Divine Mother" pops up on the screen. Visitors are invited to share their entreaties and prayers with fellow devotees via Twitter, SMS, and e-mail. Devotees in all corners of the world can thus connect to the guru on a daily basis, wherever she may be. The guru's *līla* (divine play), enacted on a global platform, is simultaneously captured on the World Wide Web for devotees' near simultaneous consumption and delectation through the mere click of a mouse, touch of a button, or tap of a touchscreen.

CYBER-SATSANG

The guru-centered community enabled and represented here is not passive but is an active and interactive one. The Amritapuri website actively invites individuals to participate in this community and express and share their guru *bhakti*. They are invited, for instance, to contribute entries to an online "Ashram diary," which compiles devotees' narratives of experiences they have had in the guru's presence, events relating to the guru that have inspired their lives, poems and articles about the guru, even drawings and sketches based on the guru's life and teachings.[13] New diary entries are regularly posted on the website, and its visitors can post comments in response. An excerpt from one such diary entry, posted on December 27, 2010, by an ashram resident by the name of Rta and titled "Supreme Love that lights up all creation," reads as follows:[14]

> My celebration of Christmas began on the beach in the late afternoon of December 24th. The waves were rushing to the shore reverberating against the rocks. The sea breeze cooled us. Eagles circled overhead. Several hundred devotees were sitting around Amma under the palms; cross-legged on the sand before her, perched on chairs and leaning against the rocks. I thought of the Fisher of Men, whose birthday we were about to celebrate. Now over two thousand years later, I was sitting with the Fisher Girl on the seashore of her birthplace. When young she had meditated here alone: now she meditates with a sea of people. I fell into silence with Amma. Ma. Om . . .

Reflections like this one, and the responses they generate, constitute, in the MAM, what is understood to be Satsang (*satsaṅga*), the sharing of beautiful experiences and thought-provoking ideas in a spirit of companionship and spiritual striving. Devotees, when they get together in real time and space, tend to engage in Satsang, usually sharing stories about the guru's glory, their experience of her love, and the impact she has had on their lives. This is understood to be activity that earns spiritual merit and burns away the effects of negative karma. Online too, Satsang is made possible via the many sites on the World Wide Web dedicated to the guru.

The website maintained at the M.A. Center in San Ramon, California, explains the meaning of Satsang as follows:

> Satsang is a Sanskrit word, meaning, a close association or companionship with a Self-Realized Soul . . . Satsang is also discussion or hearing of spiritual truths expressed by Self-Realized Masters. . . .
>
> The first and foremost type of Satsang is a direct physical, mental and intellectual relationship with the Master. In the presence of a living Master spiritual practice becomes smooth and less complicated. . . . In the scorching heat of worldliness, being in the presence of a Master is like cool breeze in the shade of a huge tree.
>
> The second type is established indirectly—by studying teachings, reflecting on and practicing the teachings. Satsang should be done daily for some time. By discussing spiritual subjects, the mind will get concentrated on God.[15]

The websites maintained by devotees in different parts of the world facilitate what is described here as the first type of Satsang in obvious ways. By enabling devotees to be in the constant (virtual) presence of their guru at all times and to connect with her in different ways, these websites in effect serve as the "huge tree" in whose shade devotees can experience the "cool breeze" that is the presence of the Master. The Amritapuri website, for instance, devotes a great many pages to the teachings of the guru, providing extensive quotes from published compilations of her teachings and from the speeches delivered by her on different occasions. It includes hundreds of pages of archived material, containing a vast amount of text, as well as a large collection of images. The website provides a search option, so that a visitor interested to find out what the guru may have had to say about a specific subject can type in the appropriate keywords and instantly access a range of entries on that subject. In this way—by accessing what are understood to be the guru's own words (in translation)—the website enables direct learning from the guru. Some websites additionally provide links to e-shops, where visitors can browse through, and purchase, the MAM's numerous publications (as well as other devotional artifacts).

The second type of Satsang is facilitated through discussion, reflection, and sharing with others. Online Satsang is enabled through such means as the Ashram Diary already noted as well as a range of other online arrangements. The "Amma UK" site, for instance, notifies visitors of an "Amma Yahoo Group," which it describes as "an informal way for devotees in the UK to exchange information, share files and pictures, and publicize Satsangs and other events."[16] Additionally, many regional centers invite visitors to their websites to subscribe to e-newsletters. These too solicit contributions in the form of articles, poems, and photographs from devotees enabling both the online expression of *bhakti*, and immersion in Satsang.

It is noteworthy that an individual in any given location can access the webpages maintained not just by the center closest to him or her but also those operated by centers in the far distance and thus may engage with the expressions of *bhakti* of fellow devotees from across the world. The network of websites focused on this guru connects devotees into a virtual community that transcends geographical divides. It also sustains a sense of what Coleman (2000: 49–71) refers to as *global orientatedness*, leading to individual and collective imaginings of a global assembly of devotees and of one's own location within this global collective.

"GETTING INVOLVED": CYBER-*SEVĀ*

The guru's mission is a humanitarian one—her stated aim is to alleviate suffering in the world. To this end, her organization engages in a range of charitable activities in the areas of health, education, social welfare, and disaster relief. The Amritapuri website quotes the guru's words as follows, encapsulating her "dream" for humanity:

> Everyone in the world should be able to sleep without fear, at least for one night. Everyone should be able to eat his fill, at least for one day. There should be at least one day when hospitals see no one admitted due to violence. By doing selfless service for at least one day, everyone should serve the poor and needy. It is Amma's prayer that at least this small dream be realised.[17]

All devotees are thus invited to contribute to the guru's humanitarian mission by participating in "selfless service" for at least one day. This service can take the form of monetary donations as well as voluntary work. This *sevā* too is a crucial expression of *bhakti* and forms part of the devotee's practice of *bhaktiyoga*.

The website run by the M.A. Center at San Ramon (http://www.amma.org), in a section detailing the guru's humanitarian initiatives, provides a link to a subsection titled "Get Involved." It outlines a range of different ways devotees can engage in acts of *sevā* and includes details about particular projects that need volunteers or donations. One such project run by devotees in the United States is called "Mother's Kitchen," where across America people come together at regular intervals to cook meals to feed the hungry and homeless.[18] The project is described as being active in thirty-eight cities, with meals served to the homeless across twenty-three states in America as well as at two sites in Canada. The Web pages list the contact details of individuals coordinating these ventures in different areas. These pages also offer detailed guidelines on how individuals can start a fresh kitchen venture in their own locality should they wish to do so, how they can raise the necessary money for this purpose, and whom they should contact in case they are in need of guidance. The virtual "network"—indeed "community"—that visitors encounter here is not an anonymous one but one whose participants have clearly defined identities and roles; the Web pages, by providing the e-mail addresses and telephone numbers of these individuals, enable interaction with any or all of these participants.

This website also solicits monetary donations from visitors,[19] which can be paid by check, money order, or credit card. An online donation form for credit card payments allows donors to contribute to as many as five different charitable projects at a time. They can choose from a drop-down menu that lists about thirty different projects ranging from "Scholarship Fund for Needy Children" to "GreenFriends."[20] Many of the projects listed are based in India and include medical, educational, and poverty alleviation initiatives. A significant number relate to disaster relief ventures around the world and include such items as "Japan Earthquake Relief," "Haiti Relief," and "Kenya Relief Fund." The website provides advice and information on how to undertake "planned giving," which includes not just monetary donations but also contributions in the form of stocks, real estate, life insurance gifts, and retirement plan gifts.[21] Additionally it provides guidance on how to bequeath property to the guru posthumously by means of a will or trust. A separate section of the website details the extensive relief efforts undertaken by the MAM over the last ten years, in India and abroad, and notes that the Mata Amritanandamayi Math has been deemed an "NGO with Special Consultative Status To the United Nations" since 2005.[22]

The M.A. Center uses other means too, besides donations, to generate resources for the organization's humanitarian projects. Orders for *pūjās*, for instance, are a means to this end. The center's website provides visitors with a link to another site where they can order *pūjās* online.[23] These *pūjās*, according to the website, are performed at Brahmasthanam temples[24] set up by the guru at different locations in India[25] and cover a wide range in terms of the deities to whom they are addressed and the benefits they are understood to confer on the client. The rates range from thirty-five to six hundred dollars. Up to five *pūjās* can be ordered simultaneously using an online order form. Payments are processed online, and customers are informed that they will receive *prāsād* (consecrated substances like flower petals and ashes distributed to devotees after the *pūjā* ritual) from one of the temples in India as confirmation that the *pūjā* has been completed. The payments, according to the website, serve a dual purpose: "All donations for the pujas are used to support Amma's numerous humanitarian projects undertaken by the Mata Amritanandamayi Math and also to cover the expenses associated with performing the pujas. . . ."[26]

The U.K. website (http://www.amma.org.uk) offers similar opportunities to visitors.[27] The U.K. website also invites volunteers to raise money for the guru's annual visit. In a section titled "Heartfelt donations towards Amma's visit costs," the authors explain their annual need for hospitality funds:

> It is now less than three weeks month [sic] until the London programme, and we are still very short of the funds required to cover the costs of hosting our beloved Amma. It is Amma's wish that the funds to cover the costs of hiring the venue etc., to enable so many people to benefit from being in her physical presence, are met by the hosting country, so that all money raised during her visit can go straight to her numerous charities.[28]

Individuals are invited to make payments to meet these hosting expenses and also to sponsor particular items required for the guru's public programs. The list of necessary supplies needing sponsors includes items such as stage, chairs and tables, decorations, flowers and fruits, and water and electricity. For many devotees, volunteering their money and efforts toward making the guru's annual visit a success is their supreme act of *sevā*. The hosting of each such event invariably takes months of planning and preparation, at the end of which time their efforts are richly rewarded when the guru arrives in their midst and affords them real-life *darśan* in the form of the long-awaited embrace.

BHAKTI TRANSFORMED?

As the foregoing discussion shows, the websites maintained by the headquarters of the MAM in Kerala and at two of its branches in the United States and United Kingdom facilitate online guru *bhakti* and guru *sevā* in a range of different ways, even when the guru is not physically present. They enable devotees to experience her, and feel her love, across vast geographical distances. They keep devotees constantly updated with news about the guru's movements and activities and enable them to participate in her spiritual and humanitarian projects. In the case of newcomers, the websites also enable their socialization into the cultural dispositions, values, and attitudes that characterize *bhakti* in the MAM. The Internet would seem particularly suited to *bhakti's* ultimate aim of eliminating the distance between devotee and the object of devotion.

Having considered some of the ways this guru-led organization mediates *bhakti* via the Internet, I will now return to the questions posed at the outset: Does the mediation of devotion via the internet in the Mata Amritanandamayi Math and Mission lead to a transformation in devotees' experience and expression of *bhaktiyoga*? To what extent can online *bhakti* be seen to acquire characteristics distinct from its offline manifestation? In attempting to answer this question, it is useful to heed the words of caution issued by Dawson and Cowan (2004). They note that the Internet has suffered from an excessively effusive press, that it has been hyped to an unrealistic degree, and that this hyperbole is not supported by the evidence on Internet mediation accumulated by social scientists. "Cyberspace," they remind us, "is not quite as unusual a place as sometimes predicted. Life in cyberspace is in continuity with so-called 'real life' . . . People are doing online pretty much what they do offline . . ." (p. 1). Equally, however, they concede that Internet mediation can allow things to be done in ways that are somewhat new and sometimes entirely innovative.

In the case of the guru-centered websites considered here, the *bhakti* that one encounters does not appear radically different from expressions of *bhakti* in offline contexts. Instead, *bhakti* in its Internet-mediated form would seem to reinforce the dispositions and cultural habitus of the offline devotional milieu in this organization. Moreover, there is nothing in these websites to suggest that the guru's online presence is intended to substitute the offline experience of *darśan* during the guru's real-life public appearances. The online *darśan* enabled by these websites is not intended to devalue the real-life, tangible, flesh-and-blood experience of being enfolded in the guru's arms; indeed, it is not even represented as an approximation of the real thing. This is not to say that the websites deem online *darśan* to be inauthentic; if anything it is intended to support and sustain real-life *darśan* by constantly reminding devotees, long after the guru's departure, of the intimacy and power of that embrace.

The mediation of devotion via the Internet, though it may not transform *bhakti*, certainly does have the potential to enhance and intensify devotional experience in the transnational and global arena where this guru and her devotees operate. The unique features of the Internet—its interactivity and global reach as well as its basis in multimedia systems and its hypertextuality—lend an immediacy, intimacy, and vibrancy to the guru–devotee engagement that may otherwise be absent when the devotee and guru are separated by significant geographical distances.

Central to guru devotion in this organization are the devotee's constant efforts to stay attuned to the guru and receptive to her love. The guru's webpages enhance this guru focus in very effective ways by bringing alive on the computer screen the guru's sacred presence, enabling devotees to see her in different contexts, to access her teachings and messages, and to keep informed, almost moment by moment, of her latest activities and campaigns. By accessing the websites dedicated to Mata Amritanandamayi, devotees can in an instant transform their computer screen, a place of mundane activity for most part, into a personal altar or shrine (Helland, 2007: 14)—a site for expressing guru *bhakti* and rendering guru *sevā*. In an instant, followers can find themselves in the guru's sacred presence. The Internet, by virtue of its multimedia features, provides a unique "sacred sensorium" (Srinivas, 2008: 76–78) where *bhaktiyoga* can be learned, practiced, shared, and performed. It offers devotees a means to partake of, enjoy, and celebrate their sacred center (the guru) both individually and collectively, through instant participation via the Internet.

This connectivity, while unlikely to serve as a substitute either for the connection that devotees experience in the guru's physical embrace or for the connection established between devotees through face-to-face interaction and collaboration, does serve three crucial purposes. First, it fills a crucial experiential gap in the days, months, or years between episodes of real contact. The Amma websites, by keeping devotees constantly mindful of and attuned to the guru and her movements, serve to affirm the guru's place at the center of their spiritual lives. Second, it secures for devotees a virtual place at the very heart of the global devotional cyber-community centered on this guru, thus allowing a translocal shared experience of *bhaktiyoga* unfettered by spatial distance and separation. And finally, it sustains a virtual as well as real devotional network that can readily be mobilized at the guru's behest, not least for fund-raising and relief efforts when disasters strike. This was the case, for instance, when Hurricane Katrina hit the Gulf of Mexico in 2005; it was so again when the Tohoku earthquake and tsunami ravaged Japan in 2011. Internet mediation of *bhakti* thus enables a global consciousness, engenders a global orientation and facilitates translocal mobilization for collective *bhakti*-fueled action.

REFERENCES

Appadurai, Arjun. 1996. *Modernity at Large: Cultural Dimensions of Globalisation*. Minneapolis: University of Minnesota Press.

Babb, Lawrence and Susan Wadley. 1995. (eds.), *Media and the Transformation of Religion in South Asia*. Philadelphia: University of Pennsylvania Press.

Beckerlegge, Gwilym. 2001. Hindu Sacred Images for the Mass Market. In Gwilym Beckerlegge (ed.), *From Sacred Text to Internet*. Aldershot, UK: Ashgate, 2001, pp. 57–115.

Brosius, Christiane. 2012. The Perfect World of BAPS. Media and Urban Dramaturgies in a Globalised Context. In John Zavos et al. (eds.), *Public Hinduisms*. London: Sage, pp. 440–462.

Castells, M. 2001. *The Internet Galaxy: Reflections on the Internet, Business and Society*. Oxford: Oxford University Press.

Coleman, Simon. 2000. *The Globalisation of Charismatic Christianity*. Cambridge, UK: Cambridge University Press.

Dawson, Lorne L. and Douglas E. Cowan. 2004. *Religion Online: Finding Faith on the Internet*. New York: Routledge.

Dwyer, Rachel. 2006. *Filming the Gods: Religion and Indian Cinema*. London: Routledge.

Helland, Christopher. 2007. Diaspora on the Electronic Frontier: Developing Virtual Connections with Sacred Homelands. *Journal of Computer-Mediated Communication* 12 (3): (3). Available at: http://jcmc.indiana.edu/vol12/issue3/helland.html (accessed January 14, 2011).

Herman, Phyllis K. 2010. Seeing the Divine through Windows: Online Darshan and Virtual Religious Experience. *Heidelberg Journal of Religions on the Internet* 4 (1): 151–178. Available at http://online.uni-hd.de/ (accessed January 14, 2011).

Inglis, Stepher R. 1995. Suitable for Framing: The Work of a Modern Master. In L. Babb and S. Wadley (eds.), *Media and the Transformation of Religion in South Asia*. Philadelphia: University of Pennsylvania Press, 1995, pp. 51–75.

Jacobs, Stephen. 2007. Virtually Sacred: The Performance of Asynchronous Cyber-Rituals in Online Spaces. *Journal of Computer Mediated Communication* 12 (3): 1103–1121. Available at: http://jcmc.indiana.edu/vol12/issue3/jacobs.html (accessed January 15, 2011).

———. 2010. *Hinduism Today*. London: Continuum.

Karapanagiotis, Nicole. 2010. Vaishnava Cyber-Puja: problems of Purity and Novel Ritual solutions. *Heidelberg Journal of Religions on the Internet* 4 (1): 179–195. Available at: http://online.uni-hd.de/ (accessed January 14, 2011).

Kim, Hanna. 2012. The BAPS Swaminarayan Sanstha on the Web. In John Davos (ed.), *Public Hinduisms*. London: Sage, 2012, pp. 303–306.

Lutgendorf, Philip. 1995. All in the Raghu Family: A Video Epic in Cultural Context. In L. Babb and S. Wadley (eds.), *Media and the Transformation of Religion in South Asia*. Philadelphia: University of Pennsylvania Press, 1995, pp. 217–253.

Mankekar, Purnima. 1999. *Screening Culture, Viewing Politics*. Durham, NC: Duke University Press.

Pinney, Christopher. 2004. *Photos of the Gods: The Printed Image and Political Struggle in India*. London: Reaktion Books.

Scheifinger, Hainz. 2008. "Hinduism and Cyberspace." *Religion* 38 (3): 233–249.

———. 2009. The Jagannath Temple and Online Darshan. *Journal of Contemporary Religion* 24 (3): 277–290.

Smith, Daniel H. 1995. Impact of "God Posters" on Hindus and Their Devotional Traditions. In L. Babb and S. Wadley (eds.), *Media and the Transformation of Religion in South Asia*. Philadelphia: University of Pennsylvania Press, pp. 24–50.

Srinivas, Smriti. 2008. *In the Presence of Sai Baba: Body, City and Memory*. Boston: Brill.

Srinivas, Tulasi. 2010. *Winged Faith: Rethinking Globalization and Religious Pluralism through the Sathya Sai Movement*. New York: Columbia University Press.

Warrier, Maya. 2005. *Hindu Selves in a Modern World: Guru Faith in the Mata Amritanandamayi Mission*. London: Routledge.

NOTES

1. See, for instance, Beckerlegge (2001); Dwyer (2006); Inglis (1995); Lutgendorf (1995), Mankeker (1999), Pinney (2004), and Smith (1995).
2. Recent studies of cyber-*pūja* and *darśan* (the act of seeing, and being seen by, a sacred image) include Jacobs (2007; 2010: 95–100), Karapanagiotis (2010), and Scheifinger (2008; 2009).
3. Studies of guru-led organizations that cursorily examine the mediation of guru *bhakti* online include S. Srinivas (2008: 105–10) and T. Srinivas (2010: 149–52). Herman (2010) provides an interesting account of the production and use of a website by a South Californian Swaminarayan temple. Also see Brosius (2012) and Kim (2012) on Swaminarayan self-representations on the Internet.
4. For a detailed discussion of this guru and her organization, see Warrier (2005).
5. I use the term *community* here in a general sense to refer to amorphous groups of people with shared experiences of online *bhakti* centered on the guru. It is noteworthy that while the vast majority of the guru's educated, middle-class devotees in India and abroad are able to partake of the "global connectivity" that the

Internet enables, a significant number lack the necessary resources for such access and participation and continue to rely on more conventional modes of experiencing *bhakti*. *Thus*, the discussion of online *bhakti* here needs to be understood in the context of what Castells (2001) terms the *digital divide* that exists in the world.

6. In Europe there is (at the time of writing) an Amma U.K. website and a website each for Ireland, France, Spain, Portugal, Italy, Belgium, Denmark, Finland, Norway, Sweden, Holland, Germany, Greece, Poland, and Russia. In the Americas there is a main U.S. website operated from the M.A. Center in San Ramon, California, separate websites for Michigan and New Mexico, as well as a website each for Canada, Brazil, Mexico, Argentina, Venezuela, and Chile. Not every country with an Amma following maintains a website. Thus, in Asia and the Middle East, while devotees maintain separate websites in Japan, Israel, Malaysia, and Singapore, there is none for Bahrain, Kuwait, Lebanon, Oman, Sri Lanka, and the United Arab Emirates, even though the main Amritapuri website lists contact details of Amma followers for each of these locations. It would appear that the initiative to set up a location-specific website comes from the followers in each geographical context.
7. http://www.amritapuri.org/amma/who (accessed March 18, 2011).
8. http://www.amritapuri.org/amma/who/darshan (accessed March 18, 2011).
9. http://www.theammashop.org/books (accessed March 28, 2011).
10. http://www.amritapuri.org/eservices (accessed March 18, 2011).
11. http://www.amritapuri.org/ (accessed March 18, 2011).
12. http://www.amritapuri.org/eservices/to-amma (accessed March 18, 2011).
13. Contributors are reminded that the editors of this diary reserve the right to select or reject and modify particular items for posting. This online devotional environment does not represent the freedom and spontaneity of expression associated with ideal-typical *bhakti*; instead it is carefully managed, controlled, and monitored by anonymous gatekeepers who carefully vet devotees' expressions of *bhakti*.
14. http://e.amritapuri.org/blogs/on/ashram-diary/ (accessed March 8, 2011).
15. http://www.amma.org/teachings/spiritual-practices/satsang.html (accessed March 18, 2011).
16. http://www.amma.org.uk/contact-us.htm (accessed March 18, 2011).
17. http://www.amritapuri.org/ (accessed March 28, 2011).
18. http://www.amma.org/humanitarian-activities/social/mothers-kitchen/index.html (accessed March 28, 2011).
19. http://www.amma.org/humanitarian-activities/get-involved/donations.html (accessed March 28, 2011).
20. https://www.amma.org/donationsapp/donationInit.do (accessed March 28, 2011).
21. http://www.ammachi.org/humanitarian-activities/get-involved/planned-giving-index.html (accessed March 28, 2011).
22. http://www.amma.org/humanitarian-activities/disaster-relief/disasterrelief.html (accessed March 28, 2011).
23. http://www.amritapuja.org/ (accessed March 28, 2011).
24. For details on the temples unique to the MAM, see Warrier (2005: 45).
25. Devotees can, if they so choose, ask the organization's in-house astrologer to determine which *pūjās* are recommended for their particular birth chart and what dates are most auspicious for the performance of these *pūjās*. The astrologer, according to the website, does the "full chart reading" only in person. The itinerary for his annual "jyotish" (astrology) tour, when he visits different centers in the United States, is produced online so that visitors can arrange to consult him. He

also makes *pūjā* recommendations by e-mail on the basis of birth charts sent to him electronically.

26. https://www.amritapuja.org/pujas/order_a_puja.htm (accessed March 28, 2011).
27. http://www.amma.org.uk/get-involved.htm (accessed March 28, 2011).
28. http://www.amma.org.uk/gi-raising-money.html (accessed March 28, 2011).

PART SIX

Nation-Builders

CHAPTER 15

Eknath Ranade, Gurus, and *Jīvanvratīs*: the Vivekananda Kendra's Promotion of the "Yoga Way of Life"

GWILYM BECKERLEGGE

INTRODUCTION: YOGA AND *SEVĀ* IN THE VIVEKANANDA KENDRA

The promotion of yoga by *Hindutva* (Hindu nationalist) organizations in India[1] represents a significant strand in the "vast historical and contextual web of yoga in the modern world" (Newcombe, 2009: 986).[2] If such an association might seem incongruous to those unfamiliar with contemporary *Hindutva*-inspired movements,[3] this would be consistent with literature on yoga's tendency to focus on "what yoga as yoga is all about" rather than on "what it has come to mean in the social and cultural context of modern India" (Alter, 1997: 309). It might also reflect the dominant preoccupation of many studies of the ideological and organizational manifestations of *Hindutva* with political impact rather than wider religious and cultural dimensions (see Alter, 2004: 143; cf. 142; Alter, 1994; Beckerlegge, 2004; Klostermaier, 2006: 3).

One way *Hindutva*-inspired organizations have extended their influence has been through the offering of *sevā* (service, in the sense of organized humanitarian service) (Beckerlegge, 2003; 2004; 2006b). Acknowledging Swami Vivekananda (1863–1902)[4] as the source of its inspiration, the Vivekananda Kendra, a lay "spiritually oriented service mission," has drawn on the traditions of not just the Ramakrishna Math and Mission, which Vivekananda established, but also the RSS (the Rashtriya Svayamsevak Sangh or National Volunteer Association), founded in 1925 by Keshab Chandra Hedgewar (1889–1940). Like the RSS (cf. Anon., 2004; Parameswaran, 1998: 4),[5] the Vivekananda Kendra[6] counts

Figure 15.1:
Front cover of Eknath Ranade's biography. (Courtesy of the Vivekananda Kendra.)

its promotion of yoga among its *sevā* activities, but the teaching of yoga is far more central to the Kendra's mission. According to P. Parameswaran (1998: 4), the Kendra's president at the time of writing, yoga is one of the Kendra's "thrust areas."

The creation of the Vivekananda Kendra was one outcome of a campaign to mark the centenary of Vivekananda's birth by establishing the Vivekananda Rock Memorial at Kanyakumari, which was instigated by the RSS and overseen by Eknath Ranade (1914–1982), formerly the general secretary of the RSS who would become the Kendra's founder.[7] Its birth was financed through the momentum gathered by the RSS's public appeal for contributions toward the cost of the memorial, which was completed in 1970, and additional funding was provided by the publication of a commemorative volume (Anon., 2005a: 171–72). Although closely supportive of the RSS and the *saṅgh parivār* (the "family" of organizations affiliated to the RSS) (see, e.g., pp. 277, 341), the Kendra is not strictly a constituent of the *parivār*. Its activities, for example, are not recorded in the RSS's database of the *saṅgh parivār*'s *sevā* projects (see note 5).

GURUS AND *JĪVANVRATĪ*

Like his own guru, Ramakrishna (c.1836–1886), Vivekananda has been acknowledged as "one of the most important modern gurus" (see, e.g., Smith, 2003: 173; Killingley, this volume) and also as having been particularly influential in the development of Modern Yoga (see De Michelis, 2007; 2008; Singleton & Byrne, 2008: 6–7).[8] It might be thought, therefore, that the origins of the Vivekananda Kendra's promotion of yoga could be explained in terms of Vivekananda's influence and the Kendra's proximity to the Ramakrishna Math and Mission and the RSS. Both these organizations have been suffused with respect for gurus, although in different ways and to different degrees.

The Ramakrishna Math maintains—although the evidence concerning Ramakrishna's own initiation and that of Vivekananda and Ramakrishna's other young disciples is equivocal (see, e.g., Beckerlegge 2006: 22–23)—that it is connected to the lineages of the Daśanāmī Order, which in turn traces its origins to Śaṅkara. The Ramakrishna Math and Mission remains to this day very much a *saṃnyāsin*-led organization, and Vivekananda's photograph (see, e.g., Figure 1.1 in this volume), together with those of Ramakrishna and Sarada Devi, Ramakrishna's wife and consort, provides a focus for *pūjā* in its centers. Keshab Chandra Hedgewar, the founder of the RSS, insisted that *svayamsevaks* (its volunteer workers) offer their loyalty to the organization and not to the person of the *sarsaṅghhālak* (supreme leader), although he demanded absolute obedience to the *sarsaṅghhālak*. Yet "more or less against his wishes, he was recognised as a guru by his disciples" (Jaffrelot, 1996: 41, also see pp. 39, 62). According to Andersen and Damle (1987: 37), ". . . The *guru* model of authority governs the leadership principle of the RSS" (cf. Bhatt & Mukta, 2000: 415; Gold cited in Jaffrelot, 1996: 43 n. 138).

Madhav Sadhashiv Golwalkar (1906–1973), Hedgewar's successor, who selected Eknath Ranade to coordinate the celebration of the centenary of Vivekananda's birth, was popularly known within the RSS as *Guruji*, a title not bestowed on other *sarsaṅghhālaks*. Golwalkar is said to have been "almost revered" by first-generation *svayamsevaks* (Kanungo, 2002: 77) and associated with ". . . the highest ideals of purity and abstinence" (quoted in Jaffrelot, 1996: 42) and strong, traditionally expressed, spiritual, and ascetic inclinations (Andersen & Damle, 1987: 41–43).

In fact, Golwalkar followed Swami Akhandananda of the Ramakrishna Math in 1936 to Bengal, where he received *dīkṣā* (initiation) from Akhandananda (Beckerlegge, 2003: 43–44). An account from within the RSS relates that Golwalkar "had the unique privilege of taking spiritual exercises, and undergoing heavy odds and ordeals to accomplish 'sadhana' as a 'Yogi' under . . . Swami Akhandanandaji" (Anon., 1956: 12). But for Akhandananda's death, Golwalkar might well have offered himself for training to enter the Ramakrishna Math rather than returning to the RSS (see Beckerlegge, 2003: 41–49). Akhandananda is reported to have practiced bodily disciplines associated with yoga ("a lot of breathing exercises" including *prāṇayāma* and *kumbhaka*; Akhandananda, 1979: 3; cf. Chetananda, 1997: 557) and to have been recognized as a yogi (e.g., Annadananda, 1993: 35, 36). It is not clear, however, whether the use of yogi here implies one who specifically practiced a visible form of yoga now associated with the popular English connotations of this term or conveys the "the wider, far more varied and layered" senses embraced by this term in Indic languages (De Michelis, 2007: 3), perhaps simply denoting somebody intent on following a spiritual discipline (*mārga*) leading to self-realization (cf. Yogananda, 1963: 13 n. 2).

Since the nineteenth century, the absolute nature of the guru's authority, and on occasion its abuse, has prompted the rejection of the authority of gurus on rational and moral grounds by various movements and thinkers. These have ranged from the Brahmo Samaj and Jiddu Krishnamurti (1895–1986), who memorably referred to Truth as a "pathless land," to the Indian Rationalist Association and literary figures such as the novelist G. V. Desani. With specific reference to yoga traditions, Georg Feuerstein (1990: 123–24) speaks of the "intense teacher-disciple relationship in traditional Yoga" and the "superlative importance of the *guru*'s role in practically all schools [of *haṭhayoga*]." However, citing early warnings in the Upaniṣads about teachers who deceive, he also notes that relatively few gurus have achieved full enlightenment and that students have been exploited. The recent global export of yoga beyond India, Feuerstein suggests, has raised questions about "the appropriateness of spiritual discipleship and the legitimacy of spiritual authority" (p. 126).

In spite of Ranade's profound respect for Vivekananda, the organization that Ranade created also sprang in part from a critique of *guru culture*. Ranade, too, wished to curb what he regarded as the excesses of the popular practice of elevating teachers to avatar-like status. His primary concern, however, was not so much to avoid the consequent danger of the abuse of power but rather to reverse what he regarded as a paralyzing trend in India of relying too heavily on "a great man" coming forward to put new ideas into action and so bring about change (Anon. 2000: 157). Motivated by his sense of the urgency of addressing the crisis he perceived was facing India by mobilizing "ordinary" people, Ranade set out to build "an extraordinary organisation, consisting of ordinary men . . ." (Anon. 2000: xix). Its achievements would rest upon teamwork, rather than gurus, beings hailed as avatars, or swamis, or even a Vivekananda or Swami Dayananda Sarasvati (Anon. 2000: 158). In the process of forming a lay organization, Ranade and his followers have asserted the value and distinct role of lay workers who adopt a life of renunciation, pointing to the limitations of *saṃnyāsins* in dealing with the everyday challenges that confront the bulk of the population (Beckerlegge, 2010: 75). The outcome was Ranade's organization of the Vivekananda Kendra as a cadre-based movement, which relies heavily on its core of *jīvanvratī* (life workers) (see Beckerlegge, 2010). According to Nivedita Bhide (2008) (a vice president of the Kendra at the time of writing), Ranade "did not establish himself or even Swami Vivekananda as the Guru of the Vivekananda Kendra. Any specific name or form of God also would have brought limitations on our capacity for representing the whole society. Therefore, Mananeeya Eknathji has seen to it that Omkar- the most effective Pratika of Ishwara would be the guide for us. . . . All the forms and the names—Namrupa—come from Omkar. Omkar indicates the inter-connectedness, inter-relatedness, inter-dependence of the existence." *Jīvanvratīs* are initiated on completion of their training in the presence of *oṃkāra*.

Ranade's precepts have been greatly influential in shaping the ethos and leadership of the Kendra. Yet his stance did not preclude him from showing respect for and seeking the guidance of swamis, particularly those of the Ramakrishna Math, and acknowledged gurus (see Beckerlegge, 2010: 72, 77), including, as we shall see, in the matter of the transmission of yogic teaching. Ranade's contemporary followers, while insisting on their distinct mission as a lay movement, in my experience are highly respectful of the Ramakrishna Math.[9]

As a lay movement, the Kendra is closer in its style of organization to the RSS than to the *saṃnyāsin*-led Ramakrishna Math and Mission while also differing from the RSS in key respects, as this chapter will illustrate. Like the early leaders of the RSS, however, it could be argued that Eknath Ranade *functioned* to an extent as a guru, if not as a teacher then in his style of leadership. This is evident, for example, in his exercise of personal charisma and authority and the selection of *jīvanvratīs* while rejecting personally and institutionally both the status of guru and many of the trappings popularly associated with guru-led movements. The nature of the Kendra's organization, with its embedded notions of leadership and authority, impinges on all aspects of its activity, including its promotion of yoga. The position adopted by Ranade, and subsequently the Kendra, stands in contrast to other Hindu movements where devotees for various reasons have also rejected the use of the title guru, for example, as a suitable basis for expressing adequately the nature of their relationship to their teacher or the ontological status of the teacher (see, e.g., Hirst & Zavos, 2011: 123). These markedly different stances, however, have not prevented the persistence in these movements of at least certain functions of a traditional style of guru leadership.

The remainder of this chapter will explore ways Eknath Ranade's criticism of the guru model of leadership has shaped the Kendra's dissemination of yoga theory and practice through modifying traditional understandings of the role of the guru and the guru–disciple relationship. The guru–disciple relationship historically has enabled the workings of *paramparā* (the oral transmission of knowledge) through *sampradāya* (lineages of chosen initiates), lineages that have often served to authenticate the authority of the guru. Such lineages have undergirded the leadership of sects and ashrams, among other Hindu institutions and, as De Michelis (2008: 19) points out, ideally and often in practice the transmission of yogic knowledge. Under Ranade's direction, the Kendra has used its cadre of *jīvanvratīs* to develop a model of delivering yoga instruction in which some echoes of the older guru–disciple model continue to reverberate. The Kendra's approach, however, is more programmatic and, in the language of recent styles of human development and training, closer to a *cascade* model, in which the flow of knowledge becomes ever more dispersed than to the *paramparā–sampradāya* model, in which the transmission of knowledge is channeled through the lineage of initiated disciples.

EKNATH RANADE'S INFLUENCE UPON THE PROMOTION OF YOGA IN THE EARLY YEARS OF THE VIVEKANANDA KENDRA

In spite of the prominence given to yoga in its activities and publications, the Vivekananda Kendra has received limited attention in studies of yoga. Sarah Strauss (2002: 244–45) gives a brief account of an untypical branch center of the Kendra in Bangalore, which was the base for a project on yoga. Strauss includes, and appears to endorse, one of her informant's negative judgment on the "strident undertones of Hindu nationalism," which he found in the Kendra.[10] Somewhat surprisingly, because the Vivekananda Kendra's members and publications refer routinely, and with a sense of pride rather than any embarrassment, to the RSS and the Ramakrishna Math and Mission as the Kendra's "two mothers," Strauss (p. 244) records that she was initially not made aware of the Kendra's historical relationship to the RSS.

Strauss's (2002) account highlights questions about the nature of the Vivekananda Kendra's relationship to both the RSS and the legacy of Vivekananda. The absence of a systematic account of the Kendra's development prior to 1986, however, creates the impression that, first, the Vivekananda Kendra emerged in an ad hoc and opportunistic manner and promoted yoga in much the same spirit (p. 245) and, second, that the Ramakrishna Math and Mission completely withdrew its support from the memorial project.[11] As the prominence given to yoga in the Kendra is attributed to its founder, I shall contextualize the movement's later activities by reviewing briefly Ranade's role in embedding yoga in the foundations of the Vivekananda Kendra.

Andersen and Damle (1987: 137–38, n. 111) assert, based on an interview with Ranade in 1970, that the idea of creating a new movement crystallized during the RSS's campaign to create the Rock Memorial. Within the Kendra, it is said that this was when Ranade came to appreciate that widespread distrust of the RSS was undermining support for the otherwise popular cause of commemorating Vivekananda's birth. Ranade's extensive published correspondence reveals that he was thinking beyond the concrete memorial by late October 1964, that he had sketched out a rationale for a new movement by early 1965, and that this was probably under active consideration by late 1967 (Anon., 2005a: 28, 55, 127–30). One can trace similarly detailed plans for the establishment of the headquarters, Vivekanandapuram, at Kanyakumari, the creation of two journals, the *Vivekananda Kendra Patrika* and *Yuva Bharati* (for young people), and the selection and training of the first cohort of trainee *jīvanvratīs*, all of which were in place by 1973.

In 1980, Ranade (Anon., 2005a: 406) referred to the Kendra's intention of initiating a major project centered on research into yoga and yoga therapy, presumably an allusion to what would become the Bangalore center. If so, this anticipated by five years the creation of the Vivekananda Kendra Yoga Anusandhana Samsthana (VK YOGAS), the Bangalore center to which Strauss refers,

Figure 15.2:
Eknath Ranade. (Courtesy of the Vivekananda Kendra.)

under the leadership of Dr. H. R. Nagendra. Nagendra had joined the Vivekananda Kendra in 1975 and, prior to moving to Bangalore, had worked for approximately ten years at the Kendra's Kanyakumari headquarters to develop yoga training and yoga therapy programs (see, e.g., Anon., 2005a: 343, 393).[12]

Ranade's correspondence suggests strongly that the teaching and promotion of yoga were seen as central to the institutional life and work of the Kendra from the outset in 1972. This was several years before Nagendra joined the Kendra and the subsequent establishment of VK YOGAS. Ranade checked on the progress of "morning Yogasana classes and the evening physical training class" at the training camp for the first cohort of intending *jīvanvratīs* in 1973, questioned a trainee who had absented himself from the *yogāsana* classes (Anon., 2005a: 239, 247), urged other Kendra supporters to begin classes in their areas, and routinely referred to yoga courses and camps organized by the Kendra. *Yuva Bharati* carried regular features on yoga from its first issue in 1973. Crucially, while the exercise of Ranade's authority in spelling out yoga's place in the movement might be reminiscent of that of a guru figure, he did not function as a guru in respect of the transmission of specific teachings concerning the practice and theory of yoga.

Ranade thought in terms of *teams* of workers in the service of the Kendra and the nation rather than seeking to establish a *sampradāya* in a traditional sense, with a lineage of chosen *individual* initiates. In one of his more extended treatments of the principles and rationale behind the Kendra's promotion of yoga, Ranade declared in a pamphlet that the Vivekananda Kendra has "yoga as its sheet anchor for the development of personality so that its life-workers can effectively use this in the service of men. . . . Thus equipped and trained, the team of workers will devote their entire life to serve our people in particular and humanity in general at all levels starting from essential needs of life, like food, shelter etc. up to imparting knowledge on Yoga."[13] In addition to being reminiscent of Vivekananda's hierarchy of service, from bodily requirements to spiritual knowledge, Ranade's pamphlet touches on a number of claims and themes commonly found in presentations of Modern Yoga, bolstered here with reference to Vivekananda and Ramakrishna before him.[14] For example, yoga is an ancient Indian science (thus universal and nondenominational in nature) whose value has now been proven through medical research and has applications in the education of the young and counteracting the pressures of contemporary society (cf. Anon. no date d: 4). Nivedita Bhide (2003: 165) explained one of the strategic implications of this perspective:

> Eknathji knew that if the "English educated class" is to be drawn for the work, then they need to be approached in such a way that it appeals to them as well as it benefits them. He felt, in the stress-ridden modern life, the "Yoga way of life" would be apt as it is based on the integral view of life. Thus, Yoga was adopted as the core of the Vivekananda Kendra.

This appears to update Vivekananda's call to service on his return to India in 1897, which similarly targeted the young and well educated. But, as we shall see, the designation "Yoga way of life" operates at two levels, referring to both the practice of the style of postural yoga, which the Kendra's outreach activities promote, and living according to the Kendra's philosophy.

> That is what "Yoga way of life" is. Yoga is not just some physical or breathing exercises but yoga is living a life in which we perceive the oneness and also employ our body-mind complex in the service of the Divine which has expressed as family, society, nation and the whole creation. This is Omkara Upasana too—to see the whole universe as the expression of that vibration Omkara. (Bhide, 2008)[15]

Yoga is consequently central to the Kendra's outreach activities (*kāryapaddhati*, system of working).

The Kendra's workers and leaders often identify Vivekananda as the directing influence on their resolve to lead a life of service (Beckerlegge, 2010). Some have explained to me that they came to know more about Eknath Ranade and his movement only once they had become involved in one of the Vivekananda Kendra's regional outreach activities (at state and district levels) of which introductory courses on yoga for adults and children are a major feature. Older Kendra workers who encountered Ranade directly spoke uniformly of the sheer impact of his charisma upon them and the subsequent course of their lives.

The provision of *yoga varga* (courses), which are routinely offered by all the Kendra's centers, is one aspect of the Kendra's methodology (together with *saṁskāra varga*, character education and training, and *swādhyāya varga*, working/thinking together for the nation). This was more than evident at the Kendra's annual Yoga Shiksha Shibir (yoga training camp), held in December 2010 at Vivekanandapuram, its headquarters at Kanyakumari.[16] Like all Kendra Yoga Shibirs, the annual camp is designed to foster the

> "propagation of Yoga way of life and to help the participants in their spiritual growth. It is also to make the participants aware of the current social situations and the responsibility of every citizen for the constructive contribution for the betterment of the society. . . ." (http://www.vkendra.org/YSS Accessed May 2011).

YOGA AND THE VIVEKANANDA KENDRA'S *KĀRYAPADDHATI*

The participants at the Shibir experienced an intensive fifteen-day program, beginning daily at 04.30 and ending at 21.00 hours. The camp incorporated the Kendra's introductory course on the theory and practice of yoga within a round of chanting and prayer, discourses, teamwork, organized recreational activities (see Pol, 2010), and other activities designed to immerse the participants in the Kendra's engagement with *karmayoga* and the task of nation-building. Participants were divided into groups ("teams") of about fifteen on the basis of linguistic preference, either Hindi or English (about a third of the participants), and thus spent substantial parts of each day in these small groups with leaders from the organizing team.[17] The organizing team was drawn primarily from the cadre, which takes responsibility for national yoga Shibirs, with some other Kendra workers. It comprised four women and nine men, led by a woman senior life worker. The *jīvanvratīs*, when not leading sessions, constantly interacted with the participants.

Following prayers and chanting from 05.15, *yogābhyās* (yoga practice) took place from 05.45 until 07.15, with a second session from 16.45 until 17.30 preceding *bhājan saṃdhyā* (evening devotional session) from 18.30 until 19.20.[18] These sessions were based on the Kendra's compact manual *Yoga: An Instruction Booklet* (Anon., 2008), which, because of its programmatic nature and structure, lends itself to use at Kendra yoga events of different lengths aimed at different audiences. Participants at this Shibir practiced *śithilīkarana vyāyāma* (loosening exercises; Anon. 1977: 4), the *āsanas* detailed in the booklet, with particular attention paid to *sūryanamaskāra* (twelve rounds of sun salutation with the appropriate mantras), a limited number of *kriyās* (*kapālabhatī*, *jala neti*, *jala dhauti*) and techniques of *prāṇayāma* and related *mudrās*.

The participants, who had to be at least eighteen years of age, came from all over India with two Europeans who were coincidentally traveling in India. Over a third of the eighty-eight participants were from Maharashtra, with the next largest concentration from the northeast (Assam, Arunachal Pradesh), where the Kendra is very active. The remainder comprised contingents of no more than five, mostly fewer, from other states. Women made up approximately a third of the group. Individuals were distributed relatively evenly across the age bands thirty and under, forty-five to sixty, and sixty-one upward (made up almost exclusively of retired men), with slightly more participants falling within the thirty-one to forty-five age range. I was informed that twenty-one of the participants, who were already involved with the Kendra's branches, had been invited to attend. Of these twenty-one, seventeen were women, the vast majority involved with the Kendra in the northeast, and nine of the twenty-one were connected to the Kendra's hospitals in Assam and Madhya Pradesh. The remaining sixty-seven participants were said to have no known previous link to the Kendra. Talking with members of this disparate cohort, I found that their motives and expectations were as varied as those anticipated by the organizers.

When I asked one of the organizing team how many of the Shibir's participants he anticipated would become more involved with the work of the

Kendra, his expectation was modest. He spoke of one participant who had already indicated a desire to train for entry into the cadre of *jīvanvratīs*. For such a person, attendance at a Yoga Shikska Shibir would be mandatory, as it would be for teachers employed in the Kendra's school, and one teacher about to take up a post was among the participants. I was told there was one other person also considering entry into the cadre. While meeting the specific need of training intending workers, the main purpose of the camp was to disseminate the Kendra's message and to attract supporters who would work for local centers by donating financially (patrons) or giving their time as workers. The Kendra's structure is unlike the RSS's *śākhā*-based (local branch) organization, which requires that members attend daily short meetings.[19] The Kendra relies heavily on its supporters to sustain the activities of local centers, which are expected to hold a monthly meeting but whose main function is to promote the conduct of *saṁskāra varga*, *swādhyāya varga*, and *yoga varga* and to celebrate specified festivals.[20]

One of the workers, who assisted with the training of the team to which I was assigned, had committed himself to giving time each year to help at the annual Yoga Shiksha Shibir. He disclosed that he hoped to open a Kendra school in his region for orphans and indigent children. The Kendra's status as a lay movement had attracted a retired man who had decided a few months earlier to dedicate the remainder of life to being a Kendra worker and declared, "I have saffron around my heart" (cf. Beckerlegge, 2010: 76–7, 82). Several participants described themselves loosely as existing supporters (financial but, I sensed, on a very ad hoc basis) of their local branch. Some of the younger participants had been directed to attend, one by his grandfather and another (who had no intention of becoming a *jīvanvratī*) by a senior worker in his local center who wished to strengthen that center's capacity to offer instruction in yoga. This is a further illustration of what I have termed the *cascade* method of yoga teaching in the Kendra.

Some participants were motivated to attend, at least in part, by the prospect of the *Kanyakumari experience* (visiting the Rock Memorial, Sunrise Beach, and the Kumārī Ammān temple) as well as by the opportunity to come into closer contact with the Kendra. This was not regarded by the organizers as in any sense unacceptable but as part of the rich spiritual experience that attendance at the Shibir offered to participants.

What was striking, although in keeping with the nature of the Shibir as an outreach event, was the number of participants with whom I spoke who confessed to having limited knowledge of the Vivekananda Kendra prior to attending the camp. Many of these, while regarding attendance at the Shibir as worthwhile, declared that they had not come with any intention of establishing a particular link with the Kendra.

Once involved in *yogābhyās*, it was obvious that some of the participants, by no means confined to a specific age range, were more experienced than others in the practice of *yogāsanas*. Some had brought their own yoga mats. Others practiced *āsanas* that had not been introduced in the Shibir's program but had been learned from each other during breaks in the formal sessions, although never as an exclusive clique. Here again it was surprising to find in conversation that some participants had identified the Shibir through a general search on the Web for yoga training. One participant expressed surprise, but not a complaint, about the emphasis placed on activities other than *yogābhyās* and the extent to which the discourses addressed yoga with an overriding emphasis on the Kendra's ideology. An indicator of the strain of the physical demands over the fifteen days of the Shibir—including the constant practice of *āsanas*, on participants who were previously unfamiliar, or less familiar, with this discipline—was the increasing number who sought chairs during the discourses and plenary events. This rather confirmed that the Shibir, while attracting a minority who attended primarily to extend their own ongoing practice of yoga, was serving a much wider purpose, as the Kendra intended, for the majority of its participants who had come with a variety of expectations. With few exceptions, the participants nevertheless displayed a seriousness and unflagging commitment throughout the Shibir.

THE TRANSMISSION OF KNOWLEDGE OF YOGIC PRACTICE AND THEORY IN THE VIVEKANANDA KENDRA

The organization of the Kendra's Shibir had much in common with features of other Shibirs identified by Alter (2008); Alter (2008: 37) describes Shibirs as typically "purely spectacular events," in which "the spectacular is . . . an integral feature of performativity," resulting from the choreographed instruction and focus on the teacher. Although the Kendra's branches do mount exhibitions of yoga practice, its annual Shibir felt intimate, partly because instruction was largely at team level and partly because the agenda driving the Shibir meant that *yogābhyās*, although a central feature, did not dominate the program.[21] Here there was no dignitary to inaugurate the Shibir by lighting an *āratī* lamp (cf. p. 41) but instead a respected elderly *jīvanvratī*. Also, in keeping with the ethos of the Vivekananda Kendra, the focus on the figure of the teacher or instructor was diffused because *yogābhyās* was not generally conducted in a plenary setting but by small clusters of teams in their own bases with their own teacher. In my grouping, the leader frequently invited different students to demonstrate a particular *āsana*, which heightened the experience of the event as a team effort in which the leader was more akin to a facilitator.

The *jīvanvratīs* induction into yoga forms part of their standard five-year training, and, as already noted, anybody considering applying to join the cadre would be expected first to attend the annual yoga training camp. Although Dr. H. R. Nagendra was involved in devising yoga training and yoga therapy at Vivekanandapuram prior to his move to Bangalore and eventual separation from the Kendra, it is the cadre through its standard training that has developed and delivered the yoga outreach program. This is cascaded down through the Kendra's various national and regional levels and is disseminated externally through the Kendra's outreach activities. It is an area in which individual *jīvanvratīs* might become more involved, for example, because of personal inclination and aptitude and the necessary communication skills. There is, however, no distinct section of yoga teachers within the cadre, and the preparation of those who take on this role remains within the responsibility of the vice president responsible for training in the Kendra. Any imparting of yogic teaching thus falls within the generic role of the *jīvanvratī* whose task is to support and lead the range of activities undertaken by the Kendra, whether in branches, more specialized centers, or particular projects. Clearly, the training received by the *jīvanvratī*, including the manner in which yogic knowledge is transmitted, and the broader generic role of the *jīvanvratī*, which embraces any teaching of yoga, are very different from corresponding elements of earlier guru–disciple, lineage-based transmissions of yogic teaching.

During the Shibir frequent allusions were made to Patañjali (who was invoked at the end of *yogābhyās*) and *aṣṭāṅgayoga*, and (as in the Kendra's publications) to Vivekananda and Sri Aurobindo in any broad definitions or characterizations of yoga (cf. Ranade, 1975). The Kendra, however, does not typically justify its practice beyond this through reference to any one school or lineage of gurus. Instead, it points to the institutional imperative laid down by its founder. When I asked *jīvanvratīs* at the Shibir what the Kendra had drawn on when first establishing its own pattern of yoga training, it became apparent that there was no collective sense of being part of a lineage. I was referred to Mr. A. Balakrishnan, a Kendra vice president at the time of writing, largely because, in addition to holding a senior office, he had been in the first cohort of trainee *jīvanvratīs* in 1973. This reliance on the personal memory of one senior *jīvanvratī* was a further illustration of the way the Kendra, being true to its ethos, does not look self-consciously to a lineage of gurus to authenticate its teaching, whether specifically in relation to yoga or more generally.

Mr. Balakrishnan recalled that the first cohort received instruction from Janardan Swami of the Yoga Bhyasi Mandal, Nagpur, who had given lectures and taken classes where the trainees practiced various *āsanas*. Mr. Balakrishnan described Janardan Swami as a "traditional" teacher of yoga who was already in his eighties at that time. In response to my question about the significance of the Nagpur location (the birthplace of the RSS), Mr. Balakrishnan confirmed that Eknath Ranade knew Janardan Swami well and that Janardan Swami had taken classes for the RSS. Beyond the RSS, Janardan Swami has been presented as embodying "that true religion," as defined by Swami Vivekananda, popularizing the teaching and practice across social divides, and promoting the view that the practice of yoga has a special contribution to make to addressing the strains of "modern society." Janardan Swami is said to have "devoted his life for the cure n [sic] sewa of ill persons by the healing power of yoga."[22] (No such claim about yoga's curative powers was made at the Shibir.)

It would seem reasonable to infer, albeit on the basis of patchy information, that personal acquaintance in Nagpur, common emphases and preoccupations, and experience of having provided classes for the RSS may well account for Janardan Swami being invited to provide classes in the theory and practice of yoga for the Kendra's first batch of trainee *jīvanvratīs*. While Janardan Swami is revered as a guru within the Yoga Bhyasi Mandal, Nagpur (see, e.g., http://www.jsyog.org/OurGuru.htm), clearly the relationship between Janardan Swami and Ranade was not that of guru and disciple, and thus no direct line of transmission was incorporated into the foundation of the Kendra to which later members might refer to justify, or authenticate the standing of, the teaching they have received. It cannot be said, however, that Ranade's role was restricted merely to delegating responsibility for inducting the first cohort of intending *jīvanvratīs* into the practice and theory of yoga to a guru who had provided a similar service for the RSS. It was Ranade who had established that the teaching of yoga would be integral to the Kendra's provision of *sevā* and thus would take on greater prominence than has been the case in the RSS and its affiliates.

There is in the Kendra an intimate connection between the advocacy of a physically beneficial practice of yoga and the enterprise of nation-building to which the RSS is similarly committed.[23] The adoption of an understanding of *yuj*—as signifying union with other members of society and, by extension, nation-building—is by no means confined to the Vivekananda Kendra, representing as it now does another reading that has been added to the expanding lexicon of contemporary yoga. Thus, as participants at the Kendra's Yoga Shiksha Shibir gathered for outdoor events, these moments were punctuated by shouts of "*Bhāratmātā ki jai*" (Hail to the Motherland!) and the singing of patriotic songs, led by the organizers (cf. Anon., 2004, Yoga).

Yet the Kendra is very different from the RSS. There is nothing akin to the RSS's flag-raising and -lowering ceremony in the Kendra, and the practice of *yogāsanas* in the Kendra is sharply differentiated from the sports and other forms of physical training undertaken by the RSS's exclusively male membership.[24] From the time of Ranade, moreover, the Kendra's positioning of yoga at the forefront of its national and regional outreach activities does not mirror the practice of the RSS. Even Ranade was associated more with *kabaddi* than yoga during his early days with the RSS (Bhide, 2003: 13; cf. 12, 14; Sirsikar, 1988: 191–92).

Alter (2004: 146) draws attention to the way "yoga is integrated into the *śākhā* drill regimen . . ." and physical strength is understood, as one aspect of "man-making," in relation to its power to generate the nation's "life force" (see also pp. 23, 148, 163, 280; cf. Alter, 1994: 562–70). Alter (2004: 148) concludes that the very goal of the RSS thus "makes it very difficult for the RSS to accommodate Yoga as Yoga." He notes, however, that the RSS has inspired several individuals to "do more with Yoga than it is able or willing to do within the framework of its own organizational structure, and something rather different from what it seeks to do in terms of its masculinist, muscular cultural agenda" (ibid.).

Is it the case that Ranade and his followers have tried "to do more with Yoga" than leaders and ideologues of the RSS? The answer to this might be implicit in the Kendra's self-characterization as a "spiritually oriented" movement (see, e.g., Bhide, 2008; Ranade, 2004). It has adopted, following Vivekananda's example, not what some within the RSS have spoken of as that movement's distinctive *sādhanā* (means to attainment, or spiritual discipline), namely, participation in the "*śākhā* technique," but instead a collective commitment to the *sādhanā* of *sevā*. A former member has noted that the RSS movement was not interested in religious orthodoxy or strict adherence to scriptures and that the "*svayamsevaks* were never asked to observe the traditional rituals of Hinduism" (Sirsikar, 1988: 200).[25]

Attempting to explain the ways the Vivekananda Kendra patently differs from the RSS in its promotion of yoga simply in terms of a different mediation of Vivekananda's influence via the Ramakrishna Math and Mission, however, is far from straightforward. Just as the Kendra, with its recruitment of men and women, differs from the RSS in leadership and organization, so too the lay Kendra differs significantly from the *saṃnyāsin*-led Ramakrishna Math and Mission, which has not placed the promotion of yoga at the forefront of its activities. But, strikingly, given the centrality of yoga to the Kendra's outreach strategy and Vivekananda's acknowledged role in the shaping of Modern Yoga, the Kendra does not present Vivekananda primarily as a yogic guru.

Members of the Kendra have readily celebrated Vivekananda's reported "triumphs" at the World's Parliament of Religions in Chicago in 1893 (see, e.g., Ranade, 1975). This was the Vivekananda who acted not only as an effective apologist on behalf of the Hindu tradition at the Parliament but also then took on the role of the first Hindu teacher to address the spiritual needs of late nineteenth-century audiences in the United States and England, subsequently providing for them a novel and influential reworking of aspects of yoga tradition in *Rāja Yoga* (1896) (see, e.g., Burger, 2006; De Michelis, 2004). It is not, however, the Vivekananda of the Parliament of Religions who has so captivated Ranade and others who have followed him in the Kendra. It is above all the powerful image of Vivekananda *in* India, "Vivekananda of Kanyakumari" (see Beckerlegge, 2008: 34), the *parivrājaka* (wandering renouncer) and nation-builder who retrospectively attributed his plan for the regeneration of India through *sevā* to a vision he reported experiencing in Kanyakumari in 1892.

In spite of the influence Vivekananda exerted after the publication of *Rāja Yoga* and devotees' reports of Vivekananda's "wonderful knowledge" of yoga and his mastery of "extraordinary Yoga powers" (His Eastern and Western Disciples, 1993: 205–6, 244–45, 459), there is little evidence of Vivekananda's systematic involvement in any one form of yoga in India prior to his first departure for the United States. In 1890, Vivekananda traveled to Ghazipur (now Uttar Pradesh) where he hoped to learn from Pavhari Baba, who was reputed to have been "initiated into the mysteries of Yoga on Mount Girnar in Kathiawar" (p. 229). It would seem that Vivekananda hoped, among other things, to receive instruction in *haṭhayoga* from Pavhari Baba to strengthen his body. Yet even then Vivekananda could refer slightingly to *haṭhayoga* (with its "queer breathing exercises" and "gymnastics") as the only kind of yoga found in Bengal, "the land of Jnana and Bhakti" (Vivekananda, 1989: 6:233).[26] When Vivekananda did offer practical instruction on the techniques of yoga in San Francisco in 1900, he declared while affirming its benefits "I have been studying [yoga] all my life and have made very little progress yet" (Vivekananda, 1989: 1:157). Without denying the intellectual contribution of gurus of the stature of Vivekananda and Sri Aurobindo (see Gleig and Flores, this volume) to the yoga renaissance, Alter (2006: 765) offers a measured assessment of the extent and significance of the direct contribution of these individuals to the development of Modern Yoga, particularly in India. As Alter points out, Vivekananda, for example, never advocated the practice of *haṭhayoga* (ibid.).

The Kendra's reading of Vivekananda's life and career does not take as the culmination of his life's work the popularizing in London and the United States of his understanding of *rājayoga* during his last decade. Thus, the text prescribed for study by participants at the Yoga Shiksha Shibir was not Vivekananda's *Rāja Yoga* but Ranade's (2006) birth centenary commemorative volume of Vivekananda's teaching, *Swami Vivekananda's Rousing Call to Hindu Nation*. In his compilation, Ranade (2006: vii, ix) drew on Vivekananda "at this critical hour in our history" to delineate "a particular frame of mind as well as certain qualities of mind and heart required of workers or 'karykartas' willing to participate in the nation-building activity." As Deepak Khaire (a *jīvanvratī* and member of the organizing team) declared at the 2010 Yoga Shiksha Shibir, "We are not born to sleep. We have a mission in life."[27]

The ethos of the Vivekananda Kendra has been profoundly affected by Eknath Ranade's urgent references to the "the need of the hour," whether linked to a threat to India's borders or a sense of malaise in Indian society now manifested particularly in the attitudes of young people. The Kendra's response to this perceived "need" has been to build its organizational life on the theory and practice of *karmayoga* as laid down by Ranade, who drew heavily in this respect upon Vivekananda's inspiration.

Participants at the Shibir were introduced through its discourses to the principles of Vivekananda's now familiar, four-fold classification of *bhakti, karma, jñāna,* and *rāja yoga* and increasingly to techniques of *prāṇayāma* and *dhyāna*.[28] But, the Kendra's credo of unremitting activism was constantly reinforced at the Shibir by the insistence that the yoga for the modern world is *karmayoga*, and that this would be the main concern of the Shibir, although other aspects of yoga tradition, including the practice of *yogāsanas*, would not be neglected. One speaker recalled that Ranade had spoken of *karmayoga* as *dāl* with a meal, while other forms of yoga were the accompanying pinch of salt. In prioritizing *karmayoga* as a means to nation-building over the self-realization of the individual (whether this is conceived metaphysically in terms of *kaivalya* or the union of *jīvātman* and *paramātman*), the Vivekananda Kendra can point to the comparable responsibility that Ramakrishna is popularly believed to have imposed on Vivekananda (Nikhilananda, 1975: 58–59).

Arguably, the daily sessions given over to teamwork and group discussion, reinforced as these were by other aspects of the Shibir's program, were more revealing of the Kendra's handling of the different strands of the composite yoga tradition than the highly visible practice of *āsanas*. It was in these settings that I came to appreciate more fully, as a participant observer, the respect in which the *jīvanvratīs* were held and the charismatic standing of certain *jīvanvratīs* in particular. Their discourses were the most eagerly anticipated and warmly received, and their very presence seemed to draw clusters of participants whenever there were breaks in the formal program.

Participants were encouraged to engage in the daily teamwork sessions, which included, for example, cleaning and serving meals as opportunities to practice, if undertaken in the right spirit, the discipline of *karmayoga*.[29] The requirement to share very simple and austere dormitory accommodation at the Shibir was also presented during the discourses as an opportunity to strive for the virtues fostered through the practice of *yama* (observances) and *niyama* (restraints). The preeminence of *karmayoga* was reinforced in the daily recitation of the Kendra Prayer in which the participants declare themselves to "have deep faith in the chosen path of Karmayoga" and pray that they may achieve their goal through their "Renunciation, Service and Self-knowledge" (Anon., 1991: 8). The recitation of the prayer was accompanied by chanting of sections of the *Bhagavad Gītā* that deal specifically with *karmayoga*. This text alone, among all texts on yoga, was held to constitute a "comprehensive guide" to yoga in addition to the status ascribed to it of being a "national book."[30] If the *Bhagavad Gītā* is a "national book," the Yoga Way of Life, according to Satish Shamrao Chowkulkar (2010: 138) (a *jīvanvratī* member of the organizing team), is nothing other than "the *Bharateeya* Way, the *Bharateeya Sanskriti*" (the Indian Way, Indian culture).

CONCLUSION

It has aptly been said that "gurus are in fact difficult to summarise" (Smith, 2003: 173). While some gurus are held to exercise authority through their personal charisma and others through the charisma attached to their role as gurus, for others this is a hereditary office. Not all gurus have been renouncers, and some have been self-styled gurus rather than authenticated through membership of an established lineage. Eknath Ranade made no claim to be a guru of modern yoga, but his style of leadership retained features that were reminiscent of the guru style of leadership of which (in some respects) he was critical. Through his charisma, exercise of authority, and influence on the selection of *jīvanvratīs,* he embedded the Yoga Way of Life in the newly formed Kendra in a fashion that is reminiscent of the functioning of guru-style leadership.

The Kendra's *jīvanvratīs*, although not constituents of a traditional *sampradāya* lineage through their initiation into the cadre, undoubtedly seek to perpetuate Ranade's authoritative vision, which placed *yoga varga* at the heart of the Kendra's *kāryapaddhati* (way of working). In so doing, I have suggested, they too have exercised style of leadership rooted, for some, in personal charisma and more generally in the respect commonly given in the context of Indian society to those who voluntarily adopt a life of renunciation.

The mission of Ranade and the *jīvanvratīs* who have led the Kendra was never to create a *sampradāya* but rather to promote their understanding of the Yoga Way of Life to connect with wider society in India and so to transform it in accord with their vision. It is hardly surprising, therefore, that the traditional model of transmission through the guru–disciple relationship has been, if not entirely superseded, then greatly modified in the process, just as the Kendra's *kāryapaddhati* has offered a more recently conceived understanding of both the role of yoga in society and the reason for disseminating knowledge of yoga theory and practice.

REFERENCES

Administrator. 2009. "Sangh Shiksha Varg," *RSS On Net*. Available at: http://rssonnet.org/index.php?option=com_content&task=view&id=103 (accessed August 2, 2010).

Akhandananda, Swami. 1979. *From Holy Wanderings to the Service of God in Man*. Mylapore, Madras: Sri Ramakrishna Math.

Alter, Joseph S. 1994. Somatic Nationalism: Indian Wrestling and Militant Hinduism. *Modern Asian Studies* 28 (3): 557–588.

———. 1997. A Therapy to Live By: Public Health, the Self and Nationalism in the Practice of a North Indian Yoga Society. *Medical Anthropology* 17 (4): 309–335.

———. 2004. *Yoga in Modern India: The Body between Science and Philosophy*. Princeton, NJ: Princeton University Press.

———. 2006. Yoga at the *Fin de Siècle*: Muscular Christianity with a "Hindu" Twist. *International Journal of the History of Sport* 23 (5): 759–776.
———. 2008. Yoga *Shivir*: Performativity and the Study of Modern Yoga. In Mark Singleton and Jean Byrne (eds.), *Yoga in the Modern World: Contemporary Perspectives*. London: Routledge, pp. 36–48.
Annadananda, Swami. 1993. *Swami Akhandananda*. Calcutta: Advaita Ashrama.
Andersen, Walter K. and Damle, Shridhar D. 1987. *The Brotherhood in Saffron*. New Delhi: Vistaar Publications.
Anon. 1956. *Shri Guruji: The Man and His Mission*. Delhi: Bharat Prakashan.
———. 1991. *The Vivekananda Kendra Prayer*. Madras: The Vivekananda Kendra Prakashan.
———. 1995. *Sevā Disha—A Statistical Outline of the Service Projects and Allied Activities Being Conducted by the R.S.S and Related Organisation*. Available at: http://www.archivesofrss.org/sewa (accessed August 8, 2010).
———. 1997. *Sevā Disha—Building an Integrated and Self Reliant Society*. Available at: http://www.archivesofrss.org/sewa (August 8, 2010).
———. 2004. *Sevā Disha 2004*. Available at: http://www.archivesofrss.org/sewa (accessed August 8, 2010).
———. 2005a. *Kendra Unfolds: Selected Letters of Mananeeya Sri Eknathji Ranade*. Chennai: The Vivekananda Kendra Prakashan.
———. 2005b [1988]. *Yoga The Science of Holistic Living* (special issue of *Vivekananda Patrika* 17/2, August 1988). Chennai: The Vivekananda Kendra Prakashan Trust.
———. 2008 [1977]. *Yoga An Instruction Booklet*. Chennai: The Vivekananda Kendra Prakashan Trust.
———. No date. *The Vivekananda Kendra Arun Jyoti, Arunachal Pradesh: Annual Report 2006–2007*. No publisher or place of publication.
———. No date b. Sangh's e-Sevāks [Article about IT Milan]. Available at: http://www.sanghparivar.org/sangh-s-e-sevāks-article-about-it-milan (accessed September 15, 2010).
Beckerlegge, Gwilym. 2000a. Swami Akhandananda's *sevāvratra* (Vow of Service) and the Earliest Expressions of Service to Humanity in the Ramakrishna Math and Mission. In Antony Copley (ed.), *Gurus and Their Followers*. New Delhi: Oxford University Press, pp. 59–82.
———. 2000b. *The Ramakrishna Mission: The Making of a Modern Hindu Movement*. New Delhi: Oxford University Press.
———. 2003. Saffron and *Sevā*: The Rashtriya Swayamsevāk Sangh's Appropriation of Swami Vivekananda. In Antony Copley (ed.), *Hinduism in Public and Private: Reform, Hindutva, Gender, Sampraday*. New Delhi: Oxford University Press, pp. 31–65.
———. 2004. The Rashtriya Swayamsevak Sangh's "Tradition of Selfless Service."In John Zavos, Andrew Wyatt, and Vernon Hewitt (eds.), *The Politics of Cultural Mobilization in India*. New Delhi: Oxford University Press, pp. 105–135.
———. 2006a. *Swami Vivekananda's Legacy of Service: A Study of the Ramakrishna Math and Mission*. New Delhi: Oxford University Press.
———. 2006b. Swami Vivekananda and the *Sangh Parivar*: Convergent or Divergent Views on Population, Religion and National Identity? *Postcolonial Studies* 9 (2): 121–135.
———. 2008. The Iconic Presence of Svāmī Vivekānanda and the Conventions of European-Style Portraiture during the Late Nineteenth Century." *International Journal of Hindu Studies* 12(1): 1–40.
———. 2010. "An Ordinary Organisation Run by Ordinary People": A Study of Leadership in the Vivekananda Kendra. *Contemporary South Asia* 18 (1): 71–88.

Bhatt, Chetan and Mukta, Parita. 2000. Introduction: Hindutva in the West: Mapping the Antinomies of Nationalism. *Ethnic and Racial Studies* 23 (3): 407–441.

Bhide, Nivedita R. 2003. *Eknathji*. Chennai: The Vivekananda Kendra Prakashan.

———. 2008. Inspiring Cum Guideline Letter. July 17. Available at: http://www.vivekanandakendra.org/english/guru-purnima.

Burger, Maya. 2006. What Price Salvation? The Exchange of Salvation Goods between India and the West. *Social Compass* 53 (1): 81–95.

Chetananda, Swami. 1997. *God Lives with Them: Life Stories of Sixteen Monastic Disciples of Sri Ramakrishna*. St. Louis, MO: Vedanta Society of St. Louis.

Chapple, Christopher K. 2008. Modern Yoga. *Religious Studies Review* 34 (2): 71–76.

Chowkulkar, Satish Shamrao. 2010. *Yoga Shastra of Bhagavad Gita*. Hyderabad: Prakash Shamrao Choukulkar and Ashok Shamrao Choukulkar.

De Michelis, Elizabeth. 2004. *A History of Modern Yoga*. London: Continuum.

———. 2007. A Preliminary Survey of Modern Yoga Studies. *Asian Medicine* 3 (1): 1–19.

———. 2008. Modern Yoga: History and Forms. In Mark Singleton and Jean Byrne (eds.), *Yoga in the Modern World: Contemporary Perspectives*. London: Routledge, pp. 17–35.

Feuerstein, Georg. 1990. Guru. In Georg Feuerstein (ed.), *Encyclopedic Dictionary of Yoga*. New York: Paragon House, pp. 123–126.

Hirst, Jacqueline Suthren and Zavos, John. 2011. *Religious Traditions in Modern South Asia*. London: Routledge.

His Eastern and Western Disciples. 1993 [1979]. *The Life of Swami Vivekananda*. 2 vols. Calcutta: Advaita Ashrama.

Jacobsen, Knut A. 2005a. Introduction: Yoga Traditions. In Knut Jacobsen (ed.), *Theory and Practice of Yoga: Essays in Honour of Gerald James Larson*. Leiden: Brill, pp. 1–27.

———. 2005b. In Kapila's Cave: A *Sāṃkhya*-Yoga Renaissance in Bengal. In Knut Jacobsen (ed.), *Theory and Practice of Yoga: Essays in Honour of Gerald James Larson*. Leiden: Brill, pp. 333–349.

Jaffrelot, Christophe. 1996. *The Hindu Nationalist Movement and Indian Politics, 1925 to the 1990s*. London: Hurst.

Kanungo, Pralay. 2002. *RSS's Tryst with Politics: From Hedgewar to Sudarshan*. Delhi: Manohar.

Klostermaier, Klaus. 2006. Hinduism—Hindutva—Hindu Dharma. In Anna King (ed.), *Indian Religions: Renaissance and Revival*. London: Equinox, pp. 3–27.

Lochtefeld, James. G. 1996. New Wine, Old Skins: The Sangh Parivar and the Transformation of Hinduism. *Religion* 26 (2): 101–118.

Nagarathna, R. and Nagendra, H. R. 2001. *Yoga Practices for Anxiety and Depression*. Bangalore: Swami Vivekananda Yoga Prakashana.

Nagendra, H. R., R. Nagarathna, and S. Telles (eds.). 2000. *Yoga Research and Applications, Proceedings of the 5th International Conference on Frontiers of Yoga Research and Applications*. Bangalore: Swami Vivekananda Yoga Prakashana.

Newcombe, Suzanne. 2009. The Development of Modern Yoga: A Survey of the Field. *Religion Compass* 3 (6): 986–1002.

Nikhilananda, Swami. 1975. *Vivekananda A Biography*. Calcutta: Advaita Ashrama.

Parameswaran, P. 1998. *Heart-Beats of the Hindu Nation*. Chennai: The Vivekananda Kendra Prakashan Trust.

———. 2000. Hindutva *Ideology—Unique and Universal*. Chennai: The Vivekananda Kendra Prakashan Trust.

Pol, Dattaram. 2010. *Krida Yoga*. Chennai: The Vivekananda Kendra Prakashan Trust.

Ranade, Eknath. 1975. *Yoga . . . The Core of the Vivekananda Kendra—A Pamphlet*. Unpublished.

———. 2004. *Sadhana of Service*. Chennai: The Vivekananda Kendra Prakashan.

———. (compiler). 2006. *Swami Vivekananda's Rousing Call to Hindu Nation*. Chennai: The Vivekananda Kendra Prakashan.

Sharma, Arvind. 2002. On Hindu, Hindustan, Hinduism and Hindutva. *Numen* 49 (1): 1–36.

Singleton, Mark and Byrne, Jean. 2008. Introduction. In Mark Singleton and Jean Byrne (eds.), *Yoga in the Modern World: Contemporary Perspectives*. London: Routledge, pp. 1–14.

Sirsikar, V.M. 1988. My Years in the R.S.S. In Eleanor Zelliot and Maxine Berntsen (eds.), *The Experience of Hinduism*. Albany: State University of New York, pp. 190–203.

Smith, David. 2003. *Hinduism and Modernity*. Oxford: Blackwell Publishing.

Strauss, Sarah. 2002. "Adapt, adjust, Accommodate": The Production of Yoga in a Transnational World. *History and Anthropology* 13 (3): 231–251.

Van der Veer, Peter. 2001. *Imperial Encounters: Religion and Modernity in India and Britain*. Princeton, NJ: Princeton University Press.

Vivekananda, Swami.1989. *The Complete Works of* Swami Vivekananda. 8 vols. Calcutta: Advaita Ashrama.

Yogananda, Parmahansa. 1963. *Autobiography of a Yogi*. London: Rider.

NOTES

1. On the Vivekananda Kendra's understanding of *Hinduism* and *Hindutva*, see, for example, Parameswaran (2000: 4). Cf. Lochtefeld (1996); Klostermaier (2006); Sharma (2002).
2. Jacobsen (2005a: 3–27), Chapple (2008); De Michelis (2007; 2008), and Newcombe (2009) provide overviews of yoga studies. Apart from where the context implies a reference to yoga as a cumulative tradition, when the term *yoga* is used in this chapter without a signifier such as *karma*, it denotes a form that typically includes elements now associated with postural yoga.
3. My preferred use of *Hindutva-inspired* is intended to signal the diversity of *Hindutva* movements.
4. See the Vivekananda Kendra's website, http:www.vkendra.org.
5. Yoga training is included in *Sevā Disha* (see Beckerlegge, 2004: 127), the RSS's database of the *saṅgh parivār*'s *sevā* activities, with Sports and Physical Training and under Healthcare; for example, Table 13.2(a) in Anon. (1995); "Transformation through Education" in Anon. (1997); "Yoga" in Anon. (2004).
6. According to "About the Vivekananda Kendra," a statement commonly found at the end of the Vivekananda Kendra's publications (including those cited in this chapter), the Kendra's workers carry out various "service activities" through a number of channels, including yoga, to achieve the goal of national regeneration.
7. Questions about the appropriate nature and extent of activism have surfaced within both the RSS and the Ramakrishna Math and Mission; for example, Vivekananda's initiative to encourage *saṃnyāsis* to spearhead the delivery of *sevā* was divisive in the early Ramakrishna Math and Mission. To understand the

character of the Vivekananda Kendra, it is important to recognise the closeness of Ranade's working relationship with Golwalkar. Both have been placed with the "traditionalists" and "ethical absolutists" in the RSS who continued in Hedgewar's path of prioritising the character-building role of the RSS rather than advocating social and political activism (Andersen & Damle, 1987: 53–54, 108–113, 251). In his admiration for Swami Akhandananda of the Ramakrishna Math, Golwalkar identified himself with the most consistent supporter of Vivekananda's attempt to institutionalize the practice of *sevā* in the Math (see Beckerlegge, 2000a) but with one also drawn to asceticism. Ranade's own admiration for Vivekananda and closeness to Golwalker, as an upholder of the "traditionalist," "ethical absolutist" camp within the RSS, I would suggest, helped to shape the Kendra's emergence as a "new character-building organisation" (Andersen & Damle, 1987: 137), which took the form, according to the Kendra's self-characterisation, of a "*spiritually* oriented service mission" (italics added, see the Vivekananda Kendra's website, http:www.vkendra.org).

8. Vivekananda's impact on the Hindu tradition and Indian national life has been hotly debated. See Beckerlegge (2000b: Part 1; 2006a: Chapters 2, 3) and, for example, De Michelis (2004) on his role in Modern Yoga.
9. The Kendra celebrates Guru Pūrṇimā. Through its adoption of *oṃkāra* as guru, *oṃkāra* encompassing all that is, the Kendra thus acknowledges and respects all gurus who have preserved the Vedic tradition.
10. This is but a further example of one selection from coexisting and contested readings of Vivekananda's mission and priorities, given in note 8. See Beckerlegge (2003; 2006b).
11. Although the Math would not take part in the political campaigning that carried the project forward, Swami Ranganathananda (a future president of the Math) advised Ranade on the foundation of a lay movement, and the Rock Memorial was consecrated by then-president of the Ramakrishna Math. Workers and supporters in both movements support the publications and functions of both movements. Several participants at the annual Yoga Shiksha Shibir, to be discussed later in this chapter, spoke of their links to the Ramakrishna Math and Mission.
12. Once established in Bangalore, VK YOGAS under Nagendra increasingly prioritized medical research into yoga (Anon., 2005b: 269–274) until becoming independent from the Vivekananda Kendra in 2000, taking the name Vivekananda Yoga Anusandhana Samsthana (VYAS). This change in institutional status and mission did not signal an ideological difference between Nagendra and the Kendra. See, for example, Nagendra et al. (2000) and Nagarathna and Nagendra (2001: iii), which acknowledges Ranade's role as "the mastermind" behind the development of their work. This now independent institution will not figure further in this chapter.
13. Taken from a word-processed version of "Yoga . . . The Core of the Vivekananda Kendra—A Pamphlet," identified as having been released by Ranade in 1975. This version of the pamphlet was provided for my use by the general secretary at a time when a further volume of Ranade's writings is being prepared. It will be cited subsequently as Ranade (1975). The pamphlet also refers, as early as 1975, to the planned creation of a "big Yoga Centre."
14. These themes run throughout *Yoga: The Science of Holistic Living*, a special issue of the Kendra's journal *The Vivekananda Kendra Patrika* (Anon., 2005b).
15. A poster the "Vivekananda Kendra Karyapaddhati" on display in the training center during the 2010 Yoga Shiksha Shibir gave as one aim of *yoga varga* "to establish Yoga way of life by organising the collective life."

16. On "camp"/Shibir (adopting the Kendra's transliteration), see Alter (2008: 36–37). I am grateful to Mr. D. Bhanudas, general secretary-cum-treasurer of Vivekanada Kendra, for arranging for me to join the annual Yoga Shiksha Shibir as a participant observer; the organizing team and participants for assimilating me into the Shibir; Mr. A. Balakrishnan, vice president of the Vivekananda Kendra, for making time for me to interview him; and the Vivekanandapuram library staff for their unfailing assistance. I am also grateful to the Spalding Trust for funding this fieldwork, which consolidated earlier visits in 2006 and 2008 funded by the British Academy.
17. This pattern closely resembles the ideal Daily Routine laid down in the Code of Conduct for the Vivekananda Kendra Workers, except that this routine stipulates work from breakfast until the evening devotional session. Document provided by the general secretary.
18. This more intimate clustering of teams according to their preference for Hindi or English provided the context for gathering the material in this chapter based on informal interviews and conversations.
19. For a fuller account of the RSS, its affiliates, and the typical pattern of *śākhā* meetings, including the practice of *yogāsanas* and physical training, see Jaffrelot (1996) and Kanungo (2002) and Sirsikar (1988) for a personal account of participation in a *śākhā*. Cf. Anon. (no date b), and Administrator (2009).
20. This information is taken from the *Vivekananda Kendra, Kanyakumari, Guidelines for branch centers*. Document supplied by general secretary.
21. It was different in scale, the level of regimentation (an element of which was present), the absence of uniforms, and the absence of any fusion of the practice of *yogāsanas* with physical training. Compare, for example, the Sangh Shiksha Varg-Tritiya Varsh, June 2009, Nagpur. See http://www.youtube.com/watch?v=UVEUJbespBo.
22. These statements about Janardan Swami were gathered from websites of very uneven quality, following Mr. Balakrishnan's reference to this teacher. See "About Us" and "Our Guru," http://www.jsyog.org/ and http://wikimapia.org/486814/Janardan-Swami-Yogabhyasi-Mandal-www-jsyog-org. Taken together, they nevertheless appear to provide a consistent picture—hence their inclusion in this study. It is perhaps telling in this context that the Vivekananda Kendra Prayer (*prārthana*) also was composed by a personal acquaintance of Ranade.
23. In this too the Kendra may claim to have drawn on Vivekananda as its authority and specifically on the making of yoga "into the unifying sign of the Indian nation" (Van der Veer, 2001: 73).
24. Cf. Kanungo (2002: 71). Physical exercise is performed by women who attend the *śākhās* of women's organizations such as the Rashtra Sevika Samiti.
25. For a brief account of devotional practice of members of the cadre in the Vivekananda Kendra, see Beckerlegge (2010: 72–73).
26. Knut Jacobsen (2005b: 333) noted that, although many of the leading Hindu religious thinkers in nineteenth- and twentieth-century Bengal showed interest in *sāṃkhyayoga*, few were practitioners of this tradition.
27. Discourse on "What Is Yoga? (1)" by Deepak Khaire, (organizing team) (the Vivekananda Kendra Annual Yoga Shiksha Shibir, Kanyakumari, December 2010).
28. As we have seen, the Kendra does not present a highly theorized presentation of yoga through its outreach work, and deliberately so (Anon., 2008: 2). Consequently, the degree to which the Kendra has assimilated Vivekananda's comprehensive fourfold model and, more specifically, his interpretation of *rājayoga*, is

harder to test than noting the extent of the Kendra's reliance on references to Vivekananda's four types and more general characterizations of yoga tradition and its value, including in relation to physical fitness.

29. Discourse (see note 23 for details) on "Karma Yoga (1)" by D. Bhanudas, general secretary.
30. Discourse (see note 23 for details) on "*Bhagavad Gītā* (1)" by Satish Shamrao Chowkulkar (organizing team).

CHAPTER 16

Swami Ramdev: Modern Yoga Revolutionary

STUART RAY SARBACKER

Yoga is Samadhi. Yoga is the spiritual philosophy of self-realization, or self-knowledge. Yoga is life philosophy. Yoga is self-discipline. Yoga is not merely physical exercise but a complete lifestyle. Yoga is the spiritual knowledge of making the soul pure and seedless. Yoga is a complete medical science. Yoga is the science of life. Yoga is the solution to all the problems of individuals, societies, countries and the world.

—Swami Ramdev, *Jeevan Darshan*

INTRODUCTION

In June 2011, a series of events unfolded in the capital city of India, New Delhi, that riveted the attention of a global audience. The New Delhi police swept in under cover of darkness to break up an anticorruption protest against the Indian federal government, killing at least one protester in the process. This action distantly echoed the interventions of police forces of the British Empire during the Indian independence movement. At the center of this spectacle was the modern yoga guru Swami Ramdev, or "Baba Ramdev," a rising star among the spiritual and political elite in India, whose agitation against corruption and so-called "black money" had captured the nation's imagination. The crowds were dispersed quickly, and Swami Ramdev was eventually arrested by the police. Though it may have been viewed as a tactical success for the police forces, it quickly became clear that the move was a political miscalculation, only bringing additional validation to Ramdev's claims of government corruption and further tarnishing the government's reputation. It also resulted in the establishment of the image of Swami Ramdev as the embodiment of the Indian—and perhaps even Gandhian—spirit, and suddenly Ramdev became the spokesperson for a broad swath of the Indian population. The police may well have won the battle, but they clearly lost the public relations war. Commentators from within India and from around the globe questioned the actions of the police and brought considerable media attention to Ramdev and his cause. The situation that played out capped a series of events that have elevated Swami Ramdev to a position of preeminent spiritual and moral authority in India, bringing the discourses and practices of yoga into the mainstream of Indian society and global consciousness in unprecedented ways.

The rise of Swami Ramdev as a paragon of modern yoga and as a modern yoga "revolutionary" represents the culmination of the projects of many of the key Indian yoga gurus over the past century. His movement links together the principle of yoga as a vehicle for public health with the mass performance of yoga as an integral praxis of Indian nationalism, ultimately aiming to simultaneously bring about the health of the individual and the health of the entire nation. His success in the public sphere is rooted in his large-scale mass media yoga campaign and the success of his *āyurvedic* products, which together have provided the cultural and economic capital for him to become a major voice and agent for change in Indian society. Yoga has long been iconic of Indian spirituality, even if practiced only by a small minority of the population. The efforts of Swami Ramdev may well bring the popularity of the practice of yoga into parity with its iconic status, bringing it into the living rooms of middle-class India on an unprecedented scale, with an eye to its ultimate dissemination across the globe.

RAMDEV'S YOUTH AND THE FORMATION OF THE DIVYA YOG TRUST AND MISSION

Yogarishi Swami Ramdevji Maharaj—"The Great Lord and Yoga-Seer Master Ramdev," popularly known as "Baba (Father) Ramdev" and as "Swami (Master) Ramdev"—was born in 1975 as Ramkishan Yadav in Syed Alipur, a village in the northern Indian state of Haryana to Shrimati Gulab Devi and Shri Ram Niwas (George & Kasturi, 2011).[1] As a member of the Yadav social class, he served as a cow herder, working in the fields for his parents. He is said to have suffered from various physical ailments, most notably a paralytic condition and boils, from which he states he found relief through the practice of yoga and his studies of nationalist writings (*Indian Express* [New Delhi], May 31, 2011; Raj, 2010: 81–82). At a young age—perhaps as early as nine—he ran away from home to join a *gurukul* (traditional Hindu student–teacher school) at Khanpur, roughly thirty kilometers from Alipur. From there, at the age of fourteen, he moved to another *gurukul* at Kalwa, where he studied with a

Figure 16.1:
Swami Ramdev. (Courtesy of WikiCommons.)

teacher who would become one of his principal gurus, Acharya Shri Baldevji. At Kalwa, he studied Sanskrit language and literature, including grammatical texts and key Hindu philosophical and religious texts, along with the formal traditions of yoga and asceticism taught in the school. Together, these studies provided a foundation for Ramdev's development as a yoga scholar and practitioner (Raj, 2010: 82). In 1992, he completed his studies at Khanpur and eventually gravitated to the Kripalu Bagh Ashram in Haridwar (George & Kasturi, 2011). Haridwār literally means "the Door of Hari (Viṣṇu)" and is also known as Hardwār, "the City of Hara (Śiva)" and as Gaṅgādwār, "the Door of Gaṅgā," being located at the point where the Ganges River emerges from the foothills of the Himalayas onto the Gangetic plain. It is one of the four locations of the highly important Hindu Kumbh Mela festival and is in proximity to Rishikesh, which is anecdotally known as the "World Capital of Yoga." Spiritual and political worlds are intimately intertwined in Haridwar, and in recent Indian history it has been an important locus for the revitalization of both religious and political campaigns (McKean, 1996: 43–45). In 1995, Ramdev would take vows of renunciation (*saṃnyāsa*) at Kripalu Bagh Ashram under its leader, Swami Shankardevji Maharaj, who would become

Ramdev's second principal guru, along with Swami Baldev of Kalwa (George & Kasturi, 2011). Ramkishan Yadav took the name Ramdev, ultimately receiving the titles "preceptor" (*ācārya*) and "master" (*svāmī* or *swāmī*), indicating his accomplishments and credentials as a teacher and practitioner under the tutelage of his aforementioned spiritual preceptors.

The Kripalu Bagh Ashram was established in 1932 by Swami Kripaludev, a former freedom fighter (Raj, 2010: 83). Kripaludev was born as Yati Kishore Chand in Mewar, Rajasthan, and had been a member of the Bang Viplav Dal, an organization of "revolutionaries" in West Bengal, and played a key role in the publication of two of their newsletters. Kripalu Dev is said to have given refuge to a revolutionary from West Bengal, Rasbihari Bose, who played a key role in a failed assassination plot against the British Viceroy Lord Charles Hardinge. Kripalu is said to have associated with a range of key figures in Indian politics in the independence movement and in Hindu nationalism, including Bal Gangadhar Tilak, Mohandas Gandhi, and Jawaharlal Nehru (Raj, 2010). As an expression of his indebtedness to the example of Kripaludev, Ramdev ultimately dedicated to him one of his key publications on yoga, *Yog: Its Philosophy and Practice* (Ramdev, 2008: iii). These connections to Indian and Hindu nationalism built on Ramdev's earlier exposures to the writings of Dayananda Saraswati, one of the key figures in the development of modern Hinduism and the founder of the Ārya Samāj, one of the driving organizational forces in Hindu nationalism. The Ārya Samāj played a key role in setting up the *gurukul* system that informed Ramdev's development as a scholar and practitioner of yoga. Its legacy runs deep in Indian politics as well as in Indian religious life (George & Kasturi, 2011). The Ārya Samāj's vision of a "modern" Hinduism, which deemphasized sectarian elements of the tradition in favor of a universalism that brings together religion and society (including politics), clearly resonated with Ramdev. Likewise, a popular narrative tells of how Ramdev was particularly inspired in his mission by the writings of Aurobindo Ghosh, known popularly as "Sri Aurobindo," a former freedom fighter and Indian nationalist from West Bengal who ultimately became a prominent yoga guru and author in Southern India (see Chapter 2, in this volume).

Ramdev is also said to have spent time during this period as a spiritual seeker and as a meditator in a cave at Gangotri, the glacial source of the Ganges River, which is a Hindu pilgrimage site strongly associated with yoga and asceticism, the holy goddess Gaṅgā, and the god Śiva (Raj, 2010: 82–83; Patañjali Yogpeeth 2012). Having come to the conclusion that his solitary practice would not allow him to fully serve his community, a narrative paralleled in the life of other key modern yoga gurus, he returned to Haridwar to become more active in passing on the teachings of yoga to a larger community (Raj, 2010: 83). According to some sources, at this time Ramdev reconnected with a former schoolmate, Acharya Balkrishna, who had been similarly pursuing a spiritual quest in the area of Gangotri (Patañjali Yogpeeth 2012). Together, they are said to have agreed to pursue the propagation of yoga (Ramdev) and *āyurveda* (Balkrishna) on the grounds that they were of great utility in securing physical and spiritual health for a universal Indian and global population (ibid.). Having returned to Kripalu Bagh Ashram in Haridwar, Ramdev and Balkrishna, along with another former fellow student, Acharya Karamveer, and Swami Shankardev, founded the Divya Yog Mandir Trust in 1995, which would serve as the platform for their mission going forward.

Ramdev already had experience in teaching yoga to the public during his studies in the *gurukul* at Halwa, where he offered free yoga courses to villagers in Haryana (Raj, 2010: 82). The Divya Yog Mandir Trust gave Ramdev a new platform to pursue an industrious program of outreach to the general public outside of the formal ashram sphere. Initially, Ramdev acted in support of Shankardev's efforts, but eventually, as Shankardev's health deteriorated, he took a lead role (George & Kasturi, 2011). A key part of their program of outreach was the performance of yoga *shivirs*, or "camps," throughout the region, which provided opportunities for Ramdev to hone his teaching skills as he exposed an ever-widening community to the practices of yoga posture (*āsana*), breath control (*prāṇāyāma*), and yoga philosophy. Yoga *shivirs* have long served as key venues in which the negotiation of traditional forms of yoga and the needs of a modern audience takes place on a large scale (Alter, 2008: 36). Yoga *shivirs* are potentially an ideal venue for the propagation of yoga teachings and techniques, as they typically are attended by a large number of people who engage in synchronous practice, providing both the immediacy of a one-on-one relationship with the guru and the "communitas," or community-building experience, of a shared ritual practice (Alter, 2008: 44). The notion of the yoga *shivir* as a "spectacle" (Alter, 2008: 38) that is watched by outsiders, often vicariously through print media, film, and television, adds an additional element in its relevance to Ramdev's career trajectory, anticipating his later ascension to yoga celebrity status as a "television guru" adored by millions of people across India. Anecdotes from this period also portray Swami Ramdev as an enthusiastically entrepreneurial proponent of both yoga and *āyurveda*, traveling by foot or motor scooter around Haridwar to distribute pamphlets about their efficacy as well as *āyurvedic* products (Raj, 2010: 82). He sought out knowledge of allopathy and other forms of medicine in an effort to bring together various healing modalities and integrate them with his yoga program (ibid.). Swami Ramdev's mission had materialized and he was pursuing it zealously, becoming the face of the Kripalu Bagh Ashram and an important religious leader in Haridwar in the process. In a short period of time, he would become the most prominent face of yoga in the entire nation, the progenitor of a "yoga revolution" that would transform Indian society and launch Ramdev into a position of profound influence in Indian society and politics.

THE RISING STAR OF YOGA

The Divya Yog Trust encapsulated the mission of Kripalu Bagh Ashram as embodied by Shankar Dev, Ramdev, and Balkrishna along with their close associate, Acharya Karamveer. The performance of yoga *shivirs* provided one of the principal ways the Divya Yog Trust's mission was carried out, and Ramdev was taking an increasing role in their leadership. In 2002, one of the owners of a prominent TV network, Sadhana TV, attended a yoga *shivir* and shortly thereafter began televising them (George & Kasturi, 2011). Following this, Ramdev moved his television show to Aastha TV, another network, where he set a record for viewership, and following his ongoing success his organization eventually established ownership of the network (Raj, 2010: 109). Ramdev's television show, "Om Yog Sadhana," has been wildly popular and successful, with some estimating that he has eighty-five million followers via his television broadcasts in multiple languages and some 170 different countries and that "hundreds of millions" have been affected or influenced by his teachings (ibid.). The television shows encapsulate the spirit of the yoga *shivir*; they typically focus on Swami Ramdev as he teaches to large crowds—sometimes numbering in the thousands—the principles of yogic *asan* (*āsana*) and *pranayam* (*prāṇāyāma*). The shows also include Ramdev sharing his ruminations on applying yoga philosophy and morality to daily life. He also instructs his audience in some basic mantra performance—such as the chanting of *oṃ* and a range of popular Vedic (Hindu) mantras—as well as more formal instruction in meditative practices referred to as *dhyan* (*dhyāna*). In a manner reminiscent of the teachings of a range of modern yoga gurus, Ramdev places significant emphasis on his understanding of how various practices of *asan* and *pranayam* affect diseases such as diabetes, heart disease, and digestive ailments and of how they target particular organs, such as the kidneys and liver. In 2010, a *New York Times* article referred to Swami Ramdev as a ". . . yogic fusion of Richard Simmons, Dr. Oz, and Oprah Winfrey, irrepressible and bursting with Vedic Wisdom" (April 18, 2010). This characterization of Ramdev encapsulates the ways his career has mirrored those of famous American TV gurus associated with fitness, health, and popular wisdom. The *shivir* format of yoga instruction was a natural interface for the television format, and as Ramdev's show met with considerable success it evolved into an extremely polished and highly produced format, perhaps comparable to the production quality found in high-profile American televangelism. A valid comparison can be made between Ramdev and American televangelists like Joel Osteen, who preaches a universalizing message of "prosperity theology," and Pat Robertson, who has become influential in U.S. politics and an important player in the global spiritual marketplace (Thomas, 2009). Ramdev's elevation to celebrity status has allowed him to negotiate the worlds of personal health and public space, forcefully promoting his vision of modern yoga as an antidote for contemporary ills of both person and nation (Chakraborty, 2006; 2007).

Within a period of less than a decade, Ramdev has become a household name, and his discourses and teachings on yoga have become a part of the everyday life of millions of people in India and around the world. Ramdev's rise as a TV guru parallels the development of his "yoga empire," institutionalized in the form of the Patañjali Yogpeeth Trust in Haridwar. The Patañjali Yogpeeth Trust was founded in 2005 and built upon the successes of the earlier Divya Yog Trust and upon Ramdev's previous successes in the propagation of yoga and *āyurveda*. The Yogpeeth, literally the "yoga seat," carries the namesake (Patañjali) of the author–compiler of the *Yogasūtras*, one of Hinduism's principal classical texts of yoga philosophy. Patañjali has served as a central figure of authority within modern yoga traditions, in part because he is viewed as a timeless representative of a pure, authoritative, and unadulterated yoga (De Michelis, 2004; Singleton, 2008: 77). He is also associated with one of the most influential formulations of yoga practice, the "eight-limbed yoga" (*aṣṭāṅgayoga*), a formulation that Ramdev and many other modern yoga gurus use to illustrate the parameters of traditional yoga practice. According to one of its promotional brochures, the Yogpeeth now serves as the institutional hub of Ramdev's organization, though the Kripalu Bagh Ashram and the Yog Mandir Trust continue to operate under the umbrella of the Patañjali Yogpeeth Trust. The mission of the trust is ". . . for the purpose of establishing Yoga in the world map, for the study and ancient research of the Vedic tradition of Yoga, and for conducting the whole gamut of activities and various projects related to Yoga" (Yogpeeth, 2011: 3). In connection with the establishment of the Patañjali Yogpeeth Trust, the Bharat Swabhiman Andolan Trust, or "India Self-Glorification Trust," was developed. Here, the spiritual resources of yoga and the health benefits of *āyurveda* are applied to the pressing problems of Indian society, from government corruption and economic imbalances to water management, poverty eradication, and population control. The Yogpeeth itself is a vast set of institutes and structures, including an *āyurvedic* hospital and dispensary, a yoga research center, a library, vision and dental clinics, laboratories, a yoga auditorium, and visitor residences and cafeterias. The Yogpeeth Trust is also the umbrella organization for numerous business endeavors: Divya Prakashan Books, Divya Yoga Sadhana DVDs and VCDs, Yog Sandesh Magazine, Divya Pharmacy, Patañjali Ayurved Ltd., and Patañjali Food and Herbal Ltd. In addition to daily yoga classes at Patañjali Yogpeeth, the facilities for hosting yoga *shivirs*—the yoga auditorium and guest residences—allow for up to ten thousand people to attend each program. The Yogpeeth has also established satellite centers with teacher training programs in virtually every major city of India, with a goal of providing a network of yoga centers that serve the entire Indian population. Ramdev has estimated that the total value of his trust stands in the vicinity of 1,100 crore rupees, which is approximately US$217 million (*Indian Express* [New Delhi], May 31, 2011). This vast wealth is drawn primarily from the donations of yoga practitioners that support Ramdev's mission and through the sale of his popular *āyurvedic* products. Though the rise of Ramdev's yoga empire has not been without controversy—some have publicly questioned his claims to the benefits of his yoga practices, the efficacy of his *āyurvedic* treatments for HIV/AIDS and cancer, and the purity of ingredients for his *āyurvedic* medicines—it nonetheless has been able to withstand criticism with remarkable durability and to keep its "brand" intact (Nanda, 2006).

The combination of the cultural capital of Ramdev's celebrity—most notably the passionate devotion of his followers to his cause—and the economic capital provided by his various trusts provides powerful support for Ramdev in his quest to spread his message of the benefits of yoga and *āyurveda* and has allowed him to become a driving force in the life of the Indian nation. In an India where medical care is often a luxury, the occurrence of diseases such as diabetes is rising, and political corruption is endemic, his message has met with considerable success at the popular level. Ramdev's friend and associate Acharya Balkrishna "sketches" Ramdev's life out in this manner:

> Rev. Swami Ramdev, a celibate since childhood, is well-versed in Sanskrit Grammar, Ayurved, and Vedic Philosophy. A Strong proponent of Indian cultural values, his practical approach to Yog, research in the field of Ayurved and services in the field of cow-breeding, have won him several thousands of followers throughout India and made him a living symbol of Indian culture. His detachment from worldly happiness and devotion to social service has made him a phenomenal character in the saintly world . . . Swamiji is a devout disciple of Acharya Shri Baldevji of Kalwa, who himself is an accomplished Yogi. He was initiated on the banks of the sacred River Ganga. He has taught in Gurukulas (traditional Indian system of education) subjects such as Ashtadhyayi, Mahabhashya, Upanishads and the six systems of Indian philosophy. Besides this, during his travels in the Himalayan mountains, he performed severe austerities in the caves of Gangotri for the realization of the SELF, and acquired several extraordinary capabilities . . . In association with his learned companion, Shri Muktanandaji Maharaj, and myself, Swami Ramdevji established Divya Yog Mandir Trust in 1995 in Kankhal (Haridwar) and began activities in health and spiritual pursuits. In the camps organized at his insistence for imparting practical lessons in the matters of health and Yoga, millions of people have taken advantage of his services and have gained immunity from various kinds of serious diseases, thus restoring good health . . . Most Amiable in nature and affectionate in attitude, Swamiji combines in himself, qualities of great learning. His extreme modesty and loving nature have won Swamiji a great multitude of followers. In a short period of about 6 or 7 years, Swamiji has acquired phenomenal success in all the activities undertaken by him and has been a source of constant and unfailing inspiration for all of us who have the good fortune of knowing and associating with him. (Ramdev, 2008: Back Cover)

RAMDEV'S VISION OF YOGA

A concise but comprehensive articulation of Ramdev's yoga program can be found in his work *Yog: Its Philosophy and Practice*, first published in Hindi in 2002 (Ramdev, 2008). It begins with a discussion of the term *Yog* and sets up a context for understanding the nature of Ramdev's teachings. Drawing on the yoga philosophy of Patañjali, he describes yoga as being "the eradication of negative moods," referring to *Yogasūtra* verse I.2, *yogaścittavṛttinirodhaḥ*, which leads to finding "solace in the merging with the soul" (p. 1). Following the commentary of Vyāsa on the *Yogasūtra* verse, in which yoga is equated with *samādhi* (contemplation), Ramdev states, "We can say that the controlled practices which result in the meeting of *Atma* and *Param-atma* (Soul and the supreme soul) is Yog" (ibid.). Drawing further from the *Yogatattva Upaniṣad*, Ramdev analyzes yoga practice as fourfold—Mantra Yog (chanting yoga), Laya Yog (devotional yoga), Hatha Yog (yoga of purification of mind and body), and Raja Yog (yoga of mental purity and illumination)—and concludes that yoga can be said to be "methods and processes which are used for attaining spirituality and devotion" (p. 2). The results of yoga include "insight to know more about the self" as the "inner powers blossom to give complete bliss and an introduction to the true self" (p. 4). Ramdev (ibid.) sketches out the implications of yoga practice:

> Practicing *Yog* revives our dormant energy. These exercises rejuvenate tissues and help new cell formation. Light *Yogic* exercises reactivate the nervous system, and regulate the blood circulation. They reinstate fresh energy in the body. According to the laws of physiology, when the body contracts and expands, energy is developed and diseases get cured. This can be achieved with the help of different *Yogic āsanas*. With the practice of *prānāyāmas* and *āsanas*, the glands and muscles of the body contract and expand, and diseases get cured naturally . . . *Yog* also keeps the veins healthy. The pancreas becomes active and produces insulin in the right quantity, which helps in curing diabetes and related diseases. Health is directly linked to the digestive system. The improper functioning of the digestive systems is the primary cause for most of the diseases. Even some serious problems like heart disease occur due to a faulty digestive system. *Yog* strengthens the entire digestion process, making every part of the body healthy, and active. Fresh air enters the lungs making them healthier which keeps diseases like asthma, respiratory problems, allergy, etc. away. Fresh air also strengthens the heart. *Yogic* exercises dissolve the fat deposits which make the body light, healthy and attractive. *Yog* is beneficial for thin and lean physique as well. Along with physical fitness, *Yog* also affects the subtle senses, the intellect and the mind. *Yog* controls the working of organs and helps the mind to detach itself. The follower of *Ashtang Yog* passes with great ease from the darkness of ignorance towards a joyous, peaceful and ever illuminated existence by

connecting with the supreme soul. 'Tādā Drashtuh Swaroope, Vsthanam'. Thus we can embark on the path of *Yog* and experience the inner happiness of connecting with the Supreme Being and attaining physical, mental, intellectual, and spiritual progress.

Ramdev's presentation of the parameters of yoga practice brings together the multiple threads constituting modern yoga practice under the aegis of *aṣṭāṅgayoga*, a trope characteristic not only of many modern yoga traditions but also of many Hindu efforts to reconcile various yoga techniques (Sarbacker, 2009; 2011). For Ramdev (2008: 9), the appeal of *aṣṭāṅgayoga* extends far beyond simply one's own physical or spiritual development; it is potentially a panacea for the ills of the entire world, a solution to humankind's deepest concerns:

> Every person in this world is craving for peace and happiness. . . . Not only individuals but every nation, the entire world is praying for world peace. . . . But nobody knows the way to bring this peace to the world. There are many solutions to these problems but no agreement has been reached and universal peace still remains a distant dream. Some people are of the opinion that a single religion in the entire world is the key to this matter. Some people propagate Christianity or Islam, on the other hand some people swear by Buddhisam [sic] or Jainism. India is overflowing with such claims, teachers and *Gurus* who make tall promises of world peace. But none of these religions or thought processes is broad enough to cover the entire world population with their philosophy. . . . Can't we have a philosophy of life that a person of any religion or nationality can follow? Can the entire world population join hands and walk on this path towards world peace? What is this magic solution that will protect each one's national pride, religious belief and is free from any selfish interest or greed? What is this magical word that promises individual's joy, peace and prosperity in their personal lives and shows them a path to world peace that they can adopt fearlessly? The word is *Yog*. The path of *Ashtang Yoga* which has been propagated by *Maharshi Patanjali* is that answer we are all looking for. It is not a cult or theory but a complete way of life. This is the only solution to our quest for world peace. *Ashtang Yog* provides us with individual and social well-being, physical fitness, intellectual awakening, mental peace and contentment of the soul.

According to Ramdev, yoga is thus an answer to the many problems of contemporary global civilization, and not simply or uniquely a personal philosophy or practice. In this respect, Ramdev's philosophy parallels the visions of early modern yoga figures such as Bhavanrao Pant, who was the key formulator of the iconic Sun Salutation (*sūryanamaskāra*), and of Mohandas Gandhi, in whom acts of asceticism on the individual level translated into changes in the fabric of society and related the microcosm of the individual's body to the macrocosm of society and the nation (Alter, 2000; Dalton, 2000: 1–29).

Ramdev further frames the practice of yoga by examining six aspects of a daily yoga routine and a sequence of elements within the *Ashtang Yog* system: (1) *ahara* (diet); (2) *nidra* (sleep); (3) *brahmacharya* (celibacy); (4) *vyayam* (exercise), which includes yoga *āsana* and *prāṇāyāma*; (5) *snan* (bath), to be performed after exercising to cool the body; and (6) *dhyan* (meditation), which includes the chanting of *oṃ* or the Gayatri mantra. This discussion includes a step-by-step analysis of each of the eight limbs, beginning with *yām* (*yama*) (self-restraint) and *niyama* (scriptural rules), followed by *āsana*, *prāṇāyāma*, *pratyāhāra* (withdrawal of senses from their objects), and the inner limbs of *dhāraṇā* (concentration), *dhyāna* (meditation), and *samādhi* (transcendental meditation). Throughout, Ramdev uses premodern traditional sources like the *Yogasūtras* and the *Haṭhayogapradīpikā* and quotations of prominent modernist teachers such as Dayananda Saraswati in the process of explaining the meaning of each element and the corresponding results of its practice. Building on this foundation, Ramdev's presentation of yoga in *Yog: Its Philosophy and Practice* includes a chapter on various *āsanas* (with static postures as well as the *Surya Namaskar* sequence), in which their benefits are described; a chapter on yogic purification practices (*ṣaṭkarman*), including *netī*, *dhautī*, and *naulī*; a chapter on practices of hand gesture (*mudrā*); and a chapter on the use of acupressure as a healing modality. The syncretic nature of Ramdev's practice of yoga is at parity with the larger scope of modern yoga traditions that have sought to bring coherence and relevance to yoga within a modern framework, negotiating a plurality of discourses and practices of the body, mind, and spirit that are drawn from a global spectrum of sources (Sarbacker, 2008). He views yoga as negotiating the dynamics of religion and science; the individual and society; and the corporeal and the spiritual, addressing the inherent tensions of modern Indian life in ways that have immediate emotional and experiential appeal.

RAMDEV'S VISION FOR THE INDIAN NATION

As is clear from the previous passages in *Yog: Its Philosophy and Practice*, Ramdev's vision of yoga is inextricably tied together with his vision for the Indian nation and for the world. The correspondence between Ramdev's spiritual and social visions is illustrated at great length in Ramdev's manifesto of social and spiritual transformation, titled *Jeevan Darshan* (View of Life). In *Jeevan Darshan*, which was published as both an independent volume by Divya Prakashan, the publisher for the Divya Yog Mandir Trust, and as a special edition of the trust's monthly magazine, *Yog Sandesh*, from March 2009, Ramdev articulates a vision of yoga nationalism that serves as the platform for his pursuit of social transformation within and through his community of yoga practitioners. In a section titled "National Religion," he argues that "there is no greater religion than duty towards the nation. There is no God greater than the nation. National interest is above everything. I will not betray the nation for my personal, political, economic and family welfare. I will contribute my body, mind, wealth, life and vote for national interest" (Ramdev, 2009: 12). Yoga has a unique place in the struggle of the nation, which Ramdev regards as the "spirit" or "praxis" of nationalism:

> I want to [associate] everyone with the religion of yoga in order to kindle in them the religion of the nation. I want to fill each one with the feeling of patriotism. After self-development with the help of yoga each morning, I want to fill myself with energy so as to help the nation's development. After self-awakening with the help of yoga, I want to take ahead the holy mission of national awakening. The question arises in a number of people's minds about the relationship between yoga and the nation's progress. So, I want to make it clear that without self-progress, the nation's progress is impossible. Hence, by self-development with the help of yoga each morning, we will be dedicated to the progress and prosperity of the nation the entire day. Yoga and nationalism are not two different philosophies but are two sides of the same coin! (pp. 13–14)

The practice of yoga might be seen as duty and devotion to the spirit of the nation, a universal religion in which respect and love are qualifications for citizenship:

> Earth is our mother and we are her children. Nation-god is the greatest god. Religion of the nation means our duty towards the nation, our responsibilities. Fulfilling them is our biggest religion. Just as irreligion and injustice are sinful, it is equally sinful to bear up with atrocity. Every individual should have gratitude, respect and pride towards the nation. . . . Those who do not love the soil, culture, civilization, and the people of the nation have no right to stay in this country. (Ramdev, 2009: 16)

Ramdev sums up his nationalist principles under the rubric of "Bharat Swabhiman Andolan," his "India self-glory movement," which articulates his mission to transform the nation at present into the "India of his dreams" via five main goals: (1) 100% voting; (2) 100% nationalist thought; (3) 100% boycott of foreign companies; (4) 100% domestic production (*swadeshi*); and (5) 100% yoga orientation in the nation (Bharat Swabhiman Andolan, 2012). These goals are augmented by five vows taken by yoga practitioners: (1) voting for patriotic and honest people; (2) uniting patriots; (3) boycotting foreign goods and purchasing domestic goods; (4) adopting nationalist thought in public while observing "Hindu, Islam, Christian, Sikh, Buddhist, Jain, etc. religious traditions" in private life; and (5) making the entire country yoga focused and removing society's ills by removing "self-confusion" (ibid.). The "India of Ramdev's Dreams" is exemplified as (1) healthy India; (2) clean India; (3) independent India through Indian lifestyle; (4) India free from hunger, unemployment, and poverty with population control; and (5) India free from political corruption and with 100% voting (ibid.). Ramdev also advocates an honoring and respecting of women in a conservative framework that links the "honor of the five mothers"—birth mother, mother India, Veda mother, mother cow, and mother Gaṅgā (Ramdev, 2009: 27–28). Among the many social ills that he sees as challenging the nation are political corruption; the use of alcohol, tobacco, and other intoxicants; consumption of sweetened and carbonated beverages and "junk food"; lack of sexual restraint among India's youth and the practice of homosexuality; a sexualized media culture; pollution and environmental degradation; and lack of access to medicine. The degree to which Ramdev embraces a conservative morality and politics might be said to be one key point that sets his movement apart from European and American traditions of "Anglophone yoga" (i.e., English-language based systems of yoga; Singleton, 2010: 9–10), many of which embrace a significantly more liberal-minded ethos and politics.

Ramdev's vision for Indian society, centered on the notion of an ascetic, participatory politics that is as strong as the level of grassroots adoption of its practice, echoes Gandhi's conceptions of *satyāgraha* and *swarāj* in numerous ways. Likewise, Ramdev's adoption of the language of *swadeśi* (literally "own country" but figuratively "self-sufficiency") echoes the views not only of Gandhi but also of an entire generation of Indian nationalists who see India's political existence as a nation as contingent upon its economic independence. Ramdev's opinion of Indian society is analogous in certain ways to Gandhi's regarding the centrality of India's village life in the health of the nation, a model of society that is arguably at odds with the modern industrial frame. However, Ramdev also advocates the use of Hindi as a national language (with additional instruction in vernacular and regional "mother tongues" such as Malayalam, Tamil, and Telugu as complementing it) and sees change at the national level as central to the transformation of Indian society (Ramdev, 2009: 30). He uses the term *Soul Power*, which encapsulates and encodes the Gandhian principle that the force of truth and spirit, rooted in ascetic practice and self-control, is a fundamental source of strength and power in the battle for social justice. Ramdev's political philosophy might be viewed as a negotiation between the universalizing missions of Gandhi's *satyāgraha* campaign and those of Bal Gangadhar Tilak's more forceful approach to Indian nationalism, a dynamic visually represented on the cover of a 2012 issue of *Yog Sandesh*, in which Ramdev's image is flanked by those of Gandhi and Tilak. Ramdev's embrace of the death penalty as a potential punishment for government corruption is often considered as qualifying his application of the Gandhian principles of *satyāgraha* and *ahiṃsā*; Ramdev argues that the number of people hurt or killed due to corruption is so staggering that it justifies such a legal recourse, both as punishment and as a deterrent (George & Kasturi, 2011; Laul, 2011). Likewise, the training of Indian military troops by the Patañjali Yogpeeth indicates parity in theory and practice between Ramdev's yoga discourse and methodology and those of the military forces in India (*The Times* [London], June 2, 2008).[2] This reflects a common critique of Ramdev: he is allied too closely to the Rashtriya Svayamsevak Sangh (Rāṣṭrīya Svayamsevak Saṅgh, RSS) and other conservative Hindu organizations to be an impartial advocate for the broader spectrum of Indian society. Ramdev's argument in response to such criticism is that he is working with whomever is willing to advocate for his causes and that his broader efforts are misconstrued in the media in ways that are unrepresentative of the scope of his diplomacy and coalition building (Laul, 2011).

RAMDEV'S ACTIVISM: ECOLOGY AND POLITICS

Two of Ramdev's most prominent interventions into the Indian social and political sphere involve his campaigns for the restoration of the Ganges River and his campaign against corruption and black money in the Indian government. In the case of the Ganges cleanup efforts, Ramdev's activism is at parity with his stated commitment to both a clean and healthy India:

> The country's land, food, water, rivers, air and sky have all become polluted, and the main cause of 50% of the diseases in India is non-cleanliness. Because of pollution in food, thought, mind and behaviour, disease, fear, corruption, crime, and anarchy is spreading in the entire country. Even sage Patañjali had pronounced cleanliness to be the first rule for a yogi. . . . To make the air, food and water pollution-free, it is important to have nationwide movements. (Ramdev, 2009: 19)

With respect to the Ganges River, Ramdev links the purity of country to the purity of Mother Ganga:

> Mother Ganga is the symbol of our devotion, faith and belief. Corrupt politicians and governments are the biggest obstacle to Mother Ganga's purity and continuity. Corruption is deeply immerged in its purity and continuity. As a result, after Naroda-Bulandseher, after the monsoons, only 2% of the Ganga water remains. 98% is dirty water comprised of sewage from toilets and waste water from factories. The Ganga that makes each of us pure, is herself getting dirty. I see purity of water more connected with human good than religion. It is my belief that only if the water, land and air of the country is pure and clean, the nation will be safe. I am resolved in my vow to clean and purify all the rivers in the entire country along with Ganga. (Ramdev, 2009: 28)

Ramdev's mission with respect to the restoration of the Ganges River took concrete form in 2008 in the form of an organization called Ganga Raksha Manch (Ganges Protection Platform). Ganga Raksha Manch embraced the slogan "Awiral Ganga, Nirmal Ganga" (flowing Ganges, pure Ganges). The organization was dedicated to the cleanup of the Ganges from its headwaters to its delta and to the procurement of national heritage status for the river (Alliance of Religions and Conservation, 2008). The principles of the movement included penalizing polluters, opposing a proposed Ganga express highway, lobbying for relocation of riverbank industries, and opposing expansion of the Theri Dam project in Uttarakhand, a very controversial project that has been ongoing for several decades (ibid.). Ramdev was joined in the inauguration of the Ganga Raksha Manch by Sri Sri Ravi Shankar, another prominent North Indian guru and prominent disciple of Maharishi Mahesh Yogi, and by representatives from the Gāyatrī Pariwār, a highly influential Hindu organization with ties to Haridwar.

Ramdev's action added to attention brought to the plight of the Ganges by the campaign of Veer Bhadra Mishra, a Brahmin priest and former engineer from Varanasi. Mishra had spearheaded a campaign to address the problems of the extraordinarily large amount of untreated sewage dumped routinely into the Ganges River and the health implications of the prevalence of harmful bacteria in the water (*Wall Street Journal* [Eastern Edition], February 13, 2010). It is likely that Ramdev's action also drew from the public outcry regarding the need to divert the Ganges in Allahabad during a recent Kumbh Mela festival, in which the degree of pollution had threatened to be prohibitive of the mass bathing in the Ganges that is at the center of the event (Singh, 2007). In the process of building his campaign, Ramdev was said to have brought together activists from both Hindu and Islamic organizations in the common cause of the restoration of the Ganges River (*IANS* [New Delhi], September 19, 2008). He was credited for being a key figure in crystallizing the movement and eventually convincing the Congress Party–led government of Manmohan Singh to commit to cleaning up the river. Manmohan Singh's government eventually agreed to pursue a US$4 billion campaign to remove all sewage sources by the year 2020 and pledged to grant the Ganges River Heritage status (*Wall Street Journal* [Eastern Edition], February 13, 2010). The movement represented an important shift in Hindu consciousness from one in which the purity of the Ganges River was unquestionable, due to its identification with the goddess Gaṅgā, to one in which Hindus have a responsibility to keep the river, and thus the goddess, clean. It also tapped deeply into a broader pan-Indian sentiment that identifies India as a nation with the Ganges River, transcending communal identity. It is interesting to note that the Bharatiya Janata Party (Bhāratīya Janatā Party, BJP), traditionally associated with conservative Hinduism, has recently taken up Ramdev's cause, leading to some speculation that they view it as a winning issue across the political spectrum (Sinha, 2011).

However, Ramdev has entered into the center of Indian consciousness via his political battle against government corruption, which drew the attention of the world media to the frontlines, if not the faultlines, of contemporary Indian politics in summer 2011. Following the high-profile political efforts of "Gandhian" activist Anna Hazare in April 2011 to pressure the Indian national government to pass the Jan Lokpal anticorruption bill, Ramdev took up his own highly publicized fast in New Delhi. Hazare had brought the world's attention to the battle against corruption in the Indian government, which he referred to as "India's second struggle for independence," setting the stage for Ramdev's emergence as a champion for the cause and for their political alliance. Ramdev's "Satyagraha Against Corruption" began on June 4, 2011, in Ram Lila Maidan in New Delhi, but was short-lived, as it was broken up by the New Delhi Police during the night of June 5. One of Ramdev's followers was killed in the process, and Ramdev escaped temporarily by disguising himself as a woman; he later claimed that he believed he was being targeted for assassination (Indian Express [New Delhi], June 26, 2011). The Indian Supreme Court would later rule that the New Delhi Police acted irresponsibly, though Ramdev was also held to be negligent, a claim that he disputed (NDTV Correspondent, 2012). It was also brought to light that the government had attempted to negotiate with Ramdev, declaring that he had agreed to postpone his action but later broke that agreement, which he vehemently denied (NDTV Correspondent, 2011). Footage of the protest was aired throughout India and abroad, leading to further elevation of Swami Ramdev's visibility in the Indian and global public eye. Ramdev continued his fast in Haridwar and eventually broke it at the appeal of religious leaders such as Shri Shri Ravi Shankar, who feared for Ramdev's life because his health had deteriorated. He was transferred to a hospital in Dehra Dun (*Indian Express* [New Delhi], June 12, 2011). Though Hazare initially distanced himself from Ramdev's action following the events at Ram Lila Maidan, in part due to suggestions of Ramdev's alliance with figures on the Hindu political right, he later pursued a new alliance with Ramdev, forging what he referred to as a "joint platform" to fight corruption (*Hindustan Times* 2012). This mutual effort was intended to encourage both Hazare and Ramdev's supporters to attend all of the functions offered by both leaders. Ramdev's stature as a representative and spokesperson for his followers, and of a greater Indian population that views itself as disenfranchised, is clearly on the rise.

Ramdev's political action against corruption has been particularly focused on the issue of "black money" and the idea of a black economy created on stolen and hidden Indian wealth. Ramdev argues that while India's "white money" economy, the money accounted for in the Indian system, is approximately 69 lakh crore rupees, or US$1.38 trillion, the black money economy is approximately 400 lakh crore rupees, or US$8 trillion (*Indian Express* [New Delhi], May 31, 2011).[3] According to Ramdev, then, corrupt politicians and industries are funneling a tremendous amount of India's wealth into overseas accounts, and the Indian people are suffering profound poverty and hunger as a result. The goal of his anticorruption movement is to recover this wealth and to punish those who would steal from the country. In the pursuit of this, he endorses a set of six principles: (1) withdraw 500 and 1000 rupee notes; (2) support the United Nations convention against corruption; (3) apply the death penalty for the corrupt to punish and deter criminals; (4) monitor and disrupt gateway servers that enable tax havens; (5) scrutinize foreign credit and debit cards; and (6) disable operations of "tax haven country" banks (Bharat Swabhiman Andolan, 2012). Ramdev's endorsement of the death penalty is a clear point of disagreement with the Gandhian model of *satyāgraha*, with its emphasis on nonviolence (*ahiṃsā*). However, Hazare has also endorsed capital punishment for the crime of corruption, perhaps placing it closer to the political mainstream than it might otherwise be regarded (*Economic Times* [Mumbai], June 24, 2011). For a public fed up with bureaucratic corruption and conscious of the profound struggle of many of those in India—if not of their own struggles—Ramdev's discourse on the need to battle corruption strikes a chord. Undoubtedly, Ramdev promises to be a driving force in the evolving public conversation over corruption.

RAMDEV AS MODERN YOGA REVOLUTIONARY

A number of factors characterize modern yoga traditions and distinguish them from their premodern precursors: among others, a rootedness in physicality or an empirical–experiential focus; an emphasis on health and well-being as distinct from, or in preparation for, the philosophical, spiritual, or religious aspect of yoga; identification of yoga as a science or as having a scientific basis; linkages to nationalism and nationalist politics; an integration of Indian and European ideas and practices centered on the body; and the commodification of yoga practices and products in the global marketplace (De Michelis, 2008; Sarbacker, 2008). Ramdev's personal narrative mirrors that of many other yoga modernists: a humble birth; an overcoming of personal health issues through an introduction to yoga; an itinerant youth and young adulthood spent studying and practicing with yoga masters; a return to the mundane world to spread the message of yoga for the sake of society; and a successful mission carried out in an entrepreneurial spirit and with a charismatic style. Ramdev's system—which can be referred to as *Divyayog* for simplification—exemplifies all of these elements in profound ways, and his yoga might be considered hypermodern given how he has forwarded and championed the principles and practices in such an idealized fashion. This is not to say that Ramdev's yoga is not also traditional or distinctly Indian in important ways. The Divyayog system draws on Ramdev's training in the *gurukul* tradition in ways that connect him to premodern practices and principles, among them the practice of renunciation, the use of practices like *ṣaṭkarman* that are rarely present in popularized forms of modern yoga, and the emphasis on the principles and medicines of *āyurveda*. Divyayog, and Ramdev's writings on it, has a distinctly Indian character; it is only secondarily an Anglophone yoga because its message is more easily translatable into Hindi and Marathi and perhaps even into Tamil and Telugu than into English. On the other hand, Ramdev clearly views his yoga as potentially a universal practice with global relevance. His work to propagate Divyayog has arguably brought yoga to its point of greatest exposure and popularity in the history of India and the world. The sheer scale of the practice of yoga under Ramdev's influence has reached a watershed moment in its history. The dream of an India brought together under the rubric of yoga has been realized on a scale that figures like Bhavanrao Pant could only have imagined. Ramdev has used the cultural and economic capital that the success of his yoga mission has reaped to shape Indian society in line with his vision of "the India of his dreams." Through the process he has, at least on a mimetic level, reached the sort of identity with the cosmos that is associated with the yogi of Indian literature—seemingly all-present and all-knowing, ever involved and invested in the events unfolding at the center of the collective life in India, with the powerful of the nation lined up at his feet (Sarbacker, 2011: 212–20). He has become a macrocosm reflected in the microcosm of his followers, who embody his discourse and praxis and for whom he stands as an expression of their collective concerns and dreams (p. 215).

Ramdev's vision of yoga as the link between the perfection of the individual and the prosperity of country and world is clear and coherent. For Ramdev, the answer to India's—and the world's—problems, both individual and communal, is found in becoming a yogi:

> By starting yoga duties along with national duties and joining the religion of yoga with the religion of the nation, we have not done any opposing work and rather have accepted yoga in a vast form. There is no doubt, confusion, illusion or hesitation in my mind regarding the duties of yoga and the nation. My intention and rules are very clear and *my intention is to bring unity and morality to divided India*. Yoga means—to unite. I want to unite the entire world with yoga as a medium. I want to first make each person in the nation a yogi. When each person in India is a yogi then he will be a youth of character; he will be a patriotic teacher or doctor; he will be an aware farmer; he will be a thoughtful chartered accountant; he will be a hardworking lawyer; he will be a soldier, security person or policeman with tradition; he will be a dutiful supervisor, worker or labourer; he will be an energetic businessman; he will be a patriotic artist or journalist; he will be a scientist dedicated to the good of the nation; he will be a healthy, active and sensitive senior citizen; he will be an intelligent and sensitive judge and advocate because it is my clear opinion that there can be no development

> of the nation without self-development. By doing and helping others do yoga, I will turn each person into a good person. I will make a mother an ideal mother. I will build such a foundation of tradition and culture and prepare ideal mothers and ideal fathers through yoga, so that children like Lord Ram and Shri Krishna are again born here. When, with the help of yoga, a self-realized person sees the society, nation, entire universe in himself, he will not cheat anyone, he won't hate anyone because he will feel that cheating or lying to another is cheating or lying to himself. It is because of self-confusion that there is corruption, dishonesty, immorality, anarchy, and insensitivity. With this yoga revolution, we will establish the age-old tradition of the sages across the globe and re-establish a kingdom of happiness, prosperity, joy, and peace. (Ramdev, 2009: 33)

In Ramdev's vision, yoga can be viewed as a *kalpavṛkṣa* (wish-fulfilling tree) and as the answer to the individual and collective needs of India—and ultimately of all humanity.

REFERENCES

Alliance of Religions and Conservation. 2008. Hindu Leaders Launch Massive Campaign to Save the Ganges. September 10. Available at: http://www.arcworld.org/news.asp?pageID=261 (accessed February 25, 2012).

Alter, J. 2000. *Gandhi's Body: Sex, Diet, and the Politics of Nationalism*, Philadelphia: University of Philadelphia Press.

———. 2008. Yoga Shivir. In *Yoga in Modern India: Contemporary Perspectives*, ed. Jean-Byrne and Mark Singleton, 36–48. New York: Routledge.

Bharat Swabhiman Andolan. 2012. Swami Ramdev Gives Easy Solutions for Black Money Issue. Available at: http://bharat-swabhiman.com/en/swami-ramdev-gives-easy-solutions-for-black-money-issue/ (accessed May 11, 2012).

Blakely, Rhys. 2008. Warrior pose turns Indian yoga soldiers into deadly foes. *The Times* (London). June 2. Available at: http://www.thetimes.co.uk/tto/news/world/article1975172.ece (accessed March 24, 2012).

Chakraborty, C. 2006. Ramdev and Somatic Nationalism: Embodying the Nation, Desiring the Global. *Economic and Political Weekly* 41 (5): 387–390.

———. 2007. The Hindu Ascetic as Fitness Instructor: Reviving Faith in Yoga. *International Journal of the History of Sport* 24(9): 1172–1186.

Dalton, D. 2000. *Mahatma Gandhi: Nonviolent Power in Action*. New York: Columbia University Press.

De Michelis, E. 2004. *A History of Modern Yoga: Patañjali and Western Esotericism*. London: Continuum.

———. 2008. Modern Yoga: History and Forms. In *Yoga in Modern India: Contemporary Perspectives*, ed. Jean Byrne and Mark Singleton, 17–35. New York: Routledge.

Divya Yog Mandir (Trust). 2012. Swami Ramdevji. Available at: http://www.divyayoga.com/introduction/swami-ramdev-ji.html (accessed March 23, 2012).

George, V.K. and Kasturi, C.S. 2011. Making of Brand Baba. *Hindustan Times*. June 11. Available at: http://www.hindustantimes.com/News-Feed/India/Making-of-brand-Baba/Article1-708369.aspx (accessed March 24, 2012).

Indo-Asian News Service (New Delhi). 2008. Ramdev's Ganga mission brings VHP, Muslim clerics together. No author listed. September 19. Available at: http://www.highbeam.com/doc/1P3-1557868791.html (accessed June 11, 2011).

Indian Express (New Delhi). 2011. There is no competition with Anna Hazare: Baba Ramdev. No author listed. May 31. Available at: http://www.indianexpress.com/news/there-is-no-competition-with-anna-hazare-baba-ramdev/797420/0 (accessed March 25, 2012).

———. 2011. Govt tried to assassinate me: Baba Ramdev. No author listed. 26 June. Available at: http://www.indianexpress.com/news/govt-tried-to-assassinate-me-baba-ramdev-808901 (accessed March 25, 2012).

———. 2011. Baba Ramdev breaks fast, vows to continue anti-graft campaign. No author listed. June 12. Available at: http:www.indianexpress.com/news/baba-ramdev-breaks-fast-vows-to-continue-antigraft-campaign/802506 (accessed March 25, 2012).

Laul, R. 2011. Godfellas I—A Series on Gurus and Their Politics. *Telekha Magazine*. June 4. Available at: http://www.tehelka.com/story_main49.asp?filename=Ne040611GODFELLAS.asp (accessed February 23, 2012).

McKean, L. 1996. *Divine Enterprise: Gurus and the Hindu Nationalist Movement*. Chicago: University of Chicago Press.

Nanda, M. 2006. How Modern Are We? Cultural Contradictions of India's Modernity. *Economic & Political Weekly* 41(6): 491–96.

NDTV Correspondent. 2011. Ramdev vs. Government Escalates, Both Say Trust Betrayed. *NDTV*. Updated June 4. Available at: http://www.ndtv.com/article/india/ramdev-vs-government-escalates-both-say-trust-betrayed-110158 (accessed May 4, 2012).

———. 2012. Ramlila Crackdown: Supreme Court Slams Govt, Delhi Police; also Pulls Up Ramdev. *NDTV*. Updated February 23. Available at: http://www.ndtv.com/article/india/ramlila-crackdown-supreme-court-slams-govt-delhi-police-also-pulls-up-ramdev-179184 (accessed March 26, 2012).

Patañjali Yogpeeth. 2011. *Patañjali Yogpeeth—An Introduction*. Haridwar: Patañjali Yogpeeth Trust.

Pinch, W. 2006. *Warrior Ascetics and Indian Empires*. New York: Cambridge University Press.

Press Trust of India (New Delhi). 2012. Anna, Ramdev to Fight Graft Together. 20 March. Available at: http://articles.economictimes.indiatimes.com/2012-03-20/news/31214795_1_anna-hazare-baba-ramdev-corruption-and-black-money (accessed June 26, 2011).

Pokharel, Krishna. 2010. India's Holy Ganges to Get a Cleanup: Government Embarks on $4 Billion Campaign to Treat Heavily Polluted Waters; Devout Hindus Revere River as 'Goddess.' Wall Street Journal. February 13. Available at: http://online.wsj.com/article/SB10001424052748704878904575031333129327818.html (accessed June 11, 2011).

Polgreen, L. 2010. Indian Who Built Yoga Empire Works on Politics. New York Times. April 18. Available at: http://www.nytimes.com/2010/04/19/world/asia/19swami.html (accessed March 24, 2012).

Ramdev, S. 2008. *Yog: Its Philosophy & Practice*. Haridwar: Divya Prakashan.

———. 2009. Jeevan Darshan. *Yog Sandesh*, (March 6), pp. 6–57.

Raj, A. 2010. *The Life and Times of Baba Ramdev*. New Delhi: Hay House Publishers.

Sarbacker, S. 2008. The Numinous and Cessative in Modern Yoga. In *Yoga in Modern India: Contemporary Perspectives*, ed. JeanByrne and Mark Singleton, 161–83. New York: Routledge.

———. 2009. *Aṣṭāṅgayoga in the Purāṇa Literature*. Paper presented at the 14th World Sanskrit Conference, Kyoto, Japan, September 1–5.

———. 2011. Power and Meaning in the Yogasūtra of Patañjali. In *Yoga Powers: Extraordinary Capacities Attained through Meditation and Concentration*, ed. Knut Jacobsen. Leiden: Brill, pp. 195–222.

Singh, K.M. 2007. *Water Woes at Allahabad's Kumbh Mela*. India Environment Portal: Knowledge for Change. February 14. Available at: http://www.indiaenvironmentportal.org.in/news/water-woes-allahabads-kumbh-mela (accessed March 26, 2012).

Sinha, Arunav. 2011. BJP sees Ganga as a hot political commodity for reigniting Ayodhya issue. *Times News Network*. July 18. Available at: http://articles.economictimes.indiatimes.com/2011-07-18/news/29787559_1_ayodhya-issue-ganga-aarti-ballia (accessed February 25, 2012).

Singleton, M.2008. The Classical Reveries of Modern Yoga: Patañjali and Constructive Orientalism. In *Yoga in Modern India: Contemporary Perspectives*, ed. Jean Byrne and Mark Singleton, 77–99. New York: Routledge.

———.2010. *Yoga Body: The Origins of Modern Posture Practice*. New York: Oxford University Press

Sjoman, N. 1996. *The Yoga Tradition of the Mysore Palace*. New Delhi: Abhinav.

Thomas, P. 2009. "Selling God/Saving Souls: Religious Commodities, Spiritual Markets and the Media." *Global Media and Communication* 5(1): 57–76.

White, D. 2009. *Sinister Yogis*. Chicago: University of Chicago Press.

NOTES

1. Not all sources are in agreement with respect to the date of his birth, a common variant being that he was born in 1965 (Raj, 2010: 81). The Patañjali Yogpeeth website (2012) has a brief biography of Ramdev but does not include his date of birth.
2. Yoga's relationship to martial arts and exercises is a long and storied one, represented in notable ways in the Indian epic literature, in medieval traditions of yoga and renunciation, and in the modern convergence of Indian martial arts, wrestling, and yoga. See, for example, Pinch (2006); Sjoman (1996); and White (2009).
3. This figure has been disputed by the Congress party in a booklet titled "The Congress View on Present Situation-1" (IANS [New Delhi], June 11, 2011).

INDEX

14235663R00234

Printed in Great Britain
by Amazon.co.uk, Ltd.,
Marston Gate.